TOMPKINS
A S S O C I A T E S
Worldwide Central Campus

8970 Southall Road
Raleigh, NC 27616
(800) 789-1257
FAX (919) 872-9666

www.tompkinsinc.com

TOTAL OPERATIONS
EXCELLENCE

INFORMATION TECHNOLOGY
IMPLEMENTATION

MATERIAL HANDLING
INTEGRATION

Offices Worldwide

THE SUPPLY CHAIN HANDBOOK

James A. Tompkins, Ph.D.
Dale Harmelink

Editors-in-Chief

TOMPKINS
PRESS

The supply chain handbook / James A. Tompkins, Dale
   Harmelink, editors-in-chief.
      p. cm.
   Includes bibliographical references and index.
   LCCN 2004095903
   ISBN 1-930426-03-8

   1. Physical distribution of goods–Management–
Handbooks, manuals, etc.   I. Tompkins, James A.
II. Harmelink, Dale A.

HF5415.7.S87 2004   658.7'88
                             QBI04-200341

ACKNOWLEDGEMENTS

This book has been a labor of love. Twice before now this book was ready to be published and then a major shift occurred in the supply chain that required further revisions. The definition of Supply Chain Excellence has been stable for a year, so it is now the right time to publish this book with a high level of certainty that we have provided the information you need.

There are four groups of people who deserve a major word of thanks for supporting this book:

1. The leadership of Tompkins Associates who have done much of the real ground-breaking design and implementation on supply chain projects. In particular, I would like to thank Jerry Smith, John Spain, Dale Harmelink, Brian Hudock, Jim Capece, John Seidl, Denny McKnight, Mike Futch, Mark Buffum, Dan Avila, Dan Hunt and Brian Upchurch for their expertise and support.
2. The Tompkins Press staff of Kami Spangenberg and Tonya Loggains, along with outside editor Ray Kulwiec.
3. The authors of the individual chapters of this book: Ken Ackerman, James Allred, Paul Bender, Jim Capece, Ralph Cox, Ben Cubitt, Mike Edenfield, Allan Fraser, Doulgas Furbush, Joe Hanna, Dale Harmelink, Jamie Heaward, Brian Hudock, Gerhardt Muller, Steve Parsley, Tom Singer, Jerry Smith, Bruce Tompkins, Gene Tyndall, Don Velhaber, Andrew White, and Patrick White. Thank you for your patience and ongoing efforts to make this book the best it can be.
4. The many clients of Tompkins Associates who have been innovators in the supply chain and allowed us to push the boundaries of supply chain success.

It is with great joy that we place this book on your desk. May your supply chain journey be exciting and fruitful, and this book contribute to your firm's pursuit of Supply Chain Excellence.

TABLE OF CONTENTS

PREFACE V

CHAPTER 1: The Supply Chain: Past, Present, and Future 1
James A. Tompkins

CHAPTER 2: Customer Satisfaction and the Supply Chain .11
James A. Tompkins

CHAPTER 3: Partnerships and the Supply Chain 19
James A. Tompkins

CHAPTER 4: Global Supply Chains 29
Paul S. Bender

CHAPTER 5: Budgeting and Planning the Supply Chain 55
Gene R. Tyndall

CHAPTER 6: Distribution Networks: Planning and Site Selection 77
Dale A. Harmelink

CHAPTER 7: Inventory Management 95
Ralph Cox

CHAPTER 8: Collaborative Planning, Forecasting, and Replenishment (CPFR) 135
Andrew White

CHAPTER 9: Distribution and Supply Chain 149
Brian Hudock

CHAPTER 10: Logistics and Manufacturing Outsourcing .175
James A. Tompkins

CHAPTER 11: Warehouse Operations 191
Brian Hudock

CHAPTER 12: Receiving and Shipping Systems 213
Kenneth ·Ackerman

CHAPTER 13: Warehouse Space and Layout Planning 223
Jerry D. Smith

CHAPTER 14: Material Handling Systems and Integration 247
Jim Capece

CHAPTER 15: Automated Storage/Retrieval Systems 279
James K. Allred and Stephen L. Parsley

CHAPTER 16: Transportation Modes 295
Gerhardt Muller

CHAPTER 17: Private Fleet 333
R. Patrick White and Joe B. Hanna

CHAPTER 18: Manufacturing Strategies for the Supply Chain 357
James A. Tompkins

CHAPTER 19: Leaning The Supply Chain 377
Bruce Tompkins

CHAPTER 20: Linking Store Replenishment To The Supply Chain 393
Don Vehlhaber

CHAPTER 21: Training and Successful Implementations 405
Jamie Heaward

CHAPTER 22: Supply Chain Execution Systems 417
Tom Singer

CHAPTER 23: Warehouse Management Systems 425
Tom Singer

CHAPTER 24: Radio Frequency Identification 439
Tom Singer

CHAPTER 25: Transportation Operations and Management 457
Ben Cubitt

CHAPTER 26: Manufacturing Execution Systems 471
Allan Fraser and Douglas Furbush

INDEX 489

PREFACE

Over the last 10 years, the supply chain has gone through an unbelievable transformation. I have worked on six books related to the supply chain during this time frame, and it is amazing how the field has evolved. Our first related title, *The Warehouse Management Handbook,* published by McGraw-Hill, laid the foundation for logistics excellence. Our second book, *The Distribution Management Handbook,* took a broader view of the logistics field and was published once again by McGraw-Hill. The technology explosion took place in logistics and so our third book was a technology upgrade of *The Warehouse Management Handbook, Second Edition,* published by Tompkins Press. This book was titled *No Boundaries: Moving Beyond Supply Chain Management* and was published by Tompkins Press. In this book I presented for the first time a clear vision of Supply Chain Excellence.

As we worked to implement this vision we learned a lot about the evolutionary nature of the journey to Supply Chain Excellence, so I rewrote the *No Boundaries* book to include this new information. This book, also published by Tompkins Press, replaced the original *No Boundaries* book and is titled *No Boundaries: Break Through to Supply Chain Excellence.*

The sixth book is the one in your hands and was written as a replacement for *The Distribution Management Handbook.* It achieves the broader context of the Supply Chain while addressing today's technological tools. So my original three books in this field— *The Warehouse Management Handbook, The Distribution Management Handbook* and *No Boundaries: Moving Beyond Supply Chain Management*—have all been replaced with updated thinking in revised editions and this exciting new book. The current line up is shown in the chart at right.

C-Level Executives — **No Boundaries** *Break Through to Supply Chain Excellence* — Management Overview/Philosophy

VP-Level Executives — **The Supply Chain Handbook** — Best Practices and Strategies

Managers — **The Warehouse Management Handbook, Second Edition** — How-To Advice and Practical Tools

This book fills an important void in the science of Supply Chain Excellence. It is our intent to continue to provide you with the tools you need to advance your organization along on the supply chain journey. It is so very important that we take to heart the reality that it is no longer about company vs. company, but today's competitive battles are supply chain vs. supply chain.

James A. Tompkins
President, Tompkins Associates, Inc.

CHAPTER 1
The Supply Chain: Past, Present, and Future

James A. Tompkins, Ph.D., President, Tompkins Associates

Much has been said and written about the supply chain and various attempts to optimize the way it functions. It seems appropriate in this introductory chapter to first improve what is meant by the term "supply chain" before identifying the path to supply chain excellence. The term "supply chain" is used to visualize the relationship, or linkage, between trading organizations. Typically it involves the flow of goods, services, and information from the raw materials level through to processing, distribution, consumption, and disposal. Each level is represented by a link, and together the links form the total supply "chain." Although materials may generally flow in one direction, starting at the raw material level, information in an effective supply chain flows in both directions.

Throughout the years, organizations and companies have viewed the supply chain through two perspectives. The first is the logistics perspective, which focuses on the internal coordination of materials. The second is Supply Chain Management (SCM), which focuses on the optimization of individual links while trying to control change. The future of the supply chain, however, does not lie in either of these limited perspectives.

How Business is Changing

The way we view business has changed. Today's supply chains face many challenges. Stock-keeping units (SKUs) continue to grow, boundaries between manufacturing and distribution are blurring, and deverticalization—a de-layering activity that creates the opposite of a vertical industry—is becoming a reality. These factors have also brought about the major supply chain challenges of the present: channel structure and relationships, customer satisfaction, information systems and technology, the global economy, and the shift from company vs. company to supply chain vs. supply chain.

To gain competitive advantage in the supply chain vs. supply chain wars, an organization must develop a strategy that first encompasses today's best supply-chain practices, and then provides a bridge for attaining best practices in the future. The strategy advocated here is to pursue the journey of the Six Levels of Supply Chain Excellence: 1) Business as Usual, 2) Link Excellence, 3) Visibility, 4) Collaboration, 5) Synthesis, and 6) Velocity.

To understand why the Six Levels of Supply Chain Excellence can ensure supply chain success today and tomorrow, it is necessary to look at the limitations of the past. This chapter discusses logistics, why SCM is not enough, what is happening today, and finally the promise of success today and tomorrow represented by the Six Levels of Supply Chain Excellence.

The Past: Logistics, Approaches, and Boundaries

Logistics focuses on the internal coordination of materials management (raw materials), material flow through production (work in progress), and physical distribution (finished goods). In other words, logistics begins with the need to order raw materials and ends when the finished goods are shipped. Change or turbulence in the supply chain from either suppliers or customers is viewed as a major irritant and efforts are put forth to minimize the effects. Historically, logistics has never looked at true integration or the issue of change. Its focus is internal.

Approaches

It is much easier to grasp an approach than it is to understand and implement a process. Therefore, many organizations have looked to approaches to help them meet supply chain challenges. An approach focus, rather than a process focus, unfortunately creates Management by Fad (MBF). When a technique or method failed, people often reached out and grabbed that latest fad approach for industry woes. First one thing, then another. First they did it, then they re-did it, then they were beyond re-doing it. They engineered, reengineered, re-reengineered, and then they were beyond re-engineering. They tried on a new technique and insisted that it fit—until the seams finally burst.

Some of the approaches they used (and may still be using) are Demand Chain Management, Demand Network Management, Demand Network Integration, Value Chain Management, Customer-Driven Demand Network, Supply Chain Coordination, Supply Chain Integration, and Demand/Supply Chain Management.

Demand Chain Management handles order management, distribution logistics, inventory replenishment, and demand planning. Its focus is the link. Demand Change Management looks downstream and focuses on only the demand aspect of the supply chain.

The *Value Chain Management* mindset goes a bit further, examining both the demand and supply requirements of the supply chain. Unfortunately, Value Chain Management is still an approach, not a process. It pursues optimization instead of meeting the true needs of continuous improvement.

Supply Chain Coordination is an integral component of supply chain design. Also, well-coordinated discrete activities are more efficient than disjointed independent action. However, Supply Chain Coordination still allows the slowest or weakest link to determine overall operating efficiency and speed of the supply chain. Most importantly, Supply Chain Coordination does not mean Supply Chain Integration, as it is still based upon link optimization.

Supply Chain Integration is viewed as producing greater technological innovation, leveraged knowledge, shared business risks, shorter cycle times (both production and design), and integration of production planning. However, like all the other approaches, it does not provide the tools for meeting today's supply chain challenges.

Demand/Supply Chain Management is similar to Value Chain Management in that it is the combination of what is seen as traditional supply components (e.g., purchasing, inventory management, MES, MRP, and process control) with what is seen as traditional demand components (e.g., demand management, planning, scheduling, sales, order fulfillment). Like SCM, Demand/Supply Chain Management is a logistics concept, and it still focuses on link optimization.

Boundaries

All the approaches described above share one characteristic: Each has boundaries.

To succeed today *and* tomorrow, supply chains cannot have boundaries. There have to be partnerships, not only link-to-link, but within the total chain, in order to accomplish the objective common to both present and future supply chains. That objective is the answer to the question all organizations ask: "How do we keep our customers happy, grow our business, and increase profitability?"

Today's Supply Chain Challenges

As discussed under the above section, "How Business is Changing," supply chain members face a number of crucial challenges today. These challenges, described below, require new ways of thinking, new strategies, and new ways of organizing business.

Channel Structure and Relationships

In today's business climate, channel structures are blurring and relationships are fluid. Industry is removing links from the supply chain, and alternate channels such as catalogs and the Internet are growing tremendously. The partnerships that corporations are establishing represent a leap over one of the highest hurdles in business: the "us versus them" mentality of supplier/customer relationships. Recent trends in commerce, such as supplier certification, are providing added value to the end product and strengthening the supply chain as a result.

Because channel structures and relationships are changing; de-layering, outsourcing, and deverticalization are now a reality. The impact these strategies have is unbelievable. Sometimes they add links to the supply chain, and sometimes they remove them. Whether they are adding or subtracting links, these strategies affect how businesses are organized.

Customer Satisfaction

Customization, customer choice, customer control, customer relationship management, and *customer-centric* are terms that are increasingly being used to describe the new supply chain focus. This view is a change from the enterprise-wide focus that characterized organizations just a few years ago. Basically, customer needs and desires are dictating what manufacturers produce—and any manufacturer that does not listen will be left behind. Thus, customer satisfaction is paramount.

Information Systems and Technology

Information Technology has moved forward faster than anyone has imagined. Ten years ago, voice mail and e-mail were rare. Intranets and extranets, video conferencing, whiteboarding, streaming, and Webcasts were nonexistent. The Internet has connected people and information more quickly and easily, and at minimal cost. The World Wide Web has evolved into a place for dialogue, relationships, and the streamlining of processes.

This levels the playing field among competitors, accelerates margin pressures, reduces the value of branding, and increases the importance of providing quality service.

Off the Web, Automatic Identification, communications technology, and business software are being standardized. Systems integrators are writing custom interfaces to allow the exchange of data between various applications. Also, middleware is creating ways to tie disparate programs and systems together, through the use of enterprise application integrators (EAI) and Web application servers.

Global Economy

The success of firms now depends heavily on their ability to reach foreign markets. Business no longer ends at the border of a particular country or continent. Politically, events of the last two decades have greatly decreased much of the isolationism that has plagued business. Trade agreements now ease the tensions and reticence between once-competing nations.

Technology also plays a role in our global economy. The Internet has made the world a much smaller place. With the speed of information and the shrinking distances that it creates between markets, the supply chains we are competing against are just as likely to be halfway around the world as they are to be across town. In many cases, when we are using the Internet to disseminate information, we may not even know its destination.

Supply Chain vs. Supply Chain

In today's marketplace, the thinking is no longer company vs. company. Today, it is "my supply chain vs. your supply chain." To deliver maximum value, customization, and satisfaction to the ultimate customer, while at the same time reducing inventory, lead-times, and costs, the supply chain must be integrated and synthesized to function as a single entity. The goal of this entity should be to satisfy the ultimate customer. If it fails to do so, each link, one by one, will go out of business by default.

Today, supply chains must make sure that they are flexible, modular, and scalable, thus being ready to change direction or reinvent themselves as the business climate changes. Supply chain leadership should ask, "How can we work with our supply chain's systems and processes to ensure that our customers receive what they want?" The answer begins with SCM, goes beyond it, and takes us into the future with Supply Chain Excellence.

Limitations of SCM

The vision of the future requires us to move beyond logistics, limited approaches, and outdated boundaries. It also requires us to examine SCM closely to see how it may be used as a building block for a process—the process of achieving Supply Chain Excellence. In other words, SCM does have a place in the supply chain and is a tool that can be used to start the process of achieving Supply Chain Excellence.

A commonly accepted definition of SCM is "the delivery of enhanced customer and economic value through synchronized management of the flow of physical goods from sourcing to consumption." The way SCM is practiced is to view the flow of physical goods from sourcing to consumption from the viewpoint of a link in the chain.

For many years, SCM has tried to be the panacea for curing deficiencies in customer service, communication, and relationships. Yet, despite all of our SCM efforts, we are still losing ground. According to a recent article in Supply Chain Management Review, "Companies are investing in software, hiring consultants, and reconfiguring their physical supply chains in order to capture the promised returns from lean supply chain management. Yet the returns from these investments can be elusive."[1]

This failing is not due to neglect of the supply chain. Instead, the reason that SCM has not yielded the desired results is because it has been treated as the *only* and *ultimate* way to make customers happy, grow business, and increase profitability when, in reality, it is part of a much bigger solution: Supply Chain Excellence. SCM is about optimizing individual links, and this is very important in the process of constructing a supply chain. However, it is not sufficient.

SCM's limitations begin with its name, which can be broken down into three parts:

1. Supply—indicates a push-only approach to production
2. Chain—indicates individual and discrete links
3. Management—implies a static environment of control and measurement

Problems are inherent in all three. "Push" no longer gets the job done, because it gives control to suppliers rather than the ultimate customer. Viewing the supply chain as individual links is also problematic. Like the practice of medicine in the past, it treats symptoms but does not try to discover a cause. For example, optimizing warehousing without taking into account other elements, such as sourcing, purchasing, production, inventory planning, transportation, and customer satisfaction may not yield the desired results. The cause of warehousing problems might not actually be related to the warehouse itself, but to something else entirely. As for management, the static, controlled environment implied by the term also suggests containment. A healthy, flowing supply chain is not contained. It cannot be, as that would make it resistant to change instead of anticipating and harnessing the power of change.

Furthermore, SCM often does not include transportation costs, link costs, customer satisfaction, quality issues, and manufacturing costs. One of the more unfathomable aspects is the exclusion of manufacturing costs. The blurring boundaries between distribution and manufacturing do not justify this exclusion. The omission of manufacturing implies little or no concern for value-adds and mass customization. Manufacturing must be part of the supply chain.

The final limitation to SCM is how it is approached—as a finite solution, when in reality it is just the beginning in the process of achieving Supply Chain Excellence. Too many companies have missed that point and implemented SCM practices and technology to operate at Level 1 of Supply Chain Excellence—Business as Usual. From several important perspectives—trust between a company and its suppliers, external teamwork and partnerships, integration of external business processes, and customer satisfaction—this approach falls short. SCM should be used as a stepping stool to climb to Level 2 of the

Six Levels of Supply Chain Excellence—Link Excellence. Why? Because Link Excellence is part of the focus of today's supply chain, along with Business as Usual and Visibility.

The Present: Business as Usual, Link Excellence, and Visibility

Business as Usual

Attaining Supply Chain Excellence is a process. As mentioned above, it has six steps, or levels. It is not important where an organization is in the process, as long as it moves up level-by-level. Level 1, the lowest level, is Business as Usual. At this level, a company works hard to maximize its individual functions. The goal of each individual department, such as finance, marketing, sales, purchasing, information technology, research and development, manufacturing, distribution, and human resources, is to be the best department in the company. Overall organizational effectiveness is not the emphasis. Each organizational element attempts to function well within its individual silo.

Six Levels of Supply Chain Excellence
Level 6: Velocity
Level 5: Synthesis
Level 4: Collaboration
Level 3: Visibility
Level 2: Link Excellence
Level 1: Business As Usual

It is important to remember that Business as Usual is just the first phase in the six-level journey. After the dot-com to dot-bomb phenomenon, it is easy to think that Business as Usual is the only thing that works. Organizations must avoid this mindset. Many dot-coms have failed, not so much because their processes were wrong, but because the companies themselves did not consider the entire supply chain. Business as Usual must be left behind once an organization starts its climb toward Supply Chain Excellence.

Link Excellence

A common mistake that organizations make is to try to achieve Supply Chain Excellence without scrutinizing their internal operations first. In actuality, no organization should approach its suppliers with the aim of developing partner relationships until it has evolved its individual link into the most efficient, effective, responsive, and holistic one that it can possibly be. Only after one's link achieves performance excellence can the pursuit of Supply Chain Excellence truly begin.

To achieve Link Excellence, companies must tear down their internal boundaries until the entire organization functions as one entity. Companies usually have numerous departments and facilities, including plants, warehouses, and distribution centers (DCs). If an organization hopes to pursue Supply Chain Excellence, it must look within itself, eliminate any boundaries between departments and facilities, and begin a never-ending journey of continuous improvement. It must have strategic and tactical initiatives at the department, plant, and link levels for design and systems. At this point, some of the initiatives can use logistics and SCM, as long as the organization remembers that neither approach will take it beyond Link Excellence. To make the leap successfuly, continuous improvement initiatives are necessary.

Visibility

Supply Chain Excellence requires everyone along the supply chain to work together. However, partners in the supply chain cannot work together if they cannot see one another. Visibility, the third level of Supply Chain Excellence, brings to light all links in the supply chain. It minimizes supply chain surprises because it provides the information that links need in order to follow the ongoing status of orders. Visibility, then, can be considered the first "real" step toward Supply Chain Excellence.

Through Visibility, organizations come to understand their roles in a supply chain and become aware of the roles of other links. An example is an electronics company with a Website that allows its customers to view circuit boards, and then funnels information about those customers to suppliers. Visibility thus requires sharing of information, which requires trust and technology.

Because Visibility is not possible without technology, selecting the right technology is critical. A business application that is suitable for Ford may not work for IBM. If someone has a wooden ladder, a metal rung will not fit it. Therefore, it is important to develop a strategic plan to acquire the right application, so that the mesmerizing bells and whistles do not distract the links to the point that they forget their true needs.

Once a supply chain achieves Visibility, it can move to Collaboration, the fourth level that is described below. Through Collaboration, the supply chain can determine how best to meet the demands of the marketplace. The supply chain thus works as a coherent whole to maximize customer satisfaction while minimizing inventories.

The Future: Collaboration, Synthesis, and Velocity

The supply chain of the future relies on innovative thought while monitoring the changing needs and desires of its customers. If it is nimble and treats even adverse events as opportunities, its future is assured. Each organization within the chain seizes the day and goes forward, secure in the knowledge that it has achieved ongoing Supply Chain Excellence. Collaboration and the levels that follow form the path to achieving this state of excellence.

Collaboration

Collaboration is achieved through the proper application of technology and true partnerships. Various Collaboration technologies exist, and, as with Visibility software, the supply chain must choose the right technology or if it hopes to collaborate properly.

True partnerships require total commitment from all the links in the supply chain. They are based on trust and a mutual desire to work as one for the benefit of the whole.

Characteristics of a true partnership are:

- A commitment to long-term relationships based on trust and a true understanding of partners' businesses.
- A belief in sharing information, planning, scheduling, risks, rewards, problems, solutions, and opportunities.

- A commitment to working together toward improvements in quality, lead-times, new product development time, and inventory accuracy and management.
- A resolution and agreement to build on each other's strengths, increase partners' businesses, and invest in the long-term partnership relationship.
- A commitment to systems integration and organizational interdependence, while still retaining individual identities in order to ensure innovation and creativity.
- The consensus that frequent and open communication at all levels of the organization must occur.
- A commitment to involving partners early in any innovations.
- A commitment to the flexibility required to ensure the best overall performance of the partnership.

Forming a true partnership requires discarding the traditional relationships common between organizations today. The objective of creating true partnerships is to create the same synergy between organizations that the Level 2 process created within an organization. This means first understanding that the term "relationship" is not synonymous with partnership. Instead, a relationship must be transformed into a partnership. This transformation requires an understanding of the following factors:

- No two relationships develop the same way.
- Relationships evolve as comfortable bonds between individuals.
- A positive chemistry must exist between two parties to create a relationship.
- Partnerships evolve from understanding hopes and dreams, and anticipating a bright future.
- Each party must know itself and understand what it is seeking from the partnership.
- Acceptance by indirectly involved parties (e.g., stockholders, government) is as important to the perpetuation of the partnership as acceptance by directly affected parties.
- The relationship, at its core, has interest in the well-being of the individual parties as well as the well-being of the partnership.
- Expectations of how the relationship will develop must be articulated.
- Compatibility is key to a long-term relationship.

Identifying potential true partners should be based on the opportunity for additional contribution to the growth and profitability of the supply chain. This applies to both a customer looking at its suppliers and a supplier looking at its customers. The focus should be on building trust, then communicating clearly, and, finally, adopting a continuous improvement process.

Synthesis

Once Collaboration is achieved, the supply chain then pursues the continuous improvement process of Synthesis so that it can harness the energy of change. It is from Synthesis that true Supply Chain Excellence is achieved, and therefore it deserves particular attention in this chapter.

Synthesis is the unification of all supply chain links to form a whole. It creates a complete pipeline from a customer perspective. The results of Synthesis are:

- Increased return on assets (ROA)—this goal is achieved by maximizing inventory turns, employee participation, and continuous improvement, while minimizing obsolete inventory.
- Improved customer satisfaction—Synthesis creates companies that are responsive to the customer's needs through customization. They understand value-added activity. They also understand the issue of flexibility and how to meet ever-changing customer requirements. And, they completely comprehend the meaning of high quality and strive to provide high value.
- Reduced costs—this goal is achieved by scrutinizing the costs of transportation, acquisition, distribution, inventory carrying, reverse logistics, packaging, and other sources of cost, and continually searching for ways to drive each of those costs down.
- An integrated supply chain—this ideal is achieved by using partnerships and communication to integrate the entire supply chain, thereby focusing on the ultimate customer.

Supply chains that reach the Synthesis level are going to have major successes. A few already have; they include Dell and Wal-Mart. Their accomplishments were achieved with patience. Synthesis is not achieved overnight. It takes time to remove the boundaries between links of a supply chain. However, if all links are visible and all trading partners collaborate, then Synthesis is within reach.

Velocity

Today's business environment demands speed. The Internet has created immediate orders, and customers expect their products to arrive almost as quickly. Velocity is Synthesis at the speed of light.

Synthesis with speed creates multi-level networks that meet these demands. They are complex entities that can meet the demands of today's economy through a combination of partnerships, flexibility, and robust design methods. The emphasis has changed from designing systems and networks that work, to designing systems and networks that not only work, but also work fast. It is the process that will achieve *ongoing* Supply Chain Excellence.

Conclusion

Supply chains that pursue the journey to Excellence are going to have major successes today and in the future. To make Supply Chain Excellence happen, it is important to be armed with knowledge. Information and knowledge will enable your organization and its supply chain to reach unparalleled levels of performance, create synthesis, and apply the right technology that can make the process happen from start to finish.

Works Consulted

[1] Reeve, James M., "The Financial Advantages of the Lean Supply Chain." *Supply Chain Management Review.* March/April 2002.

CHAPTER 2
Customer Satisfaction and the Supply Chain

James A. Tompkins, Ph.D., President, Tompkins Associates

The power in the marketplace has shifted from producers to consumers. Customer needs and desires dictate what manufacturers produce—and any organization that does not listen will not survive. Because customers are now in a position of power, customer satisfaction (CS) is paramount.

The previous chapter introduced and discussed the Six Levels of Supply Chain Excellence. The current chapter covers Six Keys to Achieving Customer Satisfaction. Briefly, they are:

1. Develop objective measures of CS.
2. Understand and identify customer tiers.
3. Understand and implement "Elements of CS."
4. Carry out the four basic supply chain customer-satisfaction strategies.
5. Practice CS Synergy.
6. Apply appropriate levels of technology for communicating CS goals and strategies across the entire supply chain.

Customer Satisfaction vs. Customer Service

The first step in the journey to achieving customer satisfaction is to understand what it is not. Customer satisfaction is not customer service. Customer service measures how well a company performs against internally generated standards called "key performance indicators" (KPIs) such as order-fill rates, on-time shipments, and order-picking accuracy.

There is often a major disconnect between internally measured customer service performance and actual customer satisfaction. KPIs are important, but meeting them does not necessarily mean that customers are being satisfied. Customers base their satisfaction on how easy it is to conduct business, taking into account such factors as quality of information available, consistency of receipt timing, and others.

For example, consider a company that has had many years of success when it suddenly experiences stagnation and loss. Company executives cannot understand why customers are so unhappy, because, according to the KPIs they have in place, their customer service is excellent.

At that company, customer service is defined as orders being shipped as ordered two days after receipt, with an order-fill rate above 90 percent. The company was shipping the orders accurately 99.2 percent of the time, getting them out within two days 99.4 percent of the time, and reaching an order fill rate of 99.7 percent (by lines). Customer complaints were infrequent. Although customer service was good, there was a feeling that customers were not happy because repeat orders were down for reasons no one could discern.

Then, consider another company that believes it has great customer satisfaction because it has created charts for fill rates, backorders, on-time deliveries, damage, and complaints. These charts impress the people at this company. Unfortunately, their clients are not impressed. When this company asked customers about their experiences, the responses included:

> "If anyone else could fill the orders for the products we need, we'd go to them."
> "This company is not reliable."
> "We place an order but receive three shipments."
> "I can't read their invoices. I have no idea what I'm supposed to be paying on this paperwork they send me."
> "I call their customer service and they put me on hold for an hour and a half and then make me talk to some stupid computer."

Both companies are suffering from an illness called "Customer Service Self-Centeredness." Customer Service Self-Centeredness takes place when a company separates the customer from service because it is too focused on KPIs. An example of such short-sightedness is a large U.S. airline that prided itself on customer service. The airline had dissatisfied customers because it constantly re-routed them to the wrong gates, and then told them they would not have time to make it to the right gate. In truth, the airline was not really interested in its customers or their satisfaction. What it was interested in was meeting and exceeding its own measure of *customer service,* which was on-time arrivals. Its method for meeting this measure was to pad its schedules with arrivals at any gate available so that even in the face of incompetence, it could appear to be on time.

The focus of "self-centered" companies is internal: they measure success by meeting quotas they set themselves. Then they can say they have excellent customer service. This self-centeredness can only be cured by a shift in thinking beyond internal KPIs and toward true customer satisfaction.

What Is Customer Satisfaction?

Customer satisfaction is the measure of a supply chain's effectiveness. It is the means by which companies in a supply chain attempt to differentiate their products, keep customers loyal, improve profits, and become the supplier of choice. In other words, it is an ongoing, escalating, process of adding value, meeting requirements, and exceeding expectations. The following section describes how all members of the supply chain can use the Six Keys to achieve ultimate customer satisfaction.

Develop Objective Measures

Customer satisfaction is a scientific process. Its formula is:

> *Customer Satisfaction = Customer Perception of the Service − Customer Expectation of Service*

The formula presupposes two critical points:

- Customer satisfaction is based on customers' perceptions and expectations, not on a self-centered view of what the customer *should* want.
- The level of customer satisfaction will change as customers' expectations change.

Customer satisfaction, then, requires the organizations in a supply chain to divest themselves of their self-interest and focus on the needs, expectations, and perceptions of those to whom they provide products and services. Because the requirements of customers change over time, companies cannot maintain customer satisfaction with the same set of services and value-adds that worked yesterday. As customers evolve in their patronage, they expect more and more to satisfy them.

The companies in a supply chain must know and be able to identify the special needs of each level of their customer base. That is to say that they must understand the hierarchy of customer tiers.

Understand and Identify Customer Tiers

No company (or supply chain) has only one kind of customer. A customer base is made up of people, and no two are alike. Each person has his or her own set of expectations, and each requires different services. Identifying the many different aspects of a company's customer base is vital. Such identification can be as broad and thorough as a company chooses, as long as one critical point drives it: Every customer is different and demands different levels of service.

Consider one grocery chain. When asked who the customers were, the reply was, "We've got lots of customers," which meant the company did not know where it made its money. It hired a market research firm to study its customers. When the study was complete, the research showed that the company had three kinds of customers: those who spent $20 a week in the store, those who spent about $75 a week, and those who spent $150 a week. Those who spent $20 a week cost the chain $3 each time they visited; those who spent $75 a week earned the chain $6 each on each visit; and those who spent $150 a week earned the chain $30 each time they came in.

Unfortunately, even though the chain learned that three levels of service were necessary, the logical idea that the customer level bringing in the most money should receive the best services was lost. Instead, the store created a special express cashier for customers spending only $20 a week, while the best customers waited in longer lines.

The grocery chain did not understand that the basic customer tier arrangement enables companies to pursue customer satisfaction in a highly focused and specialized manner. The tier structure is made up of three levels of customers with three corresponding levels of satisfaction. The first is the visitor level. "Visitors" are customers who occasionally purchase products and services but have no lasting commitment to the company. To them, satisfaction comes from the fundamental aspects of the product. These customers define satisfaction in terms of product features and cost.

The second level is the associate level. "Associates" are customers who regularly, but not exclusively, purchase a supplier's products and services. Because the associates' experiences have grown since they started out as visitors, their expectations have also increased. As they become associates, they begin to take features and cost for granted and turn their attention to quality. This is a serious challenge because different customers define quality differently.

The third level is the partner level. "Partners" are customers who have moved a company to the primary position on their lists in a product category. Through time and maintained satisfaction, they have come to the point where they always choose their preferred company first. Like associates, however, their expectations have grown, and so have their requirements for satisfaction. They still expect features, cost, and quality, but they also require new value-added support like special handling, special delivery, extra services, training, and so on. Partners are candidates for true Supply Chain Excellence evolution because they are more than customers; they are part of the supply chain and contribute to its success.

How Customer Satisfaction and the Customer Tiers Work Together

Consider a situation in which a company produces an excellent product at a competitive cost with high quality, but adds little extra value. Also, suppose the customer's perception of service was 100 points. If that customer is a visitor whose expectation of service is only 40, then, following the customer-satisfaction formula from above, satisfaction is high at 60 (100 - 40 = 60). However, if that customer is an associate who expected an excellent product, competitive cost, and high quality, and had a point value of 90, then customer satisfaction is low, only 10 (100 - 90 = 10). Or, if that customer is a partner, who expected an excellent product, competitive cost, high quality, and considerable value-added support, and had a 110-point expectation of service, then the level of satisfaction becomes -10 (100 − 110 = -10). The latter represents a customer dissatisfaction level of -10.

This example explains why the company with the previous long history of customer support is now having difficulty. As customers' expectations increase from visitor to associate to partner levels, without a corresponding increase in the the perception of service received, then satisfaction quickly becomes dissatisfaction. The company thought that customer satisfaction would remain the same if it kept the same level of service or improved it slightly. It did not try to keep pace with its customers' increased expectations. This mindset will position a company for eventual failure.

To maintain satisfaction while transforming visitors into partners, companies must know their customers well enough to see them evolving and be willing and able to evolve with them. They must keep in mind that customer satisfaction grows out of a supply chain's focus on the ultimate consumer and that all customers must become partners.

Understand and Implement Elements of Customer Satisfaction

Because customer satisfaction is a scientific process, it has specific elements that define it. These elements are grouped into three categories: pre-transaction, transaction, and post-transaction, as shown in the accompanying sidebar, "Elements of Customer Satisfaction."

A supply chain is on the path to customer satisfaction when it offers these elements. Their presence indicates that a supply chain believes that demassification of a product, rather than mass production, will be the driver of exemplary customer satisfaction. The customer becomes the co-creator of value, and ongoing customer dialogue becomes the norm. Why? Because it is good business to treat customers as individuals rather than as numbers.

To increase levels of customer satisfaction, the supply chain must ask: Who is the customer?

What does the customer want? How do we increase customer satisfaction? Without answers to these questions, the chain cannot focus on the ultimate customer, or end user.

However, these questions are not as easy to answer as they

The Elements of Customer Satisfaction

The elements that comprise customer satisfaction are organized into three separate categories, based on when they occur during the buyer-seller relationship. As listed below, these categories are classified as pre-transaction, transaction, and post-transaction.

Pre-transaction elements

Knowledge of availability

Quality sales representation

Monitored stock levels

New product and package development

Target delivery date communication

Regular review of product depth and breadth

Transaction elements

Ordering convenience	Question handling
Credit terms offered	Order cycle time and reliability
Delivery frequency	Order status information
On-time deliveries	Fill rate percentage
Order tracking capabilities	Back order percentages
Shipment shortage	Ability to handle emergency
Product substitutions	orders
Order acknowledgement	

Post-transaction elements

Invoice accuracy	Returns and adjustments
Well-stacked loads	Easy-to-read packaging
Quality of packaging	

---

might seem. It is not unusual for companies that comprise a supply chain to disagree over who the customer is. For example, is a brewery's customer the beer distributor, the retailer of the beer, or the customer who drinks the beer? Is a pharmaceutical company's customer the wholesaler of their drugs, the doctor that prescribes the drugs, the pharmacist, or the patient who needs the drugs? What about a baby food manufacturer? Is its customer the wholesaler, the retailer, the father, the mother, or the baby?

Often, a plan for providing customer satisfaction becomes mired in the various answers to this question. The companies discussing their customers need to understand that everyone in the supply chain—distributor, wholesaler, retailer, purchaser—represents customers. Each and every one of these customers has needs that must be met and exceeded. When that occurs, then the end user, the individual who buys the original product, is satisfied.

Once organizations have established who their customers are, they begin to ask what their customers want. Recently, the trend has been to believe that independent of a product's quality, the key to giving customers what they want lies in behavior and looks. Over the last two or three decades, companies have told their employees that customers want to be treated with a smile, empathy, and solutions to their complaints. But, upon reflection, shouldn't a company or organization provide a quality product delivered how and when the customer wants it so that there are no complaints?

Work with Supply Chain Partners Toward Customer Satisfaction Goals

The answer to the question, "How do we increase customer satisfaction?" is a straightforward one. A supply chain must adopt a culture of customer satisfaction based on a shared, consistent direction through the Six Levels of Supply Chain Excellence and an attitude of progressive, continuous improvement and learning. The customer satisfaction culture within a successful supply chain involves four basic steps:

- Reducing costs
- Increasing product quality
- Promoting teamwork
- Responding efficiently to customer needs

A supply chain can easily follow these steps. It can reduce costs by scrutinizing transportation, acquisition, distribution, inventory, reverse logistics, packaging, and manufacturing costs, and it can look all along the supply chain for ways to reduce costs significantly while increasing profitability. This could include simplifying and blurring the processes of manufacturing and distribution, reducing scrap and rework, and eliminating inefficient operations and delays.

Traditionally, manufacturing has done all the work and warehouses have simply stored the product. Blurring the boundaries between manufacturing and warehousing moves value-added activities closer to the customer. Also, organizations should eliminate double handling of product, increase customer responsiveness, and add more value to SKUs throughout the pipeline.

The partners in a supply chain can increase quality by encouraging the employees of every organization along the supply chain to adopt a continuous quality improvement process and to go beyond "doing it right the first time" to "doing it better every time." They can establish standards and implement process controls at all levels to achieve these standards, and can ship orders accurately without stockouts. They must reject the various quality crusades and the quality hype of the last several decades and work to understand that quality is more than just conformance to customer requirements. They must also be totally committed to complete customer satisfaction.

Teamwork between supply chain partners can be accomplished through improved planning, scheduling, and cooperative team-based improvement efforts. Organizations should ask themselves:

- What do we produce?
- Where do we get the materials to produce it?
- How do we receive the materials to produce it?
- How much do we produce?

- How do we store it?
- How do we package, label, and ship it?
- When do we ship it?
- Where do we ship it?

Interestingly, no one function, department, or company can answer these questions without help from others. It does not matter if a company is a factory that produces parts and then assembles them, or if it has deverticalized to become a virtual factory that outsources non-core competencies. Customer satisfaction increases come through teamwork. There must be a positive relationship between internal and external functions. Collaboration and cooperation must exist—with suppliers, within organizations, and with customers. Within the organization, this combination of collaboration and cooperation is called teamwork; within the supply chain, partnership.

A supply chain can respond to customer needs by reducing cycle times, increasing flexibility, and making sure that customers in trouble receive the assistance they need. One way to accomplish this is to implement postponement, either by delaying a product's customization or by relying on merge-in-transit.

An example of the former is an apparel manufacturer that produces the same dress for seven different distributors. When the supply chain partners cooperate, the warehouses receive the one dress, generic thus far, and place labels and tags on it as called for by the specific requirements of the customers. The manufacturer can concentrate on making the apparel and not tie up resources performing operations that the warehouses can do later.

Merge-in-transit is a manufacturing process used frequently in the computer industry. Components are received in the warehouse from various original equipment manufacturers (OEMs) and contract electronics manufacturers (CEMs): a keyboard from A, a CPU shell from B, a mouse from C, a hard drive from D, and so forth. Kitting and packing occur at the warehouse, based on customer specifications.

With postponement, manufacturers have fewer inventories to control, warehouses take an active role in the supply chain (unlike the traditional perception of them as a cost center), and customers receive what they want.

Practice Customer Satisfaction Synergy

Customer satisfaction synergy is the ultimate focus of supply chain partners, with both material and information flowing in a true, top-down progression that begins with the customer. The synergy is both broad and holistic. Individualism is not part of this perspective. Business systems are integrated. Products are not being delayed on the dock because no one knows what is in the container. No one is re-entering information that has already been entered by the shipping company. Instead, the partners use automatically received advanced shipment notices (ASNs), crossdocking, and vendor-managed inventory. There are no surprises because everyone is focused on the integration of the process for the total good: the satisfaction of the ultimate customer.

How is such synergy achieved? Through pursuing the journey of the Six Levels of Supply Chain Excellence. At each level, the stage is set so that partners are synergized and energized. Boundaries cease to exist. All the people involved see themselves as part of one huge team working to increase customer satisfaction.

Communicate with Appropriate Levels of Technology

In each phase of increasing customer satisfaction, communication is a key. When a company, either virtual or vertical, sets out to integrate business processes and disparate entities, it is vital that everyone communicate.

Today, numerous and varied options for communicating openly are available—from direct links to virtual private networks (VPNs), which transport data over secure Internet channels as if they were private lines. A wide range of information systems is available for strategic, tactical, and technical purposes. However, this technology is useless unless it is used to create simultaneous, instantaneous, and multi-directional communications that allow everyone involved to work at the same time rather than sequentially. This practice eliminates inventory buffers and accelerates the flow of cash. It also allows for dynamic planning, which replaces the outdated practices of long-term forecasting. It makes strategic information available to all partners so that everyone has contact with the customer and is aware of changing needs and trends.

The means of communication is not really important, although the Internet does make these types of communications easier. What is important is using technology to foster teamwork so that everyone along the supply chain communicates to achieve success. This goal is most easily attained by applying the technologies that enable the Six Levels of Supply Chain Excellence. To move up from Level 1, companies need technology solutions that allow the company to begin seeing itself as one entity instead of a group of loosely connected fiefdoms trying to outdo one another. The technology focus at Level 2 is mainly company-wide communication, with some emphasis on planning at the inventory level. At Level 3, commitment to the technology that makes internal information available not only within the company, but also to select supply chain partners, is critical. The focus of the technology at Level 4 is supply chain systems integration (as opposed to internal systems integration) with a view to sharing knowledge and building strong relationships with supply chain partners. Level 5 technology helps smooth the supply chain into an entity without silos, links, and boundaries. Since velocity is synthesis at the speed of light, the focus of the technology for Level 6 is speeding synthesis and keeping it nimble.

While the proper application of technology plays a significant role in promoting communication, it will not achieve customer satisfaction alone. The company leadership must be committed to open, honest, and clear exchanges, and must demonstrate this commitment. The partners can then respond in kind, and when this happens the whole supply chain wins.

CHAPTER 3
Partnerships and the Supply Chain

James A. Tompkins, Ph.D., President, Tompkins Associates

Partnerships are everywhere. The Internet, regulatory approval, deverticalization, and global competition are driving an explosion of partnerships worldwide. Many recent partnerships were formed between major corporations to create online trade exchanges, covering all business sectors, including automakers, biotech companies, retailers, and software makers.

A small percentage of these partnerships are succeeding. Many more are failing, especially the trade exchanges, often referred to as business-to-business (B2B) e-marketplaces. Market researchers at International Data Corp. in Framingham, Massachusetts, estimated that less than 20% of all exchanges were successful. Some of these failed marketplace partnerships were based on a communication system with all the information technology (IT) bells and whistles, created simply to satisfy the need to exploit the Internet and World Wide Web, and not with any real plan or idea of what they wanted to accomplish with their partners.

The underlying truth about why these partnerships failed and why more will fail is that they use technology and communications to foster *traditional* supplier/customer (manufacturer/wholesaler/retailer) relationships. The same has been said about efficient consumer response (ECR).[1] These relationships are not true partnerships.

True partnerships are formed within companies along the supply chain to achieve Supply Chain Excellence. As discussed in Chapter 1, Supply Chain Excellence has six levels. Briefly, they are:

Level 1 – Business as Usual. At this level, a company works hard to maximize its individual functions. The goal of individual departments is to be the best department in the company.

Level 2 – Link Excellence. To achieve Link Excellence, an organization must look within itself, eliminate any boundaries between departments and facilities, and begin a never-ending journey of continuous improvement. Its individual link must be evolved to make it the most efficient, effective, responsive, and holistic that it can possibly be.

Level 3 –Visibility. Visibility establishes the groundwork for information sharing. It minimizes supply chain surprises because it provides the information links needed to understand ongoing supply chain processes.

Level 4 – Collaboration. Collaboration is achieved through the proper application of technology and true partnerships. Through collaboration, the supply chain can determine how best to meet the demands of the marketplace. The supply chain works as a whole to maximize customer satisfaction while minimizing inventories.

Level 5 – Synthesis. Supply Chain Synthesis (SCS) is a continuous improvement process that integrates and unifies a supply chain. Synthesis harnesses the energy of change to address a turbulent marketplace and ensure customer satisfaction. It is from synthesis that true Supply Chain Excellence is achieved because it enables a supply chain to reach unparalleled levels of performance.

Level 6 – Velocity. After synthesis, the goal becomes accelerating the organization or supply chain to a higher velocity. The term velocity is used to indicate the ongoing acceleration of Supply Chain Excellence.

True partnerships have critical roles in Levels 2 through 6. Without true partnerships between departments, Link Excellence is nothing more than a pipe dream. The sharing of information necessary for Visibility means eliminating adversarial customer/supplier relationships. Collaboration is not possible without true partnerships. Synthesis and Velocity also require true partnerships. They are necessary for ensuring customer satisfaction from the original raw material provider to the ultimate, finished-product consumer, and they use IT capabilities wisely, rather than blindly, to ensure quality communications.

Best Practices and Strategies for True Partnerships

This chapter discusses the Six Strategies for Partnership Success. Representing current best practices, the strategies are: 1) Identify true partnerships, 2) Analyze true partnership requirements, 3) Create the true partnership, 4) Overcome partnership pitfalls, 5) Apply the success elements of an ongoing true partnership, and 6) Integrate true partnerships with Supply Chain Synthesis (SCS).

Identifying True Partnerships

To understand true partnerships, keep in mind:

- When similar companies in the same kind of business band together to pool their resources to conduct research, evaluate technology, or lobby for a political position, they have not created a partnership. They have created a *consortium.*
- When companies lose their independence and become one corporate entity, it is not a partnership. It is an *acquisition* or *merger.*
- When companies work together to pursue a specific, single-focused business objective, this activity is not a partnership. It is a *strategic alliance.*
- When two companies form a separate entity with joint ownership to pursue a specific business objective, they have a *joint venture,* not a partnership.
- A long-term relationship based upon trust and a mutual desire to work together for the benefit of the other partner and the partnership is a true partnership.

Thus, it takes two committed organizations to have a true partnership. Each true partnership requires a supplier and a customer who are both ready for partnership. As stated above, true partners invest in the long-term partner relationship that is based on trust and a mutual desire to work together for the benefit of the other partner and the partnership. There are no boundaries separating their abilities to share information and requirements. Both organizations in the partnership are independent, so each retains its own identity to ensure maximum innovation and creativity.

Characteristics of a True Partnership

Having defined a true partnership in general terms, we now look at its specific characteristics:

- The partners reject and resist the mindset that business relationships are based upon antagonism, leveraging, hammering, and negotiating.
- They are committed to long-term relationships based on trust and a true understanding of their partners' businesses.
- They believe in sharing of information, planning, scheduling, risks, rewards, problems, solutions, and opportunities.
- They believe in working together toward improvements in quality, lead times, new product development time, inventory accuracy and management, and cost control.
- Partners believe in building on each other's strengths, increasing each partner's business, and investing in the long-term partnership relationship. Because of this commitment, the partners will deal with fewer and fewer suppliers.
- They believe in systems integration and the interdependence of their organizations while still retaining their individual identities, thus promoting innovation and creativity.
- They believe in involving each other early in any new innovations and working with each other with the utmost flexibility to ensure the best overall performance of the partnership.

Analyzing Partnership Requirements

The core ingredients for a true partnership are: 1) CEO commitment and leadership, 2) a success/success mindset, and 3) a team-based structure.

CEO Commitment

Only a CEO has the power to commit the resources to form partnerships and to break down the barriers to acceptance. CEOs must foster climates that allow organizations to define their relationships with suppliers and customers in new and creative ways.

The CEO and the organization's executive management must make decisions that support the philosophy of continuous improvement, and they must communicate this philosophy throughout the organization as well as outside it. Choices made based on the bottom line alone send a clear message that, while the company says it wants cultural change and partnerships, in reality it is conducting business as usual. Too often, leadership gives its commitment, only to be distracted by other, short-term issues. When leadership focuses elsewhere, the partnership initiative often founders.

Another cause of partnering initiative failure is the tendency of leadership to proceed before the organization is ready. Frequently, once the initiative is identified, leaders want to charge forward and make immediate improvements. They want to launch an intense effort before everyone understands the initiative and becomes aligned with it. Leadership optimistically expects committed employees and committed suppliers to follow.

A better approach develops a strong consensus and the necessary supporting structure at the top before beginning the improvement effort. Senior leadership needs to spend time off-site working through the issues. This approach allows discussion of all concerns until there is near-total acceptance of the initiative, scope of actions, necessary cultural changes, rewards and recognition, supporting systems, and the process of implementing the mission statement.

Succeed/Succeed Mindset

A true partnership requires developing a succeed/succeed mindset. A succeed/fail (or win/lose) mindset has historically held partnerships back. Those that have this mindset believe that if someone else succeeds, then they fail, and so they do not cooperate with others. They view their partners as opponents, not allies. In a succeed/succeed partnering mindset, the supplier is totally focused on helping its customer achieve success, because the supplier believes that is the only way for both to truly succeed. Powerful relationships develop because suppliers and customers are focused on making each other successful.

Team-Based Structure

Each organization in a true partnership must develop an internal team-based structure, and then take it outside the organization. In fact, the partnering process can be thought of as the application of team-based development between organizations. The teams that consist of members from all organizations involved in the partnership develop their own identity, and the identities of suppliers/customers become blurred. Eventually, the supplier/customer distinctions disappear and the partners act as one to improve, grow, and prosper, while still maintaining their own corporate identities.

Organizations with this structure respond more quickly to change, and thus are truly able to collaborate to deliver quality and customer satisfaction at a lower cost. Team-based organizations make true partners because they are better equipped to respond to strategic opportunities.

Creating True Partnerships

A true partnership satisfies the requirements described above. It is the successful application of the collaboration process between organizations. This process takes time and requires a great deal of communication and work. The first step toward creating a partnership is moving as a "customer-driven" organization. The next step is creating invincible customer satisfaction. To move beyond the initial stages of a relationship, the partners must step up their commitments to one another. The ultimate commitment is a true partnership.

Striving to create long-term partnerships means first understanding that the term "relationship" is not synonymous with partnership. Growing a relationship into a partnership, and ultimately into an SCS partnership, means realizing that:

- No two relationships develop the same way.
- Relationships evolve as comfortable bonds between individuals.
- A positive chemistry must exist between two parties to create a relationship.
- Partnerships evolve from understanding hopes, dreams, and the anticipation of a bright future.
- All parties must know themselves and understand what they are seeking from the partnership.
- Acceptance by indirectly involved parties (e.g., stockholders, government agencies) is as important to the perpetuation of the partnership as acceptance by directly affected parties.
- The relationship, at its core, has an interest in the well-being of each party as well as the well-being of the partnership.
- Expectations of how the relationship will develop must be articulated.
- Compatibility is key to a long-term relationship.

Who Should Partner?

Identifying potential true partners should be based on the opportunity for additional contribution to profit over a five-year planning horizon. This measure applies to both a customer looking at its suppliers and a supplier looking at its customers. The focus should be on building trust, then communicating clearly, and finally, creating top level performance. This process involves continuous improvement and preparing for future challenges with a win-only attitude. As these relationships continue, the escalation of trust, openness, and success will naturally lead to the sharing of Models of Success and strategic business plans. (Models of Success are defined in the accompanying sidebar, "Models of Success—Properties and Elements.")

Part of the partnership process is chartering a Partnership Initiative Team. The purpose of this cross-functional team is to establish an official collaborative relationship,

Models of Success—Properties and Elements

In a true partnership, the escalation of trust, openness, and success will naturally lead to the sharing of Models of Success and strategic business plans. A joint Model of Success can be developed for forming compatible cultures that still retain the personality of each organization. The properties and elements of a Model of Success are as follows.

A Model of Success has seven special properties:

1. It is appropriate for the organization and for the times.
2. It sets standards of excellence and reflects high ideals.
3. It clarifies purpose and direction.
4. It inspires enthusiasm and encourages commitment.
5. It is well articulated and easily understood.
6. It reflects the uniqueness of the organization.
7. It is ambitious.

A Model of Success also defines five elements:

1. Vision—a description of where an organization is headed.
2. Mission—how to accomplish the Vision.
3. Requirements of Success—the science of an organization's business.
4. Guiding Principles—the values an organization practices as it pursues its Vision.
5. Evidence of Success—Measurable results that will demonstrate when an organization is moving toward its Vision.

determine the objectives of the partnership, and develop a mutual plan for the partnership. As a result of this effort, the identity of suppliers and customers becomes blurred until they have no boundaries—first individuals, and then teams, and then entire companies will be true partners. Without boundaries, the partners will act as a whole to improve, grow, and prosper, while maintaining their own corporate identities.

Overcoming Partnership Pitfalls

Because a partnership is a significant investment of time, money, and reputation, much is at stake. Forming a true partnership requires that traditional relationships between organizations be discarded. In these traditional, "arm's length" relationships, limited communication flows vertically within each company. "Horizontal" communication between two companies occurs only at the level of sales staff and buyers. Even then, the focus of this communication is usually on problems, not their causes and solutions, nor does it address continuous improvement. These factors contribute to extended lead times, higher operating costs, and relationships that ignore a supplier's creativity.

Applying the Success Elements of Ongoing Partnerships

The road to overcoming partnership pitfalls is built on three key elements: 1) trust, 2) communication, and 3) assimilating organizational and cultural change.

Trust is the key ingredient in a partnership; from trust, relationships grow. Without trust, there is no partnership. However, creating trust between partners takes time and happens only as a result of many positive interactions. Trust then progresses to respect, and respect fosters the willingness to listen. From this listening comes understanding, concern, participation, and finally open communications. The most important thing to remember about trust is that it does not occur between companies, but between people. Therefore, partnerships are not really about companies, but about people, and those people must be committed to making a partnering relationship work.

When employees are viewed as people who are part of the whole process, when previously proprietary information is shared, and when everyone shares the benefits of success, then employees develop trust in the organization and the cycle of success continues. When this kind of trust is developed within an organization, employees become better prepared to apply such trust to what had formerly been antagonistic relationships with customers and suppliers. This transformation represents culture change.

Communication is also a key factor in the success of partnering efforts. Today's technology makes possible an instantaneous, continuous flow of information within and between organizations. Care must be taken not to place too much emphasis on the technology, at the expense of human interaction. It is important to have frequent, planned, face-to-face interactions within the company and between partners. There have to be specific "point-of-contact" individuals at each company who are committed to keeping the lines of communication open and are prepared to anticipate potential problems.

Assimilating organizational and cultural change is the biggest challenge in creating true partnerships. It requires overcoming the paradigms that are the byproducts of organizational culture. Culture is a key component of establishing true partnerships, and must be understood and developed to achieve the desired results. Overcoming a traditional culture that takes the existing view of partnerships requires: 1) motivational leadership, 2) a cultural revolution, and 3) alignment.

Motivational Leadership

Motivational leaders create the environment necessary for a true partnership. They seek out other motivational leaders among their supply chain partners and share skills and knowledge. They also recognize that instantaneous dissemination of information among partners is critical to the success of Supply Chain Synthesis. Although motivational leadership is not a set of traits, these leaders do have the following characteristics:

- Integrity—the leader lives and tells the truth.
- Credibility—the leader is accountable, genuine, and open.
- Enthusiasm—the leader shows excitement about the future.
- Optimism—the leader focuses on success.
- Urgency—the leader knows that the only way to impact the future is to act today.
- Determination—the leader steps forward to face doubts and uncertainties, accept risk, move forward, and make real the understanding that there are no boundaries between the organization itself and the activities it must perform to ensure competitive advantage. Leaders act.

Relying on these characteristics, leaders motivate others by the way they communicate, work, and treat others. Leaders recognize the importance of effective communication. They arm people with the certainty and control that allows those individuals to harness the energy of change through direct communication and the sharing of information. When leaders make decisions, they adhere to the "three rights": the *right* decisions at the *right* time communicated to the *right* people. They enjoy their work. Finally, leaders treat others in the way that others want to be treated.

Cultural Revolution

Culture is the personality of an organization. Any attempt to change merely the inanimate portions of the supply chain—facilities, equipment, and transportation—will fail. Changes must also occur with the people involved and how they interact with one another. Revolutionizing a culture is no simple task, for an organization's existing culture will try to stifle the introduction of a new one. Those charged with the process of revolutionizing a culture must transform the rules, habits, procedures, standards, norms, rewards, language, jargon, stories, expectations, ceremonies, and titles that affect cultural conformance, organizational behavior, and organizational performance. The foundation for this revolution is a shared, consistent vision of where the organization is headed.

Alignment

In a true partnership, everyone must be aligned with a commitment to dynamic consistency, the underlying basis of which is "improve, improve, improve." If the true partnership is one between departments in an organization, what is needed is a Business Process Continuous Improvement (BPCI) philosophy. If it is one between organizations along the supply chain, what is needed is a Supply Chain Synthesis (SCS) philosophy.

BPCI is a leadership-driven process of collaboration that uses teams and a shared Model of Success to change company culture and operating style. Organizational teams are created across job functions, product classes, and organizations to consolidate, integrate, and share organizational responsibilities. These teams collaborate and create synergy to improve business processes continuously. The essence of the process is a definition of how the company functions. Once BPCI is used within one organization to achieve cultural change, companies may use it to develop a joint Model of Success for forming compatible cultures that still retain the personality of each organization.

An organization achieves alignment when it can accomplish the following:

- Connect its employees' behavior to the mission of the company, turning intentions into actions
- Link teams and processes to the changing needs of customers
- Shape business strategy with real-time information from customers
- Create a culture in which these elements all work together seamlessly

Integrating True Partnerships with Supply Chain Synthesis

Supply Chain Synthesis (SCS) takes the same alignment principles described above for a single organization, but applies them to an extra-organizational collaboration among supply chain partners. SCS is a holistic, continuous improvement process of ensuring customer satisfaction along the entire chain, from the original raw material provider to the ultimate, finished-product consumer. The seamless, "No Boundaries" connection between the raw materials producer and the ultimate customer is the essence of SCS. SCS is holistic because it is concerned with a complete chain, rather than with one link. It is a continuous improvement process that is infinite; it never stops. SCS melts the links in the supply chain into a smooth, continuous flow. Visualize a river, properly banked and channeled, that is flowing toward a goal and you are also visualizing SCS. A river has no links, and although thousands of separate, natural forces comprise it, it is seen as one entity.

An example of a true partnership is a recent alliance between Ford Motor Company and UPS in which the two partners overcame a compensation challenge. Ford and UPS Logistics Group, a subsidiary of UPS, were developing a system to reduce, by 50 percent, the time it takes for vehicles to move from the assembly line to the dealership. The effort included revamping Ford's network of road and rail carriers, and adding an information system to ease tracking of individual vehicles through a Website.

The challenge the partners faced was compensation—who would be paid for what tasks—and they came up with an innovative solution. Between 100 and 150 UPS employees and 30 and 50 Ford employees will manage the system together, and UPS will be compensated based on how it helps Ford meet speed and efficiency goals.[2] As more true partnerships are embraced in this millennium, such methods of overcoming challenges will become the norm.

A Necessary Bond

You cannot have SCS without true partnerships. As discussed above, true partnerships are based on the principle that sharing information openly, communicating requirements extensively, and involving alliances early in the process will provide competitive advantage and strength to an organization. SCS takes the concept of a true partnership and extends it beyond the organization to the supply chain. This extension increases the challenges discussed earlier, because managing relationships throughout an extended enterprise adds to the complexity of the endeavor.

True partnerships and SCS can be compared to the dates that lead to marriage. There's a meeting, then a date, then more dates. There is the time when both partners decide that they only want to date each other. If all goes well, there is an engagement and a wedding date is set. If the engagement is a success, then the wedding takes place. These steps all take time and have to be done right. Suppose you go to a bar tonight and someone who hasn't met you before asks, "Hey, want to get married?" Most likely you would think that person either wasn't serious or was crazy. If you accept the proposal, then both of you are crazy.

With SCS, the intimacy of a true partnership is among four or five partners who comprise the supply chain to be synthesized. These intimate partners are committed to the SCS process, have win/win mindsets, and have team-based structures in place. They have determined specific criteria for evaluating the partnership, as well as for evaluating potential new partners. They also know, as SCS partners, that they have a long-term relationship that must provide mutual benefit through open communication, continuous improvement, and a focus on the customer. They communicate with one another on the causes of problems, potential solutions, and achieving continuous improvement, rather than on the problems themselves. SCS partners also believe that the challenges they face—trust, communications, and culture—must be overcome to secure competitive advantage. Improved performance of the TOTAL supply chain is necessary through partnerships. The keys to partnership success are integration, information, and interaction, and it is important to benchmark partnership activity to achieve continuous improvement.

Successful SCS partnering requires alignment around shared goals. Then, building on the assumption that intra-organizational alignment has been achieved, the next step is to ensure that this spirit of cooperation and collaboration is extended throughout the supply chain. The supply chain culture must nurture SCS through teaming, true partnerships, and the proper use of the Internet and other technologies.

Works Consulted

1 Tompkins, James A., *Revolution: Take Charge Strategies for Business Success.* Raleigh, N.C.: Tompkins Press, p. 247, 1998

2 Tompkins, James A., Ph.D., *No Boundaries: Moving Beyond Supply Chain Management.* Raleigh, N.C., Tompkins Press, pp. 153-154, 2000.

CHAPTER 4
Global Supply Chains

Paul S. Bender, President, P S Bender & Company, LLC

Businesses everywhere are confronting the consequences of accelerating change brought about by two forces: a technologic revolution and globalization. This chapter focuses on the impact of globalization on the supply chain, and outlines some basic concepts required to successfully manage a supply chain in an international business environment. The topics are covered from an American perspective, but most of the issues presented apply everywhere.

The "business environment" provides a general conceptual foundation for this chapter; it outlines the fundamental principles that characterize domestic and international management; it explains the globalization process that underpins global supply chains; it outlines cultural and political considerations important in international management; and it offers guidance on multi-cultural management.

The Business Environment

It is useful to describe a business environment anywhere as composed of two elements that surround an enterprise, offering opportunities and imposing restrictions on its actions. These are the macroenvironment and the microenvironment.

The Macroenvironment

The macroenvironment includes the major long-term trends that affect business in general and an enterprise in particular and their consequences. These are demographic, economic, technological, political, and social trends. These trends and consequences are the background for strategy, and differ significantly from region to region.

Demographic trends are the foundation of business because they determine the location and characteristics of demand and of labor. There are countries with declining populations (e.g., Germany, Italy); others, where the population is stable, (e.g., Japan, China); and others, where the population is increasing (e.g., India, Brazil, Nigeria). Those differences imply substantial long-term re-alignments in the world's geographic dispersion of demand and in the location of labor pools. Another important demographic trend is age distribution. Young populations, such as those in Latin America, Southeast Asia, and Africa provide a larger proportion of active people than older populations, such as that of Japan. This impacts the type and level of demands in those economies and the tax burdens required to support an aging population. Finally, the trend toward major migrations—for example, from Africa into Europe, from Eastern Europe into Western Europe, and from Latin America and Asia into the United States—is having an important effect on the demographic and social characteristics of those regions.

Economic trends affect the structure of business. The most important economic trend today is globalization, a trend toward a worldwide economy. Another important economic trend is that most national economies are market-driven, although to different degrees and in different ways. These trends are changing drastically the characteristics of competition in every market. Long-term economic projections indicate that these trends will accelerate in the decades to come.

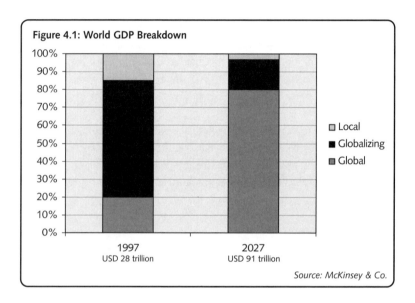

Figure 4.1: World GDP Breakdown

Source: McKinsey & Co.

Technological trends determine the characteristics of business enablers, and increasingly, are the underpinning of business models and business management. Information technology is the critical business technology today. It is changing radically the nature of products and processes, distribution channels, and demand characteristics. In this regard, we consider Internet-based and wireless business applications to be the main source of the current business revolution.

Political trends provide a framework for business by defining the conditions and restrictions under which businesses must operate. The most important political trend is that toward supra-national interdependence, with international organizations (e.g., World Trade Organization, Asean, European Union, Mercosur, NAFTA) acquiring an increasing role in regulating business affairs.

Social trends influence all aspects of business; especially demand characteristics, organizational structures, and business relationships. Cultures determine, to a large extent, what can and cannot be done in a particular country or region, regardless of technical feasibility or economic desirability. One of the most important social trends today is democratization in all organizations.

The Microenvironment

The microenvironment around an enterprise includes customers, prospects, competitors, suppliers, partners, and regulators. The interactions with those parties determine strategic, tactical, and operational issues that we outlined later in this chapter.

Domestic and Global Management

To succeed in the business environment of today and tomorrow, it is necessary to adopt a global perspective on business strategy. Even to compete in a small region within a country, it is necessary to have a global strategy defining where and how to source the products to offer there. Otherwise, a company may be unable to compete in its own traditional region with companies implementing a global strategy there. In adopting a global perspective, it is important to understand that local requirements and characteristics must be considered and respected to perform successfully. As a rule, the more strategic the problem, the more global the solution required; the more operational the problem, the more local the solution required. For these reasons, this chapter focuses on global strategic (and some tactical) issues, while providing a more localized approach to operational issues.

The Globalization Process

The globalization process is the worldwide integration and coordination of economic activities supported by global communications, a global financial system, and global logistics services. This process is the consequence of advances in information technology, such as the Internet and wireless communications, and in logistics methodology, such as just-in-time operations. Ongoing deregulation and privatization of economic activities in most countries, the existence of a global financial system, and the emergence of a worldwide market economy compound the effects of those advances. The result is a worldwide decoupling of procurement, production, distribution, and consumption of goods in space and time.

Economic globalization is transforming business and, therefore, supply chains—strategically, tactically, and operationally. It is important to understand the strategic reasons for globalization:

- *Profit from market economies.* Most economic activity in the world takes place in countries that have adopted some form of market economy. This presents excellent opportunities for companies to expand worldwide, reaching new markets that provide additional economies, and to diversify their risks geographically.
- *Confront shrinking product and process lives.* As technology shrinks the useful lives of products and processes, it is necessary for companies to reach the largest possible market to amortize their development and procurement costs as fast as possible. Global reach provides the means for selling products in the largest market available.
- *Deny sanctuary to competitors.* When an enterprise confronts competitors operating in countries where it does not operate, it provides them sanctuary there. Competitors

can sell their products in their exclusive countries at a high profit, and legally subsidize sales at a low profit in the countries where they compete against local enterprises.

- *Bypass protectionism.* In countries pursuing protectionist policies, local companies are protected from foreign competition by import tariffs. Participating in the economies of such countries can bypass their protectionism.
- *Profit from global financial systems.* Financial systems have been operating globally for decades; therefore, it is possible for companies to obtain financial support from major financial institutions worldwide and lower their financial costs.
- *Profit from global communications and media.* Worldwide communications and media are homogenizing demands for goods and services. This makes it increasingly efficient to offer similar or the same products, through similar or the same processes worldwide, thus obtaining economies of scope.
- *Establish early presence in future markets.* Many developing markets may not be large enough to support profitable current sales; however, progressive companies establish a local presence in those markets ahead of their profit threshold to preempt future competitors.
- *Profit from location economies and efficiencies.* Different countries and regions offer very different financial incentives for the location of economic activities, such as those in production and logistics facilities; these can make a substantial difference in a company's profits. Furthermore, labor costs vary significantly across the world. This is illustrated in Table 4.1 where the dimensionless index represents the ratio between a country's labor hourly rates in manufacturing and their equivalents in the United States.

The tactical reasons for globalization include:

- *Obtain cyclical and seasonal diversification.* Operating in many different national economies that are likely to be at different phases in their economic cycles and different seasons in different hemispheres, provides excellent opportunities for diversification, thus spreading a company's risk.

Table 4.1: Comparative International Labor Hourly Rates in Manufacturing (1998)

Country	Index
United States	100
Canada	85
Mexico	10
Australia	80
Hong Kong	29
Israel	65
Japan	97
South Korea	27
Singapore	42
Sri Lanka	3
Taiwan	28
Belgium	125
Finland	116
France	98
Germany	147
Ireland	72
Italy	92
Netherlands	111
Spain	65
United Kingdom	89

Source: U.S. Department of Labor, Bureau of Labor Statistics (January 2000)

- *Extend economies of scale, scope and location.* Additional markets provide additional opportunities to obtain economies of scale, scope, and location when companies manage their businesses globally.
- *Maximize outsourcing opportunities.* Companies are finding outsourcing opportunities in an increasing number of countries, and using them substantially improves their profits.
- *Maximize benefits from transfer prices.* Companies can legally profit from significant differences in corporate tax rates in different countries by setting transfer prices to maximize their profits in countries with low tax rates and minimize their profits in countries with high tax rates. Such practices must be followed carefully to ensure full compliance with the laws of all countries involved.
- *Participate in counter-trade.* Many countries have limited foreign currency reserves and resort to counter-trade practices, such as bartering, to support their imports. This is a growing and potentially profitable type of business that requires specialized knowledge and experience on the part of its practitioners. These practices have a major impact on supply chain operations, because payments are obtained in kind, not in cash, and they must be delivered to other markets to obtain cash.
- *Profit from global trade growth.* Global trade—measured by global exports—is growing much faster than any single national economy. Between 1951 and 2000, global trade grew 2000% (or 6.2% per year, compounded) while the world economy grew 700% (or 4% per year, compounded). Also, global trade is growing at an accelerating rate, while the world economy is growing at a steady rate. These trends are likely to continue for the foreseeable future.

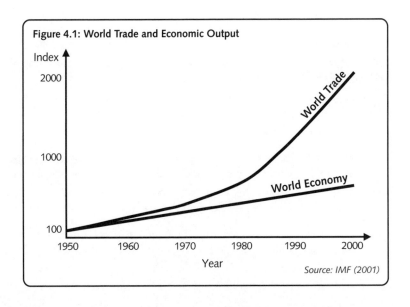

Figure 4.1: World Trade and Economic Output

Source: IMF (2001)

The operational reasons for globalization are:

- *Profit from arbitrage production and logistics capacities.* In general, companies have excess capacities at production and logistics facilities, even when they are downsizing. The reason is that capacity can only be increased or decreased in discrete increments. Thus, if excess capacities are located in countries with weaker currencies relative to the corporate currency, processing there becomes increasingly cheaper in the corporate currency; thus, corporate profits increase through long-term devaluations with respect to the corporate currency.
- *Improve customer satisfaction.* Worldwide presence enables companies to offer localized service from closer facilities. This results in better service that, in turn, increases sales.

Globalization: Advantages and Disadvantages

The process of "going global" has both advantages and disadvantages. Its main advantages are:

- Accelerated productivity when countries exploit their comparative advantages.
- Global inflation is kept low through competition.
- Open economies spur innovation and worldwide competition.
- Export-related jobs, which often pay more than other jobs.
- Low interest rates from worldwide free-flowing capital.

The disadvantages include:

- Jobs lost through company, facility, or process relocation offshore. Often workers are left with either lower paying jobs or no jobs at all. Service and white-collar jobs are increasingly vulnerable to movements offshore.
- Wages in rich countries are depressed by foreign competition. Workers in advanced countries lose their comparative advantage when companies build technically advanced facilities in low-wage countries. Some countries undergo forced re-structuring of entire economic sectors to remain competitive.
- Major changes in an enterprise's ownership and structure typically result in changes in internal vision, culture, and processes that may require people to change their work environment and habits.

Globalization is propelled by the simultaneous impacts of information technology, logistics support, and market economies. It is underpinned by an existing global financial system.

Information technology advances globalization in several ways:

- The Internet-based part of the economy is by definition global. All websites are accessible from any point in the world.
- The availability of instantaneous financial flows worldwide, in the form of electronic data, enables efficient global trade.

- The availability of instantaneous information worldwide, at low cost, enables efficient worldwide transaction processing, decision support, and customer service.
- Accelerating information technology advances shorten the useful lives of products and processes; their acquisition costs must be amortized very fast, on a world-market scale.

Logistics support advances globalization in several ways:

- International freight costs are mostly declining in real terms. Important exceptions are recent major increases in ocean transportation to and from China, and increasingly, to and from India. This situation is due to important increases in import and export volumes in those countries, and also to lack of adequate port facilities there, which results in ships having to wait for up to 30 days before loading or unloading. Since a typical ship lease costs about $100,000 per day, the impact on transportation rates is substantial.
- Worldwide, full-service logistics enterprises are emerging to confront global competition, to obtain economies of scale and scope, and to provide global services to existing customers.
- Logistics planning techniques enable worldwide, optimal facility, process, and inventory deployment and management.
- Efficient global logistics enables competitive worldwide outsourcing.

Market economies advance globalization through:

- Deregulation and privatization of logistics assets (e.g., postal services, railroads, airlines) enable the penetration of new markets by logistics operators that obtain economies of scale and scope.
- More flexible work rules create a global division of labor that fosters the decoupling of procurement, production, distribution, and consumption of goods. This results in an increasing need for global logistics support and in increasing global marketing opportunities.
- Worldwide homogenization of demand through worldwide media enables companies to sell the same or similar products, in a similar manner, in most countries, thus obtaining economies of scale and scope.

Globalization creates many issues that affect the management of global supply chains. They include governmental, marketing, financial, and operations issues.

Governmental issues affecting global supply chains include:

- Infrastructure development programs
- Regional financial incentives
- Legislation of labor, environmental, financial, and other issues
- Duties, tariffs, and drawbacks
- Regulation of vehicle sizes and weights
- Regulations affecting technical specifications of products and processes
- Regulations affecting international shipments' security

Marketing issues affecting global supply chains include:

- Customer satisfaction parameters and standards
- Marketing channels
- Pricing policies
- Packing, packaging, and labeling requirements
- Product features and product line extent
- Counter-trade
- Advertising and promotions
- Communications
- Languages
- Culture

Financial issues affecting global supply chains include:

- Financial incentives
- Fixed asset investment requirements
- Inventory investment requirements
- Taxes
- Monetary transfers
- Transfer prices
- Insurance
- Duties, tariffs, and drawbacks
- Exchange rates
- Inflation rates
- Financial transfers

Operations issues affecting global supply chains include:

- Inventory replenishment
- Facility and process deployment, capacity allocation, use, and arbitrage
- Demand allocation
- Vendor selection
- Outsourcing
- Port selection
- Border crossing selection
- Availability and quality of global logistics services
- Availability and condition of logistics infrastructure
- Availability and condition of communications infrastructure
- Security and protection of people, information, merchandise, facilities, equipment, and financial assets

Cultural and Political Considerations

Culture has been defined as the understandings that govern human interactions in a given society. It determines how people think, act, and relate. All those aspects have a major impact on local business practices and relationships.

Cultural differences vary from the superficial (e.g., greeting somebody is done in some cultures by shaking hands, while in other cultures, it is done by bowing) to the critical (most cultures include "taboos" or practices that are unacceptable). Awareness of cultural differences is of critical importance for anyone conducting international business—especially when selling. Some of the most important cultural differences to consider include:

- *Language.* In any international exchange, knowledge of the buyer's language makes an important difference in the quality and smoothness of the relationship. This applies even in large global corporations that have standardized English as their official world language.

- *Punctuality.* In the United States, Northern Europe, and Japan, punctuality is extremely important when transacting business. In other regions (e.g., some Latin, Arab, and African countries), it does not receive the same importance.

- *Information exchange.* In some cultures (e.g., France), written information exchanges are preferred to other forms; in others, (e.g., United States) oral communications are preferred.

- *Decision-making.* In some countries, decisions are typically made at the top of the organization (e.g., some Latin, Arab, and African countries), and are handed down for implementation with minimal or no discussion. In those cultures, an executive that consults subordinates may be perceived as weak and indecisive. In other cultures, (e.g., Japan, South Korea) collegial decision-making is the norm, and decisions made by one or a few people, are extremely difficult to implement.

- *Motivation.* In some countries, (e.g., United States) appealing to individual financial incentives typically results in strong cooperation, in other countries, (e.g., Japan, South Korea) appealing to group welfare works better.

- *Risk avoidance.* (i.e., the tendency to avoid highly risky alternatives in decision making). International sociological studies indicate that executives in some countries (e.g., Japan, South Korea, France) have been found to exhibit high levels of risk and uncertainty avoidance, while with executives of other countries (e.g., Singapore, United Kingdom, United States) the opposite is true.

- *Authority.* In some countries (e.g., some Latin, Arab, and African countries), an executive's authority may derive mostly from family or tribal ties, while in other countries (e.g., United States, Scandinavia, Germany) it derives mostly from position in the organization.

- *Graft.* In the United States, it is illegal to offer inducements to officials of any organization, anywhere in the world. In many other countries, there is a far more relaxed attitude toward such practices. This is an important consideration for American companies competing in foreign markets with non-American companies using such practices, frequently with the help of their governments.

In addition to cultural considerations, political considerations are critical in an international context. These include:

- *Labor relations.* Many American business practices, such as unionization and collective bargaining, are known and used in many other countries. However, even in those cases, there are important differences. For example, job security is an important issue in the United States, while in other countries it is critical: it may be almost impossible or extremely expensive to terminate an employee unless clear major cause is proven.
- *Government relations.* In the United States, lobbying is an important method of influencing legislation that affects industries or enterprises. In other countries, working together with the government may be indispensable for the success of an enterprise; for example, cooperating with government development plans for job creation, technology transfer, regional development, product content, local ownership, or management may spell the difference between success and failure in certain countries (e.g., China, Singapore, Malaysia).
- *Organization structure.* Generally, highly centralized organizations do not perform well in an international context because of the impact of cultural differences and local conditions. Although resource deployment and allocation may be centralized, the implementation of central decisions is usually best left to competent local managers.

Multi-Cultural Management Principles

Multi-cultural management is important to the success of an international business. However, it introduces significant complexity into the management process. Although this issue has many dimensions and ramifications, a few basic principles can provide the basis for an effective multi-cultural management approach:

- *Set a common language.* Among the most effective global companies are those that have standardized all communications internal to their enterprise in one single language, even when that is not the language of their country of origin. Typically English, a common language for internal communications worldwide, eliminates the time and cost of translations to different languages in different countries, and the consequences of faulty translations.
- *Establish common values.* Despite major cultural differences throughout an international organization, everyone in it must share some fundamental values that distinguish the enterprise and its relationships with customers, suppliers, and others. Foremost among these are the company's position regarding integrity and customer orientation. Other values may be needed to reflect the type of business the enterprise is in; for example, in consumer businesses, ensuring that customers get the highest value for their money may be of paramount importance.

- *Provide common basic skills.* For a company to operate internationally, its members must possess certain common basic skills for working in the "company way." Depending on the company and the regions in which it is active, these skills may range from oral and written communications in the corporate language to a specified level of proficiency in the use of computers and the Internet.
- *Foster frequent exchanges.* The best way to familiarize company members with the characteristics and needs of different regions is through employee exchange programs and exposure to other cultures. This may take the form of holding international meetings in different locations and personnel rotation among different regional offices.

The Global Supply Chain

The most important principle of successful global business management was stated by Akio Morita, Founder and ex-Chairman of Sony, as "Glocalization," or thinking and planning business on a global scale while operating at a local level.

Many of the problems encountered by companies doing business internationally derive from their lack of understanding of the heterogeneity of the world. They think, plan, and operate in "Europe" or "Asia" or "Latin America" or "Africa," not realizing that, from a business point of view, those regional distinctions are not relevant. What is relevant is the knowledge of different regional practices, within continents and within countries. Unless those differences are well understood, it is likely that major mistakes will be made assuming a uniformity of economic conditions or business practices that do not exist at all. We provide below some examples of such differences.

Europe

Within Europe, even within the European Union, countries differ widely, and within each country, there are also significant differences. Aside from major cultural differences, such as languages, local dialects, and traditions, there are specific economic differences, such as different levels of economic and technological development, and differences in standards of living. For example, there are significant differences in business tax rates among different European countries, as illustrated in Table 4.2.

Furthermore, shopping habits differ enormously within Europe and within each country. This translates into different demand characteristics for similar items in

Table 4.2: European Corporate Tax Rates (as of January 2001)

Country	Rate (%)
Austria	34.0
Belgium	40.2
Denmark	30.0
Finland	29.0
France	35.3
Germany	39.4
Greece	37.5
Ireland	20.0
Italy	40.3
Netherlands	35.0
Norway	28.0
Portugal	35.2
Spain	35.0
Sweden	28.0
Switzerland	24.7
United Kingdom	30.0

Source: European Commission (2001)

different countries and regions, as illustrated in Table 4.3.

Latin America

Within Latin America, there are major economic and cultural differences, not only among countries but also within countries. For example, in Brazil, the state of São Paulo has vastly different economic

Table 4.3: European Distribution Characteristics (for consumer goods, in 2000)

Country	Stores per 1000 People	No. of Delivery Points to Reach 95% of Market
Italy	4.8	70,000
Portugal	4.0	10,000
Spain	2.7	30,000
Belgium	1.6	600
France	1.0	300
United Kingdom	0.9	150
Germany	0.9	5,000

Source: Philippe-Pierre Dornier & Michel Fender: "La Logistique Globale"

and social characteristics than the states in Brazil's northeast or northwest; thus, doing business in São Paulo state is quite different than doing business in Amazonas, Bahia, or Mato Grosso. Similar examples can be provided for many other regions of the world.

Global Supply Chain Principles for Success

The global supply chain shares some features with the domestic supply chain. However, it also differs in important ways. We summarize below some basic principles that have proven successful in global supply chains.

- *Work with three-dimensional maps.* In continental operations, a flat, two-dimensional map of the earth is adequate for representing locations and transportation lanes. However, it is impossible to capture the characteristics of a global logistics network correctly in two dimensions. For example, in a two-dimensional map, Alaska appears at the extreme northern end of the world, in an isolated position; however, in a three-dimensional map, Alaska clearly shows up as the geographic center of air routes between North America, Europe, and East Asia.
- *Work with governments.* In most countries, the government not only establishes and polices the rules of business, but is also an active participant in the economy. For example, government ownership of railroads, airlines, banks, and industries makes it imperative that private companies engage in continuous, close relationships with those governments, beyond the lobbying activities typical in the United States.
- *Comply with multiple sets of regulations.* Working within any one country means respecting many, complex regulations. Working in many countries increases more than proportionally the number and complexity of regulations to respect. Being prepared to do so efficiently is important to smoothly operate a global supply chain.
- *Adopt the International System (IS) of measurements also known as Système International (SI).* As of 2004, of the approximately 190 countries represented in the United Nations, only three countries have not adopted the IS as their only official system of measurements: the Sultanate of Brunei, the Republic of Myanmar, and the United States of America. American companies are used to working with distances in miles,

dimensions in inches, weights in pounds, and temperatures in degrees Fahrenheit, for example. Outside the United States, those units are irrelevant, and frequently not understood. Even the way dates are abbreviated in the United States is different from the rest of the world; for example, 10 July 2004 is abbreviated 7/10/04 in the United States, but it is abbreviated 10.7.04 in Germany, and 04/07/10 in Japan, and similarly in the rest of the world. Thus, it is indispensable for American companies to train their people working in international business to use the International System (IS) of measurements and nomenclature, derived from the metric system. By the same token, it is indispensable for non-American companies to understand the measurement units and nomenclature used in the United States, to do business successfully in that country. Otherwise, communications are complicated, business opportunities may be lost, and many costly errors can arise.

- *Manage the impact of exchange rates.* Exchange rate fluctuations are typically the highest source of uncertainty in international business. Systematic hedging and the use of arbitrage in capacity deployment may benefit a company substantially.
- *Exploit inflation rate differences.* As different countries experience different inflation rates, costs in those countries grow at different rates, thereby affecting sourcing, outsourcing, and facility and process location decisions.
- *Manage the impact of taxes, duties, and drawbacks.* These are often the most important supply chain cost elements in an international business.
- *Manage the impact of transfer prices.* These are sometimes the most important sources of corporate profits in an international business.

In addition to the principles outlined above, it is important to understand some major strategic, tactical, and operational issues directly affecting the global supply chain.

Strategic Issues

- *Global vs. regional approach.* Strategy should always be developed globally, however, the best general approach is to centralize planning, control, and learning, while decentralizing execution.
- *Facility and process co-location.* A major issue in global supply chain design is how to optimally deploy facilities and, simultaneously, the processes within those facilities and any inventories needed to meet customer requirements while maximizing the benefits for the company.
- *Complementary organizations.* For a supply chain to function effectively, it is necessary for all the partners constituting the extended enterprise to structure their organizations in a complementary manner. Common processes should take place once, thus eliminating duplications that waste time and money.
- *Information technology impact.* As the Internet restructures national economies and economic sectors, it is also affecting supply chains. Exploiting Internet advantages efficiently is likely to result in the replacement of the supply chain concept by a more efficient one. We are beginning to see the emergence of global enterprises that do not rely on an integrator—as supply chains do—to organize and coordinate an extended

enterprise. Virtual enterprises self-organize dynamically by letting market forces restructure them through the Internet. They coordinate their common activities mainly through real time, Internet-based data and information exchanges.

- *Information sharing.* Sharing information and sometimes knowledge among partners, is a major feature of supply chains, enabling them to function smoothly. How to ensure that common processes work well, while protecting vital information and other resources, is a key strategic decision. It is especially important in global supply chains, where many partners have had short acquaintances and may have vastly different levels of informational sophistication.

- *Outsourcing.* Outsourcing non-core processes is a common characteristic of today's supply chains. Global supply chains add an important dimension to outsourcing by maximizing the opportunities for location economies and facilitating entry into new markets through the right outsourcing partners.

- *Security and protection.* Increasing international political volatility and especially terrorism, demand that international strategies include specific elements to protect from and mitigate the impact of those developments. An important cost in international business is that of protecting all the resources of the company: people, information, goods, facilities, equipment, and financial assets.

Tactical Issues

- *Resource allocation scope.* Resource allocation is the basic tactical decision in any enterprise. In a global supply chain there is the additional question of whether to allocate company resources to satisfy customers' demands on a global, centralized basis; or on a regional, decentralized basis. Important criteria for evaluating this issue are the commonality of products across regions, transportation times, logistics costs, and customer service requirements.

- *Design for postponement.* This is a fundamental approach that minimizes the proliferation of items in a global supply chain and optimizes process deployment. It is based on the design of products and processes so that products can be finished close to their demand locations, at minimum cost. In this manner, economies of scale are obtained by producing most of a product in a few production facilities, while local customization can be completed economically in logistics facilities.

- *Packaging and labeling.* These are simple issues in a domestic supply chain, but they become important in the global context. Different regulations, contents, and languages mean that unless packaging and labeling are handled efficiently (e.g., design for postponement) they can give rise to a major proliferation of items, and therefore high inventory investment and carrying cost.

- *Security compliance.* Ensuring that all regulations governing international shipments are observed is of major importance from the security and cost viewpoints. Containers that may carry one single item that has not been properly identified in the documentation may delay the shipment of the entire container, until all security measures have been fully respected.

Operational Issues

- *Execution synchronization with partners.* Synchronized operations across the extended enterprise are the backbone of a well-integrated, efficient supply chain. Collaborative management can ensure efficient synchronized operations.
- *The evolution of logistics services providers.* Business trends affecting industrial and commercial enterprises also affect logistics services providers, and therefore the structure and operation of global supply chains. In this sector, major changes are underway that will substantially alter the manner in which such services are provided, creating a new type of company that offers worldwide, integrated logistics services. Such companies offer to transfer and process anything, anywhere, anytime. Thus, they provide shippers a single contact for any transfer, taking full responsibility door-to-door, and ensuring rapid, reliable service. Successful logistics services providers offer all that, at a competitive and decreasing cost. Thus, shippers have access to global services through a single point of contact. Those services may include multimodal transportation, cross-docking, warehousing, product finishing, re-packaging, re-labeling, returns processing, recycling, customer-order management, inventory management, shelf replenishment, customer service, documentation generation and processing, customs clearances, advice on taxes, duties and transfer prices, consulting and engineering, insurance, and financing.
- *The logistics dimensions of security.* Logistics plays a critical role in ensuring the security of international cargo flows. In this regard, it is imperative that companies engaged in international business provide several types of logistics support:
    - *Security stocks, separate and distinct from safety stocks.* Security stocks must be established to enable the company to continue its operations despite terrorist or other forms of attack. They should never be used for any other purposes.
    - *Dispersed warehouses.* Providing multiple warehousing locations that are far apart from each other diffuses risk.
    - *Emergency transportation.* Establishing the modes and carriers to be used in case of emergency is a must in the current international environment.
    - *Customer order assistance.* Under emergency conditions, it is important to offer effective customer ordering support and steering, to provide timely, accurate information on merchandise availability and delivery terms, and suggest items and quantities to order.

International Operations

A global supply chain requires logistics, administrative, and financial support. *Logistics support* includes the transportation, handling, storage, packaging, and unitization of goods. *Administrative support* includes customer service support, customer-order management, use of free trade zones, and documentation preparation. *Financial support* includes managing exchange and inflation rates, evaluating financial incentives, establishing and managing hurdle investment rates, and processing customs duties and drawbacks. In this section, we focus on those aspects of global supply chain operations that are substantially different, or are not present at all, in domestic operations.

International Transportation Modes

International transportation modes include water (ocean, lake, river, or canal), air, railroad, truck, and sometimes pipeline. (International pipeline transportation represents a very small fraction of global merchandise transfers. Furthermore, its characteristics, and the issues associated with it, are similar to those in domestic transportation. For these reasons, we do not elaborate on it in this section.) The transportation modes used, their characteristics, and the regulations governing them depend on the specific countries involved in the movement of goods.

Ocean Transportation

Throughout the world, water transportation is typically cheaper, but also slower, than other modes. In many developing countries, it is the primary transportation choice. In developed countries, water transportation is mostly used to transport commodities with relatively low unit cost, for relatively short distances. Common examples include transportation on the Mississippi River or the Erie Canal in the United States, or the Rhine-Main-Danube (Europa) canal in Europe. Ocean transportation takes place using a variety of vessels, including:

- Bulk vessels—are oil tankers, liquid natural gas tankers, and ore-bulk-oil (OBO) tankers.
- Container vessels—carry mostly 40-foot containers, loaded and unloaded by port gantries.
- Lighter-Aboard-Ship (LASH) vessels—carry their own gantries to load and unload "lighters," which are floating containers. They load and unload containers rapidly, reducing ship turnaround time and port expenses.
- Roll-On/Roll-Off (RORO) vessels—are designed to carry self-powered vehicles (automobiles, trucks, tractors) that "roll onto" the ship at the port of loading and "roll off" the ship at the port of unloading. These vessels load and unload vehicles rapidly.
- Special vessels—have a specific design, such as refrigerated ships.

Most of the global tonnage carried by ocean is bulk cargo of commodities, such as oil, coal, and grains. The owners of vessels chartered for this purpose provide those vessels under contract to the shippers. Brokers negotiate most of those contracts, known as "fixtures," and match shippers and owners. Charter agreements are usually negotiated for a specific trip, or for several trips during a specified period, which typically is between three and twelve months. Longer agreements are rare, due to the extremely competitive nature of the ocean charter market, which induces important price variability. Brokers negotiate most of those contracts, known as "fixtures," and match shippers and owners. Charter agreements are usually negotiated for a specific trip, or for several trips during a specified period, which typically is between three and twelve months. Longer agreements are rare, due to the extremely competitive nature of the ocean charter market, which induces important price variability.

Global ocean transportation of non-bulk items other than self-propelled vehicles, concerns mainly fabricated products. These are shipped in containers and unitized typically in pallets or cartons, and are carried by ocean in scheduled vessels, and are carried by ocean in scheduled vessels. Those vessels sail between designated major ports, in given regions, such as the United States East Coast, or the European North Atlantic, or Japan, carrying cargo for many different shippers. Those vessels sail between designated major ports, in given regions, such as the United States East Coast, or the European North Atlantic, or Japan, carrying cargo for many different shippers.

Operators providing scheduled ocean transportation are organized in legal cartels, known as liner conferences. Conferences regulate the transportation of goods among their members; they agree on the ports to be served, the frequency of service, the prices to charge shippers, and the commissions to pay intermediaries, such as freight forwarders.

Three criteria form the basis for determining ocean transportation charges:

- Freight classification: based on ease of handling.
- Origin and destination: the longer the trip, the lower the cost per mile.
- Shipment size: large shipments move at lower rates per unit of weight or volume than small ones.

New ship designs may soon promote greater use of ocean transportation. The fastest freight ships available, as of 20032, travel at a maximum speed of 23 knots (approximately 26.5 miles per hour, or 42.6 kilometers per hour); that speed may be reduced to some 17 knots in heavy seas. Those ships carry up to 7,000 containers. Faster ships, capable of carrying 1,400 containers at up to 38 knots, are now being evaluated. Those ships could offer door-to-door delivery in the North Atlantic in an average of seven days, for about half the cost of air cargo deliveries requiring an average of five days.

Air Transportation

Air transportation is growing faster than any other mode in terms of ton-miles transported. Small package transfers are the fastest growing segment within global air transport. In 2000, global air transportation accounted for about 40 percent of the goods transferred worldwide, by value. This despite a transportation cost premium of about ten times the equivalent cost of ocean shipping.

Air transportation is used to support international just-in-time systems and for other purposes. Its main advantages are speed, door-door service, extremely simple documentation, and very fast customs clearances.

International air cargo transportation has two modalities: freight, and express parcels and documents. These are acquiring increasing importance because they can support global supply chains that have one or more of the following needs:

- Delivering perishable goods, such as fresh foods or flowers
- Delivering fashion items, such as apparel
- Reducing in-transit, safety, and buffer stocks
- Providing fast delivery from fewer facilities around the world
- Increasing utilization of expensive assets—such as dies—among global facilities
- Supporting new, untested markets without maintaining local stocks
- Reducing the cost of expensive packaging and crating
- Reaching places inaccessible by ocean and land transportation

The maximum size of small packages or air parcels is limited by regulations. However, the limit has been increasing, thus, the difference between a parcel and a less-than-truck-load (LTL) shipment is blurring. As a consequence, many companies that used to offer courier services are now, in effect, carrying cargo.

Virtually all air cargo is unitized in airline containers known as "unit load devices" (ULDs), or in pallets enveloped by nets. Due to the curvature of airplane fuselages, ULDs have a variety of shapes and dimensions to maximize space utilization in every airplane type. Thus, every airline accepts only containers that can be fitted efficiently in its fleet. As a consequence, more than 20 varieties of ULDs and pallets are used for air cargo.

In international air transportation, cost is not the most important consideration: service is typically more important, within limits. The reason is that airfreight is normally used to save inventorying and warehousing costs at the destination, so the magnitude and variability of lead times is critical in minimizing safety stocks.

When comparing air against ocean transportation, it is necessary to account for all costs involved. These include not only transportation across oceans, but also inland transportation at both ends, handling and storage, inventorying, documentation, packaging, and insurance costs, as well as payment collection speed (cash flow float cost). Typically, intercontinental transportation costs are higher by air than by ocean; however, all other costs tend to be lower.

Road Transportation

Road transportation is the primary mode for freight transfer in the world. International road transport is regulated by the terms established in the "Transports Internationaux Routiers" (TIR) convention, established by the United Nations Economic Commission for Europe. Its purpose is to enable merchandise transported in sealed trucks or containers to cross one or more national borders without undergoing customs examination or payment of duties until it arrives in the country of delivery. This is accomplished through a "TIR Carnet," a document showing that the trucks or containers have obtained prior approval after fulfilling the requirements established by the TIR convention.

The TIR convention started in Europe several decades ago to facilitate cargo transportation among European Union member nations. It later expanded beyond Europe to facilitate intermodal transportation on an intercontinental basis. It is currently managed by the International Road Transport Union (IRU), an organization representing the road transport sector. Other important conventions governing international road transportation are:

- Contrat de Transport International de Marchandises par Route (CMR). This governs contractual conditions for the international transportation of cargo by road.
- Articles Dangereux par Route (ADR). This governs the international road transportation of hazardous materials.

Railroad Transportation

Railroad transportation is important in continental transportation. It provides a low-cost alternative to road and air transport, although with slower, and, sometimes, less flexible and less reliable service. In all regions of the world, the fraction of freight carried by railroads has been diminishing in favor of motor and air transportation.

Europe, Japan, and the United States account for about 80 percent of the entire railroad track in the world.

In Europe and Japan, there is government pressure to use railroad transportation as a means to reduce the pollution and energy consumption associated with road and air transportation. In the United States, there is less government pressure on businesses to do so.

In the United States and Japan, the railroads are privately owned and operated. In Europe, they are government owned and operated. Thus, in Europe, railroad transportation prices do not always reflect costs, and rates are not published, although they are negotiable.

Transportation Mode Selection

Many factors, such as cost, speed, frequency of departures, space availability, service reliability, and flexibility, influence transportation mode selection. From an economic point of view, the decision is based on the tradeoff between transportation-related and inventory-related costs. For example, air transportation is faster but more expensive than ocean transportation. However, a supply chain served by air carries lower inventories at the destination, because of shorter and more reliable replenishment lead-time. The following breakeven cost equation for a given lane (origin-destination-product combination) can be used to determine which mode to use:

$$(T_{air} - T_{ocean})\, Q = (I_{ocean} - I_{air})\, U\, C$$

Where:

T_i: Unit transportation cost by mode i ($/ton)

Q: Annual quantity shipped in the lane (tons/yr)

I_i: Average inventory carried at destination when using mode i (tons)

U: Unit cost of product inventoried ($/ton)

C: unit annual inventory carrying cost (fraction/yr)

The left-hand side of the equation represents the annual transportation-related cost premium to be paid if shipping by air, while the right-hand side of the equation represents the annual savings in inventory-related costs obtained by air shipments. If the transportation premium exceeds the inventory savings, ocean should be selected. If the transportation premium is less than the inventory cost saving, then air should be selected.

The cost elements included in the equation above may contain other items. For example, transportation cost may include not only the transfer cost, but also the insurance cost and other items. Similarly, the inventory carrying cost may include not only the financial costs involved, but also other items, such as the costs of packaging and shrinkage.

The same equation can be used to compare any other modes from a cost viewpoint.

International Handling and Storage Services

International transfers typically require handling and storage services, including consolidation, break-bulk, and distribution. These take place at logistics facilities available throughout most developed countries, and mainly at seaports and airports in developing countries. Five major logistics facility types are used in international transfers:

- *Transit sheds.* These are enclosed facilities, usually at piers. They are used for temporary storage of in-transit cargo to be transferred between two vessels, typically from two different transportation modes (e.g., ship to airplane).

- *In-transit storage.* These are facilities are typically offered by railroads at seaports and airports. They allow shippers to obtain through-rates for their cargo, while performing some operations on it before embarkation. These may include re-packing, re-labeling, and crating. These facilities are mostly used to eliminate the cost of transporting the crating materials all the way from the origin.

- *Hold-on-dock storage.* These facilities are provided by carriers, usually at no additional cost, to hold cargo waiting for its scheduled sailing. This storage service can be used advantageously to consolidate cargo from many origins.

- *Public warehouses.* These facilities are used to store goods for longer periods than those allowed by the facilities mentioned before. Usually, they are used when problems arise with a shipment, such as lost documentation, export license revocation, and so forth.

- *Bonded warehouses.* These facilities are operated under customs supervision, in buildings specifically designated by the local government for that purpose. In the United States, the Secretary of the Treasury designates these warehouses, defining them as facilities "for the purpose of storing imported merchandise entered for warehousing, or taken possession of by the collector of customs, or under seizure, or for the manufacture of merchandise in hand, or for the re-packing, sorting, or cleaning of imported merchandise."

There are several types of bonded warehouses:

- Public stores, which use government-owned facilities that can be used to process the goods.
- Public bonded warehouses, which can be used by many parties, but only for the purpose of storing imported merchandise.
- Private bonded warehouses, which can only be used by the owner of the facility.
- Special bonded warehouses, which can be of any of the types listed above, but are used for a specific purpose, such as storing a specific commodity.

Packaging and Palletization

Packaging costs are always an important element in logistics operations. In the case of international shipments, packaging has a much greater importance than in domestic ones, for several reasons:

International shipments require more re-handling and travel longer than domestic ones; therefore, they are more exposed to damage and loss. International shipments require stronger, more expensive packaging than domestic shipments.

International shipments may have to travel through many different weather zones with widely different temperature and humidity levels. Thus, cargo may need additional protection from the elements.

Some countries demand that all cargo that enters their borders be packaged with specifically designated materials. For example, some countries stipulate that imports be shipped in wooden crates that are subsequently used locally for construction purposes.

Pallets used in international shipments normally conform to the metric dimensions established by the International Standards Organization (ISO). The international standard pallet sizes, and their approximate equivalents in inches, are:

- 1220 mm x 1015 mm (48.01 in. x 39.94 in.)
- 1200 mm x 1000 mm (47.23 in. x 39.35 in.)
- 1200 mm x 800 mm (47.23 in. x 31.48 in.)
- 1135 mm x 1135 mm (44.67 in. x 44.67 in.)
- 1100 mm x 1100 mm (43.29 in. x 43.29 in.)

Foreign Trade Zones

Foreign trade zones (FTZs), also known in some countries as special economic zones (SEZs), are areas designated by a country's government for the duty-free entry of goods. Since duties can be very high, the exemptions provided by FTZs are extremely important to consider when designing and operating a global supply chain.

FTZs are typically found near seaports and airports. They enable many operations, such as manufacturing, assembly, finishing, testing, consolidation, break-bulk, labeling, re-packaging, and storage—to take place without paying duties, until the goods exit the

FTZ and enter the country where it is located. If goods are re-exported to other countries, they exit the FTZ country without paying any duties.

Since the regulations governing the operation of an FTZ are local, they vary significantly from country to country, and even among regions in a country. For this reason, it is important to obtain the latest local regulations for any given FTZ.

Documentation

A major difference between domestic and international operations is the documentation needed to transfer cargo. In domestic operations, the documentation required is simple. In international operations, documentation is far more complex and those preparing it must have in-depth knowledge of the options available in such areas as goods classification, see accompanying sidebar, "Main Export and Import Documents." This is very important in the global supply chain, because the documents involved determine how each shipment is to be handled along with its associated costs, and because a significant part of the information required in them must be provided by supply-chain or logistics managers.

In all international transfers, documentation must be available with the goods at all border points. Documentation can be transmitted electronically to the point of need; however, it must be physically present before goods can pass through customs.

From a practical viewpoint, international transactions are complex, and resolving any problems with them can be extremely costly and time consuming. For this reason, it is important to ensure that full precautions are taken when preparing international documents. This is the best way to ensure that problems are minimized though a clear definition of responsibilities. When problems occur despite such precautions, good quality documentation can reduce the time and cost needed to resolve them.

The International Chamber of Commerce has standardized the terminology and definitions used in international documentation in a document known as "Incoterms." The most important terms define the responsibilities of the parties involved in international transfers of goods.

Systems of Units

It is important to note that in international operations practically all documents must be prepared in the metric units of the International System (IS). Some countries accept documents showing IS and other measurement systems; however, an increasing number of countries demand that only IS units be used in trade documentation. This is important for companies based in the United States, accustomed to using only the British system of units.

Currency Rates of Exchange

All international transactions take place in a designated currency, such as the United States dollar. However, the parties involved in the transfer of goods must pay different items, such as customs duties, in different currencies. Since most currency exchange rates are floating (i.e., their value is continuously changing) it is necessary to establish the rate used

Main Export and Import Documents

This information provided courtesy of the International Chamber of Commerce.

Export

- **Bill of Lading:** Both a receipt for cargo accepted by the carrier and a contract for transportation between the carrier and the shipper. Bills of lading are classified by carrier mode into ocean or air bills of lading, railroad waybills, and trucking pro-forma bills of lading. If a bill of lading is a "negotiable bill of lading," it may be used as an instrument of ownership—it can be bought, sold, or traded while the goods are in transit.

- **Dock Receipt:** Transfers responsibility for cargo between the domestic and international carriers involved in an international transfer. It is issued at the terminal where the transfer of goods takes place.

- **Delivery Instructions:** Provide the inland carrier with detailed instructions about the arrangements made by the shipper or forwarder to deliver the cargo to a given pier, gate, or carrier.

- **Consular Invoice:** Some countries require this document to identify and control goods shipped into them. It is prepared on special forms available at the respective consulates.

- **Commercial Invoice:** A common invoice sent by the seller to the buyer. Customs authorities use it to assess duties.

- **Certificate of Origin:** Certifies to the importing country the country of origin of the goods involved. A recognized chamber of commerce normally issues it.

- **Insurance Certificate:** Assures the consignee that insurance has been obtained covering loss or damage for in transit cargo.

- **Transmittal Letter:** A list of a shipment's details and also a record of the documentation being transmitted, including instructions for disposition of the documents and other special instructions.

- **Export Declaration:** The United States Department of Commerce requires export declarations to control exports in compliance with export licensing, and to provide export statistics.

Import

Main Import Documents provided courtesy of the United States Department of Commerce.

- **Customs Entries:** Four types of documents are needed for goods entering the United States, depending on the situation:
  - **Consumption Entry.** Contains information about the origin of the cargo, a description of it, and the estimated duties applicable to the commodity imported, payable when the entry is filed.
  - **Immediate Delivery Entry.** Expedites cargo clearance. It allows ten days for payment of estimated duty and for processing of the consumption entry. It also allows delivery of the goods before the payment of estimated duties, and allows subsequent filing of the consumption entry and duty.
  - **Immediate Transportation Entry.** Allows cargo to be transferred from the pier to any point inland by a bonded carrier, without payment of customs duties or finalization of the entry at the arrival port.
  - **Transportation and Exportation Entry.** Allows goods coming from or going to a third country to enter the United States for transshipment.

- **Carrier Certificate and Release Order:** Advises customs of the details of a shipment. With it, the carrier certifies that the company or individual named in the certificate is the owner or consignee of the cargo.

- **Delivery Order:** A consignee or the consignee's customs broker issues a delivery order to the ocean carrier to authorize the release of the cargo to the inland carrier. It includes the necessary information for the pier delivery clerk to determine whether the cargo can be transferred to the inland carrier.

- **Arrival Notice:** Notifies the receiving party of the estimated arrival date of the vessel. It contains shipment details and shows expiration date of free holding time.

- **Freight Release or Freight Bill Receipt:** Provides evidence that freight charges for the cargo have been paid. It can be used at the pier to obtain release of the cargo.

- **Special Customs Invoice:** United States Customs requires a special customs invoice when the value of the cargo exceeds a prescribed limit. The foreign exporter normally prepares it and customs uses it to determine the value of the shipment.

- **International Payments:** The choice of terms reflected in international documentation is the subject of bargaining between the seller and the buyer. It usually reflects the risks to the parties involved in the transaction, including risks of payment, loss, and damage. International payments may be made by the same cash in advance or open account methods used in domestic transactions, or by letters of credit, or drafts.

for each transaction. These variations are typically one of the most important sources of uncertainty in international trade.

It is highly advisable to hedge against unusual variations in exchange rates. Currency hedging is a practice of critical importance in international trade and should be a major concern in any such transactions. This can be accomplished through financial and legal hedging techniques. Financial hedging techniques include forward contracts, futures contracts, and currency options. Legal techniques include contractual risk-sharing terms and escape clauses. The preferred approach will vary in every case and will typically consist of a combination of financial and legal techniques; these should always be carefully evaluated with financial and legal experts.

Drawback

A consideration of great importance in international trade is the use of drawback. This is essentially a refund of duties paid on imported materials used in the manufacture of products, which are subsequently exported from the country where they were used. The purpose of drawback is to encourage manufacturing and export operations in the country receiving the imported materials by reducing their cost by the amount of the duty paid on them.

Drawback is a privilege, not a right. It requires compliance with the customs laws of the country granting it.

International Supply Chain Security Initiatives

The U.S. government has implemented several initiatives of major impact on international business. These must be understood and observed to avoid major compliance problems resulting in substantial delays, work, and additional costs. In addition, private groups have started complementary initiatives of major importance in international trade. The main initiatives are:

- *Customs-Trade Partnership Against Terrorism (C-TPAT).* Is a private-public partnership offering security guidelines for international supply chain operations. By complying with its voluntary guidelines and submitting to inspections, U.S. importers can qualify for expedited customs clearances for goods coming into the United States.
- *The 24-hour Manifest Rule.* U.S. Customs requires international carriers to submit a cargo declaration 24 hours before cargo is laden aboard a vessel at a foreign port, for destinations in the United States.
- *Automated Commercial System (ACE).* An update of the Automated Commercial System (ACS). Is an automated information system enabling the collection, processing and analysis of commercial import and export data. It allows the movement of goods through ports faster and at lower cost, as well as detection of terrorist threats.
- *Container Security Initiative (CSI).* A program of U.S. Customs to prevent international containerized cargo from being exploited by terrorists. It is designed to enhance the security of sea cargo containers.

- *Fast And Secure Trade (FAST).* Another U.S. Customs program allowing U.S. importers on the U.S. Canadian border to obtain expedited release for qualifying commercial shipments.
- *Automated Targeting System (ATS).* An information system that allows the U.S. Bureau of Customs and Border Protection (CBP) to review shipment data against information stored in law-enforcement and commercial databases, to identify potentially high-risk international shipments.
- *Smart & Secure Trade Lanes (SST).* A private initiative of the Strategic Council of Security Technology, a group of executives from port operators, major logistics technology providers, logistics consultancies, and former military and public officials. Aims to enhance the safety, security, and efficiency of cargo containers and their contents moving though international supply chains into U.S. ports.
- *International Trade Data System (ITDS).* Aims at creating a single database and processing platform for trade-related data used by more than 100 U.S. federal agencies.

Globalization and Change

There is a globalization process underway that is changing the economic and business characteristics of the world. Global supply chains are a fundamental enabler of that process.

The macroenvironment is producing major shifts in the location of economic activity. Those shifts are creating consequent adjustments in business perspective, which require the support of global supply chains. The microenvironment is being altered by the globalization process that introduces additional dimensions in it. This requires global supply chain capabilities to exploit them effectively.

Even to compete in a small geographical region, a company must have a global strategy to survive. There are substantial differences between domestic and international supply chains. There are also many additional considerations in the global supply chain. Awareness and exploitation of them is critical to manage successfully in a global environment.

Global considerations go beyond those found in any domestic environment, with consequent higher complexity. They must be fully integrated in every business in order for it to survive and prosper in the global economy. Many such considerations affect directly affect supply chain operations, and require managers to know them well and to use them proficiently. For example, preferring pallet sizes standardized by the International Standards Organization (ISO) to other sizes in United States operations may result in long-term benefits when operating a global supply chain.

The keys to global supply-chain success are the seven principles discussed in this chapter, along with specific strategic, tactical, and operational issues that should be followed. Following these key principles and issues will enable a company, along with its domestic and international trading partners, to achieve the benefits of a long-term global position of not only competitiveness, but also true leadership.

CHAPTER 5
Budgeting and Planning the Supply Chain

Gene R. Tyndall, Partner, Supply Chain Executive Advisors, LLC

Few problems threaten supply chain success today more insidiously than uncontrolled costs. Even companies known for both excellent products and services can lose money because they fail to act on significant opportunities to improve their costs—particularly overhead costs. Companies often adopt strategic imperatives such as total quality management, close-to-the-customer, and time-based management, yet fail to develop the proper information structure to support meaningful planning and budgeting that could help them achieve these strategic goals. Such information deficiency can affect the well being of the entire supply chain.

Few corporate executives are unaware of how quickly competitive pressures have intensified in recent years. The strategies for attaining market share (among them product and service innovations, emphasis on quality, speed to market, and cost considerations) are more numerous and more complex than ever. Yet many companies continue to launch new strategic initiatives without analyzing or understanding the likely profitability of these moves. Other companies are satisfied with the status quo and fail to recognize competitive opportunities. Small wonder that many of these companies end up disappointed with the results. Even worse, their supply chains run the risk of becoming less competitive.

In this complex world, those operational activities that comprise the functions of logistics, physical distribution, or materials management are being rediscovered as critical links in the supply chain. More and more companies are realizing the value of functions that support production and product sales. This value takes the form of logistics services, which are provided to internal "customers" as well as to external customers who purchase the company's products.

At the same time, there is the corresponding management obligation to better understand what the costs of the supply chain are and how they vary by activity levels (e.g., order sizes, specialized storage and handling requirements, and shipment or delivery frequencies). Studies have proven that the overall costs of the supply chain (e.g., sourcing, transporting, warehousing, ordering, distributing, servicing, and carrying materials and products, and more) range anywhere from 15 to 50 percent of sales, depending on the industry, products, and company. Today's emphasis on operational effectiveness to meet customer needs can mean bottom-line improvements if companies plan, budget, and manage costs and services properly.

ABC—The "best practices" method
The good news is that more sophisticated, adaptable, and powerful planning and budgeting methods not only exist, but also are readily available to any firm willing to try them.

Collectively these new methods are called total cost management (TCM). Total cost management focuses on activity-based costing (ABC) as the preferred method for leading companies to plan, measure, and control expenses associated with managing and monitoring supply chain processes. Before getting into the details of ABC, it is worthwhile to review some planning and budgeting principles.

Planning and Budgeting—The Framework

Since budgeting integrates logistics into the complete range of corporate and supply chain activities, it is a highly effective means of planning for integrated operations. In the past few years, formal planning has received increased emphasis by companies and managers striving to influence and control their destiny, rather than being content to react to market and business conditions. Planning, the most basic and pervasive management function, is a formal, systematic process to ensure the direction and control of the organization's future. It includes evaluating where the company is and deciding where it should go. Planning the course of action involves deciding in advance what is to be done, who is to do it, when it has to be done, and how it is to be done. These questions can be answered with strategic planning.

Strategic planning sets long-range (3-5 year) goals and objectives that focus on the company's scope (i.e., markets, products, and customers); on its competitive position, including particular strengths or weaknesses; on specific targets for company size, market share, and profitability; and on necessary resources and how they should be applied. Its methodology differs from another type of planning known as operational planning, which sets short-term objectives, primarily in financial terms, for marketing, sales, production, and the other corporate activities for the coming year. The primary element of the latter is the overall corporate budgeting process.

It is important to recognize the relationship of budgeting to strategic planning. Ideally, the budgeting process commits resources to execute the strategic plan. However, if the strategic plan is absent, the budgeting process becomes more complex, because it must identify and deal with both long- and short-term issues. Integrating planning and budgeting is therefore critical. The strategic plan provides the framework and rationale for the organization's daily decisions; thus, the budget should be responsive to the rationalization for the resources employed in supply chain activities. The budget should also provide the means of measuring performance and targets.

The first year of the strategic plan, therefore, should provide the framework for the current operating budget for supply chain functions. This interrelationship, performed effectively, provides the essential link between planning and budgeting. The functions and benefits of budgeting are covered in the sidebar, "Budgeting Basics."

The benefits of planning and budgeting are very clear. To understand the process, it is important to be aware of the types of budgets encountered during strategic planning and budgeting.

Budgeting Basics

The budgeting process serves three primary functions—planning, control, and communication—the interrelationship between these three making the process a powerful and effective management tool.

1. **Planning.** The budget is the culmination of an annual planning process, and it documents the resulting plan in financial terms. The plan describes the structured approach necessary for the corporation to meet its goals and objectives, and it helps to ensure that all corporate resources and activities are directed toward a common target.

2. **Control.** The budget provides an objective means for monitoring the organization's progress in meeting its goals. Analyzing budget variances can identify inefficiencies and other causes for deviations from the annual plan. Thus, corrective actions can be taken promptly and can be focused properly when actual results differ from expectations.

3. **Communications.** The budget provides a communication link between management and those implementing the plan. When the planning process has been completed, the budget imparts management's objectives, goals, strategies, and programs for the next year, throughout the organization. During plan implementation, monthly budget reports compare actual with planned results to communicate performance measure in a clear, concise format.

The benefits of an effective, organization-wide budgeting process go far beyond the additional focus of cost control and include:

- **Commonality of goals and objectives.** Common goals and objectives are established throughout the organization. The purpose of the organization and its specific goals can be communicated, and progress in achieving them can be monitored.

- **Periodic planning.** The preparation of the budget requires key managers to set aside time each year for planning. The budgeting process is a formal planning framework that encompasses all company activities.

- **Quantification of the plan.** The budget quantifies the activities and programs to be engaged in during the next 12 months. In addition, the benefits of each project under consideration are quantified. This enables management to review proposals, to determine which are more advantageous.

- **Effective cost control.** Periodic (e.g., monthly) variance reports provide a means to better manage and control costs. Unacceptable situations are quickly and clearly identified, and corrective action can be taken immediately.

- **Performance evaluation.** Managerial performance in each budgeting entity may be appraised objectively. Managers at each level know what is expected, so they can monitor their own progress.

Budgeting for the Supply Chain

A company's overall budget, commonly referred to as the *master budget,* is comprised of two major elements:

- The *operating budget,* or *profit plan,* which includes subsidiary budgets detailing revenues, expenses, and the resulting net income for the budget period.
- The *financial budget,* which consists of supplemental budgets for cash, the balance sheet, capital expenditures, and a statement of changes in financial position.

Budgeting for the supply chain is associated with other elements of the operating budget such as the sales, production, and cost of goods sold budgets. The assumptions used to develop these budgets provide the underlying information necessary for an effective supply chain budget. They provide information on the inbound, interfacility, and outbound flow of goods that is essential to the logistics budgeting process.

Fixed vs. Flexible Budgets

It is critical that the operating budget be flexible to accommodate the needs of the supply chain. Flexible budgets differ from fixed budgets, which are the common form for master budgets. Fixed budgets consist of revenue and cost projections for only one level of activity. Fixed-budget performance reports compare actual performance with the single level of activity reflected in the budget. If the actual level of activity turns out to be different from that underlying the fixed budget, the performance reports, of course, become less effective.

Flexible budgets, on the other hand, are based on formulas that reflect fixed and variable cost components. Thus they can be adjusted easily for activity level changes. This capability allows managers to answer the question, "What should our costs be, given the actual volume level?" More innovative companies use flexible budgeting techniques as an improved means of controlling expenses.

Figure 5.1 illustrates the overall context of planning and budgeting for the supply chain.

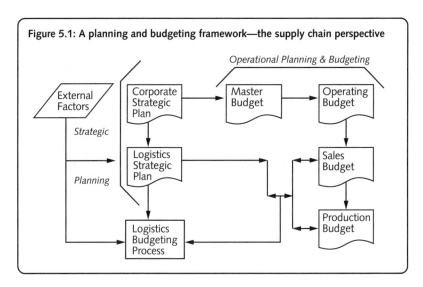

Figure 5.1: A planning and budgeting framework—the supply chain perspective

Ultimately, the goal of every company must be to provide value to customers at a profit. For customers, value is a function of three interrelated factors: cost, quality, and time. Since profitability can be achieved only if a company knows the "true" cost of its products and services, the emphasis for planning is on cost.

Cost Management Issues

Although management accounting was always intended to provide information for the internal use of managers, traditional accounting systems fail to provide relevant and timely information for managerial decision-making. Too often, traditional cost systems provide inaccurate and misleading product and service costs. Consequently, these inaccurate product costs lead to poor decisions about product lines or logistical service. Traditional cost systems also cause (at least indirectly) dysfunctional behavior by both individual employees and functional departments. Examples of such dysfunctional behavior include producing excess inventory to "absorb" overhead, or buying substandard raw material that causes poor-quality products to be manufactured. By contrast, cost management (through activity-based costing, or ABC, discussed later) provides reliable product costs. Cost management helps a company improve its products and services by reducing waste and eliminating dysfunctional behavior.

Much of the frustration with traditional cost systems stems from the fact that variances between actual costs and standard costs represent information that is too late and too aggregated to be of any use. Activities, by contrast, can be monitored directly and continuously. Cost management emphasizes the management of activities rather than the management of costs for the simple reason that activities—unlike costs—can be managed. At best, costs are only indirect measures of efficiency or effectiveness—in other words, a cost is a historical fact that cannot be changed. Something can be done in the here and now, however, to change how an activity is performed, because an activity is simply work, or a collection of tasks, that people or machines perform.

Costs remain vitally important in making strategic decisions for the supply chain. Ultimately, however, they are best managed by managing the activities that consume resources, which is the key to success in modern cost management.

Economic realities have made it necessary for most companies to operate with a "lean and mean" philosophy. In one industry after another, markets have become global, with worldwide competitors offering high-quality, low-cost goods and services. Industries previously operating under regulatory rules, which allowed them to pass all costs on to the customer, now face a changed regulatory environment. Streamlining and restructuring have become common goals in all industries.

At the same time, businesses are pressured to offer new services and new product features. Companies have worked hard to understand their customers' needsæthat understanding has in turn sparked the marketers' and product designers' imaginations and enthusiasms. Those companies that rapidly bring innovative new products and services to the market have gained a huge competitive edge. On the other hand, companies that are ineffective at quick response are extremely vulnerable if a variety war breaks out in their industry. In fact, improving the process of introducing new products and services has become a strategic objective for many companies.

Yet the proliferation of products and services can add to the complexity of getting work done throughout an organization: in engineering, in operations, in logistics, in customer service, in human resources. This complexity is one of the chief causes of rising costs everywhere.

Finally, one other factor continues to change the business environment: automation. Machines now do much of the work previously performed by a direct labor force. An increasing number of employees are now engaged in indirect or support functions. Similarly, more and more of the administrative functions are transacted with assistance from computerized information systems. This trend explains why the ratio of indirect costs to direct costs keeps rising steadily. Facing all these new challenges, executives are questioning how well their old cost techniques provide them with the information needed to make management decisions.

The Role Cost Information Plays Today

In almost all companies, accounting departments periodically (weekly, monthly, quarterly) produce a set of management reports. These reports usually appear as income statements individualized for department heads and summarized for high-level management.

Typically, such reports show budgeted amounts, actual amounts, and the difference between the two for the current period and the year-to-date. Companies using a standard cost system generate reports that show the standard cost of goods produced or services performed, along with any variances incurred. In either case, the reporting basis is the predefined cost; the budget in the first case, the standards in the second.

The major purpose of periodic management reports should be to provide managers with a means of monitoring progress toward their goals and of directing their energies to situations needing attention. Yet these reports achieve their purpose only if they organize and calculate costs in a way that reflects the true dynamics of the business. This is achieved only if the timing of the report is synchronized with underlying activity.

The traditional transition from basic logistics starts with a function that is simply measured as a percentage of gross sales moves toward a function that minimizes costs, and eventually creates an integrated function that contributes to profitability. Proper achievement of this transition requires a concerted management effort to incorporate logistics within the overall business strategy. In addition, more and more companies are providing "specialized logistics services" and view logistics as a competitive advantage. This trend places more emphasis on the complete understanding of logistics components, and on the need for improved methods of measuring and controlling logistics costs across all organizational functions.

Total costs and the supply chain

The identification, measurement, and control of total costs are fundamental to effective management. Since total costs are a decisive factor in making strategic and operating decisions, it is important to understand the tradeoffs (such as transportation versus inventory), as well as the implications of a functional focus across the entire supply chain (such as cutting purchasing costs, which results in a delay of product supply). When corporate strategic objectives are linked to the supply chain, the proper interrelationships between such functions as manufacturing capacity and inventory management can be determined to arrive at improved overall efficiency.

These improvements in time and cost are increasingly important to companies in today's environment. As supply chain innovations are created, how they are implemented determines their contribution; how they are planned and costed determines their value.

Activity-Based Costing—the "Best Practices" Solution

There are strategic plans that capitalize on business processes using technology as a tool to capture opportunities. Such opportunities will not only reduce costs, but will also provide a system of consistency in the management of the strategy to effectively control costs within internal organizations and throughout the supply chain. These plans have become known as "Total Cost Management" (TCM). The approach to TCM is "Find it, get it, keep it":

- *Find it* through a comprehensive assessment of your internal operations and external business partner relationships.
- *Get it* through effective sourcing, negotiations, and effective business partner relationships.
- *Keep it* by applying and enforcing electronically automated compliance rules and reporting measurements.

A key component of TCM is *activity-based costing*. While business process analysis is the cornerstone concept for improving management accounting, activity-based costing (or ABC) has become the catch phrase to describe the new techniques in management accounting. Activity-based costing is a technique for accumulating cost for a given cost object that represents the total economic resources required or consumed by the object. In this discussion, the term "activity-based costing" describes the specific techniques for costing business processes and for costing "objects." The objects may be products, services, product lines, service lines, customers, customer segments, or channels of distribution.

Organizations that sell goods or services already cost their products for inventory valuation or regulatory purposes. But many people who must rely on these costs for internal decision-making consider them both incomplete and distorted. They are incomplete because they include only the costs to acquire or produce the end products. They may not include any of the costs of warehousing, distribution, sales, or service. They are distorted because each product typically includes an assignment of overhead that was allocated on some arbitrary basis such as direct labor, sales dollars, machine hours, material cost, units of production, or other volume measure.

The logic of activity-based costing is simple. Companies expend resources to fund activities. They perform activities to benefit products, services, or other cost objects. The goal in activity-based costing is to mirror this causality among resources, activities, and cost objects in assigning overhead costs. For example, salaries, facility costs, and computer costs may be spent to support supply chain planning activities, which in turn support individual products or services. Thus, the cost of each product or service should reflect the cost of the supply chain planning activity required to support it.

At first glance, this ABC process may appear to require extremely elaborate data collection systems. This is not necessarily the case. Companies may want to assign overhead costs to objects more accurately, but they are also looking for ways to simplify rather than complicate the work their people do. Therefore, ABC would not require that staff members begin keeping track of how much time they spend supporting each individual product or service. Rather, ABC would make use of data that already exist as a natural consequence of the work. ABC data can be generated by scanning a computerized planning-and-control system (quite possibly, a DRP-11 system) and determining how many logistics or service-planning transactions were processed for each product. In fact, the very existence of rich databases is precisely what makes the actual implementation of ABC systems feasible.

The cost data contained in a company's general ledger are reorganized into *activity cost pools,* and the amounts in the activity cost pools are then assigned to products/services or other cost objects based on some causal factor. Once the object costing has been completed, the costs are compared to selling prices or revenues to analyze profitability by product, service customer, or other factors.

Activity-based costing occurs in two major phases. First, the costs of significant activities are determined. Then, the activity costs are assigned to products or other "objects" of interest, such as customers or services. The first phase is *activity-based process costing;* the second is *activity-based product costing* (or more accurately, *activity-based object costing*).

Activity-based process costing serves two separate purposes. First, it develops the costs of the activities identified in the business process. Second, it is a necessary intermediate step in calculating activity-based object costs. Activity-based process costing is a major link between improving the accuracy of costing and improving supply chain performance. The primary objective is to assign costs that reflect or "mirror" the physical dynamics of the business. A phrase often used to describe the underlying concept of ABC is that "the business's resources are consumed in the conduct of activities, and activities are performed in the service of products." Activity-based costing tries to manifest this two-stage dynamic environment.

Thus, activity-based process costing applies costs through a series of "activity/driver bases." The process is made up of a series of activities directed at producing an output. Activity-based process costing is therefore the precursor to activity-based product costing, and helps to facilitate performance measurements for responsibility accounting.

Activity-based product costing applies costs to products by developing cost pools within processes. The pools represent costs that vary with a common activity/driver. An important distinction to note is that activities consume resources at the process level, while products are the end result of activities. This distinction allows us to integrate activity-based process and product costing by first costing the activity where incurred (process), and second, rolling up costed activities into products.

Activity-based product costing improves the tracing of costs to products. Any costs that can be charged directly to products should be removed from the cost pools. With logistics costs of activities "outside the factory" representing as much as 40 percent of gross revenues in some industries, product cost information not integrated with total supply chain activities is quite limited.

ABC and the Supply Chain

Most supply chain functions (or activities) lend themselves to ABC. Transportation and warehousing activities—which together comprise 40 to 60 percent of typical logistics costs—can be treated as activity costs, since they primarily involve transactions that are product-related. Once the logistics activities are understood, a company must determine cycle times and costs for the activities, which can be determined through observation and by examining historical data. The factors include:

- The time (in hours and days) required to cycle from start to finish one work product
- The cost (in labor and other expenses) associated with the cycle

Figure 5.2 illustrates a sample cost and cycle time profile for labor associated with the flow of materials through the company, to delivery of one order through a particular distribution channel and finally to a customer. Note that this figure transcends the inbound-to-outbound supply chain for the company itself. It does not include comparable supply chain activities for vendors, carriers, and customers. The time line depicted in Fig. 5.2 also involves a cost associated with the dollars spent to move a product from raw material to customer delivery. This time includes "dwell activities" (such as storage, inventory, or other time-consuming activities not directly associated with flow), packaging, and labeling.

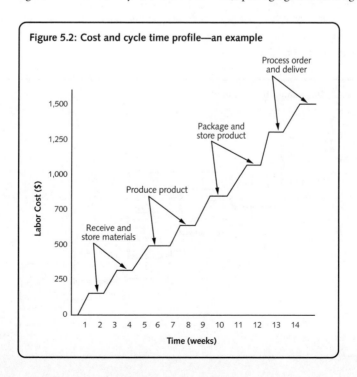

Figure 5.2: Cost and cycle time profile—an example

Similar cost and cycle time profiles can be developed for detailed activities undertaken within functions such as purchasing, order processing, warehousing, transportation, and information support. The sum of all such cost and cycle time profiles represents ABC for product groups, lines of business, distribution channels, customers, or other cost management interests.

To the extent that it is practical and costs are material, activity-based cost information should be identified and assigned to products or groups. Products incur overhead costs by requiring resource-consuming activities, including warehousing. The costs of products, then, differ according to their different actual requirements for support activities, such as warehousing.

A useful approach is to develop a "cost model," typically for one business unit, one product group, one period, and one type of distribution channel. Figure 5.3 illustrates the eight steps to follow in developing the cost flow model. These are further defined as follows:

- *Collect financial data* for the current (or past actual) period budget.
- *Identify activities* for the selected product group.
- *Develop cost flow model* by identifying, as a preliminary step, all costs that can be assigned to the product group.
- *Identify cost drivers* or events that initiate the activity and result in the cost.
- *Collect cost drivers data* including historical, budget, observed, or estimated data.
- *Calculate activity costs* per cost driver and per activity, and reconcile their scope to the sum of costs.
- *Calculate time cost of money* for each product group and distribution channel; the variables are the company's cost of capital, multiplied by the total dwell time, multiplied by total activity costs.

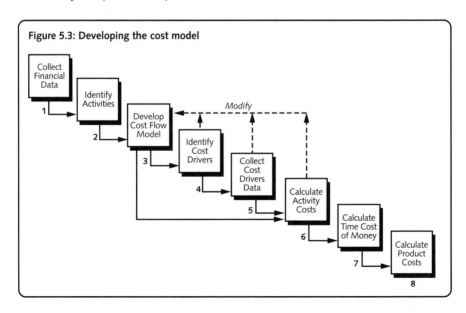

Figure 5.3: Developing the cost model

- *Calculate product costs* for their product group based on the appropriate drivers and activities. Also, calculate the margins, and compare the resulting costs with traditional product costs.

The outcome of the cost flow model can thus be evaluated in light of its comparability with the firm's traditional cost methodology, its ability to accurately calculate total product flow costs across the supply chain, and its ability to calculate other measures such as gross margin, value-added costs, and profitability. Once the cost flow model approach has been deemed appropriate, the complete ABC method can be developed for all product groups and all activities.

Cost Drivers for Supply Chain Activities

Cost drivers should be identified to determine the causes of cost incurred by supply chain activities. For example, the following are typical cost drivers for supply chain activities:

- Materials (number of stock keeping units (SKUs) and items)
- Materials supply network (number of vendors and locations)
- Materials inventory levels
- Production flexibilities
- Finished goods distribution network (number of locations)
- Finished goods inventory (products) levels
- Customer demand levels and patterns
- Customer satisfaction
- Transportation (inbound and outbound)
- Warehousing (storage and handling)

The strategies and operating policies of the company for these key cost drivers cause costs to be incurred at the activity level. It is important to understand why costs are incurred for the business, as well as how and when. Let's take a look at the three drivers at the bottom of the list in detail.

Customer Satisfaction

Several factors become important in being able to measure, determine, and control an optimum balance between cost, potential sales, and customer satisfaction. Some of the cost factors involved include:

- *Material cost.* The cost of the materials used in the product build.
- *Packaging cost.* The cost of packaging throughout the supply chain.
- *Marketing/sales cost.* The cost of initiating sales and leads, developing customer requirements, and processing orders.
- *Product development cost.* The cost of developing and designing the product, in terms of expended cost and time-to-market cost.

- *Overhead costs.* The costs associated with the manufacture of the product—tooling, capital equipment, facilities, utilities, etc.
- *Transportation cost.* The cost of the means to move the product from the last production process to the customer.
- *Storage/inventory costs.* The costs of storing and handling in-process and finished goods.
- *Service cost.* The cost of providing customer satisfaction through after-sales service and support.
- *Indirect costs.* The costs of indirect and support functions that assist in the nondirect tasks of transforming, storing, packaging, and moving the product.

Today, with increasing customer expectations, it is obvious that customer satisfaction is not free. For instance, if inventory is maintained at a high level to service the customer through all possible demand fluctuations and operating uncertainties, the results are significant downside cost ramifications. However, if inventory is maintained at a low level, the penalty may be lost sales or customer dissatisfaction.

As sales and market penetration increase, the cost to maintain optimum satisfaction levels also increases. The important task is to maintain the balance between sales and optimum service. There is an optimum level of customer satisfaction to be achieved between the sales dollar and the cost of servicing the sale. Providing optimum satisfaction levels may require increased levels of capital and working capital, but the benefits in terms of improved customer service and sales can be significant. Figure 5.4 illustrates certain supply chain issues for major tradeoffs, while Fig. 5.5 cites methods for analyzing and deciding among choices.

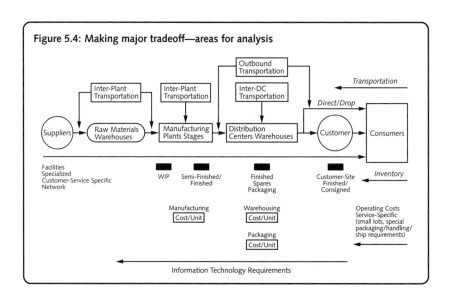

Figure 5.4: Making major tradeoff—areas for analysis

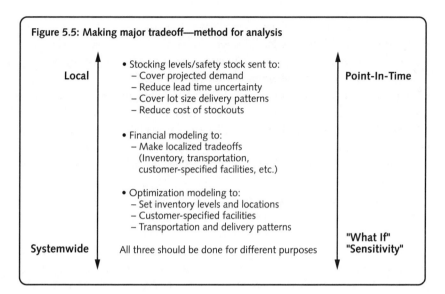

Figure 5.5: Making major tradeoff—method for analysis

Transportation

Since a company's policies for customer satisfaction affect transportation costs, transportation decisions and resulting costs must be consistent with, and must support, the overall customer service strategy. Many factors contribute to transportation costs. These include, but are not limited to, the following:

- Shipment origin and destination
- Product shipped (i.e., its value and its specific shipped characteristics, such as special handling, weight, or packaging)
- Mode of shipment (truck, rail, air, ocean, barge, or pipeline)
- Outside carrier used
- Shipment size (e.g., full truckload, full carload, or less-than-truckload)
- Shipment weight
- Frequency of shipments
- Packaging type and unit (e.g., pallet load or air container)
- Shipment routing and total distance traveled
- Shipment tracking
- Rehandling of product (e.g., consolidation or breakbulk operations)
- Origin and destination handling
- Payment terms
- Desired speed or transit time (e.g., one-day service or cheapest route)
- Special services
- Claims (loss and damage)
- Transportation of hazardous materials (e.g., routing implications, special handling charges, or insurance costs)

In determining for-hire carrier costs, several types of special charges should be identified and measured. These include line-haul charges, occasional charges for extra services (e.g., diversions, reconsignment, demurrage, and transit privileges), claims administration (including loss and damage reimbursement), and terminal overhead.

Companies using for-hire carriers normally audit freight bills to ensure that all charges are correct and that correct amounts are paid to carriers. Freight bill audits and payments can be done internally or through third party service organizations. In either case, the systems used for auditing and paying freight bills should not only ensure correct charges and accurate payments, but also provide the data required for comprehensive transportation cost management.

If a company-owned service (e.g., a private fleet) is being used, all associated costs should be identified and measured. They include maintenance, terminal, and operating costs (including driver wages and fringes), fuel and oil, interest, equipment depreciation and base, and insurance. The dynamics of the deregulated transportation industry today continually change the relative economics of private versus for-hire transportation. Companies with private fleets should periodically study the possible cost and return on investment relationships of the for-hire option.

For costing inbound transportation movements, the following circumstances or factors should be considered:

- Inbound transportation costs are often incorporated into the materials purchase cost. The freight expenses need to be separated for management and control.
- Inbound transportation movements typically consist of low-value, commodity-type materials. Companies often "forward-buy" to take advantage of lower prices; thus, shipments are typically made in large volumes that require minimal packaging and minimal special handling. These factors affect decisions concerning carrier selection, receiving practices (e.g., quality control and storage), and other factors affecting transportation costs.
- With the current emphasis on JIT deliveries, many companies may be paying premium transportation rates for more frequent and smaller inbound shipments.

For outbound movements, products typically have higher value and represent lower volumes. In addition, more emphasis is placed on customer service requirements, such as loss and damage, on-time deliveries, and packaging. These factors affect decisions about mode selection (type of transport), shipment sizes, carrier selection, and use of private fleet, which contribute to total transportation costs.

Direct assignment or allocation of costs should occur at the transaction level of detail, or otherwise at the lowest level of detail practical (such as activity). For example, freight costs associated with individual shipments should be assigned to the products and destinations on those shipments and then aggregated, or rolled up, as required for management cost-reporting purposes. Good judgment must be exercised about which costs to specifically assign versus which costs to allocate as miscellaneous, or "overhead," based on their applicability to specific activities.

Transportation costs that are incurred often relate to more than one cost object (e.g., the cost of a shipment containing two different products). The allocation base normally applied is weight or volume, although number of loads or number of shipments may be used. The choice of an allocation base should reflect, to the degree practical, the resources actually consumed by the elements to which costs are charged.

The objective in transportation costing is to have data available on all transportation-related costs, preferably organized by functional cost categories. Functional costs may be directly assigned to cost-behavior classifications (e.g., short-run variable, long-run variable, or fixed costs). This method permits effective marginal cost pricing, cost-volume-profit analysis, flexible budgeting, and variance analysis.

Time-related costs, such as depreciation, are frequently allocated based on hours of use. The total-hours computation for these time-related costs includes the total hours the equipment is normally in use (including the empty and loaded portion of the trip), including hours when the vehicle is in service but not being operated on the highway (e.g., loading and unloading time). Average hours generally are used for costing purposes. This procedure requires the development of average driving speed by zone, or geographic region, based on mileage brackets. The average can be determined based on continuous analysis of actual performance of each load. Alternatively, the average can be determined by using statistical sampling techniques.

For costs that are a function of miles operated, both loaded and empty miles should be included. The per-mile charge is determined using system averages or averages for each major traffic lane. This approach may be used to allocate other function costs (e.g., fuel and oil, tractor maintenance, tire and tubes, and accidents and insurance), depending on how they are incurred. The total cost of the load is calculated by accumulating the functional cost allocations using the hours, loads, and mile bases.

The accuracy of transportation costing can be enhanced through the use of cube or density factors, which are used jointly with the hundredweight (cost) miles-allocation base. This process enables the costing system to account for the weight, distance, and cube or density factors of the products shipped, when a combination of light and dense products are being shipped together.

Transportation information must be comprehensive enough to include all relevant costs and assets associated with transportation activities. The information should include all costs of inbound, interfacility, and outbound shipments. Both for-hire and private fleet costs should be included.

Information should be consistent across divisions and subsidiaries, to facilitate company wide decision-making. The database should include all capital assets employed (e.g., trucks and rail cars) and their related depreciation costs. This categorization should reflect key cost behavior patterns. Cost variability must be identified (e.g., fixed and variable costs must be isolated). The traditional type of expense categories (e.g., labor, materials, and fuel), and organizational classifications of cost for responsibility accounting, should be provided.

With these information requirements in mind, and with today's information technology capabilities, more companies are designing and implementing information systems for transportation management. These systems increasingly take advantage of the Internet, as well as electronic data interchange (EDI) with outside suppliers and customers.

Properly designed, a transportation information system provides simultaneous capture (single-point data entry) of important operational and financial data. These data include origin and destination of shipments, cube (volume) and weight, indicators, service indicators (e.g., times and miles), and equipment capacity utilization. Ideally, a transportation system should be designed with interfaces to distribution, purchasing, manufacturing, accounting, and other systems.

Warehousing and the Supply Chain

Storing and handling of products or materials have sometimes been characterized as non-value-adding activities, thus making them cost-adding steps in the product supply chain. The true value of warehousing, however, lies in having the right product in the right place at the right time. If the value of warehousing is evaluated continuously and the locations, types, and levels of inventories are determined scientifically, the costs of product flow (versus storage) can be identified as value-added for the business. The identification and management of these costs is fundamental to the effective management of the warehouse function, because such costs often are a factor in making logistics and distribution decisions. Moreover, warehousing costs can also have a significant impact on product or segment profitability, product cost and pricing, and ultimately corporate profitability.

Warehousing costs may exist for goods or products at various stages, including: (1) inbound materials, (2) semi-finished products at different phases of assembly, and (3) finished goods to be shipped to customers. In addition, support costs, such as those associated with people and information, are included in warehousing cost management.

Warehousing costs are sensitive to the different components that make up the supply chain. For example, the raw material used in manufacturing products, along with the sources of those materials, helps to determine the capacity and size requirements of each warehouse. Also, the physical characteristics and seasonality of finished goods can affect the volume and timing of storage requirements.

Transportation costs, a major factor in considering warehouse needs and locations, influence and interact closely with warehouse costs, depending on the need for, type, and mode of movements. In general, transportation movements (i.e., shipments from plants to warehouse) increase with additional warehouses, thus increasing transportation costs. On the other hand, additional warehouses usually reduce the cost of transporting products from warehouses to customers. Therefore, the proper balance between overall costs and needs should be determined. The costs of warehousing, however, increase with the number of warehouses. This increase includes inventory carrying costs as well as costs for labor, activities, facilities, equipment, order processing, support, and communications.

Since a company's customer satisfaction policies play a significant role in how warehousing costs are incurred, a key challenge to warehousing cost management is to ensure that warehousing strategies and decisions support the overall customer service strategy. This coordination may require programs such as postponement, build-to-order, and less-than-truckload (LTL) shipping.

Categorizing costs by specific activities is essential to determining the cost of certain warehouse practices (such as crossdock shipments) in which shipments are received and reshipped without being put in storage. It also permits the application of control methods (i.e., the managing of warehousing activities).

When there is more than one cost object involved (e.g., the cost activities to receive or ship two different products), the allocation activity costs may be directly assigned to cost behavior classifications (e.g., short-run variable costs, long-run variable costs, and fixed costs). This method permits effective marginal cost pricing, cost volume-profit analysis, flexible budgeting, and variance analysis.

These activity costs may be aggregated into the three major categories of warehousing services—handling, storage, and administration—and then allocated to products or groups. The categorization of products into a group, is based on a detailed warehouse profile that defines each group. The specific factors include the following:

- Mode of shipment
- Loading method (i.e., palletized, slip sheeted, or floor-loaded)
- Order size
- Line items per order
- Allowable stacking height
- Temperature or order control required
- Weight and dimensions per case or unit
- Cases per pallet
- Pallet size

Product grouping enables us to identify by product the "cost drivers" that contribute to non-value-adding activities (waste).

The warehousing function varies substantially among companies in its organization, objectives, and cost structure. Thus, different ABC methodologies may be applied. An effective costing system uses detailed cost information as well as numerous operational statistics regarding warehouse activities. The system is then able to trace direct product costs by activities and, therefore, to identify delay, excess, and unevenness in the product supply chain.

To a large extent, the appropriate volume of warehousing space and services needed depends on the timeliness and accuracy of information. The better the information on demand and activity costs, the fewer storage and handling services are needed. Thus, quality and timeliness of information is invaluable for effective warehousing cost management.

Information for warehousing cost management may be classified according to two distinct but related categories: (1) information on levels of inventories needed and available, and (2) information on warehousing activities. The completeness and accuracy of inventory information can affect the volume of warehousing activities required (i.e., the better the information, the lower the amount of excess storage and handling activities). Most important, this information can be updated and made available for on-line inquiry.

Effective warehousing information must be comprehensive enough to include all relevant costs and assets associated with warehousing activities. The information should include all costs of labor, work activities, equipment, inventory carrying, and facilities. Both public and private warehousing activities and costs should be included. Warehousing information should provide for measures of performance and its evaluation, and for productivity improvement. It should also support capital planning (e.g., building, leasing, or disposing of storage facilities) by identifying warehouse space requirements.

With these information requirements in mind, and with today's computer hardware and software capabilities, more companies are designing and implementing computer-based information systems for warehousing management.

Properly designed and applied, these systems provide simultaneous capture (single-point data entry) of important operational and financial data. These data include activities associated with receipts, storage, handling, shipping, labor, and equipment utilization. The warehousing information system should have interfaces with related activities (e.g., distribution, purchasing, manufacturing, and accounting systems). Figure 5.6 illustrates some of these interfaces.

Activity-based warehousing cost information contributes to management decision making about product mix, product profitability, and customer profitability. The costs of warehousing activities—whether the activities are deemed value-added or not—represent resources that can make the difference to the competitiveness of a company's products and margins.

ABC Costing for Other Activities

For functions other than customer satisfaction, transportation, and warehousing, the approach to ABC costing should be similar. Activities should be identified for each function or process. For example, in procuring packaging materials, the typical activity steps would be those shown here.

Daily:
• Issue purchase order
• Receive deliveries

Figure 5.6: A sample data flow diagram—distribution center, and related accounting activity.

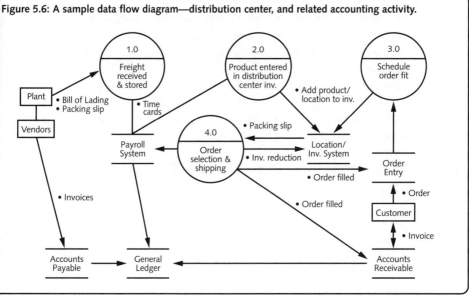

Periodically:
- Determine packaging material needs
- Determine qualified vendors
- Develop purchase specifications
- Update and evaluate sourcing strategy
- Release bids to vendors
- Select vendors
- Evaluate vendor performance

Once all the company's supply chain activities have been identified and the steps delineated, basic costs can be determined for the activities. Total cost management can then be developed for the entire supply chain.

Supply Chain Performance Measurement—The Balanced Scorecard Framework

Supply chain performance measurement is an extension of TCM that enables managers to monitor, evaluate, and improve the supply chain. It should take into account responsibility and accountability, beginning at the lowest possible level, flowing up to top management, and moving outside to the total supply chain. A key step is to review the enterprise's strategy as defined by its senior management. It is critical that there be a consistent understanding of the strategy; otherwise, a critical measure may not be incorporated into the system, which is based on the strategic goals of the enterprise. Do not assume that everyone is familiar with or understands the strategy.

A performance measurement system can be developed in a myriad ways, but one of the most effective is Kaplan and Norton's balanced scorecard approach. This approach measures performance based on four different perspectives: customer, supply chain business process (which includes internal, interfunctional, and partnership business processes), innovation and learning, and financial. It incorporates measures, both integrated and non-integrated, that motivate employees to view the success of their enterprise as something that only comes with the success of the supply chain to which the enterprise is linked. The principle of continuous improvement should apply—that is, the relentless pursuit of improvement in the delivery of value to customer. Excellence should be the ongoing goal.

Supply Chain Improvement Depends Upon Effective Cost Management

Improvements in supply chain operations cannot be gained without effective cost management of the supply chain's functions and activities. Logistics costing once focused on logistics activities (e.g., transportation, warehousing, order processing, and customer service), but this no longer applies in a world where competitive advantage is determined across the entire supply chain. TCM, with its ABC methods, must be adopted with the same rigor once applied to logistics costing.

Total cost management is a sophisticated set of approaches and techniques capable of producing significant changes and cost savings in all business processes, including logistics. Its use should be guided by the following six principles:

1. *The cost information must support the strategy.* Whether the company's strategic focus is quality, close-to-the-customer, time-based competition, or something else, good information is needed to back decisions. Lacking good information, you can't reach your strategic goals. Acquiring good cost information is the fundamental power that total cost management provides.

2. *Try to see the organization as a collection of processes, not as a set of organization charts.* In fact, the view of processes needs to capture all of the interactions among the organizational units. This means that the analytical framework should be more open to concepts of how the work really gets done, and less focused on the reporting relationships used to manage the work.

3. *Once you've made the fundamental shift in how you perceive your company, manage cost by managing activities.* Only when you focus on activities can you make sustainable changes in cost structure. TCM makes it possible to organize information in ways that point out opportunities for reducing cost—a process that depends most significantly on identifying activities and their root causes. This focus on activities is the power behind all the TCM principles: business process analysis, activity-based costing, and continuous improvement.

4. *Organize information by identifying the value of activities to your customers.* Identify improvement opportunities by determining which activities are value-added or non-value-added to your customers, and which are disproportionately costly to you.

5. *The findings of your TCM analyses must make their way into action plans.* Don't fall into the trap of simply reorganizing the numbers.

6. *Monitor the business by aligning performance measures with the critical success factors identified.* Again, the process view allows you to establish metrics for measuring and monitoring the important elements of performance.

TCM is not an objective in and of itself; rather, it's a way to support business objectives, whatever they may be. Reaching a new understanding of the company's numbers isn't the goal you should seek. Instead, focus on understanding the numbers so as to develop an information support structure that allows you to accomplish your strategic goals.

TCM, in short, is a means to an end. Cost management is the means. The end is greater competitiveness, and a world-class supply chain in the global marketplace.

Works Consulted

B. Brinker, ed., *Handbook of Cost Management,* Warren, Gorham & Lamont, Boston and New York, 1992.

Ernst & Young, *The Ernst & Young Guide to Total Cost Management,* John Wiley & Sons, New York, 1992.

Ernst & Whinney, *Corporate Profitability and Logistics: Innovative Guidelines for Executives,* Council of Logistics Management (CLM) and Institute of Management Accountants, 1987.

Christopher Gopal and Gerry Cahill, *Logistics in Manufacturing,* Business One Irwin, Homewood, Illinois, 1992.

Institute of Management Accountants, *Cost Management for Freight Transportation,* Montvale, NJ, 1990.

Institute of Management Accountants, *Cost Management for Warehousing,* Montvale, NJ, 1990.

Michigan State University, *Leading Edge Logistics: Competitive Positioning for the 1990s,* CLM, Oak Brook, IL, 1989.

Michael E. Porter, *Competitive Advantage. Crediting and Sustaining Superior Performance,* The Free Press, New York, 1985.

CHAPTER 6
Distribution Networks: Planning and Site Selection

Dale A. Harmelink, Partner, Tompkins Associates

In its simplest form, the physical distribution system can be described as a linked system of nodes (typically, stocking points). All distribution networks have these key components: stocking points, transportation, inventory management, customer service, and management information systems.

Stocking points can be distribution centers, consolidation points, terminals, ports, return centers, or other points that receive goods from production plants or suppliers or are ship-to-demand points. Their job is to receive, store, pick, and ship product. Any point through which produced material flows to reach the customer is a stocking point.

Transportation includes movement from plant to warehouse, warehouse to warehouse, and warehouse to customer.

Inventory management is the purchasing and control of products based on a market forecast. Inventories are typically a buffer between vendors, production, and the customer to permit the system to accommodate unexpected variations in demand or production. Inventory management generally consists of forecasting requirements, procuring orders, and managing what is on hand.

Customer service is responsible for handling the key interactions between the company and its customers in order to assure customer satisfaction. It involves handling customer inquiries and order changes and managing other situations that occur in the customer/supplier relationship. Customer service may also include the ordering process. In addition, it is responsible for monitoring the goals management establishes for each product or market segment, (e.g., order fill rate, delivery time).

Management information systems are any communication and/or control systems that support distribution. Their tasks range from taking incoming orders to managing fleet operations. The types of systems most distribution operations make use of are:

- *Forecasting*—converts sales projections into shipping requirements, including quantities that must be shipped on a daily or weekly basis from each location. It is typically a distribution requirements planning (DRP) computer system.
- *Budgeting*—takes place for the following fiscal year and transforms plans into cash flows and spending targets.
- *Inventory management*—includes inventory records, safety stock calculations, inventory replenishment, historical use, and reorder points.
- *Order processing and invoicing*—provides for customer order procedures, including receipts, entry, status inquiry, and invoicing.

- *Customer relationship*—provides informational support for customer service operations, including inside sales, claims handling, price quotations, order terms, and product information.
- *Multiple Order channels capability*—a system capable of supporting all order channels including primary customers, e-commerce, and secondary customers is a key to insuring all service levels remain high and costs for distribution are balanced. This includes the ability to receive orders from multiple systems as well as service them on the required levels of responsiveness and volume.
- *Warehouse management*—supports the warehouse by generating putaway and picking lists or radio frequency tasks and audit trails identifying inventory by storage location. It handles cycle counting tasks, performs lot control, and monitors warehouse performance.
- *Transportation management*—supports traffic operations by providing bills of lading and other documentation required for shipment; private fleet accounting; fleet routing, scheduling, and dispatching; fleet maintenance information; and auditing freight bills. This system also helps with scheduling and bidding services from third-party carriers, managing those loads, and invoicing and payment.

In short, management information systems process data to support the stocking points, transportation, inventory management, and customer service functions of the business.

Organizational Structures

An organizational structure ties the stocking points, transportation, inventory management, customer service, and information systems together and provides the building blocks to accomplish the corporation's objectives. Just as there are many ways to structure a network, there are many ways to structure an organization. Described next are some key considerations and principles for setting up an organization.

- *Unity of command.* This has to do with the chain of command. It is recommended that no one have more than one superior with direct authority.
- *Span of control.* To effectively manage an organization, there must be limits on the number of people a manager supervises. These limits depend on the task being performed, the type of people being supervised, and how supervision is applied, but the general rule of thumb is five to seven per manager.
- *Responsibility and authority.* Responsibility means a manager is being held accountable for the actions of his/her staff. Authority is the right of the manager to command action from a staff or discharge responsibility to it. An often-debated subject is whether managers should have equal authority and responsibility. The level of authority should be clear to the manager, so that he/she is aware of the limits of the position.

- *Line or staff.* Line functions typically refer to those activities in a distribution center that support the everyday function of the operation. Staff activities assist and/or support the functions of the overall company or a division of the company.
- *Centralized versus decentralized.* A centralized organization would have, for example, all customer service concentrated in one location, reporting to one manager. A decentralized organization would have customer service representatives at each distribution center reporting to the distribution manager of that area.

Setting up an efficient organizational structure will help the company, but it does not guarantee a successful, motivated staff. To accomplish that, an organization must espouse a winning culture as the most important part of the organization. To create a winning culture, many companies are adopting team-based continuous improvement. Only by creating a unified team will a company move toward success.

Types of Planning

There are various methods of planning or devising a scheme to guide and position the organization. This planning can be for predictable or unpredictable circumstances. Without plans, a firm risks insufficiently anticipating problems and failing to implement a solution within the required lead-time. With plans, a company becomes active rather than passive. The framework for planning is based on the types shown in Table 6.1.

Table 6.1: Types of Planning		
Type of Planning	**Reason**	**Focus**
Strategic	Determine overall objectives and resource requirements	Policy-making
Tactical	Translate the strategic objective of the distribution system into an action plan	6-18 months
Operational	Assure that specific tasks are implemented into the day-to-day operations	Five years
Contingency	Respond to emergencies	Backup

Strategic Planning

Strategic planning is the process of deciding on objectives of the firm, changing the objectives when necessary, determining resources needed to attain these objectives, and setting policies to govern the acquisition, use, and disposition of resources. The goal of strategic planning is to define the overall approach to stocking points, transportation, inventory management, customer service, and information systems and the way they relate to provide the maximum return on investment.

Strategic planning is an offensive tool designed to guard against predictable changes in requirements whose timing can be anticipated. Strategic planning is directed at forecasting needs far enough in advance to allow sufficient lead-time to efficiently meet them with resources throughout the supply chain. Granted, forecasting with a long planning horizon is a risky business, and distribution plans based on such forecasts often prove unworkable. Nevertheless, the forecast is a supply chain's best available information concerning the future, and it would be foolish not to use that information to advantage. In fact, the only way to survive the rapidly changing distribution environment today is to have good strategic plans that include shared information throughout the supply chain. Strategic planning addresses such issues as organizational structures, realignment of capacities, network planning, and impact on the environment.

Tactical Planning

The tactical planning time frame is one to two years. Its primary purpose is to plan policies and programs and set targets for both actions to be taken and the timing that will accomplish the company's long-term strategic objectives. Tactical planning must anticipate the distribution center workload to prevent overloading the primary resource—the workforce —during peak demand. The tactical plan defines how to develop the resources needed to achieve the goals in the strategic plan. For example, if a firm decides in its strategic plan that it requires a new warehouse location to enhance customer satisfaction, the tactical plan allocates resources and determines the timing. For example, here are some of the steps to follow when relocating a warehouse:

- Locate the new facility
- Sign the lease
- Design the new facility
- Modify the facility according to design
- Hire new employees
- Train employees
- Start transferring material from vendors and existing plants
- Start shipping from the new facility

Tactical planning first attempts to provide timing for each step. Second, it considers major issues, such as identifying specific skills required to accomplish the plan and the time needed for each step. Third, specific capital requirements are identified for each step. A fourth component is often the need for outside sources. In warehousing, this could mean anything from hiring a consultant to hiring a construction company. Some other types of tactical planning include inventory policies, freight rate negotiation, cost reduction, productivity improvements, and information system enhancements and additions.

Operational Planning

Operational planning can vary from daily to weekly to monthly. It implements tactical policies, plans, and programs within the framework of the distribution system to meet the company's strategic objectives. The major components of operational planning are managing resources, such as labor and capital assets, and measuring performance to aid operating efficiency and anticipate future operating issues. An operational plan incorporates the philosophies of the strategic plan and general timing of events in the tactical plan and devises the daily routine. An operational plan is, so to speak, where the rubber meets the road. Typically, it is where the planning process fails because the majority of the daily activities are routine. No priority is put on implementing the planned activities, and it becomes easy to lose sight of the planned goals. Operational planning can involve tasks such as distribution center workload scheduling; vehicle scheduling, freight consolidation planning, implementing productivity improvements and cost reductions, and operations expense budgeting.

Contingency Planning

One of the most overlooked tools that are particularly meaningful for sound distribution management is contingency planning. Contingency planning is a defensive tool used to guard against failure resulting from unpredictable changes in distribution operations. Typically, contingency planning asks "what if?" questions. For example, "What if a major supplier is on strike?" or "What if we had a recall?" The prepared manager will look to contingency planning to help counter the potentially devastating impacts of the many emergency situations that may directly involve distribution. He/she will determine in advance what course of action will be required if a given unanticipated change in requirements or circumstance occurs. Contingency planning is the opposite of the common non-planning or crisis-management ("putting out fires") approach, which entails developing a plan *after* something has occurred. The idea behind contingency planning is to significantly reduce the lead-time required to implement a plan of action. You do not wait for a fire to start before installing sprinklers in the warehouse.

Events that can adversely affect a distribution system include:

- *Energy shortages* can affect both the warehouse and the transportation system. Transportation is the most talked about distribution function that is affected, but energy shortages also affect the warehouse. On the transportation end, how do you maintain service? Do you offer less product line? Repackage to maximize loads? Warehouse energy shortages could affect lighting, heating, and material handling equipment.
- *Strikes* can occur in the company itself or at key material or services suppliers. The objectives of a strike plan will need to be determined. Items to consider are personnel and property protection; maintaining goodwill with customers, the public, and employees; and resuming operation as soon as possible. Decisions will need to be made on whether to build inventory, divert work to another plant, outsource work, lay off workers, operate with non-striking employees, or hire temporary workers.
- *Natural disasters,* such as forest fires, tornadoes, floods, or hurricanes, can result in problems such as cleaning up, resuming operations, restoring order, dealing with employees' lost wages and time, and computer backups.
- *Product recalls* can be time-consuming and expensive, so it is important to be ready to minimize cost and damage to the company's image. Items such as lot shipment

identification, lot segregation and return procedures, legal obligations, production contingencies, and public relations should be addressed.
• *Acts of violence* can occur to an enterprise or can be completely unrelated but can still have an impact, as when security concerns in September 2001 closed U.S. borders for several days and interrupted the flow of goods.

Strategic Distribution Network Planning

Distribution network planning is one of the main areas in which strategic planning is applied. A strategic distribution network plan is developed to implement business objectives over a given planning horizon. A good plan will determine the optimal network to provide the customer with the right goods in the right quantity at the right place and the right time and to minimize the total distribution cost. As the number of warehouses increases, delivery costs decrease but warehouse costs increase. This is shown in a simplified manner in Figure 6.1. The opposite is also true: as the number of warehouses decreases, delivery costs increase and warehouse costs decrease. To minimize total distribution costs, it is important to find the best balance between warehouse and transportation costs.

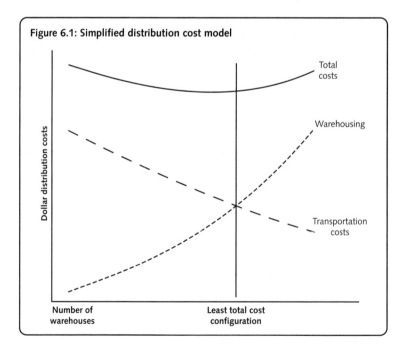

Figure 6.1: Simplified distribution cost model

The objective of strategic distribution network planning is to come up with the most economical way to ship and receive products while maintaining or increasing customer satisfaction requirements; simply put, a plan to maximize profits and optimize service. Strategic distribution network planning typically answers the following nine questions:

1. How many distribution centers should exist?
2. Where should they be?
3. How much inventory should be stocked at each?
4. Which customers should be serviced by each center?
5. How should the customers order from the center?
6. How should the distribution centers order from vendors?
7. How frequently should shipments be made to each customer?
8. What should the service levels be?
9. Which transportation methods should be used?

Factors in Strategic Distribution Network Planning

Distribution networks can range from direct shipments from the source to demand points for job-shop items to complex multisite networks. The design of a distribution network depends on factors such as type, range, and volume of products; the service area's geographic spread; level of service required; and number and type of customers. Furthermore, since distribution is a dynamic environment, it is also affected by:

- Geographic shifts in production and consumption (population shifts)
- Market segmentation, new markets, and new customer service requirements
- Cost increases in energy, plant and equipment maintenance, and labor
- Government regulation or deregulation
- Fuel and other accessorial charges
- Negotiated rate contracts
- Service requirements
- Product proliferation and product life cycle
- Competition
- Economy

Internal organizational areas such as marketing, production, and finance also affect the makeup of a distribution network. To understand how, it is important to understand their goals. Marketing seeks to maximize sales by being accessible to the customer and having plenty of inventory to minimize back orders. Production wants to minimize cost by running long lots and pushing the product out the door, so both marketing and production request more inventory and more locations to hold it. Finance wants to minimize cost and conserve cash and credit, thereby lowering inventory and the number of stocking points. With these conflicting needs, the distribution network planner must find the lowest-cost distribution network and inventory management technique that satisfies the customer and the company's objectives.

The Planning Process

Planning a distribution network is a sequential process that continually needs updating. The pitfall some companies run into is performing steps 3 through 7 before accomplishing—and understanding—steps 1 and 2, which are the most important. The planning process is only as good as the data put into its analysis, and it should:

- Document the distribution network
- Identify the delivery requirements
- Determine network operating requirements
- Develop alternative networks
- Model annual operating costs of the existing network and the alternatives
- Evaluate alternatives
- Specify the plan

Documenting the Distribution Network

The first three steps can be simultaneous. Their main goal is to understand the current system and to define the requirements of the future system. To document the existing systems, information must be collected on the distribution centers and the transportation system. It is critical to collect information from *all* sites being considered because the study could result in recommendations for closing, moving, or expanding them. The following information needs to be collected for each site:

- *Space utilization.* Determine the use of the distribution center. This will allow you to determine the amount of inventory space that will be required if this facility is to be closed when the analysis is complete. It also identifies how much more inventory could be consolidated to this location.
- *Layout and equipment.* List the equipment and layout of each facility. If you have a list available during the planning stage, it will be easier to determine the investment requirements of a new or expanded facility.
- *Warehouse operating procedures.* Understand the order picking and shipping procedures. If there are two product lines in one location, are they picked and shipped together? Understand the differences in operating methods between facilities. This may tell you why one facility achieves a higher throughput efficiency per person. Understand how replenishment orders are pulled or pushed to the distribution center.
- *Staffing levels.* Document levels by position. Understand which jobs could be consolidated. Collect labor rates by level, including fringe benefits.
- *Receiving and shipping volumes.* Understand the number of incoming and outgoing trucks and the number of docks. This will be important if the facility is required to increase throughput.
- *Building characteristics.* Collect square footage, clear height, column spacing, lighting levels, etc. for the same reason as layout information, and remember to review expansion capabilities.
- *Access to location.* Review the access to main highways. Determine if this affects freight cost.

- *Annual operating cost.* Collect lease costs, taxes, insurance, maintenance, energy costs, and other facility costs.
- *Inventory.* Collect information on inventory turns and levels, fill rates, safety stock levels, and ABC analysis. With this information, you can determine the savings to be gained by consolidating facilities. Also collect information on which and how much stock is slow moving or seasonal to help determine if it should be centralized in one location or stored in public warehouse space. Get future inventory goals.
- *Performance reporting.* Understand the performance measures for service requirements, order completeness, and shipping accuracy.

The following information should be collected for the transportation system:

- *Freight classes and discounts.* Collect the freight classes and rates used. In addition to freight classes, get the discounts by carrier or location. It is also important to understand where, and under which parameters, the discounts apply (e.g., routes, minimum weights).
- *Transportation operating procedures.* Understand how a certain mode of transport is selected and how a carrier is selected.
- *Delivery requirements.* What are the delivery requirements (days of delivery) to the customer, and how is carrier performance measured? Is order completeness measured?
- *Replenishment weight/cube.* At what weight is a trailer cubed out? Get this information from each replenishment point and for a typical load of general merchandise.

At the end of the data collection, which would benefit from site visits, a project team meeting should be held to summarize the data collected and assess each site. This assessment will give the team insight into its operation. In addition, it will discover information unknown to management that will be useful in developing alternatives.

Documenting the future distribution network requirements requires an understanding of marketing strategies and sales forecasts. Here are some questions that marketing and sales should answer:

- Are any new products coming out? From where are they sourced? What is the target market area (geographical)?
- What are the current ordering parameters? For example, what is the minimum ordering size? Are any terms of order changing (e.g., charging for expedited service)?
- What is the direction of the market (packaging changes, wholesalers, mass merchants having more volume)?
- What are the sales increases by year?
- Are there noticeable customer shifts? Are fewer customers handling more volume?
- Are geographic shifts emerging? Have sales increased by geographic region?

Identifying Delivery Requirements

One of the keys to analyzing a distribution network is delivery requirements, or the time from order placement to receipt of the shipment. If these requirements are not identifiable, a customer service gap analysis must be undertaken. The gap analysis is a series of questions directed at internal staff and customers. It aims to identify discrepancies between the level of service that will satisfy the customer and current performance. The gap analysis attempts to find out the customer's balance between service and cost. In general, is it more important to have the goods faster, or at a lower price?

Figure 6.2 shows distribution cost as it relates to days of delivery, and its effect on profits. The figure indicates that as delivery requirements are reduced, there is a point where the cost of the product and the distribution of the product will outweigh the income achieved from sales. The figure also indicates that the longer the delivery time, the higher the profits. At some point, sales sharply decline because competition exceeds both your delivery and your cost (assuming equal product quality). The key is to find the best service that also maximizes profits.

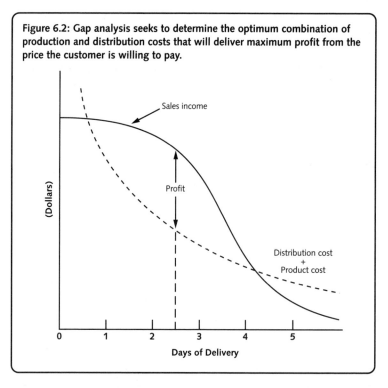

Figure 6.2: Gap analysis seeks to determine the optimum combination of production and distribution costs that will deliver maximum profit from the price the customer is willing to pay.

Network Operating Requirements

With customer service requirements understood, the next step is to determine network operating requirements. This involves determining the baseline cost and the service and performance characteristics of the current network. Key elements to be identified include:

- Current facility locations, capacity, throughput, cost, performance, flexibility, effectiveness, and efficiency
- Inbound transportation costs from plants and suppliers
- Outbound transportation costs to customers and intra-company facilities
- Current inventory levels, in-stock percentages, and inventory carrying costs
- Delivery time to customers
- Current supply points for vendors and production facilities
- Distribution of customer demand

This information provides a baseline with which alternative scenarios can be compared. Without the baseline, it is difficult to evaluate the costs and a benefit of each alternative versus the status quo.

As the baseline information is gathered, it is important that it be analyzed and validated against information available from alternate and independent sources within the company. It is not uncommon for databases or database inquiries to yield incomplete results that would potentially skew the analysis. Cost information should be compared with source documents, the general ledger or profit-and-loss statements. Volume information from production or distribution should be compared with volume information from purchasing or sales. Stakeholders who would be affected by any changes in the distribution network should also review the baseline information to make sure that it represents the world as they know it.

Developing Alternatives

Once the data has been collected and validated, the next step is developing alternative site locations and operating methods. The inputs used to determine alternatives are site visits, future requirements, database analyses, and customer service surveys. The methods used for the selection of each site will vary. The main factors influencing site location are listed in Table 6.2.

Table 6.2: Bases for Site-Location Decisions

Factor	Explanation
Supplier and Market	How quickly suppliers reach you and you reach markets (delivery days); volume, certainty and variability of supply or demand; international border issues;
Transportation	Highway access, water and rail access, weather restrictions, congestion, and road limitations; transportation penalties, premiums, or benefits
Government & utilities	Taxes, incentive programs, planning and zoning, energy cost
Labor	Unions, right-to-work laws, wages, skills available, holiday observances
Real Estate	Availability, cost per square foot; site restrictions; proximity to markets

Typically, site selection is based on the factors shown in Table 6.2, and methods are available for weighing alternative sites based on customer volumes and distance. These methods range from experience to determining the total road miles to running a network model. Network models fall into three general categories:

- Centroid (center of gravity) analysis
- Optimization models
- Simulation models

A *centroid analysis* calculates the weighted center of customer demand by using map coordinates and customer volume. It was one of the first methods used to determine site location, but it is inadequate when compared with today's modeling techniques.

Optimization models come in a wide variety of complexity and sophistication, with prices to match. They are typically linear or mixed-integer programs that are capable of determining an "optimal" distribution network based upon the data, assumptions, and parameters provided. Changes to any of the assumptions, parameters, or data will cause the model to yield a different result. They are therefore very dependent on the quality of the data and parameters and the experience of the individual performing the modeling analysis.

Simulation models, like optimization models, come in a variety of sizes and shapes. Unlike the optimization model, which starts with a set of data and gives a single answer, a simulation model will start with a single answer—a network alternative or scenario—and examine the impact on the scenario of a variety of kinds of data sets, over time. Simulation models are very useful for determining the impact of supply or demand variability, network constraints, and bottlenecks on the efficient operation of the network. Like optimization models, they are very dependent on the quality of the inputs and the skills of the modeler.

The various techniques differ largely in their ability to analyze complex networks. The planner needs to determine how important it is to include complex variables or if assumptions and averages can provide sufficient grounds for decision-making. Centroid analysis, for example, can be done on paper and assumes that transportation costs are proportional to distance, that the straight-line distance between two points is representative of actual distance, and that there is a uniform shipment size from or to each location. It ignores capacity constraints, service requirements, and differences in transportation and facility processing costs. An optimization-modeling program is more sophisticated, but it is limited to evaluating a static range of variables. If a network can be described by summarized data, or by looking individually at one or more slices in time, then an optimization model is very effective. For example, it may use an annual average in looking at the shipping volume of a facility even though there may be wide seasonal variances. Alternatively, such sensitivity analysis could be done "outside the model" to gain an understanding of the impacts of supply or demand variability. Simulation modeling is able to use actual data that reflects such variances or to include randomness in sales or supply patterns. This may better represent the volatility a company faces in the real world. The tradeoff for the increasingly complex capabilities is increasing cost.

Location is not the only decision to make. Operating methods must be considered, as well as choices like consolidating vendor shipments, centralizing slow-moving items in one place, keeping company divisions separate, and having vendors ship directly to customers. Once alternative sites have been determined, data must be collected on freight rates, warehouse cost, and labor cost for the alternative sites.

Modeling the Annual Operating Cost

Modeling software does not guarantee the right answer. Modeling should be used only as a tool to aid in the decision process. Sometimes interpretation should be pursued. The real value in distribution planning is the knowledge gained from understanding the workings of a company's distribution system and applying imagination to the model in ways that will really benefit the distribution network. Facility alternatives can be close in cost, but range widely in other factors. That makes it important to have other criteria by which to judge the modeled costs. For instance:

- Central administrative costs and order-processing costs. Typically, these costs increase with the number of warehouses. It takes more effort to coordinate and manage a larger network of facilities.
- Cycle and safety stock carrying costs. More warehouses means more total system inventory. Inventory theory supports the notion that safety stocks will increase with the number of facilities.
- Customer order-size effects. Customers who operate close to a warehouse generally tend to order more frequently and in smaller quantity than customers who are farther away. This implies that delivery costs tend to increase on a dollars-per-hundredweight basis as the number of facilities increases.
- Inter-warehouse transfer cost. The more distribution centers there are, the greater the coordination problems and the more likely the need to transfer inventory between facilities due to imbalances.
- Negotiated reduction in warehousing and delivery costs. The fewer the facilities, the greater their individual volume and the more opportunity there is to negotiate more favorable arrangements for warehousing and delivery service.

Because this chapter is concerned with the overall approach to distribution planning, it does not discuss the various techniques available to model annual operating cost. However, no matter which modeling method is used, the overall approach should closely resemble the following steps:

- *Validate the existing network.* Run a computer model to simulate the existing cost. Compare this cost with actual cost.
- *Run alternative networks.* Once the model is validated, run alternative networks for present volumes and forecasted volumes.
- *Summarize runs and rank.* Create a table to summarize cost by alternative. The table should list individual distribution center costs.

- *Summarize all annual costs and service factors.* Create a table that shows, by alternative, all cost and service factors.
- *Perform a sensitivity analysis.* Sensitivity analysis is based on the idea of setting up runs that fluctuate some components of the data. One might be a cost that is uncertain or has potential to change. By modifying this one parameter, the effect on the run can be determined.
- *Determine all investment costs associated with each alternative.* Look, for instance, at the cost of new warehouse equipment required to save space, at expansion and construction costs, or at any building modifications such as adding dock doors.

Evaluating Alternatives

An economic analysis compares the benefits of a recommended network plan with the implementation cost. To do this analysis, you must determine all the investments and savings associated with each alternative. Costs such as new warehouse equipment, construction, or any building modification should be included. Additionally, the following information must be identified: personnel relocation, severance, stock relocation, computer relocation, taxes, equipment relocation, and income from the sale of existing land and buildings.

The result of this evaluation should be the return on investment of each alternative compared with the baseline. Once this step has been taken, perform a sensitivity analysis that fluctuates various costs and savings to see which alternatives are the most stable. To round out the analysis, perform a qualitative analysis looking at factors such as customer service and ease of implementation. Once a conclusion has been reached, draw up a time-phased implementation schedule that lists the major steps involved in transferring the distribution network from the existing system to the future system.

Site Selection

Once agreement has been reached about the prime geographic area for the new facility and management has approved the strategic distribution network plan, the job of selecting the best community and site begins. This is the most difficult and time-consuming part of the planning process. Initially, there may appear to be many prospective locations. One mistake frequently made at this point is looking at sites before the overall approach has been determined. The site-selection team needs to make inquiries or get outside assistance to narrow down the potential communities because each detailed site search could take hours or even days. Support for narrowing the list of communities can come from many sources.

- *Real estate brokers* are typically tied into the multiple-listing service that lists all available property in an area. Remember, however, that brokers are compensated for a successful transaction. This may or may not create pressure that could affect the search.
- *Utility companies* are a good source of information because they typically have large service areas. However, utilities divide territories into regions and have regional sales-

people who are geared toward increasing revenues in their region. If you have decided on a particular region, though, a utility should provide an unbiased source for identifying industrial sites in the area.

- *Government agencies.* State and local government development agencies, as well as local chambers of commerce, are also reliable information sources once the decision as to community has been made. Since these people are motivated to attract new industry into their area, make sure the area is where you really want to be before relying on their advice.

- *Consultants* provide an unbiased source of advice and save many hours of time. In selecting a consultant, one important consideration is whether the individual is truly independent and objective.

The best way to narrow your selection to a few communities is to create a checklist of key requirements. If a community does not meet the requirements, eliminate it from further consideration. Some of the factors that should be on the checklist are listed in Table 6.3.

Table 6.3: Community considerations	
Labor	Unions (yes/no), availability of qualified personnel, wage levels, accident rate in area, community education or training programs, employment laws, right-to-work laws, local safety and health costs, availability of management personnel
Utilities	History of outages, rates, off-peak rates, discounts or penalties, residential rates, water conditions and chemical analysis, water, source, refuse and trash collection costs, frequency and disposal methods, communications
Community	Availability of shopping, housing availability and cost, travel and meeting facilities, news media availability, traffic levels, organizations, mail service, health facilities, protective services (fire and police), education, recreation, religious activities, cultural facilities
Exisiting Industry	Major operations in area, possible suppliers and customers, civic participation, union affiliations, environmental conditions, support to the community, number of plants gained and lost in the last five years
Local and State Government	Voting record of incumbents, annual budget, sources of revenue, annexation policies, attitude during strikes, property taxes, sales tax, financial health of state and community, amount of tax-free property, any community taxes
Miscellaneous	Weather conditions (temperature, rainfall, snowfall, humidity, days of sunshine), planning and zoning history and makeup, commercial services in area (banks, industrial distributors, office supplies, industrial repair shops)
Rail	Railroad stop-off privileges for partial loading/unloading en route, transportation demurrage charges, reciprocal switching arrangements, pickup and delivery, services, freight schedules
Highway and Truck Transportation	State laws as to truck size and weight, toll roads and bridges, condition of roads
Miscellaneous Transportation	Air: site near airport, schedule of airlines, personnel transport schedules Water: channel width and depth, terminal facilities, seasonal limitations Other: bus service, taxi service, rapid transit, auto rental agencies

Once the community list has been shortened, make site visits to view alternative lease facilities or land and buildings for sale. Before visiting each site, create another checklist that covers considerations such as zoning, topography, landscaping requirements, access to site, storm drainage, floor loadings, lighting levels, clear height, and utilities. Prioritize these considerations, and then give a grade to each site based on how well it meets the criteria. Many of the items on the list, such as utility cost, may require extensive investigation before a final evaluation can be made.

Foreign Trade Zones

One of the considerations in selecting a site is whether or not a free trade zone is applicable to your company's needs. Foreign trade zones (FTZ) or "free" trade zones are secured areas within the United States that are legally considered to be outside the country. Foreign and domestic goods may generally be stored, processed, or manufactured duty-free in the FTZ. The purpose is to attract and promote international trade and commerce. Typically, zones are operated as public utilities by states or by private companies performing under contract with public institutions that are the formal sponsors. FTZs are becoming more easily established and can be set-up in any location if the proper paperwork, procedures and controls are established and followed by the distribution operation. This is especially critical in reporting inventory ownership and transfer to point of use. are fenced-in areas with general warehouse facilities and industrial park space. They typically have access to all modes of transportation and are located in or near U.S. customs ports-of-entry. Foreign trade zones are the U.S. version of what are known internationally as *free trade zones.*

Sub-zones are adjuncts to zones and are granted to companies that cannot be accommodated in the primary zone. Each exists only for a single user, and strict criteria must be satisfied for sub-zone status. Usually a sub-zone must generate a public benefit, such as employment. Most manufacturers that assemble imported products typically fall into the sub-zone classification.

The advantages of using an FTZ are:

- Customs duty and internal revenue tax, if applicable, paid only when merchandise is transferred from a foreign trade zone to the custom territory for consumption.
- Goods may be exported from a duty and tax-free zone.
- Merchandise may remain in a zone indefinitely, whether or not subject to duty.

Any foreign goods or materials brought into a zone for any permissible activity and ultimately shipped to a third country, either in their original or a completely altered condition, are not subject to customs duties or federal exercise taxes and usually are not chargeable against quotas. Local and state authorities should be contacted about any state or local taxes. What is not always understood, and is often overlooked, is the use of zone status in exporting. Companies that intend to market their manufactured goods in other countries should research the viability of FTZ.

Any foreign or domestic merchandise not prohibited by law, whether requiring duty fees or not, may be taken into an FTZ. There are material operations that the FTZ's controlling authority may exclude, and it may deny permission to use the zone if it decides the activity or material involved is detrimental to the public interest, health, or safety. Certain agencies that license importers or issue importation permits may block zone entries. Many products subject to internal revenue tax may not be manufactured in a zone. These include alcoholic beverages, tobacco, firearms, white phosphorus material, and sugar. In addition, the manufacture of clocks and watch movements is not permitted in a zone. Retail trade is not permitted in a zone.

Success Requires Doing Your Homework

It is important to remember that a good strategic distribution network plan relies on a defined set of requirements. It should not be composed simply of ideas, thoughts, or possibilities that have not been researched and validated. Possible requirements should be defined, analyzed, and evaluated and they should result in the development of a specific set of strategic requirements. Normally, the planning horizon is stated in years. A five-year plan is typical. A good distribution network plan is also action-oriented and time-phased. Where possible, the plan should set forth very specific actions needed to meet requirements, rather than simply state the alternative actions available. The distribution network plan is based on a set of premises concerning future sales volumes, inventory levels, transportation costs, and warehouse costs. Most importantly, to get support for the plan, a detailed written document and maps should accompany the recommended action to describe and illustrate how the network will be implemented and operate.

CHAPTER 7
Inventory Management

Ralph Cox, Director, Tompkins Associates

Effective inventory management on a supply-chain scale can reduce the stocking of redundant inventories in different links in the chain. This accomplishment obviously reduces costs for partners across the chain. It also reduces the possibility of obsolete inventory becoming clogged in the pipeline, while competing supply chains are moving products to market.

Developed after World War II, and correct insofar as it went, traditional inventory management theory was philosophically limited in its view to a single link in the supply chain. The science included comparative economics to address cycle stock, the use of statistics to address safety stock, and logic to address stocking policies. Today we see inventory as an issue among multi-link chains of partners competing as a group.

The dynamics of the demand/supply interactions between links are better understood today. In particular, we understand that long-term customer satisfaction is dependent on more than the link from which the customer directly purchases product. Information availability and collaboration between multi-link supply chain partners can completely re-write the old rules, and provide levels of inventory performance not previously possible. When it is possible for an individual link to operate with little or no inventory, it will be because of the collaborative relationships developed between the upstream links and the downstream links, supported by information technology.

Inventory is in a significant state of change. A few years ago, inventory turnover[1] in the UK ranged from 2.3 to 3.4 depending on the industry, while at the same time the US range was from 2.3 to 4.7 and the range in Japan was from 1.3 to 8.5. In a recent report[2], the Warehousing Education and Research Council notes that average inventory turnover across all segments of commerce increased from 8.0 to 10.4, with an expected further increase to 13.2. At the same time, while all types of firms reported net increases, manufacturers led both retailers and wholesalers in both the rate of change and the total increase.

Regardless of length or complexity, inventory plays a central role in every supply chain. After network configuration and volume through each channel, inventory is the most fundamental characteristic of product flow from raw material supplier to ultimate consumer.

Inventory's Conflicting Roles

Inventory is not universally well understood. It is variously characterized in both positive and negative ways, depending on your viewpoint, including the following:

- An economic asset
- A non-income-producing use of capital funds

- A potential opportunity for improving cash flow
- A vehicle for serving customer needs promptly
- A buffer from customer demand fluctuation
- An insurance policy against supply disruption

Of course, all of these are true and yet none tell the complete story. Only when considered simultaneously in light of all of the quality, customer service, and economic aspects—from the viewpoints of purchasing, manufacturing, sales, and finance—does the whole story become evident.

An Asset

Assuming that it is salable, inventory is, of course, an asset in the financial sense, although an asset with no return in the traditional sense (some incremental increases in safety stock inventory, however, do provide a return in terms of increased revenue).

Above and beyond accounting's balance sheet aspects, however, inventory is an asset to business in day-to-day operations, in that it provides prompt customer service and eases workflow complexity. For purchased products, holding inventory reduces the number of purchase orders to be issued and processed through accounts payable. For manufactured products, holding inventory reduces the number of equipment changeovers or setups required to support short term customer needs—allowing a plant to produce, say 100 products, on any given day, while shipping, say 10,000 products, on the same day. Above and beyond the financial benefit, changeover reduction also significantly increases manufacturing capacity, minimizing the need for additional shifts, equipment, and/or complete plants.

But Not Really an Asset

On the other hand, inventory is not an asset in the sense that it represents a draw down on capital funds that would have otherwise been available for investments providing a satisfactory return. Most important, funds tied up in inventory may delay internal investments in core business areas that are key to the future of the business. Further, inventory can cover up a variety of sloppy practices in purchasing, warehousing, and transportation in all supply chains, as well as in production scheduling in manufacturing operations.

Objectives

The objectives of inventory management, however, are clear, and include the following:

- Direct
  - Achieve the desired customer service level
  - Minimize acquisition transaction costs
  - Minimize inventory working capital

- Indirect
  - Facilitate efficient product flow
  - Maximize profit

Inventory Strategy

At the core of inventory strategy for all supply chains is the issue of providing customers with what they want, when they want it. In manufacturing, the primary objective becomes ensuring flow to maximize equipment utilization, while in maintenance the focus becomes ensuring immediate inventory availability with little or no notice.

Then there is the matter of cost—variable purchasing, manufacturing, warehousing, and transportation expenses, as well as the working capital invested. Cost may be subordinated to customer service, but only up to a point.

Assuming that the customer requirements are known (see Demand Planning), two questions are implicit in forming an inventory strategy: "what does the customer want and when will it be needed" and "what options do we have to meet the need?"

The driving forces for inventory, therefore, are:

- The need for good service to individual customers, often in the absence of good information on individual customer needs, in terms of both product availability and timing
- Variability in demand for all individual customers, taken as a whole, having the potential to exceed short term supply capacity
- The need to eliminate, or as a minimum, control, both transaction-related expenses and working capital investment

There are several major approaches to inventory, both for meeting customer needs and controlling cost, as follows:

- Strategic
  - Reducing uncertainty through information sharing
  - Increasing responsiveness
  - Reducing the cost of surprises

- Tactical
  - Scheduling techniques
  - Holding inventory

The three strategic approaches noted are designed to address the underlying issues of inadequate planning information (lack of communication, forecasting error, etc.), acquisition lead time greater than customer lead time, and transaction cost (purchase, set-up, changeover, set-up, etc.), respectively. Or, to express it differently:

- If customer demand were known, through trustworthy, partnering relationships leading to increased visibility, then acquisition schedules could be coordinated with customer need schedules, and there would be little or no need for safety stock inventory or for cycle stock inventory.

- If delivery were more responsive by virtue of a reduced supply lead-time, then the issue of inadequate information can be mitigated to some extent. Thus, if supply lead-time is less than customer lead-time, products can be acquired more readily for specific customer orders in more instances.
- If transaction unit costs were reduced, again in the absence of adequate information, then the cost penalty for mid-stream change to meet a specific customer's needs is reduced, and less cycle stock inventory will need to be held.

To the extent that the strategic approaches cannot be completely implemented for all products, tactical approaches must be used—generally requiring some inventory, while minimizing the cost impact. The two techniques noted work in conjunction with one another, with the scheduling technique being applied first, then holding inventory being the last resort.

Inventory Constituents and Types

While inventories can be classified several ways, underlying those classifications are individual SKUs that, by virtue of their nature, are classified as having independent demand or dependent demand. Independent demand SKUs are directly affected by trends in the marketplace, while dependent demand SKUs are affected for the most part only by changes in demand for independent demand SKUs. (Some dependent demand SKUs have independent demand, as well). The need for independent demand SKUs is forecast, while the need for dependent demand SKUs is calculated, based on the bill of materials for independent demand SKUs.

Constituents

Inventories have two constituents—cycle stock and safety stock. Cycle stock is intended for routine consumption, while safety stock is intended for consumption only during the acquisition lead-time if demand is above average. The underlying driving force for cycle stock is economics, while the underlying driving force for safety stock is customer service.

Types

Inventories can be categorized based on function, permanence, and a variety of status characteristics.

Function-based

In the broadest functional sense, inventories include the following types:

- Decoupling: Inventory created to decouple supply from demand.
- Hedging: Inventory created as a hedge against possible events, including not only exceptional demand, but also, possible political instability, labor strikes, or price increases
- Anticipation: Inventory created in anticipation of known, upcoming events, including promotions, seasonal demand, and pending shutdowns

- Transportation (pipeline): "Inventory" in transit, either between purchaser and supplier or between purchaser locations.

Permanence-based

Above and beyond their function, some inventories are more permanent in nature, while others are clearly temporary. Temporary inventories, in which different SKUs are on hand at different times, include the following:

- Transportation (pipeline) inventories
- Work-in-process (WIP)

Transportation inventory is in motion, and the quantity depends on the unit volume per period and the transit time from shipment to receipt. If the product is being shipped between purchaser and supplier, transportation inventory can be reduced by using higher velocity transportation and/or by acquiring product from physically closer suppliers. Reducing transportation inventory is in conflict with minimizing transportation expenses.

While most transportation inventory is in trucks, aboard railroad cars, or on ships, staged product in a warehouse is also a type of transportation inventory, and the quantity can be determined in the same manner.

In manufacturing, WIP includes released raw materials and partially completed product. In supply chain areas external to manufacturing, WIP is inventory that is temporarily unavailable for disposition, due to the need for inspection or processing.

Permanent inventories, in which the same SKUs are expected to be on hand at essentially all times, can be further differentiated by their orientation, and include the following:

- Flow Oriented
  - Raw Materials
  - Finished Goods
  - Consumable Maintenance, Repair and Operating Supplies (MRO)

- Service Oriented
  - Spare Parts
  - Used Equipment
  - Retained Samples
  - Tools
  - Files and Records
  - Fleets of Returnable Containers
  - Fleets of Mobile Equipment – Fork Lifts, Railroad Cars, Truck Tractors, and Trailers, etc.

Flow oriented inventories are driven by product purchases and sales, while service oriented inventories are driven by a variety of factors.

Status-based

Inventories of all types routinely carry a status of some type that further defines their availability or defines their quality, disposition, control, or ownership, as follows:

- Availability-based
  – On Order, In Transit, Unloaded, Received, Available, Allocated, etc.
- Quality-based
  – On- / Off-specification, Hold for Retest, Quarantined, Waste, etc.
- Contents-based
  – Filled, Product Name, Quantity, etc.
  – Empty - Dirty, Empty - Clean, Empty - Former Product (to be refilled), etc.
- Control-based
  – Push, Pull, Vendor-managed inventory (VMI), etc.
- Ownership-based
  – If Transportation: FOB-Origination, FOB-Destination, FAS, etc.
  – If Decoupling, Hedging, or Anticipation: Paid, Consigned, etc.
- Location-based
  – Facility X, Staging Area Y, VSP, (Author: Please define VSP.) etc.

Supply Chain Location-based

None of the above characterizations are independent. For example, all or a portion of a raw materials inventory may simultaneously 1) have been acquired in anticipation; 2) be consigned; 3) be allocated; although 4) in quarantine; and 5) be located in Staging Area X in 6) Facility Y. Characterization of an inventory in different ways is useful for different purposes. Above and beyond all of the above, however, the location of the inventory in the supply chain affects both the planning for, and the expectations of performance from, any inventory. The following breakdown has been constructed to make the point that all inventories are sequential parts of supply chains, whether the flow of product is within or between organizations. This concept will be helpful in understanding, for example, how a supplier's changeover cost matters with respect to his finished goods inventory as well as to the purchaser's raw materials inventory.

- Single Link Examples (Sequential Inventories across Organizational Boundaries but within Ownership Boundaries)
  – Manufacturer
    ○ Raw Materials – WIP
    ○ WIP – Finished Goods
    ○ Finished Goods – Customer(s)
  – Value Added Distributor
    ○ Not Priced – Price Ticketed
    ○ Loose – Overwrapped, etc.

- Multiple Link Examples (Sequential Inventories across Ownership Boundaries)
  - Multiple Companies
    - Supplier – Manufacturer(s)
    - Manufacturer – Manufacturer(s)
    - Manufacturer – Retailer(s)
    - Manufacturer – Distributor(s)
    - Distributor – Distributor(s)
    - Distributor – Catalog / Internet Customer(s)
    - Distributor – Retailer(s)
    - Retailer – Customer(s)
  - Multiple Tiers Within the Same Company
    - Retail DCs – Retail Stores; Manufacturing Warehouses – Distribution Centers; Inbound Consolidation Points - Next Destinations; Last Destinations - Outbound Pool Points

Demand Forecasting

For some inventories, the opportunity exists to share information in order to replace ignorance as to upcoming demand with certainty. For the majority of inventories, however, even if the potential for information sharing exists, the near term reality limits either the quantity and/or the quality of the information, creating the need for forecasting. For those inventories that directly serve ultimate customers, information sharing is not an option and demand forecasting is a necessity.

Routine Demand

Routine demand may be characterized as having demand patterns that are uniform; constantly increasing or decreasing; seasonal; or combinations of any two of those patterns. Routine demand may be forecast relatively well for existing products having a twelve-month history and all of the methodologies are appropriate in certain applications.

Causal forecasting tools attempt to develop statistically significant correlations between past demand and its underlying driving force(s) so that future demand may be forecast based on the actions of the driving forces. Causal forecasting tools include least squares regression models and econometric models of all types, and are complex. They are almost exclusively useful for inventory in the aggregate, as opposed to individual SKUs, and beyond the needs of most users.

Naïve forecasting tools extrapolate historical demand data using simplistic (compared to causal) mathematical extrapolation for individual SKUs. Naïve models are based on the use of moving averages, which require extensive data, or exponential smoothing, which requires significantly less data.

While judgment may be applied by experienced personnel to routine demand SKUs, even with 12, 24, or 36 months of sales history available to them, the results are not exceptionally good. Compared with naïve forecasting tools, differences of 30-40% will be evident in individual time periods. Reality, of course, may be even more variable.

In routine demand forecasting, it is particularly important to address significant increases or decreases in demand that exceed preset limits. If these are not addressed, particularly before the next purchase or manufacturing work order is released, the risks of stockouts are significantly increased.

Above and beyond the type of naïve or causal model used, the planner has significant control over its application. These include:

- The length and point in time of the basis period used
- The hierarchical level at which the forecasts are to be made (supplier, product category, SKU)
- The extent to which the planner chooses to personally review seemingly extraordinary events

Very few products have demands stable enough to permit future demand to be estimated based on judgment. Discrete events, in particular, are difficult to model and negatively impact the results. Further, even with good forecasting software, the planner is routinely faced with situations that may represent the beginning of a trend, not yet fully developed, or a one-time, fluke event, never to be repeated. If the planner is incorrect in his interpretation, the result will be undesirable—a shortage of product or excess stock.

Event-based Demand

Forecasting demand associated with individual events is much more difficult than for routine demand. Sales, advertising promotions, holidays, and similar one-time events, even if repeated quarterly, semi-annually, or annually, should be forecast separately from the routine demand forecast, if the short term peak in demand exceeds the planned safety stock. If the planned safety stock in expected to be exceeded, there are several reasons for creating a separate event-based forecast for the SKU.

First, forecasting the event separately will ensure that it gets addressed directly. Second, separating the event history from routine history will ensure that the routine forecasting does not see the event demand as the beginning of a trend or demand that may reoccur. Third, if there is a stockout situation, the routine history will not have to be edited to capture the lost demand.

Inventory Reduction thru Improved Forecast Accuracy

Accurate forecasting is key to both sides of inventory management—minimizing working capital while simultaneously providing the desired level of customer service. Free, trusting, and open communications with customers is the long-term solution to the need for accurate information.

In its absence, or for ultimate consumer demand, depending on the particular software application, there may be one or a variety of ways to forecast or reforecast upcoming demand, including the following:

- Multiplying the calculated average demand by a factor to arbitrarily increase or decrease the average
- Multiplying all of the history being referenced by a factor to arbitrarily increase or decrease the historical demand for each period
- Over-riding software-identified trends
- Limiting the history being referenced to the most recent periods or to the upcoming periods in the previous year
- Modifying (correcting) history to remove one-time demand
- Entering an arbitrary demand for each upcoming period

Developing accurate forecasts depends on 1) ensuring that all forecasting personnel are well versed in all of the possible techniques available in the software application being used; 2) understanding those situations in which each of the techniques is most appropriate; 3) that information being available to remove extraordinary, one-time events from past demand and incorporate best estimates of anticipated demand for future one-time events; and forecasting personnel being free to use their best judgment, consistent with their past results.

Without historical demand data from the supplier, new products are notoriously difficult to forecast because of the absence of any sense of what to expect above and beyond generalities. Many new products are forecast based on the history of similar products. This may be a good approach, provided that the base product is selected with some care.

The important concept to recognize is that manufacturer, product family, physical characteristics, application, use, or similar points in common may have little to do with the profile or absolute values of the upcoming demand. More complex points, such as the depth of the existing product line in terms of manufacturers, models, and price points; the relative availability of the product in the market; the price; and the advertising to accompany the release may be much more useful in selecting a product(s) to mirror.

One of the most fundamental ways to improve the forecast accuracy of new products is to measure and report forecast accuracy. Forecast variance may be reported in the aggregate, or, depending on the software application, if more definitive data is needed for meaningful feedback, it may be drilled down to separate the variance for items such as regular products, very new products, very old products, and seasonal products.

Replenishment Logistics Systems

Replenishment logistics systems define how replenishment is performed in terms of order quantity and timing of orders, and thus how product flows in terms of transportation (external to facilities), and personnel and material handling equipment (within facilities). In a similar manner, they impact the nature of the profile of the on-hand balance as it moves up and down over time. Economic order quantity (EOQ) is one well known such system, of which there are many, as shown in Table 7.1.

Table 7.1: Replenishment Logistics Systems

Demand	Name	Order Timing	Order Quantity
Independent	Economic Order Quantity	Re-order Point (ROP)	Fixed – economic basis
	Fixed Order Quantity	ROP	Fixed – other basis
	Fixed Interval	Fixed Interval	Variable, to maximum, if below ROP
	Periodic Interval	Periodic Interval	Variable, to maximum, always
	Time Phased	Schedule-based	Discrete value
Dependent	Lot-for-lot	Schedule-based	Discrete value, as required for lot
	Fixed Order Quantity	Each Period	Fixed order quantity or multiple, as required for the upcoming period
	Fixed Period Quantity	Each Nth Period	Discrete value, as required for a fixed number of periods
	Period Order Quantity	Each Period	Discrete value, as required for a variable number of periods determined based on economics
	Lot-size Inventory Management Technique (LIMIT)	Each Period	Determined in the aggregate for similar products
	Least Unit Cost	Each Period	Lowest total cost per unit for the period
	Least Total Cost	Each Period	Lowest total cost for the period
	Single Period	Schedule-based	Most profitable for one-time event with unknown demand
	Part Period Balancing	Each Period	Similar to the least total cost, but compares previous and next periods for possible inclusion in the order.
	Wagner-Whitin Algorithm	Each Period	Compares all possible options

Regardless of the replenishment logistics system used, three different situations may arise relative to items on order. Using contrived figures, the three situation are shown in Table 7.2:

Table 7.2: On Order Possibilities

Acquisition Lead Time (periods)	Avg. Vol. per Period (units)	Safety Stock (units)	Order Quantity (units)	Re-order Point (units)	Situation	Comments
10	100	10	10,000	1,010	Normal	Sometimes on order
10	100	10	1,000	1,010	Re-order on receipt	Always one order open
10	100	10	100	1,010	Re-order prior to receipt	Multiple open orders

Cycle Stock

Cycle stock is designed for consumption. It is replenished as the previous replenishment order is consumed, forming a repetitive supply and demand cycle, with a total cycle time and repetition frequency that are a matter of planning. The EOQ is widely used for determination of cycle stock order quantities although, as noted above, it is only one of the possible replenishment logistics systems.

Economic Order Quantity

The EOQ represents the lowest total cost solution for a given forecast demand, incorporating both working capital and operating expenses. In addition to a number of simplifying assumptions, it is a theoretical calculation that completely ignores other aspects that must be addressed after completion of the calculation (discussed below). It is a function of the forecast demand (units per period), the unit operating expense to acquire inventory ($ per order), and the unit inventory holding cost ($ per unit per period).

EOQ Assumptions

The EOQ equation is based on the following assumptions for each SKU:

- Known demand
- Constant demand over depletion cycle
- Known acquisition transaction unit cost
- Unit transaction cost independent of order quantity
- Unit transaction cost independent of preceding SKU
- Annual transaction cost dependent on the number of orders
- Unit inventory holding cost linear function of product value

- Unit inventory holding cost linear function of quantity
- Replenishment is instantaneous
- Lead time is known
- Lead time is constant over multiple replenishment cycles

EOQs have a number of other characteristics, which are not assumptions per se, but are important to understand. They include the following:

- Unit transaction costs can be summed over sequential functions, providing that there is no convergence or divergence of product flow.
- Calculated EOQs are relatively insensitive to error.
- EOQs are ultimately a function of the ratio of the unit transaction to the unit inventory holding costs, as opposed to the specific values (i.e., if both are reduced by the same percent, the EOQ is unchanged).
- Because acquisition transaction and inventory holding costs both exist on a unit basis (per order) and an annual basis, it is important to carry the units of measure to ensure that no mistakes are made

Unit Acquisition Transaction Costs

The unit transaction cost is a deductible operating expense, and is the cost to acquire an additional order, exclusive of the value of the product itself. Transaction costs are inherently variable in nature and, although not expressed as such, are included in operating budgets.

For purchased products, transaction costs are associated with purchasing and receiving. Unit acquisition transaction costs for purchased products generally include all of the following components:

- Labor
  - Purchase order execution
  - Expediting
  - Receiving and checking
  - Putaway
  - Receiving report preparation
  - Posting to inventory
  - Invoice matching, checking, tracking, and payment
- Materials
  - Checks, envelopes, and postage, if not an electronic payment

For manufactured products, transaction costs are associated with set-up or changeover of manufacturing equipment. Unit acquisition transaction costs for manufactured products generally include most of the following components:

- Labor
  - Production scheduling
  - Manufacturing work order preparation
  - Equipment cleanup for previous SKU
  - Equipment set-up for next SKU
  - Operating crew waiting time during the above
  - Quality control testing and on-specification verification
- Materials
  - Cleanup materials
  - Manufacturing supplies which must replaced for every SKU, but are not incorporated into the product
  - Quality control supplies for testing
- Product
  - Reprocessing, disposal, or sale at reduced price of off-specification product created by the changeover
  - Raw materials or packaging materials scrapped during the changeover process
  - "Lost" gross margin for production not made during the changeover during sold-out situations, typically based on the SKU with the highest volume / lowest gross margin percent
- Other
  - Utilities consumed during the changeover period for maintaining equipment temperatures (re-heating cooled down equipment or re-cooling warmed up equipment)

The most common difficulty encountered in developing acquisition transaction costs lies in the question of whether a cost is variable as a function of the number of orders—and therefore part of the transaction cost—or fixed, and therefore not. This question occurs with respect to personnel in particular, but is also encountered for other items. The resolution lies in the question "would the total annual expense be increased if more orders were processed?" If the answer is "yes", then the item is variable and part of the transaction cost. If the answer is "no", the cost is fixed, and therefore not a transaction cost component.

Annual Acquisition Transaction Costs

On an annual basis, acquisition transaction costs are dependent on the unit transaction cost and the number of orders. For a given annual unit volume, the number of orders and the order quantities are inversely proportional—fewer large orders or numerous small orders. The annual acquisition transaction cost and order quantity relationships are as follows:

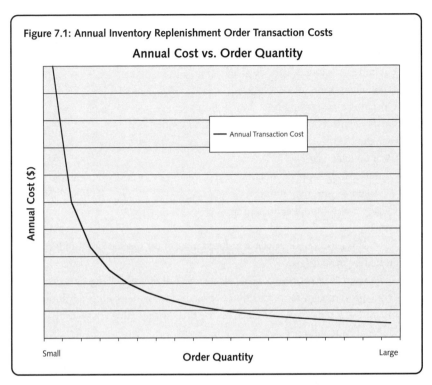

Figure 7.1: Annual Inventory Replenishment Order Transaction Costs

Annual Cost vs. Order Quantity

Unit Inventory Holding Costs

Unit inventory holding costs are more complex, and reflect the costs associated with holding inventory over a period, assumed to be a year, unless otherwise stated. They include three very different components, as follows:

- Storage—the incremental cost to store an additional unit of the SKU
- Risk—the average cost incurred per unit of the SKU in storage as a result of the product which was salable at the beginning of the period, but unsalable at the end
- Opportunity Loss—for an average unit of the SKU, the return on the working capital which would have been received if the funds had been otherwise invested

The storage and risk portions of unit inventory holding cost each have multiple components, as follows:

- Storage
  - Building rent, lease expenses, or depreciation for storage facilities
  - Property and inventory-based taxes
  - Property and inventory insurance
- Risk
  - Product lost through physical damage, deterioration, degradation, spoilage, or theft
  - Product which becomes unsalable as a result of supercession or change in market demand

The opportunity cost is not the interest rate on any borrowed funds (a common misunderstanding), but rather is the return on investment which could have been achieved, had the funds not been "tied up" in inventory. It is commonly valued at the internal threshold or hurdle rate of return for low risk capital investments.

Inventory holding costs are, therefore, entirely variable in nature, like transaction costs. However, unlike transaction costs, they are only partly in the operating budget. It is usually easier to determine each of the components as a percent per year and multiply it times the SKU's unit cost (price) to determine the unit inventory holding cost.

The most common difficulty encountered in developing unit inventory holding costs lies in the question of whether to include the cost of permanent, owned building space. While clearly not variable, many firms include it to ensure that it is used most effectively, particularly if it is inadequate to hold the complete inventory.

Annual Inventory Holding Costs
On an annual basis, inventory holding costs are dependent on the average inventory on hand. For a given annual unit volume, the average inventory on hand and the order quantities are directly proportional… smaller orders and lower inventory levels or larger orders and higher inventory levels. The annual inventory holding cost and order quantity relationships are as follows:

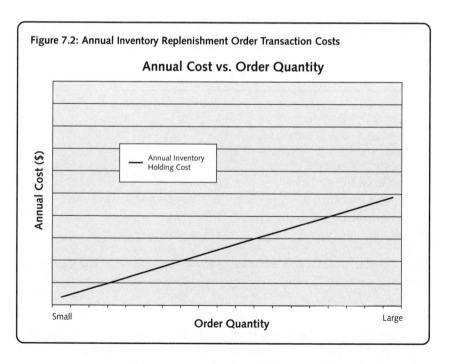

Figure 7.2: Annual Inventory Replenishment Order Transaction Costs

Theoretical EOQ Calculation

The theoretical EOQ calculation determines the order quantity that will yield the minimum total annual cost for acquisition transaction costs and inventory holding costs, as illustrated by the following:

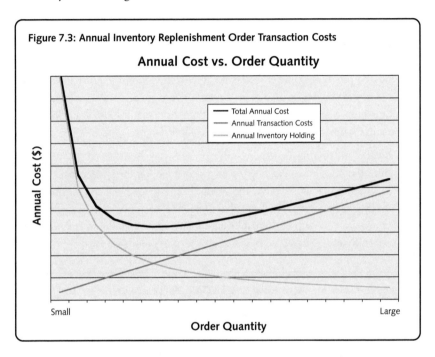

Figure 7.3: Annual Inventory Replenishment Order Transaction Costs

Annual Cost vs. Order Quantity

Theoretical EOQ Example

As an example, if an SKU had the following:

- Projected Volume: 1,000 units / period
- Current Order Size: 50 units
- Current Order Frequency   20 orders / period
- Unit Acquisition Transaction Cost: $500 / order
- Unit Inventory Holding Cost: $25 per unit per period

Such a product would have a maximum cycle stock inventory of 50 units, an average cycle stock inventory of 25 units, and a mean time between orders of 0.05 periods.

Then the EOQ would be SQRT((2 x 1,000 x 500)/25) = 200 units, where SQRT = square root.

Thus, the maximum cycle stock inventory would be 200 units; the average cycle stock inventory would be 100 units; the order frequency would be 5 orders per period; and the mean time between orders would be 0.2 periods.

Combining the annual transaction costs and annual inventory holding costs gives the total annual cost and order quantity relationships, as follows:

In the example, the current annual cost is:

- Current annual transaction cost:
  20 orders / period x $500 / order = $10,000 / period
- Current annual inventory holding cost:
  (50 units / 2) x $25 per unit per period = $ 625 / period
- Current total operating cost: $10,625 / period

And the annual cost using the theoretical EOQ is:

- Theoretical EOQ-based annual transaction cost:
  5 orders / period x $500 / order = $ 2,500 / period
- Theoretical EOQ-based annual inventory holding cost:
  (200 units / 2) x $25 per unit per period = $ 2,500 / period
- Theoretical EOQ-based total operating cost $ 5,000 / period

And so the change in annual transaction cost is:

- Current annual transaction cost: $10,000 / year
- Theoretical EOQ-based annual transaction cost: $ 2,500 / year
- Savings (Increase): $ 7,500 / year

And so the change in annual inventory holding cost is:

- Current annual inventory holding cost $ 625 / year
- Theoretical EOQ-based annual inventory holding cost: $ 2,500 / year
- Savings (Increase):   ($ 1,875 / year)

And so the reduced operating cost is:

- Current total operating cost $10,625 / period
- Theoretical EOQ-based total operating cost $ 5,000 / period
- Net Savings $ 5,625 / period

Reality Modifications

Note that the above calculation has no relation to a variety of factors, including whether or not "there is room to store that much product", the shelf life is exceeded", the quantity is a perfect multiple of full pallet quantities, etc. So, the theoretical EOQ needs to be reviewed, and possibly a different OQ assigned, based on the following:

- Any product
  - Lack of storage capacity
  - Product shelf life limits
  - Quantity not even multiple of cases or pallets
- Purchased products
  - Quantity below negotiated purchase minimum
- Manufactured products
  - Changeovers inhibit total manufacturing capacity
  - Quantity too large / too small to manufacture
- Retail products
  - Quantity smaller than retail presentation minimum

It is theoretically possible to use reductions in annual transaction costs in manufacturing to justify capital investments that would produce reduced transaction costs. However, the economics provide an acceptable rate of return only on rare occasions.

Types of Costs Used
For reference, the types of costs used in the theoretical EOQ calculations are shown in Table 7.3:

Table 7.3: Types of Costs Used in EOQ Calculations			
Type	**Components**	**Use in EOQ Calculations?**	
COGS or Direct Variable Product Cost	Purchase cost or raw materials direct processing cost up to the point of storage	**Acquisition Transaction Costs**	**Inventory Holding Costs**
+ Product Gross Margin	Overhead, taxes and profit	Yes (if sold out)	No
= Product Selling Price	Income	No	No

Reduction of Cycle Stock Inventory
Cycle stock can be reduced through reduction of the theoretical EOQ's underlying cost-sæunit acquisition transaction and unit inventory holding costs, as well as through a variety of non-EOQ-related techniques.

Unit Acquisition Transaction Cost Reduction
While cycle stock is dependent on both acquisition transaction and inventory holding costs, the most direct route to cycle stock reduction is reduction of the unit acquisition transaction cost. A 10% reduction in the unit transaction cost for an SKU will create approximately a 5% reduction in cycle stock. There are a variety of opportunities for reducing acquisition transaction costs, whether the SKU is purchased or manufactured, as follows:

- For either purchased or manufactured products
  - Reduced unloading costs
    - Dock appointment systems
  - Reduced receiving and checking costs
    - Pallet manifests / product labeling
    - Returnable and purchaser-defined packaging materials
    - Bar code data entry
    - Vendor certification programs
  - Reduced putaway costs
    - Stocking in location sequence
    - Stocking multiple SKUs per trip
    - Additional cross aisles
    - Bar code location validation
  - Other reduced receiving-related costs
    - Sale of used pallets
    - Sale of baled corrugated cases
    - Trash conveyor systems
    - Modified labor scheduling
    - Waste compactors
    - Inbound visibility software
    - Training
  - Performance improvement / continuous improvement
    - Minimum dock door turnaround time
    - Minimum shift workload carryover
- For purchased products
  - Purchasing
    - Purchasing software
    - Electronic PO transmission
    - Vendor consolidation
    - Minimum PO value rules
    - Joint replenishment
    - Training
  - Expediting
    - Advance Ship Notices (ASNs)
    - Expediting by exception
  - Accounting
    - Electronic direct payment
  - Performance improvement / continuous improvement
    - Maximum invoice accuracy
    - Minimum number of partial shipments

- For manufactured products
  - Reduced set-up changeover costs
    ◦ Product sequencing by primary parameter (diameter, paint color, family, etc.)
    ◦ Completion of previous changeover to maximum extent (parts cleaned, put away properly, etc.)
    ◦ Use of line or equipment operating personnel
    ◦ Pre-staging of raw materials
    ◦ Minimized use of tools (knobs, t-nuts, slip-in / -on, etc)
    ◦ Beginning prior to end of previous run, when possible
    ◦ Training
  - Performance improvement / continuous improvement
    ◦ Minimized Elapsed Time

Above and beyond reduced cycle stock inventory, the impact of reduced unit transaction costs will also create:

- More, smaller orders
- Reduced annual transaction costs (the unit transaction cost falls faster than the number of orders increases)
- Reduced annual inventory holding cost
- Reduced unit inventory holding cost (reduced storage)
- Increased manufacturing capacity (if ET reduced)

Unit Inventory Holding Cost Reduction

While cycle stock can be most directly reduced by reducing unit acquisition transaction costs, cycle stock can also be reduced by lowering the unit inventory holding cost, but only if it is reduced by a greater percent than the unit transaction cost. There are a few ways to reduce the inventory holding cost, as follows:

- Storage
  - Reduced aisle widths
  - Reduced number of cross aisles and storage over aisles
  - Storage mode assignments for increased space utilization
  - Re-warehousing
  - Leasing extra space in owned facilities
  - Sub-leasing extra space in leased facilities
- Risk
  - Training programs to reduce product damage
  - Increased facility security
  - Staged introduction of new SKUs

- Opportunity
  - Extended payment terms, if purchased
  - Use of early payment discounts, if purchased
- Performance Measurement / Continuous Improvement
  - Minimum shrink reduction
  - Minimum use of temporary space

Non-EOQ-related Techniques

Above and beyond the fundamental techniques noted above, there are other ways to reduce cycle stock, without any relation to the individual SKU's EOQ. These include the techniques for conversion to non-stock, discussed below under stocking policy, as well as the following:

Potentially applicable to different SKU groups in the transportation-related realm are 1) joint replenishment (purchasing multiple SKUs from a single source in a single transaction for a single destination); 2) aggregation of demand (purchasing individual SKUs from a single source in a single transaction for multiple destinations, where cross-docking and re-shipment are particularly economical or where numerous destinations are involved) or its analogy (manufacturing individual SKUs in a single run for multiple finished products); and 3) aggregation of supply (purchasing SKUs from different suppliers located in close proximity, with a group of closely coordinated transactions for a single destination, thereby facilitating maximum inbound transportation consolidation).

Worth investigating in the purchasing-related realm is reducing or eliminating negotiated purchase minimums, potentially at higher unit price, if reduced annual acquisition transaction and inventory holding costs are greater than increased annual COGS (This holds true if the purchasing personnel have no way to evaluate the total impact of the price reduction offered). Likewise, negotiating return privileges based on total purchases is always worth pursuing.

In the replenishment realm, transferring (instead of purchasing) inventory of an SKU from an overstock facility in the same tier to a facility in need of additional inventory is straightforward, providing the working capital reduced is significantly greater than the cost of the transfer. Likewise, ensuring that cycle stock overrides (full cases, full pallets, etc.) actually result in reduced total cost, considering both working capital and operating expenses, is important.

In the manufacturing realm, if an SKU's EOQ is too large to manufacture in a single run, then scheduling multiple runs sequentially will almost always reduce the total set-up/changeover cost.

Obsolete/Overstock Inventory Disposition

Non-performing inventory can take two forms: 1) truly obsolete goods that are beyond sale date or shelf life, are superceded by newer product designs, or are recalled product, and 2) functionally obsolete (overstock) merchandise whose demand is very low or non-existent. The former is easy to identify and, in general, disposition is usually addressed relatively promptly. The latter, however, is much more nebulous to define and, except in the most disciplined organizations, may remain in storage and on the balance sheet for extended periods of time.

Continuing to carry obsolete or overstock inventory reduces the availability of capital funds for attractive investments, increases labor costs if located in prime warehouse areas, and incurs storage expenses unless all facilities are owned. In addition to economic penalties, stagnant inventory effectively undermines management's credibility relative to other logistics and supply chain initiatives. Addressing obsolete and overstock inventory, therefore, is critical to progress.

When considering disposition options both economic and other factors must be considered. The economics of overstock situations should approached by comparing the discounted cash flow present values of the following:

- Maintain Status Quo
  - The current probability of sale, by year, times the current selling price
  - The product direct variable (sunk) cost
  - The ongoing costs to maintain in storage, by year
  - The probability of loss, deterioration, or damage per year times the product direct variable cost

Vs.

- Initiate Disposition
  - The revised probability of sale, by year, times the alternative selling price
  - The (original) product direct variable (sunk) cost
  - The additional cost to be incurred
  - The cost to store, by year
  - The revised probability of loss, deterioration, or damage per year times the adjusted product direct variable cost

Obviously, initiating a disposition option calls for a gain in operating profit—not just a breakeven deal, unless there are other overriding benefits. One difficulty lies in assessing the probability of sale. However, in many of the options noted, sales figures are available. In the case of liquidation, other factors must be considered, above and beyond economics. These include limitations to be placed on subsequent use or resale of the product, NAFTA certificates of origin, warranties, and others.

Two keys to a rational approach for the disposition of obsolete or overstock inventory are consistency and regularity. If the decision process varies widely from year to year or if the issue is ignored until the situation is critical, it will be difficult to reconcile the financial, marketing/sales, and operational viewpoints.

SKU Rationalization

In manufacturing, conflicting priorities reveal the following conflicting views:

- Manufacturing – wants few products, long runs, and simple changeovers
- Marketing and Sales – want many products so as to meet most or all customers' needs and allow for prompt shipments
- Finance – wants reduced inventory working capital

Obviously, underlying these viewpoints are real, conflicting needs that need to be reconciled in the best interests of the business. One of the subjects at the core of such issues is the question of SKU rationalization æ "should the product line be reduced?" and, if so, "which SKUs should be eliminated?"

Pareto curves of actual or cumulative volume, or inventory turnover vs. SKU rank, illustrate the extent to which slow-moving SKUs exacerbate the inventory, but they only provide emotional support for the discussion, as opposed to anything actionable. Of more use from a financial point of view are illustrations of the portion of annual gross margin or operating profit contributed by specific SKUs. However, the fact that an item is less profitable (as a result of either volume or selling price) than others is not necessarily a reason to drop it.

The first question that needs to be addressed is "will the company be more profitable without the item in the product line?" This brings the thought process closer to the heart of the matter, but raises some complexities. First, to what extent are sales of specific SKUs affected by the availability of other SKUs in the line? Second, how should fixed costs be considered in any economic comparison? Third, if manufacturing is at or near capacity, can additional sales of some items be increased if other SKUs are eliminated?

The extent to which the sales of SKUs are correlated is probably never a matter of full consensus. However, empirical methods such as trial removal (or introduction) of a portion of the product line in some segments of the market or in some geographical regions can be used. Market research is a possibility. Further, independently completed internal questionnaires can be a major source of information if they can be normalized to eliminate personal bias.

The matter of fixed cost, variable costs, and contribution margin can be successfully addressed using activity-based product costing, with an appropriate breakdown of expense categories and a reasonable number of activities (or by simpler methods if there are only a few different process paths through manufacturing).

The question of capacity can be addressed either by recognizing actual lost sales due to capacity limits or, if the manufacturing process is cost-effective, by assuming that infinite demand for the lowest technology product exists at a price equal to the variable cost.

With sales correlation data; fixed and variable cost and contribution margin data; and capacity data, the economics of deleting specific SKUs can be developed accurately and comprehensively. Ideally, with this economic data analysis completed, the decision(s) as to whether or not to eliminate specific SKUs will be straightforward.

However, additional questions can be raised, such as: Can the economics of the decisions for any SKUs be reversed and profit increased by reducing variable raw material, set-up, or running manufacturing costs? By increasing sales volume or selling price? By changing the nature of the sales transaction in terms of minimum order quantities, stock availability, freight basis, and return privileges?

If capacity is limited only during a portion of the year, the questions become: Can the economics be improved by modifying the production schedule? By receiving commitments from purchasers earlier? By modifying the manufacturing process? If capacity is an issue throughout the year, the question becomes: Can the economics be improved by placing products with lower gross margin relative to manufacturing capacity on allocation, and by modifying the manufacturing process?

Stocking Policy

Stocking policies define the circumstances under which purchase orders or manufacturing work orders are initiated for products.

Simple Situations

In the most basic situations, orders are initiated either 1) when the inventory is running low, i.e., working capital is invested prior to sale of the product, or, 2) with no inventory, only after receipt of an order from a customer, i.e., the product is effectively sold prior to any funds being expended.

The thought process that underlies the basic situation is a matter of logic, specifically, whether the customer's needs can be satisfied with no inventory and, if not, then inventory will be required. The two questions that need to be asked are as follows:

- Is the acquisition lead-time less than the customer lead-time?
- Are customer order quantities normally larger than (my firm's) preferred order quantities, i.e., reality modified EOQs (or their equivalent under some other replenishment logistics system which would be used if the product were to be acquired to inventory)?

In general, if the acquisition lead time is less than the customer lead time, and if the customer order quantities are normally greater than my preferred order quantities, then the product can be acquired to order. Otherwise, it will need to be acquired to inventory.

The first situation is more obvious. If my firm cannot obtain the product quicker than the customer would like to receive it, then there is no choice. The second situation is subtler. If the product is produced to inventory, then the annual (not unit) acquisition transaction costs and annual (not unit) inventory holding costs are minimized. If the product is produced to order, and the customer's order quantities are normally smaller than my preferred order quantity, then the annual transaction costs will be greater than the total annual cost had the product been produced to inventory, because the number of orders is greater. On the other hand, if the customer's order quantities are normally larger than my preferred order quantity, and the product is produced to order, not only is the annual inventory holding cost zero, but, in addition, the annual transaction cost is less than it would have been, because the number of orders is less.

Another situation that arises in determining stocking policy is how to address short-term peak customer demand requirements, which are in excess of acquisition capacity. If the periods of peak demand cannot be predicted, and the product could have otherwise been acquired to order, then it will be appropriate to hold safety stock but not cycle stock.

More Complex Situations

Many situations are more complex, and offer opportunities to reduce inventories below that which would be required if only the simple-situation thought process was employed. The more complex situations include the following:

- Purchased or Manufactured SKUs: If the SKU is subsequently assembled with other SKUs to form a finished product
- Manufactured SKUs: If the SKU is subsequently used as a component in the manufacture of two or more components or finished products

Postponement

In all of these cases, the opportunity exists to acquire product to inventory in a less-than-finished form and subsequently, after receipt of an order, to assemble, complete manufacturing, or otherwise finish the product to order. While inventories are required using this concept, the reduction in working capital compared to inventorying the SKUs, as finished products may be significant.

Inventory Reduction thru Stocking Policy

Assuming that customer needs can be met, the objectives of inventory management are satisfied to the maximum extent with no inventory. Above and beyond the postponement concept discussed above, there are several approaches to inventory reduction through stocking policies. They include:

- Conversion of SKUs to Acquired to Order (Non-stock)
- Conversion of Inventory Ownership Partially or Completely to Non-owned

To convert SKUs from acquisition to *inventory* to acquisition to *order,* it is necessary to attack the underlying issues—acquisition transaction cost, as discussed above, and acquisition lead-time. If the acquisition lead time can be reduced so that it is less than the customer lead time requirements, acquisition to order moves from impossible to merely more expensive. In a similar manner to the reduction of safety stock, discussed below, improved communications are the key to reduction in lead times. Industrial engineering and/or information technology investments can reduce the sheer length of the lead-time, however, providing suppliers with accurate forecasts well ahead of time so that the supplier's response begins well ahead of receipt of the order provides the same result.

The Supply Chain View

This thought process raises the question, "Which entity is in the best position to initiate acquisition orders, the purchaser or the supplier?" Ideally, the order initiator has full knowledge of all of the following:

- The purchaser's customer's forecasts
- The purchaser's inventory
- The supplier's inventory
- The supplier's open orders to customers other than the purchaser
- The supplier's production schedule (assumes a manufacturing supplier)

Note that, with the exception of the transportation aspect, the supplier's inventory and the purchaser's inventory may simply represent duplication. In some cases, with the support of the purchaser, the supplier is in a better position to ensure the desired level of service to the purchaser's customers with the minimum amount of purchaser's inventory. Thus, Vendor Managed Inventory (VMI) can be a very effective technique for reducing inventory levels through the conversion of numerous SKUs to acquisition to order and, as discussed below, for elimination of supplier's safety stock through reduced forecast variance.

Reducing the extent to which the inventory has been paid for by the purchaser, inventory working capital efficiency has the same financial result as conversion of SKUs to non-stock status. Such deferral of payment, whether based on a simple "net XX days" agreement or a more advanced "upon consumption," "upon sale," or "upon receipt of payment" agreement must be the result of an agreement as opposed to merely capricious behavior.

Safety Stock

Unlike cycle stock, which is related to cost, logistics, replenishment or other operational aspects, safety stock is the province of sales and marketing philosophy. It reflects the priority of management to have the SKU in stock when the customer may want to purchase it. Ideally every SKU acquired to inventory would be in stock, if desired. However, the cost to provide such a service level is prohibitive, sometimes to the extent of eliminating the product's inherent gross margin. Accordingly, the use of modified safety stock levels as a technique for reaching end-of-quarter inventory budget objectives is a wholly inappropriate practice and, assuming that the safety stock levels are being lowered, an undermining of management's marketing philosophy.

Demand Variability and Desired Customer Service Level

The safety stock level, as noted above, is a function of the desired service level (probability of being in stock) and the statistical difference over time between the expected demand and the actual demand. If the variability can be reduced, then the desired service level can be maintained with less safety stock.

The difference between expected and actual demand is normally distributed, so it may be represented by the standard deviation (SD) based on the data points during the lead-time. In practice, many software applications calculate the maximum absolute deviation (MAD) and use it as a proxy for the SD, since the computation is much simpler. Further, some advanced replenishment software applications incorporate reliability of supply into the safety stock calculation as a way of hedging some of the difference between the desired service level and the resulting fill rate.

The working capital required to support increasingly high customer service levels increases dramatically as the level rises above 95%, as shown in the following:

Figure 7.4: Safety Stock Inventory Levels

For a given desired service level, the safety stock that will provide that service level (if not undermined by other factors) is the SD multiplied by a factor based on the normal distribution. In order to estimate the increased safety-stock working capital associated with changing the service level, the current stock can be simply multiplied by the ratio of the two factors. Figure 7.5 provides percentage differences for the safety stock required for various service levels.

Differential Revenue

In some businesses, revenue is not lost if a product is out of stock when the customer desires to make a purchase. In many businesses, however, revenue is directly associated with the fill rate and the "lost" revenue can be calculated based on the forecast demand and the duration of the out-of-stock situation. In those situations, the question of the most appropriate desired service level can be considered from a return on investment

Figure 7.5: Percent Increase in Safety Stock for Customer Service Level Revisions

		To Customer Service Level														
		50.00%	84.00%	90.00%	92.50%	95.00%	96.00%	97.00%	97.50%	98.00%	98.50%	98.75%	99.00%	99.25%	99.50%	99.75%	99.90%
From Customer Service Level	50.00%	0%	NA	NA	NA	NA	NA	NA	NA	NA	NA	NA	NA	NA	NA	NA	NA
	84.00%	NA	0%	28%	44%	64%	75%	88%	96%	105%	117%	124%	133%	143%	157%	180%	209%
	90.00%	NA	-22%	0%	13%	28%	37%	47%	53%	60%	70%	75%	82%	90%	101%	119%	141%
	92.50%	NA	-31%	-11%	0%	14%	22%	31%	36%	42%	51%	56%	62%	69%	78%	94%	115%
	95.00%	NA	-39%	-22%	-12%	0%	7%	15%	20%	25%	32%	37%	42%	48%	57%	71%	88%
	96.00%	NA	-43%	-27%	-18%	-6%	0%	7%	12%	17%	24%	28%	33%	39%	47%	60%	77%
	97.00%	NA	-47%	-32%	-23%	-13%	-7%	0%	4%	9%	15%	19%	24%	29%	37%	49%	64%
	97.50%	NA	-49%	-35%	-27%	-16%	-11%	-4%	0%	5%	11%	14%	19%	24%	31%	43%	58%
	98.00%	NA	-51%	-38%	-30%	-20%	-15%	-8%	-4%	0%	6%	9%	14%	19%	25%	37%	51%
	98.50%	NA	-54%	-41%	-34%	-24%	-19%	-13%	-10%	-6%	0%	3%	7%	12%	18%	29%	42%
	98.75%	NA	-55%	-43%	-36%	-27%	-22%	-16%	-13%	-8%	-3%	0%	4%	8%	15%	25%	38%
	99.00%	NA	-57%	-45%	-38%	-30%	-25%	-19%	-16%	-12%	-7%	-4%	0%	4%	10%	20%	33%
	99.25%	NA	-59%	-47%	-41%	-33%	-28%	-23%	-19%	-16%	-11%	-8%	-4%	0%	6%	15%	27%
	99.50%	NA	-61%	-50%	-44%	-36%	-32%	-27%	-24%	-20%	-16%	-13%	-9%	-5%	0%	9%	20%
	99.75%	NA	-64%	-54%	-49%	-41%	-38%	-33%	-30%	-27%	-23%	-20%	-17%	-13%	-8%	0%	10%
	99.90%	NA	-68%	-59%	-53%	-47%	-43%	-39%	-37%	-34%	-30%	-28%	-25%	-21%	-17%	-9%	0%

standpoint, just like any other capital project. The ROI is based on the additional annual gross margin return on the increased safety stock working capital.

Fill Rate

Establishing safety stock levels for all of the SKUs at desired service levels does not necessarily mean that the resulting unit fill rate from the facility will fall easily into line. Nor will it necessarily be in the form desired, i.e., the weighted average of the SKU customer service levels. Specifically, and unfortunately, there are many situations in which the resulting unit fill rate does not rise to the desired level, including the following:

- Under-forecasting
- Late issue of replenishment orders
- Late supplier shipments or completion of manufacturing runs
- Greater than anticipated transportation time
- Less than 100% supplier fill rate
- Arrived, but not unloaded, received, or placed in storage
- In stock, but not shipped when ordered

Re-order Point

The re-order point is calculated based on the safety stock, the acquisition lead-time, and the forecast demand during the lead-time. It is an integer, and, in order-point-based replenishment logistics systems, serves as a trigger for the initiation of replenishment of purchase or manufacturing work orders.

Reduction of Safety Stock Inventory

Above and beyond the intra-company techniques for increasing forecast accuracy, safety stock reduction is a matter of improving supplier reliability and significantly modifying both the timing and understanding of customer requirements.

The improvement of supplier reliability is primarily a matter of feedback, as part of a comprehensive supplier performance measurement program, discussed below. It should be noted that the vendor fining (backcharging) processes that are part of many Supplier Compliance Agreements are counter-productive to the reduction of safety stock. The exception is if they are coupled with guaranteed purchase contract extensions or other meaningful, positive reinforcement methods for improved performance.

An additional, and less direct, technique for reducing safety stock is the reduction of lead-time. Because of the statistical basis for demand variability, the SD over a shorter lead-time will be reduced, resulting in reduced safety stock. Overrides also represent a concern for unnecessarily increasing safety stock, unless the SKU has demand is so low that the override is, for example, from an inventory level of from 1 to 2.

Class Management

Large inventories are almost always managed using a class management system for safety stock. Such an approach facilitates establishing safety stock levels across a varied range of SKUs on a dynamic basis, using pre-determined criteria.

SKU Ranking Parameters

There are a variety of possible ways to categorize SKUs and assign them to classes. The most common use a ranking system to place the SKUs in sequential, usually descending, order based on a ranking parameter. With this approach, break points can be used to easily break the SKUs into classes automatically after they are placed in sequence. The question is which criteria should be used to rank the SKUs. There are an infinite number of possibilities, some of which are as follows:

- Single parameters
  - By total revenue
  - By total gross margin
  - By percent gross margin
  - By unit volume
  - By number of customer purchase orders
  - By past late supplier receipts
  - By number of past out-of-stock situations
  - By severity of past out-of-stock situations
  - By stockout cost
- Compound parameters
  - By category revenue
  - By supplier gross margin
  - By marketing channel priority
- Complex parameters (joint ranking)
  - By total revenue and unit sales
  - By total gross margin and past out-of-stock situations

Some software applications provide ranking possibilities, although usually simple in nature. In order to get the best results, the ranking may have to be done outside the application and then interfaced to update the application with the resulting class. Above and beyond the criteria used to rank the SKUs, there are other aspects that must be considered, including the following:

- The appropriate period to use for ranking, i.e., the time period over which the past activity occurred or the forecast activity is expected to occur
- How often the ranking is to be updated and on what basis the decision is to be made
- Particular SKUs or categories which are to have their class permanently assigned independent of their ranking, for strategic marketing reasons

Number of Classes

The appropriate number of classes depends on the degree of variability in the desired safety stock levels. Three is common. However, three classes may not provide the desired degree of differentiation needed to reflect management's range of priorities. Theoretically there is no limit to the number of classes, but as a practical matter, 10 to 12 may be an upper limit. The following is a rough guide to the likely percent of SKUs in each class, depending on the number of classes:

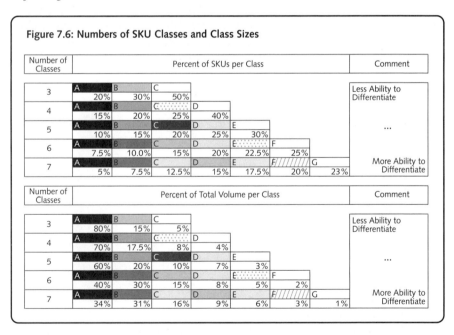

Figure 7.6: Numbers of SKU Classes and Class Sizes

Inventory Policy and Related Areas

Inventory crosses a variety of functional areas, in some cases with little or no distinction. Inventory policy is a strategic, corporate management issue with broad supply-chain ramifications, and, as shown above, has four aspects: cycle stock, stocking policy, safety stock, and replenishment logistics system. In turn, inventory policy is supported by procurement/ purchasing (sourcing, contracting, replenishment, supplier compliance agreements, supplier performance measurement, etc.), sales forecasting, and a variety of information technology and communication applications. Inventory control represents the tactical, day-to-day aspects of executing the policies, as particularly focused in replenishment order releasing, the taking of physical inventories, and cycle counting.

Cycle Counting

Cycle counting involves the frequent taking of physical inventory for very small portions of the inventory at a time, usually every day. Its value lies in:

- Detecting and reconciling inconsistencies sooner rather than later
- Reducing unnecessary stockouts
- Reducing end-of-year surprises / crises
- Making the counting function a small, integral part of the day-to-day operation, as opposed to an onerous, periodic event required by others
- Providing the ability to validate the inventory position of some SKUs much more frequently than others

There are three issues that need to be addressed in planning a cycle counting operation: 1) how often various SKUs should be counted, 2) when (during the handling operations) to complete the counting, and 3) who should perform the counting. Depending on the operation, there are pros and cons to every possibility, but the primary options include the following:

- How Often to Count Various SKUs
  - By geography on the facility
  - Using an SKU ranking method
    - Volume in $ or units
    - Lines
    - Inventory value
    - Historical variances
    - Historical reconciliation issues
- When to Perform the Counts / Validate the Perpetual Balance
  - At the time of receipt / putaway
  - At the time of forward storage replenishment
  - At the time of picking
  - At an operationally unrelated time
  - When out of stock
- Who to Complete the Counting
  - Stocking personnel
  - Forward picking replenishment personnel
  - Picking personnel

– Other warehouse personnel
– A third party

Special Situations

Multiple Facility Inventories

In supply chains, multiple facilities within the same tier which inventory essentially the same SKUs are commonly appropriate, to reduce transportation costs and/or to provide the desired response time. In such applications, the total inventory in the tier, taken in the aggregate, is a function of the square root of the number of facilities, as follows:

$$\text{INVENTORY}_{\text{EACH DC}} = \text{INVENTORY}_{\text{ONE DC}} / \text{SQRT}(N_{DCs}), \text{ or}$$

Inventory (in each DC) = Inventory (in one DC) / square root of the number of DCs in the tier

and

$$\text{INVENTORY}_{\text{TIER}} = \text{INVENTORY}_{\text{ONE DC}} \times \text{SQRT}(N_{DCs}), \text{ or}$$

Inventory (total in all DCs) = Inventory (in one DC) x square root of the number of DCs in the tier

These relationships, however, are subject to certain simplifying assumptions, the most important of which is that the volumes through each of the facilities are equal. Tables 7.4 and 7.5 illustrate numerically the impact of the equations on expanding or contracting tiers:

Table 7.4: Inventory per Single Tier DC

Number of DCs	Inventory per DC in Tier	
1	1.00	X
2	0.71	X
3	0.58	X
4	0.50	X
5	0.45	X
6	0.41	X
7	0.38	X
8	0.35	X
9	0.33	X

Table 7.5: Aggregate Inventory for Single Tier DCs

Number of DCs	Aggregate Inventory in Tier	Percent Increase over One DC in Tier	Percent Increase over One Less DC in Tier
1	1.00 X	Base	NA
2	1.41 X	41%	41%
3	1.73 X	73%	22%
4	2.00 X	100%	15%
5	2.24 X	124%	12%
6	2.45 X	145%	10%
7	2.65 X	165%	8%
8	2.83 X	183%	7%
9	3.00 X	200%	6

Tier Inventory Positioning

The question of tier positioning arises in circumstances in which there are significantly different expectations of availability for some SKUs as opposed to others. Catalog operations, which supplement traditional store retailing, are an obvious example. Similar situations occur downstream in industrial supply chains and some retail ones, and in access to spare parts for maintenance.

As with safety stock, an important question is how long the customer is willing to wait. In the case of tier placement, however, the answer is more complex in that it is not simply a matter of having the item in stock along with the associated working capital. Rather, it is a question of the relationship between sales volume and the time required to made the SKU available to the customer.

In a complex supply chain network, individual items might appropriately be held in several strategically different tiers, as follows:

Table 7.6: Distribution Tiers and Functionality

Location	Function	Response Time	Delivery
Retail shelf	Sales	Immediate	Customer
Retail store back stock	Local reserve	Minutes	Stocking personnel
Retailer's Distribution Center	Regional reserve	Days	Transportation
Supplier's Distribution Center	Regional reserve	Days	Transportation
Supplier's Manufacturing Warehouse	National reserve	Days (produced to semi-finished or finished goods inventory)	Transportation
Supplier's Manufacturing Plant	Manufacturing	Days – weeks – months if produced only to customer order	Transportation

Similarly, in a maintenance operation, consumables and spare parts may be held in different tiers, as well:

Table 7.7: Maintenance Tiers and Functionality

Location	Product Category	Function	Response Time	Delivery
In-plant Satellite Stocking Location	Consumables	Self service / free issue for commodity electrical and mechanical parts	Immediate	Maintenance personnel
Local Central Storeroom	Consumables or Spare Parts	Plant inventory	Hours	Stores personnel
Regional or National Central Storeroom	Spare Parts			
Distributor	Consumables	Local inventory	Hours to1 day	Delivery truck
Vendor's Distribution Center	Consumables	Regional reserve	Days	Common carriers

Within the manufacturing plant, the matter of tier placement may include the following:

Table 7.8: Plant and Vendors Tiers and Functionality

Location	Function	Response Time	Delivery
Plant finished goods warehouse	National reserve	Days	Common carriers
Semi-finished inventory	Assembly	Hours to days	Material handling
Work-in-process	Final manufacturing	Days	Material handling
Plant raw materials warehouse	Initial manufacturing	Immediate	Material handling
Distributor	Local reserve	Hours to 1 day	Delivery truck
Vendor's Manufacturing Warehouse	National reserve	Days (produced to semi-finished or finished goods inventory)	Common carriers
Vendor's Manufacturing Plant	Manufacturing	Days if produced only to customer order	Common carriers

The matter of tier placement is at the heart of customer service philosophy and cannot be reduced to mere economics. The economics of tier placement decisions, however, are significant in geographically large markets, or in areas in which transportation is very costly. They involve sales volume, transportation costs, and inventory working capital, and usually have the following types of relationships:

- Declining revenue as a function of increasing delivery time to the customer, due to the reduced availability
- Declining inventory requirements per SKU as a function of increasing delivery time to the customer, due to the reduced number of upstream facilities
- Increasing transportation cost per unit as a function of increasing delivery time to the customer, due to the smaller shipment size

An Additional, Sequential Tier?

Additional tiers are added to supply chain networks to provide responsiveness that would not be possible, or would be transportation cost prohibitive, otherwise. They normally handle the same SKUs as the tier immediately upstream; have more facilities than that tier; individually carry less inventory per facility than that tier; and are located closer to the destinations. While providing reduced response time to satisfy customer expectations, and possibly increasing sales volume, they increase the total inventory in the system significantly. The general form of an additional tier is as follows:

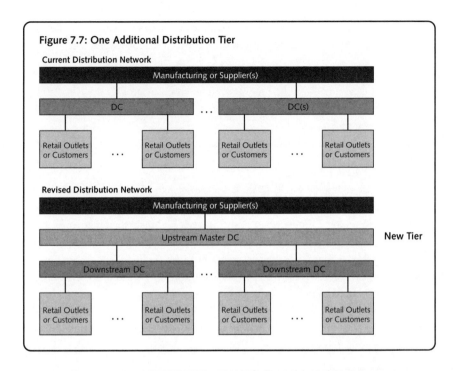

Figure 7.7: One Additional Distribution Tier

When assessing the merits of an additional tier that is not an absolute requirement, the difficulty lies in predicting the increased revenue that can be realized as a function of reduced delivery time. In this situation, the form of the economics in question, is as follows:

Does the…

	Additional revenue / year
Less	Increased COGS / year
Equals	Increased gross margin / year
Less	Additional facility expenses per year
Less	Net increase in transportation expenses per year
Less	Additional storage and risk (i.e., not opportunity) inventory holding costs
Equals	Additional net margin / year

provide an adequate return on…

	Facility capital investment
Plus	Transportation fleet capital investment, if any
Plus	Facility Capital investment, if any
Plus	Inventory working capital investment
Equals	Total capital investment

Since the exact relationship between increased revenue vs. reduced transportation time is very difficult to predict, trial facilities in some markets, with carefully selected comparative periods, are the most common approach. Further, the net inventory change may be either positive or negative depending on the relationships between the following:

- Acquisition transaction cost from the supplier vs. from an upstream DC
- Acquisition lead time from the supplier vs. from an upstream DC
- Variability of customer demand vs. regularity and consistency of DC-to-DC replenishment orders
- The number of downstream vs. upstream facilities

An Additional, Parallel Channel?

The opposite of an additional supply chain tier is the concept of splitting a supply chain network into parallel channels for different SKUs. Creating a parallel channel is possible when the required response time for part of the inventory is longer than that required for the balance of the inventory. The advantage lies in the partial or total elimination of duplicate inventories. The primary challenge lies in not incurring additional transportation expenses that overwhelm the economic advantage gained through inventory reduction.

The number of facilities in the parallel channel bears no relation to the number of facilities in the primary channel in the same tier. Depending on the required response time for the longer-delivery time SKUs, the number of facilities in the parallel channel can be as few as one. The general form of a parallel channel is as follows:

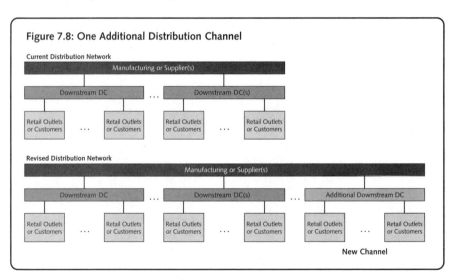

Figure 7.8: One Additional Distribution Channel

Performance Measurement and Continuous Improvement

The measurement of inventory performance, like virtually every other aspect of supply chain operations, can be approached from a variety of quality, customer service, and cost viewpoints, depending on the management priority. Further, specific measurement parameters and metrics can be developed to meet either long-term objectives or short-term issues.

Parameters

In the quality area, the emphasis is on reliability and predictability of supply and perpetual inventory accuracy. In the customer service area, the emphasis is on responsiveness, in both lead-time and fill rate. Finally, in the cost area, the emphasis is on working capital. In each of these areas, the view may be upstream, toward suppliers or manufacturing, or downstream, toward customers. Further, in a synthesized supply chain, a clear and complete view may be seen from any point along the chain.

Quality issues such as order selection accuracy and damage, customer service issues such as invoice accuracy, and cost issues such as storage cost and shrink, while closely related to inventory, are more properly measures of warehouse operations performance.

In general, the following parameters are most commonly used in measuring inventory performance:

- Quality
  - Lead Time Conformance
    ◦ During a specific period, the number of times shipments are made in the stated lead time, or less, as a percent of the total number of shipments made
  - Lead Time Variability
    ◦ During a specific period, the range of shipment times experienced relative to the stated lead time
  - Actual vs. Perpetual Inventory Balance
    ◦ At any point in time, the total inventory on hand less the perpetual inventory balance, i.e., the net adjustment required
    ◦ At any point in time, the sum of the absolute positive and negative differences between inventory on hand and the perpetual inventory, taken separately
- Customer Service
  - Unit fill rate
    ◦ During a specific period, the number of units shipped on time in the desired quantity as a percent of the total number of units ordered
  - Line item fill rate
    ◦ During a specific period, the number of SKUs shipped on time in the desired quantity as a percent of the total number of SKUs ordered
  - Order Fill Rate
    ◦ During a specific period, the number of orders shipped on time with the desired quantity of every SKU on the order as a percent of the total number of orders received
  - SKU In-stock Ratio
    ◦ At any point in time, the number of SKUs on hand, regardless of the quantity, as a percent of the total number of SKUs stocked in that location

- Financial
  - Gross Margin Return on Investment
    - During a specific period, the revenue received less the cost of the goods shipped divided by the value of the inventory on hand
  - Upstream to downstream tier Inventory Ratio
    - At any point in time, the inventory balance for a complete upstream tier as a percent of the complete inventory balance for the downstream tier being served
  - Working Capital Efficiency
    - At any point in time, the inventory which has been paid for as a percent of the total inventory, i.e., the inventory requiring working capital as a percent of the inventory in accounts payable or on consignment
  - On-hand Balance
    - At any point in time, the on-hand inventory balance less the theoretical or planned inventory balance
  - Turnover
    - During a specific period (understood to be a year unless otherwise stated) the volume shipped divided by the average inventory balance during the period

The quality, customer service, and financial parameters given above are a general guide to possible areas for measurement and reporting. In most cases, more specialized parameters need to be developed to address the specific inventories in question.

Parameter Selection, Performance Reporting, and Management Review
Parameters need to be central to improved business results, well understood by the work team, under the control of the work team whose performance is to be measured, retired (once no further improvement is possible with current infrastructure), or evolved to a more strict measure (once a superb status quo has been achieved).

Performance reports need to be line (not bar) graphs as opposed to tables of data, posted in a public place; updated on a frequency appropriate to the situation (typically monthly); easy to quickly understand (units of measure given, criteria specified, same format from period to period); and reflective of work team (not individual) performance. They should include a goal, developed (ideally) by the group whose performance is to be measured, or (in the absence of appropriate team leadership) by management. Regularity significantly reinforces both management's priority and long-term commitment.

At the time of posting, performance reports need to be reviewed with management by the team from the points of view of "what went well and how can the team replicate those situations in the future"; "what didn't go well and what can be done to avoid or rectify those situations on the future"; and "what procedural or policy changes can help."

Summary
The role of inventory policy in affecting supply-chain competitiveness must be thoroughly understood. Inventory should not be viewed as a static entity, but rather as a short duration

delay in the flow of product. As the economics underlying cycle stock and the lack of information underlying safety stock are addressed, and inventory reduced accordingly, the supply chain concept, as well as additional applications, will become more and more clear to all concerned.

Citations

1 United Nations Yearbook of Industrial Statistics

2 Warehouse Inventory Turnover, Warehousing Education and Research Council, 1100 Jorie Blvd., Suite 170, Oak Brook, IL 60523-4413

References

Inventory Management

Bernard, Paul, *Integrated Inventory Management,* 1999

James F. Cox III, et. al., *APICS Dictionary,* APICS, updated periodically

Piasecki, David J., *Inventory Accuracy: People, Processes and Technology,* 2003

Silver, Edward A., et al, *Inventory Management and Production Planning and Scheduling,* 1998

Vollman, et al, *Manufacturing Planning and Control Systems,* 1997

Supply Chain Logistics

Ballou, Ronald H., *Business Logistics Management,* 1998

Bowersox, Donald J., and Closs, David J, *Logistical Management,* 1996

Robeson, James F. and House, Robert G., Eds., *The Distribution Handbook,* 1985

Robeson. James F., and Copacino, William C.,, Eds., *The Logistics Handbook,* 1994

Schonsleben, Paul, *Integral Logistics Management,* 2000

Tompkins, James A. and Harmelink, Dale, Eds., *The Distribution Management Handbook,* 1994

Tompkins, James A., *No Boundaries,* 2000

CHAPTER 8
Collaborative Planning, Forecasting, and Replenishment (CPFR)

Andrew White, Research Analyst, Gartner Research

ERP, CRM, APS, VMI, EDI, SCM, and CPFR. There are enough acronyms in the business software market to fill an oil tanker with alphabet soup. These acronyms describe business models and their supporting software packages. One must be careful in choosing the right system/business model to address his or her company's needs. One problem is that the programs frequently overlap or only offer differing solutions to the same sets of problems. In some cases, they only address parts of problems that should be considered holistically. The software is often very expensive to buy and implement, and might even be obsolete before it is installed or paid for. This hazard is exacerbated as savvy marketers bend the meanings of these new terms to suit their own purposes.

The View From the Top

It is possible to get a handle on these issues. If you take the time to get the "50,000-foot view" of what people do at work, basic truth quickly becomes clear. Every operational activity focuses on one of three things: planning, execution, or measurement. *Planning* consists of devising or outlining a program of activities to ensure that the right products or materials will be in the right place at the right time and at the right cost, so that customers are satisfied and companies make a profit. *Execution* represents the physical creation and movement of products or materials, and *measurement* represents the counting of products, resources, materials, and activities that are relevant to the performance of the execution activity.

During the past 20 years, management leaders have focused the bulk of their time and money on efficiency in the execution and measurement functions—the physical movement of, and accounting for, goods. This is the core competency of enterprise resource planning (ERP) systems. These admittedly are important areas, but focusing exclusively on them misses the planning aspect, which is a full one-third of the big picture. ERP is about transactions: order management, purchasing, and financials even though some programs have had "bolted on" planning capabilities.

Looking beyond the four walls of your own enterprise to gather and coordinate information from suppliers, customers, shippers, and carriers has always been necessary to ensure having sufficient material on hand to make a product and fulfill customer orders. With the rise of the Internet, the performance bar has been raised. Now it is not enough to accurately and efficiently track and account for the movement of goods and their related transactions through a factory. Estimates of demand from customers, and availability of materials from suppliers, have to be far more accurate as well. Information about these issues has to flow as seamlessly as possible between you, your suppliers, your customers, and the extended value chain to your customer's customer and supplier's supplier.

Planning, Execution, and Measurement in the Value Chain

The same three processes that cover all your company's inside activities apply to your outside supply chain as well. Planning concerns itself with anticipating an order and includes all the steps that must be taken to anticipate and prepare for eventually executing it. Planning is synonymous with information. Execution is associated with the physical side of product creation and movement from one end of the value chain to the other. Measurement relates to the performance and transaction-capturing side of a business—the kinds of things ERP systems were designed to do.

To address planning issues apart from tracking and transaction functions, some software suppliers offer advanced planning and scheduling (APS) solutions. APS is a term that grew out of the finite scheduling models that were added to material requirements planning (MRP) and manufacturing resources planning (MRPII) solutions in the 1980s. However, the term has grown to include distribution, transportation, and demand optimization. It is this deep supply chain planning functionality that APS vendors offer.

The Dawn of Collaboration

APS was only the beginning of a solution. The logical next step in optimizing communication, and therefore performance across the entire supply chain, was collaboration.

Upstream supply chain collaboration concerns itself with all the customer and market-facing processes in an organization, such as collaborative forecasting (a planning function) and collaborative order processing (an execution function). Downstream supply chain collaboration, on the other hand, concerns itself with all the supply and supplier-facing processes in an organization, such as collaborative replenishment or vendor scheduling (a planning function) and collaborative MRP for plant-to-plant and plant-to-vendor execution (an execution function).

An example of a hybrid planning and execution model on the supply chain side is flow or lean manufacturing. A very forward-looking model includes the concept of electronic and wireless kanbans for automatic alert notification, which is faster than physical kanbans. Other supply chain initiatives that contributed to the evolution of collaboration include vendor-managed inventory (VMI), efficient consumer response (ECR), and quick response (QR).

Collaborative Planning, Forecasting, and Replenishment

The first steps to building a viable collaborative model took place in 1995 and 1996, when Wal-Mart and Warner-Lambert piloted electronic data interchange (EDI) and Excel-based collaborative processes. Both companies participated in determining the demand and subsequent supply plan for Listerine® Mouthwash. The pilot produced significant benefits in terms of increased service levels at Wal-Mart to meet customers' needs, lower inventory throughout the supply chain, and increased revenue to both Wal-Mart and Warner-Lambert.

At that time, the pilot focused only on the sales forecasting aspect, and there was little or no revision to the actual replenishment planning. Further, EDI was the basis for the technical sharing of data, and it was a batch process. During this period, Logility, Inc. went live with a virtually identical business model for Heineken USA using the Internet for real-time collaboration. This enabled Heineken to work with its customers in the United States to jointly derive the sales forecast at the customer (distributor) level and the replenishment order from Heineken USA.

These developments led to the establishment of Collaborative Planning, Forecasting, and Replenishment, or CPFR. The emphasis is on collaboration—the removal and elimination of barriers between trading partners. This collaboration involves sharing important plans and data across inter-company spaces.

Today, this CPFR model represents the most advanced example of a business-to-business (B2B) process that takes advantage of the Internet as a means to break down barriers between organizations. CPFR is not a process that simply uses the Internet to share information faster. It is also the first of a new breed of business processes that exploit the Internet as a tool.

CPFR represents the collaborative extensions to supply chain planning. Planning is the focal point of the relationship and represents a formal agreement between companies. Furthermore, CPFR changes the transaction and therefore the nature of the relationship between trading partners. If a feature or model fails to achieve this, it is not truly collaborative. Visionaries today see CPFR as the most advanced model available.

To help differentiate CPFR from non-collaborative processes that may call themselves collaborative, ask two questions. Does the feature or model change the transaction between partners, or does it simply speed its transfer? Do both trading partners jointly derive the information being exchanged? If the parties just send and receive data to each other, this is more likely an exchange process and not a collaborative one. If all parties submit data, and the model compares and merges the data and then synchronizes all the systems, then you have a collaborative model.

Collaboration is not achieved by the old-style partnership model of the 1980s or by simply sending and receiving EDI files faster or better.

Overview of the Nine-Step CPFR Process

The following is a summary of the nine-step CPFR model. It highlights some of the key lessons learned from early work experiences.

Step 1. Front-End Arrangement

This, the toughest step, focuses solely on the highest level of relationships between two organizations. The key concept is that senior executives from each company come to an agreement on a mutual strategy. For retailers and manufacturers, CPFR meets consumer needs by eliminating stock-outs, reducing prices, creating better assortments and more choices, and ensuring complete satisfaction.

This step is also very "soft"—it is all about organizations and people. If the collaborating organizations have divergent corporate strategies, such as cost cutting vs. market growth, the basis for CPFR will be set in sand and it will be harder to make it work. Of course, company strategies align and realign all the time. CPFR should not be seen as an "only-works-in-this-place" tool. It can act as a framework for a far more useful environment that operates between organizations.

What's new about this compared to any other agreement made between buyers and sellers? CPFR is flexible and collaborative. The agreement is that buyer and seller will agree on common metrics for the relationship so, they can measure their joint successes. In this manner, they can share in the success of the win/win solution that they achieve. Likewise, they must share in the cost.

Step 2. Joint Business Plan

The Joint Business Plan (JBP) is the operational side of the agreement between the two organizations. The JBP turns the goals and objectives of the Front-End Arrangement into real targets for real products at real locations. This level of detail includes identification of managers and planners from both companies who will determine which products are to be collaborated upon. Not all products will be managed via CPFR. There is a whole set of products and situations that lend themselves to CPFR, so companies need to be cognizant of these. Additional information is gathered here that turns the business plan and its objectives into targets that information systems can process to facilitate successful collaboration.

Collaboration is not about people reviewing all the products that they sell or buy. Collaboration is made real by agreeing on rules and regulations between buyers and sellers to automate the bulk of the business transactions. When exceptions occur, real collaboration between people takes place. Metrics are used to check the process to ensure that the automation makes sense.

Some of these rules and regulations include such things as details of the exceptions (your forecast vs. my forecast) and defining what forecast error and exception thresholds mean. The importance of having common metrics cannot be stressed enough. It is a worthless exercise if the buyer and seller use their own separate metrics to monitor the relationship. Planning has to draw out the goals of the two companies and work toward a common framework and hence, common metrics. If it turns out that two partners have divergent goals, they should cease efforts to collaborate until they can operate together more closely.

Step 3. Create Sales Forecasts

The understanding of the term "sales forecast" is very important for the relationship. This forecast represents what the buying partner thinks it will sell. If the buyer is a retailer, this is the consumer demand or point of sale (POS) forecast. If the buyer is a manufacturer (doing CPFR with a raw material or packaging supplier), it is the shipment forecast.

The value of this visibility and collaboration is clear. If the seller gets access to visibility and can be part of the process to review and agree (collaborate), then the chances of success are greatly enhanced. Visibility, as a means to information access, is one element of a successful collaboration process. However, visibility in and of itself does not result in collaboration.

In CPFR, either the buyer and seller—or both—will generate a sales forecast. Both buyer and seller have access to it and can review it with respect to the seller's ability to meet it. Integration processes are created so that information automatically flows between the buyer and seller's internal systems. In other words, the buyer's forecast is passed to the seller's planning systems for verification. Any conflicts in the seller's ability to meet the demand, or a change in demand, are the variables the companies are looking for.

Step 4. Generate Exceptions to Sales Forecasts

Assuming a business plan is in place, and assuming that buyer and seller forecasts are in line, the next logical step is to automate the approval of the forecasts' conversion to an order. This is what makes collaboration so effective—the companies collaborate on the plan so that this level of trust can be realized.

Should the forecast between buyer and seller vary, alerts are sent to interested parties and each party will review and eventually revise the disparity. This is a comprehensive step that sounds simple, but one can quickly imagine many "but-what-happens-when?" issues coming up. After implementing a CPFR process, one can quickly appreciate the level of complexity that needs to be part of the technical solutions that make CPFR possible.

Here, we refer back to the Joint Business Plan because that is where the buyer and seller captured the rules to be used to manage the relationship. In other words, for each product, parameters are set that describe what constitutes an exception and what does not. When exceptions are not present, forecasts are automatically turned into orders. When exceptions are identified, Step 5 is initiated.

Step 5. Resolve Exceptions to Sales Forecasts

This step represents a major success factor. When variances are identified, users are notified. Sometimes this requires a batch-oriented review of a report. The more advanced models today provide real time e-mail alerting capabilities. Either way, the planners end up working together to come to a conclusion. Any individual revisions to the forecasts are sent back to the CPFR solution for exception-checking again. Depending on the workflow and exception thresholds, another alert might be generated, or an order might be approved. Either way, the process automates the checking and determines the next step.

Planners may agree to disagree so a tiebreaker has to be agreed upon in the Joint Business Plan. People will not always come to an agreement, but they have to recognize that there will come a time when a mutually acceptable decision has to take place for the relationship to work. Resulting metrics will show if the decision-making process has to be changed.

The buyer and seller will operate under different calendars and have different item codes and product hierarchies. CPFR cannot and does not seek to force any of these to change. However, depending on the solution's level of sophistication, these will be rationalized and reconciled so that each user can access its data to resolve exceptions to its requirements.

Step 6. Create Order Forecasts

For those products on which there is collaboration, Step 6 should take place reasonably well. This step converts forecasts that have passed their approval windows to orders, which is another example of the type of data agreed to in the JBP. The result from the CPFR solution is a piece of information that would need to be sent to the respective ERP system or to the next step of the CPFR process.

In a typical retail/manufacturer scenario, the order forecast is generated from the buyers' purchase planning system—perhaps a distribution center-replenishment tool. In some cases where VMI might be implemented, it is possible that a seller will also be able to generate this information. Generally, order forecasts are more detailed in terms of time focus, as it is the order forecast that represents the actual inventory. Someone will pick, pack, and ship inventory according to the order forecast.

Sales forecasts also focus on products and brands—often at high levels of aggregation. Store-level CPFR is possible, but unproven. It is likely that the simplest of "order-up-to" tools or two-bin systems could produce acceptable results to manage the overall flow of product after CPFR is established. Scan-based trading does not gain the levels of improvement associated with CPFR because it simply speeds up the already established processes. If the POS forecast is of poor quality, the wrong products are replenished.

Step 7. Generate Exceptions to Order Forecasts

Step 7 is very similar in nature to Step 4 except for the fact that we are talking about a different piece of information. From the buyer's perspective, the order forecast is the inbound delivery from the seller; from the seller's perspective this is the shipment to the buyer. In past initiatives, this was *the* primary focus for the seller—this is what made up the quarterly numbers. CPFR elevates the relationship to another level that ties buyer and seller.

Exceptions here should focus on the supplier's ability to satisfy the order. In other words, it is likely that output from the seller's planning systems is shared and compared with the orders. This output might include inventory availability (ATP), product order status, plant and transportation capacity (capable to promise, or CTP), and so on. CPFR is not prescriptive—it does not mandate what data is used or who supplies it.

Step 8. Resolve Exceptions to Order Forecasts

This automated process is like Step 5 in that a resolution is sought between buyer and seller, purchase order and order management system, and planning and execution systems. This might result in a change to the order forecast, or it might result in a change in the execution plans. Either way, a resolution is achieved. If two parties agree to disagree and leave the issue unresolved, the result will materialize later in the form of poor customer service. CPFR mandates reconciliation. Both partners may dislike it, but it ensures that the relationship continues to move forward.

Step 9. Order Confirmation

Step 9 is innocuously small and yet this is the where the rubber meets the road. In fact, as practitioners in the field know, Step 9 is not a step at all. It turns out that this step is now evolving and expanding into what is being called Collaborative Transportation Management (CTM). The point is that once orders are approved, there are several other planning steps that seek to combine orders and maximize the freight aspect. CPFR did not seek to change this process. CTM does.

CPFR Deployment Options

The CPFR topology diagram describes a "hosted" model of CPFR in which a series of buyers and sellers use a "service" approach to accessing a CPFR tool. Alternative models also available today include those where a company acquires and hosts its own CPFR tool. In this case, each company would have a Web server. The point is that CPFR is so flexible that it "exists" at every potential node in a value chain.

A "hosted" topology for CPFR is where a third party hosts a CPFR solution and buyers and sellers congregate to practice CPFR. The hosting agent could be an application services provider (ASP), or net market. Individual members would not need to have their own CPFR technology.

The hosted deployment option is similar to the net market model in which a managing company hosts the solution on behalf of some of its members.

An earlier deployment model is the hub and spoke model. In this approach, one company "hosts" the technology and the partners log on to it to "do" CPFR. The good news for the hub is that they have access to their own solution and are therefore enabled to "do" CPFR with all of their key trading partners. The bad news for the spoke companies is that they have to "do" CPFR with only those partners who have the technology. In other words, they would have to interface with many different CPFR solutions.

Peer-to-Peer (P2P) CPFR is likely to become a long-term deployment model, particularly for companies that are large enough or who view collaboration as critical. Meanwhile, hub-and-spoke approaches will be used where these peers perform CPFR with tier-two partners. The mix will also include hosted offerings for mid-sized companies, and offerings via Microsoft's bCentral for small companies who can then perform CPFR with any partner.

The Current Status of CPFR

CPFR was an initiative of the Voluntary Interindustry Commerce Standards Association (VICS). Recently, the VICS CPFR group merged its operations with those of the European Efficient Consumer Response groups under the auspices of the Global Commerce Initiative (see www.globalcommerceinitiative.org), because the largest retailers and manufacturers operating in the U.S. and Europe needed a global standard to do B2B. Global CPFR is the initial priority for this group, but CPFR will prove to be just the platform, the beginnings of a collaborative framework upon which other collaborative processes will spring. In addition, other B2B and some not-so-B2B business processes will be absorbed by or, more precisely, built on top of CPFR. Examples include Collaborative Promotion Planning and Collaborative Transportation Management.

The Committee's efforts will turn to multi-tiered or "n-tier" CPFR. In this application, more than two tiers of a value chain align themselves to participate in a mutual CPFR relationship.

What is the ultimate goal of CPFR as currently envisioned? The concept is that by sharing such collaborative, one-number plans with multiple layers of the supply chain at the same time, all partners of the chain can synchronize their businesses to the real trends identified in the channel.

Today, the ultimate in the naming game is B2B Collaborative Commerce. The use of the word collaborative here represents all Internet-based processes, including planning, execution, and measurement. However, only true collaboration changes the transaction and hence the nature of the relationship between trading partners. How do you know if a process is true collaboration? Look at the data or information in question and ask, "Is this jointly derived?" If the data are jointly derived through a process, it is true collaboration. If the body of data in question has no joint component, then it is of the false collaboration model.

In summary, CPFR is an advanced business-to-business process that uses Internet technology to break down barriers between trading partners in the supply/demand value chain. Through its special focus on planning, CPFR changes the nature of the relationship between trading partners. The nine-step process that defines CPFR represents a major breakthrough in helping to achieve final supply chain (value chain) success.

Works Consulted

Tompkins, James A. *No Boundaries: Moving Beyond Supply Chain Management*. Raleigh, N.C.: Tompkins Press, 2000.

Voluntary Inter-Industry Commerce Standards Association (VICS). "CPFR Guidelines." 1998. http://www.cpfr.com.

VICS. "The Case Studies: Roadmap to CPFR." 2000. www.cpfr.com.

White, Andrew. "The Rise and Fall of the Trading Exchange." *Logility,* 1999. http://www.logility.com.

White, Andrew. "The Dating Game: Searching for Liquidity in the New Economy." *Logility,* 2000. http://www.logility.com.

CASE STUDY: HEINEKEN

Collaborative Commerce Over the Internet: CPFR In Action

Mike Edenfield, President, CEO, Logility, Inc.

The "Heineken Story" has been reported more times in the public press than any other story relating to Internet-based, business-to-business (B2B) collaborative planning. Ever since its initial pilot and implementation in late 1995, Heineken USA has been regarded as being at the forefront of value chain best practice. Even before the word "collaboration" was hot, Heineken USA was transacting business with its trading partners over the Internet.

Today collaboration is indeed hot and is imbedded in the concept and system of Collaborative Planning, Forecasting, and Replenishment (CPFR). The focus of CPFR is on the information flow between trading partners. It forces companies to see an alternative way to transact business—one that virtually eliminates the need for customer order processing, purchasing, and even enterprise resource planning (ERP).

CPFR is the first of a new wave of different processes that actually eliminate several older processes. CPFR provides a way to jointly derive data that changes the transaction and hence the relationship between trading partners.

Heineken USA

In 1994, Heineken USA was a staid beer distributor. Being family owned, the company operated in a quiet market. Growth was relatively flat—and the company had a very flat brand program with only four brands making up 26 stock keeping units. The organization was also fairly conservative with a traditional, for its time, centralized focus. Marketing was more of a concept than a reality, so the company played little part in the general market as a whole. Further, its information technology (IT) infrastructure was very basic. In 1994, personal computers were not used, and communication with everyone, customers and suppliers alike, was handled via fax. All of the beer was made in Holland and shipped to U.S. customers. Heineken was then (and still is today) a non-stock environment.

The company was focused on the trade, but because of the lack of marketing it often watched from the sidelines as the market evolved and grew. Since prohibition, the beer distributor has to be a separate organization from the beer manufacturer and retailer. To make matters worse, the U.S. operation operated independently of the parent company in Europe. This fragmented approach created a slow, static supply chain with poor customer service.

The situation was far different by 1997. In that year, the European parent company bought back the U.S. operation so that it became an operational division. This helped to better align the U.S. goals and objectives with those of the rest of the organization. The market had also changed dramatically because Americans, and in fact most of the world, drank more beer than ever before. Currently, light beers are the high growth area, but from 1993 to 1996 there was a 24% general growth in demand. This growth presented an ominous threat to any manufacturer or distributor who had outdated or inefficient supply chain systems.

During this period, Heineken's product line expanded from four brands and 26 SKUs to seven brands and 42 SKUs. Even though this may sound like a small portfolio to many, it was a massive change for Heineken and its systems. Furthermore, these numbers do not take into account additional complications created by state requirements for packaging and labeling. The company grew from being slow, reactive, and centralized to a more de-centralized, proactive organization and increased its off-premise-focused sales force from two to 30 people. Heineken has since implemented an integrated marketing plan and process, and is now supported by a state-of-the-art IT infrastructure.

More importantly, Heineken is now focused on customer service. Instead of focusing exclusively on shipping numbers and the trade, management now worries primarily about customer service issues such as planning, replenishment, and performance. After the customer service issues are handled correctly, the numbers always follow. With this integrated and outward approach, the U.S. organization plays a more important role within the overall Heineken group.

The Way it Was

Back in 1996, Heineken suffered from numerous conditions that undermined its goals and objectives, including:

- Separate and independent processes that led to distributor beer orders based on "negotiation" between the distributor and company sales people. Sales planning was independent of marketing planning and didn't necessarily support financial targets or meet minimum production runs in the brewery.
- Data collection was manually (fax) driven and inventory management was haphazard at best.
- Order processing was a manual process requiring human intervention during containerization and routing.

This fragmented series of processes supported the company's traditional view of the supply chain. The results of these fragmented processes were very clear and painful:

- Uncertain impacts on production resources
- Antiquated systems and processes
- Police-like relationships with customers and distributors
- Ineffective and inefficient communication throughout the supply chain
- Long lead times waiting for product
- Inaccurate prediction of demand
- A sales force overwhelmed with paperwork
- Inconsistent inventory management

At that time, beer was produced well in advance of actual customer orders. The company had to forecast orders using tools available at the time. The use of paper and spreadsheet tools produced a very detailed paper chain rather than a real value chain. An inordinate amount of time was spent gathering and sharing information in a slow, outdated, and unresponsive manner. IT was viewed more as a chore than as a way to exploit or deliver competitive advantage.

Relationships with customers—the beer distributors—were not strategic. In this competitive environment, Heineken was at the small, upper-end of the market for high-value or premium beers. The overall market is basically "owned" or driven by the large U.S.-based domestic brewers. The latter represent a very large share of the market, and consequently have the greatest influence on distributors. A smaller niche marketer has to be nimble and customer focused if it is to be aggressive and create greater market share. It has to deliver a service and system providing greater added value than the large producers can deliver.

The antiquated systems in use were the result of a lack of vision, and as a result the manufacturing operations in Holland were plagued by poor visibility and inaccurate forecasts. To help the manufacturing plants meet their objectives (long run times), which were different from that of the U.S. company (revenue growth), customers were subjected to long lead times. This produced a vicious circle. The longer the lead times, the poorer the forecast, which meant that lead times had to be extended even further to give the plant greater visibility, and the cycle continued. Consequently the beer inventory that should have been a customer service asset turned out to be a liability. The sales model focused on customer service included late deliveries, inadequate response, and order expediting.

This operating model was replicated across all the 450 customers in the U.S. And these 450 distributors are all very different. Several very large customers have their own ERP and supply chain systems. At the other extreme, are very small, so called "mom and pop" customers who have no computer systems to speak of other than a PC. Therefore the company's systems had to cater to all the varied type of environments in which it operated.

Consequently Heineken recognized that it needed a massive change. If it was, as an organization, to enter the late 1990s with a highly competitive, dynamic business model that could allow growth, weathering of competitive threats, and management of changing market conditions, then major change was needed.

Alice in Wonderland to the Rescue

But what should be done? Where to start? Turning to one of the classics, one can imagine a dialogue as this:

Alice: "Would you tell me, please, which way I ought to go from here?"

Cat: "That depends a good deal where you want to get to."

Alice: "I don't much care where."

Cat: "Then it doesn't matter which way you go."

Alice: "So long as I get somewhere."

Cat: "Oh, you're sure to do that, if you only walk long enough."

Heineken recognized that it had a choice. If it could not build a new, dynamic and forward-looking vision, then it mattered not what it did. With a new team in place, Heineken USA decided to build a vision, which interestingly was significantly ahead of its time. Today, this vision is known as collaborative planning, forecasting, and replenishment (CPFR). Internet-based collaboration is another name that is in use today. But when the project was started, the Internet was not even popular.

The Heineken vision started out as a "wish list" that said, "wouldn't it be nice if..."

- There was one plan, that was integrated through one central planning organization, and
- If that plan was created from the bottom-up, and
- If that common plan drove initial forecasts for all areas, and
- If those initial forecasts were made visible to distributors so they could "collaborate" and "massage" them based on local market knowledge, and
- If those "collaborative forecasts" became the basis for orders, depending on a distributor's sales patterns and inventory levels, and
- If those forecasts, sales patterns, and orders were seamlessly communicated throughout the chain, requiring minimum labor to drive the process, and
- If there was a system that facilitated the above while minimizing the impact on both Heineken USA's and the distributor's infrastructure, and
- If that system could also be used to communicate programs and promotional information to distributors, and
- If that system had a catchy acronym?

The smart answer to this question was a wholehearted yes.

Software and Partner Selection Process

Heineken USA worked with outside professionals to determine a process to select a software partner to build and meet the company's vision. The winning vendor demonstrated, live, over the Internet, a web page that encapsulated the company's vision. This software supplier had listened to the expression of company needs and presented a software tool and supporting solution that met those needs. This software provider has become a fundamental component of the company's team as it continuously looks to the future to improve what it does.

The Solution: Process Model

The process that was jointly developed looked like this:

One Number Planning: In order for all parts of the organization to synchronize their efforts, and to tie those efforts to customer needs, a "one number planning" system was needed. This meant that sales inputs, marketing plans, and financial goals and objectives would be integrated, along with the various strategic planning goals shared with the corporate parent.

The tool used has a pyramid structure embedded in the software that supports the gathering of forecasting information from remote and distributed sources, and for merging the numbers together to one, agreed-upon number. Each function in the organization then can see the one number in its own unit of measure. Generally, finance is interested in profit, sales and marketing in terms of revenue growth, and operations in terms of pallets of beer.

There is further integration with the rest of the Heineken operational systems in order to support brand quotas, regional quotas, distributor quotas, brewery forecasts for products, and overall company cash flow projections. What started out as a way to plan better turned out to be a complete business planning and management solution.

Integrated Planning: By synchronizing the forecasting process, the company began to achieve a much more highly organized and synchronized business. Sales volume planning was now part of an integrated planning process that drove brewery short-term production plans as well as longer-term capacity plans for capital investment. Finance was now part of the processes as the forecasts now represented real numbers to be achieved. Therefore, the cash flow projections that could be derived from the processes were invaluable inputs to the financial management of the organization. Integrated to all of the above are Heineken's corporate and regional marketing plans.

Collaborative Planning: The distributor customers now have an environment in which to collaborate successfully, real-time, 24-hours a day as needed via the Internet with Heineken USA. Their initial plans are submitted to the processes with Heineken's own experienced people who make recommendations. Subsequent collaborations take place until agreement is reached. From this agreed-upon sales plan the resulting (and now deterministic) replenishment plan or order forecast is also collaborated upon. The order plan takes into account the on-hand inventory status at both customer and supplier ends of the value chain.

From Order Placement to Customer Relationship Management: What began as a simple order placement system (the original name was Heineken Order Placement Systems—HOPS—and was replaced with Heineken Operational Planning Systems) has become a complete customer relationship environment, or CRM as the market now calls it. In this environment, more than just orders are placed. Customers now communicate at their leisure their most recent demand statistics and inventory status—in some cases this information is automatically updated. Then medium-term sales forecasts are shared, as are subsequent short-term replenishment orders (order forecasts). Additional data pertaining to a shared calendar of events such as period-ends, or special deals and promotions, are communicated across trading partner boundaries. This creates a unique experience for customers, and thus provides a unique competitive advantage for Heineken USA.

The Benefit is Clear

The technology employed is the Internet, which is challenging all that has gone before it. For Heineken, the challenge has paid off. In a recent survey of customers, the company experienced a 100% improvement in customer satisfaction. Now more than 70% of customers (up from 35%) said the company provides good or excellent service compared to much larger and more resourceful competitors. Recognizing that there is no room for complacency, Heineken continuously reviews its processes with a view to improving them. Another measure the company is proud of is that in random tests, it has shown it can deliver beer to a retailer shelf from a factory over 5,000 miles away, with a longer shelf-life product than that of a local microbrewer.

Technology as an Enabler

Many of the company's partners and even its own employees were very nervous about adopting the Internet back in 1995. But today, they find they are ahead of the curve. Now, several customers simply use an Internet provider account to collaborate on plans, forecasts, and replenishment orders with Heineken USA. The Internet has provided a 24x7x365 operational environment that offers the highest level of customer service. There is no down time.

The Internet also did not place heavy demands on information systems (IS) resources. The company did not have to acquire a completely new infrastructure. Several competitors had tried a more traditional IS approach in the past and had failed. With an Internet application, Heineken USA reduced the training requirements for its customers and reduced dramatically the cost of ownership associated with a traditional client/server application.

Benefits

The benefits realized in this application are very real. Cycle time, from when customer demand is recognized to when it is satisfied, has been reduced by over 67%. This is not because the beer is packed quicker, or shipped faster. It is simply that huge amounts of wasted time and inefficient processes, that previously hindered the customer relationship environment, have been eliminated. Other benefits include:

- Better Forecasting and Planning
- Self-Regulating Order Planning
  - Adjusts for inventory variance due to forecasting error
- Better Inventory Management
- Reduced Lead Times
- Fewer manual processes and procedures
- Stronger and more focused communication
- Shifted sales focus from "what goes into the warehouse" to "what leaves the warehouse"
- Perceived "Leadership"
  - GartnerGroup ieC Award
  - VICS Best in Class Logistics
  - Food Processing Achievement Award

The Use and Abuse of "Collaboration"

The Heineken story is an excellent example of the real use of the Internet for true collaboration. But what is meant by true collaboration?

It is any process that helps to: a) jointly develop or derive data or information, and b) change the transaction between partners and hence the relationship.

The Market Acceptance and Phases of CPFR

Heineken implemented what today is referred to as "hub and spoke" CPFR, which is where there is one central hub (Heineken) and all the trading partners (customers and/or suppliers) use the Heineken system to "CPFR." Those partners are not enabled to CPFR with any other partners except Heineken USA, as they are effectively "subscribing" only to the Heineken system. In order to CPFR with multiple and any partners, those partners would need to acquire their own CPFR solution. This would then create what is called "Peer to Peer" CPFR.

The latest development is that of "hosted CPFR". This arrangement provides one hub or Community, and all trading partners, customers, suppliers, and carriers go to one location to do CPFR. It is a good way for a company to implement CPFR much faster, since they do not even have to build a web site or web server.

Virtually all other major IT initiatives that have ever been pioneered required a large barrier to entry. For many years, only the largest companies could do MRP. ERP has a high price tag associated with it. Even EDI is an expensive option. Heineken has proved that a world class Customer Relationship Management model can be built using an Internet provider account at a nominal monthly charge. This is a different plan to those of the multi-million dollar, multi-year projects. Anyone who has read Intel Chairman Andy Grove's "Only the paranoid will survive" will recognize CPFR as a major, strategic inflection point. Those companies that recognize this issue will reap the rewards.

CHAPTER 9
Distribution and Supply Chain

Brian Hudock, Partner, Tompkins Associates

In the past, distribution was the focus for optimizing logistics costs and networks. It encompassed all that we could see or imagine in our world. With the globalization of the past 10 years, our world got smaller a lot quicker than anyone predicted. Gone are the days when node-to-node product movement was the focus of organizations specializing in logistics. Now that information is more readily available and the steps and partners in the supply chain increase in complexity, perfecting a single movement between any two nodes now generates smaller returns than it once did.

What is now critical is how effectively these node movements work together to synthesize the total supply chain, part of the Supply Chain Excellence process. Achieving Supply Chain Excellence involves six levels: Business as Usual (Level 1), Link Excellence (Level 2), Visibility (Level 3), Collaboration (Level 4), Synthesis (Level 5), and Velocity (Level 6). It requires an organization to start at the lowest level—Business as Usual—and move through the levels in sequence. Distribution plays a significant role at each level. (For more information on the Six Levels of Supply Chain Excellence, see Chapter 1.)

This chapter discusses the two components of distribution—warehousing and transportation—and how they are changing, what drives the distribution of product, and the distribution approaches that are commonly used today.

The Basic Distribution System

A basic distribution system consists of four points connected by a transportation system. The four points are:

- Raw materials supplier
- Manufacturing/assembly operation
- Warehouse
- End-user

Who and what the end-users are, and where the raw materials are, and how raw they are, depends on their relative positions in the supply chain. A shirt sewing operation sees the cutting operation as the supplier of raw materials and the end user as the consumer. The cutting operation sees the fabric mill as the raw materials supplier and the sewing operation as the end-user. This example of limited visibility is one of the limitations of the distribution system. The different parts of a supply chain are as important as the whole because one bad step can shut down the entire supply chain.

In a true distribution model, two key components must be controlled to make the distribution network efficient and cost effective: warehousing and transportation. The section that follows takes a closer look at warehousing and current trends for warehousing as part of distribution; distribution alone is discussed further in this chapter. (A third could be the point of consumption, but it is really a driver for order size and frequency.)

Warehousing

An old saying in warehousing is, "If there is available space, someone will eventually fill it, usually sooner rather than later." Therefore, it is not uncommon for a warehouse to be full even during slow periods. Normally, a warehouse will run out of space due to rapid growth, seasonal peaks, large discount buying, planned inventory builds for manufacturing shutdowns, facility consolidation, or even slow sales. In retail and catalog environments where seasonal planning and purchasing rely heavily on forecasts and style trends, the availability of the right merchandise to ship to the customer is the key to sales and success. Hence, planners want both a wide selection of goods and large quantities of "hot" items on hand to fill customer orders.

Generally, three types of space deficiencies occur in a warehouse. First, there is too much of the right inventory, second, there is too much of the wrong merchandise, and third, the warehouse space is poorly utilized. To address each type of space issue appropriately, one must first understand the issues. Having an abundance of the right product appears positive in terms of customer satisfaction and order fulfillment goals. Yet, as the sales staff and buyers celebrate, the warehouse operates well below established productivity and safety standards. Pallets of product are stored in aisles, stacked in dock areas, and placed on rack end caps. Or, multiple SKUs of the product are mixed in single bin locations. Blocked visibility creates safety hazards and decreases labor productivity, while inefficient multiple handling of product becomes an accepted practice. However, the right product usually moves quickly through the warehouse and space problems exist for short periods.

Too much of the wrong product often indicates that sales projections or production planning areas are incorrect. It also often indicates that the warehouse is not managing inventory levels or obsolete product properly. Unlike having too much of the right product where short inventory peaks can be dealt with using extra labor, having the wrong product requires action from management to resolve the problem. If not, the inventory remains in the warehouse for months or even years.

A good example of this lack of inventory management occurred at the warehouses of a mid-sized arts and crafts supplier. Upon reaching a full warehouse condition at both their manufacturing and distribution centers, the company brought in a consultant who, upon examination of their inventory, discovered that 600 of the 3,000 pallets at the manufacturing center had not been used in the last 12 months. At the distribution center (DC), over 400 of the 4,500 pallets on-hand had no movement in over three years. Another 500 pallets had zero activity within 12 months. Too much of the wrong product was solved with the stroke of a pen and a one-time hit to the bottom line.

Poorly utilized space, a condition usually caused by growth, and changing storage and service requirements, is common and non-exclusive of inventory type or storage conditions in the warehouse. Traditionally, warehouses are built and equipped to handle projected volumes, a set number of products, and limited unit loads. Then they are expected to adjust to customer demands and be more efficient asnd time passes. To meet these conflicting goals, warehouses generally accept long-term penalties. Examples include creating customized floor-ready merchandise for end cap displays and hand-pricing a key customer's merchandise on the piece level when goods traditionally ship in full-case quantities. Both of these actions take valuable floor space and labor away from primary warehouse functions.

Other indicators pointing to poor space utilization include low vertical space use, wide aisles (more than nine feet), multiple product SKUs in single bin locations, and/or partial unit loads being stored in full unit load locations. These types of problems should be addressed with physical layout and workstation design changes.

Often inventory excesses and general space constraints result from any of the abovementioned conditions, but the consolidation of operations or a case of continuously growing sales can create real space deficiencies. When relocation or facility expansion is not an option, three paths may be followed, including outside storage, internal warehouse redesign, or improving inventory management.

Inventory builds traditionally handle seasonal peaks or new product introductions. Demand for products such as cold weather garments that sell like hot cakes during the first significant snowfall of the season and the first release of a long-awaited music CD are prime examples of planned inventory builds. In some cases these builds are unavoidable and require temporary measures to handle the inventory peaks.

Some methods for handling these temporary builds include third party warehousing to store excess inventory or storing and shipping orders direct to customers. Unfortunately, a premium for these services is charged on short-term contracts vs. year-round deals. Several manufacturers have reduced the penalty of seasonal storage by forming alliances with companies that have different seasonal peaks but similar storage needs. For example, a sausage manufacturer that has an inventory peak in winter and spring each year to meet high summer demand for cook-outs might partner with a turkey producer that has a late summer and fall build for Thanksgiving and Christmas demand.

Another method is to store product on trailers for short periods. This method can be extremely expensive, as monthly quality trailer rental or demurrage can range widely and include drop-off charges, trailer loading and unloading labor expenses, and security. Trailer storage succeeds best when a true partnership exists with a dedicated carrier. Often the carrier will manage the freight and store trailers in its yard as part of the freight agreement. The carrier benefits by having guaranteed freight throughout the year and by being able to charge a profitable rate for all routes.

Trends for Warehousing as Part of Distribution

Over the past several years, many have predicted the demise of warehousing, especially with the evolution of concepts such as just-in-time (JIT), quick response, efficient consumer response, direct store delivery, and continuous flow distribution as part of supply chain optimization. Common themes represented by these programs have caused a number of uninformed individuals to imagine a world without stockrooms, kitting operations, wholesalers, distributors, and DCs.

We can be sure that warehouses will continue to play an important role in the logistics supply chain. Just as we can be sure that warehousing will continue to be a dynamic function, driven by market forces toward continuous improvement. In keeping with this idea, the trends that will take industry into the future:

- Focusing on the customer
- Consolidating operations
- Continuous flow of material and information
- Time compression
- Crossdocking
- Paperless warehousing
- Electronic commerce using the Internet
- Customized warehousing (secondary manufacturing)
- Third party warehousing
- The incredible shrinking order
- Automation
- Educated workforce

The following sections take a look at these trends.

Focusing on the Customer

The most successful, fastest growing, most profitable organizations talk to their customers. They understand that the customer wants increasing value at lower costs and with higher levels of information. They understand that quality is a given. Their focus on quality goes beyond production by having shipments that are consistently complete, accurate, and on time. They understand that the warehouse must add value—the utility of having the right product, at the right time, in the right form, and making that product available to the customer.

They welcome and solicit special customer requirements as opportunities to differentiate themselves from their competition. They already know how well they are doing because they have established relevant performance measures. As competitive pressures increase, customer service—and customer satisfaction—is the competitive advantage in the 21st century. The most successful companies will be those that go beyond today's standard of customer focus, to develop true partnerships with suppliers and customers that transform the arm twisting of the 1990s into information sharing, joint planning, and win/win agreements in the future.

Consolidating Operations

Industry consolidations are rising in number and speed. The word "consolidation" brings to mind a client with 44 DCs that would like to reduce that number to two. However, that is only the tip of the iceberg. Financial institutions are merging globally, as are printing companies, publishing companies, telecommunications companies, and pharmaceutical companies. The results are fewer and stronger competitors, customers, and suppliers, as well as consolidation layers such as site consolidations, company consolidations, and functional consolidations, all of which may take place at the same time.

During mergers and acquisitions, consolidation often is a natural result of an action. One company buys another and then eliminates clearly duplicated functions or sites. Consolidation, however, may also be the result of great effort and persistence. Efficient and effective transportation infrastructures and economies of scale that provide for higher throughput levels and customization also create consolidation. Redundancies become merely remnants or memories of the past.

The end results are fewer operations of greater scope and greater efficiency and a tighter network of DCs. The goal of a distribution network is shipping and receiving products while maintaining or increasing customer satisfaction requirements and decreasing costs. Companies are increasingly relying on network modeling to create a network that meets these goals. For more information on distribution networks and network modeling, see Chapter 6.

Continuous Flow of Material and Information

Today shipments are more frequent. An increase in receiving, putaway, picking, and shipping activities puts greater demands on the material handling systems used in warehouses, affecting fork trucks, conveyors, and even carts. Demands on storage systems are different. The sizes of loads that are handled and stored are shrinking. At the same time, stock keeping unit (SKU) proliferation requires more storage locations, not less. Also, consolidation has created bigger distribution centers with more orders to process daily.

Just as material flow has become more continuous, so has the flow of information. Online and even real time information systems are replacing batch systems. As the number of material handling transactions increases within and between warehouses, so too are information transactions. In this age of information, we are witnessing perhaps the greatest change in warehousing with respect to information flow. Will you be ready for the future?

Time Compression

Better, cheaper, and faster is the battle cry of the future. A wholesale supplier wants to increase service levels with same day shipments and reduce SKUs and space requirements by packing to order, all simultaneously. On the other hand, a retailer, also simultaneously, needs to balance the warehouse workload and deliver store shipments on Friday ahead of the weekend sales rush. A wholesaler is convinced that sales are maximized with the traditional end-of-the-month push. Another retail supplier ships 40 percent of its annual volume in the last month of the year. In this scenario, from a time perspective, the warehouse lives constantly on the edge, pushing the performance envelope in ways not understood by purchasing, sales, or the customer representatives that they work with. How much time can you eliminate in your supply chain to keep pace with competitors in the future?

Crossdocking

Crossdocking has existed and evolved for many years in the trucking industry, where terminal crossdocking has become the norm for cost effective operations. However, until recently, the use of crossdocking in both manufacturing and distribution warehouses had been the exception rather than the rule. The typical crossdock operation only occurred as an out-of-stock product was received or produced and directly transferred to the manufacturing line or shipping dock. This is a truly opportunistic and infrequent utilization of crossdocking.

The increasing requirement to reduce inventories and the growing trend toward smaller and fewer warehouses will likely transform the majority of facilities to predominately crossdocking operations in the future. The ability to access and process information in real time will force warehouses to handle product in this manner increasingly over time. Crossdocking is discussed in depth later in this chapter.

The Paperless Warehouse

The tracking of goods in and out of a warehouse from receipt, to putaway, to order picking, and to shipping is the function that warehouse professionals consider to be the most critical in their operations. It requires the most non-value-added resources and remains the most error-prone process, making tracking the biggest obstacle to obtaining timely data of any of the warehousing functions. One powerful trend that can be implemented to simplify and streamline the material tracking function is the movement to a paperless warehouse environment.

In principle, the paperless warehouse simply implies that all product movement is tracked electronically rather than through the old-fashioned paper trail. This eliminates the traditional errors associated with product recognition, location confirmation, data entry, and picking accuracy, while increasing tracking capabilities and reducing overall labor requirements and training.

Eliminating delays associated with secondary data entry, allows inventory to be updated and available at the time of receipt. This allows a computerized WMS to then allocate inventory to either pick locations or bulk storage locations immediately upon receipt confirmation. Inventory location moves, forward pick location replenishment, and inventory cycle counting may then be directed by the warehouse control system through the use of wireless batch or RF terminals, pick-to-light systems, and/or totally automated picking units such as AS/RS units and A-frames.

Essential to the success of the paperless warehouse is a radio frequency (RF) system. Using bar codes read by laser scanners or handheld and laptop computers with radio frequency capabilities, RF systems free data collection to go to the product instead of requiring the material handling system to move the product through a data collection point.

An RF system is basically a hub and spoke data system, with small fixed radio antennae as the hubs and radio waves as the spokes. It is a kind of cell phone system for the distribution center, letting data collection gear go where it needs to anywhere in the process without being limited by the length of a wire.

Data collection devices are numerous. They range from relatively simple handheld scanners to units with keyboards, color displays and even photographic capability. With the photo-capable unit, a worker can to an area of a warehouse where pallets have been damaged, record the incident photographically and collect and transmit data from labels on the damaged units.

Electronic Commerce Using the Internet

Business transactions on the Internet are increasing exponentially. Consumer online sales hit $47.6 billion in 2001, a 12 percent increase over 2000. On the B2B side, the average amount of materials bought online by companies jumped from 7.1 percent of all purchases in the third quarter of 2001 to 9.5 percent in the fourth quarter. With the provision of secure servers and electronic signatures, companies are discovering that much of the tempest about Web security has been eliminated.

While many experiments with B2B e-commerce have seen little success or have fallen by the wayside, one form of B2B e-commerce—the private trading exchange—has proven to be not only viable, but also long-lived. A private exchange is a Web-based point of contact that facilitates internal and external communications, transactions, and collaboration among a limited and approved group of member companies—a private e-marketplace, essentially. It takes advantage of the Internet's ready accessibility and low cost to maximize information sharing and process integration between enterprises. With private trading exchanges, companies can automate tactical and collaborative business processes and share supply requirements and availability without compromising confidentiality or security.

Recent survey findings from AMR Research indicate private exchange activity is growing among companies in the United States. Twelve percent of large and medium-sized U.S. companies have at least some limited private trading exchange technology in place, and AMR expects that to increase to 28 percent by 2003. These figures indicate that the business of electronic markets should not be considered lightly; any reticence exhibited in entering the electronic age of commerce, even with its numerous dot.com failures, will not bode well for any industry.

Customized Warehousing – Secondary Manufacturing

Millions of dollars will be lost for companies that do not prepare their warehouses to support their customers' custom packaging requests. Providing customized services is one of the fastest growing trends redefining the changing role of the warehouse. Customized warehousing services can be a simple as transferring finished goods to a unique pallet configuration or as complex as a significant portion of what we have traditionally thought of as manufacturing activities. They include any packaging or assembly enhancement to the products, or improvement to the services provided by or in the warehouse.

The reason customized warehousing has grown in popularity is because of its proven benefits, which include:

- Reduction of required warehouse space
- Minimization of the impact of SKU proliferation on the warehouse
- Increased levels of customers satisfaction (reduced back orders, increased responsiveness, enhanced customization)
- Reduced customer returns and charge backs
- Reduced SKU reconfiguration
- Reduced levels of obsolete and slow inventory
- Additional flexibility for special and/or rush orders
- Manufacturing can plan, schedule, consolidate, and balance production runs in the most economical lot sizes rather than on a SKU-by-SKU basis
- Manufacturing can minimize changeover frequency and set-up times
- Increased inventory turns

This has resulted in increasing demands on the warehouse to provide the following customized services:

- Customizing generic products in the warehouse (on-demand packaging)
- Compliance labeling
- Ticketing and bagging
- Dunnage
- Palletization

In other words, the warehouse is evolving into a "customer satisfaction center" that performs numerous customized and value-added services to products before shipment. This has created changes in four areas:

1. **Facilities**. Due to manufacturing producing generic product, manufacturing is being simplified and the amount of space required for finished goods is being reduced. At the same time, the warehouse needs more storage and working space for customization activities.
2. **Equipment**. New, different, and equipment is required for customized warehousing, as a result of changing storage requirements and the addition of some manufacturing functions to the warehouse.
3. **Technology**. To handle the demands of customization, the warehouse needs a real-time, bar code-based, radio frequency communication WMS with the functionality to kit materials, schedule production tasks, and to track work-in-progress.
4. **Labor**. Depending on the specific customized warehousing design, more labor may be required. Even if no additional labor is necessary, necessary skill sets are changing and production workers are being transferred from manufacturing to the warehouse.

Warehouses are no longer in reactive mode. They are adopting proactive processes for handling customization trends. In other words, their paradigm is shifting.

Third Party Warehousing

At some point, most companies evaluate the possibility of a third party handling all or part of the process of moving their product to the consumer. Companies returning to their core competencies and others refusing to build more space to store peak inventory have been driving the growth of third-party logistics (3PL) to date, but in the future the need to leverage capital and increase service levels will feed third party growth. As the 3PL market continues to grow, more small and medium companies will be compelled to use these services to compete effectively.

So, what is 3PL? It is the utilization of an outside firm to perform some or all of the supply chain functions presently performed internally. This involves any aspect of the logistics function. As a rule, a service provider integrates more than one function within the overall supply chain.

Third party can be narrow or broad. It can be:

- Public warehousing: leasing space in a warehouse facility in order to accommodate overflow or geographic considerations.
- Distribution: contracting a third party to handle all the distribution in a geographic area.
- Total logistics: a third party handles all the distribution. After the point of manufacturing, the third party deals with all distribution issues and sometimes even the raw materials.

Those companies and enterprises choosing to outsource logistics functions to a 3PL provider generally outsource more than warehousing. However, warehousing is generally part of a 3PL package and that has a cumulative effect on warehousing overall. The ability to reach the next level of performance with little or no capital investment will drive 3PL growth and reduce the number of warehouses owned by corporations and increase the number of warehouses leased to corporations by 3PL providers.

The Incredible Shrinking Order

Today, order sizes are shrinking while actual orders are growing. So many factors are driving the reduction of order sizes and the increase in order frequency. Better information availability, higher levels of technology, vendor-managed inventory programs, the elimination of the onsite retail warehouse, and the direct-to-store and direct-to-customer programs are making the days of mixed-pallet shipments seem like utopia. Home shopping (via Internet or similar technology) is in its infancy and yet there are companies that only exist on-line, they have no stores or outlets. The ability to ship an order of any size from one item to many is no longer a problem, but rather is a common way for many companies to do business.

Automation

Handling consolidated facilities with ever increasing volumes is not accomplished simply by adding labor. Automation, such as conveyors to move small totes and cases across long distances and to sort to the appropriate repacking station or loading dock, is just as important. In addition, the use of automated picking equipment such as A-frames and dispensers is on the rise because it improves throughput capacity of existing centers without building additional space. Automation has also replaced humans in the warehouse for heavy lifting and the non-value-added movement of goods in limited access areas of the warehouse. However, the human workforce will continue to be required to complement automation for, as we have learned, a computer can think logically and adapt to pre-defined changes in the requirements, but only the human mind can operate efficiently during the chaos following a system glitch.

The Educated Workforce

In retrospect, with the advent of new technology and automation, the warehouse appears to require less human intervention and skill. However, the level of expertise and technical skills, especially computer skills, has and will continue to increase dramatically, and the quality and education of the primary workforce must keep up. This will be accomplished by maintaining the best of the existing workforce, training workers in new technologies, and crosstraining them in all warehouse job functions.

As this discussion has demonstrated, those leading warehouse operations face steep challenges. Those same challenges offer a number of exciting opportunities. If companies can capitalize on these challenges and trends, while maximizing transportation, prospects for improved logistical opportunities will be excellent, especially for those companies seeking to achieve world-class status. The next section discusses transportation today and what practices and systems can maximize its contributions to the supply chain.

Transportation

Having the product in the right place at the right time in the right condition is a key to the success of any distribution system. How that product gets there is the key to creating customer satisfaction. Therefore, the type of customer shipped to will often dictate the mode of transportation used.

Small or consumer-direct customers will generally place small orders that are single-piece or single-case items. This type of order is shipped via a parcel carrier. Retailers or wholesale or custom manufacturers that focus on variety and a high turnover are more likely to ship mixed-pallet loads or single pallets of one item is more likely. This type of load is traditionally carried by a less-than-truckload (LTL) carrier or local delivery truck. Those supplying processors or manufacturers or those handling import and export where multiple-pallet loads of material are common generally use common carriers or private fleets. The largest and least time sensitive of these loads are shipped by rail, intermodal, and ocean vessel shipping.

Although the basic mode of transportation may be dictated by the customer and the order size, within each mode there are numerous options and cost factors that must be understood, including:

- **Volume.** The volume of shipments has a direct correlation to the overall cost of the shipments, carrier responsiveness, and quality of service. Operations that have high volumes dictate terms and discounts with the majority of parcel carriers. Those with lower volumes are often forced to use a single carrier to get any discount. This limits the service given to all customers, as some areas are not serviced as well by all carriers. Large-load shippers can reserve significant space and obtain favorable rates on rail and ocean transport also.
- **Routing.** The ability to plan and route orders to specific geographic zones can improve service levels and costs. All carriers would much rather handle a load once rather than take it through several processing centers. This is referred to as *zone skipping* in both parcel and LTL environments. Routing can also be useful when the same routes are run on a regular basis. This allows carriers to bid more precisely on the distribution routes knowing when and where the volume will be moving. The carriers may then plan and utilize the return route well in advance and maximize their backhaul potential.
- **Timeframe.** How long a load can take from order to delivery is a major driver for customer satisfaction and costs. The choice between shipping an item next day or air, vs. putting it on a long-haul trailer, must be made carefully. If a customer makes next day a requirement, then that customer should bear the extra shipping cost, unless the problem is with the originating node. Expectations should be established early and policies followed.
- **Contracts.** If the volumes, routes, and timeframe can be identified and controlled, the ability to negotiate favorable rates with all types of carriers becomes possible. It should be the goal of every organization to leverage inbound and outbound controllable shipping lanes to reduce costs on all routes.
- **Customer Expectations.** The customer or receiving node's expectations define all other aspects of transportation. A clear understanding of the timing, condition, and cost of transportation are part of business and must be part of a good distribution system.
- **Import/Export.** The product's origination and destination are critical to timing and cost. Companies should take advantage of the ability to plan ahead and manage lower-cost transportation modes to bring low-value items to customers or production. This requires long-term visibility of needs and reliable service between these nodes as well as reliable points of origin. This as well as people and technology to manage numerous languages, currencies, custom requirements, duties, and security issues.

- **Private vs. common carrier.** In addition to the above issues, companies must make the difficult decision of whether or not to operate a private fleet or contract out all shipping services. The ability to manage and control the shipping process with an internal fleet is a powerful argument from a control and service perspective, but it is often not as cost effective unless it is very well managed and the routing and volume are stable enough to allow for high trailer utilization. When operating a private fleet, the costs should be compared regularly against open bids by common carriers to monitor how the changes in business are affecting efficiency.

Managing these options and factors is best accomplished by a warehouse management system (WMS) that drives the warehouse, the transportation management system (TMS) that drives the routing and product movement between nodes, and the distribution requirements planning (DRP) system that drives the inventory requirements to optimize the overall network.

Warehouse Management System (WMS)

The primary objective of WMS technology is to allow warehouse management to manage its operations productively. Reducing and eventually eliminating uncertainty within the warehouse can achieve dramatic improvements in overall operations. By eliminating information errors and excess lead-times, improvements can be achieved in customer service, enhancement of performance measurement, and reductions in operating costs can be achieved.

A WMS also has an impact on receiving and shipping. During the receiving operation, employees no longer have to look up purchase orders and check back-order lists before receiving product. Fast receiving means reduced inventory, since the material becomes available to the facility within minutes of receipt. Manual receiving can take several days before product can be released to the floor. Shipping operations also benefit. Purchase orders (POs) can be directly downloaded to the shipping department for immediate fulfillment. Automated shipping manifests, bills of lading, and internal account documentation can all be automatically generated in a WMS.

Finally, a WMS manages and directs labor to the immediate tasks at hand. The primary benefit of labor management is the reduction of deadheading, or an empty return trip. Directing employees through a series of tasks based on each employee's location in the facility can result in shipping and receiving tasks being performed in the same cycle.

Transportation Management Systems (TMS)

There are two types of TMSs. One type manages infrastructure on a large scale, and the other helps companies make educated, efficient decisions about its private fleets and about the litany of shipping options available.

Large-scale transportation management systems are obviously at work today in our cities. Companies are achieving a similar level of synchronizationcity in their distribution and logistics operations today. Integrated WMS/TMS solutions offer the following transportation-oriented features:

- Optimization of dock space through dock door confirmation and dock staging and truck loading management
- Updateable freight rating capabilities
- Assignment of carriers based on product characteristics and rates
- Maintenance of shipper and customer discounts, special charges, stop-offs, and loading allowances
- Maximization of the shipping dollar through order consolidation, LTL pooling, lane building, and zone skipping
- Production of standard bills of lading, shipping labels, and carrier manifests
- Audit capabilities to ensure that duplicate billings and incorrect charges are eliminated or reduced

The traditional system of transportation management involved shuffling papers, making phone calls, waiting, waiting, and then waiting some more. With an integrated WMS/TMS solution, the supply chain is becoming a model of accuracy and immediacy.

Distribution Requirements Planning (DRP)

Distribution requirements planning is a logistics tool that evolved following the great success of basic materials requirements planning (MRP) and manufacturing resources planning (MRPII) systems in the manufacturing industry. DRP is a system and database used in planning and scheduling activities and developing a dynamic action plan based on a continually changing set of events. Changes in customer demands sets off chain reactions that affect inventory, warehousing, transportation, procurement and manufacturing. DRP reacts by changing and adjusting plans to suit changing conditions. Some of the benefits of using DRP and associated systems include helping to reduce inventory levels, distribution cycle times, and required warehouse space. A DRP system can also be adapted for use on almost any computer system—mainframe, mini computer, or microcomputer. In addition, information can be exchanged using networks and radio frequency devices. Through networking, the system allows all partners in the total distribution channel to work with one another using one set of numbers and with one plan.

The synthesis of 1) distribution resource planning (DRP) software, which guides the company's purchasing efforts through close scrutiny of inventory, 2) the WMS which manages the operations of the warehouse, and 3) the transportation software which determines shipment routings based on customer service issues, makes for a powerful system. Combine this system with information enablers such as auto-ID and electronic data interchange (EDI) or XML (Web based), which provide an accurate means of transferring or entering information, and the benefits to any distribution approach can be overwhelming.

Distribution Approaches

A multiple location distribution system has several points of origin and distribution known as distribution centers (DCs). In any multiple location distribution system (see Figure 9.1) a balance of inventory must be reached between the points of origin and the points of distribution. The primary goal of such distribution systems is to provide the end user (customer) with an accurate and quick response to his orders at the lowest possible cost. This is accomplished by operating the system with the minimum inventory necessary to meet the peaks and valleys of demand and minimizing transportation and space costs. At the foundation of defining inventory levels is an accurate sales forecast. Unfortunately, sales forecasts are subject to Murphy's Law—"If anything can go wrong, it will." This reality creates the need for a safety stock inventory in order to maximize customer service. Furthermore, DCs generally are not designed to handle the peak inventory level, except when sales are relatively flat. So, during peak inventory periods the product is either backed up at the plant or stored in a temporary location. These two factors: the need for safety stock and the inability to handle peak inventory levels, greatly impact the choice of a distribution system.

There are two basic approaches that can be followed to achieve a balanced inventory and to handle the required safety stock and inventory peaks. The first approach is to PUSH all the products from the plants to the DCs based on projected sales within a distribution facility region. The second approach is for the DCs to PULL products from the plants based on actual demand.

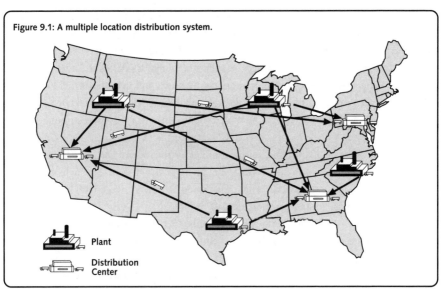

Figure 9.1: A multiple location distribution system.

Plant

Distribution
Center

PUSH Distribution System

In a PUSH system (see Figure 9.2), since all of the product is deployed based on the sales forecast for each region, an inaccurate sales forecast incurs several severe penalties, including:

- Increased safety stock
- Larger DCs
- High stock-transfer costs

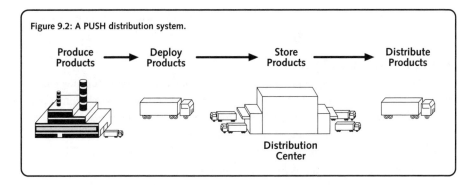

Figure 9.2: A PUSH distribution system.

The pre-order deployment of product directly increases safety stock as more DCs are added to the system. Each location must have enough safety stock to not only cover system-wide forecast inaccuracies, but also to handle the individual regional sales fluctuations. This increase in safety stock then necessitates the need for larger DCs to handle the increase in product inventory. When large regional sales fluctuations occur, products must be shipped between DCs to accommodate customer demands. These fluctuations increase the transportation costs system-wide, and additional handling and shipping costs are incurred due to an increase in material handling, shipping, product loss, and damaged material. The more points of distribution in the system, the greater the penalties incurred for unpredicted order fluctuations.

The goal of any distribution system is to improve or maintain a high customer service level. In the PUSH distribution philosophy, the penalties of higher safety stock, larger DCs, and increased safety stock are not the only penalties that a system may incur. By building a large inventory at each DC, the issue of product rotation becomes more important and the ability to utilize crossdocking is greatly reduced. Instead of crossdocking, all products must be unloaded, staged, taken to a storage location, stored, pulled from a storage location, staged, and loaded for shipment. In a crossdocking mode, all products are just unloaded, staged, and loaded for shipment. The crossdocking approach allows for the elimination of much of the material handling of the product. However, a PUSH system presents several very positive and cost saving benefits as well, including:

- Small plant warehouses
- High customer service levels
- Full-truckload plant to DC shipments

The only warehouse needed at the plants, since all products are stored at the DCs, is the area required for dock staging. This allows the plant to utilize its space for production and eliminate the need for a full warehouse staff thereby reducing costs. A high customer service level is the goal of a system and will aid in increasing future sales of the product. Finally, by having the products deployed to the regional DCs, it enables the plants to build full truckload quantities and reduce system wide transportation costs. A PUSH system functions most effectively when sales patterns are consistent, there are a low number of product codes in the system, and there are a low number of DCs.

PULL Distribution System

In a PULL distribution system (see Figure 9.3), since only production (not deployment) is based on system-wide sales forecasts, an inaccurate sales forecast has a less significant impact on the distribution side of the business. All fluctuations in demand are corrected by changing the production schedule at the plant. In a true 100% PULL environment, an order from a customer generates an order from the DC to the plants. In an ideal PULL production environment, the facility would produce the product at the time an order is received and immediately ship it. However, this type of operation would be extremely expensive to build and costly to operate. Realistically the plants will stock a buffer inventory and pull products from this buffer to ship to the DCs, who in turn receive and mix the product and ship the completed order to the customer.

A 100% PULL system utilizing large production runs incurs several penalties, including:

- Large on-site plant warehouses
- Slower order fill time (lower customer service level)
- Increased less-than-truckload shipments

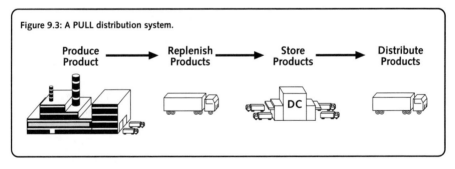

Figure 9.3: A PULL distribution system.

Produce Product → Replenish Products → Store Products → Distribute Products

The larger on-site plant warehouses occur as the majority of the system inventory is stored at the point of origin rather than at the point of distribution as in a PUSH system. These on-site plant warehouses increase the size of the plant, the plant warehouse staff, and may also reduce the plant's ability to expand production areas in the future. One way to reduce the size of the on-site warehouse is to shorten the product production runs. It is often the case that investment in production equipment to increase capacity, to improve efficiency, to reduce maintenance, and reduce changeover time is a better investment than warehouse space.

A slower order-fill time will reduce customer service in most cases. As orders take longer to get to the customer, the growth of future sales may slow or even decrease.

The final major penalty occurs when customer orders are placed—they generally do not equal full-truckload quantities. This creates the need to combine several orders when possible, which may further slow response time. When orders cannot be combined to create full-truckload quantities to a DC the transportation costs of an order increases significantly.

However, because sales forecast inaccuracies have less impact on a PULL system, the following results are experienced:

- No stock transfers between DCs
- Lower safety stock
- Lower overall system inventory
- Direct plant-to-customer shipment opportunities

The buffer inventory maintained at the plants serves as the system inventory and handles the reallocation of products to the DCs when sales fluctuations occur. This eliminates any DC-to-DC stock transfers. In addition, by storing all the inventory at the plants, the safety stock is reduced, because only system wide sales fluctuations, rather than regional and system wide sales fluctuations, affect product inventory. This in turn reduces the overall system inventory and reduces the overall required warehouse space. The final benefit of a PULL system comes from the opportunity for shipments to be made directly from the plant to the customer. On large customer orders for products from one plant, that plant can ship that order directly to the customer. This reduces transportation costs, handling costs, reduces DC traffic and improves response time and customer service level. A PULL distribution system functions most effectively in an environment with variety of production points, many points of distribution, and a high number of product codes in the system.

PUSH/PULL Distribution System

The reality of both PUSH and PULL distribution systems lies in the goal of the system, the environment in which it operates, the products stored, the available facilities, or the capital for investment. In reality, a distribution system that is between a pure PUSH and a pure PULL is often best (see Figure 9.4). A plant often has a warehouse to store a small amount of inventory and DCs often pull products from plants to adjust to sales fluctuations in a predominately PUSH environment, while plants will create full truckloads by pushing popular products to DCs and the DCs will build inventories to meet peak sales demand periods in a predominately PULL environment. In fact, in most distribution systems some combination of PUSH and PULL is the solution, which offers the most benefits including:

- Little or no DC-to-DC stock transfers
- Full-truckload shipments between plants and DCs
- Reduced overall system safety stock
- Crossdocking at DCs
- Direct plant-to-customer shipments
- High customer service levels

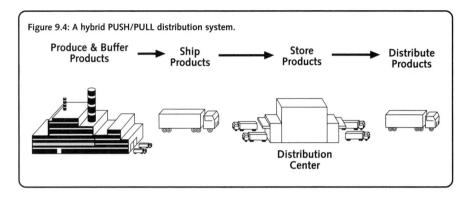

Figure 9.4: A hybrid PUSH/PULL distribution system.

In order to determine the type of distribution system that best fits each individual operating environment, a distribution strategic master plan must be done to analyze both the present and the projected factors, including:

- Transportation costs and methods
- Inventory carrying costs
- Product storage and rotational requirements
- Damage costs
- Percentage of products damaged per operation
- Expansion needs and costs
- Sales trends
- Projected growth
- Production capacity
- Production cycles
- Customer demands and needs
- Multiple industry specific factors
- Factors dictated by corporate policy

The process must also include a plan for the number of distribution points necessary or desired in future operations.

In the final analysis of any distribution system, one will find that no two systems are alike and that over any period of time any individual distribution system must adapt to various external and internal influences in order to operate efficiently. Two common and successful adaptations are crossdocking and drop shipping, both of which are discussed in the following sections.

Crossdocking

In theory, crossdocking appears so simple that it seems it could be implemented without much effort. Nothing could be further from the truth. In fact, most crossdocking failures come from an insufficient understanding of the requirements for success and a lack of planning for the execution.

Many operations have all of the physical elements in place that are required for crossdocking. In these operations, there is a temptation to implement crossdocking without developing a formal program. Since crossdocking requires that many internal and external functions work closely together, attempting to implement crossdocking without a formal program is the path to failure.

To successfully implement crossdocking, it is necessary that a formal program be set up to address each of the above categories. The formal program must include:

- Teams comprising appropriate internal and external personnel for each category
- The development of required changes
- A plan to implement these changes
- Implementation and testing of the changes
- A crossdocking implementation plan and schedule
- The implementation of a crossdocking pilot program
- Evaluation of the pilot program and the implementation of required modification
- Implementation of crossdocking
- A formal periodic review of the crossdocking operation and the implementation of appropriate improvements

Crossdocking has an additional advantage. By eliminating the storage function, one increases inventory turns, thus reducing inventory carrying costs and speeding the flow of product to the consumer.

It should be pointed out that crossdocking is not new, and many operations have engaged in "opportunistic" crossdocking. This technique involves filling existing orders with received product even when it is in storage, or shipping received product to fill back orders.

JIT (just-in-time) is crossdocking for the receipt of components or raw materials. However, crossdocking is just as applicable (possibly more so) to the shipping of finished goods. Distribution crossdocking involves the receipt of full-unit loads (pallets) and the shipping of either the same-unit loads or of unit loads composed of sorted pallets.

Terminal crossdocking is a truck sortation and consolidation of orders where unit loads that are received from two or more manufacturing or distribution operations are placed on the outbound truck so that they can be shipped to a customer at the same time.

Crossdocking can be further divided into current or future modes. In current crossdocking, material is moved directly from receiving to shipping without any intermediate staging. In future crossdocking, product is staged between receiving and shipping. The time product is staged can vary, but it would be hard to consider that an operation is actually crossdocking if product was staged for much more than a day.

The requirements for crossdocking can be broken into the following six categories:

- Partnership with other members of the supply chain
- Absolute confidence in the quality and availability of product

- Communication between supply chain members
- Communication and control within the crossdocking operation
- Personnel, equipment, and facilities
- Tactical management

These are discussed in greater detail below.

Partnering with Other Members of the Supply Chain

The fact that crossdocking involves receiving and shipping means that it involves other members of the supply chain. When one member of the supply chain implements cross-docking, it frequently results in other members incurring increased effort and cost. The tactic of forcing the other members of the supply chain to absorb this cost will, at best, result in grudging cooperation and, at worst, result in total failure.

For example, if crossdocking requires that empty trailers be staged waiting to be loaded during outbound manufacturing crossdocking, it is foolish to assume that the trucking company will absorb the cost of having the extra trailers on-site. The proper approach is to work with the trucking company to minimize the cost of providing the extra trailers and then to pay for any reasonable additional costs.

In the case of manufacturing finished goods crossdocking, the supplying member of the supply chain is the manufacturing operation. It is therefore imperative that manufacturing is consulted and that appropriate changes be made to the cost structure to account for the changes that manufacturing has to make to accommodate crossdocking.

Absolute Confidence in the Quality and Availability of Product

Crossdocking is a real time operation; therefore, it demands that material flow without interruption. The crossdocking team has to be absolutely certain that the correct product will be available when required. In addition, it is critical that product is of the correct quality. Before crossdocking is attempted:

- Set specifications for all appropriate requirements
- Communicate specifications clearly to all parties
- Ensure all parties have the opportunity to review specifications, request revisions, and agree to all requirements
- Conduct a formal test program; establish the ability of all parties to meet the requirements

Once crossdocking is established there has to be a formal analytical system that measures and tracks adherence to requirements and provides constant feedback. As in any well-managed function, it is necessary that the specifications be periodically reviewed and modified appropriately.

Communications Between Supply Chain Members

As mentioned previously, crossdocking is a real time operation; therefore, information must be immediately available. The receiving function has to know what product is on a shipment before the shipment arrives. The only way to accomplish the flow of information with sufficient speed is for the supplying operation to communicate with the receiving operation and the receiving operation to provide the trucking company with required delivery time, and the trucking company to confirm this time. The best way to create this type of communication is to achieve the Six Levels of Supply Chain Excellence, particularly Levels 3 and 4, visibility and collaboration. (For more information on this, see Chapter TBD on Supply Chain Technology.)

Communications and Control Within the Crossdocking Operation

Once material arrives at the crossdocking operation, it has to move swiftly through the facility without interruption. This requires that information is available, so that the flow is not interrupted while information is being gathered.

To accomplish the task of internal communication in a warehouse of any size or complexity, there must be a WMS with bar coding and RF communications. For a typical crossdocking operation, the WMS would require the following functionality:

- Receipt of the notification through EDI or the Web/Internet, of the shipping time, date, carrier, SKUs, quantity, and bar coding information for each order
- Receipt by EDI or the Web/Internet of order detail from the customer
- Notification by EDI or the Web/Internet of the shipping carrier pick up time, load description, destination, and delivery date and time
- Notification of the customer by EDI or the Web/Internet of shipment detail, carrier, and arrival date and time
- Selection of dock location for the receiving and shipping trucks
- Recording of the bar code on each pallet received
- Comparison of the received pallet bar code to the receiving EDI or Web/Internet application on expected receipt information
- Identification and notification of receiving variances
- Supervisory control of sortation and other equipment
- Creation and tracking of bar code and other label information for application to cases and pallets
- Direction of personnel for moving material
- Tracking and reporting of supplier and carrier performance
- Tracking and reporting of warehouse performance including labor utilization
- Planning of operations including manpower and dock utilization

Personnel, Equipment, and Facilities

Crossdocking will eliminate or greatly reduce storing and picking; however, it will increase the requirements for receiving and shipping. Before one attempts crossdocking, it is essential that these requirements be clearly understood and that sufficient resources are allocated to ensure that these requirements are met.

Given the uncertainty of transportation times, it is frequently necessary that trailers be staged before receiving and that empty trailers be staged for shipping. It is necessary to provide sufficient room to stage these trailers and that there are equipment and personnel available to move the trailers to the appropriate location. Additionally, a crossdocking operation often must have a yard tractor and trained driver.

Frequently, various workload-leveling techniques such as truck appointments have been used to reduce shipping and receiving manpower and equipment requirements. Cross-docking greatly reduces the flexibility to level workload; therefore, while total workload may remain constant, peak workload may increase significantly. It is necessary to analyze the amount, duration, and timing of this peak workload to determine how best to use dock equipment and maximize labor productivity.

If the crossdocking operation involves the break down of unit loads, case sorting, and rebuilding of unit loads, it is necessary to plan for space, equipment, and labor to perform these functions. There has to be sufficient space to stage the pallets before and after the sortation system. Sufficient personnel and/or equipment must be provided to stage pallets, de-palletize cases, re-palletize cases, and move the pallets to shipping.

The functional requirements for the sortation equipment have to be carefully developed so the equipment performs as required. At a minimum, functionality should include:

- Average and maximum throughputs
- Sortation requirements
- Software communication with the WMS
- Case label printing, application, and verification requirements
- Storage for future crossdocking functionality
- Merging requirements
- Maximum and minimum case weights and dimensions
- The location, placement tolerance, size, and symbology of existing bar code labels
- Input and output buffer storage capacity for increasing labor productivity
- Future sortation, capacity, and product requirements

Crossdocking finished products in manufacturing has the potential of significantly reducing cost and improving customer service. Frequently, to implement crossdocking in manufacturing requires significant changes in quality control methods, equipment capacity, production methods, and production scheduling.

Some production operations use finished goods inventory as a quality control hold until testing is complete. Crossdocking eliminates finished goods inventory; therefore, the product must be tested and approved as soon as it leaves production. While this may appear to be an impossible task, it can have the desirable effect of forcing an operation to address quality problems and evaluation techniques. By addressing these problems, the operation will be transformed so that quality is built-in rather than inspected-in. This is not an easy transition, but it usually more than pays for itself in increased production, reduced scrap, and improved product acceptance in the marketplace.

On the other hand, there are operations that find crossdocking to be so important that they are willing to ship unapproved product and recall the product if testing shows that it is not acceptable. Of course this can only be done if product is infrequently substandard and if there is a tested, foolproof way of having the entire defective product recalled.

It is not uncommon for some products to require significantly more of certain production resources than other products. Production capacity is calculated on average requirements and products are produced in a sequence that seeks to minimize the peak requirements of the limited resources. In crossdocking, production has less flexibility in scheduling to minimize the peak load on these resources. Therefore, before crossdocking can be implemented it may be necessary to increase the capacity of limiting resources.

Some products require aging before they can be shipped. An example is a painted product whose paint is not fully cured; thus the paint would chip if it were subjected to shipping. In this case, the only way to crossdock is to modify the operation so that the product is ready for shipment when it is produced. While modifying the process may be expensive, the advantages may well outweigh the costs. A product that will be damaged during shipping will likely be damaged during normal handling. Crossdocking will result in savings in product loss from handling. Perhaps most important, eliminating the dwell time speeds up availability of the product to the customer.

Production planning is frequently done to minimize change- over and cleanup time. For example, in the manufacture of colored products, the schedule usually starts with the lightest color and proceeds to the darkest without cleaning the equipment. Crossdocking can reduce scheduling flexibility, thus increasing the need to change over and clean up. The impact of these increases can frequently be minimized by improving the cleanup and change-over operations and/or by providing extra equipment.

Tactical Management

In many ways, tactical management is the least considered, but most important part of implementing crossdocking. With all of the planning, partnering, adding of equipment and systems, and changes in manpower, crossdocking still requires a high level of tactical execution to work. For example, no matter how well EDI works, it is still necessary for someone to actually direct the over-the-road and yard tractor drivers so that the trucks are spotted at the correct doors. When the inevitable problems crop up, there has to be someone in charge of redeploying resources and working around the problems.

Unfortunately, the need for tactical management is often neglected, and the function is added to the work of an already busy first-line supervisor. To prevent the lack of tactical management from becoming a barrier to successful crossdocking, it is imperative that supervisory workload is evaluated and if required, additional resources are provided. These additional resources can be some combination of workload shedding to other supervisors, additional supervisors, and clerical support.

By sending received goods directly to the customer and bypassing storage, crossdocking has the potential of reducing warehousing and speeding the delivery of product. While crossdocking is a simple concept that works in many operations, successful implementation requires that six categories be considered:

1. Partnering with other members of the supply chain
2. Absolute confidence in the quality and availability of product
3. Communication between supply chain members
4. Communications and control within the crossdocking operation
5. Personnel, equipment, and facilities
6. Tactical management

The successful implementation of crossdocking requires that a formal plan be established for implementation including:

1. Teams comprised of appropriate internal and external personnel for each category
2. The development of required changes
3. A plan to implement these changes
4. Implementation and testing of the changes
5. A crossdocking implementation plan and schedule
6. The implementation of a crossdocking pilot program
7. Evaluation of the pilot program and the implementation of required modification
8. Implementation of crossdocking
9. A formal periodic review of the crossdocking operation and its implementation

Drop Shipping

For those organizations that ship directly to end users in small quantities, crossdocking is not an option. However, inventory can still be minimized using other methods. One of the most common is to have suppliers ship orders directly to the customer. This is often referred to as drop shipment or supplier direct shipping. To accomplish this, there must be a very good relationship and distribution agreement, or else the supplier may eventually decide to sell directly to your customers.

Drop shipping has the benefit of eliminating one movement in the distribution system and multiple touches within the warehouse. When done properly, the customer does not even realize that the supplier, from whom it was purchased, is not shipping the product.

So which method is right and what is the perfect distribution system to use as a basis to achieve supply chain excellence?

The Perfect Distribution Model

There may not be a perfect distribution model today. Due to the changing nature of customer requirements, ever-changing technologies, and new and stronger competition, there may never be a perfect model in the future. However, trying to reach that goal is what makes distribution such a critical part of achieving Supply Chain Synthesis and Supply Chain Excellence.

Imagine if you could make a product out of the energy around you and deliver it to your customers, using matter transfer devices, when and where they wanted it on demand. The process would still be distribution. The movement of goods between point A and point B relies upon a transportation device, an order entry system, and the equipment to produce a product. It may appear perfect, but imagine the maintenance and information systems required to keep it operating. As part of a supply chain, the movement of products to the ultimate end-user must be the focus for all distribution systems supplying materials to produce the end product.

Understanding the impact of a single distribution system on the entire supply chain is critical to long-term success. To do this, one must balance all the costs in the supply chain. By taking all the individual distribution links, one can calculate out the total cost of the supply chain and determine how changes affect not only single distribution links, but also the entire supply chain.

Total cost per distribution link = Storage and Handling Costs + Order Processing/Accounting Costs + Transportation Cost + Product Conversion Cost

Total Supply Chain Cost = Sum of All Distribution Link Costs + Manufacturing Costs

Conclusion

Distribution of product is driven by customer demand and product availability. The ability to minimize cost is limited only by customer demand and information availability. It is impossible to have all products for all demands on-hand and still be profitable, but not being able to fill orders in a timely manner will quickly destroy a company's customer base. Therefore a balance between inventory, transportation, information, and product must be reached to make a distribution system work effectively. At the same time, not all the improvements within a single distribution system should be taken advantage of if they negatively impact trading partners in the supply chain moregreater than they benefit a company's distribution system. The ideal approach should maximize both for the benefit of all the links in the entire chain.

CHAPTER 10
Logistics and Manufacturing Outsourcing

James A. Tompkins, Ph.D., President, Tompkins Associates

It's no secret that the world's most successful companies—like Dell, Wal-Mart, and Sony—owe much of that success to outsourcing. As a result, in their search for increased competitiveness and success in the 21st-century global marketplace, companies are either considering outsourcing or have already decided to pursue it.

Consider a well-known casual clothing producer that decided to go the outsourcing route to boost its market share and land a lucrative contract with a large retailer like Wal-Mart. The company created a department that has the sole responsibility of managing outsourcing relationships, and that department is now the gatekeeper for all outsourcing providers that want to do business with that company. That department is largely comprised of experts on the functional competencies being outsourced who understand the outsource vs. insource question, know the solicitation process, and realize the importance of maintaining ongoing relationships with outsourcing providers. They have years of experience with outsourcing contracts, dos and don'ts, and outsourcing war wounds. Yet, despite all this effort, outsourcing is not producing the desired results and many are either frustrated or questioning the value of outsourcing altogether.

What has eluded this company—and others like it—is this: outsourcing is a management tool that shifts the organizational structure of companies. It is a business transformation process that can create great opportunity for improved performance, but it can also create great opportunity for problems, issues, and, ultimately, failure. In the search for core competencies and non-core competencies to outsource, it easy to overlook the fact that outsourcing itself is a competency. As such, it must be approached with business process knowledge and effective outsourcing processes experience to reap its full benefits.

What does this mean for the clothing producer? Truthfully, their best bet is to look for outside help. There are companies out there that have a wealth of outsourcing knowledge. They've been in the trenches for decades, before the term "outsourcing" was even coined, and they know the ropes. They realize that, for most companies, outsourcing is not a core competency, and they can offer their expertise to those that have not developed it themselves, integrating it with the knowledge and experience company insiders bring to the table.

Outsourcing outsourcing? Is that possible? Sure it is. Many companies believe that the manufacturing and logistics experts within a company are the natural choices for finding third-party manufacturing and logistics providers. In some cases, that may be true, but in most cases these experts are overwhelmed when it comes time to hand those processes over to someone outside the company. A company with outsourcing as a core competency can work with these experts, harnessing their knowledge and experience and using it to develop and manage logistics and manufacturing outsourcers and outsourcing relationships.

Emerging Trends in the Past Ten Years

For the past decade, organizations have been downsizing, right-sizing, and reengineering in efforts to improve efficiency and financial performance. These techniques have generally reduced costs and assets. However, they have not truly addressed the work that needs to be done, who is going to do it, and if it is really a core competency of the company or not.

Outsourcing, when done properly, reduces the work required of the organization and improves the efficiency and effectiveness of processes. Because some of the biggest names in business have done outsourcing properly, it is being viewed as the source of higher profitability and larger market share. As such, the percentage of companies that view outsourced manufacturing and logistics services as viable alternatives to internal operations has increased over the last 10 years. As a result, a number of trends have emerged, including:

- Increased spending for outside warehousing and outbound transportation
- Improvement in outsource provider capabilities
- Greater use of software and technology solutions
- Increased competition amongst contractors
- More short-term projects
- New products and innovations for the marketplace and
- A shift in overall management thinking about ownership and assets

These are discussed in greater detail in the sections that follow.

Increased Spending

At one time, companies sought to outsource functions like IT, HR, and mail room services and budgeted accordingly. In the past few years, however, the percentage of company budgets spent on outside warehousing and outbound transportation is on the rise. One of the reasons for this trend is the ever-increasing pace of global trade and the popularity of offshore contract electronics manufacturing. Companies are contracting with logistics consultants to untangle global supply chains, integrate and monitor international shipping, and help them navigate increasingly complicated product supply channels.

Another reason for these expenditures is that companies are learning that these operations are not necessarily core functions. Core functions are an organization's core competency, the unique business functions that allow the organization to be successful. They are the critical activities included in an organization's vision statement that allow it to thrive. For a research organization, the core function is research; for a manufacturing organization, the core function is manufacturing; and for a distribution organization, the core function is distribution. Although the research organization may also do some manufacturing and some distribution, its core function is research. In fact, the research organization may do manufacturing, distribution, finance, marketing, procurement, information technology, human resources, etc., but research remains its core function.

Interestingly, the research organization, the manufacturing organization, and the distribution organization may all be in the pharmaceutical industry, but their selected niche, their "thing," their unique business functions that are keys to driving their success are determined by how they have defined their core functions. What is left after a company defines its core functions are the non-core functions—the many other functions that need to be performed for an organization to exist. These functions can be split into tactical non-core and strategic non-core functions.

Tactical non-core functions are activities that need to be done, but unless they are really, really done poorly, they do not have an impact on an organization's bottom line. For example, in a typical organization the functions of food service, landscaping, payroll, auditing, or janitorial services are not going to have an impact on an organization's bottom line. If, however, the food service people poison your staff, the landscape people knock trees onto your facility, the payroll people embezzle your funds, the audit people allow others to misreport your income, or the janitorial people throw away important papers, then, yes, these things will have an impact on your bottom line. But for them to impact your bottom line to any serious extent, they have to be done really poorly.

Strategic non-core functions, on the other hand, are functions that, although not core, do have an impact on a company's bottom line. For example, sporting goods manufacturer Nike has realized that its competencies are branding, product design, and development. If any of these things are not done well, they will have a major adverse affect on a company's bottom line.

Logistics, information technology, marketing, and manufacturing are excellent examples of strategic non-core functions for the research organization mentioned earlier. Suppose that organization outsources both food service and logistics. If food service does not work out, the research organization fires the firm, brings another provider in, and apologizes to its staff for the first provider. If logistics does not work out, the organization has a major sunk cost in the transition costs, it has exposed its customers to bad customer service, and it may incur serious interruptions in service. The tactical non-core food service mistake is not good, but it will not really have an impact on the business. To the contrary, the strategic non-core logistics mistakes will have adversely affected the organization's bottom line, and it may well take years to recover from the impacts.

Improved Capabilities, Software Solutions, and Increased Competition

Outsourcing providers are becoming more capable, using technology and software, including the Internet and specialized applications, to create innovative solutions. At the same time, companies want to work with fewer contractors to streamline communications and reduce interactions. There is heightened competition amongst contractors due to this rationing of service providers, which has outsource providers offering an increasingly integrated set of services that cover a broader range of functions.

Take Flextronics International, for example. In September 2003, the Singapore-based company was first on the list of the top 100 contract manufacturers published by *Electronic Business*.[1] When Flextronics went public in 1994, it basically manufactured electronics components. Now the company's services range from design engineering through manufacturing and assembly to distribution and warehousing, and they also offer the installation and maintenance of communications networks.

It is important to note here that because so many companies have outsourced manufacturing to Flextronics, which is located in Singapore, many executives, pundits, and politicians tend to equate outsourcing with offshoring. This is a common mistake. Yes, many outsource providers are located overseas—in Asia or India, for example. However, outsourcing is not offshoring. Offshoring is an option, but companies need to look at the total supply chain costs and make the best decisions based on what will best achieve long-term goals.

More Short Term Projects

Another trend that has emerged in the last decade is that companies are increasingly using service providers for short-term projects rather than creating long-term relationships. This can be a good thing if a company needs a quick fix. In other words, a software company releasing a new version of its premier program that wants to offer free telephone support for a limited period is a prime candidate for successful short-term outsourcing (by using a third-party call center). The same may be said for a company that is selling a limited run of a product and decides to outsource its packaging. However, an appliance manufacturer that wants to outsource the production of one of its smaller products may be better off fostering a long-term relationship with the outsourcer so that the customer does not perceive the product as unreliable. Economics today can favor short-term outsourcing decisions, so management time, resources and capital are not expended in short term or high risk operations.

New Products and Innovation

Digital radio, expanded circuit boards, chips for mobile communications, a silicone adhesive—these are among the numerous products that have been introduced in the last few years. Nothing stops innovation. However, as much as companies want to exploit creativity and technology, they also are looking for ways to curb upfront capital investment.

Their search creates opportunities to use outsourced manufacturing and logistics to do more with less. For example, computer giant Hewlett-Packard in 2003, in an attempt to capitalize on the popularity of digital music players, tried to develop a digital music player. However, late that year, the company decided that it could get into the digital music market faster if it outsourced the player but branded it in-house. The result was a deal announced in January 2004 for HP to utilize Apple to produce iPods under the HP brand name.

Shift in Management Thinking

In the last few years, company leaders have been changing their views about ownership and control of assets. They are realizing that relinquishing the tight reins they have held on costly assets will increase growth and improve earnings. At the same time, they continue to seek the following:

- Workforce reduction
- Freedom from restrictive labor environment
- Expanded geographic coverage
- Operational flexibility
- Reduced cycle time/improved responsiveness and
- Logistics operations cost reduction

They are shifting their thinking away from simply downsizing or expanding into new areas without careful thought and planning to acquire what they seek. They have recognized that there is a second step that must follow selling off assets and shedding workers. Many of them believe that outsourcing is that step.

What Does All This Mean?

From these trends, we can draw several conclusions. First, the decision on whether to outsource or not has almost been made for many company leaders. They have no choice but to outsource. Yet, for outsourcing to work for these companies, they either must become very good at outsourcing or they must be willing to outsource the outsourcing process to experts. This is because the winner in this game is the company that is best at outsourcing. Second, competition has made outsourcing a viable option for many more companies and for many more logistics and manufacturing functions. Outsourcing is paying off in areas we didn't even dream about 10 years ago. Lastly, pressures on improved financial results have never been greater. This pressure has created a surge of interest in outsourcing functions where bottom line improvement potential exists.

The Outsourcing Process

To take the plunge into Outsourcing strategic non-core functions without a robust outsourcing process will not only prevent an organization from achieving the benefits from outsourcing, but will also result in a major setback to the organization. A solid up front effort is required to identify the functions to be outsourced, so that the right processes are considered that have the best returns. Consideration must also be given to the risks, potential benefits and market availability of the service providers. Once a good decision about what to outsource has been made, a robust process must be followed to assure achieving the benefits of outsourcing. The process we have defined consists of seven steps:

1. Defining requirements and the Request For Proposal (RFP)
2. Evaluating bids and selecting outsource partners
3. Creating outsource relationships
4. Forging the legal relationship
5. Getting started: Putting the outsource relationship in motion

6. Establishing the outsource relationship
7. Managing the outsource relationship

Step One: Defining Requirements and the Request For Proposal

The first step in the outsourcing process is to define specifically what is to be outsourced and to develop a RFP defining the functions to be outsourced. Keys to success for this step include:

1. Clearly define the scope of what is to be outsourced. Once the scope is defined, be sure that the boundaries of what is to be outsourced are clearly established.

2. Clearly set forth the goals to be achieved by outsourcing. Reasons to outsource often include:
   • Cost reduction
   • Increased customer satisfaction
   • Focus on core functions
   • Increased competitiveness
   • Release of capital
   • Reduce future investment
   • Reduce risk

3. Do not outsource to avoid an existing problem. Do not rush into outsourcing as a way to bypass poor performance. Be sure you outsource to accomplish positive goals and not to avoid negative circumstances.

4. Develop a detailed, realistic timeline for the outsource process. Identify key dates such as dates of:
   • RFP release
   • RFP response
   • Site visits
   • Short list
   • Due diligence
   • Selection
   • Term sheet signing
   • Contract signing
   • Beginning implementation
   • Completing implementation

5. Involve senior management early, often and at key decision points. Be certain senior management understands the scope, goals and timeline. Set realistic expectations. Obtain leadership support. Do not assume that today's level of performance is what is required for the service provider. The goals must fit the organization's needs over the life of the relationship.

6. Establish a benchmark of doing the functions to be outsourced. Understand the cost drivers of self-performing and service levels that will serve as a baseline for the outsourced activity.

7. Be certain the RFP provides a clear set of requirements, a clear path forward and a clear desire for innovation and creativity. Do not use the RFP to tell potential providers how to do their job. Use the RFP to tell people what needs to be done. Be certain the full range of requirements are set forth to include slow, typical and high levels of requirements.

8. Be certain that a wide range of candidates is pre-qualified before sending the RFP. Consider outsource providers as well as industry players. Perform extensive research to be certain all viable candidates are asked to bid. After qualified candidates are identified have each candidate sign a non-disclosure agreement or a confidentiality agreement prior to receiving the RFP.

9. Share the outsourcing process and timeline with each qualified provider. Be sure all candidates are given the same information and opportunity to present their best bid.

10. After sending the RFP to each candidate and receiving assurances of their desire to submit a proposal, perform a financial and business due diligence check on each potential candidate. Prepare appropriate background questions and concerns about each candidate.

Step Two: Evaluating Bids and Selecting Outsource Partners

Once the responses to the RFP are received there must be a methodical bid evaluation and provider selection process. Keys to success for conducting this process include:

1. It is important to control communications with all potential providers while the evaluation process is ongoing. A single point of contact should be communicating with the potential providers. All providers should be given the same information and all questions and answers to the providers should be handled through the contact.

2. As important as the "how" of the bid evaluation process is the "who to do the evaluation process." Having the wrong people involved in the selection can easily result in making the wrong decision. Having several people from the same department or having several people holding the same perspectives can also lead to problems. Also, people with an upfront bias should be excluded from the process. The team that will do the evaluation should come from a variety of different "touch points" with the outsourced function. This cross-functional team should have a good understanding of the function being outsourced and should ultimately be involved with the outsource provider in some capacity.

3. Evaluation criteria should be published as a portion of the RFP. The evaluation team must agree on the definitions of the criteria and the weighting of the criteria. There may be one weighting of criteria for short list selection and another for final selection. For example, short list evaluation criteria may be:
   - 50% – Solution
   - 25% – Credibility and reliability
   - 25% – Flexibility

Whereas the criteria for final selection may be:
- 10% – Quality of solution
- 15% – Comfort with ability to deliver/implement the solution
- 10% – Continuous improvement culture
- 10% – Value added services
- 15% – Cost
- 10% – Reputation/related experience
- 10% – Terms and conditions
- 10% – Open communications/culture
- 10% – Financial stability

4. The evaluation process should not be rushed. Often time pressures are present, but these pressures should not result in allowing the process to be anything other than fair, detailed and robust.

5. The evaluation process is a business decision, not a low cost or a personal preference. The process must be methodical. Neither relationships nor executive preferences should be overly emphasized. The evaluation criteria must be rigorously applied in a fair and equitable manner.

6. Care must be exhibited to do the bid evaluation and not a sales person presentation evaluation. The written bid is what should be evaluated. In a similar way, the evaluation must be done of the potential providers not of the potential providers sales team.

7. Bids are often complex. Be sure all bids address the full scope of the functions to be outsourced. Be sure the evaluation is of "apples vs. apples." Get into the details of the pricing and do the arithmetic on the pricing proposal for benchmark levels. Do not "assume" anything about the bids nor "take them at face value." Dig into the details and really understand each potential providers assumptions and approach.

8. Call at least three customers of each potential provider and obtain insights into the provider's performance. Ask a standard set of questions and be certain to obtain provider feedback on everything that gives you concern. If appropriate, go visit customers and view first-hand the provider's performance.

9. Have a clear understanding with the potential providers and the evaluation team how you will be handing short list determination, second visits and additional information requests. Be sure the short list process is followed and the evaluation team and process are maintained throughout the short list and ultimate selection process.

10. Do not tell any potential provider they are "the winner" until after a binding term sheet or contract is signed. Especially for larger outsourced contracts it is appropriate to go to detailed, binding term sheet discussions with more than one potential provider. Until a binding relationship is established, always retain more than one option.

Step Three: Creating Outsource Relationships

It is very important that everyone associated with an outsourcing relationship understand that outsourcing a function is not just buying services. Outsourcing is a business relationship that must be developed and evolved. Keys to success in creating an outsource relationship include:

1. Outsourcing is giving up internal control of a business function and trusting others to handle this function for you. Many have an intellectual understanding of this fact, but emotionally have a hard time accepting it. Outsourcing is much more than a business tool, it is a new way to think about business and thus requires a different thought process than has been the norm. Therefore, the relationship between a supplier and a customer is not the same as the relationship between a company and a provider. It is very important that everyone associated with outsourcing get these differences clearly defined in his or her own mind.

2. Early on in an outsourced relationship communication protocols must be established. All relevant parties must have a face-to-face meeting and then be encouraged to communicate frequently to establish rapport. Information about the outsource relationship must be broadly, consistently and openly presented to a cross section of people within both the company and the provider.

3. Multiple touch points between the company and the provider must be established. As early as possible the touch points must go beyond the provider's sales organization and involve the people who are actually going to do the work. People from both the company and the provider must be current on the RFP, the solution and the negotiation on the term sheet and contract.

4. As early as possible the roles and responsibilities for both the company and the provider must be established. There must be a clear understanding by all parties associated with the outsource relationship on who is doing which tasks. All boundaries for responsibilities must be explored to be sure all have the same understanding of the roles and responsibilities.

5. The chemistry between the company and the provider must be allowed to evolve. The chemistry must be positive, respectful and open. The culture of the company and the provider must be thought through and differences understood so that the relationship can evolve for both the company and the provider.

6. Trust must be growing between the company and the provider. This trust is a result of ongoing meeting of expectations. Trust begets respect, which leads to improved communications and thus greater trust. Open discussions about trust are to be encouraged.

7. An important relationship hurdle is the pricing structure that is put in place between the company and the provider. At the highest level the pricing options are:
   - Fixed cost
   - Transactional cost

- Cost plus
- Management fee

Each of these pricing options has advantages and disadvantages. It is important that both the company and the provider have a very clear understanding of how the pricing model will be applied. Surprises here can destroy relationships.

8. A second major area where surprises can destroy relationships is lack of agreement on what is meant by service levels. As early as possible the company and the provider must invest the time to get real clarity into the definition and performance measures for each service level.

9. An important relationship factor revolves around the transition of employees from the company to the provider. Doing this poorly can kill a relationship. Factors such as compensation, benefits, severance and government regulations must be clearly understood and communicated to all. Individuals to be transitioned must understand the positive aspects of moving from the periphery of the company to a core group within the provider. Each individual to be transitioned needs to have his or her own personal fears and concerns addressed.

10. The relationship between the company and the provider is often referred to as a win/win relationship. However, to make this true, both parties in the relationship must benefit when things go well. Thus, early in the relationship some form of a gain sharing or goal sharing process needs to be put in place so that the win/win relationship is not just a thought process, but in fact a reality.

Step Four: Forming the Legal Relationship

Interestingly, the better the two parties do at forming the legal relationship the less likely it is needed. But the poorer the two parties do on the legal relationship the more it is needed. If the legal relationship is done well, the success of the relationship will be measured by the accomplishment of the goals established for the outsourcing. If the legal relationship is done poorly, the protection the legal relationship provides each of the parties will be the criteria used to determine how poorly the relationship was done. Keys to success in establishing the legal relationship include:

1. The legal relationship can go through a variety of paths. Options include (in order of preference by Tompkins Associates):
   a. Binding term sheet to contract
   b. Letter of intent or non-binding term sheet to contract
   c. Letter of intent to binding term sheet to contract
   d. Contract

   Independent of which approach is used, the key players from the company and the provider and the lawyers from the company and the provider should be involved from the outset. The lead in developing the legal documentation at each step of the process should be the company. It is very important that the legal documents provide for flexibility for the relationship, as we all know the relationship and the requirements will evolve.

2. The legal relationship must clearly define the details and schedule for transition steps. Key questions that need to be answered include:
   - What assets, operations, employees, testing, and go-live transition steps need to take place and who has responsibility and accountability for these to happen?
   - What will take place if these do not happen as planned?
   - How will you know if these transitions steps occurred or not?
3. The legal relationship must clearly define each service level and the criteria to measure each. Penalties and rewards must be set forth for not meeting or exceeding these service levels.
4. The legal relationship must clearly set forth the issues on confidentiality and ownership of intellectual property and data. Specifics relating to confidentiality, intellectual property and data must be understood by all associated with the outsource relationship.
5. The legal relationship must clearly specify the frequency and content of all reporting and documentation of the relationship.
6. The legal relationship must clearly define the pricing model, the invoice terms and the payment terms. There must be a clear understanding how these issues will change and evolve over the life of the relationship.
7. The legal relationship must clearly set forth the relationship governance. The dispute resolution process and the escalation process if disputes are not resolved.
8. The legal relationship should present the ultimate dispute resolution mechanism as a three-arbitrator panel for binding arbitration. The legal relationship should define the termination guidelines, procedures and costs.
9. The legal relationship must clearly set forth the rights to audit the relationship and the responsibilities thereto.
10. The legal relationship must define the rights of approval or censure with respect to provider facilities, staff, procedures, etc.

Step Five: Getting Started or Putting the Outsource Relationship in Motion

Start-up is not easy. The go-live of an outsource relationship requires thousands of things to go well. Irrespective of all the planning, hard work, and testing, no go-live will ever be flawless. Keys to success that will simplify go live include:

1. Implement the transition plan as set forth in the contract. Methodically go through the contract and be sure each contract requirement is being meet. Methodically go through the transition plan and be sure each step has been addressed. Work the plan. Do not let time pressures or "surprises" throw you into a panic mode.

2. Do not allow yourself to say, "That is not how we have always done that." Recall you have outsourced this function and your job is no longer "how" to do something, but rather the meeting of requirements and service levels.

3. Deal with the FUD factor: Fear-Uncertainty-Doubt. People are afraid of the unknown and it is human nature to resist change. So flood the people with information. Explain to them the negative push from the prior approach as well as the positive pull to the future approach. Beware this applies to all levels within your organization.

4. Manage expectations. You will not go-live at full production speed or efficiency. The learning curve requires time to get things right. Be patient and pace the start-up expectations to realistic levels.

5. Be certain not to continue the mistakes of the past. Outreaches that were not effective, inventory that is dead, past mistakes and damaged materials need not be outsourced. Prevent past mistakes from lingering.

6. Go to the site before go-live and be familiar with the operation. Be familiar with the people. Be onsite at go-live. Communicate and encourage people. Personally lead the celebration for the success of go-live.

7. Assure accuracy of data and information at go-live. Be sure the people have the information needed to do their jobs.

8. Oversee and check the process for the creation of the first reports, service levels and invoices. Perform a "handshake" on the first edition of each of these documents. Be sure there are no surprises and both the company and the provider feel good about what is happening.

9. Be aware that there will be problems at go-live. Identify the root causes behind these problems and solve them. Fully address all early problems and be sure both the company and the provider understand the problem and the resolution.

10. Be aware that there will be people who complain and do not like the "new" way of doing things. Address all concerns and overly communicate with all involved with the complaints. Be sure all complaint cycles end with positive feedback and communications.

Step Six: Establishing the Outsource Relationship

Getting past start-up is very important but it is a long way from ultimate success. In fact, start-up is the wedding and the honeymoon. The ongoing relationship is the marriage. The reason why so many marriages fail today is because the individual parties do not adequately invest their time into the marriage. Similarly, outsourced relationships need to continue to evolve. Not investing in the outsource relationship will result in failure. Some keys to success on establishing the outsource relationship include:

1. Realize right up front that all outsource relationships are between both organizations and people. Yes, there is a contract between the company and the provider. But more important is the relationship between the people from the company and the people

from the provider. Failure to adequately invest in the people side of the relationship will result in the downfall of the relationship.

2. Regular, ongoing business planning, evolution and communications must be put in place so that both parties agree on the status of the relationship. Decisions must be made with respect to the level of and frequency of formal and informal communications and meetings.

3. Guidelines must be established and implemented for how to handle continuous improvement. An ongoing process of continuous improvement is required for all outsource relationships to flourish. Creativity and innovation must be encouraged on both sides of the relationship.

4. A rewards structure of gain sharing or goal sharing must be implemented so that both sides are motivated to participate in improving the performance of the outsource relationship.

5. A regular ongoing executive interaction effort must be put in place. Depending upon the magnitude of the relationship this may require a CEO-to-CEO regular face-to-face interaction. These interactions should have both structured status reporting activities in addition to unstructured, informal communications about the evolution of the relationship.

6. Effort must be invested in going back to the RFP and the contract and asking what surprises or changes have taken place. Problem areas should be identified. Any areas where reality is different from expectation should be reviewed. Opportunities for improvement should flow from these discussions.

7. Effort needs to be invested to review how well you are performing against the initial goals that were established for outsourcing. This needs to be much more than a cost vs. budget analysis but a full, robust analysis of the success of outsourcing.

8. A formal "lessons learned" round table meeting must take place both by the company alone on the topic of outsourcing as well as between the company and the provider on the specific outsource relationship.

9. An objective going into the relationship was a win/win relationship. The company and the provider must sit down and review how this has evolved. The fact is if both parties are not happy with the relationship, neither party will be happy with the relationship.

10. At the end of the contract term there are basically three options:
    - Bring functions back in house
    - Extend the contract
    - Take the contract out to bid

    A good outsource relationship will share thinking on these options and there will be no surprises.

Step Seven: Managing the Outsource Relationship

Like all of business the outsource relationship is alive and dynamic. Keys to success that can help the relationship to be fresh and relevant include:

1. Leadership focus, diligence and follow through on continuous improvement initiatives are very important. Staff from both the company and the provider get busy with the day-to-day routine and forget to continue to push the boundaries of continuous improvement. By leadership continuing to make this a focus, the relationship will continue to prosper.

2. On a regular basis leadership should refer back to the contract and see how it is going. Are you following the contract? If not, is this good or bad? Are you following the timelines and responsibilities included in the contract? Is there room for improvement?

3. The business that was outsourced goes through business cycles. How is the relationship and performance holding up under the changing business climate? What changes need to be made to align the outsource relationship with the evolving requirements?

4. Keep in mind how the relationship is functioning and how you could improve performance. How should service levels, budgets and incentive plans be upgraded to assure our relationship is fresh? It is important that goals for the future of the relationship be established and both the company and the provider accept these goals. Making the future better will not happen unless leadership sets the pace here.

5. Performance levels must be reviewed and kept current. Joint efforts need to be invested to see how improvements in performance levels can be achieved.

6. The customers or users of the provider's services should be brought into the process of improving the outsource relationship. A customer/user round table should be conducted to identify specific opportunities for improvement.

7. In all outsource relationships there will be an evolution of the relationship. People leave organizations, requirements change, and businesses change and the relationship must adapt and continue to evolve. A key to being sure the changes do not upset the outsource relationship is open communications. Both the company and the provider should be challenged to define opportunities to improve communications.

8. Leadership must demonstrate their ongoing commitment to the outsource relationship with their active involvement with the relationship with the investment of their time in the relationship. Ongoing relationship development meetings should be held to advance the relationship to the next level.

9. There should be no surprises in the relationship. Ongoing strategic discussions from both the company and the provider must take place to be certain the relationship stays current and focused on the correct priorities.

Developing a Core Competency in Outsourcing

Outsourcing is an awesome business solution when pursued in accordance to the guidelines presented here. Without a core competency in outsourcing, outsourcing can become a setback for many organizations. Outsourcing done well can have tremendous payback; outsourcing done poorly can bring a business to its knees. If you are in doubt about pursuing an outsourcing initiative, leverage the expertise of proven outsource process consultants. With the proper planning great benefits can follow.

Works Cited

Bill Roberts. "Top 100 Contract Manufacturers." *Electronic Business.* September 1, 2003.

CHAPTER 11
Warehouse Operations

Brian Hudock, Partner, Tompkins Associates

The four walls within which a warehouse operates no longer serve as its boundaries. The lines separating manufacturing and the warehouse, and even the warehouse/ distribution center (DC) from the customer, are blurred. Operations once completed in manufacturing plants are now completed further down the supply chain, and additional value-added services once performed in buffer warehouses have moved even farther upstream in the distribution channel.

Many trends have put new pressures on the warehouse/DC (we will refer to both the warehouse and the DC operations as warehouses for brevity). Increased emphasis on customer satisfaction and consumer demand patterns has also increased the number of unique items in a typical warehouse operation. The result is SKU proliferation. A good illustration of this is in the beverage industry. Not that long ago, the beverage aisle in a typical grocery store offered two or three flavors in 10-ounce bottles in a six-pack. Today, the typical beverage aisle offers colas (regular and diet, caffeinated and noncaffeinated), clear drinks, and fruit-flavored drinks in 6-, 12-, and 24-pack glass and plastic bottles and cans, 1-, 2-, and 3-liter bottles, juice boxes, and pouches.

A renewed emphasis on customer service has increased the number and variety of value-added services in the warehouse. Orders must be packaged and labeled specifically to meet the needs of the customer and their needs tend to force additional labor, systems, and space in the warehouse.

Workload and complexity have increased, but the time allowed to respond to customer demands has been shortened. Very quickly the standard for order cycle time is becoming same-day or overnight shipment. The compressed time schedules limit the available strategies for productivity improvement and place increased importance on the functionality and capacity of warehouse control and material handling systems.

Direct-to-consumer business has grown, although not to the levels of early projections, and single-pick customer-direct shipments have added complexity and new ways of processing orders in many warehouses.

The quest for quality has also moved from manufacturing into warehousing and distribution operations. As a result, the standards for accuracy performance have increased dramatically. Today, the average shipping accuracy in U.S. warehouses is about 99 percent while the Japanese standard of one error per 10,000 shipments is commonly accepted.

Industry consolidations are rising in number and speed. Consolidations bring great changes within the warehousing environment to integrate new products and manage the capacity and throughput of additional volume. Even if not directly affected by consolidation, there can be indirect impacts as consolidation results in fewer and stronger competitors, customers, and suppliers.

Finally, an increased concern for the preservation of the environment, the conservation of natural resources, and human safety has brought more stringent government regulations into the design and management of warehousing operations.

As complexity in the warehouse has increased, the availability of skilled labor is increasingly scarce. Historically, greater demands have been met by adding technology in the warehouse leading to the need to recruit a new breed of worker and placing higher demands on training. Language is becoming an ever-greater issue as the percentage of non-English speakers in the workforce increases.

The dot-com era proved that we had a lot to learn in the world of warehousing. Companies struggled to find the right approach to fulfilling the demands of a new kind of customer and how to design a supply chain without an understanding of what the future would look like. Clearly, the lesson learned from this is the past is no longer a good predictor of what is yet to come.

With so much change in the warehousing environment, the keys to success are flexibility, a teaming approach (internal and external to the company), a customer focus, and a continuous improvement philosophy. The planning and management of today's warehousing operations is very difficult. To cope, we must turn to simplification and process-improvement as a means of managing warehouses. Toward that end, this chapter is meant to serve as a guide for warehouse operations improvement through the application of best-practice procedures and available material handling systems for warehousing operations.

The Role of a Warehouse

In a distribution network, a warehouse may meet any of the following requirements:

1. It may hold inventory used to balance and buffer the variation between production schedules and demand. For this purpose, the warehouse is usually located near the point of manufacture and may be characterized by the flow of full pallets in and full pallets out, assuming that product size and volume warrant pallet-sized loads. A warehouse serving only this function may have demands ranging from daily to monthly replenishment of stock to the next level of distribution.

2. A warehouse may be used to accumulate and consolidate products from various points of manufacture within a single firm, or from several firms, for combined shipment to common customers. Such a warehouse may be located centrally to either the production locations or the customer base. Product movement may include full pallets in and full cases out, typically responding to regular weekly or monthly orders.

3. Warehouses may be distributed in the field, to shorten transportation distances and permit rapid response to customer demand. Frequently single items are picked, and the same item may be shipped to the customer every day.

Functions within the Warehouse

It used to be said that the functions of a warehouse could be broken into four activities: receiving, storing, picking, and shipping. That simplification does no justice to the warehouse of today. Most warehouses today can engage in:

1. Crossdocking
2. Receiving
3. Prepackaging (optional)
4. Putaway
5. Storage
6. Order picking
7. Packaging and/or pricing (optional)
8. Kitting/Customization
9. Sortation and/or accumulation
10. Packing and shipping

These functions may be defined briefly as:

1. *Crossdocking* is moving received goods directly to outbound shipping, eliminating storage, and orderpicking. It bypasses the putaway and storage steps in the warehousing environment. This can be accomplished by receiving pre-distributed orders from your supplier or through detailed planning and coordination of your inbound and outbound product. Crossdocking provides a way to minimize inventories, space, and labor in the warehouse.
2. *Receiving* is the collection of activities involved in (a) the orderly receipt of all materials coming into the warehouse, (b) providing the assurance that the quantity and quality of such materials are as ordered, and (c) disbursing materials to storage or to other organizational functions requiring them.
3. *Prepackaging* is performed in a warehouse when products are received in bulk from a supplier and subsequently packaged individually, in merchandisable quantities, or in combinations with other parts to form kits or assortments. An entire receipt of merchandise may be processed at once, or a portion may be held in bulk form to be processed later. This may be done when packaging greatly increases the storage-cube requirements or when a part is common to several kits or assortments.
4. *Putaway* is the act of placing merchandise in storage. It includes both a transportation and a placement component.
5. *Storage* is the physical containment of merchandise while it is awaiting a demand. The form of storage will depend on the size and quantity of the items in inventory and the handling characteristics of the product or its container.
6. *Order picking* is the process of removing items from storage to meet a specific demand. It represents the basic service that the warehouse provides for the customer, and is the function around which most warehouse designs are based.

7. *Packaging and/or pricing* may be done as an optional step after the picking process. As in the prepackaging function, individual items or assortments are boxed for more convenient use. Waiting until after picking to perform these functions has the advantage of providing more flexibility in the use of on-hand inventory. Individual items are available for use in any of the packaging configurations right up to the time of need. Pricing is current at the time of sale. Prepricing at manufacture or receipt into the warehouse inevitably leads to some repricing activity, as price lists are sometimes combined into a single document.

8. *Kitting/Customization* is defined as grouping, packaging or combining components together to build a final product for shipment. Kitting can be done according to three general procedures: sequential kitting, batch kitting, or zone kitting. Each procedure will impact the warehouse differently. Warehouse operations are commonly creating special product groupings for various retailers and other customers just prior to shipment to give their customers a one-of-a-kind product that no one else can offer.

9. *Sortation* of batch picks into individual orders, and accumulation of distributed picks into orders, must be done when an order has more than one item and the accumulation is not done as the picks are made.

10. *Packing and shipping* may include:
    - Checking orders for completeness
    - Packaging merchandise in an appropriate shipping container
    - Preparing shipping documents, including the packing list, address label, and bill of lading
    - Weighing orders to determine shipping charges
    - Accumulating orders by outbound carrier
    - Loading trucks

Crossdocking Operations

There are three major types of crossdocking: manufacturing, distribution, and terminal. In manufacturing crossdocking, instead of placing goods into a finished goods warehouse, they are dispatched directly to the dock for shipment. In the ideal sense, the products would be directly loaded into a waiting trailer, but often the materials do require some staging at the loading dock.

In distribution crossdocking, full-unit loads are received, but both full-unit loads and also individual cases within the loads can be crossdocked for shipment. When individual cases are crossdocked, there is often a conveyor sortation system to sort and transport the product to the appropriate outbound shipping door. Terminal crossdocking is used to consolidate orders from different suppliers into a single outbound shipment. Terminal crossdocking can be integrated into an existing distribution center where additional products are merged with warehoused products, or it may take place at a hub or terminal, where no product is warehoused and the only function of the facility is to consolidate products.

There is no "best practice" approach to the application of a crossdocking process as the benefits are based upon individual circumstances. Regardless of the type of crossdocking implemented, there is a requirement for coordination and systems integration between trading partners.

Receiving Operations

The primary objectives of a receiving system are (1) safe and efficient unloading of carriers, (2) prompt and accurate processing of receipts, (3) accurate maintenance of records and activities, and (4) rapid dispersal of receipts to appropriate locations for subsequent use, and access to material as soon as possible for order filling. Concentration on an efficient procedure to fulfill each of these functions will accomplish the objectives of a receiving system. The primary functions of a typical receiving system include:

1. Analysis of documents for planning purposes:
   - Determining approximate dates of arrival in terms of type and quantity of material
   - Scheduling carrier arrivals as much as possible
   - Furnishing carrier or incoming traffic controller with spotting information
   - Preplanning temporary storage locations
2. Unloading carriers, and clearing the bill of lading or carrier responsibility
3. Unpacking goods as necessary
4. Identifying and sorting goods
5. Checking receipts against packing slips
6. Marking records to call attention to unusual actions to be taken
7. Recording receipts on receiving slip or equivalent
8. Noting overages, shortages, and damaged goods
9. Dispersing goods received to appropriate location for subsequent use
10. Maintaining adequate and accurate records of all receiving activities

Receiving Principles

The efficient completion of each of the tasks just enumerated depends on the successful application of best-practice operating principles. The principles are meant to serve as guidelines for streamlining receiving operations. They are intended to simplify the flow of material through the receiving process, and to ensure that the minimum work content is required. In order, they are:

1. *Don't receive.* For some materials, the best receiving is no receiving. Often *drop shipping*—having the vendor ship to the customer directly—can save considerable time and labor associated with receiving and shipping. Large, bulky items lend themselves well to drop shipping. An example is a large camp and sportswear mail-order distributor, drop-shipping canoes and large tents.
2. *Prereceive.* The rationale for staging at the receiving dock, the most time- and space-intensive activity in the receiving function, is often the need to hold the material for

location assignment, or product identification. This information often can be captured ahead of time by having it communicated by the vendor at the time of shipment through advanced shipment notification (ASN).

3. *Crossdock "crossdockable" material.* Since the ultimate objective of the receiving activity is to prepare material for the shipment of orders, the fastest, most productive receiving process is crossdocking—essentially, shipping directly from the receiving dock. Palletized material with a single SKU per pallet, floor-stacked loose cases, and back-ordered merchandise are excellent candidates for crossdocking.

4. *Putaway directly to primary or reserve locations.* When material cannot be crossdocked, material handling steps can be minimized by bypassing receiving staging and putting material away directly to primary picking locations, essentially replenishing those locations from receiving. When there are no severe constraints on product rotation, this may be feasible. Otherwise, material should be directly put away to reserve locations. In direct putaway systems, the staging and inspection activities are eliminated. Hence the time, space, and labor associated with those operations are eliminated. In either case, vehicles that serve the dual purpose of truck unloading and product putaway facilitate direct putaway. For example, lift trucks can be equipped with scales, cubing devices, and on-line radio frequency (RF) terminals to streamline the unloading and putaway function. The material handling technologies that facilitate direct putaway include roller-bed trailers and extendable conveyors. In addition to pre-receiving, prequalifying vendors helps to eliminate the need for receiving staging.

5. *Stage in storage locations.* If material has to be staged, the floor space required for staging can be minimized by providing storage locations for receiving staging. Often, storage locations may be live-storage locations with locations blocked until the unit is officially received. Sometime spaces are provided over dock doors.

6. *Complete all necessary steps for efficient load decomposition and movement at receiving.* The most time we will ever have available to prepare a product for shipment is at receiving. Once the demand for the product has been received, there is precious little time available for any preparation of the material that needs to be done prior to shipment. Hence, any material processing that can be accomplished ahead of time should be accomplished, including:

   a. Prepackaging in issue increments—at a large office supplies distributor, quarter- and half-pallet loads are built at receiving in anticipation of orders being received in those quantities. Customers are encouraged to order in those quantities with quantity discounts. A large distributor of automotive aftermarket parts conducted an extensive analysis of likely order quantities. Based on that analysis, the company is now prepackaging in those popular issue increments.

   b. Applying necessary labeling and tags

   c. Cubing and weighing for storage and transport planning

7. Sort inbound materials for efficient putaway. Just as zone picking and location sequencing are effective strategies for improving order-picking productivity, inbound materials can be sorted for putaway by warehouse zone and by location sequence.

8. When possible, combine putaways and retrievals. To further streamline the putaway and retrieval process, putaway and retrieval transactions can be interleaved to reduce the amount of empty travel for industrial vehicles. This technique is especially geared for pallet storage and retrieval operations. Again, lift trucks that can unload, put away, retrieve, and load are a flexible means of executing dual commands.

9. Balance the use of resources at receiving by scheduling carriers and shifting time-consuming receipts to off-peak hours. Through computer-to-computer links, companies have improved access to schedule information on inbound and outbound loads. This information can be used to proactively schedule receipts and to provide advance shipping notice information.

10. Minimize or eliminate walking by flowing inbound material past workstations. An effective strategy for enhancing order picking productivity, especially when a variety of tasks must be performed on the retrieved material (e.g., packaging, counting, labeling), is to bring the stock to stationary order picking stations equipped with the necessary aids and information to perform the necessary tasks. The same strategy should be employed for receipts, which by their nature require special handling. Any requirements for weighing, cubing, sizing, or labeling should take place in the receiving operation. In addition, if the material is needed for an outbound order, a receiving operator can divert the case to shipping to complete a crossdocking operation.

Slotting

A critical step in maximizing warehouse operations is proper slotting of product within the warehouse. Slotting is the placement of product in a facility for the purpose of optimizing material handling and space efficiency. Travel time in a warehouse accounts for approximately 60% of all direct labor activities making it the largest target for reducing expenses. The benefits of slotting are:

1. Reduced picking labor requirements by locating the product in the optimal pick sequence

2. Reduced replenishment labor requirements by matching product unit loads with the appropriate size storage location

3. Reduced response time and improved flow by balancing workload between operators

4. Increased picking accuracy by separating similar products to avoid proximity picking errors

5. Reduced possibility of injuries by placing product in its ergonomically best location

6. Reduced product damage by organizing heavier product first in the pick path

7. Increased palletizing productivity by arranging product by case height allowing the building of tighter pallets for better trailer utilization
8. Deferred capital investment by maintaining the optimum warehouse layout and cube utilization, reducing the need for building expansion
9. Increased store level productivity by organizing product in family groups, and eliminating or reducing sorting of product for restocking at the store level

The steps in slotting are identifying your slotting goals, collecting product data, conducting a demand analysis, determining your slotting strategy, and then developing alternatives and analyzing the collected data to meet your strategy. Slotting is not just a one-time endeavor.

Order Picking

Order picking is the point in warehouse operations where intersection with customer requirements takes place. It is defined as selecting the correct item in the correct quantity from storage to satisfy customer demand. There are five levels of order picking based on the size of the unit that is being picked. They are:

- Pallet picking – retrieval of full-pallet quantities
- Layer picking – retrieval of full layers of cartons from pallets
- Case picking – retrieval of full cartons from storage
- Split-case picking – retrieval of inner packs from cartons in storage
- Broken-case picking – retrieval of individual items from storage

There are many choices when deciding the best picking methodology for your business, including: system supported or paper-based, part-to-man or man-to-part, automated or manual, and whether to pick discrete orders, pick by batch, pick by zone, wave pick or a combination. But regardless the decision of how to pick the product, there are fundamentals that apply to any circumstance. They are:

1. *Apply Pareto's Law, commonly referred to as the 80-20 rule.* In most operations, a small number of SKUs constitutes a large percentage of the inventory and throughput. By grouping these few fast-moving items together, we can reduce travel time in the warehouse during picking.
2. *Use clear, easy to read picking instructions.* This applies to computer directed picking activities. Instructions should include only the required information and be presented in the order in which it is required: location, item number, unit of measure, and quantity required. Additionally, any special labeling or packaging requirements should be included if it is a picker function rather than a packer function. If paper-based pick instructions are used, the font should be large enough to be read easily, the instructions should be spaced appropriately, and horizontal rulers should be used to assist in reading.

3. *Use pre-routed pick instructions.* The operator should be directed to pick locations in the shortest possible sequence. The inventory should be pre-allocated when the order is printed or released so that orders are not "competing" for the same inventory. The best way to do this is with RF, voice, or light directed technology vs. paper picking.

4. *Maintain an effective stock location system.* It is not possible to have an efficient order picking system without an effective stock location system.

5. *The order picker must be accountable for order accuracy.* Checkers should only be used as a random auditing function and not a quality control system. Pickers must be held accountable for their picking accuracy, with the "safety net" of a check station, there is no compelling reason for the picker to pay attention to detail. As in manufacturing, you cannot inspect quality into the product.

6. *Avoid counting.* The first step to eliminate or reduce counting is to make sure the package sizes match typical order quantities. Packages that are too large require more split and broken-case picking, and package sizes that are too small increase the amount of counting and work involved in the picking process. Another approach to solving the counting problem is to measure instead. Particularly for small items ordered in large quantities, weighing can improve productivity and accuracy.

7. *Require pick confirmation.* It is critical to order accuracy that the order picker actively verify that the quantity picked is the quantity required or the actual quantity picked is different than requested. Automatically doing this via scanning or automated pick confirmation provides even greater accuracy. In addition, this will eliminate confusion in shipping and at the customer's receiving operation. Many companies are charging vendors if they are not notified of shipment quantities correctly and in advance.

8. *Minimize paperwork.* Paperwork is a distraction during picking. It must be picked up, read, written on, and put down twice during each pick increasing the likelihood of errors. Paper should be eliminated from operations and provided only if the customer still requires it for their operations.

Order Picking Procedures

There are four basic procedures for picking orders. All order picking practices are combinations of these four procedures. In describing the alternative order picking procedures, the following terminology will be used:

- Item – a specific SKU
- Line – a single requirement for an SKU as defined on a specific picking document
- Order – customer requirements as specified by a picking document
- Pickers – the personnel responsible for selecting, counting, and delivering to shipping customer order requirements

The procedures are defined in terms of the following operating parameters:

- Pickers per order – the number of pickers that may work on a single order
- Line items per pick – the number of orders that products picked for at one time
- Periods per shift – the number of order scheduling windows there in one (eight-hour) shift

Discrete (Order) Picking

One person picks one order, one line (product) at a time. There is only one order-scheduling window during a shift. This means that orders are not scheduled and may be picked at any time on a particular day. This method is the most common because of its simplicity. It is also known as "order picking" in the purest sense. Discrete order picking has several advantages. It is the simplest for the order picker in paper-based systems, as only one picking document must be managed. As a result, the risk of picking errors or omission is reduced. In a service window environment it provides the fastest response to the customer. Accountability for accuracy is clear-cut, unless checkers are used. On the down side, it is the least productive procedure. Because the picker must complete the total order, travel time is likely to be excessive compared to other methods.

Zone Picking

The total pick area is organized into distinct sections (zones) with one person assigned to each zone. The picker that is assigned to each zone picks all the lines for each order that are located within that zone. The lines from each zone are brought to an order consolidation area where they are combined into the complete order before shipment. If the required lines are spread out across three zones, then three pickers would work on that order. Each picker only works on one order at a time and there is only one scheduling period per shift.

There are two variations of zone picking. Sequential zone picking is zone picking one zone at a time. The order is passed to the next zone for which it may (or in some cases, may not) have lines to be picked. This is sometimes referred to as a "pick and pass" method. Simultaneous zone picking is zone picking from all applicable zones independently, and then consolidating the order in a designated location as it is completed.

Zone picking is often used because of different skills or equipment associated with the equipment used in a hybrid warehouse. Pallet picking with narrow-aisle equipment, case picking from selective rack, broken-case picking from static hi-rise shelving, and broken case picking from horizontal carousels lend themselves to zones. In order to reduce travel time, a large equipment zone may be subdivided into several separate zones. A highly active storage equipment zone may be further subdivided into picking zones to reduce congestion and associated delays. In fact, it is often a good idea to size zones to balance the workload between zones.

Bucket Brigade

A variation of the zone-pick and pass methodology, except that the zones are not defined on a pick line, is the activity in each zone where the pickers travel. In the simplest terms, the order is started by picker one; picker two travels to picker one when he needs work. The place they meet is called the temporary zone break. Picker two then picks the order until picker three travels back to meet them and take over filling the order. This keeps all pickers active, eliminates backlogs between pick zones, and automatically balances the pick line on a daily basis. This can be done in paper-based systems, pick-to light, RF, or labeled picking areas.

Batch Picking

One picker picks a group of orders (batch) at the same time, one line at a time. When a product appears on more than one order, the total quantity required for all the orders combined is picked at one time, and then segregated by order. The segregation may take place while picking into totes (small items in small quantities) or transported to a designated area where they are sorted and grouped by individual order. There is only one order scheduling window per shift.

Picking more than one order at a time has a significant effect on picking productivity for case and broken case picking. In fact, the more orders a picker can effectively manage at once, the greater the productivity gain. Of course, there is a point of diminishing returns. The best candidates for batch picking are orders with few (one to four) lines and small cube. Once again, the reason for productivity improvement is the reduction in travel time. Instead of traveling throughout the warehouse to pick a single order, the picker completes several orders with a single trip. It is critical, however, that measures be taken to minimize the risk of picking and sorting errors. Computer control systems and automatic sortation are very effective.

Wave Picking

This method is similar to discrete picking in that one picker picks one order one line at a time. The difference is that a selected group of orders are scheduled for picking during a specific planning period. There is more than one order scheduling period during each shift. This means that orders may be scheduled for picking at specific times of the day. Typically this is done to coordinate the picking and shipping functions.

The following three methods are combinations of the basic procedures. As combinations, they are more complicated and thus require more control.

Zone-Batch Picking

Each picker is assigned a zone, and will pick a part of one or more orders, depending on which lines are stocked in the assigned zones. Where orders are small in terms of lines, the picker may pick the complete order in the zone. Still, only one scheduling period is used each shift.

Zone-Wave Picking

Each picker is assigned a zone, and picks all lines for all orders stocked in the assigned zone, one order at a time, with multiple scheduling periods per shift.

Zone-Batch-Wave Picking

Each picker is assigned a zone, and picks all lines for orders stocked in the assigned zone, picking more than one order at a time, with multiple scheduling periods each shift.

Table 11.1: Zone-batch-wave picking.

Procedure	Pickers per order	Line items per pick	Periods per shift
Discrete	Single	Single	Single
Zone	Multiple	Single	Single
Batch	Single	Multiple	Single
Wave	Single	Single	Multiple
Zone-Batch	Multiple	Multiple	Single
Zone-Wave	Multiple	Single	Multiple
Zone-Batch-Wave	Multiple	Multiple	Multiple

Conventional Order Picking Systems

Conventional order picking systems are those that use long established handling and storage methods, and simple control technology. The storage systems are considered to be either static (the product does not move on its own) or dynamic (the product flows by gravity when allowed to do so). Handling systems consider whether the picker travels from location to location (man-to-part) or the location moves, presenting itself to the picker (part-to-man).

Static Storage

The most common storage equipment in warehousing and distribution is the selective pallet rack (single deep) and the steel shelving unit ("clip" shelving). Used appropriately, it is an effective method for the storage and picking of all but the most popular products in a warehouse. Storage by size and popularity is critical. All too often, pallet rack is configured to provide assigned picking locations on the lower two levels, and reserve storage above. This allows the picker accessibility from the floor, but requires a prime storage location for every SKU, regardless of its popularity. This is typically a result of an ineffective control system. Shelving is typically used for storing SKUs whose inventory is small in cube. A typical shelf will hold four and one-half cubic feet of material, whereas a pallet may easily contain 64 cubic feet. Like pallet rack, shelving represents a very modest investment. The true cost of these systems must include the operating costs that result from excessive travel times during order picking.

Dynamic Storage

For the more popular products, flow rack presents an opportunity to improve picking productivity. It comes in two basic varieties: carton flow and pallet flow rack. In general, flow rack uses gravity conveyor or air flotation rails to present a unit of material to the picker at a specific (assigned) location. The carton flow rack is used for broken case picking, whereas the pallet flow rack is used for case picking. In the case of dynamic storage, popularity is measured in terms of cube. The advantage of flow rack is that a large volume of products is presented in a relatively small picking face, since both cartons and pallets are stored in-depth. The small picking face reduces the size of the zone, and therefore, the travel distance for the picker. However, there are, as always, trade-offs to consider. The equipment required is in addition to that required to store the basic inventory, and commands a premium price on a cost-per-cubic-foot-stored basis. The stock stored in flow rack is considered primary picking stock, with reserve stock stored randomly either in bulk or in pallet rack. In addition, you must consider the labor required to replenish the primary pick location. Properly applied, the additional investment and replenishment costs are justified by the savings in picking labor.

- *Man-to-part:* The most traditional material handling approaches to order picking require the picker to travel to the storage location. Without a stock location system, this involves searching as well as traveling. With a good locator system, the searching is minimal. Still, travel is a non-value-added activity and should be minimized. There are several man-to-part methods.
- *Pick-to-pallet:* The picker operates an industrial truck with a pallet. The industrial truck may be a man-up order-picker truck for picking out of pallet rack or hi-rise shelving, a pallet truck, or a pallet jack. It is commonly used for case picking and broken case picking.
- *Pick-to-cart:* The picker operates a pushcart or powered cart. This method restricts access to storage levels that can be reached from the floor. Radio frequency batch carts are available that include computer control and radio communication capabilities to improve productivity. Tugger vehicles pulling trailers can be used when the orders are large and the distance traveled is long.
- *Pick-to-belt (conveyor):* The picker is assigned a zone along a conveyor, to which he places picked items. This is commonly used with flow rack storage, and requires sortation by customer order before shipping. Applications include both case picking and broken case picking.
- *Man-aboard storage/retrieval:* The picker rides a captive aisle storage/retrieval (S/R) machine. It is an S/R machine because it rides on a rail, and is powered by an electric bus overhead. While the flexibility of being able to move between storage aisles conveniently is lost, the vehicle can operate at higher speeds than industrial trucks, thereby reducing travel time.

- *Part-to-man:* Significant productivity gains compared to man-to-part methods are possible in appropriate part-to-man applications. It is important to consider the storage considerations of each alternative, including cubic storage capacity per SKU and the replenishment requirements. Generally, the greater the portion of time that a picker spends traveling during the order picking process, the higher the return on investment. The part-to-man systems include carousels, storage conveyors, and automatic storage retrieval systems (AS/RS).

- *Horizontal carousels:* These are storage bins that rotate horizontally on a track under electric motor power. They should be considered as an alternate for static shelving. They also may be stacked to improve cube utilization, and will require either a mezzanine or a personnel-lifting device for access. Carousels up to ten-feet tall are commonly accessed by rolling ladders. Typically, a single picker will operate multiple carousels combined in a work zone or "pod". The objective is full utilization (no waiting, no traveling) of the operator as each carousel indexes independently. In practice, carousels can be in either the putaway or retrieval mode at any time.

- *Vertical carousels:* These are storage shelves that rotate vertically, always presenting a shelf to the picker at waist level. They are excellent for space utilization and organization when storing small items that are not used in large volumes.

- *Vertical storage/retrieval modules:* Similar in application to the vertical carousel, these machines move trays of parts from an overhead storage location to a single picking location at the pickers waist level. In each cycle, the S/R device returns one tray and retrieves the next.

- *AS/RS:* These systems may be thought of as a hybrid of the carousels and S/R modules, although they have been available longer than the S/R modules. They store and retrieve containers under computer or operator directed control. Those that handle heavy loads (i.e., pallets over 750 pounds each) are called large or unit load systems. Those that use trays under 750 pounds are referred to as mini-load systems. The smallest class may be referred to as micro-load systems. They handle totes or other unit loads that an operator can handle. Order picking applications for AS/RS are always "end-of-aisle," and include kitting for manufacturing.

Control Systems

Conventional order picking control systems may be characterized as paper-based and batch-process methods. They have evolved with the mainframe (host) computer where they are typically run. The logic is straightforward because it is simplistic. Orders are received up to a cut-off time on "Day 1." The orders are processed, including inventory allocation overnight, and released to the distribution center in the morning of "Day 2." Before picking can begin, the orders are printed and sorted by warehouse personnel. Pickers are given batches of orders to pick, and then they return the picking document to the office when the order is finished. The process ends with a shipment on either "Day 2" or "Day 3."

An improvement on this approach is called label picking. A label is printed for each SKU or full case with correct location address, SKU identity, and customer order number. Ideally, these are bar coded with a license plate number for automatic identification in shipping. For each line on an order, the picker reads the label, locates the stock, picks the requirement, and applies the label to the unit picked. Label picking reduces the likelihood of counting errors, especially in full-case picking. It also improves productivity by eliminating subsequent labeling and facilitating downstream sorting and palletizing.

The efficiency of traditional order picking systems can be further improved with two control system strategies.

- *Pick-to-light controls:* This control strategy uses a visual display to lead the picker through the process of picking each line in the assigned zone. It has been developed to aid picking from carousels, carton flow rack, shelving, and AS/RS. The benefits are paperless picking and order accuracy. There are many variations of this concept, including:
  - *Carousel light trees:* A column of displays is mounted adjacent to the horizontal carousel, one display per shelf. The display indicates the need for a pick from the shelf and the quantity to pick, under computer control.
  - *Carousel pick-to-tote:* When batch picking, a display is located at each of several tote positions for accumulating picks by order. The display indicates the quantity of each pick to place in each container.
  - *Flow rack pick-to-light:* A display is located in each rack bay to indicate the correct pick quantity. A pick confirmation keypad and indicator light is located at each stock location. An alternate scheme places a pick quantity display and confirmation keypad at each location.
  - *AS/RS display:* A graphical representation of the layout of a mini-load storage container is displayed along with an indication as to which compartment should be picked from and in what quantity.
- *Real-time warehouse management systems:* Radio frequency data communication links the picker to the control computer in real time. Onboard and hand-held terminals display picking instructions and provide a means of confirming or correcting picking orders. Automatic data collection is used to confirm the location and the SKU that is picked. Routing decisions are made by the control system to minimize travel in real time. The benefits are reduced travel time and delays and high order accuracy.

Automated Picking Systems

When short-term throughput requirements are very high, or the need for order accuracy is critical, or the human effort required to handle the product causes ergonomic concerns, automation of the order picking process should be considered. The automated systems all operate under computer control, receiving line-by- line instructions for each order, and retrieving the required quantity of the correct product without human interference. In most cases, stock keepers are required to replenish the stock in the order picking systems.

- *Unit-load AS/RS:* When the unit to pick is a full pallet or similar large load, the AS/RS offers complete automation from storage to retrieval, in minimal space. Unit-load AS/RSs are installed to 100 feet high with aisles only inches wider than the load to be stored. The S/R machines operate at speeds much faster than industrial trucks and travel simultaneously in the horizontal and vertical directions. They are used when inventories, throughput, and space costs are high. In totally automated systems, AS/RSs are supplied by conveyors, automated guided vehicles, or electrified monorail systems.

- *Horizontal case flow systems:* There are at least two approaches to dispensing cases or totes automatically. One uses conveyor in-feed on one side of a bank of stacked flow lanes and conveyor takeaway on the opposite side. The horizontal flow is achieved using the "walking beam" approach. The beam is installed underneath the travel path and moves up, forward, down, and back to its starting position. The stroke of the beam moves the column of cases forward. This technology was developed to store cartons of milk in a European dairy. The second approach is an adaptation of carton flow rack and a tote handling storage/retrieval device. The S/R devices riding on rails feed totes on one side of the flow lanes and retrieve them from the other.

- *Vertical case dispensers:* Case picking can also be accomplished vertically. The vertical dispenser uses gravity to dispense cases. A stream of cases is fed from a de-palletizing operation to the upper level by conveyor to a specific vertical column (tower) of tilt trays with skate wheel surfaces. Each case, in turn, cascades from the top shelf to the first empty one, thereby filling the selected tower. In the picking mode, each column dispenses a specific SKU, one case at a time, feeding a take-away conveyor. The final step in the process is palletizing and stretch-wrapping the load for shipment. Towers can vary from 10 to 100 feet, depending on pallet-case counts, and trays can handle cases of various sizes from 10 to 100 pounds.

- *Cylindrical case dispensers:* An innovative approach to automated case-picking has been developed for use in the beverage industry. It might be described as a large "slinky," after the helical coil toy that was popular in the 1960s. The equipment has a helical coil constructed of sheet metal. It is fed by a conveyor and receives cases on a last-in, first-out basis by rotating on its vertical axis. Cases may vary in length and width, but must be of a single height. Case picking occurs by indexing the unit 180 degrees to feed a second conveyor on the other side by rotating in the opposite direction from in-feed. The case dispenser can change modes (load/dispense) within 10 seconds. It is also a part of a larger system that includes de-palletizing and palletizing, all under central computer control.

- *Robotic cells:* Robots are also used for case and layer picking from pallets. Those equipped with layer equipment tooling may be used for de-palletizing for case dispensing by horizontal, vertical, or cylindrical case dispensers. Most often, the robot will be gantry mounted, where it travels overhead on rails that are supported by columns that are floor mounted. A two-axis robot can move horizontally in one direction, as well as vertically. Therefore, its work envelope is restricted to a single column of pallets. A three-axis robot adds a second horizontal direction of motion, and can pick from multiple pallets to multiple pallets. An alternate approach uses a cylindrical robot mounted on a track on the floor that allows it to move between a row of pallets providing stock for case picking and another row of pallets that are used for shipping. Whereas case-dispensing systems address the ergonomic challenges of manual case picking and are cost-justified on the basis of productivity savings, item dispensers offer high-speed picking with complete accuracy. Justification for all automation must consider the total systems cost including replenishment labor, de-palletizing systems, conveyances, dispensing equipment, computer controls, and integration.

- *Horizontal item dispensers:* These systems are very similar to the horizontal case dispensers discussed previously. They are simply built on a smaller scale. A stock-keeper manually loads horizontal magazines with product. In the picking mode, the equipment ejects units one at a time onto a belt conveyor that raises and lowers from one level to another. The conveyor delivers a complete order to a tote or carton for transportation to either a pack area or downstream picking zones. Typical applications are products for the health and beauty aids industry, with uniform size and automation-friendly packaging. Ideal applications are those where product value is high, and errors are costly.

- *A-Frame dispensers:* These systems have magazines that are arranged vertically on either side of a take-away conveyor. Each magazine holds a single column of a specific product. The system dispenses all the products required for a single order onto a moving pick-to zone on the belt conveyor. As this zone passes a dispenser, the product will be counted out and ejected onto that zone of conveyor, from the beginning of the picking module to its end, where product is transferred into a carton or tote. Pick rates are very high.

- *Dense matrix array dispensers:* An array of product magazines is positioned above the belt conveyor. Each magazine is removable for easy replenishment off-line, or fast replenishment on-line. The magazines are mounted on a double angle that allows the product to lie in a "trough" for flexibility, and directs the ejected units in the same direction as the conveyor is moving to minimize product damage. Other automated picking systems are available. For the most part, they are variations on the themes described in this section.

Sortation

Sorting systems are used to congregate material (e.g., cases, items, totes, garments) with a similar characteristic (e.g., destination, customer, store) by correctly identifying the like merchandise and transporting it to the same location. The components of a sorting system include transport systems, divert mechanisms, induction systems, identification/communication systems, and accumulation media.

Transport Systems

Conveyor systems are by far the most common mechanism for transporting merchandise through a series of diverters. Both belt, roller, and carriers on chain conveyors are used. The application of each type of conveyor depends on throughput requirements and the physical characteristics of the product being handled.

Divert Mechanisms

The wide variety of divert mechanisms available for mechanized sortation is evidence of the variety of throughput, size, and weight requirements that can be satisfied with alternative sorting systems. The divert mechanisms can be classified into four major categories: surface sorters, pop-up sorters, tilting sorters, and carrier sorters.

Induction Systems

The simplest induction is a gravity roller conveyor section placed next to the sorter. An operator codes each article as it passes this section, then pushes the article onto the moving sorting conveyor. This push-off type of induction is suitable for surface, pop-up, and tilting sorters.

When distribution systems are used for lightweight articles, the coding operator simply paces each article onto the sorter with one hand while entering the sort code on the keypad with the other. A beam of light, moving synchronously with the sorter conveyor, indicates the correct spot for the article to be placed. This type of hand induction is typical to tilt-tray sorting systems.

In some situations it is possible to induct articles automatically. A belt conveyor carries the articles past a coding operator (at a speed at which he can recognize the code), then conveys them directly onto the sorter. Throughput can be increased by adding a second coding operator, the two operators coding alternative items as they pass by.

Automated induction systems accept, orient, and deposit items on sorters without losing proper orientation. The physical induction is typically executed with a belt conveyor operating at a 45-degree angle to the direction of the sorter.

The fundamental control requirement in mechanical sorting is the ability to identify a product, a product's destination, and the product's place on the sorter. Product identification may be done manually, with induction operators reading labels related to product codes and types. The identification may be automated, with bar code or optical character recognition labels applied to or integrated into the product packaging. The product identification is then communicated by hand (with keyboard data entry), or mouth (with voice input), or automated (with bar code scanners or vision systems).

Accumulation Lanes and Chutes

The last major component in a sorting system is the mechanism used to accommodate merchandise at a discharge point. Depending on the weight and dimensions of the items and the number of divert points, the range of options for lanes and chutes is vast. For surface and pop-up sorters, accumulation lanes are usually comprised of some type of wheel or roller conveyor ranging from simple gravity flow rack or skate wheel conveyor to heavy-duty pallet roller conveyor. For tilting and carrier sorters, an even greater array of chute designs is available. Chutes are widely variable in configuration (e.g., single-lane, double-lane, drop-door) and material (e.g., metal, wood, or cloth).

Shipping Operations

Shipping typically encompasses the sortation, accumulation, consolidation, packaging, staging, and loading of outbound orders. Shipping is another space- and labor-intensive function in a distribution center. However, through direct loading of outbound trailers (crossdocking), the staging activity and the associated space, labor, and time are eliminated. The labor content in the remaining shipping activity, trailer loading, can also be minimized through the use of automated forklifts and conveyors that extend into the outbound trailers. When the staging activity cannot be eliminated, the space requirements can be minimized through rack systems.

Shipping Principles

Many of the best-practice receiving principles also apply (in reverse) to shipping, including direct loading (the reverse of direct unloading), advanced shipping notice preparation, and staging in racks. In addition, best-practice principles can be utilized for and securing loads, automated loading, and dock management, including:

1. *Select cost- and space-effective handling units:*
   a. *For loose cases.* The options for unitizing loose cases include wood (e.g., disposable, returnable, and rentable) pallets, plastic, metal, and nestable pallets. The advantages of plastic pallets over wood pallets include durability and cleanliness. Metal pallets are designed primarily for durability and weight capacity. Nestable pallets offer good space utilization during pallet storage and return, but are not very durable and have limited weight capacity. Other options for unitizing loose cases include slipsheets and roll carts. Slipsheets improve space utilization in storage systems and in trailers, but require special lift truck attachments. Roll carts facilitate the containerization of multiple items in case quantities, and facilitate material handling throughout the shipping process from order picking to packaging to checking trailer loading. The selection factors for unitizing loose cases include initial purchase cost, maintenance costs and requirements, ease of handling, impact on the environment, durability, and product protection.
   b. *For loose items.* The options for unitizing loose items include totes (nestable and collapsible) and cardboard containers. As was the case with unitizing loose cases, the selection factors include impact on the environment, initial purchase cost, life-cycle cost, cleanliness, and product protection.
2. *To minimize product damage:*
   a. *Unitize and secure loose items in cartons or totes.* In addition to providing a unit load to facilitate material handling, a means must be provided to secure material within

the unit load. For loose items in totes or cartons, those means include foam, peanuts, popcorn, bubble wrap, newsprint, and airpacks. The selection factors include initial and life-cycle cost, impact on the environment, product protection, and reusability.

b. *Unitize and secure loose cases on pallets.* Though the most popular alternative is stretch-wrapping. Velcro belts and adhesive tacking are gaining in popularity as environmentally safe means of securing loose cases on pallets.

c. *Unitize and secure loose pallets in outbound trailers.* The most common methods are bulkheads, foam pads, and plywood.

3. *Eliminate shipping staging, and direct-load outbound trailers.* As was the case in receiving, the most space- and labor-intensive activity in shipping is the staging activity. To facilitate the direct loading of pallets onto outbound trailers, pallet jacks and counterbalance lift trucks can serve as picking and loading vehicles, thus bypassing staging. To go one step further, the automating of pallet loading can be accomplished with pallet conveyor interfacing with specially designed trailer beds, to allow pallets to be automatically conveyed onto outbound trailers, with automated fork trucks, and/or automated guided vehicles. Direct, automated loading of loose cases is facilitated with an extendable conveyor.

4. *Use storage racks to minimize floor-space requirements for shipping staging.* If shipping staging is required, the floor-space requirements for staging can be minimized by staging in storage racks. Many companies use racks along the shipping wall and above dock doors to achieve this objective.

5. *Route on-site drivers through the site with a minimum of paperwork and time.* A variety of systems are now in place to improve the management of shipping and receiving docks and trailer drivers. A centralized lounge or office area should be located near the shipping and receiving operations for the drivers to report.

Integrating Material and Information Flow

The principles and systems that have been described above are designed to streamline the operations of individual functional areas within the warehouse. To complete our objective of achieving streamlined, minimum-work-content warehouse operations, the flow of materials and information must be well integrated. The principles and systems described briefly in this chapter are designed to help the reader understand the integration of material and information flow in warehouse operations.

Automatic and Paperless Communication Systems

Automated status control of material requires that the real-time awareness of the location, amount, origin, destination, and schedule of material be achieved automatically. This objective is in fact the function of automatic identification technologies, technologies that permit real time, nearly flawless, data collection. Examples of automatic identification technologies at work include:

- Fixed scanners, reading bar code labels to identify the proper destination for a carton traveling on a sortation conveyor
- Handheld laser scanners, to relay the inventory levels of a small-parts warehouse to a computer via radio frequency
- Voice recognition technology, to allow hands free communication to the computer system
- Radio frequency identification tags used to identify totes and cases without a line of sight requirement

Radio-Frequency Data Communication

Again, although not technically a member of the automatic identification systems family, hand-held and lift-truck-mounted RF terminals have become the standard for both inventory and vehicle/driver management. RF terminals incorporate a multi-character display, full keyboard, and special function keys. They communicate and receive messages on a prescribed frequency via strategically located antennae and a host computer interface unit. Beyond the basic thrust toward tighter control of inventory, improved resource utilization is most often cited in justification of these devices. Further, the increasing availability of software packages that permit RF linkage to existing plant or warehouse control systems greatly simplifies their implementation.

Voice Recognition Technology

Voice recognition software uses a series of audio and verbal inputs to indicate picks and confirm the pick has been completed. This has the advantage of being 100% hands free and flexible for multiple pick areas within the operation. The amount of system hardware is driven by the number pickers vs. pick-to-light which is driven by the number of pick locations. The disadvantage is training the system to a picker's voice and the picker to a consistent entry rhythm.

Radio Frequency Identification

Radio frequency identification (RFID) is a dynamic automatic identification and data capture technology that could replace barcode technology in certain applications. An RFID tag is a transponder that electronically transmits data. RFIDs yield better scan rates, require no line of sight, enhance sortation, and can create "smart" pallets, cases, or totes. With RFID, a company can gain full visibility of almost any product throughout the supply chain. The potential of RFID technology has not been fully tapped, and as companies realize to use RFID as a tool rather than a technology, the supply chain benefits will continue to grow.

Next-Generation Warehouse Operations

There are three main drivers that will require warehouse operations to be focused on continuous improvement: technology, complexity, and competition.

Computer systems are continuing to evolve and provide new opportunities to reduce costs and improve operations, but it can be difficult to keep up with the pace of change. Warehouse systems have made great strides in helping operations improve the operations within the four walls and supplement the functionality provided by ERP business systems, and they will continue to expand their reach up and downstream. While this will help synthesize the supply chain, the effect on warehouse operations will be dramatic and require a new level of thinking and process design. Automation within the warehouse creates new skills requirements for management and operators.

Complexity will continue to increase. The drive to smaller more frequent deliveries and growth in direct-to-consumer business is generating more, smaller orders in the warehouse with a much greater level of customization for each customer. This change in order profiles and requirements requires new methods of operation and in many cases totally different equipment, systems, and space requirements to meet the same overall demand.

Competition will not get any easier. Competitive advantage can only be realized by continually improving operations and never resting on past successes. Warehouse operations will continue to compete with existing rivals and also be challenged by new channels and external service providers. Many companies will choose to outsource their warehousing operations and pressures will continue to be placed on warehouse operations to remain a more economical and strategic asset of the company to fend off this risk.

Regardless of how your warehouse currently operates, the keys to success will be flexibility, continuous improvement, and total integration. The past is no longer a good predictor of the future. We must remain nimble to react to external demands and proactively look for ways to reduce total supply chain costs. New challenges cannot be addressed in isolation. Operations challenges will require a holistic review of not only the warehouse operations, but also the role of the warehouse as it evolves within the overall supply chain.

CHAPTER 12
Receiving and Shipping Systems

Kenneth Ackerman, President, K.B. Ackerman Company

When reduced to its essence, the business of warehousing is nothing more than managing space and time. A major portion of the time management aspect, or materials handling, is centered on the receiving and shipping functions.

In his writings on the logistics function, Professor B.J. LaLonde of Ohio State University recognizes four activities that continue to influence the warehousing industry:

- Reducing order-cycle time
- Improving quality
- Enhancing asset productivity
- Adapting to a new kind of workforce[1]

Receiving and shipping systems are closely involved in the successful achievement of all of these activities. Receiving and shipping systems are major points of emphasis in any effort to improve warehouse safety. Government studies often describe loading and unloading freight vehicles as the most dangerous work in a warehouse. A load may collapse as it is loaded or unloaded, metal or plastic bands used to seal containers may cause cuts or other injuries, industrial trucks may cause serious injury as they move across dockboards from the warehouse floor to the body of a trailer, and securing a trailer improperly can cause fatalities.

Receiving and shipping is also closely associated with warehouse security. Most of the contact between the warehouse and the outside world takes place at the shipping and receiving dock. Truck drivers employed by outside companies may be tempted to pilfer store merchandise while waiting at the dock. More seriously, both receiving and shipping systems present an opportunity for collusion theft, a partnership between a dishonest warehouse worker and a truck driver. Many theft-prevention techniques assume that collusion theft will exist with outbound shipments, taking place when the vehicle is deliberately overloaded. Such theft, however, can take place just as easily at the receiving dock when a vehicle is not completely unloaded.

The Critical Role of Receiving

Receiving is defined as the process of accepting material into the warehouse. Until a product has been physically unloaded, properly identified, and placed in a designated location, it cannot be shipped. Therefore, a serious breakdown in receiving can cause the pileup of a substantial amount of material that has arrived at the warehouse but is not ready to leave it.

Therefore, receiving holds a critical role in the warehouse and its efficient performance is the first step in operating a successful warehouse.

To expedite the receiving to shipping process, today's warehouse manager must be closely linked to information technology. Most technology systems require detailed identification, and are designed to "freeze" an item if its identity is in doubt. There are three identification challenges that must be met:

1. What is the standard shipping unit? Is it one each, one six-pack, one case, or one pallet?
2. What is the correct SKU number?
3. Does this item have affinity with one or more other items in the warehouse?

Whenever third party warehousing is involved, and sometimes even when it isn't, there is a legal aspect to receiving and shipping. Frequently, title passes from one party to another as the act of shipping or receiving is completed. For example, a common-carrier driver signs a bill of lading, and at that point, the carrier is responsible for protecting the cargo covered by this bill. On the other hand, railroads are not to blame for cargo theft from loaded boxcars that are still on a shipper's or receiver's property. Public warehouses become responsible for goods in their possession the moment they sign a bill of lading and issue a warehouse receipt. This transfer of ownership is obscured by crossdocking.

Because of the fluid nature of the operation, crossdocking tends to blur the points at which title passes. Therefore, any contract for a crossdock operation should be very specific in defining those actions that cause title to change from one party to another.

Though critical, receiving has historically been the neglected area in warehouse management. Marketing and sales people get very nervous about the shipping process because that is the action that completes a sale. However, nothing can be shipped until it is properly received, and more than one delivery operation has been seriously degraded by problems in receiving. One sign of neglect is an unreasonable time lag between physical receipt of a product and the time it is entered into the data system so it can be shipped.

There are many developments in the design of warehouse management systems that enhance the effectiveness of the receiving process. The most important of these is the advance shipping notice (ASN). This document provides information about the inbound load before the material actually arrives. A growing number of warehouse operators will refuse a load at the receiving gate if the ASN has not been received. When combined with scanning technology, the receiver who has the ASN can quickly and positively verify that the goods on the vehicle coincide with the listing of what was supposed to be shipped. The ASN should answer key questions about the loading pattern, the different SKUs (separated by item or order), and the sequence in which they are found on the vehicle.

As mentioned, clogging in the receiving function can have serious consequences. There are at least four common bottlenecks that tend to interfere with the fluid operation of a receiving system. The first of these is buyer inspections. In some retail operations, the merchandise buyer may wish to inspect the inbound shipment before approving the invoice for payment. Perhaps only that particular buyer can be certain that the quality of the product delivered conforms to the merchant's expectations. However, if the buyer is on vacation or away on business, the inbound load may remain in a staging area until the inspection is completed.

In other cases, a detailed quality-control test is involved. For example, one chain of hamburger restaurants uses a fat-content testing device to approve or disapprove every inbound load of hamburger. A random sample case is removed from the rear of the truck and unloading cannot proceed until the test is completed.

There are some pharmaceuticals and food products that must be isolated in quarantine until production quality control tests are complete. Today's information systems will allow an electronic quarantine by freezing the storage location of the inbound product until the quality control test results are received.

The receipt of returned merchandise is a slow and laborious process, and when returns are received at the same docks as other warehouse receipts, an oversupply of returns can create a bottleneck for the entire process. One answer to this is to have a totally separate receiving area for customer returns.

Conventional wisdom would have us believe that every inbound load must be staged before it can be moved to a storage location. However, one of the best ways to enhance receiving and shipping effectiveness is to adopt the practice of live unloading and loading. In a live unloading system, merchandise is moved directly from the delivering vehicle to a predesignated storage location. If any inspection is called for, that inspection is done in the storage location—not in a staging area. In a growing number of cases, inspection is eliminated by making it clearly understood that perfect quality is the vendor's responsibility. The ASN eliminates any questions about count or identification, and the vendor understands that delivery of substandard merchandise will cause the end of the relationship. Therefore, why should anything be staged on the dock?

Physical Aspects of Receiving

There are three options available to receive merchandise. Listed in order of efficiency, they are:

1. Unload the product and move it directly to an outbound vehicle (i.e., crossdocking).
2. Unload the product and move it directly to a storage slot (i.e., live unloading).
3. Stage the unloaded product at or near the receiving dock until it is inspected or checked.

The third of these is obviously the least efficient, but it may be a necessary step if narrow-aisle vehicles or other specialized lift trucks are used in the storage area. As you consider the three options, measure the number of missed opportunities to move from Step 3 to Step 2 or Step 1.

Neglect or mismanagement of the physical aspects of receiving can have serious consequences for your operation. In the absence of proper discipline, you may place damaged or off-spec materials into storage without pinpointing the responsibility for the discrepancy.

While you may hold the vendor responsible for being his own inspector, your system must be sufficiently detailed to allow the buyer to identify precisely which inbound shipment contained the off-spec material. Without an accurate counting procedure, you could sign for merchandise that you never received. The collusion thief exists by creating such situations.

Improving the effectiveness of receiving requires teamwork between the vendor and buyer. Vendors should be encouraged to load vehicles in a fashion that facilitates receiving. On the other hand, vendors who deliver loads that are extraordinarily difficult to identify and sort should be sanctioned.

To show how a serious abuse of the receiving function can paralyze a warehouse operation, consider this example. While it may seem unbelievable, this is not a fictitious incident. An e-commerce retailer retained a third-party fulfillment specialist to handle a large and highly seasonal inventory. As goods began to flow into the distribution center (DC), some vehicles contained more than 900 SKUs on a single trailer, and typically were mixed at random within the vehicle. ASNs were nonexistent, and frequently neither the warehouse operator nor his customer could identify certain items. Eventually, the backlog of unidentified merchandise grew until it exceeded 50,000 cases, all of which were piled in a "no man's land" because they could not be identified or shipped. As a result, the peak-shipping season was crippled because the fulfillment specialist was unable to ship a major portion of its inventory.

Receiving as a Process

Six steps should be followed in developing a process flow for warehouse receiving:

1. Call inbound carriers for a delivery appointment
2. Receivers should verify that ASNs are available before confirming delivery appointments
3. Assign a door for inbound loads (or staging spots for drop & hook operations)
4. Spot and secure vehicles with wheel chocks or safety hooks
5. Break cargo seals and examine the rear of the load in the presence of the delivering driver
6. Remove the load from the delivering vehicle

Total accuracy in this process is critical. An error in identification at receiving will probably cause the product to be warehoused in the wrong slot and then incorrectly shipped. A failure to discover and pinpoint responsibility for product damage may cause the loss to be borne by the warehouse operator.

Before the electronic age, a favorite debate was whether receiving should be "blind" or verified by load tally. The winners were usually those who advocated blind receiving, since this process ensured that the workers on the receiving dock would carefully count and identify the goods as they were unloaded. When ASNs and scanners are available, as they commonly are today, the checking process is performed electronically, and the debate is obsolete.

As the physical unloading process is considered, you have three options. The most common option today is to use a lift truck to remove pallets or unitized loads from the delivering vehicle. The second option, in those few cases where floor-loaded material is received, one or more workers must palletize the material according to a standard pallet pattern. This pattern is referred to as "tie and high" in the grocery product industry. The third option, often found in clothing companies, is to use a conveyor that transfers each item from the delivering vehicle to a staging area. Obviously, the first of these options allows the most efficient use of labor, and most warehouse operators prefer to change procedures to allow the handling of unitized loads.

Receiving Metrics

How do you measure the effectiveness of your receiving function? More importantly, are you measuring it at all? There are at least five methods of measuring this function:

1. How long is the time lag from the arrival of the inbound vehicle until the received product is placed in stock and ready to ship? This is commonly referred to as "dock to stock" time. In a few unfortunate operations, it is measured in days rather than hours. Your goal should be to reduce this time to minutes and eliminate the obvious waste involved in keeping unshippable merchandise in the warehouse.
2. Measure the number and percentage of receiving discrepancies. The percentage is as important as the number, since it would be normal for a high-volume operation to experience more errors than a low-volume one. It is equally important to track these discrepancies by vendor, since eventually the vendor who contributes an unusual number of irregularities should be sanctioned.
3. Measure each carrier's compliance with delivery appointments. Maintaining the dock schedule will greatly enhance the effectiveness of any warehouse, but scheduled delivery works only when the carriers cooperate. When one or more carriers demonstrate a continuing pattern of noncompliance, appropriate action should be taken.
4. Measure the time elapsed to unload each vehicle, and compare that time to the number of pieces or pounds received. This measurement will allow you to judge the effectiveness of the existing process of removing freight from the delivering vehicle. It also allows you to judge the efficiency of proposed new systems that promise to enhance this process. This measurement may also allow you to compare the efficiency of different work shifts or different warehouses.
5. Measure vendor compliance with your requirements for pallet patterns or load sequence instructions. If you have instructed the vendor to load the vehicle in a certain fashion, there should be some type of penalty when your instructions are ignored.

The venerable business proverb says: "Nothing can be managed until it is measured." Whoever wrote this must have been talking about the receiving function.

Putaway

The last step in receiving is the placement of each item in the optimum storage location. Those items that are most urgently needed may not be put away at all, but held in the dock area so that they can be shipped immediately.

Every warehouse operator should use a Pareto Analysis (i.e., the ABC system) to identify the fast movers, the "dogs," and those items that are in between. Today's information technology makes the maintenance of an accurate ABC system relatively simple. In many inventories, there is a substantial difference in the results of the analysis at different times of the year. A hot item in November may be a dog item in May.

Once an inbound item's popularity is determined, a storage planner can determine whether this item goes to a pick line, a forward pick area, or to a permanent storage slot. If it is a dog, the storage slot is in one of the least accessible areas in the warehouse. The fastest movers should stay close to the door and close to the floor.

A storage planner should specify and list location addresses for each item on the ASN, and this process should be completed before the load arrives at the warehouse. Unfortunately, a high percentage of warehouse operators do not take this step. When the storage address is not determined by management, the lift operator unloading the vehicle must also be the storage planner. When this happens, it is natural for the lift operator to find the first available hole and place the material in that location. The result is a chaotic storage pattern that contributes to continued inefficiency.

The storage planner should also recognize the opportunity to store related items together. For example, if SKU number 123 is typically shipped along with SKU 798, then it is efficient to store these two items in adjacent locations.

Ergonomic considerations are also an important part of storage planning. The fastest moving items should be kept in the golden zone, or in storage shelves that are high enough from the floor to eliminate stooping and low enough to eliminate stretching. Most people define the golden zone as that area that is no higher than the shoulders and no lower than the knees.

The Shipping Operation

Shipping might be defined as staging the unloading of vehicles for delivery to customers. A proven method of saving time in shipping is increasing the size of the typical unit that is handled. This is called unitization and represents one of the best ways to increase the efficiency of materials handling.

Increasing the size of a unit load requires some standardization of the unitized process. Unitized handling, as we know it today, started in the U.S. military during World War II. As the industrial truck was developed, its users quickly recognized that the best way to move product was to place forks on the front of the vehicle and then build a wooden platform that could be used to transport cartons or other types of cargo.

The first such platforms were skids that consisted of a wooden deck nailed across two or more vertical boards. These boards raised the platform enough to allow the forks to slide underneath the deck. As the need for stacking stability was recognized, additional boards where nailed across the bottom, and the skid evolved into a pallet. Pallets are made of wood because that is the least expensive and most plentiful building material in most places.

Pallet standardization was also fostered by the U.S. military, and huge supplies of standardized pallets were abandoned in 1945 as the war ended. Because the Australians had a particularly large supply of military pallets, they formed the Commonwealth Handling and Equipment Pool (CHEP) to utilize the surplus pallets. In this way, Australia achieved the world's first pallet standardization as a legacy of its war surplus. Standardization started in the U.S. during the 1960s, primarily by General Foods. (Its standard design specifies the size and spacing of the boards on the top and bottom deck as well as the size of the runner boards or stringers.) Because of the size and bargaining power of General Foods at that time, the grocery industry was persuaded to standardize, and the Grocery Manufacturers of America took over the job of promoting the industry standard called the "GMA pallet." While many features of this standard have since disintegrated, the size specifications remain today.

There was a time when nearly all grocery products were shipped with individual cases loaded on the floor of the vehicle, and the result was a substantial amount of time wasted in both loading and unloading. Because nearly every grocery retailer had a favorite pallet size with appropriate rack installations, any standardization of unit loads was considered to be impossible. Once the industry adopted a pallet standard, it was possible for grocery shippers to design a unitized load that was acceptable to nearly every buyer.

There are several ways to handle these unitized loads. One is a pallet exchange program in which the delivering carrier might trade 26 loaded pallets for 26 empty ones. The effectiveness of this method has deteriorated in the absence of any policing of a pallet quality standard. The carrier might deliver 26 high-quality pallets that are exchanged for pallets of very poor quality, or vice versa. Another option is the use of a carton clamp truck or a slipsheet-handling device for a load-transfer device that can switch the unitized load onto the receiver's pallet.

Industry continues its search for more cost-effective pallets, but at least the standard dimensions of 48 inches by 40 inches (1.0 m by 1.2 m) remain in general use.

Crossdocking

Crossdocking is perhaps the most exotic element in shipping. Crossdocking is a distribution system in which the freight comes in and out of the DC without ever being stored. Like many logistics concepts, the process is not as new as it might appear. Back in the days when merchandise was transported in boxcars, the process was called pool car distribution. A single carload containing shipments to several customers was sent to a distributor who unloaded the vehicle and distributed the orders. The best way to understand this popular process is to compare it to one brand of ice cream that comes in five different flavors. Just as each flavor has substantial differences, so does the cross docking operation.

The plain vanilla is the easiest and lowest cost option in crossdocking. In this case, the inbound load is segregated by the outbound order. The shipper unloads the orders in sequence, and then places them on an outbound vehicle.

The chocolate flavor is more complicated. In this case, the inbound load is segregated by SKU, but not by order. The crossdock operator must create the outbound orders either after staging a load or as the product is unloaded. This process is obviously more costly than the plain vanilla.

The lime flavor represents the inbound load that is labeled but not sorted. The shipper may have to stage the entire load on the dock so it can be sorted by outbound order and subsequently shipped.

The lemon flavor describes the inbound load that requires supplemental filling from inventory already stored in the warehouse. In this situation, the shipper combines inventory that is already in stock with merchandise found on the inbound vehicle.

The most complex flavor is raspberry. In this situation, the merchandise is neither labeled nor segregated, but loaded at random on the delivery vehicle. Obviously the time and cost of handling this product will be significantly higher than that incurred with the other flavors.

As you contemplate a crossdock operation, it is essential to consider the flavor, or process, involved. As you can see, there can be substantial differences in both the time needed and the cost involved. If you budget for plain vanilla and end up with raspberry, your operation may suffer significant financial loss.

Success Factors in Crossdocking

The three most important factors for success in crossdocking are timeliness, communication, and accuracy.[2] Regarding time, it is essential for the crossdock operator to receive detailed information about the load before the vehicle arrives. Failure to submit advanced information will usually wipe out the cost advantages of cross docking. Since the purpose of the whole operation is to save time, it is obvious that each element of crossdocking must be available on a timely basis. One of the challenges is stock-outs. If all the needed inventory is not available, the orders cannot be properly delivered. In effect, crossdocking is the coordination of receiving and delivery, and some of it is secured on a JIT (just-in-time) basis.

Complete communication is another critical factor. The ASN is absolutely necessary. Like timeliness, a communication failure can erase all the advantages of crossdocking. However, the quality of communication is every bit as important as timeliness. Sloppy or incomplete paperwork can cause serious trouble.

Finally, the work must be accurate. If the load sorting is not done properly, the shipments will not be correct. If the documentation is not accurate or incomplete, the customers will not be satisfied.

Special Forms to Support Crossdocking

In crossdocking, a pick ticket is prepared for each product code. It lists customers receiving merchandise and the quantity going to each destination. A loading tally accompanies each bill of lading and is used to control the outbound shipments. It shows where each order is within the trailer, starting with the nose and ending at the rear. A pallet record lists the number and types of pallets received and shipped; the purpose of this form is to control pallet exchange. Customers are normally billed for the cost of pallets that are not returned. The other three forms, receiving tally, bill of lading, and invoice are similar to those used in most warehouse operations.

To Check or Not to Check

The practice of checking freight at the shipping or receiving dock is a relic of the time when many workers could barely read or count. Because of the lack of these skills, a more educated person was needed to review the work. Today, the scanning process can fill the same function as the human checker did prior to the electronic age. With the capabilities available in today's information technology, it is hard to imagine a single instance where a checker is really necessary.

Congestion and the Drop & Hook Solution

A favorite complaint of today's warehouse manager is lack of adequate truck docking space. In many cases, the design of the building makes the installation of additional dock doors either very expensive or absolutely impossible. One solution is to create a trailer storage yard and use a jockey tractor to move trailers between the yard and the dock doors. However, this step also involves a method of managing the storage yard and maintaining the visibility of every trailer. Sometimes tracking devices are used to be certain that the wrong trailer is never loaded or that the proper trailer is never missing in action.

Shipping Metrics

Like receiving, the shipping operation cannot be improved until it is measured. One measurement is tracking time from the arrival of the vehicle at the warehouse property until the load is completed. This measurement can be used to combat unjustified claims for detention, and it can also be a means of tracking efforts to improve loading times. One large DC has established a standard that no driver will spend more than two hours on the property. When one and one-half hours have passed and the job is not finished, management uses every effort to expedite completion of the job.

Shipping errors should be tracked as a percent of total activity. The same can be done with damage claims as well as product damaged during the shipping process.

Carrier performance should be measured. What percent of the shipments were delivered to the customer on time? What is the frequency and amount of carrier claims? Are the customers satisfied with the carrier's service? Given the fact that transportation remains a highly competitive business, it is important to track the quality performance of outbound as well as inbound carriers.

Keeping a "Driver Friendly" Warehouse

We are destined to suffer a continuing shortage of skilled labor in the logistics area, and nowhere more severely than in the field of truck driving. In the face of this problem, some carriers have pinpointed "unfriendly" consignees and try to avoid serving them. Obviously, you should never let your warehouse build this reputation.

Here are some things you can do to improve your relationship with your carrier. First, when you establish a scheduled truck dock, be sure to honor your own schedule. You cannot expect the carrier to arrive at a prescribed time unless you demonstrate that you will also keep this appointment.

Some warehouses are easier to access than others. It may be impractical for you to move, but you can be sure that any access roads to your facility have the traffic moving counter-clockwise. In that way, the driver never has to spot a trailer from the "blind side" of the vehicle.

Finally, do whatever it takes to reduce the time that the driver spends in loading, unloading, or waiting. Wherever possible, avoid floor-loading of loose cases. If you cannot do this, consider the establishment of a drop and hook operation because it will eliminate waiting time. With the drop and hook system, a trailer is dropped in a parking lot and moved to the warehouse dock by a shuttle tractor for loading or unloading. When the operation is complete, the trailer is returned to the lot.

Summary

Receiving and shipping systems lie at the heart of every material handling operation. They should be the primary focus for both safety and security. Since nothing can be shipped until it is properly received, the efficiency of the receiving function deserves far more attention than it currently receives. Both receiving and shipping processes can be readily charted. Both can be, and should be, the subject of detailed measurements that lead to operational improvements.

Works Consulted

1 Ackerman, Kenneth, *Warehousing Forum,* Volume 7, Number 9, 1992.
2 Ibid, Volume 10, Number 9, 1995.

CHAPTER 13
Warehouse Space and Layout Planning

Jerry D. Smith, Vice President, Tompkins Associates

What is the thing one always runs out of in a warehouse? One might answer this question with the response, "Capital." In reality, though, one can get more of that and other resources if one's salesmanship skills are honed. The true response is, "Space." Of all the common denominators in warehousing, space is the primary finite resource. All too often, there is a deficiency in the planning of this key physical factor, which then hinders the operating efficiency of the warehouse. Examples of these deficiencies are products being stored in public warehousing immediately after the facility opens, or extended travel distances due to poor layout, or even something as simple as a column in the middle of an aisle. Therefore, to meet the objectives of the warehouse, proper planning of warehouse space and layout requirements is imperative. This chapter addresses the methodologies and philosophies for correct space and layout planning for the warehouse.

Space Planning for Receiving and Shipping

The most important functions of a warehouse occur on the receiving and shipping docks. This is where the control of merchandise is transferred, whether product is brought into the warehouse or taken from it. If this transfer of control is not accomplished efficiently, safely, and accurately, it is impossible for the warehouse to satisfy the customer, regardless of the quality of the other aspects of the warehouse. Unfortunately, these are also the most neglected areas of a warehouse.

An important prerequisite of efficient, safe, and accurate receiving and shipping activities is enough space in which to perform them. The following sections detail the steps necessary to provide adequate space for the dock area, first defining what materials are to be received and shipped, then determining the dock requirements and the maneuvering allowances inside the warehouse, and finally calculating the staging requirements and other dock-related requirements. This methodology should be followed to determine the space requirements of all receiving and shipping activities.

Defining the Materials Received and Shipped

The first step in space planning for receiving and shipping operations is to define what is to be accomplished; that is, to define the materials to be received or shipped and the related frequencies. Therefore, data defining the physical characteristics of the product is required. The following information is critical:

- Unit length, width, and height
- Unit cubic feet

- Unit weight
- Units per load
- Load length, width, and height
- Load weight
- Whether received on pallets or slipsheets
- Stackability
- Classification (flammable, corrosive, radioactive)

It is seldom practical to collect this data for each individual SKU, and in fact it typically is impractical, because most warehouses store thousands of different SKUs and determining the dimensional information for each would be an extremely time consuming task. If the facility being planned is new and forecasted data is used, these forecasts are inevitably wrong. Consequently, planning a warehouse based on specific item requirements is a waste of time.

A much better strategy is to establish generic categories of items and then determine the physical characteristics for representative items in each generic category. The items in a given generic category should have similar characteristics with respect to type of item and unit load received, stored, or shipped. Developing generic categories reduces the number of entries to a manageable level. Another advantage is that fluctuations in requirements for individual SKUs will have less impact because they will affect a whole generic category, not just one unit.

Determining Frequency of Activity

The frequency with which items are received and shipped should be determined by collecting the following information:

1. Receiving activity
   a. Units (or loads) per truck
   b. Frequency of receipt
   c. Unload time per truck
   d. Total trucks per day
2. Shipping activity
   a. Units (or loads) per truck
   b. Frequency of receipt
   c. Load time per truck
   d. Total trucks per day

Determining Dock Bay Requirements

After materials to be received or shipped have been defined, determine the requirements for the receiving and shipping dock bays. Three questions must be addressed:
   1. What kinds of vehicles are at the docks? To determine this, you will need to collect the type, exterior/interior length, exterior/interior width, clearance height to the top of the carrier, and height of the carrier bed off the road.

2. How many dock bays are required? Typically the answer is obtained by means of one of three techniques: guessing, waiting-line analysis, and simulation.

3. How should the dock bays be configured?

Number of Dock Bays

Of the techniques listed in No. 2, only *simulation* will consistently result in an accurate assessment of the number of dock bays required for a typical warehouse. Unfortunately, *guessing* is most commonly used. The guess is usually based on some historical experience of the guesser, such as the number of dock bays in the old warehouse or in other warehouses in the area. Although guessing may very well result in the correct answer, success can usually be attributed to luck, not knowledge. Furthermore, a warehouse plan based on guessing will rarely withstand the scrutiny of upper management.

Waiting-line analysis or *queuing theory*, is often suggested as the correct technique for determining the number of dock bays required if the time between carrier arrivals and the time to service the carriers at the warehouse vary randomly. However, this rarely is the case in most warehouse operations. Instead of being random, carrier arrivals usually follow a pattern. For instance, more trucks may be received in the first two weeks of the month than in the last two weeks, and more shipments may occur during certain parts of the week or day. Because dock activity generally does not occur in a random manner, waiting-line analysis will rarely result in an accurate determination of the number of dock bays required.

Simulation, then, is the recommended technique for warehouses in which carrier arrivals and service times are not random. Contrary to what complicated statistical models and computer programs imply, simulation is a straightforward, simple tool.

Dock Simulation

An example: XYZ Company is building a warehouse. The company has completed a receiving and shipping analysis chart which shows that truck activity tends to surge at 10 a.m. and 2 p.m. The same pattern is expected at XYZ Company's new facility.

How many receiving dock bays should XYZ Company construct, and what is the anticipated performance of this number of bays? Based on the experience of local warehouses and the anticipated volume of flow into XYZ Company, the expected time between truck arrivals from 8:00 a.m. to 10:00 a.m., from 11:00 a.m. to 2:00 p.m., and from 3:00 p.m. to 5:00 p.m. is shown in Table 13.1.

Table 13.1: Truck Arrivals.

Time Between Arrivals (hr.)	Relative Frequency	Cumulative Frequency	Random Number Range
0.25	0.02	2	0-1
0.50	0.07	9	2-8
0.75	0.22	31	9-30
1.00	0.30	61	31-60
1.25	0.27	88	61-87
1.50	0.07	95	88-95
1.75	0.04	99	95-98
2.00	0.01	100	99

The expected time between truck arrivals from 10:00 a.m. to 11:00 a.m., and from 2:00 p.m. to 3:00 p.m., is shown in Table 13.2.

Table 13.2: Truck Arrivals.

Time Between Arrivals (hr.)	Relative Frequency	Cumulative Frequency	Random Number Range
0.25	0.32	32	0-31
0.50	0.41	73	32-72
0.75	0.27	100	73-99

Experience has also shown that the time to unload a truck follows the distribution shown in Table 13.3.

Table 13.3: Unloading Times.

Unloading Times (hr.)	Relative Frequency	Cumulative Frequency	Random Number Range
0.50	0.01	1	0
1.00	0.11	12	1-11
1.50	0.20	32	12-31
2.00	0.21	53	32-52
2.50	0.20	73	53-72
3.00	0.16	89	73-88
3.50	0.08	97	89-96
4.00	0.02	99	97-98
4.50	0.01	100	99

The relative frequency columns of Tables 13.1, 13.2, and 13.3 represent the percentage of time that the interval between truck arrivals (Tables 13.1 and 13.2) and the unloading time (Table 13.3) is equal to the values indicated in column one. For example, in Table 131.1, between 8:00 a.m. and 10:00 a.m., the interval between truck arrivals will equal 0.25 hour, 2 percent of the time. These relative frequencies can be represented by assigning an appropriate range of numbers between 0 and 99. Thus, a relative frequency of 0.02 would be assigned two numbers between 0 and 99. This assignment has been made in the random-number range columns of these three tables.

Some other information required to complete the XYZ Company receiving dock simulation:

1. The dock opens at 8:00 a.m. for incoming trucks.
2. Dock personnel take breaks and eat lunch according to this schedule: break, 9:30 a.m. to 9:45 a.m., lunch, 12:00 p.m. to 12:30 p.m., break, 2:15 p.m. to 2:30 p.m.
3. The receiving dock closes to incoming trucks at 3:00 p.m. Trucks arriving after 3:00 p.m. must return the next day.
4. Dock personnel receive overtime pay for work performed after 5:00 p.m.

The simulation model to help determine the feasibility of various numbers of docks should be constructed by following these steps:

1. Generate a series of random numbers from 1 to 100. (Choose any numbers from that group.)
2. Transform the random numbers into a series of truck arrival times using Tables 13.1 and 21.2, which indicate the times at which trucks arrive.
3. Generate a series of random numbers from 1 to 100.
4. Transform the random numbers into a series of truck unloading times using Table 13.3.
5. Assume there will be three bays.
6. Assign trucks to dock bays and, if a bay is unavailable, to a queue. Unload the trucks. Perform the truck operations for the entire day and maintain statistics.
7. Determine if steady state is reached.* If so, and if more than five docks have been considered, terminate the model.
8. If steady state is reached and fewer than five dock bays have been considered, add a bay and return to step 1.
9. If steady state is not reached, return to Step 6 and simulate another day's operation.

Steady state is reached when incorporating the summary statistics for another day's simulated operation into the cumulative summary statistics has no significant impact on the cumulative summary statistics. A baseball player's batting average has achieved steady state toward the end of the season, when hitting a home run or striking out has little impact on his or her season's batting average.

Figure 13.1 presents the simulation of one day's operation of XYZ Company's receiving dock. It assumes that three dock bays are available. After the day's operation has been simulated, statistics describing the performance of the dock for that day should be summarized. They are presented in Table 13.4.

Figure 13.1: Simulation worksheet.

Truck Number	Random Number	Time Between Arrivals (Hrs.)	Time of Arrival	Random Number	Unload Time (Hrs.)
1	23	0.75	8:45 a.m.	19	1.50
2	4	0.50	9:15 a.m.	88	3.00
3	35	1.00	10:15 a.m.	52	2.00
4	16	0.25	10:30 a.m.	57	2.50
5	79	1.25	11:15 a.m.	14	1.50
6	8	0.50	11:45 a.m.	87	3.00
7	77	1.25	1:00 p.m.	77	3.00
8	89	0.25	2:30 p.m.	16	1.50
9	27	0.50	2:45 p.m.	54	2.50
10	39	0.50	3:15 p.m.	--	--

Time of Day	Dock 1	Dock 2	Dock 3	Dock 4	Dock 5	Dock 6	Queue
8:00 a.m.				1			
8:15 a.m.							
8:30 a.m.				2			
8:45 a.m.	8:45 a.m.						
9:00 a.m.				3			
9:15 a.m.		9:15 a.m.					
9:30 a.m.							
9:45 a.m.							
10:00 a.m.							
10:15 a.m.			10:15 a.m.				
10:30 a.m.	10:30 a.m.						
10:45 a.m.							
11:00 a.m.							
11:15 a.m.							11:15 a.m.
11:30 a.m.							
11:45 a.m.							11:45 a.m.
12:00 p.m.							
12:15 p.m.							

Table 13.4: Summary statistics for the three dock bays—Day one.

Average truck-waiting (queue) time (hr)	0.5
Longest truck-waiting (queue) time (hr)	1.5
Average time truck spent at warehouse (hr)	3.1
Longest time truck spent at warehouse (hr)	4.5
Average dock-bay usage (percent)	82

The simulation of the receiving dock with three dock bays is repeated for several days of operation until steady state is achieved. Then the process is repeated for receiving docks having four and five dock bays. The cumulative summary statistics for each alternative are summarized in Table 13.5.

Table 13.5: Cumulative Summary Statistics for Dock Simulation.

Factor	Number of Dock Bays		
	3	4	4
Average truck-waiting (queue) time (hr.)	0.80	0.30	0.10
Longest truck-waiting (queue) time (hr.)	1.00	0.40	0.10
Average time truck spends at warehouse (hr.)	2.80	2.30	2.10
Longest time truck spent at warehouse (hr.)	3.50	2.50	2.10
Average dock bay usage (percent)	85	65	49

Analysis of the statistics presented in Table 13.5 indicates that, as the number of dock bays increases, the carrier costs decrease, while the dock costs (the costs of dock space and unloading labor) increase because dock bay usage declines. XYZ Company owned the carriers; therefore, the cost of having an over-the-road truck sitting idle was extremely high. A four-dock-bay receiving dock was judged to be more economical than a three-dock-bay receiving dock. A comparison between four dock bays and five dock bays, however, revealed that the reduction in carrier cost gained by using five bays was not significant enough to justify the additional dock space and unloading crew. Consequently, the decision was made to construct a four-dock-bay receiving dock at the XYZ Company.

The simulation worksheet presented in Figure 13.1 is an excellent method of keeping track of carrier arrival times, load/unload times, and assignment of carriers to bays or the queue in a dock simulation. The top portion of the simulation worksheet records the random numbers, carrier arrival times, and carrier service (load/unload) times. The bottom portion of the worksheet simulates the assignment of carriers to dock bays to study the impact of having various numbers of dock bays.

Unfortunately, simulation will not give an unequivocal answer to the dock bay question. It will, however, reveal how dock performance will vary with different numbers of dock bays, and provide valuable data upon which one can base sound management decisions. Simulation is significantly more valuable than the other methods of determining the number of dock bays required.

Dock operations, particularly receiving functions, generate a tremendous amount of trash, including corrugated boxes, binding materials, broken and disposable pallets, bracing, and other packing materials. Therefore, a refuse container is a requirement. Most companies find this is ideally located at a dock door. Therefore, it is a good idea to add an additional door to the planned number of doors.

Dock Bay Configuration

The third step in determining the dock requirements is to ascertain the dock configuration. There are several basic dock types. The basic configurations are 90-degree (flush) docks and finger (staggered) docks, with the variations being whether or not they are enclosed. Another configuration that exists is the open dock.

With the 90-degree dock, the truck is positioned perpendicular to the building. The ideal configuration for a 90-degree dock is one with a relatively level driveway approach pitched slightly toward the building, as seen in Figure 13.2. The slight decline assists in holding the truck against the dock bumpers while being loaded or unloaded and also aids in drainage. In another configuration of the 90-degree dock, the driveway is depressed. This occurs when buildings are placed on grade and the driveway must be depressed to create the proper dock height. If the depressed configuration is necessary, care must be taken to ensure that the truck does not hit the building wall. In either configuration, the 90-degree dock is the most poplar of the dock options because it takes up a minimum amount of inside warehouse space. This popularity is directly attributable to the relatively high cost of inside warehouse space compared with outside space.

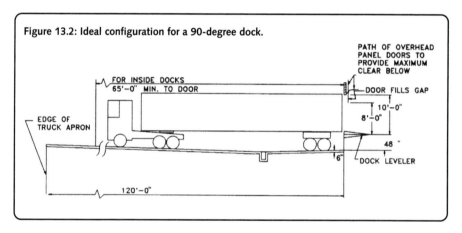

Figure 13.2: Ideal configuration for a 90-degree dock.

However, when there is limited maneuvering area between the dock and the nearest obstruction or street, then finger docks are much more attractive. Finger docks require a minimum amount of outside warehousing space, but do reduce the total available dock space and interior warehousing space. As seen in Figure 13.3, a 45-degree finger dock occupies twice as much interior space per position as a 90-degree dock.

Tables 13.6 and 13.7 provide general guidelines for required dock bay widths and apron depths for 90-degree and finger docks, respectively.

Note that the apron depths given in Tables 13.6 and 13.7 assume clockwise backing of trucks into the dock area. Trucks should enter the dock area in a counterclockwise direction of travel, to allow the truck to back into the dock in a clockwise direction. Clockwise backing enables the driver to clearly see the rear of the truck as it turns into the dock berth. By contrast, when backing counterclockwise, drivers must rely on rearview mirrors to guide their approach to the dock. At first glance this issue may appear trivial; however, experience has shown that counterclockwise backing requires the apron bay to be 20 feet deeper than the bay required for clockwise backing.

An option for either of the aforementioned dock configurations is to enclose them. The enclosure has inherent advantages. It provides excellent weather protection and accessibility to trucks, and it offers a secure environment. However, enclosing docks is expensive because of the additional construction costs and the costs associated with the extra space and the installation of an exhaust system to remove fumes from truck engines. Also, energy usage will be higher to provide lighting and heating.

The least desirable dock alternative is an open dock. However, where conditions dictate an open dock, it should have a canopy that extends to cover the work area and a minimum of 4 feet beyond. The outer edge of the canopy should have a minimum

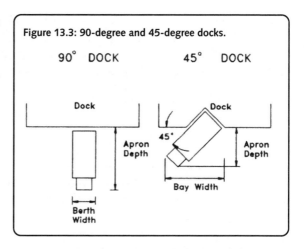

Figure 13.3: 90-degree and 45-degree docks.

Table 13.6: Space requirements for 90-degree docks.

Truck Length (ft.)	Dock Width (ft.)	Apron Depth (ft.)
40	12	43
	14	39
45	12	49
	14	46
50	12	57
	14	54
55	12	63
	14	58
60	12	63
	14	60

NOTE: Dimensions are for unobstructed docks. Where trucks must back into the dock alongside other trucks, the effective apron depths are equal to the apron depth in the third column plus the length of the truck.

Table 13.7: Space requirements for finger docks for a 65-foot truck.

Dock Width (ft.)	Finger Angle (degrees)	Apron Depth (ft.)	Bay Width (ft.)
12	10	49	66
14	10	47	67
12	30	74	62
14	30	70	64
12	45	92	54
14	45	87	56

clearance of 15 feet from the road. The dock should be wide enough to accommodate two-way traffic. To determine the proper width, take the width of the material being handled, multiply it by 4, and add the length of the dock levelers. If any staging is required on the dock, the dock width needs to be increased to accommodate it.

Maneuvering Allowances Inside the Warehouse

Directly inside the warehouse, behind the dock doors, is the maneuvering space required for a receiving or shipping dock. This space consists of two components, the first being the area occupied by the dock-leveling device, the second the aisle located between the dock-leveling device and the back edge of the staging area.

The amount of space a dock-leveling device occupies will vary according to the type used. Generally, temporary inside dock-leveling devices will occupy 3 to 7 feet, measured from the dock face. Permanent inside dock-leveling devices will require 4 to 10 feet of inside warehouse space.

The aisle behind the dock levelers allows personnel and equipment to enter and exit the carrier and travel to the appropriate staging area. This aisle should be restricted to these operations only. The existence of other traffic within the dock-maneuvering aisle will inevitably result in injuries to both dock personnel and other traffic.

The required width of the aisle depends on the type of material handling equipment. Generally, 6 to 8 feet are recommended for manual handling and for non-powered material handling equipment. For powered material handling equipment, 10 feet to 12 feet is sufficient.

Staging Area Requirements

The majority of warehouses require a staging area directly behind the dock-maneuvering aisle. The staging area for receiving serves as an immediate depository for materials unloaded from the carrier. Thus dock personnel are able to concentrate on unloading the carrier and releasing the carrier quickly. This is particularly important to companies with large investments in their private fleets. Companies that utilize common carriers can avoid demurrage or detention charges. Once the carrier has been released, a more thorough check-in can be performed.

The shipping staging area serves as an accumulation point for the merchandise that comprises a shipment. Various levels of accumulation may be established within the shipping staging area. Different types of accumulation include individual line items that make up a customer order, the customer orders making up a shipment, or shipments that go to a particular region. Activities performed within the staging area might be packing, unitizing, or verifying that the shipment is ready for loading on the carrier.

The functions performed in the staging area are easy to delineate. Determining the size of this area is another matter entirely and, if not calculated correctly, can be a source of inefficiency for the entire warehouse. The impact will be particularly severe if too little staging space is provided, because congestion will occur, as will lost product, damaged material, and erroneous shipments. Determining the amount of staging space required is contingent on the degree of control that exists over the workload of the dock area. The more uncertain the receiving or shipping workload is throughout the day, the more flexible the staging areas have to be. Thus, if a carrier arrival schedule exists and is strictly adhered to, there is a good possibility that the staging area can be limited to one truckload of material per dock bay. If not, surges in carrier activity will require that the staging area be increased.

To determine the amount of staging area needed, the same options are available as when determining the number of docks. Guessing is the most commonly adopted option and, as mentioned before, may provide the correct answer. However, one cannot expect that method to withstand any scrutiny, and it would be foolish to "take a stab" at calculating such an important area. Historical activity can be reviewed, and patterns identified, as another way of determining the amount of space required. This allows for surges in activity and for larger volumes to be accommodated. The danger is that an excess of space may be allocated, which increases construction and operating costs. Simulation, then, is the recommended technique for warehouses in which carrier arrivals and service times are not random.

The previous example for dock doors also can be used to determine the number of lanes. By assuming that the time between arrivals is the time that a lane is filled with a truckload, and that unload time is the time it takes to empty the entire load into a staging lane, one can use the same methodology to determine the number of staging lanes. One determines the size of the lane to accommodate the typical load, either a full truckload, less-than-truckload, or a UPS shipment. Then one determines the amount of time required to fill that space with the expected deliveries or picking activities and assigns that time to be the time that the lane is filled. The unload time is the time required to empty the staging lane. With this data, one can simulate the staging lane requirements. The same drawback is evident as before: simulation will not give you an unequivocal answer to the staging lane question. Simulation will, however, reveal how land utilization varies with different numbers of lanes and will give valuable data upon which one can base a sound decision.

Dock-Related Space Requirements

There are several other support activities that require space in this area and are imperative for a successful warehouse. These support activities are:

- Office area for supervision/clerical
- Quarantine area
- Empty pallet storage
- Truckers' lounge

The receiving and shipping offices must be included in the dock area. Approximately 125 ft² per person regularly occupying this area is a good rule of thumb. Clerical functions may or may not be included in this same office area, since data processing responsibilities are often combined with other activities in the warehouse.

A quarantine area is essential for accumulating material that has been rejected for any reason. This area should be separate from the main staging area, and may be used to temporarily store material that has failed a quality-control inspection, been damaged in transit, or requires a quality-control sample. The amount of space required is dependent on the type of material likely to be rejected, the specific inspection process followed, and the timeliness of the disposition of the rejected material.

A large percentage of warehouses use pallets for transporting and storing unit loads. Incoming product and shipments may or may not be palletized. Thus a pool of pallets is required. Space must be allocated, whether on the floor or on cantilevered racks above the dock doors, to accommodate this requirement.

A truckers' lounge is an area to which truck drivers are confined when not servicing their trucks. The truckers' lounge should include seating, private toilet facilities, and a telephone. General space requirements for a basic truckers' lounge are approximately 125 ft² for the first trucker and an additional 25 ft² for each additional trucker. The purpose of the lounge is to effectively control the movements of the trucker while on-site. Doing so eliminates many potential problems related to trucker safety, theft and pilferage, labor union campaigning, and warehouse employee productivity.

Space Planning for Storage Activities

Storage space planning is particularly critical because the storage activity accounts for the bulk of the space requirements of a warehouse. Inadequate storage space planning can easily result in a warehouse that is significantly larger or smaller than required. Too little storage space will result in a world of operational problems, including lost stock, blocked aisles, inaccessible material, poor housekeeping, safety problems, and low productivity. On the other hand, too much space will breed poor use of space. The familiar situation of a homeowner filling all the available closets with "essential" junk comes to mind. The result of too much space will be high space costs in the form of land, construction, energy, and equipment. To avoid these problems, storage space planning must be thought out carefully, using quantitative analysis. Understanding and pursuing the following methodology will generate a defensible assessment of storage space requirements.

Defining the Materials to be Stored

Generally, the same SKU information required for receiving and shipping can be used here. Once again, the generic categories that were identified for receiving and shipping should be used. The following additional information is needed:

- Usage (units) over time
- Popularity (times sold)
- Average inventory (units)
- Maximum inventory (units)
- Planned inventory (units)

Choosing a Storage Philosophy

There are two major storage philosophies: fixed location storage and random location storage. In fixed location storage, each SKU is always stored in a specific location, and no other SKU may occupy that location even though the location may be empty. Random location storage allows any SKU to be assigned to any available location. Thus, in a random location storage system, one could find SKU number 1 stored in location A this week and in location B next week.

Fixed-Location Storage

The simpler of the two philosophies is the fixed-location system, where all that is required is a fixed place for each SKU. Thus, when a new SKU is introduced by marketing, another location must be defined, and conversely, when a SKU is discontinued, the location is reassigned to another SKU. To initiate a stock locator system with a fixed location system, a detailed drawing showing the locations and their associated SKUs is all that is required. After a short period of time, the operators have memorized the layout and are able to go directly to the location without referring to the drawing. In large warehouses with thousands of SKUs, the operator's memory is ineffective and must be enhanced by having the location entered into the computer containing a file with each SKU and its related location. Therefore, during picks or putaways, the operator can be told where the SKU is either by a printed pick list or a radio frequency (RF) terminal.

The advantage of simplicity must be weighed against a very serious disadvantage: poor space utilization. This is due to the requirement that enough space must be provided to store the maximum amount of inventory, or inventory level, for each SKU. This, in turn, is due to the two components of inventory: reserve stock and order quantity. Reserve stock is "just in case" the incoming shipment is delayed, just in case the part is backordered, and a host of other possibilities. Therefore, the reserve stock component of inventory is constant until an emergency.

The sum of reserve stock and order quantity is the inventory level. Inventory level peaks when a shipment is received and is depleted as orders are filled against it until another shipment arrives. The total expected inventory level will be all of the reserve stock and half of the order quantity so, one must plan warehouse space for the peak periods of inventory. Thus one can easily see how the average space utilization of a fixed location storage warehouse is 50 percent before taking into account aisle losses and staging areas.

Random Location Storage

When one thinks of something done at random, the usual image is of something close to anarchy, a state where confusion reigns. In warehousing, this should never be the case. Effective random storage has a locator system identifying every SKU and its relative information (e.g., date produced, date received, lot number). With the locator system, the SKU can be placed anywhere within a designated storage area. An example might be a fast-moving SKU designated for bulk storage in close proximity to the shipping doors. Once a shipment of this SKU has been received, it may be placed in any of the available storage lanes as directed by the locator system. The locator system then tracks each SKU once it has been stored.

The locator system maintains the orderliness of the random storage warehouse. Thus, zones may be assigned to different-velocity products, with the fastest ones closest to the docks, and the slowest in remote areas of the warehouse. The obvious benefit here is a lowering of the travel distance required to pick and place inventory. Without the locator system defining these zones, a reverse ABC storage configuration occurs, which actually increases travel distance. When a SKU is received and placed in the first available location, no matter what its velocity, slower-moving items eventually will tend to occupy all the storage locations closest to the dock. Fast-moving items will migrate away from the dock, and an increase in travel distance will occur.

Why use random storage? The primary reason is that random storage permits a superior utilization of space. Since inventory may be stored anywhere (within specific guidelines), the storage system can accommodate the peaks and valleys of inventory. When one SKU has high inventory, another SKU likely will have low inventory. The advantage gained is an ability to plan space for random location systems on the *average* inventory expected.

With these tradeoffs, which alternative is best? A clear-cut decision cannot be made. The only general conclusion is that the poor use of space associated with fixed location storage is a very large factor to consider. Fixed location storage will generally require 65 percent to 85 percent more space than random location storage. The expense of developing and maintaining a material locator system for a random location storage scenario is easily justified when compared with the high cost of construction and land. However, the accessibility to material may be such a driving factor that it will be enough to offset the high cost of space. An example would be an operation with extremely small and extremely valuable items, where accountability and accessibility is imperative, such as microchip or jewelry storage. Thus, one should closely evaluate using random location storage before deciding to use fixed location storage.

Space Requirements for Alternative Storage Methods
When evaluating alternative storage equipment, the relevant costs for each must be available. Among the costs relevant to a storage alternative is space cost. To determine the space costs for a storage alternative, the space requirements must be calculated. This section presents the basic methodology for determining storage space requirements.

The space requirements of a storage alternative are directly related to the volume of material to be stored and to the use-of-space characteristics of the alternative. Use-of-space characteristics include honeycombing allowances and aisle allowances. Honeycombing allowances are the percentage of storage space lost because of ineffective use of the capability of a storage area. In other words, honeycombing occurs whenever a storage location is only partially filled with material. It may occur both horizontally and vertically. An example of honeycombing can be seen in Figure 13.4, where three lanes of bulk storage are occupied by three different SKUs (A, B, and C) and each SKU has four pallets of inventory. Thus, the capacity of the storage area is 12 pallets, assuming the pallets cannot be stacked. In the second part of Figure 13.4, an order requiring two pallets of A and one pallet of B has been picked. No other items may be placed in these three open slots, or the back pallets will be blocked. Until the remainder of the items in the lanes is picked, these open slots are considered honey-combing losses.

Similarly, vertical honey-combing can occur. Figure 13.5 shows a side view of the lane that SKU A occupies. However, in this example the assumption will be that pallets can be stacked two high and the lanes are still four deep. Therefore, SKU A has eight pallets occupying a lane. Suppose an order requiring five pallets is picked. Therefore, as can be seen in the second part of Figure 13.5, no product may be placed in those open slots without blocking pallets. Those open slots are also considered honeycombing losses. Honeycombing, while it should be minimized, must be considered a natural and allowed-for aspect of the storage process. For each storage alternative, the expected

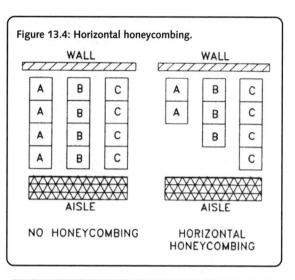

Figure 13.4: Horizontal honeycombing.

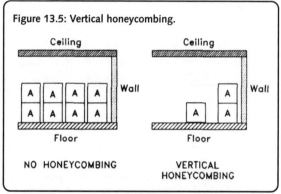

Figure 13.5: Vertical honeycombing.

Table 13.8: Honeycombing allowances.

Alternative	Honeycombing Allowance
Bulk Storage	75
Drive-In Rack	75
Flow Rack	70
Single-Deep Selective Rack	100

honeycombing allowances should be estimated and applied to the inventory. Examples of honeycombing allowances for storage equipment are included in Table 13.8.

It is obvious that warehousing is the business of storing product. However, much effort has been expended in establishing handling performance measures, such as labor perform-ance and equipment utilization. The reason for this emphasis on labor is that it has tradi-tionally been treated as a variable cost, with space cost considered as a fixed cost.

Management has tended to focus on controlling the labor cost while accepting the monthly charge for the building as inevitable. Space is as important to the total cost picture as labor, and one needs some method to determine current and future space utilization. A space standard is the benchmark that defines the amount of space required per unit of product stored. For new facilities, once a space standard has been calculated for a given class of items, using a given type of storage equipment, the total storage space can be determined for that class of items. Then, for alternative methods of storage, similar calculations can be made, and total storage space for each alternative determined.

To determine a space standard, one needs to determine the total square feet of the storage alternative "footprint" and then determine the number of unit loads that can be stored in that area. For single-deep selective rack, the formula for determining the square footage of the footprint is:

$$\text{Square feet per footprint} = \frac{A \times D}{144}$$

Where A is the length in inches of one rack opening, measured from the center of one upright to the center of the other upright, and D is one-half the aisle width, in inches, plus the depth of a single bay of rack plus one-half of the flue space. Figure 13.6 graphically depicts these dimensions. To calculate the square footage per unit load stored, determine the number of unit loads stored within the footprint and then divide into the square footage of the footprint. Thus, the formula is:

$$\text{Square feet/unit load} = \frac{\text{square feet per footprint}}{\text{quantity of unit loads stored in the footprint}}$$

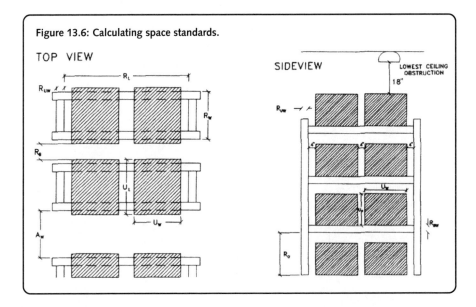

Figure 13.6: Calculating space standards.

Let's say we're calculating a space standard for a counterbalanced lift truck using single-deep selective rack. The following parameters are required:

Unit load dimensions: Length, U_L = 48"
                         Height, U_H = 50"
                         Width, U_W = 40"

Rack Dimensions: Beam width, R_W = 42"
                         Beam length, R_L = 92"
                         Back-to-back spacing, R_B = 4"
                         Upright width, R_{UW} = 3"
                         Beam height, R_{BH} = 3"
                         Rack opening height, R_O = 54"

Building dimension: Clear height, C_H = 21'
Load weight: 2500 lb
Stacking aisle width: A_W = 144"

The calculations are:

$$\text{Square feet per footprint} = \frac{[R_L + 2(\tfrac{1}{2}R_{UW})] \times (\tfrac{1}{2}A_W + U_L + \tfrac{1}{2}R_B)}{144}$$

$$= \frac{(92 + 3) \times [(\tfrac{1}{2} \times 144) + 48 + (\tfrac{1}{2} \times 4)]}{144}$$

$$= \frac{95 \times 122}{144}$$

$$= 80.5$$

To determine the number of pallets that occupy this 80.5 ft² footprint, one must calculate the number of levels of rack that can fit in the clear height of the building. The first load beam of the single-deep selective rack is 54 inches from the top of the floor. This allows 4 inches between the unit load and the bottom of the beam in order to lift the unit load. For each level above, one must add the width of the beam, thus 54 inches plus 3 inches will provide 57 inches total per level. To calculate the number of levels, it is a simple division of available clear height by the distance per level. The available clear height must have 18 inches subtracted from it for fire protection, thus the true clear height is 234 inches. The calculation is:

$$\text{Levels per bay} = \frac{(C_H \times 12) - R_O - 18}{R_O + R_{BW}}$$

$$= \frac{(21 \times 12) - 54 - 18}{54 + 3}$$

$$= 3.16$$

Therefore there are four levels: three, in addition to the first level on the floor. Each beam has two pallets. This allows 4 inches between each of the loads and the upright, as well as 4 inches between the loads. (The calculation is: 4 + 40 + 4 + 40 + 4 = 92 inches) Therefore, one can calculate the space standard for a counterbalanced lift truck using single-deep selective rack:

$$\text{Square feet per unit load} = \frac{80.5\text{ft}^2/\text{footprint}}{2 \text{ pallets/level} \times 4 \text{ levels/footprint}}$$

$$= 10.0$$

One can then determine the effects on space when using an alternative material handling method. A reach truck can operate in an 8-foot aisle as opposed to the 12-foot aisle for the counterbalanced truck. Thus, using the same calculations, the square feet per unit load would be 8.1. The tradeoff is space savings for utilizing this type of equipment vs. potential higher initial cost and limited flexibility, as it cannot load trailers. This and other types of material handling equipment will be covered in detail in other chapters.

The space standard calculated must have main and cross aisles added before it can be an accurate projection of the required footage. Main aisles allow two-way travel and, as the name implies, are heavily accessed. The cross aisle allows the material handling equipment to access another aisle without having to travel to either end. Both main and cross-aisle widths are dependent on the material handling equipment utilized.

Warehousing Layout Planning
Determining the Objectives of a Warehouse Layout
Before layout planning can begin, the specific objectives of a warehouse layout must be determined. In general, the objectives of a warehouse layout are to:

1. Use space efficiently
2. Allow the most efficient material handling
3. Provide the most economical storage in relation to costs of equipment, use of space, damage to material, and handling labor
4. Provide maximum flexibility to meet changing storage and handling requirements
5. Make the warehouse a model of good housekeeping

The objectives of both a warehouse and its layout are virtually identical. Without a good warehouse layout, it is impossible to have a good warehouse. The objective of layout planning is to arrange and coordinate the space, equipment, and labor resources of the warehouse. Poor layout planning can undermine superior space, equipment, and personnel planning.

The fourth objective of warehouse layout recognizes that warehousing exists not within a static, unchanging environment, but within a dynamic, everchanging one. If the mission of a warehouse changes, the warehouse layout should very likely change as well to adapt to the new mission. A good warehouse layout possesses the flexibility to absorb minor variances in expected storage volumes and product mixes with few or no alterations required. This flexibility allows the warehouse to function even if the forecasts on which it was planned prove to be wrong—as they so often and inevitably do.

The last objective of warehousing springs from the principle that there is efficiency in order. Good housekeeping is essential to good warehousing, and a good warehouse cannot exist without good housekeeping. Yet good housekeeping by itself will not ensure a good warehouse. If the space, equipment, personnel, and layout are not properly planned, all the housekeepers in the world could not get a warehouse to function. But poor housekeeping will surely undermine good space, equipment, personnel, and layout planning.

Following a Layout Planning Methodology

Warehouse layout planning methodology consists of two steps:

1. Generating a series of warehouse layout alternatives
2. Evaluating each alternative according to specific criteria to identify the best warehouse layout

Generating Alternative Layouts

Generating alternative warehouse layouts is as much art as it is science. The quality of the layout alternatives will largely depend on the skill and ingenuity of the layout planner. This fact is crucial to the most common approach to generating layout alternatives: template juggling. The word *juggle* means to skillfully manipulate a group of objects to obtain a desired effect. Consequently, template juggling is *the skillful manipulation of a group of templates, models, or other representations of warehouse space, equipment, and personnel in order to obtain a warehouse layout that meets its objectives.* In other words, template juggling is a trial-and-error approach to finding the proper arrangement and coordination of the physical resources of the warehouse.

The quality of the alternatives created from template juggling will depend on the creativity of the layout planner. Unfortunately, layout planners often either lack creativity or do not attempt to express their creativity. Many of them approach the problem with a preconceived idea of what the solution should be. They tend to steer the layout planning process toward that preconceived solution. As a result, creativity is stifled. The layout chosen for a new warehouse often looks exactly like the layout used in the old warehouse. Layout alternatives are generated by the creativity of the layout planner, yet many layout planners fail to harness this force.

To generate warehouse layout alternatives, follow the five steps described here:

1. *Define the location of fixed obstacles.* Some objects in a warehouse can be located only in certain places, and they can have only certain configurations. These objects should be identified and placed in the layout alternative first, before objects with more flexibility are located. Some fixed obstacles are building support columns, stairwells, elevator shafts, lavatories, sprinkler system control, heating and air-conditioning

equipment, and, in some cases, offices. Failure to consider the location of these types of items will prove disastrous. The warehousing corollary to Murphy's Law states, "If a column can be in the wrong position, it will be." Don't be the layout planner who designs a warehouse and buys the storage and material handling equipment only to find that, when the equipment is installed, the location of the building columns makes an aisle too narrow for the handling equipment.

2. *Define the location of the receiving and shipping function.* The configuration of the warehouse site may dictate the location of the receiving and shipping functions. When this is not true, however, the receiving and shipping location decision becomes an important one. Receiving and shipping are high-activity areas and should be located so as to maximize productivity, improve material flow, and properly utilize the warehouse site. The location of access roads and railroad tracks, if rail service is required, are important considerations in locating receiving and shipping.

The question of whether receiving and shipping should be located together or in different areas of the warehouse must be addressed. Common receiving and shipping docks can often result in economies of scale related to sharing space, equipment, and personnel. Separate receiving and shipping areas, may, on the other hand, be best to ensure better material control and reduce congestion.

Energy considerations are important. Where a choice exists, receiving and shipping docks should not be located on the side of the building that faces north. Avoiding this location reduces the amount of heat loss in the winter from northerly winds entering the warehouse through open dock doors. The preferred location of the receiving and shipping dock is the south side of the warehouse, with east and west as second and third choices. The particular weather patterns around each warehouse site should be examined, however, to identify the prevailing wind direction at that particular site, and the docks should be located away from the prevailing wind.

3. *Locate the storage areas and equipment, including required aisles.* The types of storage areas and equipment to be used will indicate to some extent the configuration of the storage layout and the aisle requirements. Be sure to make allowances for the fixed obstacles in the facility. Main warehouse aisles should connect the various parts of the warehouse. The cross aisle at the end of the storage area may need to be wider than the aisles within the storage area, depending on the type of material handling equipment used. For example, a side-loading fork truck that can operate with a 7-foot-wide storage aisle may require 12-foot-wide cross aisles at the ends of the storage aisles to allow maneuvering into and out of the storage aisle.

4. *Assign the material to be stored to its storage location.* This step in the generation of layout alternatives ensures that storage allowances have been made for all the items to be stored. In addition, it allows the performance of a mental simulation of the activities expected within the warehouse.

5. *Repeat the process to generate other alternatives.* Once a warehouse layout alternative has been established following the four steps just outlined, the process must be repeated many times to generate additional layout alternatives. Different layout configurations, building shapes, and equipment alternatives should be used. The creativity of the layout planner should be taxed to ensure that each succeeding layout alternative is not essentially identical to the first.

Evaluating the Alternative Layouts
A number of warehouse layout philosophies exist to serve as guidelines for the development of an effective warehouse layout. Each warehouse layout alternative should be evaluated against the specific criteria established for each of these warehouse layout philosophies.

1. *Popularity philosophy.* An Italian economist named Pareto once stated that 85 percent of the world's wealth is held by 15 percent of the people. On closer examination, Pareto's Law actually pertains to many areas other than wealth; one of these areas is warehousing. In a typical warehouse, it is not unusual to find that 85 percent of the product throughput is attributable to 15 percent of the items, that another 10 percent of the product throughput is attributable to 30 percent of the items, and that the remaining 5 percent of the product throughput is attributable to 55 percent of the items. Consequently, the warehouse contains a very small number of highly active items, often called "A items," a slightly larger number of moderately active items, called "B items," and a very large number of infrequently active items, called "C items."

    Popularity philosophy suggests that the warehouse should be planned around the small number of items that are at the center of most of the activity in the warehouse. It maintains that the materials having the greatest throughput should be located in an area that allows the most efficient material handling. Consequently, high-turnover items should be located as close as possible to the point of use.

    The popularity philosophy also suggests that the popularity of the items helps to determine the storage methods used. For example, if bulk storage is used, high-turnover items should move into and out of storage at a relatively high rate. The danger of excessive honeycombing losses will be reduced, and excellent use of space will result from the high-density storage. Low-throughput items in deep bulk storage blocks will cause severe honeycombing losses, because no other items can be stored in that location until all the low-throughput items have been removed.

2. *Similarity philosophy.* Items that are commonly received and/or shipped together should be stored together. For example, consider a retail auto parts distributor. Chances are that a customer who requires a spark plug wrench will not buy, at the same time, an exhaust system tailpipe. Chances are good, however, that a customer who buys the spark plug wrench will also require spark plugs. Because these items are typically sold (and shipped) together, they should be stored in the same area. The exhaust system tailpipe should be stored in the same area as the mufflers, brackets,

and gaskets. Certain items are commonly received together, possibly from the same vendor, and should be stored together. They will usually require similar storage and handling methods, so their consolidation in the same area will result in more efficient use of space and more efficient material handling.

An exception to the similarity philosophy arises whenever items are *so* similar that storing them close together might result in order picking and shipping errors. Examples of items that are too similar are two-way, three-way, and four-way electrical switches; they look identical, but function quite differently.

3. *Size philosophy.* The size philosophy suggests that heavy, bulky, hard-to-handle goods should be stored close to their point-of-use. The cost of handling these items is usually much greater than that of handling other items. That is an incentive to minimize the distance over which they are handled. In addition, if the ceiling height in the warehouse varies from one area to another, the heavy items should be stored in the areas with a low ceiling, and the lightweight, easy-to-handle items should be stored in the areas with a high ceiling. Available cubic space in the warehouse should be used in the most effective way while meeting restrictions on floor-loading capacity. Lightweight material can be stored at greater heights within typical floor-loading capacities than heavy materials can.

The size philosophy also asserts that the size of the storage location should fit the size of the material to be stored. Do not store a unit load of 10 cubic feet in a storage location capable of accommodating a unit load of 30 cubic feet. A variety of storage location sizes must be provided so that different items can be stored differently. In addition to looking at the physical size of an individual item, one must consider the total quantity of the item to be stored. Different storage methods and layouts will be used for storing two pallet loads of an item than will be used for storing 200 pallet loads of the same material.

4. *Product characteristics philosophy.* Some materials have certain attributes or traits that restrict or dictate the storage methods and layout used. Perishable material is quite different from nonperishable material, from a warehousing point of view. The warehouse layout must encourage good stock rotation so that limitations on shelf life are met. Oddly shaped and crushable items, subject to stacking limitations, will dictate special storage methods and layout configurations to effectively use available cubic space. Hazardous material such as explosives, corrosives, and highly flammable chemicals must be stored in accordance with government regulations. Items of high value or items commonly subject to pilferage may require increased security measures, such as isolated storage with restricted access. The warehouse layout must be adapted to provide the needed protection. The compatibility of items stored close together must also be examined. Contact between certain individually harmless materials can result in extremely hazardous reactions and/or significant product damage. Specific steps must be taken to separate incompatible materials. The easiest way to accomplish this objective is through the warehouse layout.

5. *Space utilization philosophy.* This philosophy can be broken down into four
   components:
   - a) *The conservation of space* principle asserts that the maximum amount of material
     should be concentrated within a storage area, the total cubic space available
     should be used effectively, and the potential honeycombing within the storage
     area should be minimized. Unfortunately, these objectives often conflict.
     Increased concentration of material will usually cause increased honeycombing
     allowances. Therefore, determining the proper level of space conservation is a
     matter of making tradeoffs among the objectives that maximize use of space.
   - b) *Limitations on use of space* must be identified early in the layout planning
     process. Space requirements for building support columns, trusses, sprinkler-
     system components, heating-system components, fire extinguishers and hoses,
     and emergency exits will affect the suitability of certain storage and handling
     methods and layout configurations. Floor loading capacities will restrict storage
     heights and densities.
   - c) *Material accessibility* should be included as part of the specified objectives of
     the warehouse layout. Main travel aisles should be straight and should lead
     to doors to improve maneuverability and reduce travel time. Aisles should be
     wide enough to permit efficient operation, but they should not waste space.
     Aisle widths should be tailored to the type of handling equipment using the
     aisle and the amount of traffic expected.
   - d) *The orderliness* principle emphasizes the fact that good warehouse layout plan-
     ning begins with housekeeping in mind. Aisles should be well marked with
     aisle tape or paint; otherwise, materials will begin to infringe on the aisle space
     and accessibility to material will be reduced. Void spaces within a storage area
     must be avoided, and they must be corrected when they do occur. If a storage
     area is designed to accommodate five pallets and, in the process of placing
     material into that area, one pallet infringes on the space allocated for the adja-
     cent pallet, a void space will result. Because of this, only four pallets can actu-
     ally be stored in the area designed for five pallets. The lost pallet space will not
     be regained until the entire storage area is emptied.

To evaluate the alternative warehouse layouts, each should be looked at in the light
of specified expectations relative to the layout philosophies discussed above. The layout
planner must determine which layout philosophies are most important under the specific
circumstances and attempt to maximize the extent to which the recommended layout
adheres to these philosophies.

Conclusion: Flexibility Must Be the Watchword

Remember as you incorporate the principles and guidance we've discussed here that warehousing exists within a dynamic environment. The layout chosen as the best one today
may not be as good as conditions change. The extent and timing of changing requirements

in the future should be forecast, and a warehouse master plan should be established that would effectively compensate for the changing mission of the warehouse.

Your challenge is to utilize the tools for space and layout planning to formulate an effective warehouse strategic master plan and to become one of those elite warehouse facilities that have balanced the resources of space, equipment, and labor.

CHAPTER 14
Material Handling Systems and Integration

Jim Capece, Partner, Material Handling Integration Dimension, Tompkins Associates

In the past, if your company had a highly automated distribution or manufacturing capability, you enjoyed a tremendous competitive edge in pricing, product quality, and delivery performance. Today, while that same automation capability can enable your company to enjoy the benefits of an integrated supply chain, you need it just to keep pace with your competition.

Said differently, the performance bar on distribution and manufacturing capabilities has been raised. What was once a competitive advantage is now a necessity for survival. The necessity of having an integrated supply chain has driven the need for increasingly sophisticated equipment and controls in today's distribution centers (DC). Distribution automation is now separated into two distinct enabling technologies: **Logical Automation**, the technologies and equipment that identify, track, and manage materials and products; and **Physical Automation**, the technologies and equipment that provide the movement, storage, control, and protection of materials and products. This distinction is made because it is important to separate the technologies according to their function. Some are justified by pure productivity improvements that enable supply chain integration, while other technologies are almost exclusively justified by pure labor-savings analysis. A highly automated distribution or manufacturing capability would, of course, require both logical and physical automation. The notion we are introducing here is that to have an integrated supply chain, companies need to apply at least the logical automation.

A "systems" aspect provides the necessary functionality to enable supply chain integration. Any discussion concerning material handling systems should include a discussion concerning the fundamental discipline of "integration," which is a critical element for any successful system implementation.

This chapter provides a broad overview of material handling topics, including equipment:

- *Material handling control systems:* equipment and software that manage, control, and interface with the material handling system.
- *Industrial trucks:* non-highway equipment used for intermittently moving material within a wide area.
- *Conveyors:* equipment used for continuously moving material between fixed points.
- *System integration:* the discipline of creating a tightly integrated system from the separate equipment, software, and personnel elements.

Material Handling Control Systems

The material handling control system must become a holistic process that exceeds the expectations of the ultimate user of the product involved and responds to performance feedback to continuously improve supply chain performance. This section outlines how one can begin the process of implementing a material handling control system that is capable of supporting Supply Chain Synthesis.

Distributed Architectures

The initial step is a fundamental analysis of the architecture and components needed within an organization and across the supply chain. This analysis, by necessity, will quickly lead into some form of distributed architecture. It will require an open systems environment that allows a technology infrastructure composed of individual best-of-breed products that can be effectively implemented with existing systems. Accommodating both future and legacy systems will require loosely coupled interfaces that connect and morph over time.

The infrastructure must be granular enough to allow any single product to be replaced without disrupting the architecture. There are two guidelines to follow in attempting to achieve this objective:

1. At each layer in the application technology stack, attempt standardization to make the layer directly below it exchangeable.
2. Define the interfaces based on a standard that will allow the various business and operating components to work together.

In the interest of brevity, the following component levels will be described as if they represented a single organization. However, you can develop insight into what may be required across the supply chain if you accept the notion that any level in one organization can communicate with any other level in any and all of the other members of the supply chain. Your challenge here is not technology. It is your ability to work with your supply chain members and to analyze and establish the content, methodology, organizational, and systems level of trust and timing of information flow to support the overall supply chain operation.

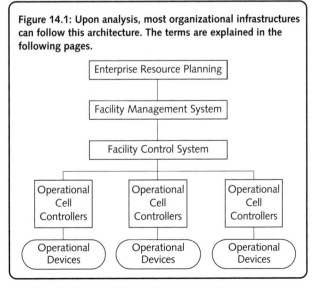

Figure 14.1: Upon analysis, most organizational infrastructures can follow this architecture. The terms are explained in the following pages.

Enterprise Resource Planning

Facility Management System

Facility Control System

Operational Cell Controllers — Operational Cell Controllers — Operational Cell Controllers

Operational Devices — Operational Devices — Operational Devices

Enterprise Resource Planning

All organizations have some form of system controls at the enterprise resource planning level. Generally, these controls provide a planning, coordination, and communication capability between the outside world and the finance, marketing, manufacturing, warehousing, and distribution parts of the organization. The tools for performing this function have changed drastically over time from pencil and paper to the Internet, relational databases, and graphical user interfaces all based on a variety of competing architectures.

As a result, several versions of the same functionality may exist within an organization at the same time, which requires a never-ending series of interfaces and upgrades. This creates a series of dissimilar legacy system components that influence the ability of an organization to meet the everyday pressures of change.

The following is a listing of some of the various communication interface methodologies used today. Most organizations will have many of the methodologies listed below embedded in their systems.

Transport Methodologies:
- Files
- Direct Table interface
- IBM MQ Series
- FTP
- HTTP
- Sockets
- COM+
- Biztalk Server
- Custom Third-Party Interfaces
- Custom Transport Methodologies

Message Formats:
- Fixed Length or Delimited Files
- SQL
- Oracle
- ODBC
- Open Data Format
- XML
- Date Streams
- RPC/SOAP
- Biztalk Framework
- Custom Data Formats

Organizations that have successfully coped with this issue have settled on a distributed computing architecture that forces physical functionality down to the lowest possible level. They have also elected to implement a single interface methodology between levels. In the future, this will facilitate a free exchange of information between all levels.

Facility Management Level

Facility Management Level

Three broad categories of facility management systems should be considered:

1. Manufacturing Management Systems
2. Warehouse Management Systems
3. Distribution Management Systems

These systems work with the ERP-level systems to determine what needs to be accomplished and when it should occur at the physical level.

Manufacturing Management Systems

The manufacturing management system (or manufacturing execution system) provides the means to implement a specific method of operation including the feedback and measurements required to identify and decide on a better method of operation. It should identify what to change and how to change it.

The key measurements to consider should include the capability to evaluate throughput, inventory, and operational expense. Throughput is the rate at which a facility generates money from sales. Inventory is the money a facility has invested to purchase items to sell. Operational expense is the money it costs a facility to convert inventory into throughput. By successfully managing and controlling a facility's productivity based on these parameters, a manufacturing management system can bring an organization closer to its goal.

A complete system generally consists of the planning, control, and reporting of:

- Production Planning
- Material Requisitioning
- Purchasing
- Receiving
- Material Tracking
- Production and Inventory Control
- Production Execution
- Financial Reporting
- Quality Assurance
- Order Tracking

Warehouse Management Systems

The warehouse management system (WMS) provides an integrated, real-time control of material movement through a warehouse facility. It is a critical execution step in the material-flow cycle. A complete WMS generally consists of the planning, control, operation, and reporting of:

- Receiving
- Storage
- Quality control

- Inventory control
- Order fulfillment
- Value-add operations
- Packaging
- Shipping

An interesting aspect that most organizations do not recognize is that "warehouse management" concepts and operating characteristics spread throughout the organization from manufacturing through distribution. Often, the systems that control and monitor these activities have been implemented at different times and with different technologies. This results in very different material management strategies being used for material movement within an organization and creates unexpected results that are difficult to detect and correct as an organization moves toward Supply Chain Synthesis.

This phenomenon is exacerbated by the fact that more and more operations are beginning to occur in what had been "warehouse only" facilities. These operations started out as simple assembly operations, but some manufacturing operations will appear in, or be integrated, with warehouse facilities as the advantage of changing a generic SKU to a customer-specific SKU becomes apparent.

This fundamental rearrangement from historically evolved methodologies to future functionality requirements will ultimately create the need for a new paradigm for operation management software that merges the operational needs of manufacturing, warehousing, and distribution. To provide the required synergy to meet the new requirements and to maintain their functional flexibility, the new systems will need to focus on collaborative capabilities and be immune to the nuances of evolving material handling solutions. Collaboration and innovative material handling solutions are essential to providing the productivity that delivers cost-effective customer satisfaction. Effective customer feedback and response controls able to affect supply chain performance are needed to ensure a continuous improvement process.

Distribution Management Systems

The distribution management system manages inventory to achieve customer satisfaction. Often confused with WMSs, the view and scope of control of distribution management systems is very different. In fact, as the concept of distribution continues to evolve from its simple form to an integrated feedback and control capability fueled by a flood of information and leveraged by technology, distribution management systems will directly impact and control the success or failure of organizations. In fully integrated form, across multiple organizations, they have the potential to be the "silver bullet" for successful implementation of Supply Chain Synthesis.

A complete distribution management system generally consists of the planning, control, operation, and reporting of:

- Freight tracking
- Freight payments
- Customs clearance
- Carrier selection
- Rate negotiation
- Vehicle leasing
- Claims processing
- Hazardous materials
- Fleet management
- Vehicle maintenance
- Driver leasing
- Insurance
- Multi-modal coordination
- Financing
- Warehousing
- Returns
- Display building
- Subassembly
- Packaging
- Kitting
- Labeling
- Order processing
- Customer Service
- Electronic data interchange
- Information systems
- Data processing
- Inventory control
- Documentation

Facility Operational Controls

The facility operational controls provide material handling equipment independence from the facility management systems. This allows both operating flexibility and some protection for technology changes over time. Implemented properly, it can also provide a degree of operating independence and a great deal of operational flexibility. The facility operational controls:

- Receive instructions from the facility management level in the form of messages and/or work orders and interpret them to execute the necessary physical operations
- Report operations results and alarm conditions, as required, to the facility management level
- Provide transaction logging for reporting and input to management or operational data warehouse applications

- Represent a comprehensive communication server that performs many of the functions that, in the past, were performed by custom interface computing hardware
- Are able to be the on-site network domain controller, if necessary, and to operate with any ODBC database
- Provide data and program redundancy for the facility and the operational cell controllers

Material handling control systems will be an integral part of how a management-level system causes items to be moved within its own organization and between outside organizations. Generally, the initiation of the process and the tracking of an event occur at the management level. The actual real-time control of physical movement and the tracking of unit moves that comprise an event occur at the various facility operational control levels. They provide real-time progress reporting on event status and completion to the management-level system.

Graphical User Interface

One of the most important elements in any system is how an operator perceives and uses the information presented to him. If information is not presented in a clear and efficient manner, the system as a whole is ineffective regardless of its technological achievement. A properly implemented facility operational control system includes a full function graphical user interface to indicate material handling equipment status and important operating conditions and to control the operation of the facility. Graphical user interfaces at the physical level are usually quite different than they are at the management levels and therefore deserve more attention.

A graphical user interface is a type of display format that enables the user to choose commands, start programs, and see lists of files and other options by pointing to pictorial representations (icons) and lists of menu items on the screen. Choices can generally be activated either with a touch screen or the keyboard or with a mouse.

A graphical user interface is also referred to as a human-machine interface (HMI) or SCADA (supervisory control and data acquisition). These are usually constructed using a specific vendor's application programming interfaces (APIs).

Operational Cell Controllers

Operational cell controllers are the computers that connect directly to the equipment they control, being either traditional program logic controllers (PLCs) or PC-based controllers.

There are two fundamental types:

1. Non-real-time cell controllers
2. Real-time controllers.

Non-real-time cell controllers do not have any real-time sense-and-respond requirements. They generally serve as floor-located operator workstations to communicate system status via the SCADA and perhaps an operator control station.

Real-time cell controllers do have a real-time sense and respond requirement. This being the case, they must conform to five basic rules of PC-based control:

1. Provide deterministic real-time performance (hard real-time control)
2. Survive failure of NT
3. Provide protection from Windows applications and drivers
4. Survive a hard disk failure
5. Use robust, reliable real-time kernels (A kernel is a software term used to describe a useful specialized software module, which can form the core functionality of a more elaborate total software solution or package. Kernels are often "reusable," which means they can form the core of multiple software solutions, sometimes addressing vastly different applications.)

Cell controllers are usually placed in cabinets that include a Windows 2000 platform using an appropriately sized color display, the necessary input/output components with drivers to support the equipment operated, and an uninterruptible power supply.

Drivers provide the communication interfaces between computer systems and specialized industrial automation equipment, and between different manufacturer's automation equipment. They can take the form of both dedicated drivers and new protocol support embedded within an OPC/DDE server (AUCS). These interfaces can be implemented with the capability to support a variety of communication methods including serial, leased-line, public telephone, cellular telephone, conventional radio, trunking radio, spread spectrum radio, satellite, TCP/IP Ethernet, arc net, and TCP/IP Ethernet terminal servers. Therefore, they have the capability to participate via Internet connectivity. This could become extremely useful in the future.

Operational Devices

Operational devices are actual drive motors, photo-eyes, or other actuators needed to physically perform the material handling function.

This is now the most volatile and changing area in the architecture. It is constantly changing with new vendors, architectures, and components. All are generally heading toward Ethernet TCP/IP connectivity, but the gateways are many and varied. They also come from a broad industrial market.

A strategic master plan for material handling systems integration cannot be implemented without knowledge of the equipment that comprises a material handling system. It is important to be aware of what is continually moving materials in wide areas as well as between two fixed points. The two sections that follow examine and discuss the two forms of equipment that handle movement—industrial trucks and conveyors.

Industrial Trucks

Industrial trucks have many classifications, taking into account the mode of locomotion (manual labor, electric-powered, internal combustion); the method of load support (platform, forks, clamps); the method of operation (manually driven or automated); and the method of control (operator-directed or computer-directed). The major types of industrial trucks are hand trucks, powered industrial trucks, and automated guided vehicle systems (AGVS).

Regardless of whether the trucks are powered manually, by an electric motor, or by an internal combustion engine, or whether they are automatically operated, there are common features that define the type of truck:

- *Platform trucks* have a wide surface for supporting the load (typically skids, cartons, and totes), whereas *fork trucks* have two narrow surfaces that support the load (typically pallets or pallet containers).
- *Low-lift trucks* lift a load four to six inches to clear the floor for transportation.
- *High-lift trucks* lift the load to stack it as well transport it.
- *Walkie* and *walkie/rider trucks* are controlled by an operator who leads or follows the truck on foot, whereas an operator, in either a standup or sit-down position, controls *rider trucks.*

Hand Trucks

A hand truck is a wheeled device that is capable of supporting a load while being manually propelled. A two-wheeled hand truck is the simplest vehicle used for handling cased goods between floor storage locations. A typical application is from storage to dock areas, and on- and off-road vehicles. A special application is the *drum truck,* specially designed to secure the upper lip of a drum while supporting the bottom rim.

Figure 14.2: Pallet jack.

A *pallet jack* (see Figure 14.2) is used to raise a pallet or skid off the floor and move it horizontally. It is versatile and is used over short distances in a relatively confined space. Another common hand truck is the *platform truck.*

This unit typically has two fixed wheels and two swivel casters for easy maneuvering. A cart is a platform truck with multiple shelves.

A *dolly* is a low platform truck with three or four swiveling wheels and a platform that may be either open or closed. The most complex type of hand truck is the *hand lift truck.* It is capable of raising loads above normal carrying heights by hydraulics actuated by a foot pump. Hand trucks are typically low-cost, maintenance-free, and relatively safe to operate. They are used for horizontal transportation where loads are light, distances are short, throughput is low, and maneuvering space is limited.

Powered Industrial Trucks

The Industrial Truck Association has established seven major classes of industrial trucks, defined in Table 14.1. These classifications represent a number of choices to the user. One is electric vs. internal combustion (IC) power.

Class I, IV, and V Trucks

IC trucks are a traditional choice for warehouse operators because their initial cost is low, but they have high annual fuel and maintenance costs due to the nature of the internal combustion engine. Electric-powered trucks are quieter and have environmental advantages because they do not emit potentially harmful exhaust gases. However, they typically require a battery charging room.

There has been a clear shift toward electric-powered trucks for indoor use, while IC trucks are clearly the choice in outdoor applications. (Diesel IC trucks are confined to outdoor use, but propane—a relatively clean burning fuel—still finds many indoor uses. Gasoline-fueled trucks are between the two and tend to be used primarily outdoors.)

The choice of tires is based on the surface conditions on which the truck will operate. Cushion tires work well on smooth, dry surfaces or where the risk of puncture is great. Where water, grease, or oil is a factor, or the surface is irregular, air-filled tires offer additional traction.

Class 1, 4, and, 5 trucks are commonly referred to as *counterbalanced trucks* (see Figure 14.3). Their design is similar to a teeter-totter: the load is suspended on the forks, the wheels behind the forks are the fulcrum, and the weight of the chassis, engine (motor), fuel (battery), and ballast keep the wheels on the ground and the load in the air.

Counterbalanced trucks are often described as *wide-aisle vehicles* because they typically require a 10- to 15-foot clear aisle for right angle stacking into storage racks or on the

Table 14.1: Industrial Truck Association Lift Truck Classifications.

Class	Description	Applications	Typical Load Capacities (lb.)	Typical Lift Heights (ft.)
I.	Electric motor rider trucks	Indoor, general-purpose	2500-12,000	16 to 18
II.	Electric motor narrow-aisle trucks	Indoor, narrow-aisle and very-narrow-aisle	2000-4500	Up to 40
III.	Electric motor hand trucks	Indoor, general-purpose	4000-8000	
IV.	Internal combustion, cushion tire	Indoor and outdoor, general-purpose	2000-15,000	Up to 20
V.	Internal combustion, pneumatic tire	Outdoor, general-purpose, paved surfaces	2000-15,000	Up to 20
VI.	Tow tractors	Indoor, long-distance	n/a	n/a
VII.	Rough-terrain lift trucks	Outdoor, construction sites	4000-20,000	Up to 20

floor. The actual dimension is a function of the truck's turning radius and the length of the load. These rider trucks are available in sit-down and stand-up versions. The stand-up version requires a narrower aisle for right angle stacking because the truck is shorter. It is a good choice when the operator must get on and off the truck frequently during the work shift. For horizontal transportation over long distances and infrequent dismounts, the sit-down version is preferred. Sit-down trucks are commonly used for loading and unloading over-the-road trailers and in bulk floor storage, since the space lost for aisles is small in relation to the depth of storage.

Class 2 Electric Motor, Narrow-Aisle Trucks

Class 2 trucks are typically stand-up riders that have a shorter chassis, which reduces the required right-angle-stacking aisle width.

Straddle trucks (see Figure 14.4) use outriggers on wheels that extend in front of the mast on either side of the forks. The load is carried between these outriggers. To pick up pallets from the floor, the outriggers must "straddle" the load unless it is placed on a support that allows the outriggers clearance underneath. For this reason and ease of operation, the bottom level of a pallet rack is typically placed on a pair of beams. The outriggers straddle the beams and permit the truck to come up flush to the face of the rack.

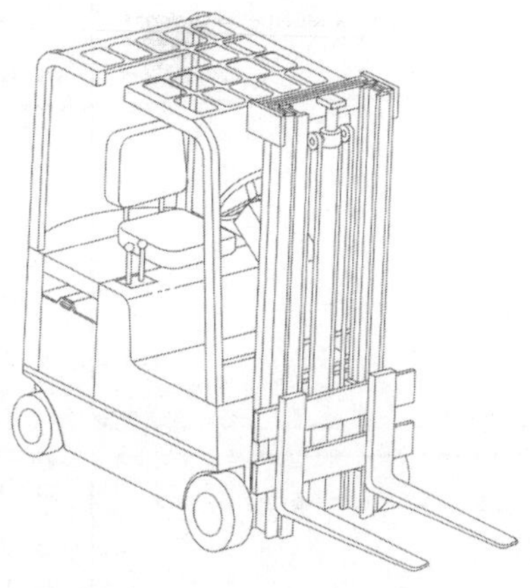

The *order picker* is a special type of straddle truck (see Figure. 14.5). It has a platform between the mast and the forks that allows the operator to control the truck (while elevated with the load) and store and retrieve goods by hand. Turns in a storage aisle are not made: wire or rail guides may be used to reduce the side clearances 4 to 6 inches. These trucks should never be used for stacking or storing pallets.

Reach trucks (see Figure 14.6) eliminate the need for a pair of beams for the bottom level of the pallet rack by incorporating either a pantograph mechanism between the mast of the truck and the backrest for the load or telescoping forks. This design also allows the operator to pick up a load too wide to fit between outriggers, because it can "reach" beyond the outriggers to pick up or deposit a load.

Figure 14.3: Counterbalanced rider truck.

Double-reach trucks provide a second pantograph extension that permits the truck to be used for storing loads two pallets deep in pallet rack. Typically, the bottom rack level is supported on a pair of beams (as for straddle truck operation). The front load is stored as in reach truck operations. The rear load requires outrigger clearance under the beams, and if necessary, a second "bite" of the pallet.

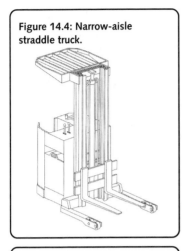

Figure 14.4: Narrow-aisle straddle truck.

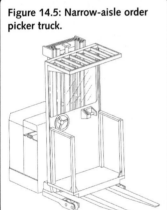

Figure 14.5: Narrow-aisle order picker truck.

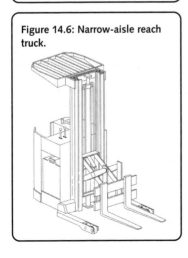

Figure 14.6: Narrow-aisle reach truck.

The first step or "bite" places the pallet as deep as possible based on the maximum extension of the reach mechanism. In the second step, the reach mechanism is retracted several inches. Then, the load is partially lifted and pushed into position. When specifying a double-reach truck, it is important to be sure that the rack opening is large enough to provide clearance for the pantograph mechanism when the load is placed in the rear position.

Class 2 also includes trucks that may be referred to as *very narrow aisle trucks.* They further reduce the width of storage aisles because their design does not require right-angle turns within the storage aisle as do wide-aisle and narrow-aisle trucks.

An order picker truck could be described as a very narrow aisle truck. These trucks operate with minimal clearances when guided by wire or rail.

Wire guidance operates by sensing the electromagnetic field produced by a wire that is embedded in the floor, through which an electric current flows. The current is provided by a "line driver," and is sensed by a device mounted underneath the truck that transmits control signals to the steering system. Wire guidance is characterized by high onboard-vehicle costs and low aisle-guidance costs, as well as a clean floor.

Rail guidance is purely mechanical. An angle iron is lagged to the floor on both sides of the aisle, and steel casters are welded to each of the four corners of the truck chassis. Rail guidance is characterized by low vehicle costs and higher aisle-guidance costs, as well as high reliability.

Swinging mast trucks (see Fig. 14.7) are designed with a special mast that rotates 90 degrees to the right and also side shifts to place a load in a rack position. These trucks require an aisle width that is the widest dimension of the truck or load, plus operating clearances on each side. The additional weight of the rotating mast requires a substantially heavier truck to achieve the same load-carrying capacity as a counterbalanced truck. Also, since these trucks can rotate only 90 degrees to the right, the operator must determine on which side of the aisle to store or retrieve the load before entering the aisle.

Turret trucks (see Figure 14.8) are able to store loads without turning in the aisle because the forks and carriage are designed to rotate (left or right) the load perpendicular to the aisle. Once rotated, the forks and carriage traverse toward the rack to place the load. Man-up and man-down versions are available. The man-up version has the advantage of locating the operator close to the load for better control and it can also be used for order picking from pallet locations. The man-down design requires a shelf-height selector or the calibration of the truck mast for the tallest storage locations, but it provides the advantage of faster operating speeds. As a result, the man-down turret truck is used in low-bay applications, and the man-up trucks are popular when the shelf height exceeds 20 to 25 feet.

Side-loader trucks (see Figure 14.9) can be either man-up or man-down. They are designed to handle long, heavy materials (pipe, sofas, lumber) that are difficult to palletize and are typically stored in cantilevered racks served by guided aisles. The truck travels in the aisle with its long axis and load parallel to the aisle. Either a pantograph or rolling mast design eliminates the need to make 90-degree turns in the aisle for storage and retrieval.

Four-directional trucks function similarly to the side-loader, but they have the additional advantage of moving along the side and then into a storage location without turning. This feature is useful when floor stacking long loads in deep lanes.

Class 2 also includes the very basic *low-lift pallet truck* (see Figure 14.10) and *pallet rider truck.* These trucks are relatively low in cost and are commonly used for loading and unloading trailers of palletized goods that do not have to be stacked or unstacked. Some are designed to carry as many as four loads at once (two high, two deep) and are both inexpensive and highly productive transportation devices.

Figure 14.7: Very-narrow-aisle swinging mast truck.

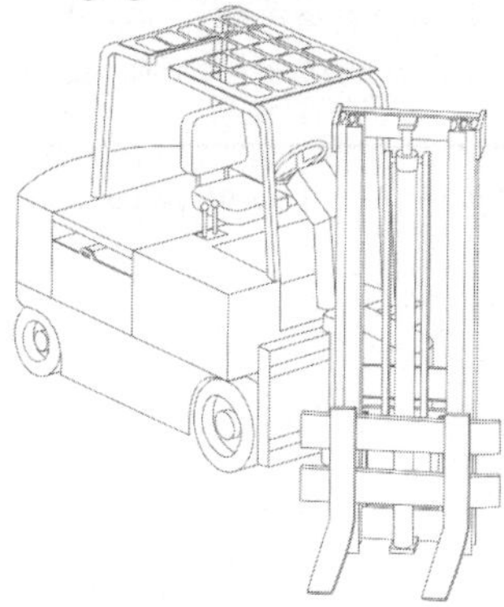

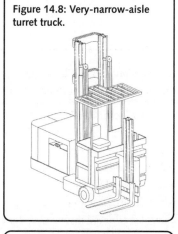

Figure 14.8: Very-narrow-aisle turret truck.

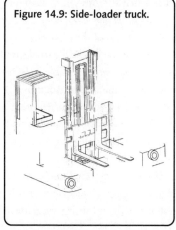

Figure 14.9: Side-loader truck.

Fixed-mast storage/retrieval trucks combine fork truck and automated storage-and-retrieval (AS/RS) machine features. They receive electric power from a bus that is mounted overhead when operating in an aisle and from batteries when they are not in an aisle. The mast extends to a guide rail at the top of each aisle, which facilitates stability and guidance of the vehicle. Faster operating speeds and simultaneous horizontal and vertical travel reduce cycle time and increase productivity. A man-up design is typical, as is a shuttle-table to store and retrieve pallets in the rack structure, similar to a storage/retrieval machine operation. The aisle widths are minimal and are based on the width of the load or the truck, whichever is greater, plus minimal clearances on each side.

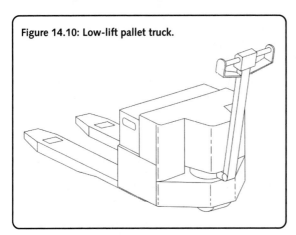

Figure 14.10: Low-lift pallet truck.

Some designs can handle storage heights up to 60 feet. They tend to be more versatile than a dedicated-aisle AS/RS machine.

Class 3 Electric Motor Hand Trucks

Class 3 trucks are characterized by a swivel control arm that allows the operator to control the truck while walking in front or behind the vehicle in the case of a "walkie," or while walking or riding in the case of the walkie/rider. This control arm is equipped with forward, reverse, lift, lower, and speed functions, as well as a dead-man brake that activates when the arm is released, allowing it to return to its normal vertical position. Directional control is achieved through horizontal rotation. Typically, there is a feature that stops the truck when the arm senses resistance when operating in reverse.

Low-lift platform trucks are used primarily for transporting skids and bins. The minimum lowered height of the platform is typically six inches. Two adaptations are common. The platform of these versatile trucks is often modified to accept customized unit loads, such as steel coils, wire and cable reels, bolts of yarn, paper flat stock, or other units with distinctive configurations. Additionally, a *low-lift walkie pallet truck* is similar to the pallet rider truck, except that it requires the operator to lead or follow the truck on foot.

Tractors are typically used to pull one to five wagons or trailers. The number depends on the drawbar pull rating of the tractor, which is intended for transporting large-volume loads over long distances.

Electric motor hand trucks are also available in straddle, reach, and counterbalanced high-lift designs. They are similar in design to the Class 2 trucks, except that they are walkie trucks and their typical lift heights are up to 15 feet.

Automated Guided Vehicle Systems

Automated Guided Vehicle Systems (AGVS) are battery-powered driverless vehicles that are controlled by computers for task assignment, path selection, and positioning. The typical AGVS has four components: one or more vehicles, pick-up/drop-off (P/D) locations, a guidance system, and the control system. Because they do not require an operator, they have low operating costs relative to powered industrial trucks, especially in a multi-shift, around-the-clock operation. However, at speeds that range from 150 feet/minute to 250 feet/minute, they are slower than typical industrial trucks that may operate from 265 feet/minute to 440 feet/minute. Economic justification is typically a tradeoff between lower operating cost and higher investment. They provide a high degree of operational discipline. They also require a higher degree of operations and maintenance support skill and knowledge relative to industrial trucks, but the difference is narrowing as electric-powered trucks are incorporating increasingly sophisticated electronic controls.

AGVS are found in the most automated, high-throughput, high-utilization distribution operations, often in conjunction with automated storage/retrieval systems (AS/RS) or for repetitive transportation over long distances. They are also used for storing high-value goods that are easily damaged with operator-controlled equipment.

Vehicle and Pickup/Delivery (P/D) Stations

There are five types of vehicles: tractors, pallet vehicles, unit-load carriers, fork vehicles, and light-load carriers.

The earliest application of AGV technology is *tractors* towing trailers. This simple design uses flatbed trailers that are loaded by fork trucks or by hand. Trailers with non-powered roller decks can be used to interface with fixed, non-powered conveyors and use manual assistance for load transfer. Trailers with powered-roller decks are less commonly used in systems with fixed powered-roller conveyors for automatic load transfer. They are powered from the tractor battery. Loading and unloading may be from either side, and each trailer can be designed to carry two loads.

Pallet vehicles are similar to the industrial pallet truck. They are typically loaded like a pallet truck, but they travel and unload themselves. After loading, the vehicle is given its next destination and placed on the guide path. Pallet delivery stations are located on spurs off the main guide path. As a truck enters a spur, it slows down to creep speed and stops at a predefined location. The truck automatically lowers the load and places the pallets on the floor. The truck restarts, backs away from the pallets, and proceeds to its next destination. Platform trucks are similar to pallet trucks, but the forks are replaced with a solid deck or platform for handling skids.

Unit load carriers are designed to handle one or two loads at a time on top of the vehicle. They are compact and highly maneuverable in both forward and reverse directions, can rotate 180 degrees in their own length, and are available as either roller top or lift-and-carry vehicles. The roller top AGV has powered rollers that can receive or discharge a conveyable unit load from or to a roller conveyor P/D stand. Power for the onboard rollers is provided by the AGV battery, and the P/D rollers may also be powered by the AGV battery or by an external power source. Lift-and-carry vehicles require loads to be placed on load stands that allow the vehicle to drive under the load. When in position, the load support lifts to clear the load from the stand and transport it to its destination. Unloading is similar, but in reverse sequence.

Fork vehicles, which come in straddle, counterbalanced, and side-loader models, allow loads to be picked up and deposited at P/D stations that are simply floor locations. They can also handle loads at a variety of levels: floor, conveyors, and racks. The straddle and counterbalanced vehicles store and unload in conjunction with right-angle turns. This maneuver requires a significant aisle width. The side loader can operate in a very narrow aisle because a right-angle turn is not necessary. However, the vehicle must leave and reenter an aisle to combine a drop-off on one side with a pickup on the other, unless the aisle is sized for 180-degree turns.

Light-load carriers are vehicles that are typically loaded and unloaded by hand. The load may be totes, cartons, or loose items.

System Controls

An AGVS control system includes an interface to a host computer, a local material handling system control computer, control software, onboard processors, a guidance system, and a means of communication between the local computer and the individual vehicles. The most basic AGVS control strategy uses an operator to enter a destination code at an on-board terminal and release the vehicle. The vehicle travels to the intended destination and waits for further instructions. The early "tugger" AGVs used this method in a centralized control hierarchy. The local material handling control computer maintained control of vehicle functions, routing, and traffic. Guidance and safety functions were at the machine level, and these vehicles were considered "dumb." In keeping with the philosophy of distributed processing, many suppliers are now using vehicles that have the onboard intelligence to receive, store, and process information. Those that have routing and traffic management functionality, and therefore can operate independently, are referred to as "smart" vehicles. All AGV control systems must provide guidance and communications, including positional control and dispatching, routing, and traffic control.

Guidance

Five techniques may be used to guide the vehicle:

1. *Inductive wire guidance* is the most commonly used method for large-load AGVs. Similar to the wire guidance used by narrow-aisle industrial trucks, a wire in the floor serves as the centerline of the travel path. A current in the wire provides an electromagnetic field. An onboard sensor measures the strength of the field and adjusts the steering mechanism to keep the vehicle centered over the wire. For reliability, the floor should be smooth and the wire must be continuous. It is becoming common for turns to be configured with wires that are at right angles. The vehicle will follow the wire to a predetermined point, leave the wire, execute a specific radius

turn under the control of an onboard processor, and then reacquire the wire as it completes the turn. This approach reduces installation costs.

2. *Optical guidance* uses tape or paint to identify the centerline of the path to the vehicle. Photocells sense the light that is reflected when an onboard light source illuminates the reflective path. Signals fed to the steering control indicate reflectance, which is maximized when the vehicle is centered over the path. Optical paths have the advantage of flexibility in that they may be easily altered. However, their lack of durability makes them suitable only in clean industrial, office, and laboratory environments.

3. *Chemical guidance* uses a phosphorus-type paint that is invisible to the eye. When illuminated by an ultraviolet light, the fluorescent particles glow, thereby identifying the path to the vehicle.

4. One of the newest vehicles, known as a "self-guided vehicle" (SGV), combines advanced *dead reckoning navigation* for general control with triangulation for corrections. The triangulation method uses infrared lasers and reflective bar codes or retro reflective targets to identify the actual location of the vehicle. It compares that with the planned location and makes appropriate adjustments.

5. *Vision systems* are the latest innovation in AGV guidance. An onboard camera records the view ahead and compares it with an image that has been programmed and stored in memory. Typically, the target image is defined as the marker lines on either side of an aisle.

Communication

The local control computer and the vehicles need a means to communicate location, task assignment, task completion, routing, and traffic conditions. Four methods of communications are available:

1. Inductive wire
2. Floor devices
3. Radio frequency transmission
4. Optical infrared

The inductive wire uses the same floor path as the guidance does, and except for when operating off-wire, communication is continuous. Floor devices may include magnets, radio frequency (RF) transponders, and additional inductive loops installed adjacent to the guide path in specific patterns and locations. Because they require the vehicle to be close enough to receive its signal, the communication is intermittent. This approach is used for determining vehicle position. RF transmission between the vehicles and system control allows continuous communication, unless dead spots exist in the facility. The use of frequency identification tags provides intermittent communication, and they can be used to identify the vehicle and receive data at P/D stations. Optical solutions typically require a line-of-sight and therefore are intermittent.

Routing

System-level control of routings uses path-switching to direct the vehicle to its destination. Inductive wire guidance systems are divided into zones that may be turned on and off. Machine-level control of routing is based on frequency selection. The AGV knows its location and is assigned a destination. A system map in memory defines the routing and signal frequency of the guide path. Internal controls monitor the correct frequency.

Traffic Control

The purpose of traffic control is to prevent collisions between vehicles. Decisions to stop, slow down, or proceed are made according to vehicle locations and the queue of pending material moves. AGV systems using dumb or semi-intelligent vehicles will locate this intelligence at the system level. Smart vehicles are able to determine the location of other vehicles internally to make stop and proceed decisions.

Carton/Tote Conveyors

A conveyor is defined by the Conveyor Equipment Manufacturers Association as:

"A horizontal, inclined, or vertical device for moving or transporting bulk materials or objects in a path, predetermined by the design of the device and having points of loading and discharge fixed, or selective...."

The definition goes on to define examples and presents a list of 109 specific conveyor types. The definition suggests two broad categories: bulk handling and object handling. Bulk handling conveyors include bucket, pneumatic, screw, trough, and vibratory designs, which are rarely used in distribution. Most distribution applications involve packaged finished goods. The packaging may be a bag, a carton, a pallet, or a drum. Sometimes loose items are conveyed using a tote or a hanger for ease of conveyance. In this chapter, the term *carton/tote load* will be used to describe the variety of discrete objects that may be conveyed. The most common types of conveyors that are applied in distribution warehousing to transport cartons or totes will fall into one of the following classifications:

1. Gravity conveyor
   a. Chute
   b. Ball transfer
   c. Wheel (skate wheel)
   d. Roller
2. Powered conveyor
   a. Belt
   b. Live roller
   c. Chain
3. Special designs
   a. Accumulation
   b. Transfer cars

c. Garments on Hanger (GOH) conveyor

d. Sortation systems

These designs and their typical applications in distribution are described in this section.

Gravity Conveyors

Chute Conveyors

A chute conveyor (see Figure 14.11) is used to change the elevation and position of a unit load and uses gravity to overcome friction. It consists of a smooth metal trough that may be straight, curved, or spiral in shape. Chutes are most often used for transporting loads over a short distance, changing the elevation of the load, and moving durable loads. Chute conveyors are often part of a sortation system and act as a transfer and accumulation device for each discharge location.

Ball Transfer Conveyors

A ball transfer is a section of conveyor that consists of an array of balls that are mounted and retained by a sheet-metal section over a bed of many smaller balls. It is used as a manual assist for purposes of changing the orientation of the unit load within a gravity conveyor configuration. Ball transfers are commonly used for in-line weigh stations, as in a parcel manifesting system. Because the bearing surface is relatively small, ball transfers may mark the surface of soft materials such as brass and wood, as well as highly polished steel. They should not be used for soft- or irregular-bottom loads such as soggy cartons, bags, pallets, drums, baskets, or crates.

Wheel Conveyors

A wheel or skate wheel conveyor (see Figure 14.12) is used to reduce the lifting force required to transport a load under manual force or gravity. It consists of small wheels that are mounted on axles. The axles are mounted in a metal frame that is perpendicular to the flow of the load. It is available in straight sections, curved sections, spurs, and switches, as well as expandable, telescoping, and portable designs. The sections are often installed at a slight decline to promote gravity flow. A wheel conveyor is appropriate for loads with a smooth and durable bottom surface. Loads with a high weight-to-hardness ratio may not roll easily. Gravity wheel conveyors are also used for supporting a pick-to container in order picking and for loading and unloading floor-loaded trailers.

Roller Conveyors

A gravity roller conveyor is used for the same purposes as the gravity wheel conveyor. It consists of rollers that are mounted on axles between supporting frames and span the full width of the conveyor. The gravity roller conveyor is available in straight, curved, and spiral sections. It is installed in both level and inclined configurations and/or where the weight or bottom surface of the load would make it difficult to roll over wheels.

Powered Conveyors

Belt Conveyors

A conveyor belt is made of rubber, plastic, leather, or metal mesh and is mounted on a drive-and-idler roller and supported by either a sheet-metal bed (slider bed) or rollers. The assembly constitutes a powered belt conveyor. As a horizontal transportation device, the belt conveyor is used for incline, decline, controlled spacing, and accurate positioning of loads. It is also used for loads with soft and irregular surfaces. It is available in straight, curved, turntable, and spiral sections.

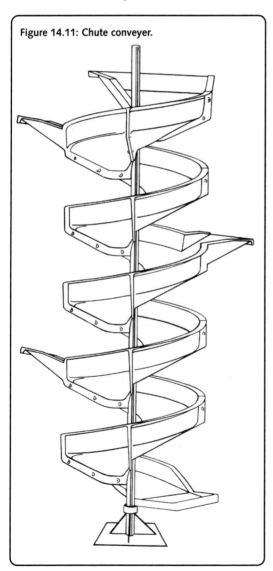

Figure 14.11: Chute conveyer.

Live-Roller Conveyor

Live roller conveyors (see Figure 14.13) consist of a series of rollers that are mounted on channels and driven by mechanical means. The driving mechanism describes the type of live roller. Light loads (those that may be lifted manually) are typically driven by a belt or O-rings. A *belt-driven* live roller conveyor uses the friction from a narrow belt that is mounted below the driven rollers and between a drive roller and a take-up roller. A *line-shaft* conveyor uses individual O-rings that wrap both the rollers and a drive shaft that runs the length of the driven section. This conveyor has the advantages of relatively low cost (due to the fact that they require fewer drives) and some degree of accumulation (slippage of rollers is encouraged by disconnecting some of the rings from the shaft). Belt-driven and line-shaft conveyors are available in straight and curved sections. They use transfers to move the load from one conveyor to another with a change in the axis of motion.

These transfers may be of pop-up roller, pusher, or puller designs. They use diverters to move the load from one conveyor to another, with no change in the axis of motion. Diverters may be of swing-arm, powered-belt, chain, or skewed/steerable wheel designs.

Emerging technology in the live-roller arena is the 24-volt motorized drive roller (MDR) conveyor (see Figure 14.14). MDR retains most of the features of line shaft or belt-driven live roller, but also adds a number of unique advantages. Instead of a conventional gear motor drive, a 24-volt DC motor, which is inside the roller, drives the zones of the conveyor. Rollers are typically 1.9 inches in diameter. Additional advantages include ease of installation, fewer spare parts, lower maintenance, and low power consumption.

Heavy loads are conveyed on a *chain-driven* live roller conveyor. Each roller has a gear, and the chains may be connected roller-to-roller or they may span several rollers. Chain-driven live roller conveyors are available in straight sections. Typically, right-angle

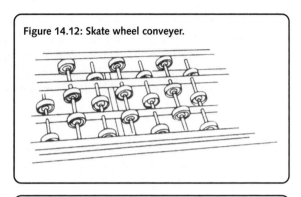

Figure 14.12: Skate wheel conveyer.

Figure 14.13: Live roller conveyer.

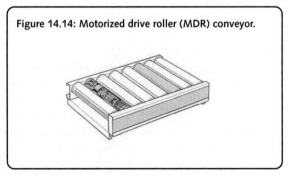

Figure 14.14: Motorized drive roller (MDR) conveyor.

transfers or turntables accomplish changes in direction and axis of motion. Power-section-to-power-section transfers use a pop-up chain conveyor that is mounted between the delivering rollers. Power-to-gravity transfers may use a pop-up tilt gravity section also mounted between the delivering rollers. Changes in direction without a change in the axis of motion are accomplished with a turntable. The delivering conveyor loads the turntable and forward motion stops until the 90-degree rotation is complete. Chain-driven live roller conveyors are used to transport pallet loads when the throughput between fixed points is high.

Chain Conveyors

Chain conveyors (see Figure 14.15) use two or more continuous strands of chain that are mounted between a drive sprocket and an idler sprocket and are supported by a low-friction continuous surface. They include sliding, rolling, pusher, and vertical designs. Chain conveyors are used to transport loads that must be carried with the runners perpendicular to the intended direction of travel. They are also used for heavy loads such as large castings, stacks of steel sheets, or steel coils. In distribution, the most common chain conveyor is the *sliding-chain* conveyor in which the chain is dragged on a wear surface with the load carried directly on the chain. Because of the higher friction of this design, it is commonly used for relatively light loads and shorter distances (e.g., right-angle transfer). Rolling chains incorporate a roller at each bushing or barrel to reduce the friction against the supporting surface and therefore can be used for heavier loads and longer conveyors. A *pusher-chain* conveyor has bars at specific intervals between two strands of chain that push the load along a slider bed. A *roller-slat* conveyor is a continuous chain that consists of rollers that span the width of the conveyor. In the slat conveyor design, fixtures or other special mechanisms can be mounted to the slat for positioning or carrying a load. *Vertical-chain* conveyors are either a reciprocating or continuous type. *Reciprocating* conveyors are used to shuttle loads between floors in a multi-story facility, and *continuous-type* chain conveyors are a variation of the roller-slat design in which gaps between slat sections provide spacing of the loads.

Special Designs

Accumulation Conveyors

The purposes of accumulation capability in a conveyor system are to:

- Buffer irregular input flow rates
- Provide continuous activity during interrupted flow
- Consolidate related or similar loads that were separated

In a distribution environment, accumulation capability is used as a part of a conveyor system that either delivers product to the warehouse or handles the loads that are created during the order fulfillment process, which includes picking, packing, and staging for shipment. Typical locations, in the context of the conveyor system, are:

- Before the intersection of two lines
- In a staging zone before a sorter

- Before induction at a sorter
- After a sortation zone
- Wherever a smooth, metered flow is required

In general, accumulation should be only in straight sections, and the length and pitch of gravity lines must be engineered according to the weight of the load.

While there are many electromechanical designs for accumulation conveyors, functionally, they come down to two: zone, or zero/minimum pressure, and continuous accumulation. Minimum pressure designs divide the conveyor into zones. Each zone has a load sensor that, when activated, will remove the power from that zone. The system controller controls the zone at the end of the accumulation line. A stationary load in the last zone removes the power from the previous zone and so on to the beginning of the line. The release from a zone-type accumulation can occur individually or in a slug of loads. Case sealers, stretch-wrap equipment, and shrink wrappers require individual release, whereas palletizers require metered slugs according to the cases per layer. Variations in line pressure and slug releases are typically due to the variance in load size relative to the zone length.

Continuous-type accumulation may take place on a gravity roller conveyor or live-roller conveyor. The first load in the line is stopped, either mechanically or by removing power from a metering section. The live-roller designs are continuously powered, but once the slug reaches critical length, the drive force is reduced either by removing power from the line or by mechanical adjustment. The mechanical adjustment reduces friction between the power source and the roller to the point where the roller does not move under the slug.

The key design parameter in live-roller continuous-type accumulation conveyor is line pressure. Crushing or buckling the slug can occur if the line pressure is too great. There are three factors to consider in determining line pressure:

1. Integrity of the load itself
2. Length of slug
3. Coefficient of friction of the conveyor

The metering section of the conveyor is designed to release a single load at a time. Release of the line may be by a sensor or by mechanical stops. Often a speed-up section is used to create a constant gap at the discharge point.

Transfer Car

A transfer car conveyor (see Figure 14.16) consists of a short section of conveyor that is mounted on a frame with wheels. The wheels are typically designed to ride on a pair of rails. Transfer cars are used to route loads from many inbound lines to many outbound lines when throughput is low. The car is loaded, it moves perpendicular to the intended direction of travel to align with the intended takeaway line, and the load is discharged. The cycle is completed when the car moves to the next line to pick up a load. The transfer car can be either manual or powered.

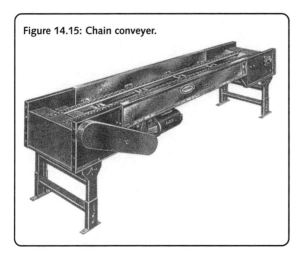

Figure 14.15: Chain conveyer.

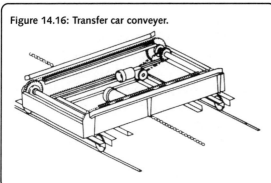

Figure 14.16: Transfer car conveyer.

Garments on Hanger (GOH) Conveyor

GOH is a method of handling garments on hangers for storage and transportation purposes and is primarily used in retail garment business. This system provides an inexpensive and flexible method of dealing with products that need to be handled gently and kept wrinkle free. A system may include a number of components.

Hanging trolleys are a specialized hanging device with wheels at each end that allow the device to move about in the system. They are generally 36 inches to 42 inches in length and are designed so that hangers will remain in place on the trolleys as they move horizontally, up inclines, and down declines.

The power rail is a simple system (similar to standard enclosed-track power systems) that transports hanging trolleys horizontally and up and down elevation changes to eliminate the need for manually moving the trolleys in the system.

Slick rail is the monorail round tubing on which the trolleys travel. The rail allows the trolleys to be pushed manually through the system, thus allowing transport and sortation to the holding lanes. Slick rail can be static (horizontal) for staging and processing of garments or slightly pitched to allow gravity fed accumulation of garments on trolleys. The trolleys can be moved from one route to a different route through the use of rail switches. The rail switches can be manually operated or can be activated electronically or pneumatically.

Operations

A typical GOH system has direct parallels to conventional carton or tote handling systems. The hanging trolleys serve the same function as a tote box that holds the garments, but usually with greater density and less product wrinkling. While in the holding or processing lanes, the garments are often inventoried, undergo QC inspection, are ticketed, and sorted into store assortments.

Because the power rails can easily transport GOH product up inclines, systems are often run overhead and consume little floor space while running a serpentine path through a facility. Typically processing of GOH is accomplished on a mezzanine that is either freestanding or supported by the GOH system supports. As compared to other systems, GOH systems are a relatively low-cost solution to garment handling problems.

Sortation Systems

Sortation systems (see Figure 14.17) are used in DCs to organize mixed products that are to be:

- Dispatched to specific storage zones
- Palletized in specific unit load configurations
- Routed to specific dock doors for shipping

Where throughput is moderate, sortation can be accomplished using powered conveyors with transfers and diverters that feed spurs consisting of gravity and chute conveyors. High-speed sortation systems handle cartons and have four subsystems: (1) merge, (2) induction, (3) sort, and (4) takeaway.

The *merge* subsystem receives product from various sources in the distribution center and provides a controlled release of cartons to the downstream sortation-induction equipment. The specific design of the merge is dependent on the number of infeed conveyors that it serves and the desired throughput rates. In general, there are two types of designs: *parallel design* and *perpendicular design*. The in feed flow-control device regulates the flow of cartons to the merge bed where cartons in two or more columns feed a funneling device. The result is that a single column of cartons feeds the induction subsystem.

The *induction* subsystem provides spacing between the cartons and identifies them individually. Operators accomplish low rates (10 cartons/minute to 40 cartons/minute) by visually identifying the carton and keys on a control console. Moderate rates (40 cartons/ minute to 80 cartons/minute) are achieved by adding manual key-entry induction stations, or by laser-scanning bar-code labels. Multiple induction stations typically require another merge between induction and sortation.

Sortation systems can provide moderate to high processing rates. High rates (from 80 up to 200

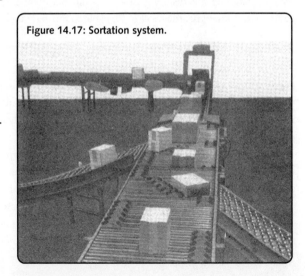

Figure 14.17: Sortation system.

cartons/minute) are accomplished by a sophisticated system. In the latter case, one to four servo-driven indexing belts release the cartons one at a time with a precise gap to a merge device. A second series of indexing belt conveyors optimizes the gap and feeds an omni-directional scanner for identification.

Using a diverter, the *sortation* subsystem divides the flow of cartons into separate streams according to a downstream destination. Once identified, the carton is tracked until it reaches the divert point, where the system controller activates the divert device. The type of divert used depends on the speed and weight of the carton. Low-rate devices include barrier-type arms, pop-up transfers, and pushers. Moderate-rate devices include pop-up skewed wheels and steerable rollers. High rates are accomplished with sliding-shoe and tilt-tray diverters. They are both fast and bi-directional. Typically sliding-shoe diverters are slat conveyors with "shoes" that slide between the slats to push or pull the load off the line. They are gentle. Tilt trays "dump" the product to either side of the line. In general, they are suitable for soft goods as well as cartons. Some designs provide a parabolic trajectory that can handle breakable goods without damage. A tilt-tray system can handle a large number of divert locations.

The takeaway conveyors must accept diverted material without affecting the sorter. The type of conveyor that is used depends on the operating rate, product mix, product weight, and product durability. Powered takeaways are either live roller or belt conveyor. They typically run faster than the sorter conveyor so that they can pull the cartons away. Due to its lower inertia, the gravity wheel conveyor is preferable to the roller conveyor. It is used with positive sortation, such as the sliding shoe diverter, as its speed of up to 350 feet/minute provides significant momentum. It is also used on slow systems. Chute conveyors are often used with tilt-tray systems where orientation is not important.

The previous sections have introduced material handling control systems and the equipment involved in the material handling process. It is important for those implementing material handling systems integration to familiarize themselves with these systems and equipment. Otherwise, they will not be able to integrate them effectively.

Pulling It All Together: Systems Integration

Systems integration is a disciplined science. Users are increasingly turning to systems integration firms to handle the complex job of creating a functional system from all of the various technologies, equipment, and software products available. At one point or another, a systems integrator is required to tie together the maze of hardware and software elements that are a part of every integrated supply chain solution.

In the past, many companies chose to integrate their own systems. This was likely done because these organizations believed their in-house resources were as good or better then the external integrators available to them. After all, systems integration is complex work, which requires an in depth understanding of a firm's "as-is" and "to be" business operations, and who would better know this than the key people working within it everyday. Two significant things have happened in the past 10 years that should cause most firms to rethink integrating themselves. First, these firms have likely gone through several rounds of downsizing. The engineering and information systems staff that formed the SWAT team responsible for these jobs are probably not around or are now absolutely consumed in running their own day-to-day operations activities. Second, the field of potential external systems integrators has significantly grown.

No one would ever consider performing heart surgery on himself to install a critical piece of human automation such as a pacemaker. Likewise, any company that needs an automated system should thoroughly assess whether in-house capabilities exist to successfully perform an automation project. Choosing the right systems integrator has become the single most important decision and requires careful consideration. Systems integrators should possess technical expertise as well as the ability to ensure unbiased access to any potential solutions. Variety, availability, convenience, quality, and affordability are key attributes to look for in choosing a systems integrator. The client should demand performance and results. This allows no margin for errors and requires enhanced sophistication and skill in material handling integration. The discipline requires a holistic approach that begins with the client, involves advanced technologies and interfaces, and demands complex engineering practices done faster than fast.

In a world that wants everything faster and with less hassle, it's naturally attractive for a service or product provider to claim to be a material handling systems integrator. To most customers, that implies one-stop shopping. Many companies who call themselves material handling systems integrators produce mixed and varied results as they implement their practice. A project might go well if led by an experienced project manager who has previously performed on similar jobs and therefore knows the majority of the pitfalls to avoid. However, even when those individuals are faced with an innovative system design, they too can fumble through the project's implementation phases.

It is not surprising that as the initial demand for material handling systems was developing and the industry was not yet ready to respond to that demand, many customers or systems users took the do-it-yourself approach. Additionally, many traditional equipment companies, with little to no understanding of material handling systems integration, saw this growing demand as an opportunity to expand their sales. Unfortunately, users who have mistakenly attempted to perform their own material handling systems integration and equipment companies who have misrepresented their capabilities have created a legacy of material handling implementation horror stories.

Here is list of some of the common pitfalls that must be avoided to achieve successful integration of your supply chain systems:

- *Trusting the success of your operation to someone other than a properly trained integration professional.* Companies that strictly manufacture equipment, although well intentioned, cannot know your business, and are usually not oriented to collecting and analyzing your full operational data. Thus, they are not as likely to create the optimal solution using best-of-breed products for your company's needs. It is important that equipment bias does not drive a systems analysis.

- *Choosing the wrong technology.* Often, people are not aware of the possibilities that exist, and the strengths and weakness of each technology select products and technologies. As a result, choosing the wrong technology, or misapplying the right technology, is common. An experienced material handling systems integrator, unbiased by its own product line, understands all of the technologies available and the appropriate applications for each.

- *Assuming that you can improve the output of your system by simply running it harder and faster.* A system should be designed and operated to meet your company's specific operational needs, and as those needs change, the entire system should be reanalyzed, perhaps using detailed simulation. Increasing the run-time often jeopardizes necessary system maintenance, which ultimately decreases system availability. Speeding up system components may not have a positive effect on the resulting output either. In fact, it can cause the component to become less reliable and thereby reducing output.

- *Applying automation to current operations without process optimization or cost- benefit analysis.* A true material handling systems integrator always looks to first simplify operations, then to maximize efficiency, and to increase return on investment (ROI). Often, trying to handle a few exceptions can drive the majority of the system's cost.

- *Underestimating the ramp-up and debug phases of a project.* Many companies commonly assume that a well-designed system will operate at peak levels shortly after commissioning. The three key elements of every system—hardware, software, and people—must be treated with equal importance. The best system will not perform as expected until properly trained personnel are allowed to develop complete competency with the system. Like the hardware and software, which should be integrated in a step-wise fashion, users should be allowed to gain confidence through a gradual process of operational ramp-up. This can be accomplished through incremental training and system usage. Your employees should be introduced to new and more complex system features and functions only after they have mastered the basics. Additionally, your system product volumes should be artificially constrained at start-up and then gradually increased until full volume is reached.

Most so-called material handling systems integrators practice the art of what we call "reactionary debugging." This is when a system is loosely defined on the front end, and the project is allowed to progress into the fabrication and installation phases without further definition. As a result, your team will have to accommodate errors later in the project, most likely during the integration phase. When this is allowed to happen, the implementation phase should be renamed the "debug phase."

For the disciplined material handling systems integrator and its clients, there is a distinct difference between the terms debug and integration. Integration is the science of bringing a system together in a logical, step-by-step fashion against a defined systems baseline using a predetermined set of integration procedures that validate the entire system's functionality along each step. The systems complexity is seen as a series of layers. The core system functions are proven, a layer is added and tested, regression tests are conducted to verify that the core function is still fully functional, another layer added, and so on. This process continues until the entire system is proven to be fully functional.

Debugging, on the other hand, is the necessary process of trying to figure out what is broken. Think of it this way—if your integration procedures were detailed enough, then debugging would not be required at all. When a new layer of function is added, it should be thin enough so as to be defined as a single function. If, after adding this layer it is determined that the new function does not work, it is easy to tell that this is what is broken. However, it is not cost effective to design integration procedures for a complex system to this level of detail, so the material handling systems integrator has to trade off how many functions to bundle in each layer. This tradeoff leads to debugging when things do not go as planned.

- *Not planning for growth or scalability.* In today's business environment, the only constant is change. The true material handling systems integrator understands this principle and therefore designs systems that are modular and scalable, and can be easily modified for technology and functionality infusion. For example, a properly designed system would support increased volume, without business interruption, by predetermining the location and connectivity of required additional equipment modules.

- *Delaying key project milestones without changing the overall project completion date.* Delaying your project's early milestones and not appropriately changing your project end date results in an unrealistically compressed scheduled of remaining tasks and sets the stage for implementation disaster. An experienced material handling systems integrator will identify and communicate potential schedule risks and offer alternatives rather than compressing the schedule.

- *Not clearly defining and testing for key systems performance characteristics.* Oftentimes, systems are installed and success is declared only to find out later that the system does not meet critical performance criteria such as peak demand throughput. To ensure that your proposed system will ultimately meet all of the expected requirements, an experienced material handling systems integrator will, based on system performance requirements, clearly define system performance testing criteria and conduct testing.

- *"Too many cooks in the kitchen" syndrome—assuming that doubling your project team staff will shorten your project time.* When a systems implementation must be accomplished in a specific timeframe, which is shorter than the typical system deployment time, it is wrong to assume that simply adding more people will shorten the cycle. In fact, an experienced integrator knows that although optimizing the deployment team size is critical in shortening deployment cycle times, there are many other ways to accomplish that objective. For example, minor changes to your operational processes can greatly eliminate time-consuming software development tasks.

Similarly, thoughtful definition of system requirements may avoid the use of customized material handling equipment.

- *Deciding to patch your existing system in order to save money instead of making a real change.* Often a company may come to the conclusion that it is less expensive to modify or add to an existing system than to implement a new one. When not supported by an unbiased system cost and benefit analysis, this conclusion could be a critical mistake. To avoid this mistake, the analysis must compare the cost of the current system upgrade against the cost of the new system. It must include a comparison of the operational and maintenance costs of both scenarios and quantitatively evaluates all other benefits of a new and improved system. It is also important to understand that the upgrade cost grows as the system is being asked to migrate further and further from its intended use.

The hallmark of a qualified material handling systems integrator is the ability to help a client organization understand the science of integration. Like any other science, this requires a solid understanding and control of the inputs and transformational processes. To deliver systems that consistently meet all performance, budgetary, and schedule objectives, an integrator must utilize an established set of fundamental processes. One of the most critical processes is project planning.

Project Planning—The Three Phases of Material Handling Systems Integration

Material handling systems integration can be broken down into three distinct phases. The term "project" is typically used to define the summation of these phases. The better you understand and define a project's phases, the higher the likelihood of your project's success. In some cases, the three phases may be clearly defined and represent months or even years of effort crossing from one phase to another. In other cases, the phases can be very poorly defined and as a result, your project team may skip a phase or transition inappropriately to another phase, creating significant project risks. The overall complexity of the Material Handling Systems Integration, the experience of your performance team, and the urgency and tolerance for risk are key factors in determining the required time for each project phase.

Phase I—The Strategic Master Plan

During this phase, the customer or mission needs are collected, defined, understood, analyzed, and documented. Potential applicable technologies are explored and traded off. Alternative system concepts are created and evaluated, and system requirements are defined and documented. It is during this phase that a recommended path forward is developed and preliminary project investments, savings, and economic justifications are determined. A project manager should be assigned, and should create and lead a multi-disciplined team throughout the subsequent project deployment phases.

Phase II—Detailed Planning

In this phase, a functional specification that documents all of the operational system requirements is developed. Material handling systems constraints, which act as filters in the next phase, are also defined, and specific technical solutions are considered and selected. During this stage, bid specifications are prepared, along with potential vendor source listings and evaluation procedures for source selections. Here, a considerable amount of vendor interaction takes place, which culminates in vendor selections. In addition, a detailed implementation schedule is created.

The entire set of documents becomes known as the "system baseline documentation" which is maintained with a process known as configuration management. This process clearly communicates to all system participants when a pending change is being considered, so that a complete set of system impacts are determined and informed change decisions are made. After a change is approved, this process ensures the proper communication of that change takes place.

During the detailed planning phase, the design team will begin conducting another process called design walkthroughs. A multi-disciplined team will participate in these walkthroughs to ensure all aspects of the system are refined concurrently. The walkthroughs accomplish several different objectives. One is to provide everyone on the design team the opportunity to become familiar with the workings of the system design; another is to take advantage of the team's experience in optimizing the design and removing risk to the client by identifying system shortfalls and correcting them. Walkthroughs are an invaluable tool that should be utilized after the system baseline has been created.

Just as in Phase I, once detailed planning is complete, the economic viability of the project must be established. The Phase II savings, investments, and economic justifications must be done at ± 5 percent accuracy to encourage executive buy-in and approval in order to move the project on to Phase III.

Phase III—Implementation

The old carpenter's adage of "measure twice, cut once" sums up the correct way to perform material handling systems integration. During this phase, various elements or subsystems are going to be procured, manufactured, developed, tested, shipped, delivered, installed, integrated, tested again, and sold to the customer. All these activities should be clearly defined and understood by all parties to avoid expectation mismatches and system implementation issues.

A detailed installation plan must be developed and followed, bringing all these system elements together in a logical fashion. By dividing the system into physical or functional areas such as the power distribution and control subsystems, the sequence of installation and integration steps may be more easily determined.

The fabrication of hardware subsystems and the development of software and control subsystems have a direct relationship to the quality of the documentation, which defines these elements. Integration tasks, which also begin as plans and procedures developed well before the hardware and software elements are available, are another key aspect that takes place during the implementation phase.

The final portion of the implementation phase, which is often overlooked, is the operational transition activities. These activities, once again, should begin early in a project with the development of an operational transition plan. This plan takes into account the operations and maintenance approach and requirements of the system.

Conclusion

Material handling today involves highly technical, engineered systems that combine fast, complex machinery and information technology that can facilitate value-added operations and contribute to supply chain excellence. Systems need to be carefully integrated with one another and with other parts of a business's operations. They must be selected and designed with an understanding of the total operation, and both information technology and physical systems have to be flexible, scalable and easily updated if they are to contribute a significant return on investment for the organization.

It is evident there is a high level of coordination required among many different people and numerous steps involved in material handling systems integration process that are critical to its success. Communication and coordination between all parties involved, such as the operators, those overseeing the entire project and the electrical and mechanical installers, is important. The result will be a successful implementation that meets the schedule and defined budget. If these steps are not taken into consideration the end result could be an overspent budget and a missed deadline. Keep these topics in mind during the design phase of any material handling project, and the project is likely to be a resounding success.

CHAPTER 15
Automated Storage/Retrieval Systems

James K. Allred, President (Retired), SK Daifuku Corporation
and Stephen L. Parsley, P.E., Principal Engineer, Daifuku America Corporation

Automated storage and retrieval systems are an important technology for improving material flow and control in factories and warehouses. They enable highly accurate, real-time management of inventories, keeping precise records of all item counts by location in storage while ensuring virtually absolute physical security of materials. Because of their ability to densely store material in often unused overhead space, AS/RS free-up large amounts of floor space, permitting major expansions in production volume without the need for new building construction. The high density of AS/RS storage buffers allows work stations or automatic processes to be located closer to their buffer stock, thus cutting work-in-process transportation distances and order filling cycle time.

The great accuracy, security and density of AS/RS often enable "just-in-time" operations because they ensure reliable and rapid delivery of every item in inventory to its point-of-use. AS/RS are easily linked to manual work stations, cells or automatic processes by conveyors, lift trucks, automatic guided vehicles, or shuttle cars. AS/RS computer control systems are usually directly connected to corporate computer systems which manage production, order fulfillment and distributionæimproving the effectiveness of these systems by providing precise real-time knowledge of inventories on hand.

Types of AS/RS Systems

Automated storage/retrieval systems (AS/RS) consist of a rail-running, robot-like vehicle called a storage/retrieval (S/R) machine (see Figure 15.1). The S/R machine operates in an aisle between two storage rack structures where the loads are deposited until retrieved. In some cases, the S/R machine can also deposit loads into positions that are actually entry points to a flow lane—that will accumulate material and then deliver it to a point of use.

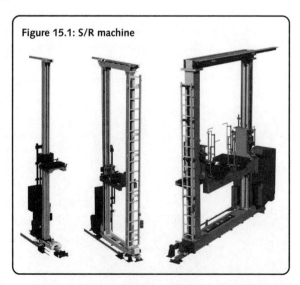

Figure 15.1: S/R machine

S/R machines are driven by a controller that may be autonomous (used to control the AS/RS system in a stand-alone fashion) or linked to a system computer controlling one or more S/R machines while tracking all inventory items in the system.

A common practice is to classify AS/RS systems as either Unit Load or Mini Load systems. Another term widely used is to refer to them as buffer systems—especially when describing the smaller box and carton handling products that belong to this family.

A Unit Load AS/RS typically handles a pallet or container that normally weighs 1000 pounds or more, with system heights ranging from 15 to over 140 feet. While lighter loads may be stored in this type of system, the use of a Unit Load design is first driven by load size, and most products handle 1000 pounds as a minimum.

Figure 15.2: Unit Load S/R

Unit Load S/R machines are normally equipped with a shuttle that reaches under the load, picking it up and transporting it to a storage position or for delivery to a retrieval output position (see Figure 15.2). While the shuttle can usually be thought of as a table on which the load will be transported, in some cases, the shuttle will be uniquely designed to interface with the bottom of the load.

Mini Load systems handle plastic or metal totes or individual cartons and are commonly installed in existing buildings, where clearances are 30 feet or less. However, they are often installed as tall as 50 feet when building clearances permit. Mini Load weight capacities for individual loads are typically 500 pounds or less—driven largely by the practicality of labor effort needed to place materials into and pick materials from the tote.

Mini Load S/R machines may have an extractor mechanism that engages a handle on the storage tote, pulling the tote from the rack structure onto the S/R machine (see Figure 15.3). Like Unit Load machines, they also frequently have shuttle mechanisms which

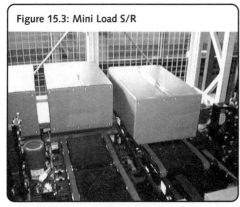

Figure 15.3: Mini Load S/R

extend a lifting platform into the rack under the load and raise, picking up the load. The differences between the extractor and shuttle-based applications revolve around density and cost. If space is severely limited, the extractor-based design allows a slightly more dense storage ratio—at the expense of a more complex mechanism and more fragile load containers. The shuttle based system will have a lower density storage ratio (because of the aperture beneath each load into which the shuttle will extend to engage the load) and may require in-rack sprinklers for fire protection, but offers a simpler technical solution that is not dependent on the critical extractor/pan interface—which can be damaged while the pan is out of the system being used at the workstation.

Load Characteristics—Important to AS/RS Success

Many factors affect the design of the storage structure of an AS/RS, but none is more fundamental than the load itself. The most important characteristics are the load weight, its footprint and its height, and the overall stability of the load. These factors define size and strength of the storage cubicle and the operating clearances that will be required to accommodate it.

The stability of the load to be stored is important. If the load is prone to shingling (where stacks of boxes on the load are easily mis-aligned through normal handling, see Figures 15.4a and 15.4b) or if the load has loose items overhanging the planned pallet footprint (i.e. open carton flaps, tags or paperwork, loose stretchwrap, etc.) these issues must be considered when qualifying the load inclusion in the system design. While most of the notorious problems in this area can be easily dealt with, some loads may not be suitable for automated handling. This is more of a practical limit than a technical one. If the majority of loads are acceptable for storage, overdesigning the system to accommodate a few abnormal conditions may negate the financial justification for the system overall.

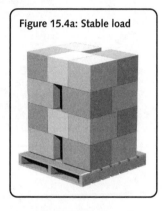

Figure 15.4a: Stable load

Figure 15.4b: Stability challenged load

If the pallet or carton is unsuitable for storage, or if loads with widely differing footprint dimensions are to be handled, it may be possible to simplify the design and reduce system cost by placing the load on a standard-sized slave pallet or tote. Slave pallets or totes are usually captive to the system and may require special collectors, dispensers, and empty pallet or tote handling equipment. But the cost of these additional devices is usually offset by the reduced cost of designing a system to accommodate a wide variety of generally non-conforming loads.

Pallet quality is very important to the success of an AS/RS. Loose or broken bottom boards, protruding nails and dimensionally variant pallets can inhibit the ability of loads to be conveyed or transferred into and out of the AS/RS storage rack. Again, a variety of products are available to address this issue, but the foundation on which the load is transported and stored is critical to the reliable operation of the system.

Rack Design Factors

Drive-through Rack

This type of rack is often called AS/RS rack. The load is supported on its edges and handled by the S/R machine's shuttle table which is extended underneath the load and picks it up from the rack arms (see Figures 15.5a and 15.5b). Since racks are designed to accommodate an individual AS/RS supplier's S/R machine, it is always necessary to consult an AS/RS supplier for assistance in configuring a rack structure. This is because each supplier's S/R machine has unique clearance heights for the lowest and highest load openings, and for load and shuttle clearances in the storage cubical. An advantage of this type of rack is that it can be used in systems were loads are stored in a multiple deep load per opening configuration.

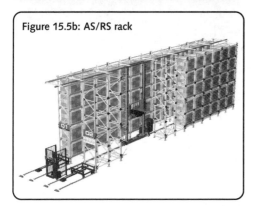

Figure 15.5a: AS/RS rack

Figure 15.5b: AS/RS rack

Euro-Pallet Rack (multi-deep storage)

This type of racking makes use of a rack design that is less expensive than drive-in racking, but requires that the load be handled on a Euro-design pallet. Again the S/R machine will have a special shuttle for this type of pallet, which sets the load on what would normally be described as post and beam racking. Multi-deep storage can sometimes be accomplished with the Euro-pallet rack, but the economies of this rack design are less significant.

Figure 15.6: S/R machine

Runout Space

At either end of the system, runout space is required. The runout at the front is determined by the length of the S/R machine, which must come partially clear of the racks in order to pick up and discharge loads (see Figure 15.6). The rear runout area is the length of the S/R machine and extends beyond the last rack column when the S/R machine serves the last bay of storage racks.

Free-standing Rack and Rack Which Supports a Building

The majority of the world's AS/RS were built with free-standing rack (structures which do not support the building) and are below 50-feet tall. Most systems higher than 60-feet are installed in rack-supported buildings; very few systems are more than 100-feet tall as building and system costs accelerate rapidly over 100 feet. Today, however, there are new products that are taking these systems to nearly 50 meters tall—gain special conditions have created this demand for height.

In a rack-supported building, the rack system becomes the framework supporting the roof deck, building siding, air conditioning system, electric power distribution system, and the fire protection system. The rack system itself is trussed together in all directions to form a highly rigid structure that can support these loads and withstand wind and snow loading. Rack structures also vary based on the eathquake zone in which erected.

The predominat consideration in choosing a rack supported design is that the installation of systems taller than 60 feet is more efficiently accomplished. The rack and cranes are installed using equipment that is often difficult to operate under existing building clearances This normally translates into a quicker, more timely installation period,

Storage/Retrieval Machine

While the storage rack itself is the operating environment for the system, the S/R machine is the basic unit of material handling. It has three motions: horizontal, vertical, and the shuttle motion into and out of the rack structure.

Operating Speeds

Systems may reach vertical speeds of up to 250 feet per minute and horizontal speeds of 300 to over 800 feet per minute. Machine speeds are often eroneously used as a qualifying attribute when making equipment selections. A very fast machine may not be able to utilize this capability in an aisle where velocity loading has made the average probably move less than needed for the crane to obtain top speed. The crane speed capabilities should be matched to system height, length, load weight and desired throughput and responsiveness since larger, higher speed (and more expensive) drives may not be required in a specific application.

Cycle Time

The AS/RS product section of the Material Handling Industry of America (MHIA) has developed a conservative formula to compute the cycle time

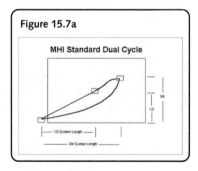

Figure 15.7a

MHI Standard Dual Cycle

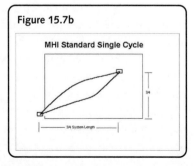

Figure 15.7b

MHI Standard Single Cycle

for both single and dual cycles. For a dual cycle (see Figure 15.7a), the S/R machine picks up the load at the home input/output station, then travels halfway down the aisle and halfway up the rack to deposit the load; the S/R machine then proceeds half of the remaining distance down the aisle, and half the remaining vertical distance to retrieve a load and return to the home station to deposit the load. For a single cycle (see Figure 15.7b), the S/R machine only does a single pick-up or a single deposit while traveling half the length of the rack and half the vertical elevation, and then returning to the home position.

This technique for measuring throughput is a good basis for starting the design of the system, but is a very conservative estimate of system capability. It ignores the impact of customary velocity loading techniques (the technique of storing more highly active loads near the home station) and it assumes there is an equal probablility among all loads that every load stored and retrieved will be transported horizontally through the system 1.5 times the system's length.

AS/RS suppliers have developed computer simulation programs in which system dimension and operational parmeters are entered, along with machine performance characteristics. A random number generator usually selects a variety of storage location combinations, and a program calculates the time to perform dual or single cycles to these selected locations. Because it more closely models the way a system will operate, this type of simulation produces a more accurate result than the MHIA formula. But the MHIA formula is still used to compare "apples to apples" in the early stages of concept comparison.

System Throughput

Overall system throughput is more complex than the simple sum of the S/R machines' performance. Factors affecting overall system performance include control strategies, the configuration of the input/output system, the purpose of the system, and the way in which the system is instructed/scheduled to be used by the operator or the host control system. AS/RS throughput requirements are often overstated, resulting in a system design that is not economically feasible and does not really suit the intended use. Care in estab-lishing accurate material flow rates is important in order to avoid over-specifying the system.

AS/RS rarely operate totally on a dual cycle basis. In fact, a realistic throughput require-ment might state, "the system is required to perform 120 stores per hour combined with 40 retrieves per hour from 7:00 a.m. to 12:00 p.m.; 120 retrieves and 40 stores per hour from 12:00 p.m. to 3:00 p.m.; and 100 stores and 60 retrieves per hour from 3:00 p.m. until 11:30 p.m." This requirement may reflect the actual operation of the facility. Careful consideration of how the system must perform in order to serve the facility is the most important first step in establishing performance requirements that are meaningful and that address the needs of the factory or distribution center (DC).

Input/Output Transportation Systems

The transportation equipment that interfaces with an AS/RS is a function of material size and weight, type of container or pallet and velocity, and distance traveled. They consist of conveyors, shuttle cars, automated guided vehicles (AGV), lift trucks, and push carts (see Figures 15.8a, 15.8b, 15.8c).

The transportation system interfaces with input and output spurs for each aisle of the system. Frequently, a load squaring operation is performed at the point of transfer, and a final positioning operation is performed at the S/R machine pickup point. A commonly used approach is an aisle transfer car that lifts the load from the main transport system and moves it into a queuing position or to the S/R machine pickup station. The S/R machine deposit station operates similarly to the pick-up station.

Load Tracking

A number of methods are used to identify and track loads moving into and out of an AS/RS storage rack. A common procedure is for the Material Handling Execution System (MHES) computer to automatically identify the load by reading a bar code or RFID tag as the load is inducted into the system. Then the MHES precisely tracks the position of the load on the transportation system as it moves, carefully maintaining load separation and "handing off" the load to the S/R machine, which stores it and reports its final location to the MHES.

Sizing and Weigh Stations

A size check to determine that the load conforms to the length and width limitations of the storage rack openings is part of most AS/RS. The height check may be either a simple go-no-go or a measurement to determine into which opening a load can be stored in a structure that supports multiple load heights (see Figure 15.9). The sizing station may also determine whether the load exceeds the

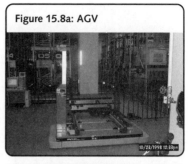

Figure 15.8a: AGV

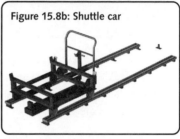

Figure 15.8b: Shuttle car

Figure 15.8c: AS/RS system

Figure 15.9: Sizing station

weight limits of the storage system. A weigh-count station is often used in conjunction with this station to establish inventory counts. When used, a section of conveyor is usually mounted on load cells that are interfaced with the control system. This method is usually used when the inventory consists of a large quantity of relatively small items and the containers have a standard or known tare weight.

AS/RS Work Stations and Ergonomics

Attention must be given to human engineering aspects of work stations. Lifters may be required to bring loads to proper working height; rotation may be required to provide access to all sides of the loads. Auxiliary lifting devices may be required if individual parts weigh more than 25 pounds. Computer screens, keyboards, or control panels need to be convenient and well-lighted to reduce fatigue and human error.

Automatic Guided Vehicles (AGV)

Although AGV system equipment can directly deliver material to the AS/RS pick-up stations and take material from the deposit stations, some conveyorization is usually required to permit load queuing and positioning.

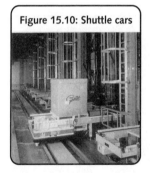

Figure 15.10: Shuttle cars

Shuttle Cars

Shuttle Cars (see Figure 15.10)are an increasingly popular way to move materials to and from an AS/RS system. They may be loop type or reciprocating. They typically operate at higher speeds than AGVs and conveyors, and are more cost-effective than conveyors in some applications. One reason for their popularity is overall application reliability. If a shuttle car is taken out of service for any reason, the remaining cars can continue to service the AS/RS. If the main conveyor across the AS/RS has any failure, the AS/RS is often inaccessible until the problem is resolved.

Specialized Systems for Large Storage Volumes and High Throughput

Double-Deep System

There are several specialized AS/RS configurations for accommodating large quantities of loads. In the double-deep Unit Load system, the S/R machine has a shuttle capable of extending the load into the second-depth storage location. This is generally used where there is a fairly small number of stockkeeping units in proportion to the total number of loads to be stored. The normal control strategy is to put two loads of the same SKU into the double cubicle to minimize the requirement to shuffle loads. (Picking up the front load and restoring it in order to access the rear load.) An overlooked issue with these systems is that vertical density is somewhat reduced (compared with a single deep system) due to the additional space that must be allowed for under each load to accommodate the larger shuttle mechanism (and its inherent deflections) needed to reach a deep load. Typically, a starting point for using a double deep design is if the loads stored to SKU ratio is greater than 9 to 1, but throughput and production lot sequencing requirements will play a larger role in this type of design.

Double Shuttle System

Two shuttles on the S/R machines are sometimes used to improve overall system through-put. Typically no more than 25 percent to 35 percent additional throughput capacity is achieved by adding a second shuttle. This is due to the fact that both shuttles can rarely store or retrieve from adjacent rack openings. Some horizontal transportation time for the S/R machine is saved, but the biggest savings is the ability to pick-up and deposit two loads at a time at the system input/output station.

Deep-Lane System

Deep-lane Unit Load storage (see Figure 15.11) is used when there are very few SKUs but a great quantity of each. A specially designed S/R machine picks up a load from an input station and transports it to the input side of a flow-through rack, which might be 10 loads deep.

Figure 15.11: Deep-lane Unit Load Storage

A similar S/R machine on the output side is used only for retrieving material on the output side. The flow-through lane ensures first-in and first-out, and provides very high-density storage, but its throughput is limited to that of the two S/R machines. A factor if gravity conveyor is to be used for the flow rack portion is the weight and conveyability of the load.

Another type of Unit Load deep lane storage uses more typical drive in rack with devices that leave the S/R machine to transport the load into the deepest position in a lane for storage—often going 10 or more storage positions deep. These systems are usually used where the entire contents of the lane will be of the same SKU, and where production lot issues will not require an adherance to FIFO inventory practices. Some systems have been built to store multiple SKU's in a lane and shuffle the inventory during off shift periods to prepare for a specific output sequence, but the applicability of this technique has been very limited. A typical indicator that this type of system might be appropriate is where the loads stored to SKU ratio is in excess of 20 to 1.

S/R Machine Controls

Positioning Systems

S/R machine positioning is usually done with binary coded plates or code bars mounted on the S/R machine for vertical positioning, and on the rack structure for horizontal positioning. Rotary shaft encoders and optical/laser sensing may also be used in conjunction with the code bars for fine positioning.

Bin Detection Systems

Infra red detectors are commonly used to sense the presence or absence of a load in the rack opening (bin) before the S/R machine is commanded to pick up or deposit a load.

Figure 15.12: End-of-Aisle Controller

10/23/1998 12:34pm

End-of-Aisle Controller

Usually a microprocessor is used as the end-of-aisle controller to manage load input and output for a specific aisle while communicating continuously with the S/R machine (see Figure 15.12). If an MHES computer is on line, the end-of-aisle controller communicates local inventory movements and system status to the host computer. The end-of-aisle controller usually contains a control panel for manually inputting S/R machine commands during maintenance procedures, and it maintains system operating data to assist in recovering from error conditions.

Communications

Messages from the end-of-aisle controller to the S/R machine are commonly sent in one of three different ways:

1. Festoon cable (often used in freezers or hazardous environments)
2. Conductors bars
3. Optical/Infrared

Computer Control System

System Computers

An AS/RS (or MHES) mini computer or micro computer usually maintains system inventory records in real-time as transactions occur. It also directs transactions, such as acceptance of loads into the system or order picking, and it commands the material handling system to move loads to and from storage. The system computer is linked directly to the end-of-aisle controllers and transportation systems controllers. The system computer often functions as a warehouse management system (WMS) with radio frequency (RF) capability directing manual order picking and other material control and warehousing operations **(Figure X5)**.

Network Management
AS/RS computers may communicate by direct serial line to lower level controllers and to the corporate host computer. Local area networks (LANS), using Ethernet are the most common method of communication enabling the system to share common network and information support infrastructures already in place in the facility.

Back Up Systems
Most AS/RS-MHES control systems have on-line backup computers which can be quickly switched on in the rare occasion of a computer failure. The inventory database maintained on disc is backed up by an appropriate on-line subsystem that will insure data preservation in the event of a problem. In the event of a power loss, Uninterruptable Power Supply (UPS) systems are used to provide temporary battery power to the system computers, permitting an orderly shutdown without the loss of data.

Software Design
Design of software for an AS/RS is complex. It requires extremely fast response times to simultaneous events occurring as loads move throughout the system. It must respond to a wide variety of possible error conditions which may affect the integrity of the inventory records. Whenever possible, pre-engineered and fully debugged software code should be used in order to minimize system checkout time.

Computer System Architecture
The architecture of a modern AS/RS computer control system using local area networks at several levels in the control system hierarchy is very imporant.

AS/RS Distribution Applications
Manual Order Picking
AS/RS are widely used for delivering loads to order picking stations (see Figure 15.13). The attractiveness of this application increases when a number of SKUs must be accessible to each operator. The system design must take into consideration the operator dwell time at the pick station to perform various functions such as weigh counting, completing shipping paperwork or packing cartons.

The design objective should be that the S/R machine increases the productivity and accuracy of the picker by eliminating travel and search time and by improving operator ergonomics. A fairly common benchmark of

Figure 15.13: Manual order picking

productivity for picking in totally manual operations is that the picking time constitutes about 17% or less of the order pickers total elapsed time. The balance of that time is spent walking to the item to be picked, transporting it to a packing station, doing packing, paperwork, and replenishment activities. With all other things being equal, using the AS/RS to bring materials to an order picker typically improves the value adding work time (actual picking) to 50% or higher depending on the other functions that must be peformed to complete the pick and distribute the material.

Automatic Order Picking

Full or partial pallet loads and cartons are often shipped directly from an AS/RS. As AS/RS speeds have increased in recent years, this is becoming an increasingly popular application.

Figure 15.14: Robotized picking

Additionally, the push to eliminate non-value adding human labor from the fulfillment process has led to robotized carton picking from pallet loads (see Figure 15.14).

Sortation

Vertical sortation of products is a natural function of an AS/RS. AS/RS offers the advantage of a large number of different SKUs which may be received, queued and released in a new specific sequence when needed to build an order.

Reserve Storage

AS/RS are frequently used for reserve storage in high-volume distribution centers where they replenish flow racks, carousels and other types of order picking systems.

Hybrid Systems

The most common mistake made in planning automation for a new warehouse or distribution center is to try and standardize on one type of system for all storage requirements. Rarely do all materials in a warehouse fit one type of storage or order picking system. Size, weight, incoming load form-factor and product velocity/order profile factors all influence the choice of a technology for storage and support of fulfillment. A starting point is to segregate items by size, function and velocity (or popularity). For example:

For:	Use:
Broken case, high movers	Case Flow Rack
Broken case picking, medium to slow movers	Mini Load AS/RS
Full case picking, high movers	Pallet Flow Rack
Full case picking, medium to slow movers	Unit Load AS/RS
Full Pallet picking and reserve storage to replenish case and broken case picking	Unit Load AS/RS

Freezers and Cold Storage

Because of the high cost of refrigeration, the density of AS/RS makes them attractive for freezer and cold storage applications. Reduced operator productivity in a cold environment is also an important factor in justifying AS/RS.

Manufacturing Applications

Manufacturing AS/RS are used primarily for staging work-in-process materials. A popular application is the receiving and buffering of purchased and fabricated parts in support of assembly operations. AS/RS is attractive because its high density and use of overhead space permits the buffer to be close to assembly stations.

Work-in-process systems may actually be a number of sub systems, each supporting a production cell or functional processing department. For example, a one-aisle system may support a number of machine tools arranged around its periphery. Material is often moved between processing steps by one AGV system or conveyor to another AS/RS module. The concept here is to stage material at or near the next work station where it will be used. In these systems, the AS/RS is really not technically a storage system, but is actually an extension of the work queue for a process step. In some systems the S/R machine directly presents the material to an automatic work station or machine tool. In other cases, the retrieved material may be conveyed a short distance to a station where a robot may pick pieces from specially designed containers to be automatically processed or assembled.

AS/RS systems may be also constructed to serve multi-story factories where they act as a buffer, horizontal transporter and elevator.

Because work-in-process materials in a factory typically spend more than 85 percent of their time in storage, physical management of these materials is increasingly being recognized as a critical factor in speeding up manufacturing cycle time and reducing inventories. Precise, physical inventory management has also become understood as the key to eliminating one of the largest preventible production delays.

Justification of AS/RS Systems

Just-In-Time Manufacturing and Distribution

Prior to the mid-1980s, AS/RS systems were used primarily to automate existing logistics processes and the primary justification factors were space savings, conventional material handling equipment savings, and material handling labor savings. Today there is an increasing realization that AS/RS and their computers are superb tools to re-engineer the way a company does business. Today's just-in-time manufacturing and distribution processes demand extremely high inventory accuracy and near perfect physical control of work-in-process material. Without this accuracy, and without the tightly controlled tolerance on when and how the material can be managed through the process, commitments to a customer are little more than statements of probability on when this requirement will be met. Because of the tight integration of these modern systems, companies do not try to justify the material handling portion of the system separately from the overall production or distribution process. Justification of AS/RS systems then increasingly includes such factors as:

- Reduced order filling cycle time
- Improved efficiency of cellular operations
- Improved customer satisfaction with smaller, more customized shipments and better shipping accuracy
- Fewer late customer deliveries
- Reduced variance within the inventory management process will result in lower inventory costs

Saves Working Capital
AS/RS can, when used to streamline the overall manufacturing or distribution process, reduce inventories, often doubling inventory turns per year. This cuts inventory investment in half and frees up working capital for other purposes.

Enables Production Expansion
Potential AS/RS users often believe they can't support an increase in production or shipping output without a major building expansion. AS/RS can utilize unused overhead space while eliminating the grid lock caused by smaller lot sizes that must move through the facilities more rapidly. AS/RS frequently permit a 50 percent expansion of output with no additional building construction required.

Saves Operating Costs
In addition to material handling labor-savings, AS/RS which are a part of a re-engineered logistics process can save:

- Carrying costs on the reduced inventory investment of at least 20 percent annually.
- Production labor—due to impact of reliable material deliveries.
- Support labor, such as material controllers, production schedulers, expediters and data entry/paper handling personnel.

Future Opportunities for AS/RS
Current factors which will affect the application and popularity of AS/RS are:

- Supply chain simplification to reduce steps, cut lot sizes, and move materials faster.
- The merging of the factory and the warehouse—(manufacturing and distribution) into one facility where semi-finished products are staged and rapidly pulled to the final assembly/order fulfillment station. Here products are "made-to-order" and shipped directly the customer.
- The practice of permitting customers to access their supplier's inventory by way of an Internet connection and automatically placing an order with no human intervention.

- Factory and warehouse workers are becoming material and production controllers with their own computer terminals that enable them to manage the flow of materials to and from their work stations.
- New production and warehousing facilities increasingly are being designed to accommodate efficient material buffering and shorter/faster material flow pipelines. This is reversing the older practice of simply building plenty of space and then letting material flow "just happen."
- DCs are now being planned which function primarily as crossdocking facilities where sorting, temporary buffering and random accessibility to all loads is required.

These trends increasingly are requiring highly reliable, very dense, flexible material buffers of all sizes which operate with speed and real-time accuracy. These are the key attributes of an AS/RS.

CHAPTER 16
Transportation Modes

Gerhardt Muller, Professor, U.S. Merchant Marine Academy, Kings Point, NY

U ntil the past few decades, transportation focused mostly on how cargo was transported and warehoused. Today, and for the foreseeable future, larger issues, such as new and emerging transportation and communication technologies, have greater influence on transportation. This has changed world trading patterns and deregulation nationally and worldwide.

Transportation can either involve a single mode or two or more modes. Examples of modes include water, air, rail, and highway. The transfer of commodities or goods between two modes is called an intermodal transfer. Although not the focus of this chapter, pipelines are also an important mode for large volumes of liquid and gas products such as oil, water, and natural gas. In certain cases, products that move through the pipeline can be considered as being warehoused until they arrive at the final destination.

Rail Transportation

In the United States, railroads that transport cargo are privately owned common carriers and must serve the general public. In most other places in the world, railroads are owned by national governments, although European railroads are now in the process of being privatized.

The railroad industry is usually grouped by size. The largest of these are Class I railroads, sometimes known as line-haul railroads, which have at least $254 million in operating revenues (Class II railroads are those that have revenues between Class I and $20 million, and Class III railroads are those with operating revenues of less than $20 million). In the areas where the line-haul carrier either does not have local access or does not operate, short-line railroads perform local distribution of rail freight and local or short-line railroad companies provide switching and terminal services, although line-haul carriers also provide these services

Fixed Right-of-Way Nationwide Network

Right-of-way restricts other railroads from using the same line, especially on lines that stretch over large distances or are in geographic areas that limit the number of rail carriers. In cases where products carried by competitors need to travel on these lines, the railroad that owns those lines would enter interline agreements. Simultaneously, the owner of that fixed-right-of-way was (and continues to be) burdened with heavy costs that include maintenance and taxes. At this time, however, no railroad has a complete nationwide network of lines that spans the country from east-to-west or north-to-south, although interline agreements do exist to perform such services.

Carrying Capacity

Most railroads have a standard fleet of rail cars. These include:

- Plain and equipped boxcars (an equipped boxcar is a modified boxcar for specialized merchandise, such as automobile parts)
- Automobile carriers
- Open and covered hopper cars that discharge bulk commodities from the bottom of the car
- Flatcars that carry trailers-on-flat-cars (TOFCs) and containers
- Refrigerator cars for commodities that require controlled temperatures
- Gondola cars with no top, a flat bottom, and fixed sides
- Tank cars for liquid cargoes, such as petroleum and petroleum products, chemicals, and occasionally even wines and other food stocks
- Double-stack cars, which have emerged with the growth of intermodalism to carry containers one on top of each other

With so many car types, the railroads can transport large-volume movements of low-value commodities over long distances at competitive rates and services. This type of carload capacity, along with a variety of equipment and car types, allows the railroads to handle almost any type of commodity, especially bulk commodities like ores, coal, grains, and now unit trains of containers and TOFCs.

Also, railroads have the unit train, which evolved from the rent-a-train concept for the movement of goods and specializes in the transport of only one commodity—usually coal, grain or containers—from origin to destination. Often, the shipper owns the cars, and the train is, in effect, rented to the particular shipper for a certain time or line. With intermodalism, double-stack unit trains could have as many as 150 cars, carrying 300 containers of different sizes. These trains often stretch one mile or more in length.

Fixed vs. Variable Costs

Railroads have a higher level of fixed costs than variable costs. Fixed costs are incurred generally no matter what the traffic volume might be, and include ownership of real estate, taxes, etc. Variable costs, on the other hand, vary or change with the volume of traffic. For example, more cargo would require more cars, locomotives, and fuel. Less demand requires more flexible or variable operations.

Labor

Until the last decade, labor was often more than half the operating expense of the railroad industry. This was especially true in cases where the number of crewmembers on each train exceeded the capability and efficiency of the technology being used. This affected the cost of owning and operating rolling stock, locomotives and communications systems. With deregulation, much of the railroad industry's labor force was eliminated, despite the sometimes-strong objections of unions. It has been argued by railroad management that flexible work rules have enabled carriers to be more competitive with other modes serving the same markets.

Fuel

Although the second largest operating expense of the railroads is fuel costs, on average, fuel costs are now around twelve percent of total operating costs and improving all the time. This is because diesel and electro-locomotives have almost entirely replaced steam locomotives, and they are more fuel-efficient than their steam counterparts, which were the workhorses until the mid-1950s. Today, steam locomotives are mainly found in museums and on short-lines that offer special tour excursions.

Service

The railroad cost structure makes it necessary to attract higher and regular volumes of traffic to take advantage of its economy of scale. In recent years, rail management has developed several service innovations to increase traffic volume such as bridge systems and increased line-haul of automobiles and trailers.

The idea of piggyback service as designed by the railroads was to increase the service levels to intermodal customers. Piggyback, which includes both TOFC and COFC (container-on-flat-car) has grown substantially in the past few decades to the point where, especially since deregulation, it ranks second behind coal in total car loadings.

TOFC

TOFC service transports highway trailers on railroad flatcars. It combines the line-haul efficiencies of railroads with the flexibility of local highway pickup and delivery service. On-time deliveries, regularly scheduled departures, and fuel efficiency of the railroads versus all-highway are the major reasons for the continued growth of TOFC service.

There are many standard TOFC plans, each providing coordinated intermodal transportation services. The trailers or tractors could be either rail-highway-shipper or consignee-owned. For example, with Plan I, a railroad hauls the trailers of a highway common carrier while the highway carrier handles the ramp-to-door service at both ends. With Plan II, the railroad transports and provides door-to-door service for its own trailers. Under Plan II 1/2, the railroad provides trailers, flatcars, and rail transportation while the shipper and consignee arrange highway pickup and delivery from the ramps. Plan II 1/2 is the most widely used. By one account, there are about fourteen such plans in operation, the number of which could rise and fall based on market service alternatives of the railroad.

COFC

Container-on-flat-car, better known as COFC, is the international form of transportation of containers by rail. It is the equivalent to domestic TOFC movements. A container, minus its chassis, is placed on a flatbed rail car after it arrives at a container yard from either the shipper or container vessel. A variation of this is where two containers are placed on top of each other, a method known as double-stack.

Domestic Containerization

Building on the concept of COFC and double-stack operations is the use of ocean containers for the transportation of domestic cargos. This is often the case when containers returning to their point of origin, say for example the Far East, could be used to carry domestic cargo if there was no cargo for that container going to the Far East. At some destination on the West Coast, the container is stripped or unloaded. The empty container, if not loaded with export cargo, is then hauled by a highway carrier to the container terminal of the steamship carrier to continue its journey to the Far East.

Alternatively, ocean containers are becoming an important factor in the domestic transportation of cargo by keeping the container in domestic service only. The advantages of on-line railroad container handling equipment for international container operations provide another cost-efficient service for domestic shippers. Domestic containers also have the added advantage of being of lighter weight (they do not have to support more than one loaded container above it for double-stack operations) and could be either smaller or larger than the standard International Standards Organization (ISO) container, which is principally used for ocean transportation.

Rail Technology

EDI and the Internet

Other forms of emerging technological advances applicable to the railroad industry include electronic data interchange (EDI) and the Internet. The need for faster, more efficient and cost effective transportation to serve the customer better requires up-to-date information for planning, booking, issuing of bills of lading, coordination and tracking of the cargo, and paying for the transportation service.

EDI was originally developed to improve the location of rail cars along the line to improve coordination of both cargo and equipment. Rapid advances in EDI extended that service by allowing both the customer and the railroad to coordinate each shipment more efficiently, and all other services that belong with the shipment.

Today, the growing acceptance of Internet services provided by the railroads has enabled shippers, often in cooperation with Intermodal Marketing Companies (IMCs), to arrange for the rail transportation of containers and trailers much like users of integrated carriers like UPS and FedEx would for small packages. This form of transportation procurement is growing in popularity as the technologies and user-friendly systems become more efficient and user-friendly.

Advanced Train Control Systems

To improve overall railroad performance, railroads, especially the line-haul carriers, are developing advanced train control systems. These systems help the coordination of rolling stock and locomotives, improve safety standards, and plan more efficient operations to accommodate seasonal cargo flows. These systems enable rail carriers to maximize the use of their assets at a level that was not possible before.

Rail Yards

Another area of tremendous improvement has been the design and operation of rail yards. This applies to both the loading/unloading of cargo and intermodal shipments, and the making up and breaking down of line haul and unit trains. Some of the more recent yards constructed are considered to be the latest examples of state-of-the-art rail yard operations anywhere.

Rolling Equipment

Equal attention has been given to the advances in rolling stock, especially in the area of improved maintenance and reducing accidents. Some of the more high-tech equipment, such as container cars and variations thereof, are very expensive. Time out for frequent repairs is costly and a drain on the bottom line.

Current Rail Issues

Mega Carriers

The railroad industry is not immune to the tremendous changes in the number of players involved. As a direct result of the wave of bankruptcies and mergers that took place because of deregulation and the ravages of economic downturns, line-haul carriers have decreased to the point where less than six such operators are still in business. Although the pace of bankruptcies and mergers has slowed in the past few years, it is reasonable to assume that head-to-head competition in the railroad industry will see the formation of mega carriers that could eventually span the nation from coast-to-coast. That could include rail lines that follow the north and south route as well. Furthermore, with the reorganization taking place with the railroads in Canada, Canadian lines could play an increasing role in the United States' railroad industry.

Vertical Integration

Recognition must also be given to the formation of railroad operations that embrace other modes and their ancillary services. For example, CSX is a railroad that owns the domestic containership line that was formerly part of SeaLand Services, and other services such as intermodal/third party logistics services. Many railroads have found that to compete, especially in high-value added services, control or entering service partnerships with other modes and ancillary services is a requirement for survival.

Highway

The transportation of intercity freight by highway carriers did not start until about 1900. Not until after World War I, however, did the industry become important as a major carrier of cargo between cities. Until then, the industry was mostly small firms and operators restricted to local and regional delivery. Today, approximately four-fifths of this nation's transportation bill—local and long haul—is attributable to the trucking industry.

The growth of intercity truck transportation was supported by technological improvements such as the pneumatic tire, more efficient engines and mechanical systems, and better roads because of increased use of passenger automobiles. Economically, the trucking industry grew because of: the decline in competitive railroad service, especially after World War II; the completion and continued upgrading of the National System of Interstate and Defense Highways, which is almost complete after almost five decades of construction; ease of access to remote areas; and deregulation of transportation in the early 1980s. That influence, however, is being challenged again today by the growth in domestic containers and trailer-on-flat-car (TOFC) service by the railroads for long haul (more than 500 to 700 miles) traffic.

The highway trucking industry makes use of an extensive road and street system that is approximately 3.9 million miles of roads and streets in the United States. Of that amount, 42,000 miles are part of the interstate and defense highway system, which was designed to connect major cities with four-lane limited access roads.

Highway Carriers

Types of Carriers

Private vs. For-hire

The private carrier provides a service to the shipper that owns or leases the vehicles and, thus does not charge a fee. The for-hire carrier charges a fee for providing service to the public.

Private carriers may transport exempt commodities for-hire, but when operating in such a capacity, the private carrier is really an exempt for-hire carrier.

Local vs. Inter-city

For-hire carriers are either local or intercity operators. As local carriers they pick up and deliver interstate freight within what is commonly called a commercial zone of a city or region as defined by the Surface Transportation Board (STB), which replaced in 1996 the Interstate Commerce Commission (ICC).

Common vs. Contract

Common carriers are required to serve the general public when the need to do so is there, at reasonable rates, and without discrimination. Contract carriers, on the other hand, serve specific shippers with whom the carriers have a contract and are therefore, not available for carrying freight for the general public.

Exempt

These for-hire carriers are specifically exempt from economic regulation by the STB. This gives them freedom from economic regulatory control by the type of commodity hauled (agricultural, lumber, etc.) or by the nature of its operation such as ancillary service to the air and ocean transportation industry. Rates charged and services provided and the numbers of vehicles used are determined strictly by market supply and demand.

Service Characteristics

Accessibility

Because almost every economic activity is accessible to highways, even in some of the remotest parts of the country, the highway carrier enjoys the best accessibility of all the modes. This is especially true in cases where transportation is limited to pick up and delivery with other modes.

Speed or Transit Time

For shipments under 500 miles, the truck can usually deliver the freight in less time than other modes. Other modes, although faster, are restricted by less frequent schedules and limited access.

Small Carrying Capacity

Trucks are often greatly disadvantaged by the total weight of the cargo and the vehicle (which is in most states no more than 80,000 pounds) and dimensions (13.5 feet high and 96"/106" wide) established by state and local highway departments. On the other hand, the smaller shipping size of the motor carrier provides the buyer and seller with the benefits of lower inventory levels and inventory carrying costs.

Safety

Although highway accidents do occur, the general result in the past decade is that through stricter law enforcement of weight limitations, speed control, vehicle safety inspections, and licensing of drivers who must adhere to strict working hours and restrictive drug and alcohol requirements, the safety of highway transportation is improving. This also affects less damage to the cargo that in turn reduces the need for excessive packaging requirements and costs.

Flexibility

Trucks have the advantage that they can be loaded and be on their way faster than most of the other modes. With rail and barge, for example, larger volumes of cargo or numbers of vehicles must be loaded before the actual transportation of the cargo can begin. Simultaneously, the number of highways or lanes trucks have available provide for faster and more efficient alternative routes when competitive pressures of shippers require this form of service.

Frequency

Because of smaller shipments, trucks can provide the shipper with more frequent shipments that can reduce inventory for the consignee, thus reducing total supply chain costs overall.

Cost Structure

Approximately 90 percent of the costs of the motor carrier industry is variable, and ten percent is fixed. Motor carriers are able to increase or decrease the number of vehicles used in short periods of time and in small increments of capacity. Most terminals, because of the short stay of the cargo, are relatively inexpensive to construct and maintain. Fixed costs are largely associated with purchasing and operating fleets and on the public side, the investment in the highway system.

Generally speaking, operating expenses, and six cents to cover interest costs and return to investors consume 94 cents of every operating dollar.

Economies of Scale

Certain economies of scale exist in the use of terminals, management specialists, and more recently, information systems. This is especially true for carriers that operate over larger geographic areas. Lower operating costs are usually a part of truck load (TL) or over the road operations, especially if there is a return load. For shorter distances and less than truck load (LTL) operations, frequent stops add to the overall cost of operation, especially in high cost areas such as some larger metropolitan regions.

Equipment and Operations

There are several types of vehicles including:

Dry van:	Standard trailer or straight truck with all sides closed, although the end of the vehicle is accessible with one or two doors. These are the most common types of vehicles.
Open top:	Top of trailer is open to allow cargo to be lifted in and out of the vehicle vertically.
Flat bed:	Trailer with flat bed or floor and no sides or top.
Tank trailer:	Haul liquids such as petroleum, liquid chemicals and waste material in liquid form.
Refrigerated:	Cargo units that provide controlled temperatures and environments.
High cube:	Trailers that have a larger than normal internal and external size, restricted only by highway safety and statutory limitations.
Special:	Special design to accommodate unique cargoes such as automobiles, heavy lifts such as machinery, and certain types of gases under heavy pressure.

Line Haul

Line haul trucks are used to haul freight long distances between shippers and consignees. The vehicle involved is typically a tractor-trailer combination of three or more axles. State regulations determine the carrying capacity and size limitations of the vehicles, a factor that often frustrates carriers when hauling cargo between states that differ in the regulations. Longer trailers that are 45, 48 and now 53 feet in length are gradually replacing standard 40-foot units. In recent years, the 53-foot unit appears to be gaining larger acceptance by carriers because of their larger cubic carrying capacity that are usually applicable to semi- and full-assembled and products.

City

Normally smaller and lighter than the line haul vehicle, city trucks are usually one self-contained unit, meaning that the truck and driver only move when the cargo is ready. These trucks are generally 20 to 25 feet in length, although small trailers 20 to 28 feet long are often used to pick up and deliver freight in inner city areas where larger truck restrictions are in force.

Terminals

Pickup and Delivery

Pickup and delivery terminals are used mainly by LTL carriers where cargo is often consolidated into larger line haul vehicles. These facilities are often located in an array of spokes that expand out from a central terminal or hub. Line-haul vehicles then travel between the hubs.

Relay/Team Driving

Under DOT and STB regulations and enforcement, drivers are permitted to drive a minimum of ten hours after eight consecutive hours off duty. At the relay terminal, one driver substitutes for another who has accumulated the minimum hours of service. (The term "slip-seat" is often used to describe this relay procedure.)

An alternative to the relay terminal is the use of a sleeper team—two drivers. While one driver drives, the other sleeps in a specially furnished bunk behind the cab. These teams have been most effective where trips are long and have many destinations, and where truck loads must reach the consignee as quickly as possible.

Types of Commodities Carried

The motor carrier industry concentrates mostly on semi-finished and finished products that move distances less than several hundred miles. Beyond that, rail transportation, especially as part of intermodal movements of trailers and containers, becomes more economical. Commodities such as live stock, food, and at an increasing rate of growth the waste industry, move by highway because of lack of alternative competitive modes and rates, and the faster and more frequent type of service that the trucking industry can provide.

Market Orientation

One of the industry's greatest advantages is that it is flexible enough to respond relatively quickly to rapid changes in the market. The smaller size of most of the carriers, especially for-hire, allows customers to receive personalized attention when and where needed. Although cost and price differences between carrier and shipper often cause sharp differences of opinion, especially when the issue of the quality of service expected and received is included in the discussion, shippers today are beginning to have a stronger bargaining position, especially in areas where the competition between carriers is intense.

Capital

The LTL segment of the industry has higher capital requirements because it must invest in terminals and freight-handling equipment that is, in most cases, not needed by the TL carrier (TL carriers usually carry cargo directly between shipper and consignee without an intermediary terminal). At the same time, special equipment carriers, such as refrigerated and heavy-lift carriers, often have larger investments than conventional freight carriers.

Rate Structures

Since deregulation, the rate structure of the motor carrier industry has been influenced mainly by several major forces of the market, namely, supply, demand, and cost of service. Before deregulation, interstate and intrastate rates were set by government regulations and/or agencies.

LTL (Less-Than-Truck Load)

LTL rates are usually much higher than TL rates because of the additional cost of handling different shipments for different customers on the same truck. Part of that rate also is allocated for the additional cost of the LTL freight terminals where individual shipments are consolidated and later broken down for further transportation to the customer.

TL (Truck Load)

TL rates reflect the economies of scale associated with almost door-to-door service for the customer. That service does not have to provide additional handling of cargo once the cargo is loaded on the truck.

Contract

Contract rates are negotiated between one or more carriers with one or more shippers for specified shipments. These specifications consider guaranteed volumes, frequency, schedules, and other factors that meet the competitive cost factors of both shippers and carriers over a relatively long period of time, including several years. The guaranteed nature of the contract allows all parties involved to better project expenses and other business variables.

Technology

Existing and emerging technologies in the trucking industry are reaching a new stage where major advances in hardware are not necessarily revolutionary as they were for the past few decades. This is not to discount the advances being made in truck operational safety and increasing fuel efficiency caused by improved body and engine design. Alternatively, the greatest leaps forward, at least in the next decade, will most likely take place in some of the software, especially communications, used by the industry to increase competitive positions.

EDI and Internet

Electronic data interchange (EDI) helps carriers and shippers track shipments throughout the movement process. EDI provides shipment status information to customers by mainframe computers, personal computers, cellular telephones, and now satellite communication and position systems. With satellite communications, not only can the company trace the exact location and perhaps route of each truck, but also cargo manifests, traffic congestion, etc., can be transmitted rapidly to one or more central offices.

Similar systems are also able to transmit information on the operating characteristics of the vehicle itself, including speed, engine performance, tire pressure, etc. Although all of this technology is expensive, the savings in the cost of actual operations, time and improvement of service to the customer, will make it cost efficient.

Like with the other modes, Internet access by shippers and suppliers of parts and services to the trucking industry is becoming a common occurrence. This allows more efficient business practices within the trucking industry but smaller carriers are not always as well equipped to handle Internet communications as the larger companies. Also, rate negotiations are often a matter that requires person-to-person communications because of strong competition between the carriers, regardless of size.

Intermodal Compatibility

Intermodalism, especially that part of the transportation and logistics management industry that involves the increased use of containers and trailers for exclusively domestic use, is becoming an important part of the trucking industry. For containers, this is especially true as double-stack service increases nationwide as the railroads make clearance improvements along their rights of way to accommodate the higher double-stack trains. At the same time, piggyback or TOFC movements could either be replaced by the double-stack operation, or, where the railroads cannot economically make improvements for double-stack operations, will encourage greater use of trailer carrying capacity because of the cost efficiencies associated with rail versus all truck operations.

Labor: Union vs. Non-union

Local and over-the-road trucking industry was until deregulation, heavily influenced by the rules established by strong unions. Usually, the industry was saddled with heavy expenses that were detrimental to its competitive position with the other modes especially rail. Since deregulation, however, the bargaining power of the unions has weakened, and in some cases, been eliminated completely. For the foreseeable future, union or non-union representation will depend on the degree of flexibility that labor and management needs for the carrier to remain in business in an ever-increasing competitive marketplace.

Water Transportation

Water transportation takes advantage of the water highways built both by nature and man. Ever since man discovered the carrying capacity of water, transportation by water has served as one of the more important means of transporting cargo and passengers.

Despite the emergence of other modes such as rail and highway, water transportation continues to be the main form of transportation, especially for bulk commodities.

Internationally, water transportation still continues to be the main form of transportation, more so for cargo than passengers. The exception, of course, is the growing popularity of cruise ships that sail from both domestic and foreign ports.

Difference Between Domestic and International

Domestic water transportation consists of all water movements where the origin and destination of the shipment is in one country. Shipments that have a foreign country as either the origin or destination are classified as international shipping.

Domestic

Domestic water transportation usually consists of three different types of service: Inland, Coastal and Intercoastal, and Great Lakes.

Inland: Inland water transportation operates over the internal network of navigable waterways such as the Mississippi, Ohio, Missouri, Tennessee, Columbia, and Hudson Rivers and other smaller arteries. Very often locks are used to compensate for areas where there is a rapid fall in height or where dams were constructed to control water levels, especially as a result of heavy rainfalls or melting of snow. These locks often restrict the length and width of vessels that use them and, as a result have an influence on volumes per vessel. Locks also are points of traffic congestion, especially if a large number of vessel movements meet at those locks at the same time and the rate of movement through them is slow.

Large bay systems such as the Delaware and Chesapeake Bays also have viable inland water transportation systems, although some of that traffic is usually connected with coastal and international transportation of cargo.

The vessels used include barges and towboats, mainly because of shallow draft restrictions. Inland water carriers dominate the north-south traffic through the central portion of the United States via the Mississippi, Missouri, and Ohio Rivers. On the West Coast, most of the navigable rivers flow in an east-to-west direction while on the East Coast; there is mixture of the two prime directions.

Coastal and Intercoastal: Coastal carriers operate along the coasts serving ports on the Atlantic or Pacific Oceans or the Gulf of Mexico. Intercoastal freight transported between East Coast and West Coast ports is in most cases via the Panama Canal. Although both use ocean-going vessels, there are some operations that use ocean-going barges, some of which have a capacity of 18,000 tons or more. The majority of the freight transported includes petroleum, both crude and refined, lumber, and bulk products such as coal and grains. The main routes are between ports along the Atlantic and the Gulf of Mexico. Oil from Alaska moves via coastal tankers to refineries along the Pacific coast.

Coastal and intercoastal operations are restricted to American flag vessels only. This regulation goes back to the earliest days of this nation's history when it was believed that, to protect American fleet operations, foreign vessels were restricted from carrying cargo and passengers between American ports. Although under constant review and discussion, the provisions of the Jones Act, the legislation which established this regulation, is still in force today. (In Europe, coastal trades are open to European Union member nation's maritime carriers—other flag carriers have to deal with more restrictive practices.)

Intercoastal water transportation used to be, before the advent of faster rail transportation, one of the primary forms of shipping cargo and passengers between coasts. The route used was via the southern tip of South America and then, later through the Panama Canal after it was opened in the early part of the century. Today, very little of intercoastal transportation is available, except for bulk shipments and in special incidences where there are disruptions in service by other modes such as the railroads because of labor unrest, etc.

Great Lakes: Often referred to as the fourth coast, the Great Lakes carriers operate along the northeastern portion of the United States and provide service between ports on the five Great Lakes that border the states of New York, Pennsylvania, Ohio, Michigan, Indiana, Illinois, Wisconsin, and Minnesota. The lake ships normally remain on the lakes, but access to Atlantic and Gulf ports is possible via the St. Lawrence Seaway. This Great Lakes-to-United States Atlantic traffic is classified as a coastal operation.

International

Despite the inroads that air transportation has made in moving high-value, low-volume cargos, the overwhelming portion (more than 90%) of international cargo still moves by water. Cargos shipped include general, bulk and neo-bulk.

In the past three decades, tremendous changes have taken place, primarily in the form of streamlining the flow of cargo through terminals and on ships. Whereas not too long ago bulk and breakbulk cargos were loaded and discharged at a relatively slower pace, modern cargo handling systems and the use of larger ships have altered international water transportation to the point where the ship is considered by many as only part of the total systems approach to transportation. Before, water transportation was often considered the main and most important of the transportation process around which everything else took second place.

Water Industry Overview

Bulk and Neo-Bulk

The major attraction of water transportation is that it is a low-cost service. Pipelines, when available as an alternative form of transportation, are still the lowest cost of transportation for liquid petroleum products. When liquid cargoes are transported by vessel, parcel tankers—vessels that carry more than one particular type of petroleum product—are considered as neo-bulk carriers. Crude petroleum is carried as a single product and is therefore considered a bulk movement.

Bulk/Unit Loads

Cargo is shipped either as bulk or in unit loads. Bulk commodities such as liquids (petroleum and petroleum products) account for the largest percent of total tonnage of domestic water commerce. Dry bulk commodities transported by water carriers are basic raw materials such as coal and coke, sand, gravel, stone, iron ore, grains, logs, lumber, waste and scrap, pulp and paper products, and if as a single vessel, automobiles. On an average ton basis, the cost to ship bulk commodities is less than other types of cargoes.

Unit loads are usually products that are finished or semi-finished. They usually come in smaller packages, which in turn are both loaded on pallets and shipped as breakbulk cargo, or in containers as containerized cargo. The cost to transport unit types of cargos is usually more expensive per ton than bulk cargos, although the actual cost is based on either a weight, volume or value basis.

Private vs. For-Hire

As with the other modes, the water transportation industry is broken down into different categories depending on whom the main customer is. Private carriers transport cargo only for the owner of the ship and cargo. In this case, bulk movements are the primary type of cargo carried by private carriers. For-hire carriers make themselves available to customers on a common carrier basis. They usually limit themselves to cargos other than bulk, but on occasion several bulk cargos can be carried on the same vessel for different shippers based on the cargo handling capabilities of the vessel and the needs of the shippers. In all cases, vessel schedules and operations meet the specific needs of the shippers or consignees and are therefore more flexible.

Common Carriers

Common carriers are mostly involved with transporting general and sometimes neo-bulk cargos. The services offered are usually on liner operations, meaning that they serve a fixed route on a published fixed schedule.

Charter or Contract Carriers

These carriers offer services to one or more parties for a particular voyage and/or time period. Although most charters are associated with bulk and neo-bulk cargos, liner operators charter vessels to compensate for gaps in fleet vessel availability. This often happens when there are surges in cargo demand or when vessels are out of service for repairs or are still being constructed. Oil companies are usually the largest charters, followed by dry bulk shippers of grains and ores. More recently, containership carriers often go on the charter market to compensate for anticipated surges in container shipments when existing fleet capacity is not available. The US military also uses chartered vessels to better manage its naval and military supply needs, especially in times of national emergencies such as the Gulf War.

Flags of Convenience

This is a situation where a ship owner registers a ship in a foreign country that offers conveniences or less restrictive requirements in the areas of taxes, manning, and safety requirements. Liberia and Panama are two of the largest nations known for flags of convenience.

Conferences and Alliances

Conferences are associations, sanctioned under American law and other international agreements that allow ocean carriers to coordinate rates, schedules and related operational practices to minimize cutthroat competition on very competitive trade routes. More recently, however, and because of changes in American maritime regulations (The Merchant Marine Act of 1984 and the Ocean Shipping Reform Act of 1998), container carriers dealing with the US have formed alliances to take better advantage of market and assets conditions. This has led to slot chartering between alliance members to maximize vessel capacity and other equipment exchange agreements.

Carriers

Vessel Sharing, Operational and Marketing Agreements

Although the number of American flag carriers has declined sharply in the past few decades, most of those still in operation continue to operate under the concept of rationalization. As discussed above, these agreements often come under the heading of alliances. Carriers such as SeaLand and American President Lines have entered into vessel sharing agreements with a number of foreign flag carriers, many of which are direct competitors on the same trade routes. Oversupply of vessel space and stiff rate competition usually results in unprofitable operations. Vessel sharing and other forms of space and marketing agreements are shared between the carriers. In some cases, these agreements have had some obvious benefits.

Alternatively, it sometimes happens that other operational factors such as terminal operations and priorities, and land transportation systems such as railroads involved with the bridge systems, cause scheduling conflicts between the carriers. This is especially true when delays in vessel arrivals, because of weather conditions and other mechanical breakdowns onboard the ship or on shore, have an impact on the respective lines' operations. This is especially critical when operations call for very close tolerances in scheduling and service demands.

NVOCCs

With the changes taking place in container steamship operations, many ocean carriers no longer wanted to become involved with more costly handling of less-than-container-load cargos. This gave rise to the growth of freight forwarders called Non Vessel Owned Common Carriers or NVOCCs. NVOCCs consolidate less-than-container-load cargos and load or stuff them in single containers. These containers are then transported to containership carriers. In return, the carriers offer the NVOCCs lower or volume rates.

The NOVCC makes a profit between the rate it charges the shipper and the rate the carrier charges the NOVCC.

Types of Vessels
Barges

Perhaps the simplest form of water transportation is a barge, which are either towed or pushed by powerful tugboats. Inland river towing operations can sometimes consist of as much as 20 barges (1,000-1,500 tons capacity or the equivalent of 15 rail cars or 60 trucks for each barge) on certain rivers such as the Mississippi and Ohio. Ocean-going barge systems are usually limited to one or two barges capable of carrying several thousand tons of cargo each. This cargo can either be bulk or in general cargo form such as container or roll-on-roll-off. Usually these operations are limited to coastal and inter-island routes using tugs that travel about 10 knots.

Tankers

Tankers carry liquid cargos such as crude oil and petroleum products. In some cases, specially designed tankers transport acids in corrosion-resistant tanks and liquefied natural gases, the latter of which are usually stored on board in very low temperature cryogenic tanks.

Some tankers, especially those that travel on large volume trade routes like the Middle East to Europe, are as big as a skyscraper. These vessels, often classified as VLCCs (Very Large Crude Carriers) and ULCCs (Ultra Large Crude Carriers) are limited to a relatively small number of ports because of their deep drafts (the distance from the keel to the waterline), some of which exceed over 100 feet. Where deep draft ports are not available, these super-sized vessels must offload into smaller tankers or permanent or floating offshore terminals.

Bulk and Neo-bulk Carriers

Bulk and neo-bulk carriers are like tankers except they carry dry bulk cargos only. Typical cargos include ores, grains, and construction aggregates. Some bulk cargos like iron ore, require specially designed cargo holding areas below deck to compensate for the extra heavy weights of these cargos. Bulk and neo-bulk carriers are smaller than VLCCs and ULCCs, mainly because the volumes carried are usually in smaller lots and require direct access to shoreside terminals. This results from more complex cargo handling equipment involved, and typically shallower channels where these shoreside facilities are located.

Breakbulk Carriers

Breakbulk carriers transport general cargo in smaller units, which must be loaded and discharged on an individual basis, usually on pallets. (Pallets are small wooden platforms about 4'x 4' and capable of receiving the fork of a fork lift vehicle to move them around on the pier and on the ship.) Up until the advent of the containership, breakbulk ships were the dominant form of water transportation for general cargo, stowing the cargo below in cargo holds and sometimes on deck. Breakbulk ships are especially useful for oversized cargos such as railroad rolling stock and locomotives.

These vessels are also labor intensive for cargo loading and unloading operations, often using 100 or more laborers on the vessel, pier and terminal area. Most breakbulk operations today are usually found in parts of the world where more efficient container handling facilities have not yet been constructed or are in limited supply.

Containerships

Containerships carry containers either below decks in so-called cells, or on deck where they are strapped down with lashing gear or other forms of securing mechanisms. The concept of containerization has been around for more than 200 years, but not until the mid-1950s did it start to develop into a major form of water transportation. On average, container ships carry about 2,000-4,000 twenty-foot equivalent units (TEUs), which, if placed end-to-end, would stretch more than six to ten miles. The cargo carrying capacity of a 2,000 TEU vessel could be as much as 20,000 tons of cargo, three to four times the carrying capacity of a typical breakbulk cargo. Because of these larger carrying capacities and the economies of scale associated with containership operations, containerships are gradually replacing breakbulk vessels on most trade routes. On major trade routes such as the North Atlantic and North Pacific, containerships are basically the only type of vessel for general cargo.

Containerships carry containers in various sizes (20, 40, 45, 48, etc.) Some container vessels are also built to carry roll-on-roll off vehicles below deck.

Ro/Ro Vessels

These vessels resemble large ferries capable of handling vehicles, which move on and off the vessel on wheels. They are especially useful on trade routes where heavy machinery and large vehicles cannot be handled by conventional ships, or in some cases, regular containerships.

Special Carriers

Additionally, these are special purpose vessels that accommodate activities that are unique to certain trade routes. This would include passenger vessels, auto carriers which can carry as many as 5,000 smaller-sized cars, offshore oil rig supply vessels, and cable-laying vessels which are becoming increasingly important as international communications rely more on underwater cables versus satellite systems. Combination vessels usually combine different types of cargos such as breakbulk and container.

Service Characteristics

Low-cost Service

Low-cost service is the major advantage of water transportation, especially for non-liquid products. (For liquid petroleum products, the pipeline is the lowest cost form of transportation, but the two forms of transportation are often not in competition with each other on most trade routes.)

Slow Speed

Transit time of water transportation is the longest (slowest speed) of all the modes that move commodities. Time is generally measured in days compared to hours for highway and air. At the same time, however, slow speed is more than compensated for because of the generally lower overall transportation cost of water transportation versus the other modes, with the exception of pipeline for liquid cargos.

Service Disruption

Winter months, periods of drought when rivers are low, siltation of navigable channels and berths, and blocking of channels because of marine accidents are some of the major disruptions that slow down, if not totally disrupt, vessel-related transportation. This is especially true on waterways that have limited access.

Vessel Size and Accessibility

Vessels must have deep enough navigable channels to reach marine terminals safely. This is not a problem for some ports because of natural geological development (Seattle, Tacoma for example). Other ports like Boston, New York and Oakland, although channel entrances from the ocean might be relatively deep, still need channels to be deepened to allow vessels to reach the terminals further up stream and along piers. The cost for dredging is becoming more expensive and environmental concerns or restrictions are also becoming a critical factor in the decision to dredge or not dredge, thus impacting the ability of a channel and port to remain competitive as vessels become larger and have deeper drafts.

Accessibility is also a factor in having a marine terminal close or even adjacent to rail and highway transportation. If other surface transportation modes are not that accessible, additional cost must be accounted for in the full development and operation of the terminal.

Cost Structure

High Variable Costs

Like motor and air carriers, water carriers do not provide their own rights of way, unless the navigable channel they use is for their own exclusive use. In these cases, carriers must pay for the construction and maintenance of that channel.

On the other hand, carriers pay user charges such as marine fuel tax surcharges, lock fees, wharfage (a charge assessed against the cargo for each ton or other measurement of cargo moved across the wharf) and dockage (a charge assessed against the vessel based on length of vessel and other criteria—which can be considered as a parking fee) for use of either government or private development provided facilities. These variable costs fluctuate based on the type and volume of the vessel.

Low Fixed Costs

Fixed costs include depreciation, amortization, and general expenses. General expenses usually exceed depreciation and amortization by a two-to-one margin.

Capital Intensive

Because vessel-related operations, with either the vessel itself or on shore, are tied increasingly to the factors of faster time with increased efficiency, investment in the water transportation industry is becoming capital intensive. That trend will continue as the demand for increased automation becomes the standard rather than the exception. Some of the larger containerships today cost as much as $100 million each, compared to the $20 million and less for earlier mid-and larger-sized breakbulk vessels.

Ports and Terminals

Warehousing and Distribution Management

Ports, especially niche ports, have recognized, especially in the past few years, that the port and its services are important to the concept of the systems approach to transportation, warehousing and logistics management, all of which are part of supply chain management. Consequently, some ports have actively embraced sophisticated electronic communications systems that tie shippers together with other port and transportation-related services. This includes forwarders, carriers, warehouse and logistics management facilitators, government agencies such as customs, etc. The goal is to streamline working relationships without having to depend on what seems to be an ever-increasing amount of paperwork.

One of the potential solutions to this information transmission problem is electronic data interchange systems (EDI) and the Internet. Port authorities play advocacy or direct roles in making sure that these types of services are available to as many participants of the transportation and logistics process.

Bridges

Bridge systems replace routes and ports of the traditional all-water system.

The principal mode of transportation across the land is the railroad, especially for containerized and dry bulk cargos. For liquid cargos like petroleum, pipelines usually are the most efficient mode. As a result, other ports and coastlines that formerly were not part of the trade route replace traditional ports that might have been the main gateways along certain coastlines. Furthermore, the time and cost of taking these bridge systems is usually faster and cheaper than the more traditional all-water routes.

There are three principle bridge systems: Land bridge, mini-bridge, and micro-bridge.

1. Land-bridge: This is where containerized cargo moving, say for example from Tokyo to Rotterdam, is transported by ship to a West Coast port like Seattle, then carried by rail to an East Coast port like Baltimore, and then reloaded aboard another vessel for the voyage to Rotterdam. This land-bridge system replaces the traditional all-ocean route via either the Panama or Suez Canal.

2. Mini-bridge: Cargo moving, for example between Tokyo and Baltimore, is transported by ship to a West Coast port like Seattle, and then moved by rail to Baltimore. In the process, ports on the East Coast—in this case it would be Baltimore—are deprived of that cargo moving across their own piers. That marine terminal activity, and all of the economic issues associated with it, would instead be gained by one of the West Coast ports.

3. Micro-bridge: Starting again, for example from Tokyo, cargo destined for inland cities like Denver, would move by container vessel to Seattle, then by rail to Denver. Formerly, the Tokyo-Denver trade route would have passed through, for example, the Panama Canal and then on to New Orleans. At New Orleans, the cargo is transferred to a barge, rail or truck or a combination of modes, to Denver. Again, as was the case with Baltimore and mini-bridge, the traditional port gateway—in this case it was a Gulf port of New Orleans—are bypassed with the resultant loss of marine terminal activity.

Alternative Modes and Trade Routes

There are also signs that once dominant routes and systems that have lost favor to the bridge systems are finding renewed interest. Some of them include:

Air-Sea

Alternative modes and trade routes appear, disappear and then reappear again because of fast changes in globalization of products and the growing flexibility of transportation systems. Examples include the replacement of all-ocean or all-air routes for certain commodities by using a combination of the two modes known as air-sea. Cargoes moving by air-sea are usually those that take advantage of the cost savings of the all-sea route that is slower, but pay a slightly higher price based on the faster service of the all-air service. Examples of such cargos are apparel starting somewhere along the Pacific Rim to a destination along the East Coast of the United States. Cargo moves by ship to Seattle where it is transferred to an airplane for the flight to New York. Such cargos might not need to be on store shelves for several weeks, but at the same time, could not afford to wait for the longer sea route and time because of market-demand pressures.

Ro/Ro and Container Barges

With better cost efficiencies associated with ocean-going barge operations on certain trade routes like the Caribbean, larger and more expensive general cargo ships like container, breakbulk and ro/ro are finding new markets for their services.

Reemergence of the Major Canals

There is also a growing interest in reestablishing the all-water route of using the Suez Canal as an alternative to land-and mini-bridge operations between the Far East and Europe and the United States. This is becoming a critical factor as the center of activity shifts from the northeastern part of Asia to Southeast Asia, thus making the route to the East Coast via the Suez shorter than the via the Pacific mini-bridge/Panama Canal route.

Mega Carriers

Deregulation, among other factors, has caused the largely tradition-bound water transportation industry to change faster than might have been the case otherwise. The result is that, after mergers, buy outs, transfer to foreign flags, and bankruptcies, the number of carriers still in the game has dwindled to the point where there are only a few players on each of the major trade routes. Except for the occasional niche carrier (automobiles, lumber and paper products, etc.) players in this new competitive environment have to be considered mega or giant companies that have the financial, operational and global-reach resources to compete with each other on a direct head-to-head basis. Those that cannot match the strengths of the mega carriers most often than not fall to the way side or must seek niche markets in which they have a competitive edge. Or they can become part of one of the alliances, which very often are dominated by the larger carriers.

Vertically Integrated Services

Vertically integrated carriers like SeaLand Services and American President Lines (APL) have either been or have absorbed other modal carriers and services in the other modes. (The international operations of SeaLand Services and the entire seagoing part of APL have been sold to foreign carriers during the latter part of the 1990s.) This was found necessary to provide their customers with what is commonly called a seamless transportation and logistics management system. Most often, these carriers are in the so-called mega carrier category because the resources to become fully vertically integrated require deep pockets and a worldwide network of services.

Intermodalism

Intermodalism is usually defined as the capability of interchange of freight, especially in containers, among the various transportation modes. The fact that the containers are of the same size in terms of width but vary in length up to 53 feet, and have common handling characteristics, permits them to be transferred from truck-to-railroad-to-air carrier-to-ocean carrier, in a complete origin-to-destination movement without once disturbing the cargo.

Transportation Only vs. Full Service

Traditional transportation of cargo, regardless of the commodity, destination, and the modes and carriers involved, concentrated mostly on the actual movement (transportation) of the cargo, and how and where it was warehoused between movements. Contracts for each of the services were usually negotiated separately.

Full service transportation, however, moves closer to what is better known as logistics or supply chain management. In this case, the transportation and warehousing/distribution (warehousing if needed; containerization is often referred to as warehousing on wheels) are joined with a higher service level of inventory control and partial value-enhancement of the product before it moves on to the customer. Certain carriers and ports like APL and Seattle have expanded their services to include this full service concept, especially as production methods become increasingly important in meeting customer needs at a more economical and efficient manner.

Handling of Goods

Cargo, regardless if it is general or in bulk, requires different handling equipment. Loose, non-containerized cargo is mostly labor intensive, relying on the use of forklifts and conveyor belts to move it from one place to the next. This process can often be made easier if the cargo is placed on pallets.

Containerized cargo, because it is unitized in a single container, moves as a single unit weighing as much as 35 tons depending on the size of the container and the allowable weights of the modes involved. Containers are loaded on and off different modes by a variety of lifting technologies. This includes container cranes, which are usually located on marine container terminals; straddle carriers, which straddle, pick up and then move the container before moving it to another location; and large forklift trucks that are usually the larger cousin of the warehouse forklift.

Dry bulk commodities, like coal, grains and ores, depend on large scoops and gravity feed shoots and loading mechanisms. Liquid cargos such as petroleum and liquefied natural gas are loaded and unloaded by pipeline.

Types of Containers

Ocean containers come in all kinds of sizes, shapes and carrying capacities. Under the International Standards Organization (ISO) classification system, ocean containers are measured in 20-foot lengths (TEUs) and are either 20- or 40-feet in length. Other container sizes used include 10-, 24-, 30-, 35- and more recently 45-, 48-, and 53-foot sizes. Most containers are 8' 6" in height. High cube containers are usually 9' 6" in height. Except for special cases, almost all containers are 8-ft wide. Nearly nine out of 10 containers are made of steel, with the remaining containers either aluminum or special materials.

The standard 20-foot/40-foot closed-top dry freight container is the most popular in use and accounts for more than half of all the containers. The remaining group of container types is mostly open-top, integral reefer, and flatrack and platform types. Other containers handle strictly liquid cargoes like concentrated fruit juices, acids and chemical products. Today, as improvements are made in minimizing damage due to condensation, some containers are built to handle bulk commodities such as coffee, raw rubber, and grains.

Labor

Automation of cargo transportation, especially containerization, is capital intensive. In most cases, capitalization reduces the amount of labor used at considerable cost savings.

With traditional breakbulk operations, several hundred laborers were used to offload and load a ship (this is especially true in parts of the world were local labor laws restrict the use of automated equipment). The time required could be as long as one or two weeks. Today, with the automation of containerization, the number of laborers needed to handle the equivalent of three to four times the amount of cargo of the more traditional cargo ship, is often less than 10 to 20 percent. The time needed to do is often as little as 24 hours.

Whereas breakbulk operations relied heavily on human muscle, container operations, except for some terminal processing operations on the pier, utilize specialized skills that take time and effort to develop. This is especially true for such specialists such as container crane operators who load and unload as much as 35 tons in one lift at speeds that could average 25-35 containers per hour.

Technology

Refinement

The technology of ocean transportation has reached the point where major breakthroughs in size and speed will be incremental at best for at least the next decade. It is true that some proposals have been made to use high-speed vessels that have the capability to move between the East Coast of the US and Europe in three and a half days, at least half of what it takes today. These specialized vessels will carry as many as 700 units. But, these vessels will most likely be the exception and will have customers who need to move their cargos faster than a conventional vessel but not at the higher expense of an all-air movement.

Instead, we will most likely see vessels that will have improved propulsion systems that use more efficient fuel mixtures and other refinements of the power plant. At the terminal, cargo will move faster on and off the vessel including container, bulk and liquid. Also, advanced navigation systems will increase safety of navigation at sea and in port. In recent years, new standards for training and watch keeping have been established at the international level, including the United States, that are designed to improve the professional standards of shipboard personal in terms of vessel navigation and operations.

Improve Flow of Activity

The biggest breakthroughs, however, will most likely come in moving the cargo through the terminal, including in some cases warehouses, faster and more efficiently. This will involve closer coordination between each phase of operation on the terminal and what takes place before and after the cargo arrives at the terminal. One version might include what is commonly called the seamless terminal, where containers discharged from a vessel will be pre-cleared by customs and then move directly through the gate without having to be placed on the terminal first. The same holds true for inbound containers. The goal will be to reduce as much as possible the time cargo remains on the terminal. This will require closer cooperation between shipper, carrier, third party services such as freight forwarders, custom house brokers, etc., and government agencies such as Customs Service, Department of Agriculture, etc.

Communications

The key, or perhaps it could be said, the glue that will bind all of these activities together is communications. With the use of faster and more powerful computers and electronic date interchange (EDI), and now the Internet, information will flow through the transportation system faster, more accurately, and with less cost. By comparison, with the evolutionary state of containerization and where it is today, it could be said that the communications revolution is still in its infancy where most of the players involved are still learning to crawl before they can walk.

Labor

Similar to other economic activities, labor will be one of the most affected due to the coming changes in transportation and supply chain management. One obvious result is that machines and automation will continue to replace most of the manual tasks involved with moving passengers and goods to, through, and out of the terminal.

At the same time, there is the continued strain between union and non-unionized work forces on and off the ship and terminal. In the United States, the larger carriers and ports still have unions. However, because of the acceptance of technological advances, combined with the recession of 1990-1992, and in some cases better labor/management relationships, there have been fewer strikes or other labor disruptions. Other parts of the globe are witnessing a similar pattern, except in countries where economic activities are still in the process of shifting from central management to one of market forces.

Skilled vs. Low or Semi-Skilled

At the same time, as it has often been said in the media and on the shop floor, skilled jobs are replacing un-skilled and in some cases semi-skilled jobs. On some of the more modern vessels today, licensed officers and certified crew-members are required to handle more operational and monitoring technology, often across several disciplines. Some ocean carriers require their officers to have dual deck and engine licenses, given that many of the engine control systems are located on the bridge of the ship in addition to the engine room.

Although this shift from muscle to brains is having a profound, perhaps permanent, impact on the number of jobs lost, many carriers, terminal operators and unions have joined forces to develop training or retraining programs that meet the technological needs of the industry as it exists today, and the shape that it will take in the future. Some carriers and terminal operators, especially in Europe and Japan, have taken the extra step of involving ship and terminal staff to be part of the technological development process right from the start. Although a full evaluation of that process is still underway, it can be argued that in most cases, this form of cooperation between management and labor has lessened the fear of technology by both management and labor. Furthermore, this dialogue has gained certain inputs that could have been missed had that input not been available.

Safety

Vessel collisions, groundings and sinkings, as well as accidents on the terminal, have always taken place. Today, however, because of faster and larger amounts of information that can be gathered, analyzed and disseminated, as well as better training, the frequency, scale and magnitude of these accidents seem to have a larger impact than what might have been known about them several decades ago. As a result, the risk to life, property and the environment receives closer attention to preventing those accidents from happening in the first place. As mentioned above, new regulations for improved standards for watch keeping and training are becoming part of international maritime scene.

This is especially true with greater use of more accurate vessel positioning technology based on advanced terrestrial and satellite navigation systems. Some of these systems have the capability of locating the position of a vessel to within several feet of its actual position.

Other improved safety measures benefit from more efficient design of vessels and shoreside equipment, and better training in all phases of operations management.

Current Issues

Drug and Alcohol Abuse

Investigation of water transportation-related accidents have seen increased incidence where the abuse of drug and alcohol were major contributors. To deal with this problem, federal agencies, like the U.S. Coast Guard and other substance abuse agencies, have instituted and followed up closely on very strict rules affecting these substances. It is more often than not that loss of job and potential banishment from the transportation industry is the penalty if found guilty. At the same time, companies and government agencies have started extensive substance abuse counseling programs designed to prevent, rather than punish, potential abusers from starting.

Air Transportation

On December 17, 1903, Orville Wright left the ground from the sand dunes of Kitty Hawk, North Carolina. As he drifted into the air, he was the pilot of what was to become the world's first controllable powered flight. That first flight covered 120 feet.

Commercial Jet Air Transportation

Perhaps one of the most dramatic breakthroughs in air transportation was the introduction of the jet plane in the late 1950s to the late 1960s. Not only did it fly faster and further than conventional propeller-driven aircraft, but its payload also increased several fold per flight. Right behind the jet came the realization that airport authorities must prepare for and construct larger airports to handle the increased volumes and sometimes frequency of passengers and cargo that these planes could handle.

With the start of jet airplanes, the air transportation industry changed dramatically almost overnight. And, for the first time, air cargo became an important player in generating revenue for carriers. Although the air transportation industry is very dependent on passenger revenues to maintain its financial viability, on average about 14 percent of operating revenues that combination passenger and cargo carriers receive, comes from cargo.

Aviation Industry

The aviation industry, as part of the larger aerospace industry, includes all the activities involved with building and flying aircraft.

Despite national and international interruptions such as downturns in the economy and the impact of military activity on transportation in general, the expectation is that aviation worldwide should grow between 4-9 percent annually. In the United States the greatest increase will most likely come from air cargo, most of which is in small packages like those handled by UPS, FedEx and others, and as businesses become more informed and take advantage of advanced logistics management concepts to serve their customers better. In Europe, in contrast with the phenomenal double-digit growth in the Far East and to a certain extent South America, aviation increases are expected to be less. Alternative competing transportation systems and closer distances between major centers of economic activity have slowed down the growth potential of the industry.

Carriers

Major

Major carriers in the United States are usually those that generate more than $1 billion or more in annual revenues. Such carriers also provide services between major population areas within the United States and with other countries. Most of the larger routes served are usually highly sensitive to price competition—especially since deregulation went into affect in the early 1980s—and use mostly large-capacity planes for longer routes that often stretch across the continent. Because of the need to increase, if not control market share, many of these airlines also serve medium-size population centers such Cleveland and New Orleans.

National

National carriers usually operate scheduled services on relatively shorter distances (Cleveland and Chicago) and in other cases large, regional areas (Cleveland and Washington). Many of these carriers are also stiff competition for the major carriers on many routes between less-populated areas and major population centers, using smaller planes. Generally speaking, these carriers usually have annual revenues between $75 million and $1 billion.

Regional and Local

These carriers operate within a particular region of the country such as the southwest corner of the United States or New England, and connect lesser-populated areas with larger population centers. These carriers are usually grouped into two categories: large ($10-$75 million) and medium (less than $10 million.) For competitive purposes, many of the major carriers, like American, own or have agreements with these smaller carriers to act as feeders.

International

Because of deregulation at both the domestic and international level, many U.S. carriers are also international carriers. They operate between the continental United States and foreign countries and between the United States and its territories. The Office of the President of the United States is usually involved in determining which carriers, both American and foreign, will be given new or expanded routes. Selection of carriers is often based on both economic and political issues, especially on routes that have the potential to generate large numbers of passengers and cargo over the years. Examples include Europe and the Far East, especially China.

Charter

Although charter carriers use the same type and size planes as national and international carriers to carry passengers and freight, they operate without fixed schedules or designated routes. They charter the entire plane to a group or companies between specified origins and destinations at agreed-to prices, schedules and other terms of limitation. In return, the customer gets a lower price for that service in place of scheduled cargo or combination air carrier.

Many of the large domestic and international air carriers are restricted to international agreements, which limit them to specific routes. To take advantage of occasional charter arrangements, many of these same carriers created charter subsidiaries. In this way, and perhaps softened somewhat by bi-lateral restrictions between the two countries involved, carriers can cover a larger range of services which are competitive with the charter market.

Small Package and Overnight Express

Since deregulation, one of the fastest growth areas in aviation has been in the small package and overnight express business. Companies such as Federal Express and United Parcel Service specialize in a service that is in most cases in direct competition with the postal services of this and other countries. They can do this because of logistical operations that start at the point where the package is picked up (usually at the shipper's own premises or central collecting points) to the final destination of the recipient. The fee for this service is usually several times what postal services might charge. In return, however, it is usually faster (overnight or two or three days later for international shipments) and more reliable.

Types of Aircraft and Service Equipment

Wide-Body vs. Short Hauls

Aircraft are usually classified by size (regular or wide-body) and short haul versus long haul. Economics and the concept of hub and spoke operations have sharply changed the role of plane sizes in the transportation of passengers and cargo. For shorter distances, or where take offs and landings are more frequent, air carriers use smaller planes like the Boeing 737. For longer distances, especially transcontinental and across the ocean, the economics favor larger wide-body planes. Although the cost of the wide-body plane is higher initially (as much as $165 million each), the cost of operation per seat-mile or cargo-mile is considerably less.

Service Characteristics

Air Transportation

Air transportation in general is usually considered to be scheduled and on fixed routes, and, therefore, categorized as common carriers of passengers and cargo. This includes most of the airline companies regardless of size and the markets they serve.

General Aviation

General aviation, on the other hand, usually serves private owners—usually corporations—use smaller aircraft and fly on a demand basis. General aviation also includes smaller pleasure aircraft.

Speed

The single most important characteristic of aviation is speed; covering larger distances in a shorter period of time when compared to alternative modes. This is especially important in today's need to move passengers and cargo almost overnight to practically any part of the world. For shorter distances, modes such as high-speed rail are strong competitors of the aviation industry. This is especially in high population density parts of the world like Europe and Japan, where large population centers are relatively close.

Flight Frequency

In addition to speed, many carriers compete on frequency of service between locations. The larger carriers, especially some of the mega carriers like American, United Airlines and Delta, have competed effectively against smaller, and in some cases, emerging airlines. Larger carriers have larger fleets and services that the smaller carriers cannot match on the same terms of competition.

Accessibility

The aviation industry also faces the growing realization that carriers, whether flying to large population centers like Los Angeles or Houston, or less dense areas like Salt Lake City, are limited by the number of airports that each of these population centers have available. On the ground, intermodal accessibly to and from the airport is another growing challenge that local communities that support their airport industries are striving to improve. Airports that offer their passengers and customers reliable transportation to and from the airport find that such services are sometimes just as important as the airplane service at the airport itself.

High Value/Low Volume

Due to the high cost of aviation service to both passengers and cargo, service is usually limited to high value/low volume clients. This, as a result, results in transporting passengers that find that the cost of transportation might be expensive, but in the total scheme of logistics/supply chain management for both passengers and cargo, time is sometimes more valuable. This is especially true when the need to arrive at a certain destination is one of the key factors to conduct important meetings or to meet manufacturing and assembly schedules that are based on tight schedules and have very little room for error.

Cost Structure

Air carriers, like motor carriers, have a cost structure that is based on high variables and low fixed costs. Approximately 80 percent of the total operating costs is variable and 20 percent is fixed. This is attributable to government investments and operation of airports and airways. The carriers pay for the use of these facilities through landing fees, which are also variable in terms of the size and weight of the aircraft and, in some cases, the number of passengers and cargo on board.

Maintenance

Maintenance of both aircraft and ground facilities also includes administration. The cost of this can reach as much as 22 percent of total operating expenses, and as a result, is subject to some of the more stringent cost reduction efforts by both carriers and airports. However, with increased pressure on reliability of service, many carriers and airports find that too many restrictions and cutbacks in maintenance could result in the loss of customers. With increased use of better materials, more efficient operations and closer attention to what the customer demands, the aviation industry has made tremendous strides in this area.

Commissions

Commissions are fees paid to travel agents and air cargo forwarders by carriers who book flights. Air cargo agents receive a percentage of the air cargo bill issued on behalf of the carrier. This commission, usually much less than ten percent of the tariff, is deducted from the air fare that the carrier charges. Many air cargo carriers continue to rely on air freight forwarders especially in cases where niche cargos and other special circumstances require the time and effort that air cargo forwarders offer, and the air carrier cannot match because of usually higher overhead expenses. More recently, air carriers, in an effort to further reduce costs, have turned to the Internet as a direct means to offer and sell air cargo service. A good example on the freight side is the Internet sites of UPS and FedEx, where shippers can book, track and pay for overnight delivery of packages.

Fuel and Labor Costs

Perhaps one of the largest cost categories that air carriers must support is in fuel and labor. In the United States, it is generally stated that for every increase of one cent in the cost of fuel, the overall cost to the industry is about $100 million. This is especially important in making the decision of what kind of aircraft to use. On average, a 747 uses about 3,300 gallons of fuel per hour while in the air, while a smaller 727 uses 1,300 gallons per hour. On the other hand, the cost per unit (passenger or cargo weight) is smaller for the larger plane than the smaller aircraft if the load factor is high enough to at least break even. Labor costs, especially since deregulation, have also received closer attention by the carriers, many of which have turned to non-union labor where this is possible because of generally lower wages and benefits needed to support that labor.

Plane Size

Plane size depends on many factors including the route being served, the number and volume of the payload (passengers and cargo) and the market being served. The largest commercial aircraft are typically the MD-11s and Boeing 747, the latter of which can carry as much as 100 tons of cargo for distances greater than 3,000 miles. Smaller aircraft, although still large, come closer in the range of carrying half that of the larger aircraft carrier, and usually specialize on routes that are much shorter and perhaps more frequent.

Routes

Air carriers specialize on routes that they are best equipped to handle. National and international carriers usually have the equipment (planes, airport facilities, etc.) to serve routes that are longer and perhaps greater in volume. They also use hub and spoke systems that allow them to take advantage of the benefits that these systems offer. Smaller local and regional carriers usually serve shorter and perhaps specialized markets such as overnight courier and small package services. Because of the competitive issues that developed from domestic and now international air transportation, many carriers are finding that they need to rationalize their route systems in cooperation with other carriers (thus the formation of alliances and so-called code sharing), thereby offering easier schedules and other services at a lower cost to the passenger and cargo.

Load Factor

Air carriers strive to maximize the load factor for each type of aircraft used on each route served by the carrier. Typically, the break-even load factor is about 60-70 percent, depending on the type of plane being used and the route. However, many carriers find that even higher load factors might not sufficiently cover all costs on particular routes, such as on the North Atlantic and cross continental, because not serving that particular market could mean the loss of customers on other routes that connect with the main route and which are usually more profitable.

Equipment Substitution

Cost of operations and competition often require carriers to switch equipment, and in some cases schedules, when the demand of the service fluctuates, often seasonally. Thus, some of the mega carriers, because of the larger range of plane types in their fleets, have the ability to switch planes to accommodate the market. Other carriers, especially regional and specialized carriers (limited niche markets such as automobile parts) might find that their operational costs do not allow them to be that flexible to allow for easy substitution, thus placing increased pressure on operational budgets.

Communications

Perhaps one area that has seen the greatest advancement in the aviation in the last decade is in communications, especially the Internet. Customers today demand faster and more accurate schedule and cost of service information to meet their own intense competitive pressures. Computers and more efficient transfer of electronic data has allowed carriers, their customers, and freight forwarders, to assess the range of services and costs available to determine the best carrier to use. Systems developed by some of the carriers, some of which have joined forces in providing this type of service, find that the key of profitable operations depend on such technology. At the same time, carriers which use these advanced communication systems are able to apply the concept of yield management to change, almost on a minute's notice, the price and schedule of a particular service as market conditions change. Communications is now also being used to book cargo faster and more accurately, but also in the case of international transportation, clear cargo through customs even before the plane lands at the foreign destination.

Airports

Most airports are developed and operated by public agencies as part of the public transportation infrastructure. Airports usually are designed and operated to accompany both passenger and cargo operations, although a few are almost exclusively cargo. Operational procedures dealing with the safe operation of the planes on the ground follow the directions and sometimes the control of government agencies, such as the Federal Aviation Administration. Other functions such as immigration, handling of food, especially imported, and clearance of passengers and cargo are the responsibilities of other agencies.

User Fees

To help pay for development, operation and maintenance, airports usually charge user fees. These user fees could include a charge for landing and take off of aircraft, usually on a set charge per weight classification (i.e., per 1,000 pounds), use of plane gates and other ramp areas where passengers and cargo are handled on and off the aircraft, passenger waiting areas, surcharges on fuel and other services, etc. Other user fees are charged to services that passengers require such as car rentals, food and other convenience stores, restaurants, etc. Cargo areas that are usually located away from the main passenger terminal area are leased to air cargo carriers and/or airfreight forwarders.

Competition

Service vs. Price

Up until perhaps the past few years, the most important issue in deciding the carrier to be selected for the transportation of passengers and cargo was price. Price, after all, was what mattered in establishing the final cost to the customer for the shipment of passengers and goods over a particular trade route.

However, as competition gained, largely as deregulation let its impact fall where it had the most impact, the issue that was beginning to receive more attention was service: service that the customer demanded or else go somewhere else. This is especially true when applied to the systems approach to transportation including logistics/supply chain management. Air transportation is one of the more costly forms of transportation, but when matched against other factors such as inventory, security, and the cost of capital among others, air transportation offers an competitive alternative.

Low Profit Margins

Open competition, primarily through deregulation and expanding markets for the services that air transportation can best provide, has placed additional strains on already stretched operations and cost structures. Low return on investment, especially investment needed to replace technologically obsolete equipment and systems, separated carriers from those who where successful in making the change from those that eventually dropped out. Deregulation made entry into the air transportation market easy, but deregulation also made the road to failure faster, and in most cases, assured if profitability was not maintained. This is particularly evident in times when there is a downturn in the economy and the resultant pressure on profits and the need to cut costs.

Mega Carrier vs. Niche

One of the direct results of deregulation, especially after the so-called fare wars, was the rise of the mega carriers. These carriers represented the winners in the almost winner-take-all sweepstakes on most of the more heavily traveled transcontinental and international routes. All other carriers, on the other hand, had to either merge, sell-out or leave the route and/or business of air transportation completely.

At the same time, there were a number of smaller carriers that were still able to offer some type of services, sometimes on the same route, but at a much smaller scale. These carriers identified and satisfied a niche in the market that the larger carriers could not fill because their overhead and other operational requirements precluded them for competing head-to-head with these smaller niche carriers.

Advanced Technologies

Advanced aerotechnologies and similar technological advances on the ground (passenger and baggage handling, faster and more efficient cargo handling, refueling, etc.) contributed greatly to lowering the unit cost of air transportation operations. Larger planes using more efficient engines resulted in lowering the unit cost of moving cargo and passengers on longer trips and in faster time. Smaller planes, especially those that have more efficient payload space and overall lower operating costs due to engine and plane design, reduced the cost of flying shorter distances. Advanced technologies increased the reliability of operations for longer periods of time, including actual flight time, thus removing the need for costly down time of the aircraft. In some cases, the need for backup equipment and planes was also reduced if not eliminated entirely.

Lower Unit Costs

Where technological advances did not compromise minimum safety regulations, either by regulation or the carrier itself, crews in the cockpit were reduced from three (captain or pilot, co-pilot, and flight engineer) to two (the flight engineer gave way to the computer).

Several decades earlier, with the gradual acceptance of the reliability of both on-board and on the ground navigation guidance systems, the navigator also lost his position.

Today, modern computers have made it possible for the plane to almost fly itself from the moment of take off to final landing. It might be said that the cockpit crew is only along for the ride. Although this is said in jest, the experience of qualified crews will in all likelihood still be needed in cases of emergency where the logic of human thought and reasoning still remains unchallenged.

Likewise, communications both on the aircraft and on the ground have reached new levels of sophistication that ensure that the information being transmitted is reliable, faster and more useful to make quick decisions when necessary.

Growing Importance of Air-Sea

Commonly referred to as the transfer of cargo between air and ocean carriers, air-sea cargo is part of the intermodal chain that takes advantage of speed and cost efficiencies of each of the modes. Such transfers usually take place without benefit of the same surface-based intermodal container because of the incompatibility of modal container characteristics (sea containers are, because of the nature of the business, heavier and stronger than air containers).

The types of cargo that usually travel by air-sea are mostly higher-value, smaller-volume consumer electronics, automated office equipment, and high-technology parts that are less time-sensitive than other airfreight. For the moment, most of these shipments travel between the Far East and Europe, although the South American/North American/European block of nations are growing on an annual basis.

Labor

Stiff competition within the air transportation industry has had a major toll on labor. Since deregulation, the American air transportation industry has actually gained jobs, most of which were on the ground. Managements were forced to seek cost economies with labor (much of which was usually union) because labor still represented sometimes more than half of the operational and administrative costs. In some cases where bankruptcies and other redistribution of air transportation related functions were massive in scale of the people employed, the consequences of lost jobs, careers and the impact on lives was Draconian. Alternatively, some of the mega carriers added employees to provide the kinds of services that expanded operations required. Many of these new jobs were often filled by non-union labor or by establishing what is commonly called tiered labor where newer employees were paid at substantially lower wages and benefits than those who might be working along side them and had longer seniority with the carrier.

Skills

The high technology nature of today's, and for that matter, the future operations call for higher levels of skills. At the root of those skills is the need for training and retraining, especially as more sophisticated communication and operational equipment is brought on line.

Current Transportation Issues

Safety

The one area where carriers and their customers cannot compromise cost is safety. The added pressure of moving larger amounts of passengers and cargo more efficiently often seeks compromises in how long a piece of equipment can go before the need of replacement or maintenance is required. Nevertheless, both labor and management realize that if the perception is there, a carrier develops a reputation for unsafe operations, some of which might include plane crashes or other forms of accidents on the ground, and the paying customers will turn elsewhere, even if it means that the cost to do so is higher.

Low Profits

All of these improvements are placing added pressure for carriers and airports to pay for them. These improvements are often costly and efforts are made by all parties to have the other players pay for them. Meanwhile, the paying customer is constantly on the lookout for lower transportation alternatives if those costs are passed on to them.

Mega Carriers

One of the few players to successfully deal with all of these new constraints on cost and the need to increase efficiency are the mega carriers. Not only are the mega carriers looking to cut costs at the airport, but also in developing innovative ways of sharing costs with other mega carriers, and in some cases, with niche carriers by coordinating schedules, sharing marketing costs, and in some cases sharing equipment through the concept of rationalization.

Emerging Trends

Changing trading patterns, technological advances, deregulation, and spreading adoption of computerization and electronic communications are fueling progress in transportation and logistics/supply chain management. The history of transportation has shown that changes in these influences sometimes require a fairly long period for commercial, financial, legal and social acceptance. Advances in transportation, and more recently in logistics management, have shown that what progress made is often part of a dynamic, lurching process.

Strategic Issues

Central to those changes are several important issues. Some of the more notable include:

Economic

Rapid changes in the world's trading patterns, something often referred to as globalization, will create new opportunities for carriers and terminal operators of all the modes to develop new business opportunities that might not have existed a few years earlier.

Ports that once served manufacturing hinterlands like the Midwest, now find that most of the cargo traffic has shifted from bulk and semi-bulk to one of finished and semi-finished products that are more efficiently handled in containers. For these ports, massive investments in capital container handling facilities are required to at least maintain a credible market share of that traffic.

Meanwhile, other transportation centers which find it difficult, if not impossible, to play a central role in transportation then they once did, must look for alternative uses for once active modal and intermodal facilities. San Diego did. At the dawn of containerization, the Port of San Diego realized that the shifts in economic trading patterns and expanded use of containers to move those cargos could no longer support the traditional water and rail transportation services of that port city. A tough decision was made which upon retrospect could be considered a success today. Where large terminal facilities once dotted the city's waterfront, mixed use recreational, residential and small commercial activities today contribute to the social and economic well being of that city. Other transportation centers and ports are now making the same decisions, sometimes reluctantly.

Social and Demographic

Shifts in economic centers of activity that take place within nations and now more often among nations themselves, affect the social and demographic growth and sometimes decline of regions. These shifts place considerable strain on the existing infrastructure. Major transportation centers like Los Angeles and Long Beach are stretching economic, environmental and limited land resources to accommodate the expanded growth of cargo, which continues to pass across their marine, rail and highway terminals and access routes. On the other hand, once prosperous ports like Philadelphia, which once served the social and industrial heart land of this country, now find that many of their transportation facilities are underutilized, and alternative uses for these properties must be found.

Energy

The cost of energy is still a major concern for carriers of all modes in determining the most efficient equipment to use and routes to be served. Now, however, the growing concern of energy's impact on the environment has forced both the carriers and the communities in which they operate to reevaluate the need to remain competitive versus the need to preserve the environment. The answer perhaps lies somewhere between the two points of view.

Governments and Deregulation

Governments in most parts of the globe have started deregulating many of their economic activities, most notably transportation. The United States was the first of the larger countries to fully embrace deregulation across the transportation field. The process has been painful in many cases, but basically it has made its role in the utilization of emerging technologies a leader. Other nations, and now trading blocks like the European Union, have placed close attention to the lessons learned from the American experience with deregulation. These lessons will also serve as the basis for other experiments in deregulation now taking place in Latin America and parts of the Far East.

It should be cautioned here, however, that regardless of how far deregulation has gone, there are still elements of regulation that remain. This is particularly true with safety. It can be argued that regulation dealing with safety in the transportation industry has become perhaps more restrictive than was the case a decade ago.

Mega Carriers and Niche Players

Deregulation of the transportation industry nationally and internationally has spawned the growth of mega carriers that face each other in head-to-head competition. This form of battle will affect each of the modes. Meanwhile, there will be many parts of the field of competition that are better served by niche players. Niche players will fill the needs of the transportation customer that the mega carriers are not willing or even capable of serving.

Human Resources

Any discussion about changes expected to take place in transportation would be incomplete without at least some mention of the roles played by technical operators and decision makers who operate and control the various activities involved. Until recently, each operation of any transportation system had its usual cadre of skilled and semi-skilled operators. In some cases, this still remains the primary method of operation, especially in large multi-layered companies that stretch across several modes and functions.

Now, however, there is the slow but visible realization that the systems approach to providing a service no longer allows for specialists to remain isolated from the rest of the system or organization. Intermodalism, as opposed to intramodal transportation, is more dependent on personnel who are informed about many different operations, sometimes affecting more than one mode. This is critical to most sectors of the industry, where being flexible is crucial to accommodate fast changes in business activity and patterns.

To some extent, the challenge of improving the caliber of personnel in transportation and logistics management is being met through formal organizational and college-level education programs and professional seminars. But this will only be part of the solution. What also is needed is a period in the early stages of training when the individual person gains actual field experience in all operations contributing to overall operations. The Europeans and the Japanese have known this for a long time.

Bibliography

Transportation in America, Eno Foundation for Transportation, Washington, DC (annual reports)

Coyle, Bardi, Novak, *Transportation, 5th Edition*, South-Western Publishing Company, 2000.

Coyle, Bardi, and Langly, *The Management of Business Logistics, 6th Edition*, Minneapolis/St.Paul, West Publishing Company, 1996.

Muller, Gerhardt, *Intermodal Freight Transportation, 4th Edition*, Eno Transportation Foundation, Washington, D.C., Virginia, 1999

Stock and Lambert, *Strategic Logistics Management*, 2nd Edition, Homeward, Illinois, Richard D. Irwin, 1987

Journal of Commerce, Recent Editions

Wells, Alexander, *Air Transportation: A Management Perspective* 2nd Edition, Belmont, California, Wadsworth Publishing Company, 1989.

CHAPTER 17
Private Fleet

R. Patrick White, CTP, WhiteTrans Solutions, Inc.
Joe B. Hanna, Ph.D., Auburn University

A private fleet is a fleet that provides transportation services to its own company.[1] For example, Wal-Mart Inc. utilizes a private fleet operation to provide transportation from retail distribution centers to retail stores. Some firms operate their own fleet, and others choose to hire outside carriers or use a combination of the two. Due primarily to the lower barriers to entry and the limited capital requirements necessary to run a motor carrier operation (relative to the other modes of transportation), many private fleets are comprised of trucks. However, private fleets do exist for the other modes of transportation.

A private fleet provides control, but it also subjects an organization to all of the management challenges encountered in operating a carrier, such as backhauls, lane imbalances, driver turnover, pallet return, container utilization, rail car repositioning, and more. The decision to use private fleet often hinges on accessibility to specialized equipment and the need for tight control over delivery. If an immediate and unexpected need arises, the transportation manager can redirect the fleet to meet company needs. This control over transportation assets creates increased flexibility in scheduling and routing.

One goal of the firms that use private fleets is to transport enough volume to achieve economies of scale and operate a fleet for less than it costs to hire the service. Economies of scale effectively means that per unit fixed costs decrease as volume increases.[2] One question each company must answer is the following: At what volume is private carriage less expensive than for-hire or mixed carriage?[3] For-hire carriage typically reduces the ability to control assets, but leaves the worry of vehicle utilization to the carrier's management. Mixed fleet, which is the use of both private and for-hire carriage, may realize the advantages of both, but it also brings with it the disadvantages of both.[4]

Sometimes it is difficult to find a for-hire carrier to provide a specific service. In other words, if an organization cannot find someone else to do the work the way it wants it done, it may have to do it itself. Therefore, many techniques aimed at improving private fleet efficiency are available to fleet managers. Not only are potential profit opportunities available from external entities requiring transportation services, many private fleet operators are now also focusing on the coordination of inbound and outbound traffic flows. For example, coordinating traffic flows allows a manager to deliver an outbound load to its' destination and return with a loaded truck carrying a shipment inbound from a supplier. This coordination can reduce the delivered cost of inbound products by eliminating the third-party transportation cost associated with the inbound delivery. Private carriers also occasionally hire out to other companies if excess capacity exists, further reducing transportation costs and improving fleet efficiency. This chapter introduces and discusses the advantages and disadvantages of a private fleet operation, examines the key issues private fleet managers face today, and introduces the alternatives to a private fleet.

Advantages and Disadvantages[5]

One key disadvantage of private carriage is the large amount of initial capital investment required.[6] Capital used to acquire and maintain a private fleet means less capital for other business opportunities. Managing a private fleet can also prove to be problematic for some companies. To meet the legal definition of a private carrier, the firm cannot have transportation as their primary business. At the same time, if transportation is not the company's primary business, management may lack the skills necessary to run an effective transportation operation. Other principle advantages and disadvantages of private fleet include:

Advantages	Disadvantages
-Maximum control	-Requires capital
-Flexible scheduling	-Technology changes
-Tailored deliveries	-Growth inhibited
-Image enhancer	-Low ROI
-Special services	-Administrative costs

To address the differences of each and make the correct choice, companies must understand the unique characteristics of their business. The company's primary mission and vision must drive the choice, and this starts with a business plan.

The Business Plan

A business plan can be defined as a document that convincingly demonstrates that the business can sell enough of its products and services (as in the case of the fleet) to make a satisfactory profit (or savings) and be attractive to potential backers.[7] A private fleet is a business within a business. It has suppliers and customers. It has expenses and revenues (in the form of cost savings or real dollars). People with varying skill sets participate in this business. Some form of capital investment or initial resource commitment is necessary for it to operate. Therefore, it must have a business plan that includes performance measures and accountability.

The Document

The business plan must be a dynamic document that can change quickly as dictated by major shifts in business direction. A strategic business plan is useless if it is developed and then placed on a shelf to collect dust. To be effective, it should be dog-eared and with additions and corrections throughout. This is because the plan is re-visited regularly to help direct the business and allow for alterations that parallel the changes in the marketplace. The plan should be both strategic and tactical in nature. It must also be shared with those charged with adherence to its guidelines.

Profitability

To demonstrate profitability convincingly, success must be consistent over time. Success comes in two parts. First, the service provided by the fleet must conform to the acceptable standards of internal and external customers. Second, the cost of operating the fleet must be competitive with the alternatives.

Please note two key words here: one is *acceptable* and the other is *competitive*. Why are we not talking about *superior* service and *lowest cost* alternative? Because this is a mistake many firms make when assessing the value of the private fleet. Too often, companies define service levels. To find out what is needed, companies must ask their customers. What's acceptable to them is what matters, not the company's perceptions of what is acceptable or expected of them; this is discussed in more detail later in this chapter. And, by the way, acceptable service levels should be negotiable. There is a direct correlation between the levels of service and the cost of those levels. As cost is squeezed out of the system, there is a significant possibility that service will decline accordingly. The value private fleet adds to the business goes far beyond cost. That's the selling point that should be stressed and supported by management.

Potential Backers

Companies make commitments to owners, private or public, and to the financial community. The accuracy of these commitments can determine the life or death of the company. The fleet, as a part of the company, must also make service and financial commitments. The results of these affect the integrity of the company as does sales volume and profit. Therefore, accuracy and consistency are key attributes that determine the success of the fleet and the company.

Business Plan Contents

It is not the purpose of this chapter to delve too deeply into the business plan. But, it is noteworthy to advise the reader of its contents. A solid plan contains:

- A business environmental analysis
  - How we are doing today?
  - Do we have accurate metrics?
  - Do we know who our customers are?
  - Do we know who our suppliers are?

- A production element
  - What is it that we do?
  - Will we be doing it tomorrow?
  - Can someone else do it?

- A quality element
  - How well do we do our jobs?
  - Are we on time?
  - What makes us the carrier of choice?

- A support training element
  - Regulated training
  - On-the-job training
  - Cross-training
  - Preparing people for tomorrow

- A cost element
  - What are the cost drivers?
  - The numbers
  - Method of costing—legacy vs. activity based

- An operating plan
  - How are we to get it all done?

- Resources needed
- Measure of success

A business plan that contains these elements and answers these questions will help put things in perspective when it comes time to decide whether or not to use private fleet.

Understanding True Costs

The decision to outsource fleet is often made because top management or fleet management does not understand the true cost of operating the fleet.[8] It is natural to decide to eliminate something that is not easily understood. It is easy to understand the bottom line of for-hire carrier costs because it is stated in absolute cost to deliver to a specific customer. Change a variable, and the result is a new cost. The same theory applies to fleet cost. Unfortunately, the normal breakdown of costs is by line item and is not equivalent to the cost to deliver to a customer.

Understanding costs means breaking down fixed and variable costs so that they specifically apply to each activity in the distribution system—from order processing all the way to the time spent at each customer. Companies often use an allocation process that does not accurately reflect the amount of services received. Often, recruitment, equipment acquisition, claims, accidents, dispatching, and office support costs are overlooked in the cost analysis and allocation process. Therefore, care must be exercised to identify charges that come in the form of charge-backs from corporate for such things as technology support, engineering support, and general office support. The fleet manager must understand these charges and their origin. It is also the manager's responsibility to challenge those expenses that should not be charged to their functional unit.

Fortunately, in many companies, the person occupying the private fleet management position is someone with multiple skills and responsibilities. Today's fleet manager is well versed in:

- Warehousing, shipping, and receiving
- Materials management

- For-hire carrier management
- Purchasing
- Vehicle specifications
- Legal and regulatory compliance
- Contract negotiations
- Labor relations
- Strategic and tactical planning
- Finance
- Customer service
- Human resource management
- The environment

The fleet manager is also a member of a larger management team and has his/her compensation partially based on the success of other departments within the company. The fleet manager is critical to the process of understanding costs and operations, as well as gathering information.

Information for fully understanding an operation should come from a variety of sources. First, management should tour the firm's facilities and observe each operation. Significant information can be obtained by simply watching the work process. Done properly, the exercise should show workers that management is concerned about improving conditions.

Second, management should either conduct interviews or focus groups with workers. Management can then understand better the problems faced by workers in each area of the organization. Employees know their jobs better than anyone else, so they have information that is vital to improving any process. Whether the employees are empowered or management delegates, improving any process requires the active cooperation and participation of line workers and supervisors. Most organizations benefit from including employees in the decision-making process. Empowerment also promotes a teamwork approach to the work environment.

Third, management should study the flow of each process. The use of a flowchart may help. In many cases, work processes were designed before significant updates had been adopted. Revisiting the original flow of each process may uncover potential problem areas. These areas should be examined closely; and if the problems are significant, the operation should become a candidate for reengineering.[9]

Each of the above cannot only add significant understanding of the overall process, but it can serve as a basis for implementing effective activity-based costing (ABC) and activity-based management systems.

Activity-Based Costing

Identifying key cost drivers by activity measures the profitability of customers and the services they receive. An ABC system develops information about cost drivers and the causal relationships these drivers have with overhead resource consumption.[10] Any activity that relates to a cost is considered to be a cost driver. A more accurate picture of expenses makes it far easier for a manager to make strategic decisions about conventional cost centers.[11]

ABC systems outperform more traditional approaches because they generally provide better operational information.[12] They also have another advantage: they identify activities that add significant cost but little value or vice versa to the private fleet function. These can then be critically examined and re-designed to improve efficiency.[13] Accurate or true costs to service specific customers can then be developed. Furthermore, service and cost levels can more accurately be analyzed for each customer, improving strategic management capabilities.

Activity-Based Management

If a company does not use an effective cost analysis process, the decisions made about the value of the fleet and the customers will be emotional rather than rational basis. Born from the effective cost analysis tools described above, many companies are now practicing activity-based management (ABM). ABM is a broad management concept designed to help manage costs.

The focus of ABM is to increase understanding of operations. The organization is examined to determine:

1) What tasks combine to produce an activity
2) What activities combine to produce a process
3) If the processes combines to create the desired result. ABM focuses on understanding the operation and implementing strategies to continually improve processes.[14] ABM has activity-based costing as one of its primary tools.

Effective understanding of true costs and operations that comes from ABC and ABM will provide managers with the ammunition necessary for deciding whether or not to use private fleet.

Profit or Cost Center

When examining the performance of a company, external analysts typically look at the income statement, balance sheet, and statement of cash flows. However, internally, managers prefer a more detailed breakdown of performance by functional area of the firm (e.g., logistics or private fleet portion of the logistics function). A profit center and a cost center are two very common analytical tools used to help assess internal performance of a particular functional area. The concept of a *profit center* is generally more easily understood than a cost center. Profit centers more closely parallel the standard business model. Evaluating success in a profit center is a matter of bottom line evaluation—earned a profit, didn't earn a profit—good, bad. This is not as simple as it seems, however. If the functional unit does not directly generate revenue, a system must be implemented to assign a reasonable amount of revenue to the function. Furthermore, private fleets are often asked to do things "out of necessity" or "just this once" or "in case of an emergency." It is very easy to get caught up in "taking one for the team" or "being a team player."

As discussed previously, unless those responsible for tracking costs fully understand all cost drivers, profits erode, and the private fleet then may seem less competitive than alternate modes, which may not be able to accomplish those "unusual" requests. Great care must be taken to document the blips on the radar screen and, where possible, assess compensatory charges. This not only helps explain the results of the profit center analysis but also points to the importance of the private fleet under certain circumstances.

The danger in being a *cost center* is the terminology itself. It implies necessary evil. In business training, students are taught early in the curriculum that costs are bad because they reduce profits. In a business downturn, the first command is to reduce costs. No matter what the problem is, the solution is to reduce costs. People forget that without costs, there is no profit because there is no business. Costs are not a necessary evil; they are just a necessary part of business. It is how a company manages costs that make the difference between business success and failure.

Managing a cost center requires a deeper knowledge of the structure and key drivers of cost. Being judged on a cost center approach is somewhat like running a race alone. The runner believes he or she is winning because there is no apparent competition. Special requests for emergency transportation support tend to be more readily accepted as "value added services." Failure to account for these when conducting due diligence variance analysis can be the one brick that topples the load.

Even though it is seldom necessary, it is a good practice to track *what it would have cost* to handle emergency transportation support by the lowest cost alternative method. As for backhauls, many of them, like normal load hauling, have no actual revenue dollars attached where the company's ingredients, materials, and supplies are involved. Usually, what happens is the company gets the freight savings benefit from a change in Free On Board (F.O.B.) terms. For example, the terms of sale are usually changed from F.O.B. destination to F.O.B. origin if the private fleet picks up the product and delivers it to its destination. As a result, no third-party freight is required, reducing the delivered cost of the item. Often those in the functional unit that receive the benefit of "free" inbound transportation forget the cost savings. Here again, sound business practice is to track these non-revenue activities as *what it would have cost.*

Key Fleet Costs

To implement an effective profit or cost center approach to the internal examination of a particular functional area, key costs of the functional unit must be understood. The private fleet is no exception. Regardless of the type of accounting a company uses or whether it is organized as a profit or cost center, several costs are typical of most private fleet operations. Labor is usually one of the most significant operating costs of a private fleet. These can include regular and overtime wages, fringe benefits, FICA tax, worker's compensation, lease payments, and travel and layover allowances.

Fuel costs are also a significant operating cost for most private fleets. Private fleet managers cannot control this expense; however, they can plan for it and attempt to minimize fuel cost fluctuation with fuel hedging programs for short-term operations, fuel purchasing programs or long-term purchasing contracts, and occasionally, fuel surcharges. The latter are common when purchasing external transportation services but have limited practical application in the operation of a private fleet. Other key operating costs can include maintenance costs, highway user fees, office and garage expenses, interest expenses, and insurance premiums. Depreciation is also a significant expense, however; it is worth noting that depreciation expense is not a cash expense and, therefore, its impact should be viewed slightly differently from cash expenses.

Clearly, private fleet operations cost money and are not right for every business situation. Management may examine these costs and feel they are excessive given the amount of value being created for the organization. If this is the case, management may elect to outsource the transportation function. Management will often justify their position by claiming the organization should return to its core competency or focus on what it does best. For example, a company operating retail stores throughout the U.S. and servicing those stores with a private fleet might make the argument that the core competency of the company is retail sales, not logistics. As a result, management may argue that transportation services should be outsourced to reduce costs and place control of the transportation function in the hands of someone whose core competency is transportation.

The Core Business Cop-out

Outsourcing is part of the current trend of contracting support services. Over the last 10 years, some practitioners have urged businesses to contract with specialists unless the activity in question is a "core competence," which confers competitive advantage. The most popular argument for outsourcing is that a company does not possess the expertise to perform the function internally.[15] Alternatively, some activities may remain in the corporate walls if the company can either: 1) perform the service more economically than outside specialists (e.g., provide the service cheaper because of high volume levels) or 2) somehow justify retaining the service internally (e.g., improved customer service, required level of control).

Several processes can assist management in the outsourcing decision. The oldest and most direct is the straight cost comparison. The buyer determines the present value of the price to purchase a good or service and compares that to the present value of the cost of doing the job internally. As discussed previously, corporate accounting practices typically do not isolate all the costs for making a particular part or serving a specific customer. Furthermore, the direct cost approach ignores the non-price expenses associated with purchasing, such as finding the supplier, negotiating the agreement, processing and paying the purchase order, and so forth. The purchase price vs. standard cost comparison also ignores the critical strategic implications of the make-or-buy decision.[16] Outsourcing can lead to loss of important expertise and control. While other methods of analysis may be used when examining the decision to perform internally or purchase externally, the final decision must be based on an examination of the goals and objectives of the company and which method better serves these goals. It helps those making the decision are familiar with the alternatives to private fleet.

Alternatives to Private Fleet

Business, customer satisfaction, history, and emotions are among the reasons why companies choose to be in or out of the private fleet arena. To make intelligent decisions about transportation, companies must be knowledgeable about the alternatives to private fleet carriage. Also, this decision does not, and most often should not, have to be all or nothing. Performance is at its best when competition is most evident. This section examines the alternatives to private fleet.

Customer Pick-up

Customer pick-up is a provision that allows a customer to arrange for pick-up of a product from a supplier. Usually, a company with a private fleet is looking to reduce or eliminate empty backhaul. Picking up product from the supplier can be a backhaul opportunity which helps consolidate inbound and outbound traffic and increase the efficiency of the private fleet. Used properly, customer pick-up, or load exchange, can strengthen the relationship between supplier and customer. If is not managed properly, however, it can be a disaster. Depending on the terms of sale, which should define where ownership of the goods transfers, the transportation might be off-invoice pricing, contract carriage, or as private carriage for the customer.

When entering into this type of relationship, the negotiating parties must lay all the cards on the table and share information openly and honestly, so that there are no surprises down the road. An overlay lane analysis, for example, can be used to show the proper allocation of loads to be handled by each party. Consider this: if there are 20 loads delivered each week to destination "A" and the customer can only supply 10 to 15 trucks on a weekly basis, a decision must be made regarding the remaining loads. Remember, the same level of service expectation exists no matter who actually performs the transportation. By comparing lanes, the negotiating parties can see other imbalances and decide how to divide up those loads to their mutual benefit. Therefore, communication will be ongoing critical factor in the successful movement of the 20 loads.

Open-market Carrier Selection

Oftentimes open market carriers have excess capacity and are looking to optimize their asset utilization and generate additional revenue. Shippers in need of transportation services are matched with carriers having excess capacity. This type of transportation relationship is not based on a long-term mutual relationship but rather one of mutual benefit to each party in the short term. In theory, open market carriers have the lowest transportation costs. Companies bid on each load in each traffic lane and the award goes to the lowest bidder.

This alternative has various disadvantages, however. The carriers are looking for the highest revenue loads and will drop a company for a higher paying load on a daily basis.

It is also difficult to establish relationships that foster good customer relations and loyalty. Service issues are more likely to arise because the emphasis is on lower costs. When equipment and manpower become scarce, the carriers will give their attention to those loads with the highest revenue. This concept also requires daily monitoring to make sure all the loads covered.

Core Carrier Concept

This alternative uses a limited number of carriers mutually committed to a specific number of loads and pre-determined service expectations. When utilized in a support role or as a stand-alone carrier choice, this alternative has competitive advantages similar to those of a private fleet. Companies should select the carriers in this group carefully to ensure that they understand what is expected of them and that there is competition from either the private fleet or the other members of the core carrier team.

Measuring performance openly and honestly is a solid way of maintaining high standards among the group. As innovations take place, the relationship is constantly transformed and upgraded. When one carrier introduces an innovation, it does not take long for the others to realize they need to step up as well. This can be particularly advantageous from a technology standpoint.

Dedicated Carriage

A dedicated carrier typically allocates an agreed upon number of transportation assets to a customer. By offering to dedicate certain transportation assets to the customer, the carrier shows a commitment to the relationship. If certain assets are dedicated specifically to a customer, the likelihood of satisfying unique customer needs (e.g., emergency shipments, unplanned demand for transportation services, expedited shipments, etc) tend to increase. Many carriers today are willing to make equipment and manpower commitments to shippers who will enter into long-term relationships whereby a relatively fixed number of loads are consistently available. If the relationship starts out amicably, this can be a good alternative to the private fleet.

Dedicated carriage is similar to a private fleet. An obvious advantage is the alleviation of managerial responsibilities for those loads handled by the dedicated carrier. Loads not handled by the dedicated carrier are still the responsibility of the private fleet. They must still be dispatched by someone in the organization, but these dispatching duties can usually be done at a lower level than management.

A downside to the dedicated carrier concept is that a wall is placed between the company and the day-to-day carrier management function. That's a good news/bad news situation, depending on how well the negotiations were handled and what form of reporting takes place and the frequency of such reporting. Trust is critical in this relationship.

Third Party Logistics

Third party logistics (3PL) is the outsourcing of transportation functions to another carrier, one that specializes in transportation. If the proper carrier is selected, this can effectively eliminate the worries associated with daily transportation function. The company that outsources transportation remains responsible for ensuring that laws are obeyed in the fulfillment of the transportation function. Oversight is still a vital role of the company.[17]

With 3PL, a company gets expertise and overhead cost dissemination from a carrier with many clients that can continually upgrade service and cost saving techniques not readily available to a private fleet. The 3PL will also take over many of the other transportation functions, such as load make-up and the booking of LTL and other miscellaneous shipments. They effectively become the company's transportation department.

3PL has its disadvantages, also. Like the dedicated option, the level of control is often vague because of the measurable distance between the manufacturing facility and the transportation group. Usually, these are on separate properties. Also, if the present 3PL is not working out, changing to a new one is not so easy.

Without a competently performed purchasing process that begins with a thorough search of third-party logistics sources, a detailed request for proposal, and a properly conducted analysis of potential sources, the purchase of third-party logistics services is likely to fail. Therefore, it is critical that a team of individuals, each of whom brings a different perspective to the situation, carefully and completely plans and executes the process. The communication lines must remain open at all times.

Fourth Party Logistics

Fourth party logistics (4PL) is relatively new and has been described in a number of ways including "watchdog" and "director." In short, 4PLs serve as the firm that oversees operations and serves as the master integrator of multiple firms working together to provide logistics services. Done effectively, a 4 PL can help lead to improved supply chain performance by helping to optimize overall supply chain operations.

Since the concept of fourth party logistics is relatively new, it is not yet clear what level of impact this concept will have on logistics practitioners. Basically, it adds another layer to the transportation process. The advantage of 4PL is that experts are monitoring the 3PL for the things for which a company would still be held responsible or accountable.

The reason to outsource the private fleet should not be that it is not part of the core business; the reason should be that it could be done more effectively outside. Companies can avoid the core competency trap by treating the transportation function as an integral part of the production process, granting it all the attention, care, and sound business practice it deserves. This can be accomplished by re-aligning corporate culture.

Re-aligning Corporate Culture

For the costing, operational, and philosophical changes necessary for the sound decision making that leads to private fleet or outsourcing, it is often necessary to re-align corporate culture. In *Calvin and Hobbes*, a comic strip about a cynical little boy who has conversations with his toy tiger, Calvin boasts about not being responsible for anything and claims everything is someone else's fault. He concludes by saying how much he "loves the culture of victim-hood." Adopting Calvin's philosophy saves employees from having to involve themselves in uncomfortable areas or put their professional reputations on the line.

This philosophy allows employees to hide in their functional safe zones and puts them out of touch and cam put their company out of business.

Getting involved in other areas of the company is uncomfortable for many people. A sound practice is to enlist the use of an "outside eye," that is, a trusted person not associated directly with the department, and run ideas by them to see if they were communicated clearly and understood. Management can then reach out to more people with a more comfortable zone of communication. Transportation workers tend to have their own vernacular, which includes acronyms clearly understood within the industry, but not outside. Avoiding these terms when communicating outside a domain is paramount if communication is to be effective between functional units of a company.

One of noted author and lecturer Tom Peter's most popular expressions is about people "going horizontal." This changes the vertical communication structure of a company. Once this breakthrough is made, the lines are open to two-way communication, paving the way to more clarity in the purpose, the mission, the vision, the direction, and the objectives of the company.

The fleet objectives are no exception. It is the fleet manager's responsibility to be proactive in determining the expectations for the fleet, both internally and externally. The manager must also have a structure in place that successfully communicates the costs associated with the services provided and ensures that the fleet's key initiatives reflect the goals, objectives, and financial structure of the company. A critical rule is: When communicating financial results, use the company's measure—cost per case, barrel, gallon, pound, and so forth. Avoid cost-per-mile and other internal support measures. It is also important to remember that certain transportation terminology and measurement techniques may have little meaning or value to individuals representing other functional units in the company.

When corporate culture is re-aligned, introducing new concepts and technology or changing the company's direction becomes easier. A company's employees will embrace change with enthusiasm because they understand that in the 21st century, business must operate at the speed of light. Given the rise of the Internet and e-commerce as major conduits for doing business, a flexible corporate culture that adapts easily to new processes and methodologies is critical to a company's success.

The Impact of E-commerce on Private Fleet

Internet technology has impacted the way companies operate, changing the manner in which they fulfill orders, deliver product, and define high-quality customer service.[18] One major impact of the Internet, and especially the World Wide Web, is that it has reduced geographic barriers by connecting everyone who has Internet access. Internet technology benefits firms in many ways, however; it is unclear what positive impacts may exist for private fleet managers. Undoubtedly, technology advances are likely to alter some private fleet management practices; however, Dale Hayes, Vice President of E-commerce for UPS accurately states, "E-commerce does not substitute for the basics of business. You still have to perform, and perform flawlessly, the basic services that customers want."

This will most certainly continue to be true for private fleet managers charged with successfully handling, transporting, and delivering their company's goods in an efficient and timely manner.

The role of private fleet management may change as companies implement innovative strategies that exploit Internet technology. For example, scheduling via the Internet may improve the information exchange between dispatchers and drivers, creating a more efficient scheduling system. Improved scheduling efficiencies should translate into higher customer satisfaction levels while simultaneously reducing transaction cost and creating cost savings. In the future, effective Internet systems designed for private fleet operations may well allow managers and even customers to have "cradle-to-grave" tracking and oversight capabilities at their fingertips, such as shipment tracking, regular and revised scheduling, load tendering, expedited or emergency shipment routing, and automated document completion.

When used properly, these developments will contribute to improving external and internal customer relationships, which are critical to the success of private fleet. John Naisbitt, in his book, *Megatrends*, points out that the global economy has changed into an information society.[19] As a result, companies that perform rather than produce dominate it. Customers focus on quality more than any other factor. If quality service is not an internal mantra, a company has little chance of providing it to its customers. Exceptional service is not something someone turns on and off at a whim. It must be so ingrained into the fabric of the whole organization.[20]

External and Internal Customer Relationships

It is obvious that the people who buy a company's products are its external customers, but there is another group of customers that is just as important to the success of a company's business and may be a private fleet's primary customers. These customers are internal customers and, even though they are key players in a company's growth and success, often they are subjected to confrontational behavior.

Think for a moment of all the people in an organization that have contact with one another on a regular basis. Do they get along? How do they view others' roles in the organization? How do others view theirs? Are the relationships adversarial and confrontational? How do they discuss one another internally and externally? How these issues are managed can have a major impact on the overall success of the business.

As Joan Cannie points out in her book, *Keeping Customers for Life*, top management is just now realizing that customer service is a strategic process.[21] The customers themselves define customer satisfaction. Therefore, to achieve the highest levels of customer satisfaction, companies need to learn to listen to the customers. It is important to meet customers' needs as they see them because it differentiates a company or, in the case of internal customers, a department from the competition. Unhappy customers can be very expensive. Look at some statistics from Robert Desatnick's book, *Managing to Keep the Customer:*[22]

- 96 percent of unhappy customers never complain about customer service.
- 90 percent of those dissatisfied just do not come back.
- 13 percent of those unhappy customers will tell of their experience to at least twenty other people.

During a recent tour of a Millican plant, one member of the tour noticed a sign posted in the facility that said, "Quality is not the absence of defects as defined by management, but the presence of value as defined by the customer." At the same time, quality is inherently subjective by nature and the question of what constitutes good or poor service is not easy to answer.[23] For more than a decade, service researchers have conducted extensive research to determine what criteria customers use across industries to evaluate service quality.[24] After extensive refinement, they developed five service quality dimensions that can be measured to help determine an organization's adeptness in providing quality service:

- *Reliability* – The ability to provide what is promised, dependably and accurately.
- *Responsiveness* – The willingness to help customers promptly.
- *Assurance* - The ability to convey trust, competence, and confidence.
- *Empathy* – The degree of caring and individualized attention given to customers.
- *Tangibles* – The physical appearance of facilities and equipment and how easily the paperwork flows.

To achieve these dimensions, a company should:

- Put its house in order.
- Ensure that its employees know exactly what to do and how to do it.
- Have written policies covering most situations.
- Put new employees through customer satisfaction training.
- Provide ongoing customer satisfaction training.
- Recognize the value of internal customers
- Measure the effectiveness of training by identifying those qualities that meet the criteria for good customer service using surveys and other measurement instruments where appropriate.

Reliable and efficient equipment also plays a role in achieving internal and external customer satisfaction. Proper equipment maintenance and savvy equipment acquisitions, therefore, can assure the infrastructure necessary for satisfying the customer.

Equipment Maintenance

In the past, fleets commonly did their maintenance in-house. It was a hand-in-glove fit with in-house hauling. If it made sense to haul, it made sense to do the repairs. And, it did make sense. The engines were much simpler and the capital expenditures were incrementally low due to having facilities housing the fleet, anyway. Large fleets with multiple facilities can still do an excellent job of in-house repairs. Also, capturing the data for maintaining good repair records is much easier with this method.

Over time, however, engines have become more complex. Diagnostic tools are expensive. Training to keep up with changes is expensive. Frequency of repairs is reduced. Overhead is rising. Therefore, the current shift is to use some form of leased equipment or seek some other method of handling the maintenance. At the same time, according to *Transport Topics*,[25] the industry-wide shortage of qualified mechanics is affecting the decision to outsource. Carriers and fleets are considering holding on to what they have rather than risking poor service from shops that lack competent service personnel. Hiring, training and retaining mechanics is becoming systemic. Fewer people are entering the field and the pool of mechanics is shrinking.

To lure fleets to outsource, two equipment manufacturers—Freightliner Corp. and Volvo Trucks North America—have forged alliances with truck-stop chains to offer routine maintenance and warranty work in order to minimize downtime for carriers, including private fleets. Many truck dealers keep their maintenance shops open 24/7 to accommodate the round-the-clock pickup and delivery schedules of trucking customers. For many dealers, contract maintenance is one of the best ways to retain customer loyalty. Some franchisees are taking their shops on the road using a specially equipped service truck to provide on-site maintenance service for fleets. Other options include:

- *Independent network.* Depending on the territory served, an option is to make arrangements with many independent repair facilities throughout the territory on an open charge basis so that drivers do not carry large amounts of cash. The problem with this method is consistency, control, and quality of work, as well as performance and manufacturers' warranties.

- *Nationwide repair networks.* These networks are willing to operate on a purchase order system with direct billing. Drivers can dial a toll-free number, advising the service operator of the driver's location. The service then locates a nearby repair facility under contract to do the repairs. While the work performed is usually of a better quality, warranties are still a problem.

- *Nationwide vendor repair network.* This system uses the manufacturer's facilities throughout the territory. Purchase order, direct billing warranty, and potentially guaranteed prices are a benefit. These facilities can also generate reports for tracking maintenance. A problem does exist with the number of facilities available to do the work, but this is a viable option that typically provides quality and consistency of work.

- *Lease company facilities.* This can work even if the company is not a lessor. These facilities usually are more numerous than those of the manufacturer and provide quality service at negotiable rates. Repair records and reports are a valuable tool in the maintenance program and are usually well kept with this type of service.

Regardless of which method is used, the process of finding the option best suited to an individual operation should be a careful and thorough undertaking. Saving money is not necessarily the primary motive for outsourcing maintenance. Often it is the loss of a key maintenance manager or simply the decision of the owner not to spend time on the problems related to maintenance. The primary goal is to minimize downtime and maximize the utilization of assets as a reasonable cost.

Equipment Acquisition Strategies[26]

Outright buying of equipment is on the wane. However, in certain cases, buying is still a viable option. Trailers, which are normally held for longer periods of time and need very little technological improvement over time, are still more likely to be purchased than leased.[27] Where there are technological improvements, these are more easily added or retrofitted than with power equipment.

In the case of most power equipment, payback comes in the form of maximizing utilization or putting as many miles on them as quickly as possible. Occasionally, companies that specialize in short-haul operations and tend to hold equipment longer can benefit from buying vs. leasing. However, in most cases, purchasing power equipment is not a viable solution because value is lost in a relatively short period of time when it is compared to the capital outlay involved. There is also the matter of having cash available to purchase the needed equipment.

Leasing creates a continuous stream of newer and more technologically advanced equipment acquisitions without any capital outlay up front. As equipment improves through technology, it becomes more economical to operate. Having newer equipment on the road may be safer and is also good advertising for the company because its logo is often on the sides of the vehicles. There is a cadre of options in leasing designed to fit almost any situation. The common types of leases are:

- *Full-service lease.* This term has been loosely used to describe all-encompassing leases, but in today's terminology may not mean a lease at all. Full-service lessors are becoming more maintenance oriented, offering guaranteed maintenance agreements instead. The most popular form of full-service lease is the TRAC lease.

- *Terminal rental adjustment clause (TRAC) leases.* TRAC leases are operating leases whereby the lessee (the user) guarantees the residual value of the equipment at the end of the lease. If the equipment sells for more, the lessee gets the gain; if it sells for less, the lessee makes up the difference to the lesser. It is in the mutual interest of both parties to see that the units are kept in good condition.

- *Operating leases.* This is commonly known as the fair market value lease and is the lease full-service lessors and finance lease companies are most likely to use. The most attractive feature of the operating lease is its walk-away provision, which removes any resale risk to the lessee, thus avoiding the taxable event of ordinary income tax imposed on the sale of the vehicle. An operating lease must meet four simple rules as required by the Financial Accounting Standards Board (FASB):
  - Ownership does not transfer automatically to the lessee at the end of the lease.
  - There can be no bargain purchase option.
  - The initial lease term cannot exceed 75 percent of the economic life of the vehicle, including any subsequent users.
  - The present value of the lease payments cannot exceed 90% of the actual cash price of the vehicle, using the lessee's incremental cost of borrowing or the implicit rate of the lease.

- *Capital lease.* If the lease does not meet one or more requirements of an operating lease (see four FASB rules above), it is classified as a capital lease. In this case, the equipment being leased appears on the lessee's balance sheet as an asset and depreciates (amortizes) over a specific period. The annual depreciation expense is recognized on the income statement and the value of the asset is presented on the balance sheet each year by being "written down" over the life of the asset. Ownership is transferred at a fixed price and it is treated similar to a loan.

To buy or lease is largely a matter of on or off-balance sheet financing.[28] Also important is how accounting treats different types of leases and their legal implications. Various leases are accounted for in different ways, resulting in a different short- and long-term impact on the company's financial statements. Also, several additional accounting treatment regulations and IRS rulings can impact a decision to lease or buy equipment. Therefore, anyone considering leasing equipment should consult his or her company's finance/accounting and legal departments for advice in this area. The legal departments should also be consulted for other reasons, such as assuring compliance with regulatory bodies.

Legal and Regulatory Compliance

As previously mentioned, to be classified as a private carrier, a company's primary business must *not* be transportation. In other words, transportation must be incidental to the primary business purpose of the firm. Private carriers typically serve their company by hauling materials inbound, outbound, or both, supporting the primary business activity of the firm. Until 1996, the federal government strictly enforced rules and regulations that prohibited private carriers from hauling public goods for a fee. However, the Interstate Commerce Commission (ICC) Termination Act of 1995 dramatically relaxed these rules, making it relatively easy for a private fleet operator to obtain authority to haul another entity's goods.

Typically, private fleets are not subject to economic regulation. Nevertheless, fleet operators must comply with various non-economic regulations including hazardous material requirements, employee and vehicle safety standards, and other legal and regulatory restrictions and standards. Unfortunately, compliance with some of these non-economic regulations can become an economic or financial issue for many private fleet operators. Legal and regulatory requirements can include compliance with various government agencies like the Department of Transportation (DOT), Environmental Protection Agency (EPA), the Occupational Health and Safety Administration (OSHA) and others who have oversight responsibility for rules and regulations that may pertain to a transportation operation.

Complying with EPA regulations is critical. The federal government sets the guidelines for environmental compliance in its sentencing guidelines for corporate crimes. The rules were originally developed for antitrust and fraud violations. No operation is exempt from these guidelines. Companies with private fleets must have an environmental protection program in place that includes:

- Waste management
- Pollution prevention
- Operating permits
- Hazardous material storage
- Emergency response
- Property liability
- Violation reporting
- Record keeping[29]

It is important for private fleet managers to familiarize themselves with these issues and work closely with whoever is designated to have direct responsibility over them. Failure to deal with these issues can have dire consequences, including possible prison sentences under certain circumstances. So, it is serious business.

The EPA guidelines suggest the following be included in a company's program:

- *Commitment.* This usually is in the form of a policy statement. The statement merely sets the tone for how the company intends to operate as a good citizen in the community. It is a guiding principle.

- *Defined responsibilities.* These detail exactly who is responsible for what issues. This should be in writing and readily available. Do not leave this document to chance and hope it is never needed. Should a problem arise, there is not time to try to figure out who is in charge.

- *Specific procedures and controls.* This is the "if something happens, what do we do about it and what are we doing to prevent it" section of the guidelines.

- *Communication and training.* Employees must be made aware of their responsibilities and be trained on proper procedures. They should have a list of whom to call and under what circumstances.

- *Records and documentation.* Proper record keeping is always critical, especially in instances of such importance. It should be clearly stated what documents are required, who will keep them, and for how long.

- *Auditing and reviews.* The only way to ensure compliance is to test the system.

- *Enforcement.* This section states the consequences for those individuals who violate the rules outlined in the program. It also serves as a deterrent to non-compliance.

- *Program review and revision.* The rules do change. It is important to keep abreast of them and make the appropriate adjustments to the program. Again, communication and training play an important role.

The following actions can help a company develop an environmental program:

1. Assess the situation. How extensive is the current environmental protection plan? Is it proactive or merely compliant? Or, does it exist at all?

2. Determine goals and objectives that tie directly to the desired needs and results.

3. Ensure cross-functional participation. Each area affected should have a representative on board. The experience and input from members of different backgrounds serve as a checks and balances system to keep the program active and current.

4. Obtain top management support and backing. The support should come in the form of a policy statement from upper-level management. This adds the credibility and enforcement authority required to place the appropriate emphasis to the program.

The result is the security of knowing that the environment program will hold up under EPA scrutiny. Under similar scrutiny from OSHA is a private fleet's safety program. Violating OSHA regulations is a serious matter, but other internal reasons exist for making sure a sound safety program is in place.

A recurring nightmare for fleet managers is seeing their equipment mangled and tying up traffic with the report that someone has died because of the accident on the 6:00 p.m. news. While the fault may matter legally, as far as company image is concerned, whether or not the company's equipment caused the accident is irrelevant. One accident and a company's private fleet department may be in jeopardy. Legal liability and worker's compensation are typically the two strongest arguments for getting rid of the private fleet. Companies feel that exposure is minimized when they use an outside carrier. Liability can still be assessed to the company, but at least the equipment with the company logo is not on the news.

Outside carrier or no, ancillary costs will mount. According to the National Safety Council (NSC), the economic cost of each fatality is just under $1 million when considering lost productivity and the expenses in dealing with the accident. Each injury resulting from an accident costs an average of $34,000 and property damages average $6,400 per accident. In the work place, approximately 5,000 workers are killed each year. That comes to approximately 4 fatalities for every 100,000 workers. In the transportation sector the rate is approximately 12 fatalities for every 100,000 workers. This impact is huge.

The four main categories of accidents are:

• Motor vehicle accidents
• Employee injuries
• General liability and property damage
• Off-job injuries

Motor vehicle accidents usually account for the greatest frequency and financial exposure, with employee injuries not far behind. Off-job injuries, while they don't command as much attention, can be an expensive proposition to the employee in the form of lost wages and to the company in the form of lost productivity and other hidden costs, including:

• Reduced efficiency due to employee's reaction to the accident, involved or not.
• Finding a replacement for the injured employee
• Time spent responding to the accident
• Employee's lost earnings potential
• Damage to customer relations due to delays in delivery
• Damage to stockholder and investor confidence in the company management
• Damaged public or community image
• Fines and increased regulatory pressure
• Overhead with no offsetting productivity
• Emotional cost from depression, anxiety, and stress that lingers

Private fleet operations should emphasize safety if they want to remain part of a company. To accomplish this, the company's strategic plan must include a written safety program that includes:

• Commitment
• Assigned responsibilities
• Company rules
• Hazard analysis
• Hazard control programs and safety procedures

• Emergency and accident response
• Training
• Auditing and inspection
• Employee incentives and enforcement
• Record keeping and reports
• Program evaluation

Part of this system includes imposing severe consequences for failure to meet safety standards and practices.

In ensuring regulatory compliance, be it environmental or safety, a private fleet manager often needs the skills of a human resource manager.[30] Managing a fleet requires the understanding of and compliance with government regulations, accepted policies, and practices. Successful fleet managers, therefore, attention must pay careful attention to the following and how they might affect fleet management:

• *Job descriptions.* Investing time in formalizing detailed job descriptions is the first step to setting expectations and defining accountability.

• *Departmental policies and procedures.* Written policies in the form of a handbook communicate things such as the company/department mission, expectations, benefits and rules of conduct. This is an opportunity to advise the employee of those areas the members of the company or department feels are important to the well being of the employees as they perform their daily tasks.

• *Regulatory compliance.* Penalties for non-compliance can apply to the violator as well as the employer. Stressing the importance of compliance sets the accountability standards. Many regulatory agencies at both the federal and state level have a vested interest in how business is conducted. There is joint responsibility. Ensuring that the employee has the knowledge and the interest in compliance and communicating that the company/department shares in that responsibility removes any doubt as to the seriousness of the regulations and the commitment of the company/department to upholding them.

• *Recruiting and hiring.* Looking first within the organization indicates a willingness to reward those who have already made a commitment to the organization and creates an atmosphere of loyalty. Another source of hiring is to encourage current employees to help in the recruiting process through a recommendation plan and rewarding participation with an employee bonus. This system rewards current employees for bringing onboard prospects for which they would personally vouch. The employee must understand that to earn the bonus, the new hire must meet all the criteria and stay for a specified time. A third method is to approach and build a relationship with driver training schools, or create one in-house. This can add a degree of professionalism to the job. Once candidates have been identified, it is time to work closely with the human resource department to ensure the hiring process meets all the guidelines of the company.

- *Training.* Getting started on the right track is important to the company, department and the new employee. New employee orientations are an effective method of communicating in a non-stressful environment. It is easier for the employee to ask questions and gain a better understanding of expectations prior to actually performing work. The next phase is to provide new employee job training. This provides job-specific training to ensure the job gets done the "company way." Along the way, there should be continuous training in the areas of regulated requirements, on-the-job, safety, crosstraining (where applicable), and training for tomorrow's job requirements and potential advancement.

The fact that a fleet manager should be aware of these elements and use them as he or she conducts fleet business does not mean that he or she is expected to replace the company's human resource department. This is appropriate functional knowledge that allows a fleet manager to make sure that private fleet operations and employees comply with accepted policies and practices.

Conclusion

This chapter has introduced the reader to many of the key issues involved in operating a private fleet; however, there is no substitute for experience. As logistics practice progresses and we move towards fully integrated systems and Supply Chain Excellence, new challenges and opportunities will undoubtedly arise for private fleet managers. How we respond to these challenges and opportunities will not only help determine how our discipline is perceived by others, our response will have a significant impact on the operating performance and business success of the entities we represent.

References

[1]Coyle, John J., Edward J. Bardi, and Robert A. Novack (2000) *Transportation*, 5th Edition, South-Western College Publishing, New York, NY.

[2]Byrns, Ralph T. and Gerald W. Stone (1984), *Economics*, 2nd edition, Glenview, Illinois: Scott, Foresman and Company.

[3]Maltz, Arnold B. and Lisa M. Ellram (1997), "Total Cost of Relationship: An Analytical Framework for the Logistics Outsourcing Decision," *Journal of Business Logistics*, Vol. 18, No. 1, pp. 45-66.

[4]Bloomberg, David J., Stephen A. LeMay, and Joe B. Hanna (2001), *The Essentials of Logistics*, 1st Edition, Prentice-Hall Publishing, Saddle Brook, NJ.

[5]Vercillo, Tony (2000), *Transportation Professionals Handbook*, Chapter 1, pp. 1.

[6]Bowersox, Donald J. and David J. Closs (1996), *Logistical Management*, New York, McGraw-Hill.

[7]Gumpert, David E., (1990), How to Really Create a Successful Business Plan, Software Publishing, Boston, MA.

[8]The Outsourcing Institute (1997), "The Outsourcing Index: Management Summary," Second Edition, from http://www.outsourcing.com/news/dnb, (December).

[9]Lambert, Douglas and Robert Armitage (1990), "Integrating Marketing and Logistics for Increased Profit," *Business*, Vol. 40 (July-September), pp. 22-29.

[10]Harrington, Lisa (1995), "It's Time To Rethink Your Logistics Costing." *Transportation & Distribution*, Vol. 36, Issue 7 (July), pp. 27-30.

[11]Miller, John A. (1996) *Implementing Activity-Based Management in Daily Operations*. New York, NY: John Wiley & Son, Inc.

[12]Kaplan, Robert S. "Yesterday's Accounting Undermines Production." *Harvard Business Review*, 62, No. 4 (July-August 1984), pp. 95-101.

[13]Roth, Harold and Faye Borthick (1991), "Are You Distorting Costs by Violating ABC Assumptions" *Management Accounting*, Vol. 73 (November), pp. 39-42.

[14]Sharman, Paul (1993), "Activity-Based Management: A Growing Practice" *CMA Magazine* (March), pp. 21-22.

[15]Prahalad, C. K. and Gary Hamel (1990), "The Core Competence of the Corporation," *Harvard Business Review*, (May/June), pp. 79-91.

[16]Venkatesan, Ravi (1992), "Strategic Sourcing: To Make or not To Make," *Harvard Business Review*, Vol. 70, No. 6, pp. 98-107.

[17]Sink, Harry L. and C. John Langley, Jr. (1997), "A Managerial Framework for the Acquisition of Third-Party Logistics Services," *Journal of Business Logistics*, Vol. 18, No. 2, pp. 163-189.

[18]Ricker, F. R. and Ravi Kalakota (1999) "Order Fulfillment: The Hidden Key to E-Commerce Success," *Supply Chain Management Review*, (Fall), pp. 103-114.

[19]Naisbitt, John a> (1984), *Megatrends*, New York, Morrow.

[20]LaLonde, Bernard, Martha C. Cooper, and Thomas G. Noordeweier (1988), *Customer Service: A Management Perspective*, Oak Brook, IL: Council of Logistics Management.

[21]Cannie, Joan K. (1991), *Keeping Customers For Life*, American Management Association, New York, N.Y.

[22]Desatnick, Robert L. (1993), *Managing to Keep the Customer* in The Jossey-Bass Management Series, San Francisco, CA.

[23]Bitner, Mary Jo, Bernard H. Booms, and Mary Stanfield Tetreault (1990), "The Service Encounter: Diagnosing Favorable and Unfavorable Incidents," *Journal of Marketing*, Vol. 54, pp. 71-84.

[24]Parasuraman, A., Valarie Zeithaml, and Leonard L. Berry (1988), "SERVQUAL: A Multiple Item Scale for Measuring Customer Perceptions of Service Quality," *Journal of Retailing*, Vol. 64, No. 1, pp. 12-40; Parasuraman, A., Valarie Zeithaml, and Leonard L. Berry (1985), "A Conceptual Model of Service Quality and Its Implications for Future Research," *Journal of Marketing*, Vol. 49, (Fall), pp. 41-50.

[25]Anonymous (2001), "Mechanic Shortage," *Transport Topics: The National Newspaper of the Trucking Industry*, Week of March 12th, pp. 17.

[26]Paul, Mark (2000), *Transportation Professionals Handbook*, Chapter 3, pp. 33.

[27]John, George and Barton A. Weitz (1988), "Forward Integration into Distribution: An Empirical Test of Transaction Cost Analysis," *Journal of Law, Economics, and Organization*, Vol. 4, No. 2, (Fall), pp 337-355.

[28]Pahler, Arnold J. and Joseph E. Mori (1998), *Advanced Accounting: Concepts and Practice*, 3rd Edition, Harcourt Brace Jovanovich, Publishers, New York, NY.

[29]Mutschler, Peter (2000), *Transportation Professionals Handbook*, Chapter twenty-two, pp. 269.

[30]Higgins, Ken (2000), *Transportation Professionals Handbook*, Chapter twenty-three, pp. 293, and Mutschler, Peter, (2000), *Transportation Professionals Handbook*, Chapter twenty-four, pp. 319.

CHAPTER 18
Manufacturing Strategies for the Supply Chain

James A. Tompkins, Ph.D., President, Tompkins Associates

Manufacturing, as we know it, has changed. Thanks to e-business, companies can no longer focus only on creating the highest-quality products. They must now also make sure that items are produced and delivered in the form desired and as quickly as possible. Traditional manufacturing practices can no longer secure competitive advantage in the war of supply chain vs. supply chain.

Yesterday's traditional factories are becoming today's focused factories, which are defined around a product family that requires similar manufacturing equipment. Physical factories are becoming virtual factories—virtual enterprises that gather, organize, select, synthesize, and distribute information and parts with information technology, be it electronic data interchange (EDI), wireless, the Internet, or a combination of all three. They are products of focused factories, deverticalization, and the ease of sharing information. Also, direct-to-consumer delivery channels, customer satisfaction, product customization, shorter cycle and lead-times, and smaller lot sizes are critical as more and more companies and customers look to the Web to provide instant products and information.

Because mass production alone cannot provide the speed and customization today's customers require, it is time to use new manufacturing strategies in the supply chain. To achieve success and competitive advantage, all manufacturing companies in a supply chain must reduce costs, minimize process failures, globalize their operations, and improve quality. Successful companies must prepare themselves to satisfy tomorrow's customer. In short, they must become Future Capable Companies.

A Future Capable Company is a manufacturing company that responds to the forces of change while using the proper application of technology. It not only focuses on the best solutions for today's requirements, but it also focuses on tomorrow's solutions. It moves from one peak level of performance to the next, ensuring success at each stop ("Peak to Peak to Peak"). A Future Capable Company has clear-cut strategies for producing quality products, satisfying customers, increasing its return on assets, reducing costs, and identifying manufacturing as a strategic strength and important link in the synthesized supply chain. These strategies are based on the 12 Requirements of Success for a Future Capable Company, which are:

1. Cost Strategy
2. Customer Satisfaction
3. Global Strategy
4. Speed

5. Change and Certainty
6. Control
7. Balance
8. Quality
9. Maintenance
10. Human Capital
11. Continuous Improvement
12. Synthesis

Strategy 1: Cost

The Cost Requirement of Success states that a Future Capable Company (FCC) must scrutinize all costs of transportation, acquisition, distribution, inventory, reverse logistics, packaging, and manufacturing. The company must look all along the supply chain for ways to reduce costs significantly while increasing profitability. Cost reductions of two percent, five percent, or even 10 percent are not significant. Significant reductions may start at about 20 percent, but ideally, they should range from 40 percent to 60 percent.

The first step in significant cost reduction is documenting present costs. This documentation must accurately and precisely define and detail the costs. Examples of the costs to be identified include:

• Space utilization
• Equipment
• Warehousing/storage/inventory
• Direct and indirect labor
• Receiving and shipping
• Plant and building
• Annual operating expense (e.g., taxes, insurance, maintenance, energy expenditures)
• Manufacturing
• Materials

The next step is to examine each type of cost. For example, an organization can examine its manufacturing costs by asking:

• What percentage of our manufacturing costs is direct labor? Material? Overhead?
• What are the definitions of direct and indirect labor? Can indirect labor be allocated directly to certain products?
• How is overtime handled? Is this done properly?
• What costs are included in the overhead? Are they fixed or variable, and are they fairly allocated?
• Are there costs buried in overhead that would be more accurately allocated to materials (e.g., packaging materials)?
• How is rework handled? Does this properly reflect the actual cost allocation?

- Why do material losses occur?
- How are material yield, salvage, and waste costs allocated?

Manufacturing companies should ask questions similar to these for each type of cost identified, to understand how the costs relate to one another and to uncover hidden costs. Once the details of present manufacturing costs are understood, specific cost-reduction goals should be established and communicated throughout the organization, using the following methodology:

- Identify duplicate and unnecessary costs, redundant functions, and wasteful spending. This step allows an organization to identify potential areas for significantly reducing costs.
- Identify and document alternative cost-reduction measures. The organization should consider a wide range of alternatives and leave no avenue unexplored. Many of these measures should focus on one of the other 11 Requirements of Success.
- Evaluate alternative cost-reduction measures, from both economic and qualitative aspects.
- Select and specify the recommended cost-reduction measures. Organize the justifiable alternatives, identified in the previous step, into an improvement plan that is sold to management and supply chain members, and then implemented.
- Update the cost-reduction measures. Future Capable Company cost reduction is based on the motto "improve, improve, improve." Therefore, the measures cannot be implemented once and the process then abandoned. The organization should periodically benchmark implemented cost-reduction performance against anticipated cost-reduction performance. Corrective action should be taken when necessary. Most importantly, the organization should look for cost-reduction opportunities throughout the supply chain on an ongoing basis.

Strategy 2: Customer Satisfaction

Customer satisfaction is an ongoing, escalating process of meeting customer requirements and exceeding customer expectations. Customer satisfaction requires a company and its supply chain to divest itself of self-interest and focus on the needs, expectations, and perceptions of those to whom they provide products. Manufacturers in a supply chain must continually seek information about their customers' needs and expectations, track how they change, and implement processes to address those changes. Ask and answer one important question: "What does our customer want?" The answer to that question leads to more questions, including:

- What do we produce?
- Where do we get the materials to produce it?
- How do we receive the materials to produce it?
- How much do we produce?

- How do we store it?
- How do we package, label, and ship it?
- When do we ship it?
- Where do we ship it?

The answers to these questions create a clear, easily understood, and measurable definition of the level of quality and reliability a customer expects in exchange for the price paid. This definition, in turn, must be communicated to everyone involved in the supply of that product. Everyone must clearly understand the customer's expectations so that they can be economically achieved.

Specific elements define customer satisfaction. These elements are grouped into three categories: pre-transaction, transaction, and post-transaction. *Pre-transaction elements* are non-availability advisement, quality sales representations, monitored stock levels, consulting about new product and package development, target delivery dates, communications, and regular review of product depth and breadth. *Transaction elements* are ordering convenience, order acknowledgement, credit terms offered, questions handled, delivery frequency, order cycle time and reliability, on-time deliveries, order status information, order tracking capabilities, fill rate percentage, shipment shortage, back-order percentages, product substitutions, and emergency order handling. *Post-transaction elements* are invoice accuracy, returns and adjustments, well-stacked loads, quality packaging, and easy-to read labeling.

If a supply chain offers these elements, then it is on the path to customer satisfaction. The elements allow the customer to take ownership of the product and service, and they promote ongoing dialogue. They also indicate that the company believes that it is good business to treat customers as individuals rather than as demographics.

Strategy 3: Global

Developing a global strategy begins with one question: Do we have a global supply chain in place? A global supply chain is the core component of a successful strategy. If the manufacturing companies in the supply chain have a global supply chain in place that was developed with a strategic planning methodology, then they are ahead of the game. If a company does not have a global supply chain based on strategic planning, the steps to correct the situation are as follows:

- Document the present supply chain and its costs. Collect information about space utilization, layout and equipment, operating procedures, staffing and activity levels, building characteristics, access to location, annual operating costs, inventory, and performance reporting.
- Identify customer satisfaction requirements. Delivery requirements (time from order placement to receipt of shipment) are key data requirements for analyzing a supply chain. Therefore, data on freight classes and discounts, transportation procedures, and delivery requirements should be collected. Then, a customer satisfaction gap analysis

must be undertaken. The gap analysis is a series of questions directed at both staff and customers. The purpose is to identify discrepancies between customer perception of satisfaction and satisfaction requirements. Another key to customer satisfaction is to fully understand the marketing strategy and have access to sales forecasts.

- Establish an order history database. The database of orders that are to be modeled can be established while the existing supply chain is being documented. This information should include ship-to-locations, shipment weight, products ordered, and the quantity ordered. Once the data is established, the next step should be to validate the data. Also, it is a good idea to prepare a summary report (sales, cases sold, weight shipped) for a "sanity check" to ensure that all the data reflects reality.

- Develop alternative supply chains. The input used to determine alternatives consists of site visits, projections of future requirements, database analysis, and customer satisfaction surveys. The methods used for the selection of each alternative will vary. Operating methods must be evaluated. Furthermore, consideration must also be given to criteria such as consolidating vendor shipments, centralizing slow-moving items in one place, keeping company divisions separate, and having direct shipment by vendors. Once alternatives are determined, data must be collected on freight rates, warehouse costs, and labor costs.

- Model annual operating costs. Determine all the investments and savings associated with each alternative. Costs such as new equipment, construction, or building modification should be included.

- Evaluate alternatives. The result should be each alternative's after tax return on investment compared with the baseline. Once this step is completed, perform a sensitivity analysis on the results. Then, to round out the analysis, perform a qualitative evaluation that examines factors like flexibility, modularity, adaptability, customer satisfaction, and ease of implementation.

- Specify the plan. After reaching a conclusion, establish a time-phased implementation schedule that lists the major steps involved in transferring the supply chain from the existing system to the future system.

The final step in the global supply chain planning process is selling the results to top management, who must be able to see the impact of the strategy on the total business. Not only should this communication express the finances relating to operating costs, but to overall sales and customer satisfaction as well.

A global supply chain is not a finite entity. It must be flexible enough to respond to change while maintaining and continuously improving its global outreach. Fortunately, the global connectivity created by the Internet can lighten the burden. Communications can now be sent to any area in the world in real time. The Internet can also help:

- Promote a focus on employees as assets rather than expenses. They have the knowledge to gain efficiencies or expand markets as a result of serving (via the Internet) on cross-boundary, global teams

- Master customer relationship management through technology investments that link companies in different countries to the ultimate consumer
- Meld together business processes practiced in various worldwide hubs
- Create a place for the customer in the information infrastructure, no matter where that customer resides
- Manage virtual structures and create new financial models for them
- Design new compensation plans for employees across the globe
- Create security for safe navigation across Web-based business communities in different hemispheres
- Leverage various media to create brand and process recognition any place in the world

Strategy 4: Speed

Speed, in the form of short lead-times, is critical to the success of a supply chain. Three types of lead-times must be reduced: customer lead-time, production lead-time, and manufacturing lead-time.

Customer lead-time is that time between customer ordering and customer receipt. The procedures to follow are:

- Document present customer lead-time by gathering data from a number of sources within the organization. Create a process map for the process that records the times for each activity. This process map should accurately document actual occurrences, not standard operating procedures. Hard data is necessary if a company is truly dedicated to reducing customer lead-times.
- Perform a competitive analysis by researching competitors' customer lead-times, as well as those of partners. This research should be global. The more a company can learn about what its partners and competitors are doing and how lead-times differ globally, the better prepared it will be when it sets its lead-time reduction goals. Comparing data, creating charts, and conducting gap analyses are all excellent methods for analysis.
- Establish goals by first analyzing the process map that documents present customer lead-time, and then rethinking the methods of doing business. This can be accomplished by recording the goals for each activity on the map. The total of goals for each activity should surpass the reduction required to achieve the overall level of improvement you require.
- Identify bottlenecks (constraints that lengthen the time to perform an activity and create longer lead-times) by examining the activities on the map and including customer lead-times in the process.
- Create broad-based teams that focus on specific sets of activities to eliminate bottlenecks. These teams should have the authority to change business methods to achieve new lead-time goals. They should also emphasize: 1) simplification of products, processes, organizational structures, systems, procedures, and methods; 2) teamwork

through elimination of all boundaries and practicing clear and straightforward communications; and 3) certainty through clear schedules and a disciplined, predictable approach.

Production lead-time is the time that transpires from the ordering of all materials for production until the last manufacturing operation is complete. Manufacturing lead-time is the time from the first manufacturing operation until the last manufacturing operation is complete. The two are intertwined, because the keys to reducing manufacturing lead-time—reducing lot sizes and setup times—also cut production lead-time.

Lot sizes should be reduced as follows:

- Document present lot sizes
- Identify specific lot sizes to be reduced
- Calculate the economic lot size
- Reduce setup times by following the Toyota production system developed by the Toyota Motor Corporation technique and concepts (see below)
- Identify alternative methods for handling the economic lot size between operations
- Evaluate alternative methods for efficient material handling
- Justify the investment required to reduce setup times and to efficiently handle materials, with the savings resulting from the reduction in lot size
- Define and obtain support for specific improvement plans
- Implement the reduced setup time and the material handling equipment as justified and begin production of reduced lot sizes

Reduced setup time concepts developed by the Toyota Motor Corporation are:

- Separate the internal setup (setup activities that must occur inside a machine and require that it be down) from the external setup (setup activities that can occur external to the machine, while it is in operation). Ensure that all external setup operations are complete before the machine is taken out of production. Only internal setup activities should be performed when the machine is down.
- Convert as much of the internal setup as possible to external setup. By altering the machine or the setup activities, the total setup time can be minimized.
- Eliminate the adjustment process. By altering the machines or the setup, a standard or automatic setting can be established that eliminates the need for adjustment.
- Abolish the setup. Standardizing parts can lead to an elimination of setup. Another approach is to have parallel operations performing different activities. Switching a mechanism makes use of only the operations that apply specifically to each product.

To apply these concepts, organizations should standardize external setup actions and machines, use quick fasteners, use supplementary tools, consider multi-person setup crews, and automate the setup process. Reducing setup times makes a reality of high-variety, high-productivity, low-inventory, and small-production-lot-size manufacturing.

Strategy 5: Change and Certainty

No longer can a company afford to play down the power of the Internet, nor can it afford to try to predict what's coming next. The supply chain is not in a steady state. Manufacturing must be dynamic—a process that harnesses the energy of change. Harnessing change means adopting a continuous improvement process that permanently rekindles individual creativity and responsibility. It also creates a transformation of a company's internal and external relationships into relationships with no boundaries. At the same time, manufacturers must maximize certainty to create quiet, order, and stability so that harmony and continuity will exist in an error-free, disruption-free, crisis-free environment. There is no room in the Future Capable Company for sloppy product development schedules, quality problems, maintenance problems, unreliable employees or partners, untimely vendor shipments, or crises.

Manufacturers in a supply chain must respond to change with:

- Flexibility—the ability to handle a variety of requirements. Flexible organizations are those able to produce a variety of products without changing their methods of operation. Their systems are "soft" and "friendly" rather than "hard" or "rigid." They have focused factories, versatile equipment, and multi-skilled employees.
- Modularity—dealing with changes in volume, rather than variety. Modular operations are those that can produce more or less of a product without changing their method. As a result, systems must cooperate efficiently over a wide range of operating rates. Modularity requires modular facilities, modular focused departments in all modular facilities, and time modularity.
- Upgradability—the ability, with a minimum amount of downtime, to gracefully incorporate advances in equipment, systems, and technology. With an accelerated rate of change, it is no longer economical to replace entire systems. Instead, the system should be able to move to the next level without stumbling and with little downtime.
- Adaptability—provides the setting for flexibility, modularity, and upgradability. An organization may think that everything it has planned will work. An adaptive environment allows the organization to respond to changes. It takes into consideration the implications of schedules, calendars, cycles, and peaks. It allows a system to work well at 9:15 a.m. on a Tuesday during the summer's slow season and at 2:30 p.m. on a Friday during peak demand times. The design, from an operations perspective, must allow it to work for a one-hour, two-hour, or two-week time frame. Adaptability allows an organization to adjust to differing levels of product demand. If an organization builds adaptability into its plans, processes, and systems, it will rarely be caught by surprise.

- Selective operability—the ability to operate in segments, allowing for implementation of one segment at a time without degradation of an overall system. This requires understanding how each segment operates so that if something goes wrong, an organization can answer questions such as: "How did this take place? What has this done to our level of customer satisfaction?" Selective operability also allows organizations to put contingency plans in place. A company that locates its distribution center on the North Carolina coast must plan for hurricanes so that other sites are not affected when a power outage, flooding, or roof damage occurs. If the company has a site in Wisconsin, it must be prepared for blizzards so that they do not affect production in a West Coast manufacturing plant. This approach can be tricky, because a focus on segments could easily be misinterpreted as a focus on the individual links inherent in Supply Chain Management (SCM). It is not SCM, however, because selective operability continues to view the chain as a whole entity. It is only by looking at the flow from start to finish that a company can make contingency plans to prevent the flow from coming to a grinding halt in the middle.
- Automation supportability—the ability to support, integrate, and interface with neighboring elements. The future promises more and more automation. Processes and functions that are not automated now soon will be. Implementation will be piecemeal, and non-automated elements must support this type of implementation.

Managing certainty requires establishing, accepting, and following standards of performance. Having activities conform to well-established and clear standards makes errors, disruptions, and crises rare. Therefore, each organization in the supply chain must define the events that have caused surprises, crises, or changes in plans. This review helps determine the standards needed, which include those for:

- Product quality
- Delivery schedule
- Delivery quantity
- Process performance
- Process duration
- Equipment downtime
- Setup duration
- Production methodology
- Part tolerances
- Packaging

Once the standards are established, they must be communicated and conformance to them must be monitored. The variability allowed in these standards must be considerably less than with traditional manufacturing. Only when tight standards are established and achieved, can an environment of certainty be established. If there is a lack of conformance somewhere in the company, its cause must be investigated and a plan developed to rectify the situation. A methodology for developing a plan is:

- Identify methods to obtain conformance
- Evaluate alternatives
- Define a plan to obtain conformance
- Obtain support for the plan
- Implement the plan

Strategy 6: Control

Achieving control can appear daunting, since the accelerating rate of change creates the impression that events are either already beyond our control or spiraling in that direction. However, control is possible with the following elements:

- A straightforward and transparent production and inventory control system based on the theory of constraints (TOC). This approach involves defining the products, families, and options to be produced; specifying a production plan; defining when materials and capacity should be present to meet the production plan; scheduling material delivery from vendors; scheduling focused factories; monitoring schedule adherence; and identifying and eliminating bottlenecks.
- Efficient material flow—It starts with the definition of the material and the flow, which is achieved by adding "why" into the material flow equation, which looks like this: {WHY) X (WHAT + WHERE + WHEN)} => (HOW + WHO). Once an organization knows the material and the flow, it can design the material handling system by pursuing these steps:
1. Define the objectives and the scope of the material handling system.
2. Establish the material flow requirements.
3. Generate alternative material handling system designs for meeting the material flow requirements.
4. Evaluate alternative material handling system designs.
5. Select the preferred material handling system design.
6. Establish an implementation plan.
7. Obtain support for the implementation t plan.
8. Implement the preferred material handling system.
9. Audit systems performance and refine as necessary.
- Up-to-date and upgradable material tracking and control. This must be a simple, real-time system using AutoID, EDI, and the Internet. A material tracking and control system team should be created and given the responsibility of leading the material tracking and control systems efforts through the following steps:
1. Document the present material tracking and control system. Define the present operating procedures and the computer system interfaces.

2. Establish a functional specification. In other words, explain the overall operation and the specific tasks to be performed by the updated and upgraded material tracking and control system.

3. Define alternative approaches to update the material tracking and control system to accomplish the functional specifications within the context of the overall material tracking and control system approach and the overall computer system architecture.

4. Evaluate the alternative approaches. Consider not only the economics of the alternative approaches but also such factors as risk, reliability, modularity, flexibility, ease of installation, response time, maintainability, and fail-safe position.

5. Select the best approach. Identify a pilot project to install, test, debug, and refine the updated material tracking and control system.

6. Develop a plan to implement the pilot project and a plan to implement the updated material tracking and control system.

7. Obtain support for pursuing the pilot project and the updated material tracking and control system.

8. Implement the pilot project.

9. Audit the pilot project's performance. Provide relevant feedback and make required changes.

10. Implement the full-scale, updated and upgradable material tracking and control system. Audit results to ensure that functional specifications have been met.

- Simplified processes. This step involves reducing complexities and increasing understanding. Straightforward and transparent production, inventory control, efficient material flow, and current and upgradable material tracking and control can always be improved. A continuous examination of the processes will result in streamlining and a clearer understanding of process elements.

Strategy 7: Balance

The first step in achieving balanced manufacturing in a supply chain is to document present work in progress (WIP) inventory because it is a symptom of unbalanced operations. Once that has been done, the following questions need to be addressed:

- What is the potential for reducing setup times? Have some reductions been implemented?
- Have production lot sizes been reduced? What is the potential for reducing them? (One-piece flow, lot size of one)? Have some reductions been accomplished?
- What potential exists for maximizing certainty in operations? Has this been accomplished?
- What opportunities exist for the creation of focused departments and focused factories? Have focused operations principles been implemented?

- Do production lots continuously flow through manufacturing operations? Are all WIP inventory buffers justifiable? Are WIP inventory buffers hesitations in the continuous flow of materials? Are high-turnover or low-turnover items involved?
- Have the proper procedures been put in place to maximize sequential flow? How can WIP inventory be reduced by implementing sequential flow?
- Have standards of performance been established, accepted, and followed for each operation, focused department, and focused factory? How can the standards of performance be more rigorously pursued?
- Have the Just-in-Time operational costs been analyzed? Is there a proper understanding of the trade-off between operating costs and balance?
- Have capacity bottlenecks been properly analyzed? Has the issue of balance been properly addressed, both before and after the capacity bottleneck?
- Why does WIP inventory exist? Are all WIP inventories justifiable?

No manufacturing operation will ever achieve total balance. Instead, the objective should be to achieve greater balance. Answering the above questions allows manufacturers in the supply chain to prioritize opportunities; identify and evaluate alternatives; and define, approve, and implement improvement plans. Combining these activities with continuous improvement will lead to greater and greater balance.

Strategy 8: Quality

In today's supply chain, the methods for achieving quality must be progressive. In other words, quality must be:

- Top-down, driven from an awareness and commitment perspective
- Bottom-up, driven from a measurement and reporting perspective
- Customer-driven from a requirements perspective

To accomplish these quality goals, the following steps should be taken:

- Know the customer. Identify the customer. Understand the customer's business. Adopt the customer's perspective.
- Define customer requirements. Communicate with the customer. Obtain a clear definition of requirements. Make sure all parties involved share the same customer expectations.
- Assess and document the supply chain's present quality performance. Compare this performance against customer requirements. Identify areas where customer expectations are not exceeded.
- Identify problems. Investigate performance shortfalls and define the reasons for them. Communicate with all parties involved to understand the shortfalls.
- Specify alternative solutions. Break communication barriers and traditional constraints to identify creative potential solutions. Be certain each alternative solution

solves the problems, rather than just relocating them. Document the operating characteristics of each alternative solution. Verify that each alternative solution exceeds customer requirements.

- Evaluate alternative solutions. Perform economic and qualitative evaluation of each alternative solution. Identify the best solution to each performance shortfall.
- Establish improvement plans. Translate the selected solutions into an action plan. Obtain support for the action plan.
- Implement improvement plans. Install equipment, train personnel, and debug the installation of the solution. Ensure the solution's performance in exceeding customer requirements.
- Audit results. Verify that performance exceeds customer expectations.

For this quality improvement methodology to succeed, it must be a broad-based, participative effort involving upper management, middle management, purchasing, product development, engineering, marketing, supervision, shop-floor personnel, vendors, and customers throughout the supply chain.

Strategy 9: Maintenance

Today's supply chain cannot tolerate process failures. To minimize such failures, a maintenance strategy must be a top priority. Without effective maintenance, machines and systems will fail. The supply chain's maintenance strategy should 1) be based on the 25 Requirements for Effective Maintenance Leadership, 2) use three maintenance best practices (reliability, preventive maintenance, and predictive maintenance), and 3) include planning for maintenance excellence.

The 25 Requirements for Effective Maintenance Leadership are:

1. View maintenance as a priority
2. Develop leadership and technical understanding
3. Develop PRIDE —*People Really Interested in Developing Excellence* in maintenance
4. Recognize the importance of the maintenance profession
5. Increase capability of maintenance personnel
6. Initiate craft skills development to enhance human capital
7. Develop adaptability and versatility
8. Promote teamwork
9. Establish effective maintenance planning and scheduling
10. Make maintenance and manufacturing operations a partnership for profits
11. Develop pride in ownership
12. Improve equipment effectiveness
13. Partner maintenance and engineering
14. Continuously improve reliability and maintainability
15. Design for modularity
16. Manage life-cycle cost and obsolescence

17. Create value-adding redundancy
18. Minimize uncertainty and eliminate root causes
19. Maximize use of computerized maintenance management (CMM) and enterprise asset management (EAM)
20. Use maintenance information to manage the business of maintenance
21. Ensure an effective maintenance storeroom operation
22. Establish the spare parts inventory as the cornerstone for effective maintenance
23. Establish a safe and productive working environment
24. Aggressively support compliance with environmental, health, and safety requirements
25. Continuously evaluate, measure, and improve maintenance performance and service

Reliability means focusing on improving maintainability, not on asset performance. The key is to apply reliability centered maintenance (RCM) and continuous reliability improvement (CRI). Key elements of RCM include:

- Analyzing and deciding what must be done to ensure excellent performance
- Defining user expectations for primary performance parameters such as output, throughput, speed, range, and carrying capacity
- Defining what users want in terms of risk, safety, environmental integrity, quality of output, control, comfort, economy of operation, and customer satisfaction
- Identifying the state of failures, ways that assets can fail, and the consequences of those failures
- Conducting failure modes and effects analysis (FMEA) to identify all the events likely to cause each failed state
- Identify a suitable reliability management policy for dealing with each failure mode in light of its consequences

CRI goes well beyond the traditional approaches found in RCM, which focuses primarily on the physical asset. CRI is a total maintenance improvement process that supports the Future Capable Company. To focus the team processes on continuous reliability improvement opportunities, CRI considers the following:

- Physical asset—Use of reliability improvement technologies, reliability-centered maintenance, preventive/predictive maintenance, and knowledge-based expert systems for maintenance of physical assets. Asset facilitation is used to gain maximum capacity at the lowest possible life-cycle cost.
- MRO material resources—Effective MRO parts, supplies, and materials for quality repair with effective storeroom operations and procurement processes.

- Information resources—Quality information resources for maintenance management and control including computerized maintenance management systems (CMMS), EAM, enterprise resource planning (ERP), vendor, and customer.
- Craft resources—Quality craft skill improvements for the people who support customer satisfaction throughout the supply chain.
- Operator resources—The added value of equipment operators instilled with pride in ownership to support maintenance at the most important level—the manufacturing shop floor.
- Synergistic team processes—Leadership-driven groups providing effective teaming that multiplies people assets

The goal of reliability is not only to reduce failure rates, but also to eliminate root causes of failure. This means developing a reliability improvement policy that includes two of today's best practices: preventive maintenance and predictive maintenance.

Preventive Maintenance (PM) is an interval-based surveillance method in which periodic inspections are performed on equipment to determine the wear on components and sub-systems. When wear has advanced to a degree that warrants correction, maintenance is performed on the asset. The corrective maintenance can be performed at the time of the inspection or later as part of planned maintenance. The decision depends on the length of shutdown required for the repair.

Consider the impact of shutting down the operation for the repair vs. how immediate the need is for repair. If the worn component allows the asset to operate without major damage, then repairs may be postponed until they can be planned and scheduled. A PM system increases the probability that the equipment should perform as expected without failure until the next inspection.

Determining the interval between inspections requires considering the history of maintenance for the equipment in each unique operation. Ultimately, intervals between PM inspections should be guided by a number of resources. These include manufacturer's recommendations, feedback information from repair history of breakdowns, and the subjective knowledge of the maintenance crafts people and supervisors who maintain the asset on a daily basis. Equipment operators may also be a good source of information.

A central characteristic of preventive maintenance is that in most major applications, the asset must be shut down for inspection. The loss of operational time when significant preventive maintenance inspections are made is one of the reasons PM programs are often less than successful. This is especially true in applications where there are few redundant units and equipment must operate at 100 percent of capacity. In some situations, the loss from shutdown is considered too high a penalty, and preventive maintenance inspections are resisted. The truth is, though, that preventive maintenance, when properly applied, unquestionably increases overall equipment availability and is a key contributor to improved reliability.

In contrast to preventive maintenance, predictive maintenance (PdM) is a condition-based system. PdM measures some output from equipment that is related to the degeneration of the asset, a component, or sub-system. For example, vibration analysis equipment might measure metal fatigue on the face of a rolling element bearing. As deterioration progresses, the amplitude of vibration increases. At some critical value, the vibration analyzer concludes that corrective action should be taken to avoid catastrophic failure.

PdM usually permits discrete measurements, which may be compared with some predefined limit (baseline) or may be tracked using statistical control charting. When an anomaly is observed, a warning is provided in sufficient time to analyze the nature of the problem and take corrective action to avoid failure. Thus, PdM contributes to the same central objective for increased reliability. With early detection of wear, you can plan for and take corrective action to retard the rate of wear, prevent or minimize the impact of failure, and predict failure. The corrective maintenance restores the component or sub-assembly, and the asset operates with a greater probability of trouble-free performance.

A principal advantage of PdM is the capability it offers the user to perform inspections while the equipment is operating. In fact, in order to reflect routine operating conditions, the technique requires taking measurements when the equipment is normally loaded in its production environment. Since the machine does not have to be removed from the production cycle, there is no shutdown penalty.

The nature of the operation should determine which methods are most effective. In practice, it takes some combination of PM and PdM to ensure maximum reliability. The percentage of each varies with the type of equipment used and the percent of the time the equipment is operating. When comparing the cost advantages of PdM over PM, consider production downtime costs, maintenance labor costs, maintenance materials costs, and the cost of holding spare parts in inventory.

Planning for maintenance excellence requires planning at both the strategic level and at the shop-floor level. Without effective planning and scheduling, maintenance operations continue to operate in a reactive, fire-fighting mode that wastes their most valuable resource—craft time. Implementing the following six-step plan of action should ensure success of maintenance and the total operation:

- Evaluate the current state of maintenance
- Determine strengths and weaknesses
- Determine potential results from improvement opportunities
- Develop and implement a strategic maintenance plan
- Validate results and return on investment
- Continually improve reliability

Strategy 10: Human Capital

Maximizing human capital requires a long-term, consistent effort. It also includes:

- A lasting commitment to employees
- The confidence of all employees in this commitment
- The development of all employees
- A mutual trust among all employees
- The cooperation and teamwork of all employees

To create this environment, the supply chain fosters Future Capable Leadership, Cultural Revolution, development, and trust.

Future Capable Leadership is energetic, passionate, intense, and determined leadership characterized by integrity, credibility, enthusiasm, optimism, and urgency. Future Capable Leaders motivate others because they adhere to personal work policies that result in working hard and smart.

Cultural Revolution occurs through the ongoing transformation of rules, habits, procedures, standards, norms, rewards, language, stories, expectations, ceremonies, and titles—in short, all the elements that affect employee screening and retention, cultural evolution, organizational behavior, and, finally, organizational performance. For a cultural revolution to be successful, an evolution of understanding the new path for each employee is critical and will help dissipate organizational resistance. Re-recruitment is also essential to ensure enthusiasm and support for the organization's cultural revolution. It involves improving the work conditions, benefits, culture, and perks offered to all existing employees. Re-recruitment results in higher loyalty, retention, and an essence of inclusion.

Development is characterized by three types necessary for maximizing human capital: visionary development, general development, and specific development. *Visionary development* is the basic foundation upon which happy and motivated employees evolve. This foundation is the basic beliefs, the bedrocks, philosophies of business and requirements of company success. *General developmental* needs are categorized as general knowledge development and general skills development. *Specific developmental* needs are programs designed for special groups of individuals. For example, network administrators will require a specific program when a new system is installed; maintenance will require one when a new machine is installed; marketing and sales will require a specific developmental program when a new product is introduced.

Trust must be present for a human capital strategy to work. When trust exists, employees and managers respect each other. From respect comes a sincere desire to listen, which results in an understanding of the other's perspective. Understanding results in a concern for another's well being; concern grows into a collaborative style that allows management and employees to openly discuss goals and directions. This approach leads to success, which gives way to a positive reinforcement that makes employees happy and motivates them to work for further reinforcement.

Strategy 11: Continuous Improvement

To practice Continuous Improvement, a supply chain must understand collaboration and cooperation—with suppliers, within organizations, and with customers. Within the organization, that's called teamwork. Within the supply chain, it's called partnership. Creating the right kinds of teamwork and partnership requires following these guiding principles:

- All organizational units and supply chain links must be 100 percent directed toward the success of the whole supply chain.
- There can be no adversarial relationships within the organization or the supply chain.
- All organizational units must function as a cohesive, collective whole.
- An environment where every employee is motivated and happy will eliminate the we-vs.-they problem that undermines teamwork and partnerships.

The Continuous Improvement Success Path Forward is the methodology for establishing continuous improvement once collaboration and cooperation within and between supply chain organizations have been established. This path forward has the following steps:

- Establish a Continuous Improvement steering team and Continuous Improvement teams
- Conduct customer and supplier roundtables
- Define continuous improvement vision and evidence of success
- Define prioritized opportunities for improvement
- Implement continuous improvement team recommendations
- Assess evidence of success
- Define new prioritized opportunities for improvement

Continuous improvement is a dynamic process; like a river, it is always moving. That means a supply chain should move with it and make sure its Continuous Improvement efforts can keep up with the motion.

Strategy 12: Synthesis

Supply Chain Excellence cannot be achieved without a synthesized supply chain. Supply Chain Synthesis (SCS) requires design, planning, and execution.

Supply chain design comprises network, inventory, transportation, and customer-satisfaction designs. There is no single, best design for an integrated supply chain, but there are principles that can provide guidance for a Future Capable Company designing such a system with its supply chain partners. The design team should:

- View the supply chain design activity as an integrated process and appoint an SCS leader to oversee it

- Conduct regular sales and operations planning meetings that continuously review performance and operating concerns
- Operate with a single forecast and replenishment plan, not separate plans for finance, sales, logistics, and manufacturing
- Centralize process administration as well as the planning for inventory and replenishment requirements, but leave responsibility for forecasting and weekly/daily line scheduling close to the source
- Build flexibility into the system through SCS manufacturing, quick setup and changeover capabilities, cellular manufacturing, "postponement" principles, and a rapid and efficient planning cycle time
- Use decision-support tools, real-time information, and integrated software in the design process

Supply chain planning follows design. It is a detailed planning process created to meet the needs identified in the design process. It plans for the placement of the right materials at the right location at the right time. In many supply chain situations, the partners work well together on the design stage but become bogged down in the planning stage. In some cases, they focus on software and not on synthesis. Supply chain partners must focus on results, with planning that covers demand, events, inventory, replenishment, manufacturing, and transportation.

Demand planning is a method of forecasting based on past orders. *Event planning* is forecasting based on the one-time events. *Inventory planning* identifies the optimal balance between inventory and desired levels of customer satisfaction based on industry best practices. *Replenishment planning* determines the proper timing to achieve the inventory plan. *Manufacturing planning* involves the scheduling of manufacturing operations, and *Transportation planning* puts in place the procedures to bring the supply chain to life. That is, it provides the logistics connectivity among all levels of the supply chain. These various components of supply chain planning must be linked and cumulative (e.g., demand planning and event planning should be used to drive inventory planning, which in turn should drive replenishment planning, etc.) for SCS to be achieved.

Supply chain execution is the final part of the process. Execution involves the systems that address SCS in real time: order, warehouse, transportation, and manufacturing management. The Internet plays a role in the process as well—it is the communications vehicle that provides the link between supply chain planning and execution. *Order management* accepts orders and passes them to the appropriate systems for fulfillment. *Warehouse management systems* support the activities of the storage facility. *Transportation management systems* focus on controlling costs and managing inbound, outbound, and intra-supply-chain goods movement. *Manufacturing management* ensures the efficiency and effectiveness of manufacturing operations. *Asset management* is the maintenance of assets that support supply chain execution without incurring downtime caused by unreliable equipment.

The results of supply chain execution affect supply chain planning because real-world events can change even the best-laid plans. It is good to review the supply chain planning components regularly and adjust them if execution warrants it. Supply chain planning in turn determines supply chain execution, and if it is altered, then the execution methods must also be altered.

During supply chain planning and execution, businesses must look outward. External applications—e-commerce, customer relationship management, and supply chains with industry-specific applications—are part of both planning and execution. Thus, the latter require the following elements:

- A focus on the customer
- An acceptance of partnering
- An aggressive adaptation of technology, such as e-commerce
- A belief in the teaming process
- A focus on synchronized performance measures
- An openness to creativity and innovation
- A belief in the importance of having no boundaries between the links of the chain

Creating a synthesized supply chain, then, requires an inward beginning and an outward growth. An organization that is synthesized internally and has used the correct processes to achieve that synthesis can then turn outward to the supply chain.

Manufacturing as a Supply Chain Strength

Today's customer-centric and global business environment does not allow us to accept assumptions blindly, because all assumptions at some point will be wrong. Changes in the way customers shop and what they want when they do shop are coming too rapidly and furiously. Manufacturers must be ready to make big changes in the way they view and conduct business. They must accept the fact that boundaries and channels are blurring, thanks to the sweeping changes of the last decade. And, they must understand that business can no longer be contained in a huge factory that owns raw materials plants, manufactures parts from those raw materials, assembles them, creates buffer stock from the assemblies, and ships them to the warehouse. Instead, manufacturers must embrace the idea of the virtual factory, with manufacturing functionalities existing in every link in the supply chain. They also have to recognize that suppliers, manufacturers, and customers must cooperate and collaborate to survive in the war of supply chain vs. supply chain. In this manner they will successfully make the journey to Supply Chain Excellence, which ensures customer satisfaction from the level of the original raw material provider to that of the ultimate, finished-product consumer. By using the strategies outlined in this chapter, manufacturers and their supply chains stand a good chance of succeeding in these exhilarating times.

CHAPTER 19
Leaning The Supply Chain

Bruce Tompkins, Principal, Tompkins Associates

Lean manufacturing, simply defined, is the elimination of waste from manufacturing processes. Leaning the supply chain, likewise, is the elimination of waste from all aspects of the supply chain, from suppliers to end consumers. Manufacturing processes and supply chain processes are value-added, non-value-added, or non-value-added but necessary.

Value-added processes mold, transform, or otherwise change raw materials into a finished product. *Non-value-added* activities do not increase the value of the product in the eyes of the consumer, and typically include transporting materials, conducting inspections, bar coding, and other internal processes. Not all non-value-adding activities can be eliminated. *Non-value-added* but necessary activities are needed for the overall process to work. An example is a final product inspection to ensure adherence to government regulations.

In traditional operations, non-value-added activities can occupy up to 90% of the resources, but are the focus of few improvement efforts. Traditional organizations typically focus on squeezing value-added activities to reduce costs. Examples include speeding up machinery and asking employees to work harder or faster. These methods may work temporarily, but ultimately will fail to get the desired results. Accident rates may increase, union issues occur, and over-taxed equipment breaks down. Lean focuses instead on reducing non-value-adding activities.

The purpose of lean systems today, however, is not simply to minimize waste, but also to foster employee creativity, teamwork, and initiative. It is possible to perform at a higher level with fewer resources. The cliché "work smarter, not harder" epitomizes what lean is all about. Lean works by focusing only on the activities that contribute toward output and by eliminating those that do not. Many companies have adopted lean techniques because they are not viewed like the optional "quality" programs of the 1980s. Lean is a strategy necessary for survival in today's cost competitive marketplace.

The beauty of the lean approach is that it is fairly simple to understand and may be implemented by any organization, with the right attitude in place, at all levels. The attitude of "we will work as a team to be the best," replaces the attitude of "I will look out for my own self-interests, even if it means doing nothing and staying out of sight," an attitude too often adopted by management, as well as the workforce.

Lean concepts were originally implemented at the manufacturing company—or link level. However, today more and more companies are incorporating lean concepts into their respective supply chains. The combined synergy, bias for action, cost savings, and reduced lead times produce results that are difficult to beat.

The History of Lean

During the U.S. occupation after World War II, Japanese companies struggled to rebuild their factories and resume production of consumer goods. To maximize output and minimize the time and investment required to design and manufacture automobiles, Toyota Motor Company developed an approach to manufacturing called "lean".

Rather than squeezing value-added activities to reduce costs, T. Ohno of Toyota decided that eliminating non-value-added activities, otherwise known as waste, would be more productive. Toyota management recognized that upwards of 70 percent of all activities in their manufacturing environment did not contribute directly to transforming raw materials into a finished product. Furthermore, they also realized that the traditional management solution to manufacturing problems was not optimal. Utilizing the knowledge, experience, and creativity of all employees resulted in a much higher level of performance.

The company developed a strong supply chain through very close relationships. Suppliers in many cases relocated adjacent or very close to the Toyota plants, in order to maximize service levels, reduce delivery times, and minimize uncertainty.

Eliminating waste paved the way to adopting the "pull" concept at Toyota. Instead of "pushing" materials from one department (or company) to the next, the items are pulled as needed. A downside to this approach might be a need for storing materials ("buffer" storage) at Department A until they are needed and pulled by Department B. However, by instituting the "just in time" (JIT) manufacturing concept, Toyota was able to reduce buffer storage by delaying producing the item until actually needed downstream.

Toyota achieved similar results when plants were built in the United States. Camry manufacturing at the Georgetown, Kentucky plant is a good example of how one side of the supply chain has focused in one geographic area. Mercedes (Tuscaloosa, Ala.), BMW (Greer, S.C.), Honda (Marysville, Ohio) and Nissan (Smyrna, Tenn.) have moved in the same direction with their respective North American manufacturing locations. The performance of these plants mimics the results achieved in Japan with respect to productivity and cost. This leads to the conclusion that the cost problems in American and European plants were more tied to management practices than labor rates.

Globally, companies began adopting lean manufacturing after Toyota proved it was successful if implemented correctly. Executing lean quickly through Kaizen, or short discreet projects, was Toyota's methodology of choice. After spreading to other companies in Japan, lean continued westward to the United States, primarily within the automobile industry. In the United States, Ford Motor Company discovered and began strongly promoting lean in the late 1970s and early 1980s. In conjunction with their Q1 program, Ford and its suppliers experienced much success with lean concepts.

In 1984, an MIT study group found that lean manufacturing was the most effective production system, much better than mass production. Since the 1990s, it has been used worldwide, although many U.S. industries have been slow to adopt it.

Lean Thinking for the Supply Chain

Although lean thinking is typically applied to manufacturing, lean techniques and focus are applicable anywhere there are processes to improve, including the entire supply chain. A lean supply chain is one that produces just what and how much is needed, when it is needed, and where it is needed.

The underlying theme in lean thinking is to produce more or do more with fewer resources while giving the end customer exactly what he or she wants. This means focusing on each product and its value stream. To do this, organizations must be ready to ask which activities truly create value and which ones are wasteful. The most important thing to remember is that lean is not simply about eliminating waste—it is about eliminating waste *and* enhancing value.

The Concepts of Value and Waste

Value, in the context of lean, is defined as something that the customer is willing to pay for. Value-adding activities transform materials and information into something a customer wants. Non-value-adding activities consume resources, but do not directly contribute to the end result desired by the customer. Waste, therefore, is defined as anything that does not add value from the customer's perspective. Examples of process wastes are defective products, overproduction, inventories, excess motion, processing steps, transportation, and waiting.

Consider the non-manufacturing example of a flight to the Bahamas. The value-adding part of that process is the actual flight itself. The non-value-added parts of that process are driving to the airport, parking at the airport, walking to the terminal, walking to check-in, waiting in line at check-in, walking to the security check, and so on. Many times the non-value-added time far exceeds the value added time in this type of process. Where should our improvement efforts be focused—on the non value-added steps or on making the plane fly faster?

Understanding the difference between value and waste and value-added and non-value-added processes is critical to understanding lean. Sometimes it is not easy to discern the difference when looking at an entire supply chain. The best way is to look at the components of the supply chain and apply lean thinking to each one and determine how to link the processes to reduce waste.

Applying Lean Concepts to the Supply Chain

Throughout its history, those who have developed and used lean have been working to perfect the system. In the process, they have come to realize that lean is a concept that should not be confined to the shop floor level or within a single company. Instead, organizations should apply lean principles to the entire supply chain to ensure supply chain success and excellence.

Lean principles focus on creating value by:

- Specifying value from the end customer's perspective
- Determining a value system by:
  - ➤ Identifying all of the steps required to create value
  - ➤ Mapping the value stream
  - ➤ Challenging every step by asking why five times
- Lining up value, creating steps so they occur in rapid sequence
- Creating flow with capable, available, and adequate processes
- Pulling materials, parts, products, and information from customers
- Continuously improving to reduce and eliminate waste

Of these principles, mapping the value stream, "waste" reduction, creating flow, and pull processes bear closer examination.

Mapping the Value Stream

The value stream consists of the value-adding activities required to design, order, and provide a product from concept to launch, order to delivery, and raw materials to customers. To develop a value stream map for a product, you select a product family and collect process information. Then, you map the steps in sequence and by information flows; this is called a current-state map. The current-state map provides a clear picture of the processing steps and information flow for the process as it exists today. Next, you search the map for improvement opportunities using the concepts of lean, and create a future-state map. The latter is the vision of the future for the process or supply chain you are creating. This future-state map helps you to visualize the roadmap to get from the current state to the future state.

Mapping the value stream for the supply chain is a similar process. However, the current-state map includes product flow, transportation links, defects and delivery, time and steps, and information flow. After creating the current-state map for the supply chain's value stream, supply chain partners should scrutinize it for bottlenecks, waste, and methods of process improvement. They should use what they discover to create future-state maps for the supply chain. An ideal-state map can also be created that provides a vision of how the supply chain could look if perfect integration of all components were to occur. This is in effect an entitlement map for the supply chain process.

Here's how it works: A current-state map might indicate that flow within facilities is well defined, but that transportation methods between facilities create excess inventory and are not cost effective. The current state map may also show a weakness in the information flow that is causing wasted efforts. The future-state map could show how to create flow between facilities, leveling pull within each facility, and eliminating waste. The method for leveling pull might be to install frequent transport runs. Information flow could be improved by installing a Web-based process to allow real-time flow of information between all supply chain partners as demand changes. The ideal-state map could consist of a compressed value system, relocated operations, a win-win-win situation for all organizations involved, and a synthesized supply chain.

"Waste" Reduction

The "waste" reduction process begins with the question "What can we do to improve?" Some answers to that question include:

- Stop defective products at their source
- Flow processes together or change the physical relationship of components of the process to one another.
- Eliminate excess material handling or costly handling steps
- Eliminate or reduce pointless process steps
- Reduce the time spent waiting for parts, orders, other people, or information

In manufacturing environments these waste reductions create the benefits of reduced manufacturing cycle time, reduced labor expenditures, improved product quality, space savings, reduced inventory, and quicker response to the customer. When waste is reduced or eliminated across the supply chain, the supply chain's cycle time is improved, labor and staff costs are reduced, product quality and delivery are improved, inventories are reduced and customer lead-times are shortened. The net effect is the entire supply chain is more efficient and responsive to customer needs.

Creating Flow

An important goal of lean is to flow products to and from all operations in a level, continuous manner and in the smallest quantity that the process can support. One piece/continuous flow is the methodology used to accomplish this goal. For example, to create one-piece/continuous flow in the manufacturing process, you might move operations next to each other in sequence to create a production cell. This cellular layout flows products from one operation to another in batches of one on a continuous basis. To create a cell you must:

- Define families of parts with similar processes
- Locate equipment in sequence with minimum physical separation
- Produce and move parts in the smallest lots possible, approaching one
- Produce at the rate of customer demand or tact time

The tact time is the rate of customer demand for a product. It can be thought of as the pulse or drum beat at which the process must operate to satisfy customer needs.

In a similar way the supply chain can also be configured to create flow. Where today excessive transportation is required to move materials and information from one point in the chain to another, we can link the processes physically or electronically to create flow.

When continuous flow is achieved, costs and time will be reduced for the entire supply chain. While linking points in the chain together is more difficult for the supply chain than within a facility, the benefits are tremendous. These benefits are what have led so many automotive suppliers to locate close to their supply points.

Pull Processes in Manufacturing and the Supply Chain

The key to pull in manufacturing is to produce only what the customer needs when the customer needs it. This means balancing production with demand and producing and flowing material in response to real demand—not on a schedule based on a forecast. Thus, manufacturing must be capable of responding to changing demand and executing on the factory floor based on signals from customers.

Pull systems rely on visual records or signals from the customer or a Kanban. Another product of Japanese industry, Kanban is a form of visual management that signals each successive step in a process as illustrated in Figure 19.1.

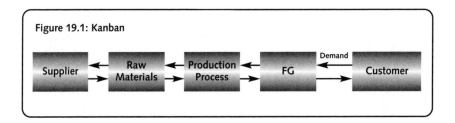

Figure 19.1: Kanban

A Kanban signal is used at each step of the process to tell the process what quantity of material is needed by a subsequent step to meet the needs of the customer. It signals when to move or produce, controls material flow, and helps determine whether the process is functioning under normal conditions. The Kanban system works best with a stable demand and product mix, short manufacturing cycle times, and high levels of quality and process reliability.

The concepts of pull and Kanban systems apply to the supply chain as well as to manufacturing processes. Material can be pulled from one point in the supply chain to the next based on customer demand. The use of pull processes across the supply chain can greatly reduce the complexity of the process and increase its speed and effectiveness.

With an understanding of the lean principles of waste reduction, flow and pull, you're ready to begin creating a lean supply chain.

Components of the Lean Supply Chain

The major components of the lean supply chain are:

- Lean suppliers
- Lean procurement
- Lean manufacturing

• Lean warehousing
• Lean transportation
• Lean customers

Lean Suppliers

Lean suppliers are able to respond to changes. Their prices are generally lower due to the efficiencies of lean, and their quality is improved to the point that incoming inspection at the next link is not needed. Lean suppliers deliver on time and their culture is one of continuous improvement.

To develop lean suppliers, organizations should include suppliers in their value stream. They should encourage suppliers to make the lean transformation and involve them in lean activities. This will help them fix problems and share savings. In turn, they can help their suppliers and set continually declining price targets and increasing quality goals.

Lean Procurement

Some lean procurement processes are e-procurement and automated procurement. E-procurement conducts transactions, strategic sourcing, bidding, and reverse auctions over Internet lines or on the Web. Automated procurement uses software that removes the human element from multiple procurement functions and integrates with financials.

The key to lean procurement is visibility. Suppliers must be able to "see" into their customers' operations and customers must be able to "see" into their suppliers' operations. Organizations should map the current value stream, and together create a future value stream in the procurement process. They should create a flow of information while establishing a pull of information.

Lean Manufacturing

Lean manufacturing systems produce what the customer wants, in the quantity the customer wants, when the customer wants it, and with minimum resources. Lean efforts typically start in manufacturing because they free up resources for continuous improvement in other areas, and create a pull on the rest of the organization. Applying lean concepts to manufacturing typically presents the greatest opportunity for cost reduction and quality improvement, however, many organizations have received huge benefits from lean concepts in other functions.

Lean Warehousing

Lean warehousing means eliminating non-value added steps and waste in product storage processes. Typical warehousing functions are:

• Receiving
• Put-away/storing
• Replenishment
• Picking

- Packing
- Shipping

Warehousing waste can be found throughout the storage process including:

- Defective products which create returns
- Overproduction or over shipment
- Excess inventories which require additional space and reduce warehousing efficiency
- Excess motion and handling
- Processing steps
- Transportation
- Waiting for parts, materials and information
- Information processes

Each step in the warehousing process should be examined critically to see where unnecessary, repetitive, and non-value-added activities might be so that they may be eliminated.

Lean Transportation

Lean concepts in transportation include:

- Core carrier programs
- Improved transportation administrative processes
- Optimized mode selection—pooling orders
- Combined multi-stop truckloads
- Crossdocking
- Right sizing equipment
- Import/export transportation processes
- Inbound transportationæbackhauls
- Supply chain process improvement
- Automated transaction steps

The keys to accomplishing the concepts above include reducing waste in processes, eliminating non-value-added activities, mapping the value stream, creating flow, and using pull processes.

Lean Customers

Lean customers understand their business needs and therefore can specify meaningful requirements. They value speed and flexibility and expect high levels of delivery performance and quality. Lean customers are interested in establishing effective partnerships—they are always seeking methods of continuous improvement in the total supply chain to reduce costs. Lean customers expect value from the products they purchase and provide value to the consumers who they interact with.

Requirements for the Lean Supply Chain

The requirements for a lean supply chain are the total understanding of the supply chain's elements, communication and alignment of business partners, and an attitude of continuous improvement.

Total understanding of supply chain elements—All elements of the supply chain must be fully understood before lean improvements may be made. The relationships between the elements, or the links, should be developed based on their specific attributes and their relationships to one another. This includes documenting systems and the relationships between systems. For this purpose, the mapping process is useful in visualizing the complex relationships and information flow that exist between supply chain partners.

Once the relationships are clearly known, we must define supply chain measures of success, or metrics that will relate directly to the values, mission, goals, and objectives of the organization. After these measures of success are defined and agreed upon, a baseline of performance, or "stake in the ground," must be established for them. To measure future performance through continuous improvement, the organization must know not only where it has been, but also where it is currently.

Communication and alignment—When you set out to integrate business processes and disparate entities in the supply chain, effective communication is key. The communication must be simultaneous, instantaneous, and multi-directional to allow all supply chain partners to work at the same time rather than sequentially. This approach eliminates inventory buffers and accelerates the flow of cash. It also allows for dynamic planning, which replaces the outdated practices of long-term forecasting. Strategic information is made available to all partners, so that all have contact with the customer and are aware of changing needs and trends. They can then respond in unison to these needs and trends.

Electronic connectivity via the Internet provides the backbone for this communication. This will greatly reduce transaction costs as orders, invoices, and payments are handled electronically, and inventories are kept low through vendor-managed inventory programs. The key is ensuring the continuous flow of information, and to use the information and communications methodology to create alignment.

An organization achieves alignment when it can accomplish the following:

- Connect its employees' behavior to the mission of the company, turning intentions into actions
- Link teams and processes to the changing needs of customers
- Shape business strategy with real-time information from customers
- Create a culture in which these elements all work together seamlessly

The same principles apply to an extra-organizational collaboration among supply chain partners. In the lean supply chain, the seamless connection between the producer of raw materials and the ultimate customer is critical. Customers and end consumers will feel any breakdown in supply chain communications, because extra inventory is not available to cover such lapses.

Continuous improvement—The cornerstone of supply chain continuous improvement programs is collaboration through teamwork and partnerships. Such collaboration requires following these guiding principles:

- All organizational units and supply chain links must be 100 percent directed toward the success of the whole supply chain.
- There can be no adversarial relationships within the organization or the supply chain.
- All organizational units must function as a cohesive, collective whole.
- An environment where every employee is motivated and happy will eliminate the "we vs. them" problem that undermines teamwork.

Once the collaboration and cooperation within and between supply chain organizations have been established, the following steps should be taken for continuous improvement:

- Establish a continuous improvement steering team and continuous improvement teams
- Conduct customer and supplier roundtables
- Define continuous improvement vision and evidence of success
- Define prioritized opportunities for improvement
- Implement continuous improvement team recommendations
- Assess evidence of success
- Define new prioritized opportunities for improvement

Continuous improvement is a dynamic process. The key is to keep searching for ways to improve relationships, processes, and products.

Lean Supply Chain Lessons Learned

It is important to remember that when working to lean the supply chain, a successful implementation will always have minor "hiccups" or disruptions at the onset. The hiccups are a part of the learning process. If the process is the correct one, however, these minor issues will slowly disappear over time. Confidence and enthusiasm will replace skepticism and fear. These attitudes will spread quickly and others at all levels will become curious and interested in participating. Some of the lessons learned to prevent hiccups in lean implementation include the following:

The right team structure—A critical first step is selecting the right team members and team leader to accomplish supply chain lean implementation. Because a successful team should be representative of the entire supply chain, skill sets should be diverse but must include a good working knowledge of lean concepts. Difficulties may arise if top and middle management infiltrate a lean implementation team in an attempt to help, but end up dictating how things will be done. Under such conditions, other team members cannot get their ideas heard, and eventually stop participating.

To prevent this intervention, an important question that must be asked early in the team-building process is, "Do we have the right players?" The right players must meet three criteria:

1. They must want to be a part of the team.
2. They must have the abilities the team requires.
3. They must be truly committed to the success of the team.

It is also important that everyone on the team meet the following specific criteria:

- Shared vision—All team players have a consistent vision of where the team is headed.
- Shared values—All team players adopt and adhere to a level of business ethics and honesty beyond levels that have been traditionally viewed as the norm. A code of ethics is not a book of dos and don'ts, but is the moral fiber of the team players. High ethical standards may result in the loss of some short-term opportunities, but in the long run, they will provide a basis for teamwork and trust.
- Shared expectations—There are no surprises for team players. The team has well defined and understood expectations that are shared by all team players and serve as the basis for teamwork.
- Shared commitment—There is no such thing as a part-time team player. Team players are committed to the team and dedicated to mutual success and cooperation.
- Shared confidence—Each team player has confidence in all other team players.
- Shared responsibility—Communications, involvement, and interactions are frequent. Team players share responsibility for success and failure. Team players are accountable for their efforts and for the team's performance.
- Shared rewards—All team players benefit from the team's success.

Creating an implementation roadmap—The lean supply chain must be initiated from top management and executed with a team-based process. Top management must be capable of evaluating the current-state map and, with the help of the implementation team, create a future-state map that moves the supply chain closer to the ideal of lean. The roadmap becomes the task list required to move the current processes to the future state. It must be detailed enough to allow the implementation team to execute the tasks, but general enough to be flexible as the environment changes and needs change. The roadmap must be reviewed and updated periodically to ensure that it still accurately reflects top management's strategic objectives and aligns resources effectively.

Management commitment—A lean supply chain implementation will often start strongly, then wither as problems and difficult issues arise. In some cases, the formula for success has been put together to make it happen. The commitment is present, the resources are present, and successes are happening. However, time or priorities may change, meetings are missed, assignments go uncompleted, and eventually the diluted motivation filters throughout the organization. The teams eventually stop meeting and the entire process dies.

In other cases, there was never a commitment to begin with. Top management was impressed with a book or a seminar and directed others to begin lean activities, or an off-site executive forced it on everyone, including the location manager. For a short period of time, the process may succeed. As the executive loses interest, and as the location managers see an opening for withdrawal, the process begins to fail.

What is needed to ensure that this is not how the story ends is to identify a high-level individual to champion the lean transformation. Picking the right person is key to keeping the momentum going and instilling the discipline to follow the process. All of the top managers must have a common vision of continuous improvement and be held accountable for the overall success of the process.

Allocating resources—Although a lean supply chain attempts to minimize resources of all types, most lean transitions that fail do so because of a lack of adequate resources. Facilitators and lean experts are an absolute requirement, but they do not have to be dedicated to this function only. Internal resources are needed to keep the attitude and process going strong. If internal resources are not developed, the lean process will lose momentum. Also, internal leaders must emerge to manage and continuously improve the process.

Training and preparation—Many times an outside expert will be hired to provide training, but this person is often given too much responsibility for implementation and continuous improvement of the lean supply chain. If the "expert" does not transfer knowledge to the team and develop in-house leaders, the learning process will not grow and the pace of improvement will slow down.

Many companies feel that they cannot afford an expert and as a result, middle or low-level managers are assigned responsibility for the transition process. In this situation, resources are available, but not necessarily the right ones. This is the worse of the two situations, because important decisions will be made with very limited knowledge. These people will be directed to read a book, and then "make it happen." The chances of true success are reduced in this environment.

Setting expectations—A high level of motivation is always a good thing, but directed inappropriately it could result in failure. The most common, and most costly, mistake is attempting to implement lean concepts into a supply chain before an appropriate knowledge base is in place. For example, many companies have moved to JIT prematurely, with the result that inventory levels have been reduced so low, that orders cannot be filled. The systems supporting a move such as JIT must first be in place before benefits may be realized.

Leaning a supply chain is not a goal in itself. The goal should be continuous improvement and employee enrichment. Implementing a lean supply chain because other companies are also doing it is a trap that many eager managers fall into. Lean is an action-based program and cannot take place on its own. All members of the would-be lean organization must contribute to its success.

Small successes should be followed by larger successes. Working up to large improvements is always the best strategy. In only a few cases will a large success result early in a new application of lean to a supply chain. The potential for problems is overwhelming. Also, many employees do not have experience and confidence working in a team-based environment. Only through experience and confidence will an organization thrive in a team-based improvement culture and take advantage of the benefits of a lean supply chain.

Benefits of Lean Systems

The benefits of a lean supply chain include the following:

Speed and responsiveness to customers—Lean systems will allow a supply chain not only to be lighter, but also faster. As the culture of lean takes over the entire supply chain, all links increase their velocity. A culture of rapid response and faster decisions becomes the expectation and the norm. This does not mean that decisions are made without careful thought. It simply means that a "bias for action" becomes the new corporate culture and anything less will not be tolerated. Slow response or no response becomes the exception, rather than the rule.

Reduced inventories—In the lean paradigm, inventory is considered waste. Many would argue this point, but manufacturing may take place efficiently with little or no raw material, work in process (WIP), or finished goods inventory. Eliminating finished goods inventory is less complicated than having no raw material inventory. WIP is somewhere in between.

Many companies today produce directly into trailers and maintain no other finished goods inventory. All quality inspections and checks are performed within the process, rather than after production is complete. In this true make-to-order scenario, all goods are shipped directly to the next link in the supply chain when the trailer is full, and overproduction is not possible and cannot be tolerated. No space is designated to store finished goods. The system is not designed to carry them.

Applying one-piece flow and pull systems reduces WIP dramatically. A Kanban or visual signal for more goods to be moved forward to the next process can accomplish this procedure. Although the ultimate goal is to eliminate WIP totally, minimal WIP is normally the result. Bottleneck elimination is one goal of a lean supply chain, but a bottleneck will always exist to some degree. As a result, WIP must always exist in front of a bottleneck or the bottleneck operation will be starved and will stop.

Raw material inventory is a different matter. Although the leanest organizations have arranged JIT deliveries to support manufacturing, this approach requires the absolute highest degree of competency and coordination within the supply chain.

Reduced costs—Traditional mass production tries to minimize unit costs by increasing total production over the life cycle of the product. High development costs are the result of this model. To recover the enormous development and initial capital costs sunk into the product before it was produced, mass producers forecast and run long production cycles for each SKU. Consumer preferences and variety suffer in this scenario. Costs still need to be minimized, but not at the expense of what more sophisticated consumers now demand.

Lean concepts have proven that companies may use half the traditional resources to produce products. These resources include labor, space, capital, inventory, and material handling. Fewer resources translate directly to less costs. These minimized resources are not related to automation. Surveys have shown an inverse relationship between level of automation and effectiveness, including quality levels.

Improved customer satisfaction—Lean promotes minimizing new product development time and expense. This delivers the product to market faster, making it easier to incorporate current requirements into the product. Lean also promotes the use of less capital-intensive machines, tools, and fixtures, which results in more flexibility and less initial cost to recover. As a result, product life cycles may be shorter and newer developments incorporated in newer versions of the product more frequently. Profitability does not suffer and brand loyalty is increased, as customers prefer to buy products and services from a perceived innovator.

Supply chain as a competitive weapon—A strong supply chain enables the member companies to align themselves with each other and to coordinate their continuous improvement efforts. This synthesis enables even small firms to participate in the results of lean efforts. Competitive advantage and leadership in the global marketplace can only be gained by applying lean principles to the supply chain. Thought, commitment, planning, collaboration, and a path forward are required.

Path Forward to a Lean Supply Chain

Lean is a cooperative process for survival and for success. Supply chains that want to grow and continue to improve must adopt lean. Lean is an attitude of continuous improvement with a bias for action. The concepts of lean apply to all elements of the supply chain, including support departments such as product development, quality, human resources, marketing, finance, purchasing, and distribution. The challenge is to bring all of these areas out of their traditional silos and make them work together to reduce waste and flow, and for the continued growth and success of the organization. Duplication and a lack of appropriate and timely communication run rampant in these traditional organizations. A lean supply chain is proactive and plans for the unexpected by positioning all resources for effectiveness. Downturns in demand can be addressed without layoffs or significant productivity losses.

Leaning "other" areas presents a larger challenge than it does in manufacturing. Supervisors and factory workers embrace change that results in making their lives less complicated and more successful. In the hierarchy of support areas, it is more challenging for the people to understand how lean can benefit them. The answer is simple: What benefits the organization as a whole benefits the supply chain.

Because the Internet provides us with unprecedented opportunities for sharing information and conducting transactions across the supply chain, companies should have a sense of urgency about adopting lean concepts. But all chain partners have to be on the same playing field, and the lean concept is intended to let everyone reach new levels of efficiency and effectiveness. Supply chains should not delay—it's urgent to act now to implement lean concepts in the supply chain.

CHAPTER 20
Linking Store Replenishment To The Supply Chain

Don Vehlhaber, President, SPI Consulting

I n the latter half of the 20th century, two distinct replenishment strategies for retail stores evolved. One relied upon a centralized buying concept that "pushed" goods to the stores, and the other entailed a decentralized ordering structure that "pulled" goods through the supply pipeline. The specialty, apparel and general merchandise segments of the consumer products industry came to utilize the former and the grocery and drugstore sectors primarily embraced the latter concept.

Early Systems Support

Prior to the 1950s, replenishment of goods for "pull" structured retail segments was largely intuitive, relying on a manual review of stock to determine what to reorder. Indeed, this concept continued for over four decades, at least at the store level. However, in the 1950s, an energetic, creative and entrepreneurial Princeton alumnus Mr. Charles C. Fitzmorris, Jr. (who made his fortune importing cuckoo clocks from Germany and reportedly coined the well-known advertising banner "Peter Paul Mounds – Indescribably Delicious"), was the owner of the Benner Tea Company—a wholesale and retail grocery operation. He obviously inherited his colorful nature from his father, the former Chicago Police Commissioner during Prohibition and who, in 1901, traveled around the world in 60 days, 13 hours and 2 minutes. In any event, Fitzmorris, Jr. engaged the IBM Software Services division to write a software application, using functional requirements that he had developed, to facilitate purchase of replenishment merchandise using historical warehouse withdrawals as the basis for forecasting product demand. In addition to the purchase management system, a warehouse management system was also developed that automated the manual stock ledgers that heretofore were the basis for warehouse inventory management. Eventually, a labor management module, utilizing integrated engineered labor standards for individual task assignment, performance tracking and variance reporting was developed. Finally, an automated store order management module, that facilitated store orders billing, inventory commitment and rules-based product allocation (whenever sufficient inventory levels were not available to satisfy total store orders demand), was also developed for the Benner Tea Company by IBM, again using Mr. Fitzmorris's operational requirements.

Fitzmorris eventually sold the Benner Tea Company to Germany's largest grocery chain, and Aldi Stores thus apparently became the first completely foreign-owned grocery chain in the United States. Mr. Fitzmorris retained title to the software applications utilized at the Benner Tea Company upon leaving Aldi Stores, and he then started

Worldwide Chain Store Systems, Inc. (WCSS) to market the new software applications to the worldwide grocery industry. The effort was highly successful, and achieved significant cost savings benefits for the grocery and drug chains. By the early 1990s, WCSS had achieved grocery chain industry penetration to the point that over 46 percent of the total industry retail sales dollars were processed through one or more of the WCSS system modules. Indeed, WCSS spawned several derivative software offerings in the marketplace including BACG Marwood—subsequently known as the now defunct Armiture, OMI and Dallas Systems—which later became a part of EXE (all of which were started by former WCSS employees) and all of which had their genesis in the original WCSS software applications functionality. It is remarkable that three of the four companies offering theses automated operational systems to the industry continue to exist in the marketplace today. The competitive environment formed by these systems offerings not only spread these pioneering systems to the entire world marketplace, but also resulted in significant enhancements in their functional capabilities. For example, the forecasted demand derived from historical warehouse withdrawals for individual items was eventually accumulated by vendor and was then used to suggest purchase orders based on up to five different ordering strategies and balanced by vendor minimums and maximums associated with truckload case capacities, weight restrictions and cubic volume (more commonly known as "load building"). Likewise, the slotting of products in the warehouse came to be driven by optimum X, Y and Z coordinates (length, width and height) location calculations based on movement volumes (faster moving products were slotted to lower levels of storage racks), travel
distance from receiving doors (like movement volumes were grouped closer together) and proximity of overflow storage to home slotting locations to optimize order selection productivity and associated receipt, storage and selection labor efficiency.

Next Generation Systems

These sophisticated applications bred a new generation of integrated systems that not only took functionality across all consumer products industry segments to new levels, but also spurred the development of ever increasing computer hardware and peripheral equipment capabilities (in 1990, IBM held a 20 percent share of WCSS, and subsequently purchased the entire company). Smaller, faster, more powerful engines running increasingly complex and functionally rich software modules became the norm and new technological breakthroughs were announced at increasingly shorter time intervals. Centralized mainframes were augmented by new mid-size computers that distributed processing for specific operational needs and eventually the personal computer (PC) brought computing power and enabling software into the hands of virtually every worker within the corporation, and linked workers together into local and wide area networks to share applications and data resources.

The Advent Of Forward Buying In Food And Drug

In 1974, President Richard Nixon imposed a wage-price freeze to combat rampant inflation in the United States, and food industry manufacturers were quick to establish a base price, before the controls actually went into effect, that was considerably higher than the previous "going rate," to get around the governmental restrictions on raising prices. The concept of "deal" offerings, including increasing discounts for volume purchase brackets, off-invoice allowances, bill-backs, and many other creative ways of lowering artificially high list pricing, created a demand for an automated system module that would track the various deal offerings and analyze the carrying costs and optimum purchase level for individual products subject to the various active deals (sometimes a given item would have several deal offerings active at the same time—these became known as "nested" deals). The practice of "investment buying" or "forward buying" was thus introduced to the industry, and system functionality to address calculation of the return on inventory investment (ROII) of the various time supply alternatives of individual items was initiated. In addition, "diverter buying", a process where one purchasing entity would pool orders from other entities (one buying region would purchase for several other regions within a chain—ultimately known as "corporate" buying, or where a cooperative buying group would procure merchandise for several co-op members or alliance partners, etc.) thus allowing all the associated entities to take advantage of the better price discounts associated with higher volume buying levels or other deal offerings, was also enabled. Over a span of some 25 years, a significant inefficiency within the industry resulted from these practices and many a warehouse structure was built solely to store investment inventories. Of course, the basic demand structure at the consumer level did not really change, so many wasteful promotional practices, such as coupons (less than one percent of all coupons produced in the United States are actually redeemed; and the number of annual coupons produced, if laid end-to-end has been estimated to circle the earth at the equator up to seven times) came into play to help move these artificially inflated inventories.

Efficiencies Of "Quick Response" In Apparel And General Merchandise

Meanwhile, the advent of the Quick Response (QR) movement for "push" style retailers in the specialty, apparel and general merchandise industries proved very successful in the late 1970s and early 1980s. Likewise, the Japanese concept of "Just-in-Time" raw materials supply to manufacturers also became popular about the same time. When the efficiencies of the two concepts became apparent, especially as illustrated by the phenomenal success of the then upstart Wal-Mart chain and their suppliers, the food and drug industries responded by engaging McKinsey Associates to study the potential impact of the QR and Just-in-Time movements on the grocery and drug consumer goods segments. McKinsey responded that the "pull" industry segments were at great risk because of the inefficiencies that had accumulated over the years. Alarmed by the findings, the industry commissioned what was to become known as the Efficient Consumer Response (ECR) study. The report indicated that over $30 billion in savings could result from improvement in four strategic areas: Efficient Product Introduction (at the time, over 80 percent of all new product introductions were failing within six months of introduction), Efficient Replenishment (the grocery model was anything but, with the wasteful forward buying practices), Efficient Promotion (the coupon problem, along with several other issues, such as the seasonal and repetitive event calendars that basically taught the consumer to buy only when items were heavily promoted) and Efficient Assortments (more about this later). Eventually the QR and ECR concepts began to blur the demarcation between traditional "push" and "pull" structures as more and more retailers and suppliers implemented the various components of the two strategies. Instead of sending all merchandise out to the stores immediately after processing, traditional "push" retailers began to hold back some merchandise (known as "pool stock") to replenish the "hot-hand" stores that were selling product at a torrid pace verses a more tepid pace at other stores. In turn, traditional "push" retailers began engaging in cross-docking tactics that amounted to an immediate flowing of some goods directly to stores instead of warehousing them. The concept of Supply Chain Management became firmly entrenched.

The Birth Of Demand Chain Management

By the 1990s, the advances in computer technology storage capacities and processing speeds made possible, for the first time, the concept of forecasting demand for individual products at the store level. The idea of Demand Chain Management was conceived, to extend the traditional supply chain that heretofore relied upon historical warehouse withdrawals, to drive the replenishment process to the individual retail store. By feeding historical point-of-sale (POS) data into the demand forecasting system modules, retailers have now begun to determine optimum replenishment orders for individual stores; they then upload this information into the traditional warehouse or distribution center replenishment forecasting systems to derive suggested purchase orders for manufacturer's goods based upon consumer purchase patterns at POS.

To illustrate the difference, let's consider the following example: Assume that a retailer operates two stores and orders 100 cases of product for shipment into the warehouse or distribution center (DC). Fifty cases of product are then shipped to each store from the DC. Store "A" sells all 50 cases of product it received, but Store "B" sells only five cases. What should be replenished? Under the concept of using historical warehouse withdrawal information as the driver for demand forecasting, the identified replenishment need is likely to be 100 cases of product, as this quantity has been previously withdrawn from the original 100 cases of supply to the DC. And yet, common sense tells us that this should not be the response at all! While it is true that Store A is out of stock on the particular item, Store B still has a more than adequate supply based on historical sales of the product. Certainly we need to replenish Store A. Perhaps the correct answer, then, is to buy 50 more cases of product from the manufacturer, ship it to the DC, then have the DC in turn ship all 50 cases to Store A to replenish their stock. Yet this seems to be a less than satisfactory response as well, as the DC will still be devoid of any merchandise to replenish either store's future needs, and Store A is likely to sell out again during the same time frame that Store B sells five more cases based upon historical volume patterns. Thus, Store A will again go out of stock, while Store B will still have 40 cases of product available for sale. One can readily see that the issue is more complex that originally perceived. The correct answer seems to favor the idea of using historical product POS data for each individual store to derive the actual need for replenishment. This lends credence to the idea that 100 cases should not be split equally to the stores in the first place. Store A sells the item at a pace 10 times that of Store B, so perhaps 100 cases received by the DC should be split 91 cases to Store A and nine cases to Store B. Then again, perhaps 34 cases should be held in reserve in the DC and 60 cases sent to Store A while 6 cases are sent to Store B.

Balance Of Many Factors

Through this example, we can readily see that satisfaction of individual store stock replenishment needs must be balanced against such factors as individual store movement versus other stores to better balance customer service levels, and reserve stock levels must take into account equal store time supplies which, in turn, are driven by corresponding corporate procurement vendor and item review cycles, reorder strategies and vendor order delivery time variances (assuming similar replenishment time frames from DC to each store). We must also carry more safety stock at the DC level if there is a significant variance in vendor delivery cycles; if the average re-supply time from a vendor is two weeks, but on one occasion the replacement order is received within one day of purchase order placement, and on another occasion the delivery is not made for four weeks, then the average delivery cycle calculation is indeed correct, but the variance requires us to accommodate the late order delivery by ensuring an extra two weeks of safety stock is maintained at the DC to replenish high volume stores in time to avoid disruption to the consumer service level.

Through this albeit simplistic example, one can readily see the advantages in optimizing and integrating the stock levels at all locations within the supply pipeline, from the stores back to the DC, from the DC to the wholesale/distributor and then back to the manufacturer; indeed, one must go all the way back to the raw materials suppliers to the manufacturer to optimize the individual product supply pipeline. And obviously, the process becomes more complex as more items, more vendors, and more stores are added to the mix.

The Complexity Of Retail

Couple this to the variations in the consumer base as well, and the overall complexity becomes overwhelming. Stores are obviously located in differing geographies, and the shoppers that visit those stores also vary in demographics and psychographic purchasing triggers. There may be economic (one consumer owns a car, another takes the bus), age (one consumer family has children and buys diapers, another has an empty nest and no need for such products) or ethnic differences in the consumer base for any given store, likewise there may be differing motivations for buying one product over another (one consumer buys wine with a cheese purchase, another is a tea-totaler).

How can a retailer cope with these infinite variations? Many different theories have been tried. The concept of category management, which facilitates the management of individual products by grouping them by like characteristics or attributes (which was born in the traditional "pull" retailer environment) has been embraced by the "push" segments. Likewise, customer relationship management, originally conceived by the airline industry frequent flyer programs, is now firmly embedded in virtually all of the consumer products industry segments.

The Power Cube

But it is the integration and interaction of these concepts wherein the true value lies. If one indeed accepts the need to begin at the consumer and work backward through the supply chain to optimize inventory levels throughout the pipeline (Demand Chain Management or Supply Chain Synthesis), then the logical viewpoint is that of a cube comprised of the three dimensional axes of consumers, products and stores. Furthermore, this "Power Cube™" (trademark of SPI Consulting International, Inc. 2003) can be broken into even smaller "cubes within the cube" via segmentation of the axes into varying degrees of importance; i.e., the ranking of customers from top to bottom of purchase transactions, the ranking of products from top to bottom movement, and the ranking of stores from top to bottom producers.

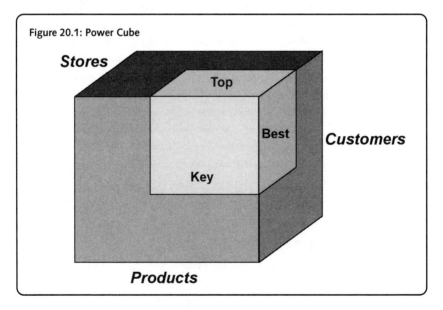

Figure 20.1: Power Cube

Thus, we can have the "Diamond" cube of the best customers, key products and top stores, to the next level of the "Platinum" cube, on to the "Gold" cube, the "Silver" cube and the "Bronze" cube, or any other variations we may want to consider. By segmenting in this manner, we achieve a workable clustering, one that can be analyzed in comparison to the next grouping, average grouping, etc. This concept results in a practical solution to an otherwise infinite tangle of possibilities.

Decision Making Utilizing The Power Cube

Through the use of this methodology, decisions can be made about what products to carry in which stores, how well the selected assortment is serving the needs of the individual store shoppers, and the success of these strategies can then be measured in terms of customer retention rates. If customers cannot find what they want when they visit a particular store, they may very well continue to shop the store if they are able to find the vast majority of what they came to the store to buy in the first place; however, if they cannot find many of the items they are looking for, the most likely result will be that they will take their patronage elsewhere.

A highly sophisticated software application, using transactional point-of-sale information (called T-log data) can interpret the various combinations of customers and products within a given store and this information can be rolled up to chain level and expressed in terms of the aforementioned cubes. Thus, the ECR concept of Efficient Assortments can be achieved through proper analysis of POS data utilizing the cube format. Coupled with other devices such as quadrant and contribution analysis, one can readily discern the specific assortment (called a "custom mix") that is optimal for a given store or grouping of stores (a "cluster").

Answers To Key Questions

Proper utilization of the Power Cube concept facilitates the answers to such questions as:

- How many of our best customers from last year are still our best customers this year? What percentage stopped shopping in our stores? How many of the best customers did we lose last year and how many have we gained or converted from other profile levels this year?
- What items or categories do we carry that are Cash Cows for us? Which ones are Dogs? Are we effectively drawing traffic into the stores by properly promoting Traffic Builders? Are we increasing market basket sales through in-store promotions of Sleepers?
- Why did some stores outperform others in the same category? Are we effectively allocating shelf space to key categories and items? What items perform the best across the parameters of unit sales, dollar sales, gross margin dollars, and gross margin percent? How is our in-stock inventory balance on these items? How are we doing versus our competitors on shelf stock-outs? Are we better at certain times of the day?
- What is the best grouping of stores and the best assortment for these stores based upon key shopper profiles?
- How much do our best shoppers spend per store visit? How often do they visit a store? How much more do our best customers spend per visit than our average customers?

- Can we increase sales by five percent if 20 percent of our average customers move up to our best customer level? What would happen if half of our average customers stopped shopping our stores?
- How important is [category] to our best and better customers than it is to our average customers?

Expected Benefits

Proper execution and utilization of the Power Cube concept should lead to significant benefits, especially in the areas of:

- Improved sales from better understanding of the shopping patterns of the five levels of customer profiles—increased market basket size and lower shelf stock-outs.
- Increased margin from improved knowledge of what items customers will always purchase at full price (never promote these items for less than full price) and from more targeted promotions to store- or cluster-specific customer bases.
- Lower inventory levels because of less investment in slower moving items and more investment in faster moving items, resulting in increased inventory turnover.

Indeed, retailers are already achieving significant benefits, as evidenced by these actual implementations of some, or all of, the Power Cube concept:

- A top five automotive aftermarket retailer completed a proof of concept test of store clustering and custom mix assortments for the back-room categories that captured a 1.3 percent increase in sales on more than $1 billion of hardparts sales, a 2.5 percent overall margin increase, and a reduction of over $13 million of inventory. Total benefit should approach $38 million.
- A top five supermarket retailer identified improvements in chain-wide inventory replenishment forecasting that projected over $22 million of benefits. Later, they revised the estimate up to $300 million!
- A Northeast supermarket retailer completed a retail sales and inventory optimization assessment of non-perishables items that projected a 10 percent increase in sales, 25 percent margin average margin increase, a 25 percent increase in inventory turnover and a 30-35 percent inventory reduction. Actual benefits to date verified the projected turnover increase and documented a 35 percent inventory reduction.
- A major mass merchandiser generated five new category assortments, assigned the new assortments to 15 test stores and kept the old assortment in 25 test stores. The results were reported in Supermarket News and included a 32.5 percent sales increase, a 46 percent inventory reduction and an 11 percent improvement in category turn.

Calculation Of Appropriate Store Stock

Optimization of individual store or cluster-based assortments is the first step in determination of WHAT to carry (Products) for WHOM (Customers) and WHERE (Stores). The next consideration should be WHEN to replenish (Time Supply) and HOW

MUCH (Quantities) is needed to support the desired time supply. Calculation of the appropriate level of stock for each item in the tailored assortment for a given store must take into consideration the store layout and physical shelf space available in that store. Space should be allocated by product category and by individual item in comparison to all other categories and items. Proper space allocation should also result in optimized stocking labor costs.

The required space to accommodate a particular equal time supply of merchandise for a given store can be identified by the more sophisticated space management systems available in the marketplace using shelf depth, required product facings (and product stacking options, if any) and individual product dimensional data. Several iterations may be required to balance the time supply of merchandise to the available linear footage of shelving available in the store. Also, adjustments may have to be made to faster versus slower moving items (too much space may be required by a high velocity item, therefore the time supply may be adjusted with the corresponding need to restock the item more frequently).

Through the use of the Power Cube concept, individual item service levels can be determined. Stock levels for items frequently purchased by Diamond and Platinum customers should be set on a "never out" program of 100 percent service levels to the customer. On the other hand, items that are infrequently purchased by Bronze or Silver customers (the bottom 5 percent of all items, for example) may occasionally run out of stock with minimal consequences to store performance. The calculation of optimum stocking levels should take the customer/item service levels into consideration.

Once the space allocation issue has been resolved, the next step is to monitor the velocity of individual items to determine when to replenish the product. The increasing use of store perpetual inventory systems, coupled with point of sale data and store receipt systems has made the use of computer assisted, or even computer generated, ordering (CAO or CGO) a viable alternative for many retailers.

Data Warehousing, Data Mining And The Concept Of Performance Management

The complexity of the retail equation, coupled with the volume of data to be analyzed and synthesized, has necessitated a fundamental shift from transactional-centric to information-centric thinking. The underlying foundation is that of a business model which provides collaboration and informational linkages that drive intelligent action and predicable/consistent decisions throughout the organization. This is the impetus behind a new class of software, hardware, and decision support processes/capabilities that help organizations manage performance in a methodical and coordinated manner.

If improved operational performance management is the strategy, then methodologies and process for structuring the analysis of information, and decisions linked to that information, are the keys to managing the performance of the entire organization. Performance Management focuses on understanding, optimizing, and aligning actions and decisions to

The Supply Chain Handbook

ensure the collaboration and empowerment of all individuals across the business network. This enables everyone to work collaboratively across strategic, tactical, and operational levels and to align actions to ensure optimal performance.

The resulting technical infrastructure is the Data Warehouse and Decision Support hardware and software that operate on a "single version of the truth;" i.e., a data warehouse that accumulates and stores all pertinent data regarding the inter-relationship of customers, products and stores data. Decision support tools access the data warehouse to enable analysis activity.

Cultural Change

The larger challenge is not just the technology and how software will evolve toward performance management, but how organizations will transition their culture and methods in this direction. Established executive and organizational politics can, and sometimes do, impact the transformation into a performance-driven culture. Enlightened organizations are addressing this issue with executive mandates and introducing new solutions that leverage collaboration. The move to metric-driven applications that can coordinate and communicate direction and progress on performance goals is rapidly increasing.

The significant investments that have made in existing software, hardware, and resources aren't always aligned to performance management. The enterprise application and application development projects are perfect examples of where many organizations are caught in never-ending upgrades and maintenance just to automate or speed up transaction-level operations. Spending in this area can certainly provide some efficiency, Organizations taking a more "holistic view", will focus investments that will optimize and align the processes and behavior throughout the organization to achieve critical financial and organizational goals.

The core principles and goals of performance management are the following:

- **Efficiency**: The ability to optimize the operations and actions of the organization, individuals, and business processes to ensure they result in the desired outcome and defined business goals
- **Quality**: The ability to continuously improve the quality of relationships, processes, and products or services to fully leverage quality practices or methodologies to maximize the value of resources and assets
- **Value**: The ability to create and manage assets in order to create a long-term ROI for maximizing stakeholder return and increasing business value.

Performance management is a critical foundation for organizations to manage their business and optimize their effective use of resources to reach profitability. No matter how small or large the deployment, performance management is the means to optimize your business and empower everyone to make the right decisions and actions. Creating and capturing knowledge and information across the organization can build long-term value for stakeholders. This is now possible by applying performance management principles

402

to your future technology investments. Achieving the goals of performance management for your organization is now in front of you, with the ability to build an environment for success. The proper implementation, tuning, training and use of Data Warehouse technology is now more critical to achieving the success and realizing the ROI that is available but often under-realized.

Conclusion

The historical progress made by retailers, particularly in the past ten years, has been phenomenal. But the pace of improvement has greatly accelerated, and the need for individual retailers to "keep up" has increased dramatically. No longer is it safe to wait for "the bugs to be worked out" of a new concept. By the time that happens, it may be too late to catch up with the competition. The dynamics of the industry require the savvy retail operator to embrace the new reality and align their organizations, and the inherent cultures, to the fact of constant improvement within the structure of performance improvement and management, and to implement the new realities immediately.

CHAPTER 21
Training and Successful Implementations

Jamie Heaward, Project Consultant, Tompkins Associates

"Performance is the most critical issue in training and development today. Companies of all types and sizes are aspiring to become high performance organizations." (Gill, 2000, p.2)

For every system implementation that succeeds, there is at least one that fails or could have performed better. Despite popular belief, a design flaw is not typically the main cause of an unsuccessful implementation. Rather, it's that the operators aren't using the system effectively.

Very often, people can make or break a system. They must be brought in early in the life of the project, and must be given extensive, hands-on training before the system goes live. Otherwise, even with the best technology in place, the odds of system failure are high if the people component in systems is not given proper attention.

By incorporating a comprehensive and strategic training program into their implementation plan, companies can motivate and challenge employees to learn the ins and outs of complex system to ensure successful implementation. Among "best practice" training methods is Competency-Based Performance Improvement (CBPI). This chapter emphasizes the benefits and steps needed to utilize CBPI in a systems-implementation environment.

It is important to realize that in today's world of supply chain partnering and collaboration, the success of a complex system is more than just an issue within one company. By having an impact on inventories and customer service and satisfaction, the system can affect more than one level in the chain. In some cases, personnel from different parts of the chain may be involved in the actual functioning of at least part of the system. Thus, appropriate training, which translates to successful system operation, is a supply chain issue.

Overview

Although there are many approaches to training, an effective program must go beyond teaching employees a specific skill. Instead, from a current best-practices standpoint, it should focus on continuous education and understanding of business processes. It is from this concept that CBPI has emerged. CBPI is a systematic approach to analyzing and improving performance in organizations. It provides individuals sufficient information about their work, enables an organization and the individual to measure progress and success, and focuses on continuous education and new employee training.

The CBPI process is especially effective in work environments because it helps businesses manage performance improvement over a diverse array of disciplines that interact and interrelate with a new application. This approach contrasts with simply walking potential users through screens without their understanding the implications of what they are doing within those screens. CBPI testing enables employers to determine whether an individual understands the material and can utilize the information on the job.

In addition, competency testing also provides feedback to administrators regarding quality of the test. If individuals taking the test consistently provide incorrect answers in one area, it's usually an indication that the training program isn't working effectively and/or the test questions aren't effectively measuring the material that was being taught. This data enables performance improvement administrators to fine-tune their training approach.

CBPI also provides resources to facilitate continuous improvement. No successful performance improvement program is static. Businesses must continue to evaluate and reevaluate the effectiveness of their training programs and leverage emerging technologies and new information to remain on the cutting edge. CBPI enables the continuous improvement process to flourish and businesses to stay competitive.

In addition to its ability to change with the evolution of the company, other benefits of a CBPI approach include:

- Increased work force flexibility
- Increased work force competency
- Increased productivity
- Improved customer service
- Increased organizational commitment
- Increased decision making at the lowest appropriate level
- Reduced turnover and absenteeism
- Increased work force participation
- Increased work force self-esteem

Establishing Your Team and Objectives

"Training programs should not be designed or delivered based on what is 'Nice to know'. Instead, training should be time efficient and focused carefully on what people must know or do to perform their work more successfully." (King, King, and Rothwell, 2001, p.4)

When you are beginning to set up your training program, you must first look at your resources. Who will you be working with to make your training program a success? Without a strong team, you will not be able to have a rewarding training experience. Collaboratively with the client, you will want to establish a team of individuals who will have the following characteristics:

- Good communications skills
- Ability to provide feedback
- Good understanding of the culture and people
- Public speaking
- Must be an employee in good standing
- Demonstrate a strong understanding of the business processes and operations of the area in which they will provide training.

This team will be working under your direction to make the training a fun and rewarding experience for all to attend.

With your team established, you are now ready to begin defining your objectives.

"Simply stated, behavior objectives are statements that describe the kind of performance learners should be capable of at the end of the training period." (ASTD, 2000, p.2)

You must have a clear direction, in order to know how to move forward. Defining your objectives helps you define the framework for your training program. Correctly written objectives will allow you to create your outline for all classes, define your role in the training environment, and will help you determine the best form of assessment.

Below are a list of questions you will want to ask yourself and the team:

1. What is the purpose of this instruction?
2. What can the learner do to demonstrate he understands the materials?
3. How can you assess if the learner has mastered the content?
4. What type of content and performance are specified in the objectives?

(Morrison, Ross, and Kemp, 2001, p.85)

When you think you have come to a portion where you believe you have good objectives written, be sure that all your objectives contain the following characteristics:

- They are observable and measurable; that is they describe behaviors that can be seen and evaluated.
- They are results oriented, clearly worded, and specific.
- They focus only on certain aspects of the job.
- They can be measured with both qualitative and quantitative criteria
- They are action-oriented statements outlining both specific activity and measurement of performance.
- They are written in terms of performance. Instructors and students are then able to select the most appropriate activities to help students achieve objectives.
- They communicate a picture of a successful learner.
- They indicate a minimum level of performance that is acceptable. Some objectives state a specific time limit or degree of accuracy.
- They can be separated into two categories: those that describe the learners' actions and those that describe actions demonstrating attitudes.

(ASTD, 2000, p.6)

Who and What Will You Be Training?

Your team has been established with a core group of individuals that know who you will be training, better than anyone. You will want to rely heavily on your team in order to learn as much as you can about the learners, so that the training experience is successful for all.

One thing that we do know for every client is that you are working with adult learners. The audience for your class should be the basis for what your training program will look like. Malcolm Knowles, sometimes known as the "Father of Adult Education" was the educator who first identified the traits of adult learners. So we must keep the following characteristics in mind when beginning the design of our program for the adult learners:

1. The training must be setup in a way that the learners feel they are directed themselves. The role of the trainer is a facilitator. The difference being they are there as a guide for the learners, not just telling them all the answers. But through discovery and activities, letting the learner understand the processes.

2. In all of our implementations, the employees already have a baseline for how the workflow works; they are just typically learning a new training program. Because of this the session must be set up where they can build on their knowledge and experiences.

3. One of Knowle's characteristics that is key for our environment is to have the training relevancy-oriented. The learners must understand why they are having this new system, how it will enable them to do their jobs better, and what impacts it will have on how they are performing their jobs currently.

4. Adults are practical. As we can all relate to, we want to know why we are participating in a training program; up front you must tell the learners why they are attending the class.

5. Lastly, show respect to your learners. Instructors must make sure that they recognize that all the learners bring different experiences and knowledge to the class.

(Lieb, S, 1991, VISION)

As is true with all training programs, you will want to do a Needs Assessment to determine what are the exact areas that are needed for training. Fortunately for our situation, we are typically providing training on all operational areas that are affected by the new system. In order to determine what areas are affected, you will want to do a comprehensive evaluation of their current operation.

As you begin to learn more about whom you will be training, you will want to develop a matrix that you can fill out appropriately. This will allow you to know what classes will need to be developed, how many people are to be trained in that area, and the total number of times you will need to offer that class. I like to refer to this matrix as the Competence Based Development (CBD) Matrix. See below for an example of one that we have used in the past.

> **Don't Focus Too Narrowly**
>
> It is very important not to exclude non-systems related competencies when developing a comprehensive training program and especially when dealing with a start-up operation. Being too systems-centric can exclude other critical pieces of the operation, thereby creating gaps in the overall process and preventing employees from achieving stage three of employment, which is helping others to do the work. Competency in corporate culture, company policies, safety, effective leadership and other areas will be key to long-term success.

After you have defined your needs, a customized curriculum based on your operations will need to be developed. As this is developed you need to take into account your business plan and your workplace culture to design a holistic program that will truly be effective.

Table 21.1: Competence Based Development Matrix.

Employee	Trainer	Super User	Pre-Receiving (TPM)	Receiving	VAS	Put to Light
Suzie Smith	X					
Todd Heaward		X				
Ray Fisher				X		
John Riley						X
Jamie Heaward				X		
Marisela Del Cid			X	X		
Theresa Zustovich				X		
Jim Tompkins						
Tiffany Burns						X
Kristin Brown					X	

Delivery Method

"While interest in technology-based delivery is obvious, it is unlikely that classroom training will ever become obsolete. One reason is that training participants want a 'human touch,' which cannot be easily given by technology-based training delivery media. A second reason is that classroom training methods are generally more effective than technology-based methods for teaching people how to interact with other people. A third reason is that people in groups are more creative than they are as individuals, which makes group settings like classrooms ideal places to poll the knowledge of people to solve problems and discover new knowledge." (King, King, and Rothwell (2001, p.4)

There are a number of training delivery methods available today. For any successful training program, you will want to use a combination of methods to address all learning styles. Education tools can include traditional audio and video, printed manuals, workbooks, and job aids, as well as Web-based training and interactive media. Technology based-instruction is the latest trend in training enhancements.

"If you rely only on one training method–such as lecture–the training may be of limited value. Individuals learn in different ways, and using multiple methods will increase the likelihood that learners will have been touched by at least one of these methods." (King, King, and Rothwell, 2001, p.277)

During an implementation, you will have learned that all of your attendees are coming from different backgrounds and different education levels. This is where you have to use varying methods, reaching out to all attendees. This does not mean you need to use *all* delivery methods that are available, this means you need to work to shake things up in the classroom and during on the job training. In most of our classes we have had the time to first begin in the classroom. The attendees get firsthand experience with the new system, by getting themselves familiar with the new screens, and possible operational changes. This setup is similar to a computer lab design. In this phase of the training, you are allowing the learners to watch you perform a task, allowing them to practice the task, and then working with a partner on various activities.

Another very popular method is On-The-Job training. There are varying reviews of this method, as sometimes it is not performed correctly, therefore the training fails.

"Structured OJT allows the learner to acquire skills and knowledge needed to perform the job through a series of structured or planned activities at the work site. All activities are performed under the careful observation and supervision of the OJT instructor." (Craig, 2000, p. 748)

Below is a list of benefits of On-the-Job Training. But these benefits are not valuable if the training did not have true examples for the operational area, guided assistance through the process, and effective training manuals and aides to follow-up the training.

1. Allows the learner to experience the day-to-day realities of the job which provides an opportunity to identify problems or discrepancies and enhance present job methods and procedures
2. Eliminates the transfer-of-training problem experiences in other training methodologies since learning is done in the actual workplace.
3. Increases learner's confidence and productiveness by allowing them to work at their own rate.

(Craig, 2000, p. 749)

To reiterate how OJT should be used with this type of implementation, you will not want this to be your first method of training. You will first want to bring the attendees into a training environment where they can see the system and make themselves aware of all the new things that the system will allow them to do. You will want them to have had significant experience, through activities, simulations, and working as a team. All this must be done before you work with them on the floor. The key to working with them on the floor is to bring them back out into their comfort zone. You want them to see how the new system works live in their environment.

Developing Materials

"In most cases, instructional designers should prepare materials for individualized use first and then modify them, as necessary, for group use. Learner-centered, individually paced instruction usually requires more complete learning instructions than group paced instructions, making modifications for group use relatively simple." (Rothwell, 1998, p.244)

Once you have determined your needs and how you would like to deliver your training program, it is time to develop the training. You will start this process by developing the Training Manual. Included in your training manual you will need to have the following:

- Objectives
- Agenda
- Table of Contents
- Content Pages (with room enough for adequate notes)
- Glossary of Terms
- Tables and Charts that are referenced in the text
- Exercises which cover material presented in the class
- Evaluation form for the attendees to complete upon completion

Objective

Your objective should already be clearly defined. When you initially worked with your team to establish your objectives, you should incorporate the same ones here.

Agenda

The agenda should be derived straight from your objectives. What do you want to achieve with this particular course? What do you want the students to be able to demonstrate when finished? You do not have to get too specific with your agenda, in case you have to make modifications as you are going. But you will want to give the attendees a time frame and an overview for the areas you would like to cover with them.

Table of Contents

Pull out the major areas you will be covering. You do not have to list every piece you are covering; you just need to highlight the major areas. Make the table of contents something easy that they can reference once the class is complete.

Content Pages

This is the critical portion of the manual. You want to be careful with how much information you put on each page. You want to give them all the information, but you do not want the pages to seem overwhelming. Screenshots are highly effective in order to give the best understanding.

Reference Material

In the end you will want to reference all the pictures and graphs that you may have used. If there is any explanation necessary for any of the pictures, this is where you will want to make notes of that.

Exercises

Exercises are critical for the users once the class is complete. You want to provide the learner with plenty of exercises during the class, as well as ones for them to practice on their own.

Glossary

There are many new terms with most implementations. Many times this is where most of the confusion can arise. A well-written glossary will be a very important tool for the trainees to use later.

Evaluation

The last thing you will want included will be your evaluation. We will get more into this in the next section, but this is where you want to give your trainees a chance to let you know what they think of the class, and possible ways that it can be improved.

"Handouts, including manuals and workbooks, are an often neglected visual aid. Be sure that your handouts support the major points of the presentation, that they are clear and can be used as job aids or as references to refresh people's memories in the future." (Piskurich and Beckschi, 2000, p. 80)

Evaluation

"Most common reason for evaluation is to determine the effectiveness of a program and the ways in which it can be improved." (Piskurich and Beckschi, 2000, p. 135)

There are two types of evaluation that must be administered, Reaction and Learning Evaluation:

Reaction Evaluation—This measures the trainees' attitude about the training. It does not measure learning. This evaluation can be accomplished with a questionnaire or a follow-up interview. See the next page for a good example of this evaluation.
Learning Evaluation—This measures the level of learning that took place. This is normally done with written tests. In order to measure the amount of learning that took place due to the training, it is useful to have a pre-session test and a post-session test.

Types of tests include:
• Quiz
• Skill Drills
• Case Study
• Interactive Simulation
• Laboratory
(Elengold, L, 2001, p. 6)

When you are writing a learning evaluation, you must always have the objectives in mind, as you will want to test on the objectives for the course. It is usually up to the trainer and the client for how they would like the tests to be administered. However, since this type of training environment usually starts out in a classroom setting and then OJT, Laboratory and Skill Drills usually are the best forms to allow the trainees to really show what they learned and let you see it in the work setting. You can design these questions so they

---

The information derived from your evaluation will be used to improve this course. Your cooperation will be greatly appreciated.

NAME (Optional): _____ DATE: _____

COURSE: _____ INSTRUCTOR(S): _____

Please circle the appropriate number that reflects your response to the following:

	Excellent	Very Good	Good	Fair	Poor
1. Effectiveness of course material:					
Training Materials	5	4	3	2	1
Skills Practice	5	4	3	2	1
Class Discussions	5	4	3	2	1
2. Effectiveness of instructor:					
Knowledge of Subject	5	4	3	2	1
Presentation/Communications Skills	5	4	3	2	1
Pace of Program	5	4	3	2	1
3. Objectives and skills to be attained were clearly stated.	5	4	3	2	1
4. The material covered in this program is relevant to my role/job.	5	4	3	2	1
5. Overall rating of the course	5	4	3	2	1

6. What did you find most beneficial about today's training?

_____
_____

7. What did you find least beneficial about today's training?

_____
_____

8. What will get in the way of you using these skills back on the job?

_____
_____

9. What other resources would be helpful to you in using these skills back on the job?

_____
_____

10. Other comments or suggestions for improvement.

_____
_____

are fill-in-the-blank answers, which allows the trainee to work through the new steps, and fill-in the answers as they go.

A few more questions to ask yourself when designing your evaluation:

1. Reaction and planned action: what are the participant's reaction to the program and what do they plan to do with the material?
2. Learning: what skills, knowledge, or attitudes have changed and by how much?
3. Job applications: did participants apply on the job what they learned?
4. Business Results: did the on-the-job application produce measurable results?
5. Return on Investment: did the monetary value of the results exceeds the cost for the program?

(Craig (2000), p. 316)

Implementation of the Training Program

Upon completion of the previously described steps, the training team is now ready to begin implementation of the training program. Many times the core team that developed the training will need to pass along the information to other managers or leads who will be performing the training for their group. This is a typical scenario in a large working environment where there are a lot of employees who need to attend training sessions.

In this case, implementation begins with a "Train-the-Trainer" program. You will want to start this program off by allowing the soon-to-be trainers the opportunity to learn great tips on how to be a trainer, things not to do as trainers, and ways to keep the class ongoing even if some things do not work out as planned. Below is a list of characteristics to keep in mind:

Good Qualities for a Trainer
- Good understanding of the existing operations
- Familiarity or a good level of comfort with computers
- Good communication skills
- Patience
- Desire to implement a successful program
- Responds well to questions
- Stays on track
- Willing to provide an open learning environment

A few things NOT to do
- Start late
- Lose your cool
- Fake what you know
- Let the conversation stray
- Give too much information

The train-the-trainer session should be filled with time for the trainers to have practice in front of the group, working through the training documents that will be used in the training classes, and opportunity for them to make suggestions with any area they see that may need improvement.

Upon completion of the train-the-trainer class, learner evaluations should be administered to the trainers. Both the trainer's performance and the validity of the learner's evaluation questions are then reviewed with the trainers and the training team in a joint meeting. Clarifications to existing questions and other changes to the training test program can be performed at this time.

The formal training process is now ready to begin. The training material and competency testing questions should be finalized and ready to distribute to the users. Below are a few more things to keep in mind during the sessions:

- *Trainer to student ratio*—Students will be less prone to ask questions in a large class environment. This may be due to the herding phenomenon where no one wants to speak up, or because the trainer may have to answer many questions and either cuts off valuable discussion or rushes to cover the required material in the allotted time. Most successful training programs have small trainer/student ratios to encourage questions.
- *Review segment at the start of each training session*—This is necessary to ensure that students understand the basic tools they need to use in the upcoming session. This provides the opportunity for all students within the group to start from the same knowledge base.
- *Material covered per training session*—Limit the amount of new material covered in each training session. Cover a reasonable amount of material so the trainees are not overwhelmed with new material and have time to assimilate the material they have already learned.
- *Training session duration*—Training sessions are typically most successful when the time is broken up over several days. Most successful training programs spread the training over a period of one to two weeks, scheduling training in two- to three-hour segments each day.
- *Active Learning*—This keeps the learners active and encourages self-motivation. Active learning also enhances retention.
- *Reinforcement*—Positive reinforcement encourages learners to respond and facilitates active learning.

(Elengold, L, 2001, p. 6)

The objectives of the training program are presented to the trainees during the orientation to the training sessions. The trainees are presented with a copy of the matrix so they can understand the required areas of focus in order to carry out their job responsibilities or new company policies. Upon completion of training for specific job titles, the trainers may administer the learning evaluation. The tests should be evaluated and feedback given immediately after the trainee takes the test. Time should be allocated to allow the students to review material they have not mastered. It is vital to provide this feedback as soon as possible after the test has been taken because it is at this time that the trainee is most focused on the program. You will know you have a successful training program if you achieve the following results:

- Employees are truly learning and retaining information
- Training efforts result in a workforce with clearly defined objectives and expectations
- Employees understand the need for Performance Improvement and buy in to what they are learning
- Mechanisms are in place for employee feedback and continuous improvement

Training is Key to Successful Implementations

With the onset of new technology and as employees take on additional responsibilities, a static approach to training isn't effective in today's marketplace, especially in a system-driven environment. Instead, a well-designed competency model that focuses on roles and performance, not on behavior, is a proven and viable solution for successful implementation projects.

It is very important not to exclude non-systems related competencies when developing a comprehensive performance improvement program and especially when dealing with a start-up operation. Being too systems-centric can allow other critical pieces of the operation to be excluded, thereby creating gaps in the overall process. Demonstrated competency and a path forward for continuous improvement for the workforce are key to a company's long-term success.

References

Caffarella, R., & Merriam, S. (1999) *Learning in adulthood.* San-Francisco, CA: Jossey-Bass Publishers.

Carey, L., & Dick, W. (1996). *The systematic design of instruction.* New York, NY: LONGMAN.

Craig, R. (1996). *The ASTD training & development handbook.* New York, NY: McGraw-Hill.

Elengold, L. (2001). "Teach SME's to Design Training." Columbia, MD: ASTD

Galagan, R. (2001). Mission e-possible. *Training and Development,* 55, 46-54

Gill, S. (2000). "Linking Training to Performance Goals." Alexandria, VA: ASTD

King, S, King M, and Rothwell, W. (2001). *The Complete Guide to Training Delivery.* Broadway, NY: Amacom.

Morrison, G, Ross, S, Kemp, J. (2001). *Designing Efffective Instruction.* New York, NY. John Wiley & Sons, Inc.

Piskurich, G, & Beckschi, P. (2000). *The ASTD Handbook of Training Design and Delivery.* New York, NY: McGraw-Hill.

Pratt, D., (1998) *Five perspectives on teaching in adult and higher education.* Malabar: Krieger Publishing Company

Rothwell, W, & Kazanas, H. (1998). *Mastering the Instuctional Design Process.* San Francisco, CA. Jossey-Bass/Pfeiffer

Smith, M. (1999). *Adult education.* [Available Online] http://www.infed.org/lifelonglearning/

(2000). *Write Better Behavior Objectives.* [Available Online] http://www.astd.org

CHAPTER 22
Supply Chain Execution Systems

Tom Singer, Principal, Tompkins Associates

Execution is the process of implementing actions or decisions according to a predefined set of instructions or rules. Supply Chain Execution (SCE) systems support the movement of inventory between entities within the supply chain. This movement is produced by transactions generated in other systems such as ERP, Supply Chain Planning, and Order Management applications. In this manner SCE software execute or support the inventory movement actions or decisions generated by external sources. They are truly execution systems.

SCE is a category of application software that addresses the fulfillment and delivery of product between supplier and customer. Its components focus on optimizing this movement within a distribution center and between adjacent points within the supply chain. SCE solutions provide tools that enable enterprises to reduce distribution labor, transportation, and inventory carrying costs. They help organizations utilize storage space and equipment more efficiently. They provide instruments that allow operations to reduce delivery time and increase visibility with trading partners. SCE systems help supply chains succeed by reducing distribution costs and increasing customer satisfaction.

SCE systems do not improve the efficiency and flow of the supply chain. They provide enterprises with the tools to pursue these goals. Their implementation cycles can be long, costly, and complex. Poorly installed they can wreck havoc within a distribution operation. But when properly implemented and combined with sound business and operational practices, they can produce a tremendous return on investment and significantly increase customer satisfaction. The can make the difference between success and failure for a supply chain.

Solution Types
The SCE family encompasses several distinct software applications. SCE solutions types include:

- Warehouse Management Systems (WMS)
- Transportation Management Systems (TMS)
- Labor Management Systems (LMS)
- Slotting Applications
- Supply Chain Visibility

In addition to these solution types, many SCE vendors augment their offerings with add-on modules. These auxiliary functions include activity costing, reporting, and multi-site order management.

SCE's core components are WMS and TMS. A WMS directs inventory movements within a distribution center. A TMS supports inventory movements from a distribution facility to delivery points within the supply chain. The other SCE solution types address optimization of specific distribution aspects, or provide visibility on inventory and order status between points within the supply chain.

The boundaries of the SCE family are not rigidly fixed. They can blur into other Supply Chain Management and Enterprise software categories. Even the individual SCE solution types can encroach upon each other. A WMS can provide TMS functionality. A TMS package may offer shipment status visibility over the Internet. Despite how the definitions are structured, all SCE solution types address the fulfillment and delivery of orders. They do so by providing functionality to help direct, manage or optimize inventory movement within the supply chain.

Warehouse Management Systems (WMS)

A WMS package helps manage activities within the four walls of a distribution center. It fulfills orders captured by Order Management Systems (OMS), ERP sales and customer service modules, and commercial Web sites. It provides functionality to manage receiving, storage, picking, packing, and shipping operations. It can also support inventory control, returns processing, replenishment, order consolidation, shipping document preparation, and yard management.

WMS packages provide extensive four-wall inventory visibility and tracking capabilities. Moveable inventory loads are typically identified by the physical and systematic application of a bar-coded serialized license plate number (LPN). WMS applications employ wireless Radio Frequency (RF) technology that provides works with the ability to capture product movement in real time by scanning load LPNs and target locations. Receipts, putaways and picks can also be instantaneously verified through scans of item, location, and LPN bar codes.

WMS solutions are more than transaction processing engines. They provide tools to help distribution operations optimize warehouse activities and storage utilization. Most WMS packages provide sophisticated wave management and order release functionality that allow operations to release orders for processing according to capacity, service needs, and picking requirements. Other tools include:

- System directed moves where workers are directed to putaway or pull loads in a manner that minimizes travel, maximizes storage consolidation, and enforces warehouse zoning requirements
- Replenishment of pick locations from reserve stock based on user-defined rules such as min/max levels and order demand

- Configurable inventory allocation methods that support lot control, product rotation rules, and operational efficiencies
- Batch and zone picking methods that allow pickers to pull product for multiple orders per pick face visit
- Container cubing routines that select carton types prior to picking according to user-defined rules such as volume, weight, and product type
- Work order management utilities that support value-added services such as price ticketing, item kitting, and special packaging
- Task management capabilities where work is automatically assigned to floor personnel based on proximity, equipment type, and other configurable rules.

By providing intelligent, comprehensive support for warehousing operations, a WMS can help reduce distribution costs, decrease order cycle times, increase inventory accuracy, and increase customer satisfaction. They also enable distribution operations to rapidly and efficiently respond to the ever-changing flow of the supply chain.

Transportation Management Systems (TMS)

A TMS package supports the delivery of shipments from a distribution facility to customers or other points within the supply chain. Some TMS packages also provide the ability to manage in-bound logistics for raw materials, outsourced goods, and customer returns. TMS solutions provide functionality to help manage all major aspects of delivery logistics from carrier selection to freight bill auditing.

The major objective of most TMS implementations is to reduce transportation costs. Carrier and freight rating is the principal tool that a TMS provides distribution operations pursuing this goal. Most TMS packages provide sophisticated carrier selection capabilities that account for rate, service requirements, and consolidation opportunities.

TMS packages typically provide multi-modal support that accommodates each carrier's unique shipping requirements as well as customer-specific discounts. Their rating engines can select the most cost-effective carrier given delivery date, product restrictions, and accessorial service requirements. Once a carrier has been determined, a TMS can produce all required shipping documentation including container labels, packing slips, manifests, and bills of lading.

Most TMS solutions support both small parcel and contract carriers. They eliminate the need to have separate carrier-provided manifesting systems by connecting directly to carrier backend systems for electronic manifest submittal and package routing. They can support the generation and transmittal of Advanced Shipping Notices (ASN) to trading partners.

In addition to carrier rating and selection, TMS solutions provide other functions that enable companies to streamline distribution operations and reduce transportation costs. These capabilities include:

- Identification of order consolidation, and zone skipping and pooling opportunities to further reduce shipping costs

- Load planning techniques that accommodate freight characteristics, weights and volumes, and stop sequencing that help ensure each load is shipped in the most efficient manner
- Freight claims processing to aid in prompt and accurate settlement of carrier claims
- Electronic freight payment and auditing routines to reduce the cost of processing carrier invoices while helping to ensure that payments accurately reflect services tendered
- Export functionality that supports customs requirements and export documentation such as commercial invoices and certificates of origin.

A TMS enables a distribution operation to automate many aspects of its transportation functions. In addition to helping achieve freight cost reductions, a TMS allows operations to streamline manual-intensive planning and documentation preparation activities. It can eliminate the need to outsource freight claims and payment auditing functions. It can provide greater control and visibility of shipments from origination through final delivery.

Labor Management Systems (LMS)

While warehouse Labor Management Systems (LMS) do not directly support inventory movement within the supply chain, they help distribution operations optimize their labor utilization. Since labor represents a major portion of supply chain execution costs, a LMS can directly contribute to the overall efficiency of a supply chain. Depending on the situation, a LMS can enable a distribution operation to achieve substantial reductions in labor costs through productivity improvements and effective planning.

LMS packages are work measurement tools that provide the capability to define the discrete tasks and the associated time values are that inherent in a specific warehouse work activity. They provide the means to calculate standard time values for preferred work methods. Using a LMS, a distribution operation can establish a baseline standard for each of its work functions from inbound receiving to outbound trailer loading. Advanced LMS packages provide functionality to develop engineered standards that are based on elemental steps and modifying conditions. They account for travel time, location, equipment, and product weight and cube variations. They accommodate direct and indirect labor activities.

Distribution operations use LMS solutions to define how work should be done. An LMS can help an organization identify labor inefficiencies and develop proper work methods. But most LMS solutions are not limited to defining work methods and labor standards. They typically provide the ability to report actual activity time by employee against standard values. They usually provide this functionality through an interface to a WMS package. This interface feeds a LMS package actual activity start and stop times by employee.

When interfaced to a WMS package a LMS becomes a productivity tracking and labor-planning tool. It can:

- Compare employee performance across functional areas accounting for operational differences and specific conditions

- Identify inefficient practices, ineffective supervision, and substandard employee performance
- Provide a reporting mechanism to support employee incentive programs
- Assess workload against available staff resources.

LMS solutions can provide very favorable returns on investment (ROI) for many distribution operations. But they tend to suffer a preconceived conception that they are a secondary system rather than a mission critical solution. Many distribution operations devote their energies and political capital to WMS, TMS and supply chain visibility applications in the belief that only these solutions can generate an acceptable ROI. LMS is viewed as a nice-to-have application that is frequently pushed to the background. This type of thinking ignores the fact that labor makes up a huge portion of distribution costs. For many operations a LMS can provide a ROI greater than other SCE applications.

Slotting Applications

Slotting packages are another SCE application type that addresses the efficiency of warehouse operations rather than directly supporting supply chain product movement. They provide functionality to help ensure that inventory is optimally located within a distribution center. They recommend pick slots and storage locations based on product velocity, product characteristics, and storage attributes. They enable distribution operations to increase storage utilization and labor efficiency.

Slotting is the process of determining inventory pick locations within a warehouse. How effectively a distribution operation slots product has a direct impact on its distribution costs. An inefficient slotting strategy wastes storage space and can lead to unnecessary facility expansions or off-site storage. It can also yield excessive pick travel times that increase labor costs. By using a slotting package a distribution operation can help ensure that product is optimally slotted within their distribution center.

A slotting package is an analytical tool that requires numerous data elements to generate slotting plans. These elements can be divided into three basic categories:

- Product velocity – picks and moves per time period
- Product characteristics – weight, volume, inventory class, and storage requirements (e.g. temperature, special handling)
- Storage characteristics – location coordinates and dimensions, equipment requirements, accessibility, and special attributes (e.g. refrigerated, safety factors).

Most slotting packages can accommodate product velocity from both historic and forecasted perspectives. All three data categories are typically downloaded from an external system such as an ERP or WMS package.

Most slotting solutions provide graphical representations of slotting plans. These views can be used to identify incorrectly slotted product and perform "what-if" analysis on plan variations. Slotting applications allow distribution operations to quickly regenerate slotting plans in response to changing customer demand. Many packages provide WMS interfaces that support plan uploads allowing WMS tasking functionality to automatically slot product according to plan requirements.

Supply Chain Visibility

Most SCE applications operate within the four walls of a distribution center. Even a TMS package, which manages the shipping requirements for multiple delivery points still focuses primarily on the needs of one operation. However, other supply chain points are dependent on the supply chain execution activities of a specific distribution center. A distribution operation that can view supplier activities can more effectively manage its own workload. Supply chain visibility applications provide organizations the ability to view activity beyond their own four walls and coordinate order fulfillment and delivery with trading partners throughout the supply chain.

Supply chain visibility packages share information generated by an organization's supply chain applications with other trading partners. They provide the means for external entities to view order status and stock levels within a distribution center. They enable organizations to track shipment status and coordinate work plans with anticipated delivery times. They offer distribution operations advance alerts about external fulfillment and delivery discrepancies that directly impact their effectiveness.

Supply chain visibility applications automate the flow of information between trading partners. Traditionally this information is transmitted via telephone, letter, and fax. This flow is manually intensive and does not typically provide timely and comprehensive views of supply chain data. Electronic Data Interchange (EDI) applications automate the informational flow of certain supply chain transactions. But EDI is costly to implement and operate. It also tends to provide a static snapshot view of information.

Supply chain visibility packages typically automate the flow of supply chain information by publishing data generated by other supply chain applications over the Internet. This data is usually extracted from the various application sources and stored in a standalone database designed specifically for query actions. Using a web browser, internal and external users can view the stored supply chain transactions in near real-time mode. Advanced supply chain visibility packages offer collaborative functionality and event-triggered messaging between trading partners.

Supply chain visibility applications provide a secure link into an organization's supply chain systems. Views can be tailored to meet the specific needs of trading partners without compromising the integrity or confidentiality of source data. By employing web-based architectures, they provide cost effective system deployment and operations. They enable key supply chain information to flow between trading partners in an efficient and unobtrusive manner.

Auxiliary Functions

Selected WMS and TMS functionality can also be found in standalone SCE applications. These applications are tailored to meet specific supply chain processes such as trailer load planning, small parcel manifesting, and Advance Shipment Notification (ASN) generation.

Some applications address wider operational needs but fall short of full WMS or TMS functionality. An example of this solution type is a shipping system that supports best way freight rating and documentation preparation without providing load planning, order consolidation, and freight claim and auditing features. These limited-feature, standalone applications are typically designed for smaller operations that cannot cost justify a full WMS or TMS package. However, larger operations may employ these tools to supplement legacy system or ERP functionality.

Auxiliary functions can also be designed to extend the functionality of core SCE solutions. These applications are frequently developed and marketed by SCE vendors as optional add-ons to their core packages. They address specific operational or information needs that are not typically deemed as core WMS or TMS functionality. These applications can be categories as follows:

- *Activity-Based Costing* – WMS packages capture transactional data on most warehousing operations. But they typically cannot tell service costs by area, function, or customer. Activity-Base Costing modules provide this analytical capability. They are typically sold to Third-Party Logistics (3PL) providers and operations that supply special handling and valued-add services.
- *Business Intelligence* – WMS and TMS packages usually provide a wide variety of standard reports and inquiries. But these informational sources present data in an aggregate text format that is not well suited for rapid decision-making and issue identification. They also do not present key data elements from external systems. Business Intelligence solutions provide graphical and analytical tools that extend the value of supply chain data. These solutions employ a separate database tailored specifically for inquiry and analysis. Their graphical presentation format supports key performance indicator (KPI) generation and event driven alerts.
- *Integration Tools* – SCE applications need to communicate with external systems and each other. This integration is developed through custom code, application programming interface (API) libraries, and third-party integration toolset providers. Some SCE vendors offer their own tool sets or resell third-party solutions that are pre-configured to work with their core applications.
- *Multi-Site Order and Shipment Management* – Organizations with multiple distribution centers frequently need the ability to allocate orders to specific warehouses based on product availability and proximity to the customer. This need may not be fulfilled by their OMS or ERP packages. Some WMS vendors offer this multi-site order management capability as an add-on module that sits between OMS/ERP packages and their solution.

Similarly, TMS packages seek to optimize shipments from one distribution center to multiple delivery points. But operations utilizing LTL and contract carrier services may be able to achieve further cost reductions by pooling their shipments or providing backhaul opportunities for other operations. Some TMS vendors provide this capability through "merge-in-transit" solutions.

Solution Providers and Trends

The SCE marketplace is pursued by a wide variety of vendors. WMS and TMS vendors are frequently classified according to the customer industry types that their packages best address. All SCE vendors can be classified according to price. Higher priced solutions typically offer richer functionality and support larger operations than lower priced packages. The breadth of their solutions can further categorize SCE vendors. Some vendors pursue only one solution type, while others offer comprehensive product suites.

No vendor dominates the SCE marketplace. Few vendors can claim a double-digit market share. These vendors tend to have comprehensive SCE suites that address the needs of multiple vertical industries. But many other firms offer a single solution tailored to fit a narrow price point and industry type. Reputation and marketing are as important to a vendor's success as functionality and technology.

Many ERP vendors also address the SCE marketplace by offering warehousing modules. These vendors are primarily targeting their core customer base by offering a SCE solution that is tightly integrated with their entire product suite. Their offerings put additional competitive pressures on the marketplace. Pure SCE vendors position themselves against ERP encroachment as "best-of-breed" solutions providers offering rich functionality and highly configurable applications. But ERP vendors have a natural constituency seeking out-of-the-box integration.

The competitive nature of the marketplace is generating a constant pressure for consolidation and contractions. Successful vendors are acquiring other firms to either complement their product suites or to buy off their primary competition. Marginally successful firms are having an increasingly harder time making the investment required to stay competitive. Vendors with older technology and lagging functionality are being forced from the active marketplace.

Changing supply chain practices are also pressuring SCE vendors to enhance and extend their product suites. Supply chains are continually being pulled toward a more made-to-order, just-in-time basis. While operational optimization is still important, flexibility and collaboration have become critical success factors. SCE vendors are being pressed to deliver highly configurable solutions and rapid implementation cycles without sacrificing optimization.

While the competitive dynamics of the marketplace have intensified, the need for SCE solutions continues to grow. Distribution operations that cannot fulfill and deliver orders in an optimal manner endanger the success of the enterprise. Supply chains that cannot execute will not succeed.

CHAPTER 23
Warehouse Management Systems

Tom Singer, Principal, Tompkins Associates

Information drives supply chains. Companies invest considerable sums of money in information systems that share data between trading partners. Supply chains seek competitive advantages by implementing supply chain planning, supplier relationship management, e-procurement, and collaboration software solutions. But for most supply chains, visibility and collaboration is meaningless without effective and efficient processes and information flows within warehouses and distribution centers (DC).

Warehouse management systems (WMS) address the internal operations of a DC or warehouse. They are generally categorized as Supply Chain Execution (SCE) solutions. As an execution system, a WMS controls the daily activities within the four walls of a DC or warehouse. From receiving to material storage to picking to shipping, WMS packages provide the ability to direct warehouse activities and material flows.

There are numerous commercially available WMS packages each tailored in functionality, processing power and price for specific types of operations. But they all share a common focus on controlling inventory movement within the four walls of a distribution facility. They instruct workers to perform specific tasks in the most efficient manner. They help facilities maximize their storage utilization. They help ensure that the right product is shipped in a timely manner. They provide operations with the ability to perform value-added services that they would otherwise not be able to supply in a cost-effective manner.

While not every distribution facility requires a WMS, those that do can substantially increase operational effectiveness and customer satisfaction through its implementation. These improvements do not stop at the four walls of the DC or warehouse. They permeate throughout the supply chain. WMS solutions can provide detailed information needed for effective Supply Chain Synthesis (SCS) and distribution excellence. In this respect WMS solutions help drive supply chains.

Evolution

The WMS software industry predates the development of most other Supply Chain Management solutions. Its roots can be found in the development of inventory control and management software packages. The first commercial WMS solutions appeared in the 1980s and were fueled by decreasing computer cost/performance ratios. The practicality and acceptance of these solutions was also driven by the development of two Automatic Data Collection (ADC) technologies; bar codes and radio frequency (RF) communications.

Bar coding provided the ability to encode identification data in machine-readable formats. This made it possible for end-users to scan product numbers, location codes and other warehouse identifiers instead of manually keying the information. RF communications provided warehouse personnel with the mobility to perform daily tasks. Hand-held and vehicle mounted terminals enabled WMS solutions to communicate directly with workers on a real-time basis.

While neither technology is essential or appropriate for certain situations, their development and acceptance have allowed WMS solutions to evolve into true execution systems. They provided WMS software with the means to direct warehouse personnel in high volume transaction environments and provided the mechanism to increase reliability and accuracy while reducing processing costs. ADC technology made it possible for many operations to increase productivity and efficiency through the implementation of WMS software.

Bar coding also enabled other developments that significantly fueled the growth and acceptance of WMS solutions: compliance labeling and Advance Shipment Notices (ASNs). Both developments grew out of the desire of large retailers to automate their inbound receiving processes. Compliance labels provided human-readable text and bar-coded information to help assist in the disposition of inbound material. ASNs provided case-level detailed data transmitted in advance of shipments through Electronic Data Interchange (EDI) networks. WMS software that took advantage of these techniques substantially improved the efficiency and accuracy of inbound receiving. An inbound shipment could quickly be received against an ASN by scanning bar-coded identifiers on cases and pallets.

Not only did compliance labeling and ASNs spur large distributors to adopt WMS technology, they also propagated WMS solutions among smaller suppliers. Large retailers started to pressure their suppliers to adhere to compliance labeling standards and provide ASN data. Many WMS packages were implemented primarily in response to compliance labeling initiatives.

Many other factors contributed to growth and acceptance of WMS software solutions. But the driving factor behind this rise was the competitive forces of the marketplace. Companies needed to reduce operating costs of their distribution facilities while being pressured to expedite shipments. Companies also needed to reduce inventory levels while struggling to meet increasing customer service expectations. WMS technology provided distribution operations with a tool to meet these demands.

Software developers and vendors initially responded to the demand for WMS solutions with custom solutions. While these early implementations were finely tuned to the operational requirements of their target facility, they were costly and required long implementation timelines. Relatively few operations could justify the price of a custom solution.

However, some custom solution developers began to market their software code and experience to other companies usually within the same vertical industry or operations type. With each subsequent sale the vendor developed additional custom code. Any custom code that was deemed marketable to other operations was incorporated into the base package.

It is from these origins that the WMS software industry evolved. Today most WMS vendors offer true software packages that can be configured to meet most of the operational needs of a distribution facility. Since the need for custom code has been reduced, the cost and timeline of WMS implementations has declined over the years. However, many WMS packages are still modified to meet the specific operational requirements of customers. This is especially true for high-end packages implemented in complex operational environments.

Other software vendors have begun to pursue the WMS marketplace. Shipping and manifesting, and stock locator system vendors have enhanced their product lines with WMS functionality targeting smaller operations. ERP vendors are also adding or enhancing their warehousing modules to directly compete with 'best-of-breed' WMS vendors.

Supply Chain Position

While they are focused on the internal operations of a distribution facility, WMS solutions play a key role in the movement of materials and information throughout the supply chain. Their exact role and interface points may vary, but their general position within supply systems is relatively well defined.

Figure 23.1 illustrates how a WMS can interact with other supply chain and business systems. A WMS fulfills sales and production orders created in an ERP or Order Management System (OMS) package. The ERP or OMS typically manages aggregate warehouse inventory, releasing orders to the WMS based upon material availability within the ERP/ OMS. The WMS manages inventory at the warehouse location level and directs all product movement.

ERP and purchasing systems also send in-bound purchase orders to the WMS. This information is typically conveyed through Advanced Shipment Notices (ASN) at the purchase order, SKU, or case level. All changes in inventory quantity and status are transmitted from the WMS to ERP, OMS, and purchasing system. This includes receipts, shipments, and inventory adjustment. WMS shipment data can also be used to create outbound ASNs for customer facilities.

Companies use Supply Chain Planning (SCP) solutions to help predict demand and required material supply levels over a specified planning period. SCP solutions typically interact directly with ERP and OMS systems pulling current demand and supply data, and producing forecasts. These forecasts are used to produce production, replenishment, and transfer orders within the distribution network. These orders are downloaded from the ERP and OMS systems to the WMS.

The WMS also feeds Supply Change Event Management solutions with near real-time order and inventory status information. Supply chain collaboration, visibility, and decision support systems use this information to support collaborative planning and customer service functions. Collaborative solutions can also support the creation and transmission of ASN data for inbound shipments to the warehouse.

WMS packages are able to interact with other SCE solutions. Its activity transactions directly feed Labor Management Systems (LMS) that report on labor performance. Interfacing a WMS with a Transportation Management System (TMS) can reduce transportation costs. The WMS or ERP/OMS downloads open orders to the TMS, which selects the best-

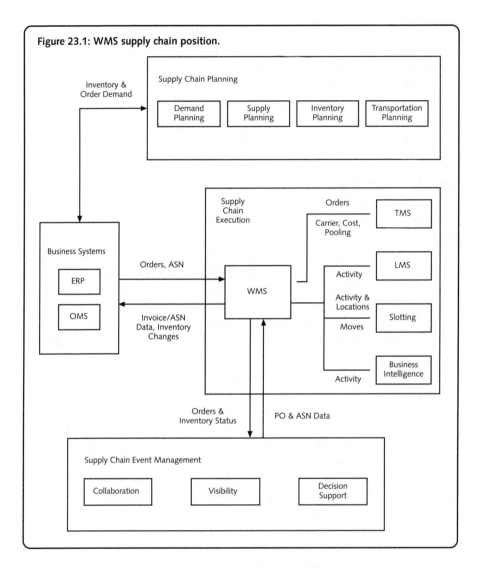

Figure 23.1: WMS supply chain position.

cost carrier, and identifies consolidation, pooling, and zone skipping opportunities. This information is sent back to the WMS, which is used to pick and ship the orders.

A WMS can also feed a Business Intelligence (BI) package with detailed activity, inventory, and order status information. The BI solution graphically presents summary views and reports based on this information to warehouse management. It can also be used to analyze trends and send alert messages based on predefined conditions.

Functionality

While they share common characteristics, WMS packages vary significantly in functionality they provide according to the target audience and price tag. At the most elemental level they support core warehousing operations such as receiving, storage, picking/packing, and shipping. But how they perform these functions and their ability to be configured to support specific operational requirements can significantly vary. Also, there are other functional areas such as work order processing and yard management that may or may not be supported by a particular package.

Probably the clearest way to view WMS functionality is to follow product flow and activities from the receiving dock through outbound trailer loading. There are also management and support processes to consider. From this perspective WMS functionality can be categorized as follows:

- *Yard/dock management*—Shipments come into and depart from distribution facilities through marshaling yards and dock doors. A WMS package can provide functionality to help track and direct trailer/container movement and schedule dock door appointments.

- *Receiving*—Receiving functionality provides tools to help receive inbound shipments against purchase orders, shipment manifests, or electronically provided ASN records. It can also provide inbound shipment quality control and inspection processes. In addition, WMS Receiving modules are typically used to process customer returns.

- *Storage*—A WMS package is used to control and track material movement within the four walls of a distribution center. This requires the ability to define various types of locations including bulk/reserve, pick, overflow, and staging. WMS storage functionality allows characteristics to be assigned to locations to control product movement between locations, and to optimize space utilization.

  WMS provides systematic procedures to storage product in reserve and pick locations. These procedures include putaway options, which are used to move product from the receiving dock to a storage location. They also include replenishment processes that direct material from bulk/reserve locations to pick faces.

- *Inventory management*—WMS packages typically provide processes to manage inventory at the location level. These may include physical count, cycle count, and inventory adjustment options.

- *Work order and value added services*—Some WMS packages provide functionality to support basic assembly, kitting, product stickering, and other value-added services. This functionality is typically incorporated in a work-order module that provides the ability to define a bill-of-material (BOM) that lists specific material requirements for a final assembly, or accepts the BOM from an external ERP system.

  These BOMs are assigned to work orders that are used to manage the production process. BOM items are consumed upon usage and final items created through a receiving process.

- *Order processing*—Order processing addresses the release of outbound orders to the warehouse for picking and shipping. Its key components are inventory allocation and order release. Allocation involves the location-specific commitment of inventory to meet order needs. It can accommodate FIFO, lot control, and best-pick method rules. Order release dictates how the warehouse floor receives work. It can also support order consolidation, cartonization, and shipment document production.

Some WMS packages furnish wave processing capabilities that allow a warehouse to schedule and release work according to a variety of user-defined criteria that reflect the day-to-day needs of the facility. WMS packages may also provide capacity control functionality that helps ensure that work is released in manageable portions.

- *Picking*—WMS packages typically provide a variety of picking alternatives to support different product, container types, order volume, equipment, and layout variations in facilities. Key differences in picking processes center on how orders are assigned to and completed by pickers. Variations supported may include discrete, batch, and zone picking. Picks may be performed by using paper pick lists, shipping labels, radio frequency (RF) terminals, and automated picking devices interfaced to the WMS.
- *Shipping*—Shipping is the last set of activities in the order fulfillment process. It centers on the consolidation of orders by carrier type and their preparation for tendering. The types of activities required are dependent on the carriers used. Some WMS packages provide parcel-manifesting modules that support carriers like UPS, FedEx, and USPS.

WMS packages also vary in their support for common and fleet carriers. Some provide comprehensive freight management functionality that aids in carrier selection, lane building, freight rating, and shipping documentation preparation.

Task Management

All WMS packages provide the ability to manually assign work tasks to warehouse employees. For example, an individual worker may initiate a putaway or pick task by scanning a label. However, this manual method may not provide optimal labor utilization. Some WMS packages address this issue by providing task management functionality where the system directs workers to perform specific activities.

Task management functionality is typically based on facility-defined rule sets that account for layout, equipment, and skill variations. Using these rules, the system can assign a task to a worker based on proximity, equipment, and priority. It also eliminates the need to return to a central point after task completion to pick up another work assignment. By interleaving tasks the system minimizes unproductive travel time.

Management Reporting

A WMS package collects and processes a considerable amount of operation data. So it is not surprising that most WMS vendors provide numerous management reports. These reports provide detailed information on all functional areas supported by the system. They can be used to monitor receiving, stock, order, and shipping activity. Some packages also provide third-party billing and employee performance reporting capabilities.

Systems Administration

Like any business system, a WMS package must provide system administration functions. These include user security, configuration rules, printer definition, and option parameter maintenance. System administration also encompasses data purging and archiving, diagnostic routines, import/export functions, and database maintenance routines.

Benefits

Companies implement WMS packages for a variety of reasons. But they are basically driven by the desire to reduce operating costs and improve customer service. The value and relevance of any potential benefit will vary between operations. Every company considering using WMS technology needs to carefully delineate and quantify their prospective benefits.

A WMS can help a distribution facility reduce operating costs in numerous ways. Generally, most companies focus on obtaining labor cost savings and increasing space utilization. They seek to increase the efficiency of their receiving, putaway, picking, and shipping operations. A WMS can provide more efficient methods to perform a particular task. Its putaway, replenishment and picking activities can be configured so that storage capacity is used in the most efficient manner. It can also assign tasks to workers so that travel and unproductive time is minimized. It provides tools that allow management to effectively control and schedule work on the warehouse floor.

A WMS can help increase inventory and order accuracy. Positive verification of each product movement through a bar code scan increases the likelihood that inventory is where it is supposed to be, thus reducing the time spent searching for inventory. It also helps ensure shipments match what the customers actually ordered. This reduces subsequent rework and customer chargebacks. In addition, a WMS can provide opportunities to consolidate outbound orders enabling an operation to save on shipping costs.

Some companies pursue WMS technology to achieve customer service gains viewing the investment as a necessary cost of business. Reducing order turnaround time and increasing fill rates are frequent implementation goals. Some firms are attracted to a WMS solution because it will provide them the ability to perform new value added services such as assortment packaging or customer stickering in a cost efficient manner. A major customer will sometimes drive their suppliers towards implementing a WMS through compliance labeling and ASN requirements.

Since a WMS captures activity information as it occurs in the warehouse, it can be a critical feed to supply chain collaboration and visibility applications. Companies implementing a WMS can provide their customers a more timely view of inventory and order status thus allowing the customer to optimize their operational processes and business decisions.

Return on investment (ROI) varies among industry, operation size, and business objectives. But 18 to 24 months is a commonly cited ROI objective for single site WMS implementations. However, many companies make the decision to invest in a WMS primarily on customer service objectives and requirements.

Architecture and Platform

Like other business systems, WMS packages tend to be classified according to the systems architecture they employ. Generally they fall into three primary camps:

- *Legacy*—the WMS application and database run on mainframe or midrange computer. The application is typically written in a 3rd generation programming language such as Cobol or RPG. Users access applications through character-based terminals or PCs using terminal emulation software.
- *Client/server*—the database and some application services run on back-end servers. Users access applications through Graphical User Interface (GUI) client software running on a desktop PC. Client software may also provide some application services and business rules processing. Applications may be written using a variety of tools including C++, Visual Basic, and other development tools.
- *Web-based*—the WMS is designed to run over the Internet with users accessing desktop functionality through a Web browser. All services, inventing the application, database, and Web, run on backend servers.

Some WMS vendors advertise that their packages are Web enabled. This means that they supply software that allows some or all of their desktop functionality to be accessed by a Web browser. Their core structure is still either legacy or client/server. Web enabled solutions vary in the look and feel that they present to browser users. Some appear to the user as if they were designed for the Web, while others merely reformat a character-based presentation for browser access.

Platform is another term that is frequently employed to describe systems structure required for a WMS package. It identifies either the type of computer (e.g., IBM AS/400, Sun, HP) or operating system (e.g., Unix, Windows 2000) needed to run the package. Some packages are categorized as open systems solutions meaning that they can run on multiple platforms. The type of database software (e.g., Oracle, SQL Server, DB2) employed is also used to classify WMS packages.

Architecture and platform usually play a secondary role in the WMS selection process. A company might give additional preference to a package if its architecture and platform matches their existing IT infrastructure because it can provide a lower total cost of ownership (TCO). Computer systems require hardware, administrative, and support resources. Selecting a package that fits within an existing IT infrastructure allows a company to leverage existing resources.

Architecture can also be viewed in terms of the hardware components and network needed for a WMS solution. These components will vary by package type and operational needs. The basic components can be categorized as follows:

- *Servers*—computers used to provide application, communication, and database services
- *Workstations*—desktop PCs and terminals that may have an attached bar code scanner
- *RF terminals*—mobile handheld and vehicle-mounted terminals that usually come with an attached or integrated bar code scanner.

- *Printers*—label, report and laser printers used to produce pick lists, shipping labels, bill of lading documents, and other reports/documents
- *Network*—cabling, routers, switches and other equipment used to connect servers, terminals, and other devices
- *RF network*—access points, base stations, and communication servers used to connect RF devices to the rest of the network
- *Material handling equipment and control systems*—automated material handling systems that move or process material. These systems typically execute tasks received from the WMS and provide back status updates.

Mobile access for warehouse employees is a prerequisite of many WMS installations. Most WMS software vendors provide this functionality through Radio Frequency (RF) terminals. These devices are typically PC-DOS computers that use character-based terminal emulation like VT100 or IBM 5250 to present services to users. Some packages provide mobile functionality using Windows-CE or palm-compatible devices.

The physical components that comprise a WMS solution will vary according to the software package, transaction load, operational flow, and material handling system that are involved. Figure 23.2 represents a possible configuration for a client/server system. An Ethernet network provides the connectivity backbone for the various components. A server running a commercial database management system like Oracle or SQL-Server is the central information repository for the system.

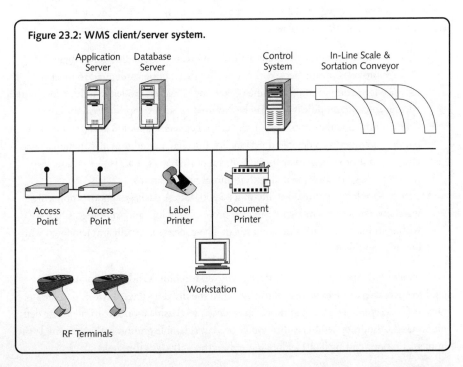

Figure 23.2: WMS client/server system.

Application Server   Database Server   Control System   In-Line Scale & Sortation Conveyor

Access Point   Access Point   Label Printer   Document Printer

Workstation

RF Terminals

Application software that provide business logic processing and presentation services reside on an application server and desktop PCs. Users access WMS functionality through desktop PCs or RF terminals connected to the network through access points. Shipping labels and documents print on networked thermal and laser printers.

Once an order is picked, outbound cartons are placed on a conveyor line. A control system records each carton's weight as an in-line scale captures it. The WMS is interfaced to the control system sending it carton data and receiving back carton weight. The control system uses the WMS-provided carton data to divert cartons to the appropriate shipping lane.

Marketplace

While there has been some consolidation over recent years, the WMS marketplace is still highly fragmented with a wide variety of vendors pursing different customer niches. These vendors can be classified by several different schemes that account for vertical industry specialty, functionality, architecture, peak transactions handled, customer revenue, and implementation costs. Industry analysts and vendors typically talk about a three-tier concept to differentiate the marketplace.

This tier concept can be applied to various classification schemes, but it is typically used in the context of total implementation cost. Total implementation cost includes software license, hardware, modifications, and consulting services. There is a correlation between price and other factors. Generally a top-tier package from an implementation cost perspective is a functionally rich solution capable of supporting high-volume operations.

While the precise category definitions vary among analysts, WMS packages can be classified according to tiers as follows:

- *Tier 1*—implementation costs are typically in excess of $500,000 for a single site. Package provides comprehensive functionality that can be configured to meet specific needs of complex, high volume operation. However, moderate to high levels of custom software modifications may be required to achieve operational objectives.
- *Tier 2*—implementation costs typically range between $200,000 and $500,000. A package provides considerable functionality, but may not address all functional areas and may not provide as many options in supported areas as a Tier 1 solution. Typically, a package is implemented with minimal modifications.
- *Tier 3*—implementation costs are under $200,000. A package supports only core warehouse functions (receiving, storage, order processing, and shipping). Options within an individual function are limited. The package is usually implemented without any modifications.

In practice, the boundary lines between tiers tend to blur. Vendors within each tier tend to encroach on adjacent tiers' territory. Since the dividing lines between tiers are not universally accepted, vendors can move up or down in classification according to the definition used. Also, the Tier 1 classification covers considerable ground with some single site implementations costing considerably more than the $500,000 threshold.

Market share is another classification method. It is usually stated as the percentage of overall WMS revenues represented by a vendor's total sales. In these terms only a couple of vendors can claim a double-digit market share. The majority of major vendors can only report single digit market shares.

WMS market share can be somewhat misleading. Few major WMS vendors offer only WMS solutions. They supplement their revenues with TMS, LMS, supply chain collaboration, and other supply chain solution sales. Most vendors are privately owned reporting their revenues on a voluntary basis.

ERP vendors that offer their own Warehouse Modules (WM) to supplement their product lines further complicate the WMS marketplace. Early ERP WM solutions offered limited functionality and capability when compared to 'best-of-breed' WMS packages. But ERP vendors are actively working to close the gap. They are specifically targeting their own customer base by offering the potential for a lower total cost of ownership.

Trends

The WMS industry has evolved considerably over the past decade. Top-tier WMS packages can address practically every internal operational aspect of a distribution facility. While WMS vendors will continue to add and refine their functionality, many will find it hard to dramatically increase the warehousing capabilities of their already functionally rich product. However, competitive market forces will require vendors to continue to make enhancements to their overall product line in order to maintain or increase market share. These efforts will focus on:

- *Using the Web as the primary delivery device for user services.* Vendors are beginning to Web-enable their products or re-write them to operate as pure Web-based applications. End-users access functionality through a standard Web browser. This approach offers customers lower deployment and administration costs by eliminating the need to install special client-side software.
- *Integrating other SCE applications into their product lines.* WMS vendors are rapidly becoming total SCE vendors by offering integrated TMS, LMS, supply chain collaboration and decision support solutions. While many vendors will offer these other SCE solutions on a stand-alone basis, their real targets will be existing customers or prospects seeking a total integrated solution.
- *Providing standard interfaces for ERP, MHE, and supply chain integration.* Many vendors offer standard interfaces to major ERP packages. They also support material handling equipment (MHE) integration to their packages. But WMS integration is still a custom development proposition for many implementations. Furthermore, overall supply chain information needs keep increasing the number of interface "touch points" for a WMS solution. Vendors are starting to offer integration tool sets to reduce costs and timelines.
- *Moving to a more packaged software approach.* Most top-tier WMS packages provide sophisticated configuration mechanisms that allow customers to tune the package

to meet its specific operational needs. However, many WMS implementations still require costly custom software modifications. Some vendors are trying to remove the need for modifications by incorporating business logic scripting, screen flow scripting, report writers, and label designers into their packages. Vendors are also seeking to reduce overall implementation timeline by developing configuration templates, enhancing technical documentation, and standardizing training material.

Other trends are beginning to impact the industry and the ways businesses employ WMS technology. Application Service Provider (ASP) solutions are becoming more viable and attractive. Under this model, the customer leases access to a WMS package that is installed on a third-party service organization's data center.

Another area of prospective change is how warehouse floor personnel interact with the system and confirm product movement. Most mobile transactions are recorded on a RF terminal though keyboard entry or bar code scans. Voice technology provides an alternative where user and application communicate verbally. Radio frequency identification (RFID) offers an alternative to bar codes and scanners. RFID tags attached to product and locations allow passive confirmation of moves thus eliminating the need for manual bar code scans. Falling costs will continue to make these technologies more attractive.

Challenges

Despite industry advancements, WMS implementation still remains a costly, high-risk proposition for many firms. Stories of WMS cost overruns and botched implementations are still commonplace. But potential cost savings and customer service gains will continue to pressure businesses to embrace WMS technology. This pressure will permeate all different operation types and facilities sizes. It will not stop with new and existing paper-based facilities, but also compel existing WMS sites to revisit their utilization and effectiveness.

While the industry matures toward a packaged software and services model, companies are still going to face numerous challenges in pursuing WMS technology. These include:

- *Selecting the right package.* As the industry evolves toward a more packaged software approach, companies will shy away from lengthy request-for-proposal processes in favor of more rapid selections. Some organizations will confuse rapid selection for merely buying according to vendor reputation and price. Failure to first adequately define current and future operational requirements can have disastrous results. It can lead to excessive cost overruns and under-performing implementations. An organization must first be able to clearly state its business requirements before it can intelligently select a package. It must be able to enumerate the prospective benefits, so that it can justify the expenditure.

- *Optimizing operations for current and future business environment.* While operational improvements are a frequent WMS implementation goal, there is a natural tendency after acquisition to try to make the WMS solution fit existing operational flows and procedures. In most situations the only way to achieve true operational gains from an implementation is through optimizing processes rather than merely applying technology. Companies that are unwilling to review and redesign processes to take advantage of a new system's capabilities tend to have an under-performing implementation.

- *Allocating proper resources.* WMS implementations tend to be complex projects. They impact every aspect of a distribution facility including layout, procedures, people, mechanization, and other systems. They require a strong project management team capable of defining and administering all the numerous tasks inherent in the overall process. They also require adequate resources to perform these tasks. Too frequently organizations try to staff WMS implementations solely with operations personnel who must also tend to the daily business of receiving and shipping material. When the inevitable conflicts for attention occur, it is usually the implementation task that suffers.

- *Providing an effective training program.* WMS implementations are as much about people as they are about technology. Training is one of the key cornerstones for a successful implementation. However, it is an area that frequently does not receive proper attention. Most software vendors provide limited "train-the-trainer" courses. It is the customer's responsibility to make sure that its work force receives adequate training in the new system and procedures. This means developing and institutionalizing a comprehensive training program complete with appropriate training material and competency metrics.

- *Preparing the facility for the new system.* Physical facilities preparation is also an important aspect of a WMS implementation. It entails location delineation and numbering, storage re-configuration, bar code labeling, product slotting, workstation design and installation, material handling equipment integration, and computer equipment installation. It can be a time-consuming and challenging task to operations that must prepare their warehouse while continuing to ship product.

- *Providing a thorough test process.* WMS implementations are typically highly complicated propositions. There are numerous data elements and parameters that must be precisely defined and correctly entered. There may also be custom software modifications and interfaces that add an extra level of complexity. Failure to execute a thorough test plan to validate that all these components are working properly is an invitation to disaster. This plan must be systematic and multi-tiered covering unit, systems, integration, and stress and acceptance testing.

While the WMS industry has matured, the potential benefits that WMS solutions can bring are more alluring today than in the past decades. Despite the costs and challenges, the return on investment for a WMS is still extremely attractive to many operations. Successful supply chains cannot afford to ignore the potential gains that WMS packages can generate within the four walls of their distribution facilities. If information drives the supply chain, then WMS solutions are definitely the main pumps.

CHAPTER 24
Radio Frequency Identification

Tom Singer, Principal, Tompkins Associates

Radio Frequency Identification (RFID) is hardly a new concept. In many areas it is already a mainstream technology—it is used every day to pay tolls, secure building access, control manufacturing subassembly movement and track assets. Until recently, its impact in supply chain management has been limited to niche roles like reusable container tracking. This has been primarily due to cost barriers as well as a lack of accepted standards, technology challenges and performance limitations.

Another automatic identification method, bar coding, already has an established position in the supply chain. From warehouse management systems (WMS) to point of sales (POS) applications, supply chain solutions depend on bar codes to track and control inventory. The need to supplant or augment bar codes with RFID technology has not been overwhelming. But as many supply chain professionals realize, this is beginning to change.

Interest in applying RFID to supply chain solutions has intensified mostly due to work done over the past few years by large retailers, consumer goods companies, academic research institutions, and automatic identification solution providers. These organizations believe that tremendous cost savings can be realized in the supply chain through the use of RFID technology. Spurred on by this belief, major retailers and government agencies have begun to issue RFID compliance mandates to their suppliers. These directives are accelerating the development of industry standards as well as attracting more and more RFID solution providers. This provides the potential for major breakthroughs in the cost and technological barriers that have limited the application of RFID in supply chain solutions. What has been a niche player throughout the 1990s now promises to be an arena of intense focus over the next decade.

With awareness of RFID technology and its possibilities also comes uncertainty. Many logistics operations understand that RFID is poised to make a major impact on the supply chain world. At the same time, they are also unsure exactly how this technology can affect and benefit the way they do business. Precise questions about its benefits, costs and integration issues can be difficult to answer. Furthermore, the pace at which RFID technology will actually work its way into the supply chain is still unclear. Even as standards and compliance mandates solidify, questions can still remain murky on the precise cost and benefits that can be gained from integrating RFID into a particular supply chain operation.

In certain respects, the current state of RFID in the supply chain world resembles the early days of bar coding. Compliance mandates will undoubtedly accelerate the breakdown of current technology and cost barriers. Each RFID solution provider will pump out case studies and trade journal articles that position its application of the technology in the supply chain as a best practice. But RFID's present state bears some similarity to the position of the Internet in the supply chain during the 1990s. There is considerable hype about cost savings and the potential reach of the technology. There is also a multitude of different vendors and solutions chasing a market whose exact shape and size can only be speculated at this point in time. No one can guarantee how successful any given vision will be in the coming years.

Despite the uncertainty, there are compelling reasons to take a close look at RFID that go well beyond current compliance mandates. Although existing cost and performance issues present significant challenges in using the technology in supply chain applications, RFID still can produce a positive return on investment in numerous situations. Even if it can't be currently justified for a specific situation, its evolutionary pace is such that it may become feasible in a relatively short time. While its precise long-term impact can be debated, RFID has the potential to dramatically increase the efficiency of supply chain operations.

It is no wonder that logistics operations are scrambling to figure out where their enterprises should be on the RFID curve. While major retailers, the media and auto identification vendors have certainly fueled this interest, the limitations of existing supply chain systems present a compelling reason to take a look at RFID. Bar coding is a proven, well-established technology. But bar coding requires a line-of-sight scan that can add additional labor, introduce extra processing steps, and reduce the accuracy and rapidity of information flow in a supply chain application. RFID's promise of a scan-free supply chain is too attractive to ignore.

Coming to grips with RFID is no easy matter—it takes a combination of hard work, a desire to improve operations, an open mind and some skepticism. The first step in this process is obtaining a basic understanding of RFID's components, benefits, current challenges and potential uses in applications. Once this step has been taken, the really difficult strategic and tactical questions about RFID can be addressed.

Basic Components

RFID does not present a single technological face to the world. Its elemental building blocks vary according to the applications they are designed to address. One vendor's solution may or may not interoperate with another vendor's equipment and tags. In some respects, RFID is similar to bar coding at a component level. An RFID tag can be equated to a bar code label—RFID obtains information from tags through a reader and antenna, while bar coding depends on a laser or CCD scan. But this analogy is an oversimplification. RFID-enabled applications can do things that bar code-based systems cannot. To understand what RFID can do in the supply chain, one needs to have a basic grasp of the components that make up an RFID application.

Tags

All automatic identification technologies require a medium to store information that will subsequently be retrieved by various applications for processing. RFID uses tags to electronically encode information. These tags come in a variety of sizes and designs and there are numerous types, each tailored to meet specific application requirements. All tags have two key components: an integrated circuit (IC) chip and an antenna. Information is stored on the chip and transmitted to the outside world via the antenna. The chip and antenna can be laminated on plastic cards, encapsulated in protective housings or embedded in label stock.

While some RFID chips are able to store significant amounts of information, most are designed to record a single identifier, much like a bar code. Tags also differ in their power sources and how they send/receive information to/from readers. Tags are generally categorized by:

- *Active or Passive.* RFID tags can be classified as either active or passive. This classification denotes the tag's power source and how the tag sends information to readers. Active tags have their own internal transmitter powered by an onboard battery. Passive tags are powered by the external reader's signal. The reader's transmission energizes the tag's antenna, which in turn resonates back a corresponding signal.

  Because they contain their own power source and transmitter, active tags generally support greater read distances than passive tags. But this added internal complexity means that they cost more. While passive tags are structurally simpler, they can require more powerful reader signals. Furthermore, the read distance of a passive tag is directly related to the reader's field strength or wattage. The more powerful a reader, the longer its tag read range. Government regulations restrict reader transmission wattage. Passive readers that must communicate with tags at their maximum read range typically need every watt available. Active reader signals are able to get by with a fraction of this amount since their corresponding tags have their own power sources.

  A semi-passive tag has an internal power source, but still relies on the external reader's transmission field to send its data stream. Its internal power source is typically used to support an onboard processor or sensor. With this added capability, semi-passive tags can track temperature variations for perishable goods or capture servicing information for warranty and preventive maintenance management.

- *Frequency.* RFID tags and readers are typically designed to transmit data on a fixed frequency band. Frequency impacts both read rate and distance. Lower frequency tags typically have shorter read distances and slower data transfer rates than higher frequency tags. Passive tag frequencies are generally classified as one of the following:

	Frequency	Maximum Read Distance	Typical Applications
Low (LF)	125 KHz	< 1.5 Feet	Security access, electronic payment
High (HF)	13.56 MHz	< 3 Feet	Tote tracking, asset management, smart shelves
Ultra-High (UHF)	860-928 MHz	6-10 Feet	Case and pallet tracking
Microwave	2.45 or 5.8 GHz	6-10 Feet	Custom solutions

Popular active tag frequencies range from 100MHz to 1GHz with maximum read ranges measured in hundreds of feet. Active tags can be found in trailer, inter-modal container and railcar tracking applications. They are also used in toll collection systems. Once again, read distances for passive tags are impacted by the strength of the reader's signal. They are also affected by a multitude of environment (e.g. type of material being tracked or background interference) and deployment (e.g. orientation of tag to reader antenna or length of time tag is in reader's field) factors.

- *Storage Method.* Tag designs also vary in how information is encoded and stored on them. These storage methods can be categorized as read/write, write once/read many and read-only. Read/write tags allow information to be recorded multiple times. As the name suggests, write once/read many or WORM tags can only be programmed a single time. However, this encoding can occur on demand. Read-only tags are encoded with data during their manufacturing process. Read/write tags are generally the most expensive variety.

- *Auxiliary Capabilities.* Some tags contain microprocessors and sensors capable of performing specialized tasks. These tasks may include monitoring temperature variations that an object may encounter in storage or capturing service information on a reusable container shared among trading partners. These specialized tags can send out alerts when spoilage conditions exist, or when product is improperly stored or handled.

Readers

An RFID reader or interrogator retrieves information stored on a tag through a radio frequency signal picked up by the reader's antenna. How this data signal is generated depends on the tag being read. An active reader receives signals broadcasted by the tag's internal RF transmitter. Some active tags broadcast their signals continuously without regard to whether there is a reader within receiving range. Other active tags require a prompt signal from a reader before broadcasting their data stream.

A passive reader transmits a signal strong enough to energize the target tag's antenna and circuitry. The tag resonates the signal back to the reader in a slightly modified form that is decoded to extract the data stream. Since they provide the energy for the tag's transmission, passive readers must have a considerably more powerful signal than active readers.

RFID readers play the same basic role as bar code scanners, although a bar code scanner generally captures information one bar code at a time. On the other hand, a radio frequency (RF) reader is capable of reading multiple tags within its transmission field. RFID readers come in two basic configurations: mobile and fixed. Mobile readers are usually employed as peripheral devices on handheld or vehicle-mounted terminals. As such, they can work in the same manner as tethered or integrated bar code scanners by capturing a single identifier as an associate moves an object. Fixed readers may support one or more external antennas. The reader and antenna may also be contained in a single housing. Fixed readers are typically deployed in portal-like arrays where tagged product is read by moving it through the portal. The portal concept is ideal for receiving and shipping dock doors where a pallet of tagged cases can be automatically read as a forklift driver passes through the door.

A reader encodes and decodes data transmitted through a microprocessor and firmware. How a specific reader and tag type communicate is governed by an explicit protocol. Consequently, a reader may not be able to communicate with a particular tag type or protocol even if they use the same frequency band. Some readers can only communicate with one manufacturer's proprietary tag or a single standard protocol. Other readers are considered "agile," which means that they are capable of interrogating multiple tag frequencies and protocols.

Software

Information collected by RFID readers must be correctly interpreted before it's passed to an application system. An individual tag can respond multiple times to a reader's signal. When multiple tags are within the reader's transmission range, the result is a cacophony of responses that must be managed and processed in an orderly manner. This is the job of RFID software and middleware that resides on data capture devices or on specialized controllers and servers.

The exact function that RFID software performs varies according to the application that it is designed to support. At a basic level, RFID software manages readers and how they interact with tags. But much more can be involved than simply passing data between host applications and readers. Consider the scenario where a pallet of individually tagged cases is moved through a receiving door reader portal. RFID software must control reader/tag communication in a manner that ensures each tag on the pallet is registered only once within an allotted timeframe.

RFID software can serve as a basic traffic cop that monitors a network of readers so that only a single instance of a tag's identifier is sent to an upstream application whenever the tag is within range. In another scenario it might provide processing logic that conditionally communicates with outside applications based on the state of all the tags that it's monitoring. Depending on the application, there may be different types of RFID software each dedicated to performing a specific task. The term "savant" is frequently used to identify this distributed or specialized RFID software.

Standards and the EPC Network

While RFID solutions have been available for years, the lack of prevailing standards has hindered its adoption in supply chain applications. Solutions tended to be based on proprietary technology—tags and readers from one RFID vendor did not interoperate with other vendors' offerings. These proprietary solutions might be suitable for specialized, closed-loop systems, but they are hardly conducive to applications where goods and information must be shared among trading partners.

Like the early days of bar coding, vendors, major distributors, trade associations and academia have pushed for the development of industry standards as a means to propagate the technology. The International Standards Organization (ISO) has responded by issuing standards for specific tag types. ISO standards govern how readers and tags communicate, which is commonly called the "air interface." Tags and readers that are compliant to the same ISO RFID standard are able to exchange data regardless of their manufacturer.

There are a number of different ISO RFID standards covering different frequencies and communication methods. Each has characteristics that make it suitable for a particular application set. These characteristics include data transfer rate, read range, and susceptibility to various environment conditions. ISO RFID standards are typically proposed by one or more manufacturer seeking to address a particular need. Like other ISO standards, they can go through a lengthy review and approval process.

EPCglobal is another standards organization that addresses RFID technology. EPCglobal, a joint venture between EAN International and the Uniform Code Council. Its roots can be traced back to work done by the Auto-ID Center at the Massachusetts Institute of Technology in conjunction with major retailers and consumer packaging goods companies. Like ISO, EPCglobal publishes air interface standards, but also govern data content, usage and software.

EPCglobal standards are centered on the concept of an electronic product code (EPC) that uniquely identifies objects. An "object" can be a pallet, case, individual SKU, asset or location. Like a UPC code, an EPC can identify both manufacturer and SKU. But it also contains a unique serial number of two size variations: a 64-bit and 96-bit EPC. Each variation starts with a header that determines the remaining field elements which supports the encoding of different data identifiers. These include:

- Serialized Global Trade Identification Number (SGTIN)
- Serialized Shipping Container Code (SSCC)
- Serialized Global Location Number (SGLN)
- Global Returnable Asset Identifier (GRAI)
- Global Individual Asset Identifier (GIAI)
- General Identifier (GID)

These identifiers are employed according to the object being identified. An SSCC can be used to identify a mixed SKU pallet or carton. A SGTIN can be used to track a single SKU pallet or case, while a GID can be employed to uniquely identify individual items. The elements that comprise a GID are:

Element	Size	Available Numbers
Header	8-bits	
General Manager (Company)	28-bits	~268M
Object Class (Item)	24-bits	~16M
Serial Number	36-bits	~68B

The concepts and standards published by EPCglobal go well beyond air interface specifications and supply chain object identification. They provide the basis for a network that governs how information is exchanged between entities in the supply chain. The key elements of this EPC network are:

- Savant: Distributed software that manages EPC data received from readers and controls the flow of information between readers and supply chain applications.
- Object Name Service (ONS): Network service used to locate where information is stored for a specific EPC. This location could be a local or remote server accessed through the Internet.
- Physical Markup Language (PML): The language used to convey detailed product information between supply chain applications over the EPC network.

The EPC Network is designed to share information over the Internet. Conceptually, it allows one organization to locate and retrieve detailed product information stored on servers maintained by another firm for any given EPC. ONS provides the appropriate network address or URL for where the information is stored, and PML provides the means for the requesting application to retrieve the information.

The EPC Network provides a vision for RFID that goes well beyond traditional automatic identification technologies. It provides the structure to track product movement throughout the supply chain. Properly maintained and updated PML servers can provide complete item-level history from the manufacturer to the end-user.

While there is solid acceptance of the EPC in supply chain applications, initial compliance mandates have eschewed the concept of the EPC Network in favor of other private networks for sharing data between trading partners. Like traditional ASNs, these efforts are concentrating on sharing information point-to-point rather than across the entire supply chain. This doesn't mean that the EPC Network won't eventually play a prominent role in the supply chain—it only implies that the future is still very much open.

Benefits

According to many of its proponents, RFID promises to save billions of dollars through increased distribution efficiency and reduced shrinkage, and will radically change the way the supply chain works. But even the most fervent supporter must admit that the potential benefits will vary greatly among supply chain operations. While some promises may seem a bit over-optimistic, RFID does provide significant advantages over bar coding. Before any organization can seriously contemplate using RFID to support its operations, it should have a firm understanding of the benefits that the technology can provide.

Improved Efficiency

The primary reason that major retailers and distributors are interested in RFID is that they believe it can save them money by making their operations more efficient. These companies already employ sophisticated systems that utilize bar codes. They require their suppliers to apply bar coded labels on shipments and transmit ASNs so that they do not have to manually identify product on the receiving dock. Even though they effectively utilize bar codes, they believe that RFID will allow them to make their distribution operations even more efficient.

While bar coding allows distribution organizations to improve their operational efficiency, the technology requires a line-of-sight scan to complete a transaction. Warehouse employees, as part of material movements, typically perform these scans with handheld or vehicle mounted units. Although the effort involved is dependent on the operation being performed, the process of acquiring and scanning bar codes still takes time and labor. Even if this additional labor costs only $.05 per scan, the total cost of all the required scans in a busy distribution center (DC) can be surprising large.

Receiving is frequently cited as an operation that can benefit greatly from RFID. The labor saved is directly related to the type of receiving performed. Since case-level receiving requires more scans, it should benefit more from RFID than pallet-level operations. In either case, the concept is fairly clear-cut. Pallet or case tags are automatically read as product is moved through an RFID portal at the receiving dock. The amount of labor saved equates to the time it takes to locate each bar-coded label and scan it. Because the portal can read multiple tags almost simultaneously, the labor savings from receiving a pallet of tagged cases can be substantial.

This labor savings is not restricted to just the actual scan time. Operations personnel can spend considerable time positioning product so that the bar code labels can subsequently be read. It is not uncommon to see case-level shipping operations where associates build outbound pallets with all case labels facing outward so that they can be scanned prior to loading. Using RFID, pallets can be built and cases stacked regardless of label orientation. Furthermore, cases can be placed in interior pallet regions since RFID does not require a line-of-sight scan. The potential labor savings are not restricted to manual operations. RFID can save money in automated DCs by eliminating the need to manually position cases on a conveyor line to face in-line scanners or replacing costly tunnel scanners with a single reader.

The value of the potential labor savings varies between operations. RFID receiving at the pallet level may mean more to a flow-through operation than a receive-store-pick warehouse. An operation that must do considerable inbound quality inspections may benefit less than another facility with a less stringent quality assurance program.

While receiving and shipping are common areas of interest for RFID deployment, an entirely scan-free operation is the ultimate goal from an efficiency perspective. The ability to verify putaways, replenishments, picks, counts and other warehouse activities without scanning a bar code can provide significant labor savings and improve product flow. Operations that need to capture additional information when performing inventory transactions may be able to gain even greater efficiencies by employing item-level EPC tags. For example, a pharmaceutical each pick operation may be able to forgo the scan or entry of lot numbers by utilizing EPC tags. While the practicality of these scan-free visions may not be immediately obtainable for a specific operation, they illustrate the cost savings potential of the technology.

Increased Accuracy

Because they provide near-perfect identification of objects, bar code-based systems can be extremely accurate. But they typically have one common weak point—they depend upon an operator to actually perform the scan. Consequently, inventory still gets lost and mis-shipments still occur because a warehouse associate performed an inventory move without performing the corresponding scan transaction. RFID has the ability to provide an inventory tracking mechanism that is not dependent on human-initiated scans. Transactions can be automatically recorded as product is moved within the warehouse.

Outbound load confirmation is a good example of how RFID can improve accuracy. In a bar code-based system, outbound cases might be systematically tied to a single bar coded license plate as they are palletized. This license plate is then scanned as the pallet is loaded onto a trailer. This is an accurate method of confirming shipment loads as long as the pallet builder scans or records each case as it is palletized. An RFID alternative that reads all case tags on a pallet as it is moved through an outbound door would eliminate both the need for the palletizing scan and the error that would occur if the scan did not take place. This may allow further labor savings by eliminating the need to audit the outbound lane for stray cases. Of course, this all presumes that an RFID tag was applied to each outbound case. Any case without a readable tag can be loaded without a load confirmation being recorded.

Given enough tags and readers, RFID can provide the ability to track all inventory movements within a DC. All physical moves could be systematically tracked without the need for an operator to record the transactions in the system. Mis-picks and erroneous putaways where the wrong bar code is confirmed could be eliminated. Cost and technological barriers currently make this level of tracking impractical for most operations, but it is a theoretical possibility that could become a reality sometime in the near future.

RFID can also be employed in tandem with other technologies to improve accuracy. For example, voice recognition and pick-to-light are viable technologies for many picking operations. But they do not prevent warehouse personnel from erroneously taking product from the wrong pick face or putting picked items in the wrong carton or tote. RFID can help supplement these solutions by automatically verifying that the correct transaction was performed.

Increased Throughput

Manual bar code scanning can be a disruptive process. It requires a worker to perform a specific transaction that may not be part of the natural flow of material. An operator performing a multi-step inventory move must stop at specific points in the process to scan one or more bar codes. This slows down the movement of material through a DC.

RFID has a passive nature. A worker need not interrupt his/her workflow to stop and scan bar codes. A transaction can be automatically captured by moving product through a reader portal, or by picking up a pallet with a vehicle that has an attached reader. Inventory can be tracked without breaking the rhythm an operation. By eliminating scans, product can move more quickly through a facility.

Reduced Inventory

Because RFID can help improve efficiency, accuracy and throughput, it can also help take inventory out of an operation. It can help reduce shrinkage by enabling a more accurate tracking of inventory. A more accurate inventory combined with a more efficient operation can enable a distribution operation to reduce safety stock and improve order fill rates.

RFID's ability to reduce inventory is not limited to internal distribution operations. It can help improve accuracy and velocity throughout an entire supply chain from supplier to retail store. Information on inventory levels and movements can also be shared more rapidly between trading partners and key points within a supply chain. The effect of these factors can be a general reduction of inventory throughout a supply chain.

Visibility

The EPC Network offers the potential to truly extend and enhance product visibility beyond the four walls of a DC. While traditional EDI provides a mechanism to share information between trading partners, RFID and the EPC Network can provide the basis for tighter collaboration and greater visibility throughout the entire supply chain. Through PML servers, an administrating organization such as a manufacturer can provide a central repository for product information. This repository can contain item-level information that is updated on a near real-time basis as an item moves through the supply chain.

The EPC Network can provide extended product visibility from manufacturing through final sale and beyond. The trading partner performing the transaction can post each product move or action as it happens on the appropriate PML server. A manufacturer could use this facility to track and maintain warranty information. It would allow a transportation consolidator to alert shipment recipients of the status of each case in the hub as it is being processed. It could also be used to support product catalog synchronization between supplier and distributor eliminating the need to maintain customer or vendor item number cross-reference tables.

Lot tracking is an excellent example of how this extended visibility can benefit a supply chain. Consider the process that a pharmaceutical manufacturer must go through to recall a specific SKU lot. Their existing supply chain systems probably only identify the immediate recipient of the lot. This recipient could be a wholesaler, hospital/clinic, drug store or retailer who in turn distributes the product to other entities in the supply chain. An individual item could go through many intermediate destinations before ending up in the hands of the final customer.

The EPC Network could be used as a facilitator to track the movement of the pharmaceutical manufacturer's products throughout the supply chain. If the need arises to recall a specific lot, the manufacturer could reference a PML server to determine the last known location for each item in the lot. This concept could also be used to support pedigree paper regulations that require drug wholesalers to provide a record of each entity in the supply chain that has handled the controlled item being resold.

The above visions are dependant on acceptance and active participation in the EPC Network by all relevant trading partners in a supply chain. These entities must enhance their systems and products to support this type of information flow. They must overcome existing technological challenges and barriers to wide-scale RFID systems deployment. The EPC Network is currently more concept than reality. The pace at which it will evolve will vary according to industry type. For example, the appeal of this type of visibility probably means more to the pharmaceutical industry than it does to building products firms.

Security
Since RFID can passively track the movement of an individual object, it can be used in a similar manner as sensormatic and other loss-prevention technology to help reduce theft. Retailers, distributors and manufacturers can employ RFID portals by exits to detect unauthorized product movement. EPC tags can double as both product identifiers for POS and distribution systems and loss-prevention tags for security systems. However, RFID tags are susceptible to interference—a thin sheet of metal foil can easily block the signal from many tag types.

Product authentication is another area that may prompt enterprises to turn to RFID for greater security. If every object has a unique identifier and detailed information on the object is stored in a PML server, any purchaser can validate the object's authenticity by interrogating its EPC tag. This would provide some manufacturers with a powerful tool to combat product counterfeiting.

The Challenges
Given the current state of RFID technology, its challenges and potential barriers can make RFID impractical for many situations. Like any other application of technology, RFID must produce an acceptable return on investment and meet production level performance criteria in order to be a viable solution for any supply chain implementation. But RFID is evolving at a fairly brisk pace—what is an insurmountable barrier today may or may not be an issue tomorrow.

Performance
RFID readers can fail to correctly read tags for a variety of reasons. Distance and tag orientation to the reader can prevent a successful read. Certain materials like metal or liquid can distort or weaken RFID signals. Packaging and the surrounding environment as well as product handling may affect read success rate. Electromagnetic background noise generated by other equipment can also present problems. Even the speed that tags move past readers impacts the ability to successfully capture reads.

Furthermore, these performance factors vary in importance according to the tag type being used. For example, a low frequency tag might be a good choice for tracking air conditioners if the reads can be performed discretely and at a short range. But the same tag would probably not be suitable for capturing outbound load confirmations for apparel shipments by driving a pallet of tagged cases through a door portal. A UHF tag is a better fit for this situation.

RFID vendors like to tout the abilities of the technology by demonstrating multiple reads of tagged cases on a cart being pulled through a portal. It is one thing to successfully read a dozen tags applied to empty cardboard boxes in a controlled environment. But it is an entirely different proposition to attempt to read 40 tags applied to palletized cases of soup as they are being driven onto a trailer. Tag type, packaging, product characteristics and other environmental conditions must be properly addressed to ensure success. This may require more work and a significantly greater investment than RFID vendors typically admit.

Cost

The compliance plans of major RFID drivers are predicated on inexpensive tags. Passive tags costs currently range from $.20 to over $10 per tag depending on tag type and quantity ordered. Earlier work done by the Auto-ID Center at MIT has identified a $.05 tag as the cost threshold needed to make RFID practical for widespread use in the supply chain. Recent advances in tag manufacturing promise to dramatically reduce tag costs. Compliance mandates have rekindled the interest of chip manufacturers in RFID. Tag costs will continue to decrease, but the rate of this decline cannot be predicted with any certainty.

Tags are only a part of the overall picture of RFID costs. Tags still must be applied to objects by some sort of mounting media or by embedding the tag in the material. Tags require readers. RFID readers vary in costs but are still generally more expensive than laser scanners. While reader costs will drop as demand spurs production, it is still a major investment for any RFID application. Furthermore, performance factors may drive other costs with prospective RFID users forced to redesign packaging or retrofit facilities to make their application work.

Evolutionary Pace

The potential benefits of RFID and the EPC Network are quite compelling. But there is still more concept than reality in many of the visions put forth by their proponents. Many existing technological and economic hurdles will be overcome as momentum builds for RFID supply chain applications. No one can determine how quickly this will happen with any degree of certainty. Furthermore, the ultimate outcome may not entirely match the current visions.

RFID will continue to evolve in the supply chain at a pace dictated by cost, performance and trading community acceptance. Compliance plans may have given the latter a considerable boost. But this hardly means that acceptance throughout the supply chain is assured. Certain issues may be difficult to surmount. For example, privacy concerns about item tagging may cause many retailers to shy away from this level of RFID tracking. This aversion may be driven more by public perception than technical reasons. If this happens, the future of RFID will look different than one where retail item-level tracking is an acceptable goal.

Redesigning Processes

While RFID can be used in lieu of bar codes, many potential efficiency and accuracy gains will only be obtained by using it in a different manner than bar code-based systems. The main advantage of RFID over bar codes is that it allows object identification in a non-intrusive manner. However, many existing supply chain applications require direct capture of bar codes through user-initiated scans. A truly scan-free warehouse will require different processes than one that relies on bar codes.

RFID receiving may be an extremely attractive prospect for many distribution operations. But real productivity gains will probably come more from making it a more flow-through process than by merely substituting an RFID read for a bar code scan. Implementing a flow-through receiving process may require changes in an operation's shipment check-in, quality, verification, special handling and vendor performance monitoring procedures.

Integration

Given existing challenges, RFID is hardly a plug-and-play solution. It can require considerable planning, engineering and tuning to make it work in a production environment. While this integration process should get easier as RFID solutions mature, any organization currently contemplating an RFID project should be prepared to devote significant resources to make the solution work. Since its usage is not widespread in the supply chain, skilled RFID integration resources are still relatively scarce, which means that many firms will have to turn to third party integrators for assistance.

Software Applications

Like other automatic identification technologies, RFID is deployed to support specific software applications. RFID can find its way into distribution operations through custom applications or commercially available software. Many supply chain execution software vendors are currently or planning to incorporate RFID support into their products. Warehouse, transportation, labor and visibility applications are all potential candidates for RFID.

Since handheld terminals and computers are available with integrated RFID readers, any solution that utilizes bar codes can claim to be RFID-enabled by substituting tags for bar codes. However, many RFID benefits can only be obtained by designing or adapting applications to work with the unique features offered by the technology. Whether as a customized solution or a commercially available package, RFID will work its way into the supply chain through a variety of application types.

Compliance

Wal-Mart and Department of Defense (DoD) RFID mandates have already sparked a new software market for RFID compliance solutions. These applications are typically designed to work with existing warehouse management modules and ERP systems. They basically allow tag identifiers to be systematically associated with carton and pallet contents. The result is an ASN that is transmitted to the trading partner.

Unless a supplier ships exclusively to Wal-Mart or DoD, the compliance application must also account for customers that do not require RFID tags. One approach is to tag every shipment. While this method offers operational and systems simplicity, the extra cost of applying unnecessary tags can be overwhelming. Many suppliers will be faced with applying compliance tags at the back end of their shipping process. This can entail significant operational and material handling equipment flow changes that must balance efficiency and investment costs with compliance dictates.

Both WMS vendors and standalone solution providers are pursuing the compliance market. However, several WMS vendors do not restrict their compliance initiatives to their own product line and offer standalone solutions that can be integrated with ERP systems and other WMS packages.

Scan-Free Distribution

While compliance will drive some distribution operations into utilizing RFID, others will be drawn by the potential operational benefits. Even those suppliers forced to adopt RFID by their customers will look to leverage the technology within their four walls. Many of these firms will first look to employ RFID to improve specific warehousing activities like receiving and load confirmation. This functionality will either be deployed as add-on applications interfaced to existing warehousing systems or by native support provided by a specific WMS package.

Under these initial deployment scenarios, RFID will coexist with bar codes. An operation might receive and load using RFID, but locate and pick by scanning bar codes. However, the ultimate goal is to replace all bar code scanning with tag readers. All product movement transactions from putway to outbound staging would be tracked and directed via RFID tags.

One way to achieve this scan-free vision with existing applications is to use pre-coded tags and mobile terminals with RFID readers. While this approach provides certain benefits, many other gains will only be achieved by redesigning applications to take full advantage of the non-intrusive nature of RFID. The advantages of redesigning a cycle count routine to take full advantage of RFID are fairly apparent. But the benefits of revamping other functions are more subtle.

Consider full case picking where the user is currently directed to perform the pull via a handheld RF terminal. The user verifies the pull by scanning the case bar code and systematically associates the case to an outbound pallet by scanning the pallet's bar code. An RFID-enabled case picking routine could eliminate the need for these two scan points. The RF terminal would still display the pick location but would automatically advance to the next pick once the correct case has been placed on the pallet.

Making an existing WMS solution truly RFID-enabled will require a fair amount of redesign and coding. Although most top-tier WMS vendors are moving in this direction, it will probably be an evolutionary process where RFID capability is gradually added to packages over successive versions. The pace of this process is dependent on how quickly the technological challenges are addressed as well as the general acceptance of using RFID to support warehousing operations.

Closed-Loop Tracking

Until compliance changes the landscape, the most common use of RFID within the supply chain is for closed-loop asset tracking. This application type utilizes RFID to track or control the location of an asset. The asset might be a trailer in the yard or a reusable container that travels between fixed points in the supply chain. Closed-loop RFID applications are generally employed when bar coding is impractical due to environmental considerations or the process flow is better suited for a scan-free solution. Since it usually involves significantly fewer tags, its costs dynamics are typically more favorable than pallet- and case-level product tracking.

Closed-loop RFID tracking applications can be used to support either manual or mechanized asset movement. Many material handling equipment vendors provide RFID readers as well as fixed laser scanners for their systems. Applying RFID tags to conveyable totes might provide an attractive alternative to bar codes in certain situations.

Real-Time Location

A scan-free RFID application tracks product movement using stationary portals and mobile RFID readers. It cannot help locate an object if it is moved outside of the reach of these devices. This same shortcoming exists in WMS solutions that rely on bar coding. While scanning is an extremely accurate method of identification and verification, bar coding does not prevent warehouse personnel from moving product outside of the system. An RFID-enabled WMS can help improve accuracy by reducing errors like the wrong target location being scanned. But it is not going to prevent someone who doesn't have an RFID reader from physically moving a pallet or case without identifying the new location to the system.

This deficiency can be overcome with enough tags, readers and special software. Real-time locator systems continuously track each tagged object's physical location within the coverage area. Given their high cost and existing technological challenges, real-time locator systems may not be viable for most operations for many years, if ever. However, they can already be found in certain specialty applications such as yard management systems (YMS).

Some YMS packages can track trailer movement through real-time locator technology. Active RFID tags are applied to each trailer as it enters the yard. The application systematically locates the trailer's position in the yard through an antenna array. Yard jockeys are not required to enter or scan trailer and location identifiers whenever the trailer is moved. The tag is removed when the trailer leaves the yard. Since only a small number of tags are needed, the investment for this type of solution may be eminently justifiable for certain operations.

Supply Chain Integration

RFID's potential to improve supply chain operations is not restricted to the four walls of a DC. The concept of an EPC Network provides the framework for increasing supply chain visibility and integration well beyond the level available from current solutions. If each tagged item's movements are posted to a PML server in near real-time from the manufacturer to the final customer, then a whole new world of productivity gains is open to the entire supply chain. The retailer, wholesaler, manufacturer and even the manufacturer's suppliers can simultaneously monitor store sales at the item level. RFID and the EPC Network can improve product recall, warranty management and return processes throughout the supply chain. This is definitely a long-range vision that may never pan out for certain supply chains. However, its potential is strong enough to keep others moving in this direction.

Moving Ahead

Despite recent developments, RFID's future in the supply chain is not entirely clear. Although many challenges must be overcome before its use becomes commonplace, the potential impact of RFID is huge. Even if the ultimate visions of its most ardent supporters fail to materialize, RFID will still have an enormous influence on supply chain operations over the next decade.

Enterprises cannot afford to ignore RFID in the supply chain. This doesn't mean that every logistics operation should aggressively pursue RFID applications. Like any emerging technology, there is a proper point in time for an organization to adopt the new tool. The exact timing of this adoption point depends on many variables. An enterprise that moves too quickly or slowly can risk its competitive position.

Logistics operations need to address the potential uses of RFID in a systematic manner. Given the technology's current state in the supply chain, this is not as easy as it sounds. It requires work. Specifically, logistics operations need to:

- *Build an RFID knowledge base.* RFID is a complex proposition. It is not a 'plug-and-play' technology. The first step in moving ahead with RFID is to develop a firm grasp of its components, benefits, challenges and applications. Since the technology is still evolving, this will be an on-going process. The trade and industry media, solution providers, industry organizations and EPCglobal are good resources.
- *Maintain a strategic outlook.* Enterprises need to account for RFID in their strategic supply chain planning process. This doesn't mean that every organization needs to have a formal RFID plan. However, every logistics operation should assess RFID's potential impact on its strategic and tactical plans.
- *Understand that RFID is not just another form of bar coding.* Any organization that only seeks to employ RFID in the same manner as bar codes risks missing out on the real benefits that the technology can generate. RFID should be implemented in conjunction with process redesign that leverages the technology's benefits and fully addresses its challenges. Be prepared to look at everything from packaging to facility layout because it can directly affect the success of an RFID rollout.
- *Recognize that bar codes and RFID will coexist.* Perhaps RFID will eventually replace bar codes as the primary identifier in supply chain systems. But it is much more likely that RFID and bar codes will coexist for many years—if not indefinitely. An operation may use RFID for pallet and case movements, but still rely on bar codes for item transactions. A distributor receiving RFID-tagged product from larger vendors may still be processing bar coded shipments from smaller suppliers. This dual approach will entail additional processing, hardware and software costs for years to come.
- *Make the proper investment in the design process.* Implementing RFID is not a pure technology project. Because RFID has so many operational, product and systems touch points, it is essential that all impacted areas have representation on the design

team. Give careful consideration to project scope so that each potential touch point is adequately addressed. Take the time and effort to thoroughly delineate each prospective benefit and challenge.

- *Have realistic expectations.* RFID is still an evolving technology. In many ways it is still rough around the edges when it comes to supply chain applications. Any logistics operation contemplating an RFID project should be realistic in their assessment of the potential benefits, costs and difficulties. While this may seem obvious, it may not be so easy to follow as momentum for the technology grows. Any operation undertaking an RFID project should be prepared for many challenges.

- *Look not just at today, but toward tomorrow.* RFID is a long-term investment proposition that should be evaluated in the context of the entire supply chain. Wal-Mart and other RFID leaders are not pushing into this new frontier because they simply want to implement flow-through receiving—they see many potential solutions that are not currently viable. They believe that the technology will continue to mature and cost dynamics improve in part because they are pushing the leading edge. Many early adopters do not see any real gain on their initial steps, but they are positioning for far greater returns further down the road.

- *Be prepared to contend with more information.* RFID and the EPC Network can provide an abundance of information down to the item level in near real time. While all this information will greatly enhance supply chain visibility and collaboration, it does present significant information systems challenges. Many supply chain operations are already awash with information. RFID promises to grow this data reservoir into an ocean. This growth will stress existing system infrastructures.

Each enterprise and supply chain must determine their position on the RFID adoption curve. Some need to be early adopters, while others should wait until the technology fully matures. Most will fall somewhere in between. Figuring out the when, where and how is not an easy proposition. But the stakes are too high not to try.

CHAPTER 25
Transportation Operations and Management

Ben Cubitt, Principal, Tompkins Associates

Transportation is the "logistics in motion" that connects your raw materials vendors to your plants, your component manufacturing centers to your finished goods assembly centers, your production/assembly points to your distribution centers (DCs), and your plants/DCs to your customers. It is as essential as any function of the supply chain. How product is moved from point A to point B can make or break the entire supply-chain effort.

The Transportation Opportunity

In the 1990s, hundreds of businesses optimized their warehouses by implementing best practices in a number of areas. Companies created strategic warehouse designs and installed warehouse management system (WMS) programs. Organizations looked to logistics managers to streamline these operations by raising efficiency and reducing costs while maintaining the highest levels of customer satisfaction. Optimizing warehouse operations is an important step in that process, but one of the best opportunities to achieve these improvements is through transportation.

Gaining visibility into your transportation operations all the way from raw materials vendors to your end customers will open the door for communication, process development, and management skills that can be leveraged in other areas like inventory management and procurement. A bonus is that many of the more advanced supply chain visibility tools gaining rapid acceptance in the marketplace are either part of a suite of applications that combines WMS and transportation management system (TMS) functions or have transportation management and optimization as their base functionality. This acknowledges the fact that transportation is the critical bond to upstream and downstream links in your supply chain.

Where The Money Is

To appreciate the size of the opportunity that transportation presents, it is necessary to understand the size of transportation spending. North American freight expenditures are almost $600 billion annually, with 80 percent spent on motor freight. Within that segment, the highly fragmented for-hire business of hauling full truckloads (TL) of consignments accounts for more than half of expenditures. The rest is divided among carriers who take less-than-truckload (LTL) shipments and smaller private fleets and parcel carriers.

Transportation is by far the largest logistics expense area for most companies. Surveys done by the Council of Logistics Management (CLM) have estimated that logistics expense represents about 9 percent of the U.S. gross domestic product and that transportation spending by itself is 6 percent of GDP. The table at right shows each of the major areas of logistics and the estimated annual expenditures in the United States for each area.

Companies in every industry understand that transportation is too large a segment of the economy and their business to ignore. Senior management is focusing on transportation because a dollar saved on transportation goes straight to the bottom line. Corporate hierarchies are beginning to see how important the transportation role is and to understand that improvements in transportation operations are often very fast to implement and require little or no capital investment.

Table 25.1: U.S. Business Logistics System Cost is the Equivalent of 8.7% of GDP in 2002 ($ billion)

Carrying Costs	
Interest	23
Taxes, Obsolescence, Depreciation, Ins.	197
Warehousing	78
Subtotal	298
Transportation Costs	
Motor Carriers	
Truck – Intercity	300
Truck – Local	162
Subtotal	462
Other Carriers	
Railroads, Water, Oil Pipelines, Air, Forwarders	109
Shipper Related Costs	6
Logistics Admin	35
TOTAL LOGISTICS COSTS	**910**

Source: 14th Annual "State of Logistics Report", Cass Information Systems and ProLogis, June 2, 2003.

The Structure of Transportation

Transportation management and optimization strives to deliver outstanding customer service at the lowest possible cost. To do this transportation managers need to have a comprehensive and detailed view of all of their transportation activities. Data is what drives transportation optimization. Data must be accurate, timely, and comprehensive. For example, having the weight of each shipment is not sufficient if the cube is what drives trailer and container utilization. Four basic factors are critical to transportation cost optimization:

- Geographic Distribution of Product—distance traveled from plant or warehouse
- Equipment Utilization—how efficiently is equipment loaded?
- Mode Selection—Truckload/Rail/Intermodal/LTL
- Shipment Cost—Cost per mile, cwt., etc. charged by carrier

Networks
The first factor that affects the transportation operation is distance. This includes the range a product is moved to and from a plant or warehouse and is influenced by the type of products each warehouse stores. Finding the best arrangements of facilities and the goods that will be moved is called network optimization.

To begin network optimization, one must establish how long it has been since the network was rationalized. Next, an analyst should determine if facilities are well located. A network optimization analysis will find the most cost-effective and customer- service capable locations and the right number of facilities for the network. It is possible that, because of corporate acquisitions and other events, it may have been some time since an overall analysis of shipping modes, routes and profiles was done. A complete network analysis will determine if goods are moving at optimal cost and service performance.

Another step is to look at how much time has passed since the inventory was rationalized. This involves establishing the most economical network locations for holding inventory. This step must determine whether all products should be held in all locations, or if some items would be better kept in only certain facilities. In many industries today this means segregating inventory into low and high volume DC's, each with it's own specialized DC design, layout, use of MHE (material handling equipment) and processes.

Equipment Utilization

The second factor is equipment utilization. Are tractors and trailers being monitored for how effectively the full cube or weight capacity is utilized? Is specialized equipment used if it will facilitate improved load planning – high cube trailers, lighter tractors to allow max gross load capacity, 53-foot trailers, 40-foot containers? Have packaging and or pallet configurations been evaluated and modified to assist in improved trailer and container utilization?

If the network uses a private fleet, there should be policies to allow for the dual use of tractors. Avoid assigning equipment to individuals, as dual tractor use can significantly impact the number of available tractors. An analyst must look at the use of the entire transportation fleet, however, not just individual trucks. Is using a private fleet the most economical approach? Is the private fleet making use of vendor inbound freight or returns for backhauls to fill "empty miles?" How long has it been since the fleet was cost-justified? Analyze to determine the proper ratio of private fleet to common carriage—publicly available carriers—but do not jump to conclusions. Sometimes, it is beneficial to use both methods.

Transportation Modes

Technically, there are five transportation modes: highway, rail, air, water, and pipeline. Highway is by far the most common mode and the easiest to use as it does not require the specialized equipment and knowledge that characterize the other modes. The highway mode has three sub-groups: truckload (TL), less-than-truckload (LTL) and small-package delivery. Whenever a more expensive mode is used, from expedited air freight to parcel to LTL, transportation managers should aggressively look for any opportunity to migrate from higher cost modes to less expensive modes. At the most basic level this means converting next day air to ground, ground parcel to pool shipments, LTL to pool points or multi-stop truckload shipments, truckload shipments to intermodal and intermodal or truckload to rail. While every order cannot be converted and each mode has its proper role in a shipper's transportation operations, mode optimization is the single largest cost opportunity for most shippers. Strategies to achieve mode optimization include consolidating shipments, gaining increased visibility and planning over multiple days of shipments, using customer incentives to encourage full truckload orders and use of a TMS to improve shipment consolidation and load planning.

Shipment Costs

Once your network has been rationalized and optimized, your planning is yielding loads that maximize the cube or weight on your outbound trailers and you have moved as much freight as possible up the mode optimization scale, you then must execute these shipments in the most cost effective manner. Your performance here is driven by good rate and contract negotiation as well as optimal carrier selection. Shipment costs are best controlled by regular carrier bids that both identify market competitive rates for every lane and mode, but also standardize and minimize accessorial fees. The most successful freight bids achieve low cost capacity with strong carriers and also help both the shipper and carrier reduce administrative cost. The lowest total costs may not be the absolute lowest cost quoted for a lane, but the lowest cost with a proven carrier that can offer both capacity and compliance with all other requirements.

Once a decision has been made about how to transport products, questions remain about with whom to ship. A manager trying to drive down costs needs to ask how long it has been since freight prices were last "shopped" and how long it has been since the carrier base was analyzed. Periodically, an analyst must review contracts and consider using alternate carriers. What discounts are available? Discounts to which carriers agreed in the past may be outdated if a shipper has achieved growth and is giving the carrier much more business today. What charges is the company that is shipping goods paying for extra services? Those payments, such as inside delivery charges, also may have been outdated by company growth or other changes.

Current and Future Transportation Spending

As discussed earlier, motor freight receives the bulk of transportation spending in the United States. More than 80 percent of America's freight is shipped by truck, and motor carrier shipments approach $500 billion in annual expenditures. The charts below show how much is spent on each mode and what the growth trends are. These figures result from a survey of CLM members.

The expected growth in ocean and small package shipments highlights two of the strongest trends in supply chain management today: the growth of consumer-direct shipments and the growth in world trade. As exports and imports continue to grow, ocean freight will continue to see explosive growth and become a much more important area of focused transportation management for many companies. Many factors are driving the surge in small package and express services, including just-in-time inventory replenishment and e-commerce direct-to-consumer shipments. When companies consolidate DCs, it can lead to smaller shipments being moved via express and parcel services rather than local deliveries by a private or other dedicated fleet.

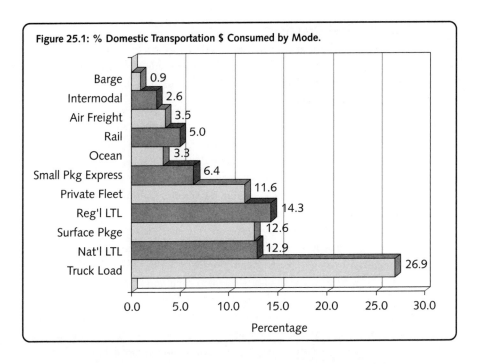

Figure 25.1: % Domestic Transportation $ Consumed by Mode.

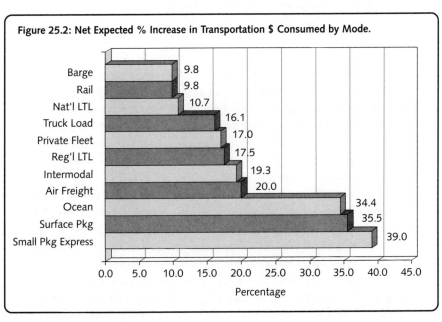

Figure 25.2: Net Expected % Increase in Transportation $ Consumed by Mode.

Transportation Best Practices

Effective transportation optimization matches the service requirements with the lowest possible cost transportation strategy. To achieve this, transportation managers need to be aware of the established and emerging industry best practices. In the following sections these best practices are identified and briefly discussed.

Established Fundamentals—The Basics of Transportation Operations

- *Implement a core carrier program in all areas of your transportation operations.* Core carrier programs have been around for years and are the most generally accepted of all transportation best practices, and for good reason. They are easy to implement and provide an immediate payback. Even in the age of online bidding and excess carrier capacity, a strong core carrier program continues to prove itself at companies both small and large. Dealing with fewer carriers reduces the administrative burden and cost of carrier management, while capitalizing on the most basic of transportation economics—trading increased volume for lower prices. Do you have more than a handful of trusted partners handling the bulk of your loads? Do you have some carriers that only handle one or a few select lanes? When it comes to carriers less is more. Leverage your total freight buy and turn your carriers into key partners committed to improving service and lowering your total cost of transportation operations.
- *Solidify your rate/tariff administration.* Are all your shipments moving on carriers where you have established base rates, fuel surcharge programs and contracts? This will not only keep you out of court, but also ensure that you consistently move your freight at the lowest possible cost. Well-constructed and properly managed contracts ensure that you set the terms for your transportation purchases. Companies that spend tremendous energy and time negotiating raw materials purchases on the most favorable possible terms enter into carrier-supplied freight contracts that are clearly on the carriers' terms. A good contract helps you document your costs and makes it easier to be certain you are paying market prices. They also help you avoid the dangers of inflating your costs by poorly evaluated and administered add-on costs like accessorial charges, fuel surcharges, minimums and other hard-to-track critical components of your total freight budget.
- *Reduce administrative costs.* How many people does it take your company to select, communicate with, pay and manage your carriers? Are you following established best practices in all areas of freight and carrier administration? Does it seem like the computer revolution passed this area by? Do you pay freight bills by generating, receiving and matching manual bills from multiple carriers, all with different formats, tariffs and procedures? Cast a critical eye on this significant cost center, learn what the industry leaders are doing and cut the fat. Automated load tendering, web-based tracking/tracing shipments, a system to measure carrier performance, invoice-less freight payment, proactive transit damage programs and outsourcing the processing of returns are all examples of how some companies have approached improvements in this area.

Leading Edge Tactical Practices

- *Optimize mode selection.* The smaller the shipment, the greater the cost, is the bedrock rule of transportation economics. What do you do until the day all of your customers agree to buy in full truckload quantity? You pool orders going the same way at the same time into the lowest cost mode possible. Shipment consolidation is the single biggest opportunity before every shipper. Small parcel shippers can pool orders for zone skipping; LTL shippers can pool their small shipments through inbound or outbound crossdocks, consolidation hubs or combine them into multi-stop truck-load shipments; truckload shipments can be shipped via intermodal carriers or in some situations on railroads. Rationalize your private fleet operations and determine if outsourcing is an option.

- *Maximize equipment utilization.* Are you paying for too much equipment or com-promising for equipment that is smaller than you really need? This is the very essence of low hanging fruit. Are your carriers supplying 48-foot trailers because that is what they have available on that day? Shipping a load from the East Coast to the West Coast on a 48- instead of a 53-foot trailer, inflates your shipping costs by well over 10 percent in most cases. On the flip side of the equation, are you using 40-foot containers for your import/export shipments when a 20-foot container generally fits your orders? Using the right equipment and utilizing a good transportation manage-ment system (TMS) or routing system to make sure that the full cube or available weight capacity is utilized is one of the quickest and least complicated ways to take significant cost out of your transportation operations. Plan for the right size of equipment, make sure that is what your carriers provide and then fully utilize the cube/weight capacity.

- *Bid lanes/freight.* Bidding freight is not out of sync with your core carrier program goals. A well conceived and fairly executed freight bid, whether it is an annual com-prehensive bid or daily spot bids of excess freight, can actually complement your existing core carrier program. Your partners get to see shipment volume they had never been exposed to before, an improved view of your total operations and this matching of your requirements with true carrier capacity leads to the lowest possible costs. The Web's improved communication and immediate data access capabilities have made freight bids even more critical and effective.

- *Manage import/export operations.* It truly is a global market and today that means most companies are either major importers, exporters or have extensive operations in both areas. The days when these cross-ocean movements were easy to ignore and carrying limited cost penalties for poorly executed strategies are over for most companies. It can all seem very difficult to grasp for the firm trying to get their ocean legs under them. If you don't have these skills in house, find a partner that can help you learn to navigate these new waters. Gain control of your global freight movements—first learn how much you are truly spending (unbundle freight costs from your materials import costs)—and then learn how to manage and optimize these costs. By the way, no matter how difficult and hard to grasp this is, it's important to do it and do it now.

- *Optimize your inbound freight.* Take control of this "last frontier" of your transportation operations and leverage your operation to save money not only in your inbound shipments, but also to lower rates across all your shipments. Too many companies fail to recognize how large their inbound freight bill is, since these costs are often hidden as part of the total material cost. Since the vendor is often just adding the freight on as an additional charge, or even using freight as a profit center, they have little or no motivation to control or reduce these costs. Convert as many of these shipments as make sense from prepaid to collect, optimize them by consolidating them from LTL into truckload shipments or move as fleet backhauls on your private or contract fleet. Taking control of your inbound shipments can also help relieve congestion at your distribution centers (DCs), greatly assist in reducing inventory and improve your visibility and control of inbound materials. Most TMSs are starting to focus on inbound optimization and shippers have more options than before to assist them in the planning and execution of a comprehensive inbound freight management program.

Emerging Industry Best Practices

- *Use TMS to optimize mode and carrier selection.* This strategy really belongs below our first category, "established transportation fundamentals." Among the larger, more leading-edge shippers TMS systems have been implemented for many years. Still, TMS implementation rates fall well below that of other advanced decision support systems like WMS, APS and even ERP. Due to this hard-to-explain, slow implementation rate, TMS falls under emerging best practices for far too many companies. Despite the fact that TMS has perhaps the quickest implementation time, fastest return on investment and lowest capital investment of the various supply chain optimization packages, companies both large and small continue to lag in implementing these critical systems. And those companies that have implemented a TMS often fail to implement all the modules or sub-optimize the full capabilities of these systems by only employing them for outbound shipments, or only at a few large plants, DCs or divisions. This is hard to believe, when TMS systems have consistently demonstrated the ability to lower transportation costs by as much as 10 to 15 percent of annual freight budgets.
- *Leverage partners' capabilities.* You've beaten down rates as low as you can, truckload carriers are failing in record numbers and still the pressure is on from above to keep taking cost out of the budget. Stop treating your carriers like the competition and start viewing them as the critical supply chain partners they are. Talk to your core carriers, find out how they can help you achieve your most important goals, challenge them to work with you to overcome constraints and make them a critical strong link in your supply chain. You'll be amazed to find out how that same LTL company you take for granted now can help you take advantage of the Web, reduce your administrative burden and, yes, lower costs. Some companies even find that there is so much potential there that it makes sense to have a permanent member of their best carrier's staff on-site to help them exploit these opportunities.

- *Manage freight globally across all plants and divisions.* Freight optimization is based on viewing as much of your freight as you can and consolidating shipments wherever possible. Obviously, this means across all existing plants, DCs and divisions. This maximizes your ability to consolidate shipments, utilize continuous moves, match inbound and outbound lanes, etc. This emerging strategy has been greatly accelerated by the tremendous increase in mergers and acquisitions. You have spent years optimizing all your transportation operations and solidifying your supply chain, when your company announces that it has just purchased their major domestic competitor. Now you are back at square one, you need to merge your core carriers, decide what TMS will survive and employ it across the entire operation, identify ways to eliminate redundant costs and in other ways move to view your "global freight opportunities" and optimize across your new supply chain.

- *Synthesize your operations with supply chain partners.* This extends optimization outside your organization to your partners up and down the supply chain. Many companies have started by working with their suppliers, as they perceive this is where they have the greatest leverage and best opportunity for a quick payback. Those companies that want to truly bring added value to their customers are reaching out to them and seeking ways to lower costs across the chain and use these savings to either compete more effectively or increase margins. The most leading edge companies have reached outside their own supply chain to create a community of shippers that can share core carriers, pool shipments to eliminate costly under-utilized cube on domestic trailers and ocean containers, and in other ways leverage their combined networks and freight budgets to dramatically lower costs. This is one area where new Web-based companies actually offer services that do not currently exist and are ahead of most of their potential customers in identifying a need and creating a system to fill it. Taking advantage of the Web to synthesize your supply chain is the new frontier of freight optimization.

Transportation Rates and Bidding

The transportation spending that we have been discussing once took place in a highly regulated and very convoluted marketplace. Deregulation of motor carrier rates has now gone through multiple waves of loosening and sometimes elimination of virtually every regulation. Shippers and carriers once had to file negotiated rates with the former Interstate Commerce Commission. Now, they are free to reach any rates, tariffs, and accessorial charges upon which they can agree.

There are six basic components in the total cost of transportation for shippers:

1. The underlying tariff, or schedule of rates
2. The application of the National Motor Freight Classification (NMFC) class rating, which is determined by the transportation industry, and the rules covering the material being shipped (applies primarily to LTL shipments)
3. The weight and/or cube of the shipment

4. The origin and destination of the shipment
5. The required service level (next day, second day, time definite, etc)
6. Any pricing agreements in place between the shipper and the carrier

Rate Increases and Classification

Motor transport costs are impacted significantly by how your freight is rated or what "freight classification" it falls under. Each product (or commodity) is assigned a National Motor Freight Classification (NMFC) class (from 50 to 500), which impacts the eventual rate negotiated, especially for LTL shipments. Companies can simplify their rate administration and freight payment process and usually lower costs by negotiating a freight-all-kinds (FAK) classification. An FAK classification flattens the NMFC classes that a carrier can apply to the products you ship. Often shippers are able to negotiate a two-tiered FAK, all freight below for example class 100 is rated at a class 65 and anything above 100 is rated at actual class. There is much to be gained from learning more about rates and tariffs.

How to Lower Transportation Costs – Actual Cost Negotiated

If it truly is a "free and unregulated market," then how effectively you can negotiate and manage the rates that your carriers agree to will be one of the greatest contributing factors to how effectively you are able to manage transportation costs. The critical steps to negotiating and managing carrier freight rates are outlined below:

1. Understand and document your current operations and costs
2. Identify what your service requirements are by customer, market, product and other segments of your business
3. Develop your negotiating strategies (freight bids, core carrier program, combined inbound and outbound freight bids, length and terms of contracts, level of freight volume to commit, mode optimization, etc)
4. Conduct bids and/or annual reviews
5. Finalize rates and contracts

Freight Bids

Annual bids to achieve lower freight costs have been gaining favor among shippers, both large and small. With the new technology offered by Web-based bid facilitation companies and services, the use of bids has expanded to even more shippers and also now includes automated spot bids for excess freight or even a significant portion of a shippers' regular daily freight.

Spot Bids

Spot bids are less common than annual or other periodic freight bids and must balance most shippers' need to guarantee capacity with a group of core carriers against the potential cost savings of frequent spot bids. Most shippers use a group of core carriers to ensure that they have capacity to move their loads, especially at the traditionally tight capacity period of month, quarter and year-end shipping surges. Still, many shippers have begun to use a number of effective strategies to achieve significant cost savings while still maintaining good relations with their core carriers. Two of the more popular "spot bid" tactics are:

- *Spot bids for "excess freight"*—when a shipper receives a very large order or has a spike in volume, they bid this "excess volume" on a spot basis. The bulk of their daily volume continues to be tendered to their dedicated core carriers, but they can use the spot bid to identify current market excess capacity and often achieve significantly lower costs.
- *Internal "Spot Bids"*—some of the most exciting developments in carrier optimization have been to automate the daily tendering process to both speed the match up of loads with carrier capacity, but also to do this at the lowest possible rate. In the past, shippers would have to perform a "tendering chain" where loads were first tendered to the "primary carrier" for that lane, then if they rejected the load or "timed out" (for most shippers a 30 or 45 minute time limit where if the carrier does not respond they then automatically tender to the next carrier on their list), then to secondary carriers in order of descending price/service preference until the load was covered. This might often involve three or four automatic tenders (via fax, EDI or email), then the shipment planner would take over and begin calling carriers to try and get the load covered. This process was both time consuming and did not identify the lowest cost carrier option. Today's best systems will often tender the load to the primary carrier and if they do not take the load, then it is then "mass tendered" to all of the carriers in the shipper's files for that lane and every carrier responds within 30 minutes on whether they can handle the load. The system then selects the carrier with the lowest cost on the "approved" list that has "bid" on the lane to move that shipment. This modified "bid" has the advantages of 1) offering the load to the primary carrier for that lane first 2) quickly identifying all secondary carriers that have availability and 3) selecting the lowest cost carrier from that group based on their established rates (not a true "spot bid"). This process achieves low costs but maintains the integrity of the volume commitment to primary carriers and the established rates submitted annually by all other carriers.

The Annual or Periodic Bid Process

The quality of the data provided to a carrier on volume, shipper profile (DC dock hours, product characteristics, etc.) and other critical bid information is the most significant contributing factor to both the quality of the bids received and usually the shipper's ability to achieve optimal pricing. Time spent preparing a well-constructed, accurate and detailed bid is critical to the success of a shipper's bid process.

Accessorial Charges

Negotiating, updating and maintaining cost effective and accurate rates is a daunting challenge. Shippers must negotiate rates with each carrier to achieve the lowest possible transportation costs and creativity in these rate negotiations, while creating complexity, also results in lower costs. A certain amount of variability in rating schemes and terms by carrier and mode is not only acceptable but also necessary. Still, the goal of every shipper should be to standardize and minimize whenever possible. The best way to accomplish this is to have your own standard freight contracts and have carriers quote according to your contract terms and conditions, rather than trying to administer a multitude of individual carrier contracts, each with it's own rate schemes, terms and accessorial charge addendums. Using your own standard contract allows a shipper to take advantage of many best practices that have developed over the years. These include eliminating certain accessorial charges that either you negotiate not to pay or that do not apply to your industry, setting a low fixed charge for many accessorial charges, establishing your own standard fuel surcharge program that every carrier will use or having all carriers quote in a standard format or use a standard tariff (especially effective for LTL pricing). Efforts to standardize and minimize your carrier contracts and charges will both greatly ease your freight payment process and result in lower overall transportation costs.

Fuel Surcharge (FSC) Programs

The use of FSC programs is very common for both TL and LTL shipments. Most shippers agree to such charges and they help maintain consistent rates as the cost of fuel fluctuates, while still providing carriers the same margin on the shipments they move. These surcharges are now viewed as a necessary and unavoidable expense by most shippers. How these charges are calculated still varies significantly from shipper to shipper. The first decision is whether a shipper will pay each carrier according to a schedule set by that carrier or whether they will provide a standard program for all of their carriers to follow. The clear best practice is to standardize on one program and ask every carrier to execute the surcharges against that payment table. This both helps keep the surcharge at the lowest possible levels (as shippers are almost never able to pass this along to their end customers and thus it becomes a straight "hit" to the bottom line), and eases the additional strain on the freight payment process.

A good FSC should work for both the carrier and the shipper. The surcharge schedule should also include rebates from the carrier when fuel costs go below the baseline established.

Transportation Staffing and Training

Well-trained and experienced transportation operations personnel are always in demand and in short supply. Traditionally, transportation staff up to the supervisor or even manager level were people who started in the shipping department as loaders, billing clerks or shipping clerks. Those with the most ability and ambition learned how to handle the day-to-day aspects of the job with extensive "on the job training," and as others retired or left their positions advanced to jobs with more and more responsibility.

As the logistics function grew and the scope of the job changed as companies grew, many transportation supervisors and managers took advantage of the additional training offered by participation in professional associations and course offered by the many universities with strong logistics and transportation programs. This continued development of "home grown" transportation staff and the influx of many new college graduates with newly minted "logistics" degrees from universities with solid programs, had a tremendous positive impact on many companies' transportation operations.

Still many companies, large and small, found it very difficult and expensive to hire, train and develop professional transportation staffs at each of their major plants and distribution centers. To improve the control, visibility into operations, cost accountability and performance of their individual plants and divisions, as well as the corporation itself, companies have attempted to achieve continued success in a number of ways:

- *Corporate Transportation Groups*—by concentrating either their most experienced or best-educated transportation professionals in a corporate group, companies felt they could both monitor and influence their many plants and divisions without having to invest in large and well trained staffs at every location. These groups typically have a senior manager (usually a Director or Vice President) and then managers for each major mode (a TL manager/group, an LTL manager/group, Rail, etc). These groups often standardize contract language and terms, monitor and report performance on a regular basis (usually monthly/quarterly/annual), conduct major initiatives that might span divisions (freight bids, select a TMS, etc) and act as internal consultants for the organization.

- *Outsourcing*—some companies have decided that transportation is not one of their core competencies and that they should not develop the staff expertise within their own organization. The companies that have made this decision have pursued outsourcing all or parts of their transportation management. This has also been a quick and less costly way for companies to obtain access to the latest TMS functionality. Like all outsourcing, this can often be a all or nothing strategy, as once it is outsourced companies no longer retain a core staff with these capabilities and it can be difficult to ever bring back in-house if the outsourcing does not produce the desired results.

- *Load Control Centers*—as companies have automated their operations, especially after the implementation of a TMS, they find that it is possible to consolidate the transportation planning and optimization for multiple locations and divisions out of a central "Load Control Center" of "LCC." These LCCs are staffed with the most experienced and effective transportation personnel from around the company and are execution focused. Advocates of Load Control Centers claim that they improve carrier management, achieve consistent and unbiased freight dispatching, standardize freight payment and drive continuous improvement through the use of enhanced transportation metrics. They use the increased visibility provided by the TMS and their knowledge of best practices to achieve the maximum possible carrier and shipment optimization across all of the company's operations. Originally, most of these LCCs operated on a "plan centrally" and "execute locally" philosophy, but as technology has improved this has migrated to the point that in some companies almost every aspect of the transportation operations are handled from the LCC. This has allowed both a significant reduction in the staff required to execute transportation across the company and the concentration of resources so that training and development can be maximized.

Transportation Optimization

Everyone involved in transportation planning, optimization, and execution is focused on two areas: making sure companies meet or exceed customers' expectations and doing it at the lowest possible cost. It can be a very difficult balancing act. Cut costs too much and service may slip. Let service at any cost become the accepted standard and the company may spend its way out of business. Often, service requirements are poorly defined and companies pay for a level of service that their customers neither demand nor expect.

In November 2001, the Logistics Institute at the Georgia Institute of Technology asked representatives from 17 companies a number of questions about transportation. When the executives were asked what were the most important performance indicators, they answered:

1. On-time pick-up and delivery
2. Total transportation costs
3. Quality / damage claims
4. Safety
5. Asset utilization (fleet, cube, etc)
6. Perfect documentation
7. Communication (info sharing, tracking, customer feedback, etc)
8. Turnover of transportation personnel
9. Customer complaints

The survey also asked the participants, "What are the top criteria for choosing a carrier?" The top two responses were:

- On-time delivery
- Cost

Clearly, cost and service drive transportation management. Everything else supports these critical focus areas. This is the essence of what transportation optimization seeks to achieve.

Logistics Trends

It is likely that the logistics function—and ultimately the transportation manager—will be impacted in coming years by reductions in the number of DCs as a dynamic economic environment forces mergers and reduced investments in new DCs. Vendor direct-to-store, vendor direct-to-customer, vendor picked store orders crossdocked at a retailers DC and pool distribution will continue to increase, thus bypassing traditional DC functions. Web-based direct to consumer shipments will also continue to grow, both for web-only shippers and traditional brick and mortar companies that begin to offer web-direct customer access.

In this first decade of the new millennium, the efficient movement of product offers the greatest opportunity to reduce costs and improve customer satisfaction. The logistics function will continue to evolve, and transportation will offer the greatest opportunity for reducing costs and improving customer satisfaction. Transportation offers many untapped opportunities in operations and systems.

CHAPTER 26
Manufacturing Execution Systems

Allan Fraser and Douglas Furbush, Teradyne, Inc.

J ust as product designers have computer-aided design systems, and finance professionals have electronic accounting systems, operations personnel have their own set of software applications tailored to their needs. These manufacturing operating systems are called Manufacturing Execution Systems (MES).

Let us begin our exploration of the execution portion of the supply chain, and the systems that support operations personnel in the production of finished goods, by breaking down the three-letter acronym MES into its component parts. The Shorter Oxford English Dictionary defines each of these terms:

- *Manufacture*—to work up material into forms suitable for use
- *Execution*—the action of carrying out or carrying into effect; accomplishment
- *System*—an organized or connected group of objects

The Manufacturing Execution Systems Association's (MESA) definition of Manufacturing Execution Systems is as follows:

"Manufacturing Execution Systems (MES) deliver information that enables the optimization of production activities from order launch to finished goods. Using current and accurate data, MES guides, initiates, responds to, and reports on plant activities as they occur. The resulting rapid response to changing conditions, coupled with a focus on reducing non-value-added activities, drives effective plant operations and processes. MES improves the return on operational assets as well as on-time delivery, inventory turns, gross margin, and cash flow performance. MES provides mission-critical information about production activities across the enterprise and supply chain via bi-directional communications."

MESA is a not-for-profit trade organization whose mission is "to serve the manufacturing operations and management community and to provide thought leadership on the application of MES in order to contribute toward the improvement of production companies' competitive capabilities." MESA's Website, located at **http://www.mesa.org**, is an excellent source of information on manufacturing execution systems.

The dictionary definition for execution is especially vital, as more than anything else, accomplishing the goals of a manufacturing organization takes place on the factory floor by the people who are responsible for making things happen. A company can have the best product designs, or the best financial management systems, but without manufacturing all of these efforts are for naught.

More than any other single component of a supply chain, it is in manufacturing that all of the imperfections in a product development process and all of the disconnects between different parts of an organization get ironed out. These issues get sorted out in manufacturing for one simple reason—if they did not, no product would ship out the door and the supply chain would break. At its best, manufacturing is like a well-oiled engine functioning at top speed and delivering goods that power the rest of the enterprise. In manufacturing, however, if you make a mistake, or worse yet, set up a machine to make hundreds of mistakes per hour, it is very difficult to hide the "bone pile" of scrapped product that needs to be re-worked. In manufacturing, if you underestimate the amount of capacity needed to produce a product, you cannot hide the unfilled orders that are piling up at the door, or the extra workers you must pay overtime in order to meet your scheduled delivery commitments and keep the supply chain humming. Manufacturing is a daunting yet ennobling challenge and a critical link in the supply chain. The potential to make a tangible difference on a daily basis in the life of an organization is the continuing challenge and source of satisfaction for manufacturing people everywhere.

The History of MES

As with most software applications, the first manufacturing execution systems were written by end-users. Applications that had some of the characteristics of modern MESs can be traced back to the late 1970s. However it was not until the widespread adoption of Unix workstations in the 1980s that sufficient computer power became widely available on the shop floor to drive these types of systems. The client-server computing paradigm in the 1980s set the stage for the emergence of a distinct set of commercially available packaged software applications identified as MESs. In the 1990s, PCs increased in power to such an extent and the Windows NT operating systems provided a sufficient reliability that the first PC-based MESs came into existence. Today, there are many vendors offering commercially available MESs on a wide variety of hardware and software platforms.

One indication that the MES market has reached maturity is that there are now several vendors who offer MES packages tailored to meet the needs of specific vertical markets such as electronics manufacturing.

MESA has identified eleven core functionalities of an MES as shown in Figure 26.1. Each of these functionalities taken individually will help a manufacturer meet its cost, quality, and schedule goals. However, when combined, they leverage each other and provide additional benefits of operating in an integrated fashion where "the whole is greater than the sum of its parts." Even if you outsource some or all of your manufacturing, you will be impacted by your manufacturer's use of an MES. In fact, you may be *more* impacted by your supplier's MES if you outsource manufacturing than if you retain captive manufacturing capability within your own organization.

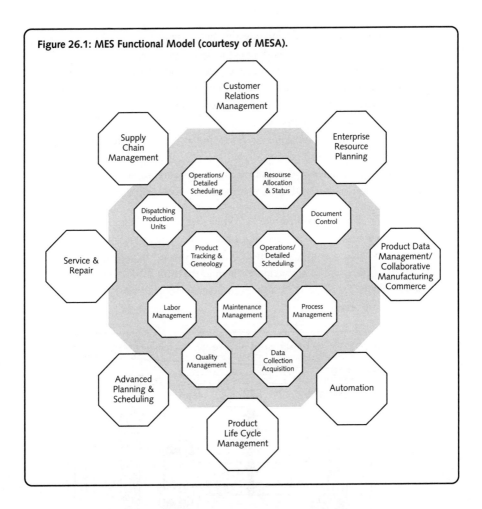

Figure 26.1: MES Functional Model (courtesy of MESA).

The eleven core MES functionalities are:

1. Operations/detail scheduling—sequencing and timing activities for optimized plant performance based on finite capacities of the resources
2. Resource allocation and status—guiding what people, machines, tools, and materials should do, and tracking what they are currently doing or have just done
3. Dispatching production units—giving the command to send materials or orders to certain parts of the plant to begin a process or step
4. Document control—managing and distributing information on products, processes, designs, or orders, as well as gathering certification statements of work and conditions
5. Product tracking and genealogy—monitoring the progress of units, batches, or lots of output to create a full history of the product
6. Performance analysis—comparing measured results in the plant to goals and metrics set by the corporation, customers, or regulatory bodies

7. Labor management – tracking and directing the use of operations personnel during a shift based on qualifications, work patterns, and business needs
8. Maintenance management—planning and executing appropriate activities to keep equipment and other capital assets in the plant performing to goal
9. Process management—directing the flow of work in the plant based on planned and actual production activities
10. Quality management—recording, tracking, and analyzing product and process characteristics against engineering ideals
11. Data collection/acquisition—monitoring, gathering, and organizing data about the processes, materials, and operations from people, machines, or controls

The four major plant systems that usually complement an MES are: enterprise resource planning (ERP) systems, automation systems, product life cycle management (PLM) systems, and customer relationship management (CRM) systems. MESs are usually located between an ERP system and an automation system in the plant. ERP, PLM, and CRM systems are usually linked to an MES at the plant level, but operate on a global basis throughout the enterprise.

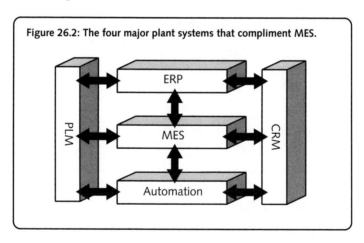

Figure 26.2: The four major plant systems that compliment MES.

ERP Systems

Most large- and many medium-sized companies today have either an ERP or an MRPII system. Commercial ERP systems started appearing in the early 1980s and represented an evolution from the traditional materials planning role of MRP (1960s) and MRPII (1970s) systems to include finance and other core application modules such as human resources and project planning. The main attribute of an ERP system is that it is a single integrated system with a single database in which all transactions cause an associated financial transaction to occur in the background. This financial snapshot capability provides upper management with a very detailed look at the company's operations on a daily basis. For example, suppose an order was shipped to a customer. Without an ERP system a company would have to update several separate systems: an order management system indicating that an order was shipped, a materials system indicating that the parts used to build that order had been consumed, an accounting system to indicate that an invoice needed to be generated to go along with the order, and perhaps a customer relationship management system indicating to both the sales force and customer support that this order had been shipped. All of these systems would have to be updated by sharing information between systems, or more typically, by re-entering the same information into each separate system. This type of scenario causes many headaches, including wrong, out of date, and inconsistent data in each system and requires additional staff to reconcile the data in these multiple systems. If this company had implemented an ERP system and an order shipped then all of the systems would be updated at the same time according to the business rules established for transactions, and the data for all these transactions would reside in a single database, eliminating re-keying errors and developing multiple-system interfaces. In addition, for the company with the ERP system, a financial update would have occurred when the order shipped, perhaps charging the manufacturing costs to the appropriate cost centers and updating the revenue realized for that product. Due to the tight integration with finance, with little or no extra effort required on the part of the worker, ERP systems can provide a very detailed, up-to-the-minute financial picture of an organization. It is literally possible to close the books on a daily or weekly basis and thus avoid some of the financial surprises that upset investors. However, as anyone who has ever implemented any large enterprise software system knows, these systems are not without their pitfalls. First and foremost, they often require that a company change its way of doing business in order to fit into a business model that can be represented in the ERP system software. This is a process than can literally take years to accomplish and is error-prone. Things that fall through the cracks in the design phase become painfully obvious once the system goes live and often cause workers to revert to the old way of doing things to keep product shipping on schedule. The other issue with ERP systems is that they need to be implemented in a comprehensive fashion to achieve the substantial benefits of having a single integrated system. Implementing one or two modules by themselves is no different than implementing one or two point solutions—the benefits of having a single integrated system are lost.

Automation Systems

Automation systems cover a wide variety of data collection and process control systems. These range from a simple programmable logic control (PLC) device controlling a single process, to complex distributed control systems with thousands of inputs controlling an entire plant. If an ERP system can be thought of as the brains of a plant, and an MES can be thought of as the central nervous system of a plant, then an automation system can be thought of as the sensory inputs of a plant. All of the plant floor data that automatically gets collected by an MES flows through an automation system. However, an automaton system can do much more than merely collect data. An automation system can actually control the flow of production by using either hard automation or soft automation. Hard automation describes physical devices such as relays that move to a different position to control the flow of goods through production. Soft automation accomplishes the same goals as hard automation, but with soft automation more of the process logic is embedded in software than in hardware. This makes soft automation systems easier to adapt to a variety of situations since it is usually easier to re-configure a software program than it is to re-configure a piece of hardware.

Automation systems obtain their inputs by a variety of means. A discrete or digital sensor may send a +24 VDC (volts direct current) signal that is translated into a 0 or +5 VDC transistor/transistor logic (TTL) signal by a voltage adaptor. An analog signal such as a temperature measurement may be translated into a 4-20 mA current signal to drive a temperature regulating feedback control system. Many automation systems interface with an MES via a serial communication interface. RS-232 and RS-485 are two of the most common serial communication protocol standards used today.

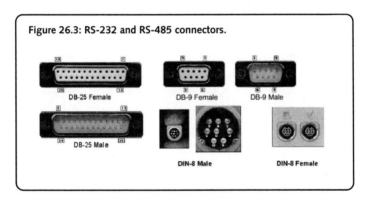

Figure 26.3: RS-232 and RS-485 connectors.

DB-25 Female   DB-9 Female   DB-9 Male

DB-25 Male

DIN-8 Male   DIN-8 Female

Increasingly, individual pieces of equipment are being integrated into local area networks (LANs) using the Telnet Communication Protocol/Internet Protocol (TCP/IP) standard. Having their own TCP/IP address makes it easy for these machines to publish selected data to the World Wide Web. The equipment can accomplish this by sending eXtensible mark-up language (XML) messages to a hypertext transfer protocol (HTTP) socket. A user then simply browses to the equipment's Web page as indicated by a universal resource locator (URL) and views the data published by the equipment.

Automation systems used to control a process may be categorized as being either closed-loop feedback systems or open-loop feedback systems. Closed-loop feedback systems use information that is measured as part of the process to control the feedback signal to the system in order to improve its performance. One of the simplest examples of a closed-loop feedback system is a person driving their car down the road. If the driver notices the car starting to veer to the left (measured signal) then the driver will move the steering wheel to move the car to the right (feedback signal).

Many continuous manufacturing processes, such as chemical and some types of food processing, use closed-loop feedback control systems to tightly regulate their manufacturing processes. A characteristic of these types of automated control systems is that they typically operate in the 50-200 ms time range.

It is important to note that MESs are not typically used for this type of millisecond control. MESs are typically used to enforce a higher level of process control such as product routing control or statistical process control.

Product Life Cycle Management Systems

MESs interface with PLM systems in order to acquire the computer aided design (CAD) data used to develop the recipes to drive the automated, semi-automated, or manual equipment in a manufacturing plant. Managing multiple product revision builds and speeding the implementation of engineering change orders (ECOs) on the shop floor with their associated routing and recipe changes are two important features of an MES as it relates to a PLM system.

Customer Relationship Management Systems

MESs interface with CRM systems to provide a detailed history of the process steps and repair actions completed for a particular product or batch. It may be valuable for a service technician to be able to view actual unit history while diagnosing a problem in the field. Data from an MES is often fed into a corporate data warehouse for reporting. These data warehouses can be mined to provide important linkages between manufacturing processes, product design characteristics, and field service issues.

Now that you have an overview of the four main systems that interact with an MES, let us discuss the eleven core functionalities of an MES in more detail.

Operations/Detail Scheduling

Traditionally, MRP and ERP systems have assigned work to plants based on the assumption that the plant has infinite capacity. Obviously this is a wrong assumption. This infinite capacity scheduling method is used to explode a products' bill-of-materials (BOM), by breaking down higher-level assemblies into their constituent sub-assemblies and component parts, and ensuring that all sub-assemblies and component parts are ordered from their suppliers with sufficient lead-time so that all material will be on-hand for the start of the scheduled product build. This is how demand signals get pushed back up the supply chain. One of the drawbacks to this method of scheduling is that actual plant capacity decisions, critical to meeting capable-to-promise dates, must be made outside of the realm of the ERP or MRP system.

Examining the factors that affect plant capacity in more detail provides some interesting insight into the operation of a manufacturing plant. One of the main factors that affects plant performance is the amount of time spent setting up (or washing down) equipment to change from building one product to building another product. This changeover time is highly dependent on the particular type of manufacturing performed, but everyone agrees that the less time that is spent changing equipment over the better. The daily schedule is the main factor that drives equipment changeover. The exact assignment of products, not only to production lines but also to individual machines on certain lines, is critical in increasing the output of the entire plant. To accomplish this important task, an MES maintains a detailed model of the actual plant resources (human and machine) that are available.

Combining the model of actual plant capacity with the current status of each resource and the routing requirements of a given product allows an MES to assign a product to be built in the most efficient manner while factoring in the actual (or finite) capacity of the plant.

Resource Allocation and Status

Since an MES knows the exact process steps required to build a particular product, and it also knows which steps a particular product has been through, MESs are typically used to guide both the human and non-human resources on a production line as to what steps need to be performed to build a particular product. Since MESs have such a fine-grained view of the factory floor they are also almost always used to report resource status and performance as well as order location and status back to other systems (accounting, order management). This is a unique feature of an MES that is enabled by the detailed view that MESs have of both the processes and the products on the shop floor. MESs are often tied into plant floor data collection, quality, or supervisory control and data acquisition (SCADA) systems to collect both process and product data with little or no human intervention.

Dispatching Production Units

Since MESs know both resource availability on the plant floor and the status of any particular order, they are well suited to be able to issue commands to materials management systems to send material to a particular location on the shop floor, or to send a product to the correct location in order to start its next step. Orders may be pushed from the last completed step to the next step, or they may be pulled by the current operation from the last completed operation. The next process step for a product may even be dependent on the status of a test performed at the previous process step. This type of conditional routing is usually used for complex, highly engineered products that are built in automated production environments. There are a myriad of manufacturing methods used today, as manufacturers continually strive to squeeze more production out of a given set of variable and fixed resources in order to reduce costs while meeting their quality and delivery schedules. Most MESs can be configured to work in many different types of manufacturing environments.

Document Control

MESs are the means used to achieve a paperless shop floor environment. The advantages of using computers to control both the contents and the distribution of documents to the shop floor include: making sure that the correct drawing, procedure, or instructions accompany each order; implementing engineering change orders; and assuring that the correct product assurance tests have been performed so that all product non-conformance issues have been resolved prior to shipping. Compliance to manufacturing procedures and product assurance tests is critical in the food and pharmaceutical industries, as well as other industries subject to government regulation or affecting public health and safety. In many manufacturing environments today, updating and distributing drawings and process instructions by hand is simply too error prone and takes too long to be a viable business practice. With the increasing speed of the entire supply chain (many electronics products can lose as much as 10% of their value each week they sit in inventory), MESs are often required to keep up with the ever-increasing frequency of product and process changes.

Product Tracking and Genealogy

Many products today are serialized, that is they have a unique bar code (2D or 3D) identifying them. These barcodes become the means by which all sorts of information about the product (and all of the sub-assemblies it contains and all of the components they contain) may be recorded and stored for future use. In industries having high product liability, such as power plants, aircraft engines, and medical devices, this genealogy or family history information is recorded, stored, and maintained for many years. If an issue arises in the field this allows similar units to be identified as part of a targeted recall. With ever increasing consumer sophistication and awareness, and businesses increasing sensitivity to liability issues, if a product recall is necessary then it must be possible to quickly and accurately identify similar units or else a company may be severely impacted. Even when it is not a safety concern, tracking a product's genealogy allows companies to see the performance of its products over time and provides critical data for both the field service department that needs to repair the product, and the design group that is working on improving the next version of the product.

Performance Analysis

Since it has a detailed view of plant operations, an MES is ideally positioned to collect all of the raw data needed to measure actual plant performance. When this actual performance data is compared with the desired plant performance, an accurate real time picture of plant operation emerges that can be used by plant management to make adjustments to operations to eliminate bottlenecks and increase efficiency

If an ERP system can be characterized as the brains of an organization, telling an organization what to do, and a Controls system can be characterized as the sensory input organs of an organization, the eyes and ears and nose, telling the organization what is actually happening in the manufacturing environment, then an MES can be characterized as the central nervous system of an organization, telling an organization how to react to its environment to achieve the desired results. With increased outsourcing, the performance of a plant with respect to a particular customer's products or set of products is now being shared in real time with that customer via the Web. This sharing of highly sensitive product and process raises many privacy concerns. Both the customer's product data and the manufacturer's process data must be kept confidential. In some cases the contract manufacturer may even be building a competitive product on that same line during a different shift.

Labor Management

Since MES has a clear view of who is performing what operation on which product at what time, it is natural to use an MES to track labor usage during product building to drive activity-based costing systems or during a shift to track actual time spent working for time-card calculations. It is the always-on, high-reliability aspect of an MES that permits it to be used to track sensitive data like number of hours worked, or to ascertain whether or not a particular operator is qualified to perform a certain operation or work on a particular machine.

Maintenance Management

Maintenance management systems today are focused on keeping equipment running and preventing expensive unscheduled downtime. An MES can monitor the status of all the equipment on the shop floor and send a page to a supervisor when a piece of equipment goes down unexpectedly. An MES can also be used to drive a maintenance management system by reporting how many cycles or operations a machine has actually performed. In addition to the main piece of machinery itself, an MES can track consumables usage on a piece of equipment and equipment tooling use as well. This is a valuable feature of an MES as it is often these lower cost items that keep an entire piece of equipment (or even an entire production line) from running.

Process Management

Since an MES knows the routes to be used to build a product in a discrete manufacturing environment, or the settings to be used to control a process in a continuous process flow manufacturing environment, and since an MES knows the actual status of all the resources on the shop floor, it follows that it can be used to direct the flow of work around a bottle-necked machine to another machine that can perform the equivalent process step or function. This integration of what is possible with what is actually occurring on the floor and the ability to respond in real time when issues arise is one the hallmarks of an MES.

Quality Management

The ability to combine data collection with statistical process control and real time alarming are some of the characteristics of a typical quality management system. In a laboratory environment a quality management system may be known as a laboratory information management system (LIMS). An MES includes these traditional quality management system functions but increases their utility by integrating the appropriate disposition of products with non-conformances according to the current manufacturing business rules. This is due to the fact that an MES maintains an overall view of the routings throughout the entire manufacturing process. Having a complete view of both a product's build history and the current state of the product in terms of its conformance to a set of functional tests means that a quality management system that is integrated with an MES can provide more value than a point solution. Similar to the case with genealogy, calculating and storing not only traditional statistical process control charts but also parametric data enable a manufacturer to relate the performance of a product in the field to a key set of product and process parameters, allowing them to gain insight into their operations and improve their manufacturing processes over time.

Data Collection/Acquisition

Data collection systems are used to collect data from an individual process or group of processes in a plant. Supervisory control and data acquisition (SCADA) systems collect data and provide some degree of process control, usually for an individual machine or a set of similar machines grouped together into a work cell. Data collection may occur when a certain event occurs on a piece of equipment (event-based), such as when a production unit is started or completed, or it may occur at specific time intervals (time-based) such as at the beginning or end of a shift. Two main types of data may be collected. These are attribute data and parametric data. Attribute data is used to indicate a binary go/no-go condition such as pass or fail, or one of a set of possible conditions, such as color. Parametric data is used to indicate analog measurements such as power output per channel or temperature. Many manufacturers today collect both attribute and parametric data associated not only with the actual production unit itself, but also parametric data about the process used to manufacture the unit. This process data is often collected via an automation system associated with a particular production unit or lot of units in a manufacturing execution system, and then summarized and archived in a data warehouse system for future reference by design, manufacturing, and service personnel.

SCE and the Internet

Today, all you have to do is pick up any news magazine and you are likely to find a discussion on the Internet, B2B, B2C, e-commerce, e-business, e-fulfillment, or the supply chain. But, what are all of these concepts referring to? Is it about purchasing goods or services, bids for goods or services, configuring your own products, or is it electronic purchase orders?

Let's start by defining some of the terms and acronyms. B2B (business-to-business) describes communications between companies and some equate it to being the supply chain. B2C (business-to-consumer) describes communications between a company and a consumer, such as someone buying a PC over the Internet. The supply chain covers both of these scenarios all the way down to the component suppliers of raw materials. When you consider the complexity of many customers, many OEMs, and many suppliers you can see why people are calling this a supply Web.

This is where it starts getting more complex. One definition of "e-commerce" describes the activities of a B2C as the "face" of an OEM or catalog company that deals with the public. For example—a company that sells to the public will set up an Internet site that you can interface with to pick and choose your product and even purchase it over the Internet. This also means it includes some of the various activities in the back-office such as credit checks, purchase orders, invoicing, and sending orders to ERP systems to drive production on the shop floor via an MES.

This is where "e-fulfillment" comes into play with checking stock on the shelf, in stores, trucking, distribution locations, and warehousing sites—all the logistical functions required to get your product to you when you want it.

The term "e-business" has been used to mean all of the above including the supply chain. However, there is much more to e-commerce than meets the eye on a web page! E-commerce takes on real meaning in the context of the execution of the orders on the plant floor. It doesn't matter how many hits you get on your Website—if you can't ship a high-quality product, at the right cost, in a timely manner, then your customers are only a mouse click away from your competition. These are the critical steps that companies need to execute flawlessly to realize the potential of e-business. The execution piece is where most companies fail to correctly estimate the amount of effort required to be competitive today.

Now lets take a minute to consider all the activities that are required in a manufacturing execution system in order to support e-business. As an example we will use the case of a manufacturer who is going to build and sell a personal computer.

First we need to know how the product is built. We need the designs from a CAD system—the drawings describing its design, assembly, and the type of components or raw materials needed. We need a list of the components—its bill-of-materials (BOM), and how it is assembled. We need a list of the processes it must go through and in which order they must be done. This is called a routing. A routing includes the path of processes (operations/tasks) that must be completed, including quality acceptance and process control specifications. The routing and quality testing all require that the correct specifications are available to build and test the product within acceptable standards. Materials are based on available components with certain characteristics and tolerances. Typically these are called out in a component configuration and from specific qualified vendors. And all of this information is required before you even start manufacturing the product!

Assume we have multiple facilities worldwide and have to manage our manufacturing capacities and follow best-in-class business practices. Added to our equation are cost-reductions, faster time-to-market measures, and making continuous process improvements. If all of this information is available in an electronic format, can it be e-mailed to the facility that will make the assembly? While this certainly represents a big time improvement over physically mailing drawings and specifications, many translation issues with entering information into the systems that control the processes and performing the quality testing still exist. Traditionally both product design data and process specification data is re-keyed into disconnected factory information systems many times in order to provide all of the plant-floor systems with the data they need to accomplish a product build. This re-keying of data from one system to the other is one of the main sources of production errors. For example, a recent National Institute of Standards study in the U.S. found that over $1 billion a year is lost due to data-transfer errors in the U.S. automotive industry's supply chain. When information is found to be incorrect or missing it can be handled in several ways. Some of it can be derived, some of it can be assumed, but usually someone must contact the original equipment manufacturer and have them send the correct data. Even when this data translation process is automated, you may end up with so many integration points between the various systems that it becomes very difficult to change or upgrade legacy software applications.

Next, we need to assemble the personal computer we are building. We need to build it to the correct specifications, using the correct components and raw materials, and we need to ensure that it is assembled correctly and functions properly. Even when you have the drawings, component call-outs, and quality test procedures you may still need to translate them for input to your assembly, test, and inspection equipment and operators. Operator instructions may need to be translated into a number of different languages.

Assume we are now building our personal computers—does the end customer need to know anything? This is where the World Wide Web is so important in providing the ability to share information and provide real time feedback. Manufacturers who provide real time visibility into their shop floors are now addressing customer inquiries such as "Where is my order" and "Will it be on-time?" via the World Wide Web.

Now, what about changes in the works? Engineering change orders (ECOs), process change notices (PCNs), substitute parts, and customer order changes are all part of today's increasingly dynamic manufacturing environment. How fast you can react to changes in the product, process, or customer orders can make the difference between success and failure in today's business environment.

Once we have started shipping products then how do we deal with units returned from the field? Having access to the as-planned and as-built product data for a particular PC helps us to diagnose and repair problems. Field service reports are also a valuable source of input for the designers working on the next version of the product.

MES and the Supply Chain – Supply Chain Execution Systems

Where does MES fit into a company's supply chain? The Supply Chain Council publishes the Supply Chain Operations Reference (SCOR) model that details all of the activities that take place throughout a company's supply chain. MES directly fulfills the "make" and "return" functions of the supply chain, and it indirectly impacts the plan, source, and delivery functions.

A supply chain cannot function without effective communication. The quick flow of accurate and complete information is a key characteristic of an efficient supply chain that has zero latency.

The ability to quickly accept new products and introduce them, while accommodating constant changes in demand, changes in design, changes in manufacturing processes, and changes in component vendors are characteristics of a company that has optimized its supply chain. The increasing pace of change is making agility a hallmark of today's successful manufacturers.

Once a product is built, it is no longer just the physical product that is delivered to an end customer. The information about the product being built, including parametric testing results, product configuration, and genealogy information, are components of the product data package and are becoming an increasingly important deliverable along with the physical product itself.

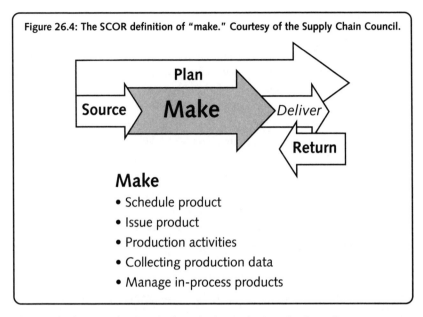

Figure 26.4: The SCOR definition of "make." Courtesy of the Supply Chain Council.

Make
- Schedule product
- Issue product
- Production activities
- Collecting production data
- Manage in-process products

The supply chain can be described as a high-speed network of suppliers, contract manufacturers, original equipment manufacturers, and customers interacting at lightning speed to supply each other with material and information covering all aspects of production from your supplier's suppliers to your customer's customers.

A complete supply chain cannot function without manufacturing execution system functionality fulfilling the critical make functions.

Supply Chain Execution Requires Teamwork

Many original equipment manufacturers (OEMs) are providing their contract managers with drawings, parts lists, authorized vendor lists (AVLs), and authorized manufacturer lists (AMLs) on the various products they have contracted to be built. This information affects may different departments from contracts, to purchasing, to engineering, to planning, to production, to receiving, to quality, to shipping, and others. This is why teamwork is so important in any business. Now, when we add in the dimension of the supply chain we see that this effort multiplies due to the additional number of companies involved. This multiple company participation greatly increases the complexity of supply chain interactions, especially when a make-to-order manufacturing strategy is being driven by a mass customization product strategy.

Today every company's data is (at least) a little bit different, and exactly what they want to do with that data also differs. Most large companies have CAD, product data management (PDM), and supply chain execution (SCE) systems that generate tremendous amounts of data. This data is usually generated in a proprietary, non-standard format that is a function of the application used to generate the data. If an original equipment manufacturer wants to share data with one of their contractors then they both must agree on the communication

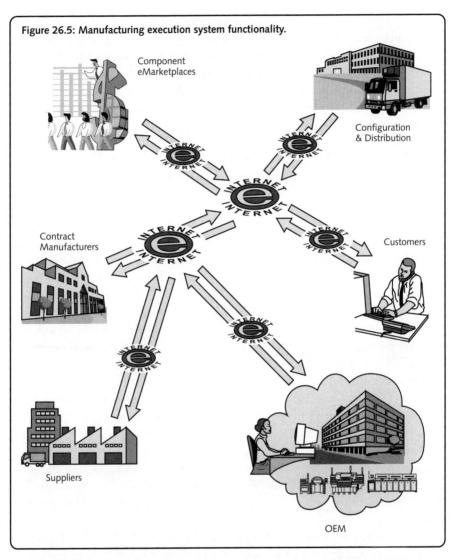

Figure 26.5: Manufacturing execution system functionality.

Component eMarketplaces

Configuration & Distribution

Contract Manufacturers

Customers

Suppliers

OEM

mechanism used (e.g., ftp or http), the format of the data to be sent (XML or ASCII text files) and, most importantly, the meaning of the data to be sent and the business rules for interpreting it. Now imagine that this sub-contractor has many OEM customers to deal with, and each one uses its own proprietary data format. This means that the subcontractor must support multiple data streams and formats for each of their customers! This almost always means that the data must be extracted from the contractors own internal information systems and formatted and sent to each original equipment manufacturer in a different manner. Things are no better for the OEM that has many different sub-contractors and different customers of its own. It is easy to see why the cost of integrating a typical factory information system today is three-to-five times the initial purchase price. Now imagine that you are an

OEM who wants to ramp up three new contract manufacturers for a period of six months to deal with increased demand for the busy holiday season and then ramp back down again. If it takes too long to integrate your supply chain with the contract manufacturer's supply chain then you may miss the entire market window. Now imagine you want to do this several times a year in different parts of the globe for closer proximity to local suppliers and local distribution channels and other regional economic advantages. This is a high-hurdle, but one that can be overtaken.

The Future of Supply Chain Execution Systems

The world is constantly changing and a framework is needed to systematically embrace change and find new and better ways to manage the supply chain and ensure success for your business.

All functions in an organization, including product design, process quality, customer service, logistics, and support must be tightly integrated in order to deliver the full benefits of an SCE. The entire supply chain is only as strong as its weakest link—and the weakest link that you are dependent on may not be your company, but a supplier to one of your sub-contractors. With the increasing inter-dependency of the individual parts of the whole supply chain, companies that can assemble the strongest overall supply chain will have the best chance of success. Indeed, even today there are manufacturing companies who tout their information infrastructure as a competitive advantage in helping them exceed their customer's expectations. With more manufacturing functions outsourced to third-party or contract manufacturers, the entire supply chain is more scattered and involves a larger number of companies. Any break in one individual piece of the supply chain can have a significant effect on the rest of the supply chain. One risk is that the supply chain in medium and large corporations grows too complex for any one person or group of people to fully understand all the different pieces and their interconnections. Future trends include perturbation analysis, which will determine the ripple effect that seemingly small changes in one part of a supply chain can have on an entire system. Failure modes effects analysis (FMEA) will expose the levels of risk to supply chain operations posed by different error scenarios.

Also, computing will become more ubiquitous and distributed. This means that both people and other computers will have access to the Internet and all of its secure, private, variations on an almost continuous basis. Furthermore, supply chain execution systems will continue to operate in this new world of fully wired and always connected businesses.

If anything, trustworthy partners whom you admit into your supply chain will become even more valuable, as trust is a key element of any relationship, and the close supply chain relationships that will be required to achieve competitive advantage in the future will require even closer contact and hence greater levels of trust between business partners.

In the future, collaborative supply chain execution systems, as well as other supply chain components, will have access to a shared, distributed, always-on, intelligent business model. These vertical industry models will be based on standard, common languages that define not only syntax but semantics as well. They will allow much richer two-way conversations, such as negotiation, between business object agents than is possible today.

The ownership of this shared model will raise many intellectual property concerns. As manufacturers shed their ability to manufacture in-house, and contract manufacturers move upstream by offering design services and downstream by offering warranty services, the traditional boundaries between manufacturing enterprises will continue to disappear. Different pieces of this shared business intelligence model will be able to be accessed by people and systems with different levels of security clearances. These security clearances will be based on the level of trust granted to the person or system requesting access. The need for greater supply chain responsiveness will continue to drive greater inter-connectedness between different companies' supply chains. This same inter-connectedness increases the amount of harm that can be brought to a company's business by a malicious partner.

Supply chain execution systems will become even more important as companies strive to improve their operational efficiency by collaborating with their supply chain partners and provide them with greater visibility to the shop floor in order to improve available-to-promise due date planning based on actual capacity and to identify production bottlenecks in real time.

Companies in the future will still need to know how builds are progressing, where problems lie in product design and manufacturing processes, which suppliers are being utilized, and each product's as-built genealogy is to trace products, reduce recalls, and perform corrective actions quickly. Future engineering changes will still need to be integrated on the shop floor with as little disruption to current operations as possible.

Supply chain execution systems will still be used to collect data from the shop floor and link the various islands of automation into a single integrated real time system.

The more functionality and partners a company adds to its supply chain, the greater will be its complexity. To combat this complexity we will start to see alliances of groups of companies fulfilling larger and larger pieces of supply chain functionality. In all supply chains, large and small, execution systems will continue to be the enabler that keeps a company's entire supply chain—and business—running smoothly.

Works Cited

1 RosettaNet/IPC/NEMI at the eConcert meeting April 24, 2001. Excerpts from the press release.

INDEX

ABC analysis, 85

Accumulation, 193-194, 207-209, 232, 264-266, 268-270

Activity-based costing, 56, 59, 61-62, 74, 337-338, 423, 480

Airfreight, 46, 325, 327

Air transportation

    carriers, 26, 43, 48, 51-52, 63, 68, 78, 127-128, 135, 148, 158-161, 195, 197, 208, 216-217, 222, 225, 229, 232, 261-262, 295-313, 315-316, 318-330, 333, 341-342, 347, 349, 419, 430, 457-460, 462-468

    deregulation of, 300, 330, 465

Aisles, 113-114, 150-151, 203, 206, 234, 240, 242, 245, 257-259

Automated Guided Vehicle Systems (AGVS), 255, 261-262, 286

Automatic Identification, 4, 205, 210-211, 439-440, 445, 451

Backhaul, 159, 341, 423

Bar code

    radio frequency, 78, 154, 156, 161, 196, 203, 205, 211, 235, 263, 288, 418, 425, 430, 433, 436, 439, 441-443, 445, 447, 449, 451, 453, 455

Barges, 306, 310, 314

Bays, 224-225, 227-229, 306

Benchmarking, 27, 180, 182, 238, 289, 359

Bill of Lading, 51, 194-195, 214, 221, 433

Breakbulk carriers, 310

Bridges, 91, 313

Bulk cargo, 44

Canals, 314

Carousel, 204-205

Carrier rates, 465

Carrying capacity, 296, 301-302, 305, 311, 370

Case flow rack, 290

Centroid analysis, 88

Chain conveyor, 267-268

Chute conveyor, 265

Clear height, 84, 92, 239

Common carrier, 160, 297, 308

Containerization, 144, 209, 298, 311, 315-316, 318, 329

Continuous flow, 24, 26, 152-153, 368, 382, 385

Continuous improvement, 2, 6, 8-9, 16, 19-21, 23-24, 26-27, 74, 79, 113-115, 130, 152, 182, 187-188, 192, 211-212, 251, 358, 364, 368, 374, 383-386, 388, 390, 406, 415-416, 469

Contract carriers, 300, 308, 419

Contract rates, 304

Control systems, 77, 133, 201, 204, 211, 247-248, 253, 262, 272, 279, 289, 298, 318, 366, 433, 475-477

Conveyors, 153, 158, 196, 204, 206, 208-209, 247, 254, 261-262, 264-269, 271-272, 279, 285-286

Cost

distribution, 0-2, 5-6, 9, 16, 29-31, 35, 40, 48, 55, 61, 63-65, 70, 72-73, 77-93, 101, 121, 127, 129-130, 133, 136, 140, 149-155, 157-167, 169, 171-173, 176-178, 191-192, 194, 202, 204, 208-209, 216, 219, 226, 247, 249-251, 261, 264-265, 268, 271, 277, 283-284, 289-292, 295, 313, 333, 336, 355-356, 358, 365, 390, 396, 417-427, 429, 431, 435, 437, 445-446, 448-449, 451-452, 457-458, 464, 469-470, 478, 482, 486

of labor, 29, 32, 35, 72, 160, 217, 280, 307, 316, 446

of transportation, 9, 69, 92, 99, 103, 158-159, 161, 170, 297-298, 300, 306-307, 311-314, 322, 325, 328, 333, 341-342, 350, 358, 457-458, 460, 462-463, 465, 470

of warehousing, 5, 61, 70-72, 152, 192, 213, 241, 396

Crossdock, 71, 154, 171, 196, 214, 220

Cycle counting, 78, 125, 154

Data capture, 211, 443

Deregulation, 31, 35, 83, 295-297, 299-300, 304-305, 315, 320-321, 323, 325-330, 465

Distribution center, 73, 78-81, 84, 89, 127, 150, 155, 191, 194, 204, 209, 216, 271, 284, 290, 365, 396, 417-418, 421-423, 429, 446

Distribution network, 65, 82-90, 93, 150, 153, 192, 427

Dock, 17, 51, 90, 113, 150, 154, 158, 161, 163, 169-170, 194-196, 209-210, 213, 215-218, 220-225, 227-234, 236, 242, 255, 271, 429, 442, 445-446, 467

Double deep rack, 287

Drive-in rack, 237

Electronic Data Interchange (EDI), 70, 135-137, 148, 161, 169, 171, 252, 298, 305, 313, 318, 357, 366, 422, 426, 448, 467

Industrial trucks, 203, 206, 213, 247, 254-256, 261-262

Inflation, 34, 36, 41, 43, 395

Information systems, 1, 3, 18, 60, 70, 72, 77-79, 138, 147, 153, 173, 215, 252, 273, 302, 425, 455, 458, 482, 485

Information technology, 3, 6, 19, 30-31, 34-35, 41, 70, 95, 119, 125, 143, 176-177, 214, 218, 221, 278, 357

Inspection, 99, 196, 215, 234, 270, 353, 371, 377, 383, 429, 483

Installation, 178, 221, 231, 263, 267, 274, 277, 283, 367, 369, 437

Integration, 2, 5, 8, 17-18, 21, 27, 31, 139, 146, 155, 195, 207, 210, 212, 247, 249, 251, 253-255, 257, 259, 261, 263, 265, 267, 269, 271-278, 291, 299, 356, 380, 398, 423-424, 435, 437, 439, 451, 453, 475, 480, 482

Intercontinental, 46

Intermodal, 46, 158, 295, 297-299, 303, 305, 322, 327, 329, 331, 442, 459, 463

International Standards Organization (ISO), 49, 53, 298, 316, 443-444

Invoicing, 77-78, 481

Just-in-time, 31, 45, 152, 167, 220, 279, 291, 368, 395, 424, 460

Labor management, 160, 393, 417, 420, 427, 474, 480

Labor standards, 393, 420

Layout, 84, 151, 198, 205, 223, 225, 227, 229, 231, 233, 235, 237, 239-246, 360, 381, 401, 430, 437, 454, 459

Less-than-truckload, 46, 67, 71, 158, 164, 233, 457, 459

Lift trucks, 196-197, 210, 215, 256, 279, 285

Line haul, 299, 302-303

Logistics

    inbound, 57-58, 65, 68-70, 87, 101, 113, 115, 140, 159, 193, 196-197, 214-218, 220, 222, 269, 317, 333, 339, 341, 349, 375, 384, 420, 426-427, 429, 446, 459, 463-466

    outbound, 57-58, 65, 68-69, 87, 101, 159, 167-168, 176, 193-194, 197, 209-210, 213, 215, 220-222, 269, 333, 341, 349, 375, 420, 427, 429, 431, 434, 446-447, 449, 452, 460, 463-466

    third party, 68, 126, 141, 151-152, 157, 214, 317, 342, 451

    trends, 3, 18, 29-30, 33, 43, 98, 103, 142, 150, 152, 155, 157-158, 166, 176, 179, 191, 293, 328, 385, 424, 428, 435-436, 460, 470, 486

Materials management, 2, 55, 336, 478

Mezzanines, 204, 271

Mode, 45-47, 51, 67-68, 70-71, 85, 114, 157-159, 163, 185, 204, 206-207, 254, 295, 313, 330, 370, 372, 384, 422, 458-461, 463-464, 466-467, 469

Modeling, 88-89, 153

Motor carrier, 301, 303-304, 333, 460, 465

Multimodal, 43

Network analysis, 459

Operating budget, 56-58, 109
Operational planning, 56, 80-81, 146
Order entry, 173
Order picking, 84, 154, 193, 197-200, 202-205, 209, 244, 259, 265, 288-290
Order scheduling, 200-201
Outsourcing, 3, 33, 35-36, 41-42, 175-181, 183-185, 187, 189, 340, 342-343, 348, 354-355, 462-463, 469, 479
Overhead, 55, 59, 61-62, 64, 66, 68-69, 112, 203-204, 206, 260, 271, 279, 291-292, 323, 326, 337, 343, 347, 352, 358

Packaging, 9, 15-16, 36, 42-43, 46, 48-49, 63, 65-68, 72-73, 85, 107, 113, 138, 143, 155-156, 178, 193-194, 197-198, 207-209, 251-252, 264, 301, 358, 360, 365, 419, 431, 444, 449-450, 454, 459
Packing, 17, 36, 153, 193-195, 229, 232, 268, 289-290, 384, 418-419
Pallet, 49, 53, 67, 71, 111, 113, 155, 169, 196-198, 200, 202-203, 206, 209-210, 214, 217, 219, 221, 233, 237, 244-245, 255, 257-261, 264, 268, 280-282, 285, 290, 333, 441-444, 446-447, 449, 451-454, 459
Palletization, 49, 156
Per-mile charge, 69
Performance measures, 75, 85, 152, 184, 237, 334, 376
Physical inventory, 125, 291
Picking, 78, 84, 125, 153-154, 158, 169, 193-194, 196-207, 209-210, 233, 244, 259, 265, 268, 280, 286, 288-290, 341, 383, 388, 418-419, 425, 429-431, 447, 452
Private carrier, 300, 334, 349
Private fleets, 68, 158, 160, 232, 333, 338-339, 347, 350, 457
Procurement, 31, 35, 161, 176-177, 298, 370, 382-383, 397, 457
Product life cycle, 83, 474, 477
Production planning, 2, 133, 150, 171, 250
Productivity, 34, 72, 80-81, 150, 170, 191, 196-199, 201, 203-205, 207, 213, 234, 242, 247, 250-251, 260, 289-291, 352, 378, 390, 394, 406, 420, 426, 451, 453
Push/pull, 165-166
Putaway, 78, 106, 113, 125, 153-154, 193, 196-197, 204, 218, 418, 429-431

Quality, 4-5, 8-9, 11, 14-16, 20-22, 36-37, 50, 55, 58, 68, 71, 74, 86, 88, 96, 100-101, 107, 130-132, 140, 151-152, 158-159, 167-168, 170, 172, 182, 191, 193, 199, 213, 215, 219-220, 222-223, 241, 247, 250, 273, 277, 281, 303, 335, 345-347, 356-358, 360, 364-365, 368-371, 377, 381-384, 389-390, 402, 406, 429, 446, 451, 467, 470, 472, 474, 478, 480, 482-484, 486

Rack, 150, 200, 202-203, 205-206, 209, 219, 237-240, 257-260, 279-285, 287-288, 290

Radio-frequency identification (RFID), 211, 285, 436, 439-455

Rail, 26, 67, 69, 87, 91, 158-159, 203, 242, 257-258, 260, 270, 295-299, 301, 303, 305-307, 310, 312-314, 322, 329, 333, 459, 469

Rates, 11-12, 32-36, 39, 41, 43-45, 47, 50, 52, 68, 84-85, 89, 91, 159, 161, 207, 211, 268, 271-272, 284, 296, 300, 303-304, 309, 347-348, 361, 364, 371, 377-378, 399, 431, 441, 448, 460, 462, 464-468

Receiving, 51-52, 68, 84, 106, 113, 118, 137, 153, 159-160, 167-170, 181, 193, 195-197, 199, 205, 209-210, 213-225, 227-229, 232-234, 242, 250, 291, 310, 336, 358, 383, 394, 409, 418, 420, 425-426, 428-431, 434, 437, 442-443, 445-446, 451-452, 454-455, 462, 484

Replenishment, 2, 36, 43, 47, 77, 84-85, 103-106, 108-110, 113, 115, 118, 120-122, 125, 130, 135-137, 139, 141, 143, 145-147, 154, 192, 197, 203-204, 207, 290, 375, 383, 393, 395-397, 399-401, 403, 418, 427, 429, 431, 460

Request for Proposal (RFP), 179-181, 183, 187, 343

Reserve stock, 203, 235, 397, 418

Safety, 43, 46, 53, 77, 85, 89, 91, 93, 95-98, 102, 105, 119-124, 127, 133, 150, 162-163, 165, 192, 199, 213, 216, 222, 234, 262, 298, 301-302, 304, 309, 317, 319, 326, 328, 330, 350-354, 370, 397, 408, 421, 448, 470, 479

Shipping, 11, 17, 45, 47, 71-72, 77, 80, 84-85, 88, 96, 143, 151, 153-154, 158-161, 163, 166-172, 176, 191, 193-197, 199, 201, 203, 205, 207, 209-210, 213-215, 217-219, 221-225, 232-235, 242, 244, 251, 271, 289, 292, 301, 306-307, 309, 336, 358, 384, 418-419, 422-423, 425, 427, 429-431, 433-434, 437, 442, 444, 446, 451, 459-460, 463, 466, 468, 475, 478, 483-484

Site selection, 77, 79, 81, 83, 85, 87, 89-91, 93

Sortation, 167, 169-170, 193-194, 201, 203, 207-209, 211, 265, 269-272, 290

Space planning, 223, 234

Standards, 11, 16, 23, 25, 36, 39, 49, 53, 60, 141-142, 150, 191, 238, 298, 316-317, 319, 335, 342, 349-350, 353, 365, 368, 373, 387, 393, 420, 426, 439, 443-444, 476, 482

Stock keeping units (SKUs), 1, 16, 65, 98-99, 101-102, 105, 107-110, 112-115, 117-120, 122-128, 130-131, 143, 150-151, 153, 156, 169, 191, 196, 198-199, 202, 204-206, 214, 216, 218, 220, 224, 234-237, 251, 286-287, 289-290, 390, 427, 444, 448

Storage, 43, 46, 48-49, 55, 63, 65, 68, 70-72, 78, 108, 112, 114, 116, 122, 125, 129, 131, 151, 153-154, 156, 163, 166-167, 170-171, 173, 193, 195-198, 200, 202-206, 209-210, 215, 218, 221, 233-238, 240-245, 247, 250, 255-260, 270-271, 279-288, 290-291, 350, 375, 378, 383-384, 394, 396, 417-418, 421, 425, 428-429, 431, 434, 437, 442

Strategic master plan, 166, 246, 254, 276

Supply/demand, 142
Systems implementation, 275

Tariffs, 32, 35-36, 462, 465-466
Tax, 29, 33, 39, 91-93, 312, 339, 349, 361
Team-based continuous improvement, 79
Terminals, 77, 154, 196, 205, 211, 293, 301-304, 307, 310, 312-313, 316, 329, 426, 430, 432-434, 442, 451-452
Theft, 108, 213-214, 234, 449
Third party logistics, 342
Total cost management (TCM), 56, 61, 73-75
Trailers, 99, 151, 168, 170, 196, 203, 209-210, 221, 240, 257, 259-261, 265, 297-298, 302-303, 305, 348, 389, 459-460, 463, 465
Truckload (TL), 67, 163, 233, 302, 304, 394, 457, 459-460, 463-464, 468-469

Unit load, 46, 151, 204, 209-210, 218, 224, 238-240, 244, 261, 265, 271, 280, 286-287, 290
Universal product code (UPC), 444

Variable cost, 58, 116-117, 237
Vendor selection, 36
Voice recognition, 211, 447

Warehouse control system (WCS), 154
Warehousing, 5, 16, 43, 46, 48, 55, 61, 63-65, 70-72, 74-75, 80, 89, 95-97, 133, 149-157, 161, 171, 176, 178, 191-193, 202, 212-214, 222-223, 230, 235, 237, 240-245, 249, 251-252, 264, 289, 293, 313, 315, 336, 383-384, 396, 401, 419, 423-424, 427-428, 435, 452, 458, 482